THE
TYPOGRAPHICAL
ASSOCIATION

THE
TYPOGRAPHICAL
ASSOCIATION

ORIGINS AND HISTORY
UP TO 1949

A. E. MUSSON, M.A.

ASSISTANT LECTURER IN ECONOMIC HISTORY
IN THE UNIVERSITY OF MANCHESTER

GEOFFREY CUMBERLEGE
OXFORD UNIVERSITY PRESS
LONDON NEW YORK TORONTO

1954

Oxford University Press, Amen House, London E.C.4
GLASGOW NEW YORK TORONTO MELBOURNE WELLINGTON
BOMBAY CALCUTTA MADRAS KARACHI CAPE TOWN IBADAN
Geoffrey Cumberlege, Publisher to the University

———

PRINTED IN GREAT BRITAIN

PREFACE

Towards the end of 1948 the Economic History Department of the University of Manchester was approached by Mr. H. Riding, Typographical Association General Secretary, with reference to the writing of a history of the Association on the occasion of its centenary. Through the kindness of Professor Redford I was given the opportunity of undertaking this interesting task. It soon became evident, however, that the available material was far too voluminous to permit of the history's publication in 1949; that its writing would, in fact, take several years if it was to be worthily carried out. To this the T.A. Executive Council agreed. I can only hope that their trust in me has not been misplaced.

My aim has been to tell 'a plain, unvarnished tale' of the development of trade unionism in the provincial letterpress printing industry from the earliest 'chapels' and trade societies down to the national Association of the present day. The book is not a laudatory account of the kind which usually appears at a centenary: in it will be found criticism as well as praise. The Association has given me open access to all its records and an entirely free hand to write the history as I found it. The views expressed herein are entirely my own, without any influence or censorship by the Association.

It would have been almost impossible, or at any rate very confusing, to have written a general chronological history of the Association covering all its various aspects, and I have therefore arranged the history under subject headings—relations with employers, wages and hours, apprentices, &c.—in order to provide an intelligible and connected account of Association policy in each of these fields. This mode of treatment, however, has itself several defects. It involves not only much more work for the historian, but also a certain amount of overlapping and cross-references. Moreover, division into separate compartments is unreal historically. To get an idea of day-to-day Association affairs, the reader should visualize the minute-books of Council meetings with their collection of miscellaneous matters from branches all over the country.

The main sources for the history are to be found, of course, in the T.A. headquarters at 'Beechwood', Oak Drive, Fallowfield, Manchester, in the innumerable large volumes of minutes, half-yearly and special reports, reports of conferences with employers and other unions, branch circulars, memorials, rule-books, wage-scales, delegate meeting reports, *Typographical Circulars*, and masses of statistics and miscellaneous papers accumulated over the past hundred years and more, which fill the filing cabinets and cellars of 'Beechwood'. In addition, the Manchester Typographical Society has kindly allowed me to browse through its minutes and reports, going back to the early nineteenth century, while I have to thank the London Society of Compositors for placing at my disposal papers dating from the late eighteenth century. I am also indebted to Mr. Turner Berry, of the St. Bride's Institute, for the use of various rare trade-union periodicals and reports. Some of the earliest trade society documents are in the British Museum or the Goldsmiths' Library (London University).

The reports and *Bulletin* of the Printing and Kindred Trades' Federation, the reports, Year Books, and *Members' Circular* of the British Federation of Master Printers, the reports of the Linotype Users' Association and its successor, the Newspaper Society, with its *Monthly Circular* and *Newspaper World*, have also provided a great deal of information. Many references to numerous other trade periodicals and to newspapers and press directories will also be found. The reports of Royal Commissions and Parliamentary Committees, the Censuses of Population and Production, and the *Ministry of Labour Gazette* have been mines of facts and figures. The various works of Mr. Ellic Howe have also been of considerable assistance, while any trade-union historian must acknowledge his debt to Sidney and Beatrice Webb.

I have to thank Professor Redford both for the opportunity of writing this history and for a great deal of sage advice. I also wish to express my great appreciation of the kindness and constant helpfulness of Mr. Riding, Mr. Blackburn, Mr. Joseph, Mr. Bonfield, and all the other T.A. officials and staff at 'Beechwood'. Mr. B. W. Clapp, of the Economic History Department at Manchester, very kindly read through some of the proofs and suggested various improvements. I am also greatly obliged to the Oxford University Press, not only for their admirable production of this book, but also for compiling the index. To Mr. Charles Batey, the University Printer, I am especially thankful for several corrections in the technical passages on printing machinery. Above all, I must thank my wife, who not only provided constant encouragement, but also typed the whole copy.

A. E. MUSSON

CONTENTS

PART III

THE TYPOGRAPHICAL ASSOCIATION
1914–49

ABBREVIATIONS

E.C.	Executive Council.
R.C.	Representative Council.
D.M.	Delegate Meeting.
T.A.	Typographical Association.
L.S.C.	London Society of Compositors.
P.M.M.T.S.	Printing Machine Managers' Trade Society.
A.C.P.	Association of Correctors of the Press.
S.T.A.	Scottish Typographical Association.
D.T.P.S.	Dublin Typographical and Provident Society.
N.S.O.P. & A.	National Society of Operative Printers and Assistants.
N.U.P.B. & P.W.	National Union of Printing, Bookbinding and Paper Workers.
P. & K.T.F.	Printing and Kindred Trades' Federation.
L.U.A.	Linotype Users' Association.
M.U.A.	Monotype Users' Association.
B.F.M.P.	British Federation of Master Printers.
I.M.P.A.	Irish Master Printers' Association.
L.N.P.A.	London Newspapers' Provincial Association.
N.P.A.	Newspaper Proprietors' Association.
J.I.C.	Joint Industrial Council.
J.L.C.	Joint Labour Committee.
N.A.T.	National Arbitration Tribunal.

PART I

TRADE UNIONISM IN THE PROVINCIAL PRINTING INDUSTRY BEFORE 1849

—————————·⋐✸⋑·—————————

I

THE EARLY PRINTING INDUSTRY AND TRADE SOCIETY ORIGINS

THE roots of trade unionism in the printing industry lie deep in the customs and regulations of the craft gilds. Trade unionism developed mainly as a result of two interconnected factors: economic revolution—the creation of a class of lifelong wage-earners, separated from the raw material, product, and instruments of production—and the breakdown of the Mercantilist policy of State regulation and protection, in face of commercial and industrial expansion and the spirit of *laissez-faire*. But

it is not among the farm servants, miners, or general labourers, ill-paid and ill-treated as they were, that the early trade unions arose. The formation of independent associations to resist the will of employers requires the possession of a certain degree of independence and strength of character. Thus we find the earliest trade unions arising among journeymen whose skill and standard of life had been for centuries encouraged and protected by legal and customary regulations as to apprenticeship, and by the limitation of their numbers which the high premiums and other conditions must have involved.[1]

Journeymen printers, for example, like other skilled handicraftsmen, were steeped in gild tradition, men as a rule of superior education and almost aristocratic exclusiveness, better trained and better paid than the mass of wage-earners. Their apprenticeship regulations, their high premiums and entrance fees long maintained a virtual monopoly of this craft in the hands of skilled tradesmen, in whose ranks the masters

[1] Webb, S. and B., *History of Trade Unionism* (1920), p. 44.

themselves had, for the most part, served their apprenticeship. Their trade clubs were, in fact, divided by a wider gulf from the majority of manual workers than from the class of their small capitalist employers.

Trade unionism in the printing industry was not, moreover, a product of the 'factory system', of large-scale works and mechanization. It developed years before there was any 'industrial revolution' in the trade, in the days of hand-press and hand composition, in small offices employing a mere handful of men.

It is impossible, therefore, to understand trade unionism among journeymen printers in the nineteenth century without an examination of their ancient craft traditions and of the industrial development and structure of their trade. Printing has always been a most conservative trade: its terminology, its technical development, its 'chapel' customs, its apprenticeship system all attest to this fact. Much of this conservatism went into typographical trade unionism, which was primarily concerned with preserving a traditional standard of life amongst workmen who were carrying on their trade in a way which would not have unduly surprised Caxton.

The main factor in the development of printing in this country until nearly the end of the seventeenth century was the control exercised over it by the State and the Stationers' Company. It was part of 'Mercantilist' policy at that time to regulate *all* industries, usually through the craft gilds or, as they were now becoming, livery companies. The Stationers', incorporated in 1557, was one of many such companies. As, however, printing possessed dangerous possibilities of religious and political sedition, Government control over it was especially severe. The orders of the Company were reinforced by Star Chamber decrees and Acts of Parliament, rigorously restricting the number and location of printers, the number of their presses and apprentices, and imposing a strict licensing or censorship. It was not until the end of the seventeenth century that the industry was free to expand, and even then the newspaper press was restricted by the Stamp Acts.

Number and Location of Printing Offices

William Caxton set up the first printing office in England in 1476, in Westminster Abbey. During the following eighty years printing presses were established not only in Westminster and London, but also at the universities of Oxford and Cambridge and in several other provincial towns, usually in the vicinity of ecclesiastical buildings—at Southwark,

St. Albans, York, Tavistock, Abingdon, Ipswich, Worcester, Canterbury, and Norwich.

In 1557, however, the Stationers' Company was incorporated and given an almost complete monopoly of printing, with extensive powers of regulation. No one was to practise 'the art or mistery of printing' except members of the Company or persons licensed by letters patent, and the master and wardens were empowered to search for and destroy anything printed 'contrary to the form of any statute act, or proclamation'. Their monopolistic control was strengthened by grants of privileges, patents, or copyrights to individual members of the Company.

State Regulation was made even more severe by a Star Chamber decree in 1586. Provincial printing, apart from illegal clandestine presses, was abruptly ended: except at the two universities, there was to be no printing whatsoever 'but only in the City of London or the suburbs thereof'. Moreover, printing in London was severely restricted. The industry there was not on a large scale. There were only twenty-one printers in London in 1583, owning fifty-three presses in all. Yet the Star Chamber forbade the setting up of any more presses 'till the excessive multitude of printers having presses already set up, be abated' to such number as the Archbishop of Canterbury and the Bishop of London should think sufficient. No one was to print anything unless it was licensed by the same authorities. Printers, binders, and vendors alike were to be imprisoned for offences against the regulations, presses were to be destroyed, and unlicensed books confiscated wherever found by the Stationers' Company, to whom execution of the decree was entrusted.

It seems probable, however, that this restriction was evaded, for in 1615 an order was made by the Court of the Stationers' Company that only twenty-two master printers should exercise their craft in London. This also had little effect and, in view of the increased output of political and religious works of a seditious character, another Star Chamber decree was issued in 1637, limiting the number of master printers to twenty. The former regulations regarding limitation of presses, licensing of books, protection of privileges and patents, &c., were reinforced, with various additions and alterations.

The abolition of the Star Chamber in 1641 meant the lapse of its decrees and left the printing industry suddenly freed from restrictions in a period of intense political and religious controversy. A host of 'diurnals', 'newsbooks', 'mercuries', and pamphlets appeared during the Civil War, despite Parliamentary Ordinances in 1643 and 1647 reinstituting the licensing system. By 1649 there were about sixty printers in

London, not including those producing unlicensed publications, and presses were at work in several provincial towns. Further harsh restrictions were imposed, however, under the Commonwealth and Protectorate and few more presses seem to have been established.

In 1660 there were still about sixty master printers in London, but the Restoration was quickly followed by the Licensing Act (1662), largely a re-enactment of the 1637 Star Chamber decree and again restricting the number of London master printers to twenty. One small development was permitted: printing could now be carried on in York; otherwise it was still restricted to London and the two universities. A new office, the Surveyorship of the Imprimery and Printing Presses, was established to secure enforcement of the Act. After the Great Fire (1666), however, the Act was practically a dead letter: its restrictions were openly ignored and new men continued to set up presses—though still, with few exceptions, only in London.

After the 1688 Revolution the Licensing Act was allowed to lapse permanently (1695), leaving the printing industry at last free to expand in the provinces. Presses were set up in Bristol (1695), Shrewsbury and Plymouth (1696), Exeter (1698), and Norwich (1701), and by 1725 had also been established in Gosport, Newcastle, Worcester, Gateshead, Nottingham, Stamford, Chester, Liverpool, Salisbury, Birmingham, Bury St. Edmunds, Canterbury, Ipswich, Cirencester, Leeds, Manchester, Derby, Northampton—in fact, in almost every town of any size.

Most of these began by printing a newspaper. There has been much controversy as to which was the earliest provincial newspaper; but it now seems established that the *Norwich Post* (1701) was the first, followed by the *Bristol Post-Boy* (1702). Exeter was also early in the field with *Jos. Bliss's Exeter Post-Boy* (1707). Several more newspapers were published in these towns in the first two decades of the eighteenth century. Other early newspapers in other towns were the *Worcester Postman* (1709), *Nottingham Post* (1710), *Newcastle Courant* (1711), *Liverpool Courant* (1712), *Stamford Mercury* (1713), and *Salisbury Postman* (1715). Soon nearly every provincial town of importance had its local newspaper. They were all weeklies or bi-weeklies. No provincial dailies were established until the middle of the next century.[1]

The limited expansion of the printing industry in this period was due not only to State and gild restrictions, but also to the limited market for books, newspapers, and printed matter. The population of England and Wales was only about six millions at the beginning of the eighteenth

[1] The first London daily, the *Daily Courant*, was started in 1702.

century and only a small minority was literate. There was also, as yet, little demand for printed matter from trade and industry.

Size of Printing Offices

The average printing office was, throughout this period, a very small affair. The twenty-one London printers of 1583 had altogether only fifty-three presses. Christopher Barker, Printer to the Queen and owner of one of the most considerable businesses of the sixteenth century, ran only five presses. In 1615, by decree of Star Chamber, a limit was set on the number of presses: the three patentees being excluded, of the other nineteen master printers fourteen were restricted to two presses each and five to one. This regulation was somewhat modified by the 1637 decree, which laid down that no printer should have more than two presses, except those who had been master or upper warden of the Stationers' Company; these could keep three, but no more without sanction of the Archbishop of Canterbury or Bishop of London.

This order lapsed in the Civil War, but was confirmed by the Licensing Act of 1662. The Act, as we have seen, was practically a dead letter, but the average printing office, nevertheless, remained very small. A survey of London presses in 1668 showed the King's Printer with six, two printers with five, three with four, five with three, nine with two, and six with only one. The King's Printer employed eighteen workmen and the other larger offices from seven to thirteen, but most had less than half a dozen, several only one or two, and two apparently none.

After 1695 the arbitrary restriction on the number of presses which any master printer might have was removed. But the limited demand for literature and other printed matter still precluded any very great expansion in the size of firms. The average printing house remained very small, especially in the provinces, the master often doing most of the work himself. We do begin to find a few larger firms in London, but even these employed no more than about fifty men in the mid-eighteenth century.

Output was not increased by any very remarkable technical development. The primitive wooden presses of Gutenberg's day had been improved by various German printers and, in 1620, by William Blaeu of Amsterdam, but no notable improvement on this Dutch press was made until 1798. The compositor's equipment also remained unchanged: in 1760, and for over a century to come, it still included the type cases, composing stick, bodkin, galleys, and other ancient accessories of hand composition.

Industrial Regulations

We have already seen the control exercised by the State and Stationers' Company over the number of printers and presses. Similar authoritarian regulations governed other matters, such as apprenticeship, wages, hours, and working conditions.

Thus, in 1576, we find the Company appointing searchers to find out 'how many prentices every printer keepeth, and whether they be his own or other man's; and whether any be kept in work that is neither prentice, journeyman, nor a brother admitted'. Numerous fines attest to the performance of these duties—the limitation of the number of apprentices, restriction of 'turnovers', and exclusion of 'illegal men' or 'foreigners', who had not served a seven years' apprenticeship to the trade.

The Star Chamber decree of 1586 strictly limited the number of apprentices that each master might take. The Queen's Printer was allowed six, the Master and Wardens of the Stationers' Company three each, the Liverymen two, and the ordinary Freemen or Yeomanry one.

The main purpose of these restrictions was to limit the number of printers and preserve the Company's monopoly. They were also aimed at preventing the excessive employment of juvenile labour, cheap competition, and unemployment. The seven years' servitude sought, in addition, to ensure sound technical training and good workmanship.

In 1587 the Stationers' Court issued *Certen orders concerning printinge* in answer to complaints from the journeymen. Their chief aim was to prevent unemployment. It was ordered that 'no formes of letters be kept standing to the prejudice of the workmen at any time', and that no impression of any book was to exceed 1,250 copies, with an additional 250 if set in nonpareil or brevier; if further copies were required, then the work must be completely reset. It was further laid down that no apprentice was to be employed at case or press should any journeyman lack employment; that the number of apprentices indentured by each master should not exceed the maximum defined by the Star Chamber decree of 1586; and that demands for wage increases by the journeymen were to be submitted to the Court. The journeymen were warned, however, against beginning 'any new suit, petition, or complaint' to the Court, on pain of losing the present concessions.

A similar set of regulations was issued by the Court in 1635, dealing with apprenticeship, expulsion of 'foreigners', enforcement of established wage rates, curtailment of cheap juvenile labour, and regulation of casual employment, holidays, and working conditions.

The Star Chamber decree of 1637 supplemented and reinforced the earlier regulations regarding the number of printers, presses, and apprentices and also dealt with the problem of unemployment again, laying down that master printers might be forced by the officers of the Stationers' Company to take on unemployed journeymen. The Government was not, however, concerned so much about the welfare of the journeymen as 'the secret printing in corners' largely 'caused for want of orderly employment for journeymen printers'.

With the breakdown of the centralized system of Government in 1641 and the lapse of the Star Chamber decrees, the extensive State control of industry broke down and was never fully re-established. The Licensing Act in 1662 embodied certain of the old regulations, but the machinery no longer existed to enforce them. The Revolution of 1688 and the lapse of the Licensing Act in 1695 resulted in the gradual decay of the policy of State regulation. Parliament did, it is true, exert itself spasmodically to enforce wage rates and apprenticeship restrictions, but on the whole 'the eighteenth century was nearly a blank period in the history of direct regulation of industrial conditions by the State'.[1] This was due not only to the breakdown of the centralized machinery of Government, but also to the expansion of trade and industry, the growing wealth and influence of the commercial and industrial classes, the rising spirit of individualism, competition, and *laissez-faire*.

The authority of the Stationers' Company also declined in the eighteenth century and its regulations were extensively evaded or ignored. In the provinces, where printing offices were rapidly springing up, it had little or no control. Many of its regulations, however, were inherited by the trade societies and became the basis of their rules.

Growth of Organization among Journeymen Printers

The Stationers' Company, like other craft gilds, comprised both employers and employed, masters as well as journeymen and apprentices, but it was not long before a gulf developed between them. The restriction of the number of printers, the granting of patents, and the evolution of gild government tended to place power in the hands of a small oligarchy of master printers and to create a body of permanent wage-earners. Already, in the sixteenth century, there existed a class of life-long journeymen, who, together with the smaller masters, formed the 'Yeomanry', with outlook and interests different from and often opposed

---

[1] Bland, Brown, and Tawney, *English Economic History: Select Documents* (1914), p. 543.

to those of the wealthier masters in the 'Livery', from amongst whom were chosen the Master, Wardens, and Court of Assistants who governed the Company. At an early date, as we have seen, they developed typically proletarian grievances, strikingly similar to those of the later trade unions—against unemployment, excessive numbers of apprentices, 'turnovers', 'foreigners', and low wages—and frequently co-operated to present their complaints to the Stationers' Court.

An excellent example of such united action is provided by *The Case and Proposals of the Free Journeymen Printers in and about London, humbly submitted to Consideration*, in 1666.[1] In this document, presented to the Stationers' Court, it was declared that

Whereas, there are at this present, in and about the city of London, to the number of a hundred and forty workmen printers, or thereabouts, who have served seven years to the art of printing, under lawful master printers, and are reduced to great necessity and temptations for want of lawful imployment, occasioned partly by the encroachment of forreigners, and partly by supernumerary apprentices and turn-overs, which have increased the number almost to twice as many in the whole, as would be sufficient to discharge all the publick and lawful work of the kingdom. The work-men printers above mentioned, have unanimously agreed upon, and presumed humbly to offer these proposals following; always submitting themselves to what other course or provision soever authority shall judge more expedient for their redress.

1. That no forreigners (that is to say) such an one as hath not served seven years to the art of printing, under a lawful master printer, as an apprentice, may be entertained or imployed by any master printer for the time to come.

2. That a provision be made to hinder the increase of apprentices, and a limitation appointed as to the number; the said restraint and limitation to take effect and commence from the present session of Parliament.

3. That no turn-overs be received by any master printer, but from a master printer; and that no master printer turning over any apprentice to another master printer, may be permitted to take any other apprentice in his place, till the full time of the said apprentice so turned over be expired: For otherwise, the restraint and limitation of apprentices will be evaded, and the number supplyed by turn-overs; under which name is understood, such persons as being bound apprentices to one master are turned over to serve the residue of the time with another.

This petition might well have been written by a printing trade union of the nineteenth century. The insistence upon a seven years' apprentice-

---

[1] This petition, now in the British Museum, is reprinted in L. Brentano's introduction to Smith, J. T., *English Gilds* (1870), p. clxi, and also in Howe, E., *The London Compositor* (1947), p. 111.

ship, the exclusion of 'foreigners', the restriction of apprentices and turn-overs—these were to form some of the most important and ceaselessly reiterated topics in the minute-books and annual reports of the later trade unions. In the seventeenth century, however, though the journey-men had undoubtedly organized themselves, their organization was still subordinate to the Stationers' Court and they themselves were still in-cluded within the framework of the Company. The Court, moreover, gave ear to their appeals and passed regulations to protect their interests. But during the eighteenth century, as the authority and regulations of the Stationers' Company lost their force, leaving the journeymen unpro-tected, it was only to be expected that they would establish their own independent organizations.

Developments in provincial towns are shrouded in obscurity. The rule of the Stationers' Company was confined to London and, apart from customary regulations, printing in the provinces must have grown up unrestricted. Here, too, a class of permanent journeymen developed, although, after the lapse of the Licensing Act in 1695, there was no restriction on the number of master printers and an enterprising journey-man could, at no great cost, establish a small business. It is probable, therefore, that journeymen printers' associations, ephemeral in charac-ter or disguised as friendly societies, may have developed in some of the larger provincial towns in the first half of the eighteenth century, although there is no actual evidence of trade-union activity until the last decade.

Throughout the eighteenth century workmen's trade organizations were punished under the common law of conspiracy. Statutes were also passed to put down 'combinations' in particular trades. The State still claimed to regulate trade and industry, to give some sort of protection to journeymen by laying down wage rates and apprenticeship restrictions and dealing with the problem of unemployment. In the second half of the century, however, State regulation became increasingly spasmodic, leaving journeymen practically unprotected, in a period of rapid indus-trial change. The system of out-door apprenticeship was utilized by employers to secure cheap labour; there was a relaxation of the seven years' servitude and formal binding in many places; wages and hours were left unregulated. Journeymen printers—a skilled, comparatively well-paid, and intelligent section of the working classes—would naturally combine to protect themselves, having behind them time-honoured craft traditions on which to base their claims. The one-sided State policy of the time, however, though abandoning the system of industrial

regulation and protection in the interests of employers, still most unfairly penalized workmen in their efforts to safeguard themselves by their trade 'combinations'. Such organizations, therefore, were usually secret or disguised as friendly societies and were often short-lived; early documentary evidence about them is naturally very scanty.

Journeymen printers had long possessed, in their ancient workshop organization known as the 'chapel', a democratic institution which naturally lent itself to trade-union organization. The 'chapel', in fact, still forms the basic unit or 'cell' of present-day trade unionism in the printing trade. It 'may possibly be nearly as old as the introduction of printing into this country'.[1] The earliest surviving description of a 'chapel', Joseph Moxon's account of the 'Ancient Customs used in a Printing House' in his *Mechanick Exercises* (1683), states that 'every Printing-house is by Custom of time out of mind, called a Chappel; and all the Workmen that belong to it are Members of the Chappel; and the Oldest Freeman is Father of the Chappel'. Moxon suggested that 'the stile was originally conferred upon it by the courtesie of some great Churchman, or men (doubtless when Chappels were in more veneration than of late years they have been here in England) who for the Books of Divinity that proceeded from a Printing-house, gave it the Reverend Title of Chappel'.

He goes on to describe the 'Customs and By-Laws made and intended for the well and good government of the Chappel, and for the more Civil and orderly deportment of all its Members while in the Chappel'. There were rules against swearing, fighting, abusive language, and drunkenness in chapel, and penalties for leaving candles burning at night, dropping a composing stick or press ball, leaving letters lying on the floor, &c. The penalty for breach of any of these customs and by-laws was 'in Printer Language called a Solace. And the Judges of these Solaces, and other Controversies relating to the Chappel, or any of its Members, was plurality of Votes in the Chappel. It being asserted as a Maxim, that the Chappel cannot Err.' The 'solaces' or fines varied from a halfpenny to a shilling. 'If a delinquent proved Obstinate or Refractory, and would not pay his Solace', then the workmen took him by force, laid him athwart the correcting-stone, and gave him a beating.

Other solaces were often imposed for offences such as suggesting sending for drink or spending the 'Chappel money' before Saturday night, playing quadrats, singing in chapel, &c.

These fines had a social as well as a disciplinary purpose in that they

[1] Webb, S. and B., op. cit., p. 27.

went to form a weekly fund for the 'Chappel Drink'. It was also a recognized custom that every new workman should pay half-a-crown, 'which is called his Benvenue', to the Chapel. An apprentice had to pay half-a-crown when bound, another when made free, and a third, if he continued as a journeyman in the same house, before becoming a member of the chapel. If he married, he again paid half-a-crown, and on the birth of a son, a shilling, of a daughter, sixpence. All this money, apparently, was spent on drink.

Moxon also describes other chapel rules and customs, such as the regulation against 'smouting' and the traditional 'Way-goose', or annual feast, provided by each master printer for his journeymen.

Thomas Gent, the eighteenth-century York master printer, gives an alternative explanation in his *Life* for the origin of the name chapel, 'printing rooms being called such, because first begun to be practised in one at Westminster Abbey'. Mr. Howe hazards a guess that 'the word is of French origin, and introduced into our technical vocabulary by French journeymen working in London in the sixteenth century'.[1] An alternative explanation might be that it was connected with a travesty of Church ritual. The following description in 1740 of the ceremonial in a printers' chapel lends some support to this view:[2]

'When a Printer first sets up, if it is an House that was never used for Printing before, the Part designed for that Purpose is consecrated, which is performed by the Senior Freeman the Master employs, who is the Father or Dean of the Chapel, and the chief Ceremony is drinking success to the Master, sprinkling the walls with strong beer, and singing the Cuz's Anthem.' There follows an account of the Chapel 'Laws', and penalties imposed for their breach, 'which an obstinate Member sometimes refuses to pay; upon which it is left to the Majority of the Chapel, in Convocation assembled, whether he shall be continued any longer a Chappellonian; and if his Sentence is to be discontinued, he is then declared a Brimstone; that is, an excommunicated Person'.

[1] Howe, E., *The London Society of Compositors* (1948), p. 32. Other words derived from the French are 'companionship' (French *compagnonnage*), the names for different sizes of type (minion, nonpareil, &c.), the 'bienvenue' paid by new members of the chapel, &c.

[2] *The Country Journal: or, The Craftsman*, 24 May 1740. Reprinted in *The Gentleman's Magazine*, vol. x (1740), pp. 239–40. The author agrees with Thomas Gent in his explanation of the origin of the term 'chapel': because 'the first Printing Press in England was set up in a chapel in Westminster Abbey . . . from whence that Part of the House, which is assigned for Printing, hath been ever since called a Chapel, and constituted in an ecclesiastical Manner, with diverse religious Rites and Ceremonies'.

The ordination of a new apprentice is described as follows:

When a Boy is to be bound Apprentice, before he is admitted a Chappel-lonian, it is necessary for him to be made a Cuz, or Deacon; in the Perform-ance of which there are a great many Ceremonies. The Chappellonians walk three Times round the Room, their right Arms being put thro' the Lappets of their Coats; the Boy who is to be made a Cuz carrying a wooden Sword before them. Then the Boy kneels, and the Father of the Chapel, after exhorting him to be observant of his Business, and not to betray the secrets of the Workmen, squeezes a Spunge of strong Beer over his Head, and gives him a Title, which is generally that of Duke of some Place of the least Reputation near which he lives, or did live before. . . . Whilst the Boy is upon his Knees, all the Chappellonians, with their right Arms put through the Lappets of their Coats, as before, walk round him, singing the Cuz's Anthem, which is done by adding all the Vowels to the Con-sonants in the following Manner.

Ba-ba; Be-be; Bi-bi; Ba-be-bi; Bo-bo; Ba-be-bi-bo; Bu-bu; Ba-be-bi-bo-bu—And so through the rest of the Consonants.

'There are several other Solemnities', the account concludes, 'of the same Kind, belonging to a Printing-Chapel; but these are sufficient to shew the sacred Institution of it, and the Reverence that is due to it.'

Thomas Gent gives a similar description of this amazing initiation ceremony. Benjamin Franklin, who worked in the London printing trade in 1725, describes how he was 'excommunicate' for refusing to pay his 'bien venu'.

Beer-drinking was clearly a prominent feature of chapel customs. Franklin describes what a considerable part it played in the lives of his fellow workmen. In the office where he worked there was an ale-house boy in constant attendance and Franklin's companion at the press drank, each day, 'a pint before breakfast, a pint at breakfast with his bread and cheese, a pint in the afternoon about six o'clock, and another when he had done his day's work . . . and had four or five shillings to pay out of his wages every Saturday night for that vile Liquor'.

This strong propensity for drink, together with the social solidarity and customs of the chapel, may well have been a most important factor in the formation of early trade societies in the printing industry. A com-bination of two or three such chapels and the choice of a public-house as the official headquarters for the Saturday night meetings were all that was required for the establishment of a regular friendly society. The chapel, moreover, provided experience of democratic organization, with rules, customs, and penalties enforced by vote of the majority.

There is no concrete evidence, however, of trade societies in the printing trade till towards the end of the eighteenth century. It is probable, however, that some sort of 'tramp-relief' system grew up at an earlier date, with the expansion of printing in the provinces. Journeymen in printing and other trades frequently tramped the country looking for work and arrangements were made in most towns for their relief. Thus we find Thomas Gent describing how, as early as 1714–15, members of 'the fraternity' passing through York 'received assistance' from the printers there. Such relief, no doubt, was not yet systematic, but might well lead to the establishment of a tramping society, which could easily pass into a national trade union.

II

THE BACKGROUND TO TRADE UNIONISM IN THE PRINTING INDUSTRY
1750–1850

THE printing industry of 1750 was still almost medieval. The small master was the typical figure, usually working himself and perhaps employing one or two journeymen and apprentices. Though a class of permanent journeymen existed, the amount of capital necessary to set up as a small master presented no insuperable barrier to the thrifty workman. The permanent journeymen were almost certainly class conscious, but there is no positive evidence of separate trade-union organization as yet; in London, the Stationers' Company still legislated for masters and men alike. Technically, there had been little development since Caxton's time, nor was it needed to satisfy the comparatively limited market. Provincial printing had developed in the first half of the eighteenth century, but was completely dwarfed by the London trade.

The Industrial Revolution was to bring considerable change and development and, ultimately, to transform the industry. But the 'revolution' in the printing trade was a very long and gradual process. Perhaps the most important effects of the Industrial Revolution in this period were indirect. A greatly increased market resulted from the growth of industry and commerce. Large-scale and complex organization necessitated increased quantities of printed matter. Newspapers became an essential source of commercial information, while competition brought a development of advertising. The market was also expanded by transport improvements, first by the turnpikes and canals, then by the railways. The rapid growth of population, together with the gradual decline in illiteracy, the increasing thirst for 'enlightenment' and the 'diffusion of useful knowledge', created new markets for literature of every kind. The development of free trade ideas and competition brought about the gradual collapse of industrial control by State and craft gild— an important factor in the development of trade unionism. The growth of a powerful middle class, eager for political power, and the creation of a large body of industrial wage-earners, suffering from a sense of oppression—the vast social changes, in fact, brought about by the Industrial Revolution—were reflected in the political sphere, and increased political activity caused an outburst of Liberal and Radical newspapers and periodicals. Free Trade brought first the reduction and then the abolition of the advertisement, newspaper stamp, and paper duties. The introduction of the penny post in 1840 was of immense advantage to printers and publishers.

The direct effects of the Industrial Revolution were confined, in this period, almost exclusively to the press department. There was, in fact, a one-sided development, which mechanized press-work, but left hand composition practically unaffected until the last quarter of the nineteenth century. Iron and steam formed the basis of the Industrial Revolution. Both were applied to the printing press in the early nineteenth century. The Earl of Stanhope's iron press (1798) was stronger and more accurate than the old wooden press and allowed a bigger sheet to be printed, with less effort. Various 'improved' Stanhope presses, such as the 'Columbian', 'Albion', and 'Imperial', were brought out in the first quarter of the nineteenth century. The Stanhope press did little, however, to increase the rate of output, which remained at about 250 impressions per hour. The first revolutionary development in the printing industry was the invention of a cylinder printing machine, driven by steam. William Nicholson appears to have been the pioneer. About 1790 he designed machines to print from type placed on either a flat bed or a cylinder, impression to be given by another cylinder and inking to be done automatically by rollers. Thus he discovered the fundamental principles on which all later machines, both reciprocating and rotary, have been constructed. He failed, however, to develop his ideas. The first successful printing machine was that of Friedrich Koenig, a native of Saxony, who, with financial assistance from Bensley, Taylor, and other well-known London printers, patented and manufactured in the years 1810–12 a cylinder press capable of over 1,000 impressions per hour. The essential principles of this machine are still incorporated in flat-bed presses today: reciprocating movement of the type bed, impression by means of a cylinder, and automatic inking of the forme.

John Walter II, proprietor of *The Times*, quickly realized the immense advantages to be derived in newspaper printing from Koenig's invention and installed two of his machines, with the result that on 28 November 1814 *The Times* was for the first time 'printed by steam'. The machine used was a double cylinder, printing simultaneously two copies of a forme on one side only, with an output of 1,800 impressions an hour.

Various improvements on Koenig's machine were soon introduced.

Its mechanism was considerably simplified and its output increased by Cowper and Applegarth, who, in 1827, invented and installed in *The Times* office a four-feeder machine, printing both sides of a sheet at once at the rate of 5,000 copies an hour.

In 1848 Applegarth brought out an eight-feeder, also for *The Times*. In this, the Vertical Printing Machine, the reciprocating movement of the forme was changed to a rotary one. A machine embodying the rotary principle had, as we have seen, been designed by Nicholson in 1790. Later inventors had also realized the advantages of the rotary system, but had never successfully put their ideas into practice. It was not until the forties that practical rotary machines were built, by Applegarth and the American firm of Hoe. Modern rotary machines print from curved stereotype plates; but at the time when Applegarth invented his eight-feeder the method of making curved moulds by the 'flong' process had only recently been invented and was not yet widely introduced. Applegarth, therefore, as Nicholson had suggested, fixed ordinary type upon a central cylinder, round which rotated eight other, smaller, impression cylinders, sheets being fed in from eight different feed-boards placed horizontally round the machine. Hence his invention was known as a 'type-revolving machine'.

The Hoe ten-feeder was built on exactly the same principle, but had the type cylinder placed horizontally and embodied an improved method of fastening type to the central cylinder, which gave a better printing surface and allowed greater speed of rotation. It was first used in America in 1845. In 1856 *Lloyd's Weekly Newspaper* put in a six-feeder Hoe, which was such an obvious improvement on the Applegarth that the proprietors of *The Times* at once ordered a pair of ten-feeders, each capable of 20,000 impressions per hour. Soon, curved stereotype plates could be cast and fitted on the central cylinder, thus enabling printers to duplicate formes and run several machines at the same time.

These revolutionary developments, however, were almost entirely confined, in the first half of the nineteenth century, to London daily newspaper offices, particularly *The Times*, where speed and quantity of output were vitally important. In the provinces—where no daily newspapers were published until the fifties and printing was confined to small weeklies, or bi-weeklies in the larger towns, and jobbing—there was no necessity for these mammoth multi-cylinder machines. Provincial offices were amply served by iron hand-presses and single-cylinder machines. Many of the small shops were still using old wooden hand-presses. The scanty evidence suggests, in fact, that power-driven printing machinery had been introduced in only the larger towns, such as Manchester, Liverpool, Leeds, Edinburgh, Glasgow, and Dublin, and that, even there, it was confined to a few offices.

The advent of iron machinery and steam had brought revolutionary developments in the press department during the first half of the nineteenth century. There were no such startling changes in composition. The compositor of 1850 still had to set every *en* of type by hand and distribute used matter back into the cases as soon as they became empty. There was thus a state of disequilibrium in the industry. Several attempts had, however, been made at solving the problem of mechanical composition. The earliest was that of an American, Dr. William Church, who was granted a patent in 1822. In his composing machine, the types were first arranged into narrow boxes or 'slips', each individual slip containing a great number of types of the same letter. These were placed in the upper part of the composing machine. The machine was fitted with four rows of keys. Pressure on any of these lettered keys would actuate a release mechanism and push a type, corresponding to that key, from the appropriate slip into a curved channel, down which it would slide into a box serving the purpose of a composing-stick.

Church's invention proved a failure, but it formed the basis of later attempts at mechanical composition. There is a description in the *Compositors' Chronicle* of a similar invention in 1840 by Young and Delcambre. This machine had 'created considerable excitement in the printing profession', but its defects were numerous. Distribution, the arrangement of the type in boxes, the feeding of the machine, and justification—all these processes still had to be done by hand, so that the machine required seven or eight persons to keep it going. Composition was also imperfect, letters got into 'pie', proofs were foul, and extra reading and correction were therefore required.

The successive failures of the machine are recorded in the trade-union periodicals of the forties.[1] It was used in the metropolis during the years 1841–4 to set two weekly newspapers, the *London Phalanx* and the *Family Herald*, and also one or two books, including *The Anatomy of Sleep*. But it proved a costly failure, despite the employment of cheap boy and girl labour. Trial of the machines was not restricted to the metropolis, for we hear in February 1844 that 'at Derby, three of them have been tried for many weeks, and have been pronounced useless'. Moreover, another machine, similar in design to that of Young and

[1] *Compositors' Chronicle* and *Printer*.

Delcambre, had been invented and tried out in Hull by a Swede, Captain Rosenberg, who also invented a distributing machine. Both proved failures, however, and little more is heard of mechanical composition until the late sixties.

Thus, throughout the period up to 1850, we have to deal with hand compositors, still carrying on their trade in a fashion centuries old, steeped in craft gild traditions and comparatively undisturbed by any 'industrial revolution' of their art. In the provinces, moreover, there was as yet no differentiation between compositors and pressmen: an apprentice was taught to be a printer, to work at both case and press, whereas in the more highly developed metropolitan trade specialization developed and compositors, pressmen, and machinemen became distinct, each with their own trade society.

The application of iron and steam to the printing press and attempts at mechanical composition were not the only developments in the industry during this period. The invention of the paper-making machine by the Frenchman, Louis Robert, in 1799, improved and successfully developed in England by the brothers Fourdrinier after 1803, was of great importance in providing cheaper and more plentiful supplies of paper. The discovery of chlorine bleaching by another Frenchman, Berthollet, in 1785, reduced the time required for bleaching from about six months to a few days. Accompanying these inventions were others in the printing industry itself. Stereotyping, by Lord Stanhope's plaster-of-Paris method, was developed after about 1800, and by the Kronheim 'flong' or papier-mâché method in the 1840's. Lithographic printing was discovered in 1798 by the Bavarian, Senefelder, who came to England in 1801 to obtain a patent and develop the process. Anastatic printing was introduced in the 1840's, together with 'galvanic engraving' or electrotyping. None of the new processes, however, came into anything like extensive use before 1850. Descriptions of them are to be found in the *Compositors' Chronicle* and *Printer* but the typographical societies made no apparent effort to absorb the new elements, which gradually developed their own trade organizations.

The Census Abstracts of 1831, 1841, and 1851 give a good picture of the printing industry's structure in the first half of the nineteenth century. They show that the number of printers over twenty years of age in the United Kingdom rose from just over 9,000 (London 4,000) in 1831 to nearly 20,000 (London 8,000) in 1851.[1] The industry was

---

[1] These figures include, apparently, all persons employed in the printing trade. There was no occupational sub-classification of 'printers'.

obviously expanding rapidly. Moreover, although it was still concentrated mainly in London and, to a lesser degree, in a few large provincial towns, offices were scattered over the whole country: nearly every small town had its printing office, turning out a local paper in addition to jobbing work. The average printing office, however, was a very small affair. The 1851 Census Abstract shows that the great majority of master printers employed from one to six men, though a fair number had ten, twenty, or even fifty, and a few large firms, mostly in London, as many as a hundred, or even two hundred.

Trade unions in the provincial printing industry dealt, then, not with a massed proletariat of factory workers, but with small handfuls of men in innumerable offices in different towns scattered all over the United Kingdom. From this fact arose many of their chief characteristics—their tramp-relief system, the strength of their local customs, the variations in local wage rates, hours, and apprentice regulations, and the amazing number of their petty strikes. Hence, also, arose such constitutional problems as the choice and location of a central Executive, legislation by Delegate Meeting, and the harmonization of branch independence with Association laws and government. It says much for their organizing ability that, in this period, they succeeded in establishing a 'National Typographical Association', which for four years extended over the whole United Kingdom.

A few great cities, however, with their sprinkling of large capitalist employers and concentration of journeymen wage-earners, formed the backbone of typographical trade unionism. Local societies existed, indeed, in many small towns, but generally speaking it was in the less industrialized areas, in the scores of country towns, that trade unionism was weakest, wages were low, and apprentices multiplied.

We have seen that, as early as the sixteenth century, a class of lifelong journeymen existed and that it was among such permanent wage-earners that trade unionism developed. But printing still remained, to a great extent, a skilled handicraft, carried on with small capital, in which a thrifty and industrious workman could 'set up for himself'. The trade was expanding rapidly and there were numerous opportunities for enterprising journeymen. Many reputable firms of the present day trace their origin to small beginnings in the first half of the nineteenth century. But it was only by cutting prices and employing apprentices that the majority of small masters were able to compete with larger, wealthier, and more efficient firms.

The trade unions, therefore, constantly denounced the under-cutting, over-working, apprentice-taking small masters, who had risen from the journeymen's ranks. These small 'unfair' offices were perhaps the greatest obstacle to trade unionism in the nineteenth century. They were extremely difficult to 'organize', being so numerous and often in out-of-the-way places. Moreover, the union was weakened by the ease with which journeymen could become masters. Many of the most enterprising members, including numerous branch secretaries and Executive members, left the ranks and, on becoming masters, frequently forgot their trade-union principles and became the worst employers and the bitterest opponents of their erstwhile brethren.

The industry had, however, long possessed a body of permanent wage-earners. Most journeymen did not have the requisite enterprise or thrift to start 'on their own'. Those who did had a hard struggle in the fierce competition of the time. Most small masters lived a hand-to-mouth existence and many failed. Journeymen were, in fact, better off as wage-earners than as precarious small masters—being amongst the best-paid of industrial operatives. Wages were highest in London, where, after 1810, the established rate for book-work and jobbing was 36s. per week, while daily news hands earned as much as from £2. 8s. to £3. 18s. per week. Printers in provincial towns nowhere received such high rates as were paid in London. There was also considerable variation from town to town, wages being highest in the large cities, lowest in the country towns. In Manchester the 'stab wages were 30s. per week, in Sheffield 28s., Cambridge 27s., Leeds 26s., York 24s., while in many smaller towns they were as low as 20s., or even less, particularly in Ireland. On piece-work much higher wages were often received.

Most of these wage rates were the result of advances won during the Revolutionary and Napoleonic Wars. Few attempts were made in the period 1815–50 to raise them. Effort was concentrated on maintaining them, for many employers considered that they should be reduced, in view of the fall in the cost of living. The situation in the printing trade confirms Professor Clapham's general statement on wage rates in this period:

A great wartime rise; a post-war fall, less than the rise, often very much less; then comparative stability, is the general formula for the years 1790–1850. . . . The war rise . . . had not been so great as the rise in the cost of living between 1790 and 1810–15; but its approximate maintenance left the skilled tradesmen relatively well off in such periods of cheap food as 1832–6, 1842–6, and, above all, in 1848–50.

But 'for the bad years, [1826–7], 1838–41, and 1847, the picture is different'.[1]

The printing industry suffered severely from these periodic trade depressions, which brought widespread unemployment and distress. The root causes of depression, naturally, were not always clearly perceived and trade-union reports and periodicals contain long, bitter, and indiscriminate denunciations of grasping master printers, the evils of competition, apprentice labour, 'rats', the land-owning legislature, and the Corn Laws, as well as of such innovations as machinery, stereotyping, and the 'condensed' mode of printing. These factors did, no doubt, contribute to distress. Some printers, however, well-educated, sensible men, with a good knowledge of current economics, were not without insight into more deep-seated causes. There is almost no trace among typographical societies of the blind rage and violence which characterized the lower grades of labour, the handloom weavers, the frame-work knitters, and the Chartist 'physical force' men, in periods of social distress. Printers tended to more practical measures, to apprentice restriction, exclusion of 'foreigners', curtailment of hours and overtime, agitation against the newspaper stamp, paper, and advertisement duties, tramp relief and unemployment funds, schemes of co-operative production, and assisted emigration.

But although printers often saw the causes of their distress and attempted to relieve it, great hardship was inevitable in periods of trade depression. There were also sharp fluctuations in the printing industry even during years of general prosperity. The wage rates given above are apt, therefore, to present a misleading picture, when a large proportion of the trade was often out of work for long periods in each year. It was stated in the *Typographical Gazette* of May 1846 that 'more than half the journeymen are unemployed during a portion of the year', and trade-union statistics invariably show between one-third and one-fifth of the members as out of work or casuals. Average wages, therefore, were a good deal lower than the established rates, sometimes as low as 10s. or 15s. per week, taking the whole year round.

Even so, however, printers were better paid than most other workmen. They belonged, in fact, to the upper ranks of the working classes and were very conscious of the fact. We constantly find them referring to members as the 'gentlemen' of such-and-such an office and to the printing trade as their 'profession', a profession which, they considered,

[1] Clapham, J. H., *An Economic History of Modern Britain* (1930), vol. i, pp. 548–9.

was 'worthy of being ranked as the aristocracy of the working classes'.[1] The *Compositors' Chronicle* stated that one of its aims was to 'maintain the claims of the profession to that rank among the industrious classes of Britain to which it is entitled, from its intellectual character and superior usefulness'.

In a changing world, printers were fond of looking back on 'the good old days'. There are several references to 'the boasted privilege to which we lay claim, of having the honour of wearing a sword and cocked hat'. Printers belonged, apparently, to 'a profession whose members are "gentlemen" by act of Parliament, and are privileged to wear their swords when attending the levees at the Castle'. These pretensions were wearing a bit thin in the first half of the nineteenth century, but it was still felt by some that printing was a 'genteel' trade. Compositors were particularly conscious of the intellectual character of their profession, in an age when a third of the men and half the women could not even sign their names in the marriage register.

Printers' trade societies thus retained, throughout the first half of the nineteenth century, a good deal of the aristocratic spirit and exclusiveness of the eighteenth. 'The customary enforcement of the apprenticeship regulations prescribed by the Elizabethan Statute, and the high premiums long maintained a virtual monopoly of the better paid handicrafts in the hands of an almost hereditary caste of "tradesmen" in whose ranks the employers themselves had, for the most part, served their apprenticeship.'[2]

This monopoly, however, had begun to break down even in the eighteenth century, as control by the State and Stationers' Company decayed, as the industry expanded and competition grew, as the old apprenticeship regulations broke down and more boys were brought in to meet the demand for labour. Efforts at apprentice-restriction by the trade societies were doomed to failure: it was impossible to prevent the rapid expansion of the industry and the Census figures show that from 1831 to 1851 the number of printers in the United Kingdom more than doubled. Thus, in spite of trade-union efforts, the labour force was constantly diluted, which inevitably tended to break down the old exclusive and aristocratic attitude.

Printers, moreover, found themselves increasingly faced with the same threats from capitalism, competition, and mechanical innovations as other industrial wage-earners. For these various reasons, there is

---

[1] *Typographical Gazette*, No. 3, June 1846.
[2] Webb, S. and B., op. cit., p. 45.

visible amongst them a growing solidarity with other sections of the working class. There exists still an aloofness which prevents them taking part in the revolutionary unionism of the early 1830's, in the Chartist Movement, or in the National Association of United Trades in the forties. But they definitely felt themselves one with the long-suffering labouring class, and made numerous subscriptions to other societies or trades who were suffering from oppression.

III

THE DEVELOPMENT OF TRADE UNIONISM IN THE PROVINCIAL PRINTING INDUSTRY UP TO 1830

THE expansion of the printing industry in the second half of the eighteenth century and the breakdown of State and gild regulations brought a threat to the journeymen's customary standard of life. Hitherto, wage rates and apprenticeship regulations had been enforced by Statute or by the Stationers' Company; there was even an authoritarian control over details of manufacture and working conditions. Now the journeymen were left unprotected, at a critical period in the industry. It is true that there had long been a body of permanent journeymen, excluded by the gild oligarchy from participation in the government of the Company; that there had been complaints against this exclusiveness, against 'small wages' and the increase of apprentices as early as the sixteenth century, complaints which had been echoed right down to the present period; and that there had long been a tendency towards separate organization by the journeymen. But it was not, apparently, until the Industrial Revolution, with the accompanying expansion of the printing industry, growth of competition, and rapid influx of apprentices, that the journeymen began to form their own organizations. Another factor, which figures prominently in the trade documents of the period, was the sharp rise in the cost of living during the Revolutionary and Napoleonic Wars.

The earliest information we possess of trade unionism among printers comes from London. It appears that 'there is no evidence pointing to the existence of a London compositors' trade union until the end of the eighteenth century'.[1] But from 1785, at least, the journeymen formed an organization, though probably not continuous, to secure wage advances, regulate working hours, and enforce the customary apprenticeship regulations. Agitation on these questions went on throughout the war years, 1793–1815, and has left a considerable amount of documentary evidence.

There is no such detailed information with regard to early unionism among provincial printers, but it is clear that during the war years

[1] Howe, E., and Waite, H. E., *The London Society of Compositors* (1948), p. 26.

journeymen in the larger provincial towns were imitating their metropolitan brethren in establishing trade societies for mutual protection and to secure increased wages. The rise in the cost of living and the other factors which led to the establishment of the London Society had similar effects in the provinces, where, moreover, the journeymen frequently justified their demands by reference to the London advances. When, for example, the Edinburgh compositors memorialized their employers for an advance in 1803, they pointed out that wage increases had already been granted to the London men 'in consequence of the continual variations in the price of provisions and the rate of living'. Similarly, when the journeymen printers of Manchester memorialized their employers for increased wages in 1810, they pointed out 'that a material advance has taken place, for some time, in London, Dublin, Liverpool, Bristol, and other leading towns throughout the United Kingdom'. They requested an increase which would give 'stab hands 35s. per week, with overtime payment of 7d. per hour; compositors on piece-work, 6d. per 1,000 ens; and pressmen, 6½d. per hour. These demands, however, must have been either refused or modified, or there were post-war reductions, for in 1825 the Manchester Society had not yet established a regular piece-scale, while the 'stab wages of the town were only 30s. per week. This was not, apparently, the first time the Manchester men had taken such action, for they pointed out 'that there is no instance on record of the Master Printers giving to the Journeymen a rise unsolicited', having, it would seem, had to ask for advances in the past.

There was, quite definitely, a printers' trade society in Manchester at this time. The earliest rule book extant in 1897, dated 1825, bore on its title-page the words 'Instituted November, 1797',[1] and in the *Compositors' Chronicle* for March 1843 there is a letter from R. Roberts, one of the actual founders of the Manchester Society and for many years its secretary, stating that it 'was established in the year 1797, for the protection of journeymen's rights'. The Manchester Society was one of the earliest, if not the earliest, of provincial typographical societies. It was the oldest society in the Northern Union (established 1830), older, that is, than those in Liverpool, Leeds, Sheffield, and the other forty-odd branches.

The Minutes and Half Yearly Reports of the Manchester Society are almost the sole source of information for the early development of

[1] Dickson, J. J., *Manchester Typographical Society Centenary: A Souvenir* (Manchester, 1897).

trade unionism in the provincial printing industry; but, unfortunately, there are none of these in existence prior to 1825. Two resolutions, passed in 1826 and 1827 respectively, provide evidence as to the number of societies then in existence. The first was, 'that . . . the allowance to Tramps with tickets from old established societies, be four, instead of five shillings; and those from minor Societies, such as Preston, Wigan, Warrington, Bolton, Rochdale, Blackburn, Macclesfield, and Hanley, to receive 2/6d.' The second laid down 'that hereafter, the Allowances to Tramps with Tickets from the undermentioned places shall be as follows: Those from Dublin, Glasgow, Liverpool, Leeds, Sheffield and Bristol [doubtless the 'old established societies' of the first resolution] to receive 4s. Those with Tickets from every other part of the United Kingdom, 2/6d.'

It is clear that by 1826 'old established' typographical societies existed in nearly all the chief cities of the United Kingdom and that even in the smaller towns, particularly in Lancashire, journeymen printers were organized. These societies, moreover, were linked together by a tramp-relief system. 'Tickets' or 'tramp cards' were given to unemployed or strike members who desired to leave town in search of employment. It was also customary to give such members 'travelling money' or 'relief allowed upon leaving town', which they had to refund in the event of their returning within a certain specified period. In Manchester, this travelling allowance varied in the early years, but was fixed in 1839 at 10s. for a single and 15s. for a married man. No relief, other than purely voluntary assistance, was given to a member's wife and family while he was 'on the road'.

On arrival in another society town, travellers presented their cards to the local secretary, who would give them 'tramp allowance'—enough for bed and breakfast in the 'society house'. Assistance to secure employment was also given, while tramps were warned against entry into any 'unfair' offices. If the tramp found work he had to return the allowance given him, but if no employment was to be had he moved on to the next town, since he could secure relief only once in each town within twelve months, all payments being entered on his card. After this period had elapsed his card had to be renewed, often at a lower rate of relief.

Tramp relief was confined to 'fair' trade society members. Discrimination in Manchester between the amount paid to tramps from large cities and those from 'minor societies' was due to the fact that the latter could afford to give only a very small allowance and their tramps, consequently, were not paid the full rate of relief in Manchester. In some small places tramps received as little as 9d. or 1s.

This tramp-relief system obviously forged links between the various societies. Many journeymen printers, at some time in their life, took to the road—sometimes of necessity, sometimes to widen their experience—and thus became familiar with men and customs in other towns. The system also gave rise to correspondence with regard to cards and admission of members. The former were apt to be forged, to have dates and names altered or payments erased, and it was often necessary to write to other towns to check their authenticity. Moreover, tramps often went into 'unfair' houses or were otherwise suspect and it was necessary to warn other societies and to check up on tramps before their admission. Warnings of strikes were also sent to other towns, in order to secure the co-operation of their members, and mutual assistance was often given in periods of trade depression. This co-operation between individual societies was to lead to the formation of the Northern Union (1830) and the National Typographical Association (1844).

The Manchester Minutes provide a clear picture of the principles and functioning of an individual typographical society in this period. It may be more than a coincidence that the earliest Minutes extant date from July 1825, just after the repeal of the Combination Laws: the Society may possibly have kept no Minutes prior to that date and conducted its affairs on somewhat underground lines. In that year, however, it springs full-grown into view, with its Committee of Management, its monthly, quarterly, and special General Meetings, its President, Secretary, and Treasurer, as well as minor officers, such as Beer Stewards and Door-keepers. These officials, together with the Committee, were elected every quarter. There was, however, no great scrambling for office, which involved arduous and poorly paid duties.[1] Members often refused, in fact, to accept office and were fined in consequence. It proved so difficult to get volunteers for election to the Committee that a resolution had to be passed in 1826 that all members should 'serve on the Committee, in rotation', on pain of being fined sixpence. This system proved so distasteful, however, that the Society eventually reverted to the elective system.

Obviously, there must have been a great deal of apathy among members of the Society, or at least an unwillingness to participate actively in trade affairs. Voting figures show that rarely more than one-fifth, and often as few as one-tenth, of the members attended monthly

[1] In 1832 the Secretary received £2 and the Treasurer 16s. annually.

meetings. The constant arrears of subscriptions tell a similar story of indifference. We find certain men, of undoubted zeal and ability, continually elected to office and becoming almost permanent officials. Robert Roberts, for example, was secretary of the Manchester Society from 1825 at least, perhaps from the establishment of the Society in 1797, until 1834.

These men performed their amateur, part-time duties in the evenings, in a public-house. The landlord would provide a room for Society meetings and reaped his profit from the beer consumed, if he was not paid a rent. The 'society house' was often changed, usually on account of 'the badness of the ale', a frequent source of complaint. Members were permitted a regular allowance of ale on monthly nights, which gave rise to one of the largest items in the Society's expenditure. There must have been a few hectic interludes at these meetings, for, in spite of rules against threatening and abusive language, fighting, and drunkenness, brawls often occurred and offending members had to be thrown out. The Minutes reflect, as a rule, considerable dignity and decorum, but it must have been difficult at times to transact Society business.

The main trade principles of the Manchester Society were enforcement of the seven years' servitude, exclusion of 'foreigners', apprentice restriction, regulation of wages and hours, and punishment of 'rats' or 'unfair' hands. The Committee adopted a very autocratic tone towards erring members, who were summoned before the Committee and ordered to correct their behaviour, or were heavily fined, or even expelled from the Society.

A rigorous control was exercised over admission to the Society. Those who had not served a full seven years' apprenticeship to letterpress printing were automatically excluded, and there are numerous instances of members being ordered to give notice unless certain 'foreigners' were dismissed, or being fined for working with men who had 'no recognised right to the trade'. All legitimate printers, however, were expected to join the Society soon after arrival in town or on completion of their apprenticeship, and those who 'held aloof' longer than three months were fined. Members were not, apparently, allowed to work with non-members, though this rule was frequently infringed.

The Society also tried to restrict the number of apprentices. In 1828, for example, numerous Committee meetings were held to consider what action should be taken against employers who were taking 'an unlimited number of Apprentices' and often employing no journeymen. Several restrictive regulations were suggested, but the time was considered unpropitious for their enforcement and no fixed rule was established until after the foundation of the Northern Union. Instead, chapels were urged to protest, 'in a respectful and suitable manner', against the introduction of extra apprentices and to point out the injurious consequences of boy labour to both employer and employed. Many masters, apparently, agreed with the journeymen, but the evil persisted, especially in the smaller offices. In 1829, therefore, it was decided that members should refuse to take employment 'in any office where no men are regularly employed, and the number of Apprentices is more than two'. During the early thirties the Society began to award monetary compensation to members refusing work in such houses, while those who went in were expelled as 'rats'.

The Society also attempted, as we have seen, to regulate wage rates.[1] Most Manchester offices were on 'stab and 'the establishment of the town' in 1825 was 30s. per week. *The Manchester Gazette*, however, was on piece-work, which was strongly condemned by the Society 'as eminently calculated to engender rancour and bad feeling amongst the workmen; to reduce the number of hands that should be employed . . . and in every sense detrimental to the interests of the profession'. The Society decided, therefore, to procure its abolition, or at least to resist its introduction into other news offices. The men on the *Gazette* refused to obey the Society and were consequently expelled, but in spite of the Society's opposition piece-work was introduced on several papers. The Society therefore attempted to regulate piece rates, deciding that 6d. per 1,000 ens should be the price for minion and 7d. for nonpareil, though it is not clear whether these rates were successfully enforced.

Steady opposition to the piece system was manifested by the Manchester Society throughout the nineteenth century, Manchester being notorious as a staunch 'stab town. A number of other towns, however, preferred piece-work to 'stab and there was a continual conflict of opinion in regard to the respective merits and demerits of the two systems.

No journeyman was admitted into the Manchester Society unless he was receiving the established wages of the town. The Society also kept a constant check on wages paid in the various offices. Those paying less than the recognized rate were condemned as 'unfair' and the men in them as 'rats'.

Hours were also subject to Society regulation. It is not clear what the working hours were in Manchester at this time, but in Leeds, according

[1] See above, p. 25.

to the local scale of 1826, the 'stab hours were 'twelve hours a day, including meal hours (that is, half an hour for breakfast, one hour dinner, and half an hour for tea). . . . All over-hours to be paid sixpence per hour.' At York, in 1836, the 'stab hours were 'from 7 to 7 o'clock, with 6d. per hour over-hours'.[1] A 12-hour working day, with 2 hours for meals, or 59 working hours per week, seems to have been the custom in most towns. Some of the larger societies were also attempting to secure a 'fixed and defined' working day, with extra payment for all overtime.

Typographical societies almost invariably adopted a moderate and conciliatory attitude towards employers in disputes and relations between masters and men were, on the whole, fairly good. In 1841, for example, the Manchester secretary spoke of 'the feeling of respect and goodwill shown towards us by our employers', due to the fact that 'in every dispute we have had with them, it has ever been our study to adopt a course of quiet, respectful, but determined conduct. Reason and justice have prevailed, where threatening and intimidation would have failed.' In the event of failure to settle a dispute by deputation and argument, the men were merely withdrawn after a fortnight's notice. The house was then 'closed' and no society man was to accept work in such an 'unfair' office, on pain of being heavily fined or even expelled.

These strikes were petty affairs, rarely involving more than one office. Employers very seldom combined against the men, owing to the barriers of competition, and the only large-scale 'turn-out' during the whole of this period was that in Edinburgh in 1847, when thirty-eight employers combined to 'lock-out' 200 men.[2] Nevertheless, these petty strikes caused considerable hardship to the few men involved and it was only fair to see that members did not suffer unduly for having made 'a sacrifice in the interest of the profession'. We therefore find in the Minutes of the Manchester Society early references to strike payments. At first these were not systematic, but it eventually became the rule to pay 30s. per week, full 'stab wages, to strike hands.

Other large societies also adopted the system of weekly strike payments, but the more usual course was to 'back' the tramp-cards of strike hands, that is, to write the circumstances of their sacrifice on the back, so that other societies would give them additional, usually double, relief in the event of their having to leave town in search of employment.

Efforts were also made by the Manchester Society to relieve its out-

---

[1] The *London Scale of Prices* (1836) provides the above information regarding Leeds and York.   [2] See below, pp. 66–67.

of-work members. Tramp relief was the normal method, but in periods of widespread unemployment it broke down and additional assistance became necessary. At first emergency funds were raised, but in 1844 a permanent relief or out-of-work fund was established, with a subscription of 3*d.* per week from fully employed members, to provide the out-of-work with 7*s.* per week.

Relief, however, was a mere palliative. What the unemployed wanted was work. The restriction of apprentices and exclusion of 'foreigners' were mainly intended to secure work for qualified journeymen. The Society also tried to prevent 'strangers' working in the town when any members were out of employment. 'Smooting' was also forbidden and the Society attempted to reduce 'systematic' overtime in order to secure work for more hands.

The Manchester Society was not a trade society alone, but a benefit society as well. In addition to unemployed relief it had established sick and burial funds, the former providing weekly payments to members off work through illness, together with 'the medicine and professional attendance of a respectable surgeon', the latter lump sums on the death of members or their wives.

These various benefits were common to most large societies. In Dublin, for example, in the 1830's, strike, unemployed, tramp, and funeral allowances were being paid. In addition, the Dublin Society had an emigration fund, the earliest of which the present writer has found trace, providing allowances of £4 for emigrants to England and £8 to America. Emigration was frequently advocated in the trade periodicals of the 1840's as a means of equating the supply of labour to the demand, but few other typographical societies seem to have actually established a fund for the purpose until the fifties.

London provided additional benefits. In 1827, for example, there was established in the metropolis a 'Printers' Pension Society' for superannuated members, while in the forties a 'Printers' Asylum' or 'Almshouse' was founded for the aged poor. Liverpool appears to have been the only other city with a printers' pension society.

Typographical societies do not appear to have suffered much from the prevailing system of repressive legislation against trade unions. George White, clerk to Hume's Committee on the Combination Laws in 1824, asserted that the Act of 1800 had 'been in general a dead letter upon those artisans upon whom it was intended to have an effect—namely, the shoemakers, printers, papermakers, shipbuilders, tailors, etc., who have had their regular societies and houses of call, as though no such Act was in existence'.[1] Our examination into the activities of printers' societies in the first quarter of the nineteenth century amply confirms his opinion as regards this particular trade. Journeymen printers in this period formed societies in practically all the large cities and in many of the lesser towns, and seem to have negotiated quite openly with their employers on matters of wages, hours, and apprentices. This was due partly, no doubt, to the tradition of such corporate action which existed among skilled handicraftsmen, and to the fact that there was, in the majority of instances, little difference of social status between masters and men, the former usually having served their apprenticeship among the journeymen and most offices being small. It was also due to the fact that 'in the skilled handicrafts . . . we find even under repressive laws, no unlawful oaths, seditious emblems or other common paraphernalia of secret societies'.[2] Journeymen printers usually adopted a 'correct' attitude of respect and moderation towards their employers. They also restricted themselves exclusively to trade matters and had no air of political or social conspiracy about them.

Nevertheless, there were a few instances of prosecution against printers' trade societies in this period, like that of the London pressmen in 1798 and of *The Times* compositors in 1810, in each case for 'conspiracy', the accused men being found guilty and imprisoned. These were the martyrs of trade unionism in the printing industry. There may possibly have been other prosecutions, which might account for the paucity of information for this period—societies being driven underground until after the repeal of the Combination Laws in 1825. But when the great increase in the number of societies and the known instances of wages negotiations are taken into consideration, it seems that, on the whole, typographical societies suffered little from the law.

[1] Webb, S. and B., op. cit., p. 77.
[2] Ibid., p. 84.

IV

TRADE UNIONISM IN THE PROVINCIAL PRINTING INDUSTRY
1830–48

The Northern Typographical Union, 1830–44

WE have seen in the previous chapter how, early in the nineteenth century, typographical societies in various towns all over the country were linked together by the tramp-relief system, how they were all actuated by certain common principles, and how they assisted each other in the event of serious dispute or distress. These connexions, this association in the pursuit of common objects, led naturally to the establishment of the Northern Typographical Union in 1830, a Union which eventually came to comprise over forty towns, mainly in the north of England, particularly in Lancashire and Yorkshire, but also extending as far south as Gloucester and Monmouth.

The movement towards 'greater unionism'—towards national unions of workers in particular trades—was general in the late twenties and early thirties of the nineteenth century, particularly among the Lancashire and Yorkshire textile and building operatives. In 1829, for example, the National Union of Cotton Spinners was established, in 1830 the Potters' Union, and in 1832 the Builders' Union. Journeymen printers shared in this movement, which, so far as their particular trade is concerned, began in the early months of 1830 and centred in Lancashire.[1] It 'arose from the inadequacy of the isolated efforts of single societies . . . to stem the continued encroachments of employers and to prevent the reduction of wages'. There was at that time 'no limitation to the number of apprentices, and men were working for whatever remuneration they could obtain'. Robert Roberts, therefore, and other leading members of the Manchester Society, 'seeing the necessity of union', decided to communicate with other societies 'in Lancashire and its neighbourhood' with regard to a meeting. Favourable replies were received from Liverpool, Preston, Sheffield, and one or two other towns and a meeting was therefore held in Manchester on

[1] This account of the origin of the Northern Union is drawn from the Manchester T.S. Minutes, the *Compositors' Chronicle*, No. 12, Aug. 1841, and No. 32, Mar. 1843, the *Typographical Gazette*, No. 1, April 1846, and the *Typographical Circular*, Feb. 1877.

D

13 September 1830, attended by seven representatives, who drew up rules for the establishment of a Northern Typographical Union.

The Northern Union, then, started in a small way, with a mere handful of societies. Little more than an agreement on general principles would seem to have been reached in 1830, for it was not until late in the next year, at a second Delegate Meeting in Manchester, that the Union received a financial basis. It was then decided that each member should contribute sixpence 'towards defraying the expenses incurred during the past year by the Northern Typographical Union' and that, in future, a regular subscription of twopence per member per month should be paid into the central fund of the Union.[1] It seems to have taken two or three years to get the Union firmly on its feet, years in which the Manchester Society and its veteran secretary, Robert Roberts, played a leading part. The Union's headquarters, however, were in Liverpool, where the Committee of Management and the General Secretary, John Backhouse, remained until late in 1844, when the Northern Union was merged into the National Typographical Association.

The Union survived the first few critical years and, as trade and trade unionism boomed in the years 1832–6, its membership grew. By 1834 it had thirty-six branches and 628 members, by 1837 forty-three branches and 783 members.[2] During the next seven years, however, years of trade depression, when unemployment figures rose and many national unions collapsed, provincial printers had a hard struggle to maintain their organization. The cost of tramp relief rose rapidly, strikes became more frequent, and expenditure began to exceed income. Subscriptions had to be increased and levies imposed, yet deficits continued. Many members deserted the Union or refused to pay their subscriptions, while others 'ratted' and a number of the smaller societies collapsed. Nevertheless, the Union kept its head above water and even

---

[1] Members had to pay much higher *local* subscriptions, e.g. in Manchester, 1s. 6d. per month.

[2] N.U. Half-Yearly Reports. By the early forties the Union included the following towns: Birmingham, Blackburn, Bolton, Bradford, Cardiff, Cheltenham, Chester, Chesterfield, Derby, Doncaster, Durham, Gloucester, Halifax, Hereford, Huddersfield, Hull, Isle of Man, Kendal, Kidderminster, Kirkby Lonsdale, Lancaster, Leamington, Leeds, Leicester, Liverpool, Macclesfield, Manchester, Merthyr Tydfil, Monmouth, Newcastle-under-Lyme, Northampton, Nottingham, Potteries, Preston, Sheffield, Shrewsbury, South Shields, Stafford, Sunderland, Wakefield, Warwick, Wigan, Wolverhampton, Worcester, and York. In addition small towns were often included in the jurisdiction of larger ones, e.g. Rochdale and Stockport in that of Manchester.

increased its membership slightly. The following figures illustrate its progress up to 1840:

Date	Branches	Members	Income			Expenditure			Strike allowance		
			£	s.	d.	£	s.	d.	£	s.	d.
1834	36	628	64	7	2	42	3	2	22	10	0
1837	43	783	104	15	6	62	10	8	13	3	0
1838	40	893	144	6	2½	82	15	2	42	7	6
1839	42	942	131	10	6	225	10	2	120	19	6
1840	44	984	200	14	6	209	19	3	110	1	3

It is difficult to estimate accurately what proportion of provincial journeymen printers joined the Northern Union. Its operations were restricted to the English provinces, particularly the north. Scotland and Ireland established their own unions in 1836—the Scottish Typographical Association and the Irish Typographical Union—on principles very similar to those of the Northern Union. London also remained independent. The Union did not, moreover, include all English provincial societies. The *Printer* estimated in June 1844 that, apart from the four big typographical unions (the Northern Union, London Union of Compositors, Scottish Association, and Irish Union), there were about twenty 'recognized societies', while the London 'Report on the National Typographical Association' of September 1844 stated that these 'independent or unconnected societies' numbered twenty-six.

According to statistics laid before the Northern Union Delegate Meeting of 1842, there were at that time 978 members and 248 'non-society men' in towns connected with the Union. Thus it is clear that at least one-quarter to one-third of journeymen printers in Northern Union branches were non-members. There were, in fact, scores of 'unfair' houses in these towns: it was stated in 1844 that 'in only fourteen towns in the Northern Union, there are no less than fifty-three prohibited or unfair houses'. Even in 'fair' houses, moreover, non-unionists were frequently employed. Furthermore, in a great many English provincial towns the Northern Union had no branches. It is doubtful, therefore, whether the Union included a half of provincial compositors.

We will now examine the Northern Union's structure, policy, and achievements under the following heads: (1) Government. (2) Regulation of hours and wages. (3) Apprentice restriction. (4) Attitude towards machinery. (5) Strikes. (6) Tramp relief.

(1) *Government of the Northern Union*

The Northern Union was presented with the problem of combining central control with local autonomy. Although local societies were prepared to surrender a certain amount of sovereignty, in order to secure general co-operation in apprentice restriction and maintenance of wage rates, with the backing of a central fund, they still preserved a strong spirit of independence in local affairs. It was a continual difficulty, therefore, to decide what were local matters and what the concern of the central government.

Typographical societies had always recognized the democratic principle that all members had equal rights, that all should have an equal voice in society affairs, that 'what concerned all should be decided by all'. This principle found practical expression in rule by general meeting. But it was obviously impossible to frame laws for the scattered branches of a federal union by general meeting of the trade. Resort was therefore had to Delegate Meetings. Initiative, however, still remained with the individual members and branches: any member could put forward proposals, which were discussed at special branch meetings and, if adopted, placed on the Delegate Meeting agenda. Delegates were also instructed how to vote: branch members merely delegated their collective voice to an elected representative.

The Northern Union had been established by a Delegate Meeting in 1830. Another was held in 1831, but the next was not until 1836. A gap of four years also followed before the next in 1840, but it was then decided 'that a meeting of delegates take place not later than once in two years'. In accordance with this rule, Delegate Meetings were held in 1842 and 1844. Such an assembly held supreme legislative power.

It was necessary, however, to have some central body to administer the rules established by Delegate Meeting, to receive Union subscriptions and dispense the funds, to investigate disputes and award strike pay, to report 'closed' houses and 'rats', and exercise a general supervision over tramp relief. This executive power was placed in the hands of a 'governing branch', chosen by Delegate Meeting. The Union could not support the expense of a representative central committee, which would, moreover, at a time when the first railways were only just being built, have been very difficult to convene and slow to act. Liverpool was the governing branch of the Northern Union throughout the period 1830–44. The central executive consisted of a General Secretary, Treasurer, and Committee of Management, composed of nine members.

The Secretary was chosen by Delegate Meeting, the Treasurer and Committee elected annually 'by the society where the Secretary resides'. The Union, like the local societies, did not possess a staff of professional officials. Even the General Secretary was an amateur, a working journeyman and part-time official, who received only £26 per annum in 1840 and probably a good deal less in earlier years. He was distinct, however, from the local secretary, though it is probable that the local treasurer and committee were also Treasurer and Committee of the Union. The Union officials, like those in the branches, were more or less permanent, or at least continuously elected to office: John Backhouse was Secretary for the whole fourteen years of the Union's existence. The same names also recur on the Committee.

The Union subscription was, as we have seen, 2d. per member per month in the early years, but was later increased to 3d. and finally, in 1840, to 4d. per month. The Executive were also empowered in 1842 to impose levies in case of emergency.

In spite of Delegate Meetings, Committee of Management, Union rules and subscriptions, local societies still to a great extent managed their own affairs. They made their own local rules, had their own officials, committee, and general meetings, decided their own rates of subscription and tramp relief, administered their own unemployment, sick, and burial funds, and, in the larger towns, made their own strike payments. Railways and the penny post undoubtedly aided centralized organization, but in a Union composed of scattered towns and myriads of small offices a considerable degree of local autonomy was inevitable. Moreover, as we have seen, there was not as yet the financial basis or experience for a professional central administration.

Local independence, however, made it difficult to secure united action and obedience to the decisions of the Union Committee and Delegate Meetings. The larger branches, particularly Manchester, strongly objected to any interference in what they considered to be local affairs. The Union possessed certain general regulations regarding wages, hours, and apprentices, and had also a central fund for strike payments, but the powers of the Executive Committee were very limited, amounting to little more than general supervision over trade affairs. The Union was, in many ways, little more than a tramping society. The *Printer* stated, in fact, in 1844, that the Northern Union was such 'only in name', comprising 'some thirty or forty societies united together without any general principles or laws for their government, but each society acting as it thinks best. Even on those points in

which they profess to be guided by the committee of management, some of the larger societies claim to act independently of such authority.'

The 'chapel', of course, with its 'father' and 'clerk' and its workshop rules, still remained the basic cell of typographical trade unionism.

(2) *Regulation of Hours and Wages*

We have already seen individual societies trying to regulate the hours of labour. These isolated attempts do not appear to have been very successful, 'many employers requiring their men to work an indefinite number of hours without any remuneration whatever beyond their regular wages'. The Northern Union Delegate Meeting of 1836 therefore decided to establish a general rule 'that fifty-nine hours' labour per week be the standard for the members of the Union; and if employed on the Sunday, the mode of charge to be the same as the London scale; and if required to work after ten o'clock in the evening, or before five in the morning, one shilling extra to be charged; and if required to labour a greater number of hours than fifty-nine, sixpence per hour for such overtime shall be charged'. Thus the Union attempted to establish a standard working *week*, with overtime payment for all hours over 59. There was also a suggestion, in the 'night shilling', of a 'normal' working *day*, with extra payment for all time worked before or after defined daily hours.

There seem to have been relatively few differences between masters and men with regard to hours of labour in this period, though it is evident that abuses did exist. There is an interesting article in the *Typographical Gazette* (August 1846) on 'Hours of labour in the printing profession', from which it appears that the hours of piece hands were almost completely unregulated, fluctuating 'according to the briskness or depression of business', and that the defined hours of 'stab hands were merely 'nominal', as many as 20 or 30 hours often being worked at a stretch, particularly on the publication nights of weekly newspapers or to complete rush orders in jobbing offices. The writer maintained that 'long hours, night labour, and, too often, ill-ventilated work rooms' caused ill health and premature debility among printers, a statement confirmed by later medical evidence.

For this reason and also to secure work for unemployed hands, many unionists sought to restrict the amount of overtime worked. It was proposed at the Delegate Meeting of 1842 'that a strict inquiry should be instituted into . . . working out of time, as many are known to work from three to four, and some even five to six hours' overtime per day, whilst numbers of unemployed men are walking the streets'. But the meeting considered that it was 'quite impossible' to curtail or abolish overtime. 'Doubtless it was desirable to equalise employment, but it was not practicable', owing to fluctuations in the printing trade.

By 1830, when the Northern Union was established, a number of individual societies had secured 'established' wages and piece-work scales, but there was extraordinary variation from town to town. It was not until the Delegate Meeting of 1836 that an attempt was made not only to secure a definite minimum rate in each town, but also to reduce the existing variation to a certain uniformity. The Committee of Management was then instructed 'to divide the Northern Union into four districts for piece and establishment work' and try to secure uniform wage rates for each. The attempt, however, proved a complete failure; in fact the Committee never seriously persisted in it. In their Sixth Annual Report (December 1836) they pointed out the 'almost inter-minable correspondence' that would be required and that the Union funds could not stand the strain of the inevitable wage disputes, in which they would almost certainly be defeated owing to the large numbers of tramps and 'rats'. The idea of wages districts, they con-sidered, was 'premature'. They would 'attempt no more at present than to assist the societies in those towns in which wages are much too low, to raise them to a reasonable rate'.

The four districts still existed at the end of 1840, but had proved 'entirely useless'. The Union continued, however, its attempt to secure 'established' wage rates in each town. In estimating the degree of suc-cess or failure attending its efforts, we are faced by conflicting evidence. In 1841 Robert Roberts, of Manchester, maintained that, since the forma-tion of the Northern Union, 'we have been enabled to receive a pretty adequate remuneration for our labour'. The General Secretary of the Northern Union also stated at the end of 1840 that 'within the last three or four years . . . an increase has been obtained in the rate of wages'. It was further pointed out, in 1842, 'that in those towns where union prevails, and men are associated in defence of their labour—there and there alone is the rate of wages such as will procure a decent mainten-ance; whilst in every other part, where no associations exist, printers have but a beggarly allowance, varying from £1 to 12s., and some few instances might be found where men do not receive more than 1s. or 1s. 6d. per day'.

Numerous instances could be quoted from the trade periodicals of the forties in support of this statement. There is no doubt that the

minimum 'stab rates and piece-scales of the various towns were established as a result of agitation by the trade societies, which acted as a
bulwark against wage reductions and succeeded, on the whole, in maintaining 'war-time' rates during the years 1815–50 and even, here and
there, securing small increases. There is no doubt, also, that wages
were highest in the large industrial cities, where unionism was strong, and
lowest in the country towns, where it was weak or non-existent. But
there is also good ground for believing that printers' wage rates owed
as much to 'natural' economic forces as to trade-union action. Composition was a skilled art, requiring reasonably educated and intelligent
workmen, of whom there was a limited supply in the first half of the
nineteenth century, but for whom there was an increasing demand,
owing to the expansion of the industry. The variation in wage rates
between the large cities and small towns was largely due to variation in
the cost of living. The quantity and pressure of work were also less in
small country towns and usually of a kind requiring less skill. Neither
the Northern Union nor any succeeding typographical association, down
to the present day, has ever been able to establish a uniform standard
of wages for the whole country. Moreover, the 'established' wage rates
of the Northern Union were not paid in hundreds of non-society houses,
while cheap apprentice labour was everywhere rife.

There was a good deal of controversy in this period over the relative
merits of the establishment, or 'stab, and piece-work systems. A few
societies in the Northern Union had piece-work scales, but most provincial towns were on the 'stab system. 'The "piece" is confined to the
metropolis and a few other large towns', it was stated in 1846, 'while
country offices but rarely adopt the system.' Both 'stab and piece came
in for considerable criticism. The chief objection against the 'stab
system, the payment of standard weekly wages, was that it placed
the idle, incompetent journeyman on a level with the skilful and
conscientious—that it was unfair both to superior workmen and to
employers, since it required 'equal remuneration for all', regardless of
ability or effort. The piece system, on the other hand, its advocates
pointed out, gave 'remuneration according to the amount of work
actually performed. . . . Each man is paid the amount he earns, and
every grade of ability or skill has its full reward.' Under the 'stab system
employers tended to 'weed out' indifferent workmen and impose
'task-work', to secure the maximum output for the minimum wages.
Less skilful workmen, therefore, were often unemployed and either
became a burden on the Union funds or went into 'unfair' houses at less

than the established wages. High 'stab rates, in fact, caused many employers to make their offices non-society and to employ cheap apprentice labour.

That many master printers were opposed to minimum 'stab rates is clear from the evidence given before the Select Committee on Combinations in 1838. While prepared to pay good wages to competent workmen, they strongly objected to 'the same rate of wages for all', preferring to pay a man 'what he was worth'.

To these objections the Northern Union gave the following answer: 'First, that we do not seek to force any man on an employer, and, consequently, if the employer be not satisfied, he has always his remedy by discharging the individual, or placing him upon piece-work; and, secondly, that we do not insist upon a maximum, but a minimum standard: we do not say an employer shall not give more than a certain sum, but that he shall not give less.' There is, undoubtedly, much to be said for establishing a reasonable minimum standard of living, which has always been the aim of all trade unions. Unfortunately this minimum tends to become a maximum: employers refuse to pay more than the established rates and workmen are jealous of any of their fellows who get more than they do. Moreover, the fact that an employer can discharge an incompetent workman leaves unions with the problem of such 'rejects', who are unable to get work at established wages and therefore tend to enter 'unfair' houses at lower rates.

Disputes, however, were just as frequent over piece prices as over 'stab wages, and there were endless differences in regard to the innumerable 'extras' for difficult matter and as to what was the 'property' of house or piece hands. There were also petty jealousies and bickerings among the men about division of the 'fat'. Piece hands suffered from the system of 'mixed' offices, in which both 'stab and piece hands were employed, the former getting most of the 'fat'; or, alternatively, hands might be switched from piece to 'stab, or vice versa, according to the class of work, whether 'fat' or 'lean'.[1] The 'stab system had the great merit of being uniform and simple and much less liable to produce friction and disputes. The hours of piece hands, moreover, were often undefined and there was a great deal of 'standing for copy'. There was also a tendency on piece-work for quality to be sacrificed to quantity and for the men to produce 'scamped' work. Piece-work tended to make men greedy for high pay packets and thus to work at high speed

---

[1] To prevent this, the Northern Union established a rule that a fortnight's notice of such changes must be given.

and all hours, regardless of the fact that they were putting others out of a job. It was far more likely, in fact, to create unemployment than the 'stab system.

(3) *Apprentice Restriction*

The 'apprentice problem' was one of the greatest facing the Northern Union. Many employers exploited cheap apprentice labour: it was not at all unusual to find offices with as many as half a dozen or more apprentices and only two or three journeymen; in many there were no journeymen at all, merely the master and a few apprentices. Moreover, many men working as journeymen printers had never 'served their time' to the trade, or had not been properly bound apprentices, or had served less than seven years.

To oppose these evils the Northern Union tried to limit the number of apprentices in each office, to enforce a seven years' servitude and legal binding, and to exclude 'foreigners'.

The Manchester Society, which had previously been unable to establish a fixed rule for the limitation of apprentices, decided in 1834 'that . . . no Office in this town shall be deemed fair, where there are a greater number of Apprentices than two, unless in those Offices where they are in the habit of employing four Journeymen regularly, when the number of Apprentices may be increased to three, but on no account to have more. Where more are now bound, the introduction of others shall be resisted till the number be brought to the prescribed limits.' This resolution was adopted by the Northern Union Delegate Meeting of 1836. Its restrictions were to be applied in all towns belonging to the Union. Hitherto, few, if any, societies had succeeded in their isolated efforts at apprentice limitation. It was now hoped that associated strength and the Union fund would secure the enforcement of a general rule.

The policy of apprentice restriction was justified in an 'Address to the Printers of Wales' in 1841. This 'Address' pointed out that 'there are at present a vast number of printers more than the wants of the community require; the consequence of which is, that many have but partial, and many more no employment'. This 'superabundance of hands' also resulted in lowered wage rates, 'ratting', and other evils. 'Self-preservation' was therefore the motive and justification of their restrictive policy. But restriction was also for the good of the apprentices themselves, who, in the present state of the trade, were likely to find themselves, at the expiration of their seven years' servitude, thrown badly trained into an overstocked market. The Union also pointed out to employers that journeymen 'execute more work in a given space of time, damage much less type, and cause the employer less expense and trouble' than apprentices, that boy labour tended to produce incompetent workmen, and that it was but a cheap form of competition, which 'honourable' employers should assist the journeymen to stamp out. Similar arguments could be multiplied, for apprentice restriction was an endless topic throughout this period.

The Union placed equal emphasis on the seven years' servitude: no one was to be admitted unless he could produce a legal indenture. Strikes often occurred against the employment of 'foreigners' or 'illegal men'. The Union also tried to deal with the problem of 'runaway apprentices' or 'turnovers'. Apprentices became fairly proficient after two or three years' training and many, instead of serving out their time on a small pittance, preferred to 'run away' to another master, where they could earn higher wages. They would 'traverse the trade in search of the most profitable employment' and might, in a few years, change masters half a dozen times. In each case there was no legal 'turnover' from one master to the next and the runaways were not, therefore, bound to any employer. They might carry on like this, underworking legally qualified journeymen, until they were as much as twenty-six years of age. The Union legislated against the practice, but without much apparent success.

At the Delegate Meeting in 1842 the Manchester Society proposed a stiffening of the apprentice restriction rule in small offices. The ensuing discussion is interesting as illustrating the results of the previous policy and general feeling on the subject at the time. The Manchester delegates declared that their society had on the whole been successful in applying the present restriction, 'except in small offices': these were the bane of the Union, the cause of the existing unemployment. It was true that 'the returns they had received of the number of men and boys in the various towns, proved that the proportion of lads was greater upon the whole than the regulations of the Northern Union allowed. Still, . . . a great good had been effected, and it was worthy of consideration whether something more might not be done.'

The general feeling of the meeting, however, was against further restriction, which 'they had not the power to carry out'. It was considered that 'the old rule should be enforced before they thought of a new one . . . there was a town in connection with the Union, in which there were 41 men and 61 boys. . . . In Leeds five apprentices were allowed. . . . In York and Doncaster, the present principle was not carried out. . . . In Derby, too, the same laxity prevailed.' Most of the 'unfair' offices were caused by the present rule and further restriction would increase their number. It would cause numerous strikes, which would be disastrous in the existing unemployment and bankrupt state of the Union funds. The proposition was therefore rejected.

It is obvious that the attempt at apprentice restriction was not proving very successful, particularly in the smaller towns and offices. This state of affairs is confirmed by other evidence, though conflicting statements were often made. It was stated in 1840 that 'there are still in many places a disproportionate number of apprentices', and at the end of 1841 John Backhouse confessed 'that there are at this time nearly as many apprentices in our business as there are journeymen in regular employment. . . . The want of a due limitation in a great portion of the United Kingdom is woefully apparent at the present period.' The chief blame, he asserted, lay on Scotland, London, and Wales, where there was practically no restriction on the number of apprentices—a fact which rendered the Northern Union's efforts at limitation futile. The situation remained the same at the end of 1842, when it was stated that 'the malady of the apprenticeship system is still in full vigour . . . notwithstanding all the efforts . . . which have been made'. Scores of instances could be cited from the trade reports and periodicals in support of these general statements.

There are various reasons for this failure. Apprentice restriction led to numerous strikes, the 'closing' of offices to Union members, and the influx of 'rat' labour. Many felt it a hardship to sacrifice their situations on that account, particularly in times of unemployment, and therefore acquiesced in violation of the rule. The basic cause of failure, however, was that restriction simply could not be enforced in the face of expanding industry, competition, and population.

Many employers sympathized with the men. Master printers giving evidence before the Select Committee on Combinations in 1838 considered 'there was some necessity to protect the men in a fair way' and 'not to have such a number of apprentices trained', so that 'men, having got a good education, and having served seven years, should not be obliged to hunt the world for employment'. They also approved of restriction because it helped to 'keep up the respectability of the business' and kept out 'those of an inferior grade'. Many 'respectable' employers disapproved of small masters who were using apprentices as 'cheap labour' and thereby 'overstocking the trade'. But they strongly opposed arbitrary regulation by the journeymen.

Members of the Select Committee, advocates of a 'free-labour' policy, suggested some telling arguments against restriction. Printers' wages, they considered, were maintained by a 'monopoly', while other workers were earning low wages or were unemployed. Education and technical ability would provide automatic limitation on entry without trade society barriers. All who could learn the trade should be permitted entry, if a demand for their labour existed. There should be none but 'natural checks against over-stocking the market, instead of persons associating to exclude their fellow-beings'.

There is no doubt that the Union's apprentice rule was restrictive, more suited to a static economy than to the rapidly expanding and competitive industry of the nineteenth century. It was, in fact, a heritage of the craft gilds, with their medieval, monopolistic outlook. Nevertheless, we can hardly blame the Union for its attempt to maintain a traditional standard of life in a time of fierce undercutting competition and trade fluctuations, which often brought widespread unemployment and distress.

(4) *Attitude Towards Machinery*

At the time when steam-power was first applied to printing a very strong feeling existed in the minds of the working class against the introduction of machinery, which, it was felt, tended merely to benefit the capitalist and deprived the working man of his right to labour by throwing him out of employment. Pressmen naturally shared with other handicraftsmen this fear and hatred of mechanical innovations. John Walter II had, for this reason, erected Koenig's printing machine secretly in a separate building adjoining *The Times* office, for fear that the pressmen might, like the 'Luddites' in the textile trade, smash the offensive machinery. The London pressmen maintained for many years a stubborn but vain opposition to steam printing. Their intransigence merely brought in 'irregular' labour, mechanics and others who had never served an apprenticeship to printing. There was thus created a new class called 'machinemen', 'machine minders', or 'machine managers', who eventually (1839) established their own organization, the London Printing Machine Managers' Trade Society.

Printing machinery was introduced several years later into the provincial trade and there is evidence of similar opposition. We hear, for example, in 1842, that the Manchester Society had 'engaged in useless strikes—ruinous, ridiculous, and unjust contests against the employment of machinery'. There is, however, no evidence of violent opposition or machine breaking. Although the machines gradually displaced hand-pressmen, they created added employment for hand compositors. Opposition was futile, in any case, and typographical societies were forced to modify their attitude so as to maintain control over the press department. The Manchester Society required the machines to be worked by its members and even passed a rule that 'on any printing machine used . . . none but journeymen or apprentices shall be employed in *feeding* the machine'. But this rule was expunged in 1847, the committee considering it 'hardship and injustice that apprentices to the printing business should be compelled to waste their time in feeding machines'. Employers were therefore 'allowed to employ such persons as they may think proper to feed machines', but these people, labourers or unbound boys and girls, were 'not allowed to interfere in any other manner in connection with the machine, or in any other department of the printing business'.

Even 'machine-minding' or 'managing' was regarded by journeymen printers as somewhat degrading and consequently some of the larger employers, using several machines, began to bind apprentices exclusively to that department, thus creating a specialized class of 'machinemen'. Specialization was inevitable as the industry expanded, but throughout the second half of the century 'twicing' was common: the great majority of firms had only one or two machines, worked intermittently by compositors. Not till some time had elapsed after the introduction of machinery in the provinces did machine minders exist to any extent as a separate class.

The Northern Union followed the policy laid down by the Manchester Society in regard to printing machines. It was decided in 1840 'that no person attending a printing machine, who has not served a seven years' apprenticeship to either press or case, shall be admitted a member of any society of the union'. This rule did not attempt to confine the working of the machines to journeymen members, but merely excluded from the Union such 'machinemen' as were not 'legal' printers. Manchester attempted to maintain control over the machine department, but in most other towns the 'machinemen', where they existed, were unorganized and outside the society, regarded by the compositors as an inferior class of mere mechanics and labourers.

Composing machinery affected the printing trade hardly at all during the first half of the nineteenth century, but where composing machines were introduced hand compositors strongly opposed them. They were regarded as a 'much dreaded novelty', a 'mechanical spectre', and denounced as 'wretched abortions'. The *Compositors' Chronicle* made a bitter attack upon 'the introduction of machinery into those branches of labour which previously afforded sustenance to honest and honourable workmen', thereby causing unemployment, lowered wages, untold misery, and a spirit of discontent. It was feared that compositors might be reduced to the condition of the handloom weavers. The *Printer* pointed out that composing machinery 'must, if successful, deprive the labouring man of his subsistence'. There was also a fear that skilled labour would be ousted by cheaper women and boys. For this reason the Midland Board of the National Typographical Association (successor of the Northern Union) would only sanction the introduction of Rosenberg's machine at Hull 'provided the established wages of the town are paid and the legal limitation of apprentices observed'. The trade-union periodicals gleefully reported the successive failures of composing machines.

(5) *Strikes*

Our survey of Union policy in regard to wages, hours, and apprentices has shown that there was fruitful ground for dispute between masters and men. Strikes were, in fact, frequent and the number of 'unfair' offices considerable. Many employers were strongly opposed to the 'tyranny' exercised by the printers' trade societies. The *Oxford Herald*, for example, declared that

among the various conspiracies by which the freedom of trade and freedom of labour have been resisted, few have been more vexatious or unreasonable than that of letter-press printers. The rate of wages, the proportion of apprentices, and every minute point in the management of the business, they pretend to regulate. They prohibit any distinction between the skilful and the bungler, the indolent and the industrious. A certain amount of wages must be paid to all alike. . . . Again, if a man, however excellent his character, or however valuable to his employer, becomes obnoxious to the conspirators, he must be hunted from the trade. . . . In short, their interference and dictation are perfectly intolerable to any employer of ordinary independence of feeling.[1]

Under the circumstances, it is not surprising that there were innumerable strikes.

The Northern Union committee cannot, however, justly be accused, as they were by some employers, of deliberately fostering disputes.

[1] *Oxford Herald*, 6 July 1843.

They invariably adopted a cautious, conciliatory policy and were opposed to unjustifiable strikes. Thus it was resolved at Manchester in 1836 'that every means shall be adopted by the central committee and local societies to prevent strikes, they being hereby declared to be generally injurious to the trade, and that all parties shall strive as much as possible (consistent with honour) to prevent such disagreeable consequences, and endeavour as speedily as possible to bring matters to a good understanding between employers and journeymen'. It was a rule of the Northern Union 'that, to avoid the injustice frequently arising from acting on *ex parte* statements, in all cases of dispute, wherever practicable, the society shall hear the statement of the employer on the subject'. The Union's aims, it was urged, 'can be most effectually accomplished by our always exhibiting peaceful conduct, and allowing justice, reason, and unanimity to preside in our counsels'. There was nothing revolutionary or aggressive about the Northern Union. Its motto was 'United to protect, but not combined to injure'.

Nevertheless, when an important principle was involved it was often impossible to avoid a strike, in which case the Union sought to recompense members who 'sacrificed their situations in the interests of the profession'. This was, in fact, the main purpose of the central fund. The Union was to give added strength to local societies in 'resisting reductions of wage-rates, the taking a disproportionate number of apprentices', or other 'injustices'. It seems likely that some sort of strike payment existed from the Union's foundation. In 1837 it was £2, increased in 1840 to £4, paid in instalments of from 15s. to £1 per week, or in one lump sum if the strike hand wished to leave town. In addition to this sum, strike hands were entitled to double relief on tramp. Secretaries were to 'state on the back of their cards the cause of leaving their situations, and request that every facility may be afforded them in getting employment'.

It was proposed by the Wolverhampton Society in 1837 that a 'sinking fund' should be established to provide weekly allowances to strike hands, instead of a lump sum and a 'backed' card, but the Union committee decided it would be too expensive. Several of the larger branches, however, supplemented the Union strike allowance, or even established local strike funds to provide weekly allowances.

We have already noticed the friction which was apt to arise between the central committee and local societies. This was particularly visible in the question of strike decisions. The Executive strove constantly to maintain control, but found it difficult to curb local independence.

Quite often societies started strikes 'upon trivial causes', swayed by local feeling, contrary to the declared policy of the Union.

The Union rule was not clear as to where ultimate responsibility lay. It stated

that whenever a dispute may arise between the employer and the employed . . . respecting a reduction of wages, apprentices or any other matter involving the interests of the profession, the secretary of such society shall transmit to the secretary of this Union, a correct, clear, and full statement thereof; stating whether pecuniary aid is wanting, signed by the officers of the said society. The secretary of the Union shall then consult the committee of management on the case, and act as he may be advised.

This was liable to conflicting interpretations. The *Compositors' Chronicle*, for example, asserted in 1842 that 'the laws of the Northern Union do not forbid them [local societies] to strike without the consent of the committee of management—they only require that the particulars of a dispute should be sent to headquarters'. This lack of central control was 'productive of innumerable disputes'. Such an interpretation, however, was rebutted by the secretary of the Halifax Society, who maintained 'that no local society could strike . . . without having, whilst the matter was merely in dispute, consulted the Union secretary and the committee of management, and it is also certain that if they so acted they would not be granted the usual allowance in case of strike'.

This, it seems, was the more usual interpretation of the rule. Nevertheless, and despite the Union's declared policy, strikes were frequent, though mostly petty affairs, involving only one office and a few hands. The majority proved unsuccessful, owing to the influx of 'rats', especially tramps. The paltry strike allowance was insufficient compensation for the sacrifice of a situation and many men 'stayed in', while in periods of widespread unemployment and distress, such as 1836-43, tramp relief did little to relieve hardship and failed to prevent many men accepting situations in 'unfair' houses or entering those where strikes were going on.

The General Secretary issued a 'monthly Circular' giving details of strikes, the names of 'unfair' houses, non-members, and 'rats', information about tramps, &c. There are references to this Circular in the minutes of the Manchester Society as early as 1834, but no copy appears to have survived. It was the forerunner of the *Typographical Societies' Monthly Circular* established in 1852, which became the *Provincial Typographical Circular* in 1875 and the *Typographical Circular* in 1877.

(6) *Tramp Relief*

Tramp relief had linked typographical societies together long before the Northern Union was established. Relief was therefore given by Northern Union branches not only on each other's cards, but also on those of the London, Scottish, and Irish Unions and all other 'recognized' societies.

The amount of relief was individually determined by the various societies and varied from 9*d*. in the smallest to 5*s*. in the largest, the average being about 1*s*. 6*d*. No tramp was relieved twice in the same town within twelve months. Even so, tramp relief was a heavy burden on small societies. It was therefore decided in 1838 to establish a Reimbursement Fund in order 'to equalise the burden of relieving tramps'. Each member had to contribute 1*d*. per month to this fund, from which small societies (with less than forty members) could claim reimbursement of all tramp relief expenditure above 9*d*. per member per month.

The total amount of relief, however, was still trifling. It was stated in 1841 that 'if a tramp were to call upon the whole of our Societies, the utmost amount he would get is £2. 19*s*. for the first twelve months: if he should be so unfortunate as not to obtain one month's employment [the minimum period for acquiring membership] in a town where there is a Society during that period, and be obliged to travel a second year with the same card, he would not be able to obtain above half that sum'.

Other trades had different tramp-relief systems—'by the mile' or 'by the day'—and there was some argument among printers as to which method was best. The mileage system was discussed at the Delegate Meetings in 1840 and 1842, but rejected as impracticable.

The number of men on tramp varied with trade fluctuations. Even in periods of brisk business there was a good deal of tramping, but depression brought 'hordes' on the roads. The number of tramps relieved by the Manchester Society varied from 110 in 1835 to 340 in 1841. They naturally made for cities such as Manchester and Liverpool, where the largest amount of relief was given and where there was most chance of work; but as only one allowance was to be had in each place tramps were forced to move from town to town in search of relief and employment. All societies, therefore, had their share of tramps. But the Northern Union area, comprising over forty societies in towns close together, was obviously a much better hunting ground for tramps than the south of

England, where there were very few societies. Thus the Northern Union, with a smaller membership than that of the London Union, had to bear a far heavier burden of tramp relief—a great grievance among provincial printers. London, on the other hand, complained that the tramp system enabled the provinces to export their unemployed to the metropolis.

Tramp figures provide evidence of considerable mobility among journeymen printers in this period. It was not unusual for a tramp to perform a 'grand tour' of the three kingdoms, particularly in periods of depression, when employment was nowhere to be found. This 'floating' labour force was of great importance in strikes. Tramp relief was intended not merely to relieve distress and help the unemployed to find work, but also to keep them faithful to the Union and out of 'unfair' houses. But the amount of relief was extremely small and a tramp might, in a bad period, be on the road for months, suffering considerable hardships, with no more than a few days' casual employment. Unfair houses presented great temptations to men so circumstanced: hence the influx of tramps which ruined so many strikes.

Tramp relief was open to considerable fraud and abuse. To prevent 'imposition of any kind by worthless members of the profession in search of employment', branch secretaries were to report cases of forged cards, erasures, neglect of work, or 'ratting' to the General Secretary, who would warn all known societies to stop further relief to the guilty parties. The names of these 'worthless characters' were frequently printed in Northern Union circulars and annual reports and in the trade periodicals. Tramps, in fact, acquired an almost proverbial reputation for being idle, dissolute, and inferior workmen. The system certainly tended to foster 'professional roadsters'. On the other hand, there were 'many instances of men who have tramped long and hard, and yet have never . . . brought the least disgrace upon their own characters, or upon the profession'. The misconduct of a few, no doubt, resulted in exaggerated statements about all tramps.

Apart from voluntary chapel aid and occasional branch relief funds, the tramp system was the only method of unemployed relief in this period, except in a few large towns, which, in the early forties, established their own systems of weekly allowances. Its inadequacy, however, became increasingly obvious in the trade depression of 1836–43. Not only was it open to many abuses, but also involved great hardships. A man had to tramp the country in all weathers, hopelessly looking for work, suffering severe privations, often falling ill, degraded and demoralized in lodging houses, while his family was left destitute at home to fall on parish relief. No wonder, then, that men refused to come out on strike, or that tramps often went into 'unfair' offices.

It was the problem of unemployment, the inadequacy of tramp relief, and the closely connected failure of strikes that, more than anything else, led to the attempts at reorganization of printers' unions in the early 'forties which finally resulted in the foundation of the National Typographical Association.

Events Leading up to the Foundation of the National Typographical Association

Throughout the first four decades of the nineteenth century there was frequent co-operation between the various typographical societies in the British Isles—in London, the English provinces, Scotland, and Ireland. They were linked together by feelings of brotherhood, common principles, and the tramp-relief system, and often assisted each other in strikes or trade depression. Co-operation became much closer after the establishment of the Northern Union (1830), the London Union of Compositors (1834), the Scottish Association and Irish Union (1836). Not only was there frequent correspondence between them, but their officials met at Northern Union Delegate Meetings, to which representatives from all independent societies were invited.

The idea naturally arose, therefore, of a union of all printers in the United Kingdom. This was suggested at least as early as 1840, when the Northern Union put forward the following proposals: firstly, 'that a general sinking fund for the United Kingdom . . . should be established', to provide assistance in strikes, and, secondly, that the Unions should 'consider whether it is not advisable to connect the London, Irish and Scotch Unions with the Northern Union, and what steps are necessary for that purpose'. Nothing, however, came of these proposals.

Nearly all the following suggestions for reorganization and more extended union arose out of the failure to deal with the problem of the unemployed—the breakdown of the tramp-relief system and the failure of strikes. It was in vain that rules were passed against 'ratting', warnings issued, names published, and tramp cards detained. The paltry strike allowance and tramp relief were insufficient to retain the loyalty of out-of-work members.

These failures led 'A Northern Unionist', writing in the *Compositors'* *Chronicle* in 1841, to urge the abolition of tramping and the adoption in its stead of regular weekly allowances to the unemployed and strike hands in their own towns. He pointed out that it was unreasonable and unjust to send a man on tramp from town to town, leaving his wife and family at home, when trade was so bad that there was no hope of finding work. Weekly out-of-work payments in their own towns would keep men true to the Union, while haphazard tramping could be replaced by unemployment returns to headquarters and a system of labour direction. More effective safeguards and punishments could also be provided against fraud and neglect of work.

The increased financial burden was to be met by 'consolidation' of the separate unions into 'one body or association', divided into districts, under a central executive, which would exercise stronger control over strike decisions.

The *Compositors' Chronicle* strongly supported these proposals. John Backhouse, General Secretary of the Northern Union, also approved of them, but pointed out the great expense they would involve, especially in periods of trade depression.

That some sort of reorganization was necessary seemed clear from the Northern Union's annual report. The increased subscription of 4d. per month had proved insufficient, expenditure had exceeded income, funds were exhausted, and a levy had to be imposed. The number of tramps had been 'great, beyond all former example', almost every society had exhausted its funds in relief payments, and expenditure on reimbursement Account was nearly twice the income, thus necessitating borrowing from the General Fund. Owing to the lack of funds and the number of unemployed and 'rat' hands, strikes had failed and apprentices multiplied. The Committee was well aware that trade depression was mainly responsible for these misfortunes, but felt that some improvement might be made by reorganization.

The greatest objection to the new plan was that the proposed unemployed and strike allowances would be too costly and contributions too high. The industrious would have to support the idle and dissolute. Moreover, by restricting movement the proposed scheme would cause the unemployed to stagnate in their own towns without going out to find work. The new organization would also be unwieldy and impracticable.

The Liverpool Society therefore put forward an alternative scheme in 1842, for a 'General Tramping Reimbursement Fund' including all the various unions. Tramping should not be abolished: instead, its burdens should be more equally distributed. The provinces were spending far more in relieving London cards than London was in relieving theirs: London should bear its fair share of the expense, by contributing to a General Reimbursement Fund.

Here, then, were the two plans put forward to solve the present difficulties: one for a complete reorganization by amalgamation and division into districts, with weekly out-of-work and strike payments; the other for reform of the tramping system only, by equalizing the burdens of relief expenditure. Both were to be given a trial, the latter in 1842, when a General Reimbursement Fund was established, the former in 1844, with the foundation of the National Typographical Association. Both were to fail and in 1848 the streams of trade-union history in the printing trade were to return to their old channels.

The Liverpool scheme for a 'General Tramping Reimbursement Fund' was strongly supported at the Northern Union Delegate Meeting in June 1842, before representatives from all important typographical societies in the United Kingdom. Statistics revealed the inequality of tramp-relief burdens borne by the London and Northern Unions. The Scottish and Irish Unions, however, were bearing their fair share of tramp relief and were therefore excluded from the plan. It was decided that Northern Union members should, as hitherto, each contribute a penny, London members two-pence, to the Reimbursement Fund, in order to relieve the financial burden on small societies.

It is obvious that this plan would not solve the acute problems of the time. It might do something to relieve the financial burdens of the Northern Union; it might also succeed in raising slightly the amount of relief given to tramps; but it would not cope with the problems of the unemployed and 'ratting'. It merely re-enacted, more stringently, the old safeguards against fraud and entry into 'unfair' or 'strike' houses. Furthermore, it failed to secure the support of the London Union, which, in spite of plenipotentiary powers given to its delegates, rejected the scheme on their return.

The trade's problems, therefore, remained unsolved. A suggestion had been put forward at the Delegate Meeting on the lines of the plan proposed by 'Northern Unionist', but seems hardly to have been considered, in view of the general feeling in favour of a reimbursement fund. Now, when the latter misfired, a number of remedies were suggested, all more or less variations upon the 'Northern Unionist' theme. Thus, in the *Compositors' Chronicle* of November 1842 R. Davies, of Liverpool, a member of the Northern Union committee, put forward a scheme for 'General Union', a 'Proposed Plan of sustaining Members of the Profession who have relinquished their situations in defence of Trade

Principles, by the adoption of a Consolidated Fund, embracing the London, Northern, Scotch and Irish Unions'. He pointed out that £4 and a backed card were utterly inadequate compensation to strike hands and that larger societies in the Northern Union were already providing weekly strike pay. He did not, however, propose any radical reorganization: the unions were to remain separate, but to assist each other in strikes by levies paid into a 'Consolidated Fund'.

Davies stated that 'the Secretary, Mr. Backhouse, and the Committee of Management . . . have given their unqualified approval to the general principle of this plan'. The *Compositors' Chronicle* also approved of the idea, but considered the proposed means inadequate and also urged reform or abolition of the tramping system.

The Northern Union's Annual Report for 1842 further emphasized the need for new measures. The situation had worsened in the past year. The present subscription was 'totally inadequate'. The number of unemployed had resulted in reduced income, while expenditure had risen on tramp relief and strikes, so that there was a large deficit, in spite of a levy and a loan from the Dublin Society. Several small branches had collapsed. Obviously these were evils which no trade union could cure: they were caused neither by apprentice labour nor grasping employers, but by prolonged trade depression. Nevertheless, the journeymen sought salvation in reorganization, in wider union.

The details of Davies's 'Proposed Plan' were clearly unsatisfactory, but its main principle of supporting strike hands by weekly allowances and his idea of a 'General Union' based on this principle secured wide support. Thomas Houghton, of the Preston Society, writing in the *Compositors' Chronicle* under the pen-name 'Argus', accepted these basic ideas, but himself propounded a much sounder scheme of reorganization. He maintained that 'a general union, to be effective, must be formed on the principle of a sinking fund', otherwise 'there would be no funds in hand when it was known a strike would take place'. Thus a fund raised by levies during strikes would be insufficient. Houghton also proposed the abolition of the tramp system and its replacement by weekly allowances to the unemployed, as well as to strike hands. An increased subscription would, of course, be necessary; a shilling per week he estimated.

The Northern Union's Annual Report for 1843 officially condemned the tramping system and supported this scheme. The whole question was to be discussed at the Delegate Meeting in the summer of 1844.

Before this meeting took place further plans were put forward in the *Printer*, all advocating 'General Union', abolition of tramping, and payment of weekly allowances to unemployed and strike hands. 'Our relative position and mutual dependence upon each other', it was urged, 'are no longer determinable by the claims of nationality, nor bounded by geographical limitation. Partial operations have hitherto failed from the want of concentrated force and the inability to maintain our principles from paucity of support.' A 'General Union' or 'Amalgamation' of all typographical societies would bring success.

The National Typographical Association, 1844–8

The 'Printers' Parliament' at Derby on Monday, 15 July 1844, was the largest Delegate Meeting of printers that had ever been held. After four days' discussion a plan of amalgamation was unanimously agreed on, to come into operation on 1 January 1845. Its basis was a proposition put forward by the Preston Society in which Thomas Houghton expounded his previous proposals for 'General Union'.

It was decided 'that this Association be called the National Typographical Association, and shall consist of all typographical societies and printers (who have served a seven years' apprenticeship) of fair character in the United Kingdom; and that the principle upon which it shall be based be impartial justice to all with whom it may co-operate or oppose'. As a writer in the *Printer* put it, 'This is a good title. . . . It is not a "Union"—oh no! That term is offensive to ears polite: it is not sectional, nor provincial, but a "National" Association.' Moreover, a union could not be maintained unless it did 'justice' to its members: weekly out-of-work and strike payments were therefore provided. The Association would also maintain 'justice' in its dealings with employers: non-aggression, moderation, and conciliation were to be its characteristics.

The objects of the Association were 'to advance the interests of the typographical profession, and to improve the social condition of its members'. The subscription was to be 6*d*. per week for the fully employed, proportionately less for those partially employed, and nothing for the unemployed. New members were to pay an entrance fee of 5*s*. and would also be fined if guilty of having 'held aloof' or of 'unfair' practices.

The Association was divided into five geographical districts. England was split into three—the South-eastern, South-western, and Midland Districts, while Scotland became the Northern and Ireland the

Western District. These divisions were not, of course, new: the Northern and Western corresponded to the existing Scottish and Irish Unions, the Midland covered roughly the same area as the Northern Union, the South-eastern was dominated by London, while the South-western was the embodiment of previous hopes for a 'Western Union'.

Each district was to be governed by a District Board, consisting of seven (later nine) members, 'elected from the society named for that purpose by a delegate meeting': each district, in other words, was to have its 'governing branch'. It was eventually decided that the district centres should be London (South-eastern), Bristol (South-western), Liverpool (Midland), Dublin (Western), and Edinburgh (Northern). Each District Board was to appoint its own secretary and treasurer. These were still working journeymen and only part-time officials, secretarial salaries varying from £8 to £20 per annum. They and the Board members had nearly all been active as officers or committee-men in their Unions or local societies. Thus there was no break in continuity of government.

Each Board was to be 'arbiter of every question affecting the interests of the Association' in its district, that is, of questions which were beyond the powers of branches to decide, such as threatened strikes. It was also to have control over the surplus money left over from Association subscriptions after branches had met such liabilities as unemployment and strike payments, salaries, &c. The aggregate amount accumulated in the various districts would be the Association's capital. District Boards would, in case of need, remit money to branches to meet claims for unemployed or strike payments. Should a District Board itself require funds, it was to apply to the General Secretary, who would communicate the fact to the other Boards.

The individual Boards were competent to decide 'questions affecting a district only'. Important matters such as strike decisions had to be dealt with by the Executive. There was, however, no central committee for the whole Association. The Executive consisted of the five District Boards, in whom, collectively, resided 'the whole judicial and executive power of the Association'. The Association was, in fact, a rather loose federation of districts which still preserved a good deal of their old independence and autonomy. Co-ordination was achieved by means of a General Corresponding Secretary, to whom all important questions requiring Executive decision were transmitted by the various District Boards. He submitted the facts to all the other Boards, who, after consideration, sent back to him their individual decisions. Each Board had one vote and a majority of such votes constituted the decision of the Executive, which was made known to the District Board concerned by the General Secretary.

This organization was extremely cumbersome, requiring a tremendous amount of postal communication, involving long delays and encouraging friction, not only between the various Boards, but also between them and the General Secretary. The latter was the king-pin of the whole organization, a kind of one-man central office. He was meant to be a mere 'go-between', but inevitably acquired considerable influence and power, which aroused jealousies and suspicions and fears of dictatorial action. The office was held by our old friend John Backhouse, ex-Secretary of the Northern Union, at a salary of £25 per year. Even his was an amateur, spare-time office.

Obviously there was considerable feeling against centralization. The different districts still retained their varying customs. Their policies in regard to apprentice restriction, for example, differed widely: the Midland District tried to maintain the old Northern Union rule, while in London there was no rule at all; no general regulation was made on the subject. Neither did the Association attempt to secure any uniformity in wage rates and hours. Nevertheless, it was a great step forward in harmonizing the aims and co-ordinating the actions of the hitherto separate Unions.

Local societies still retained a good deal of independence. Each was to 'elect its own members, appoint its own officers, watch over the interests of the profession in its town, and aid by all means in its power in carrying out the general objects of the Association'. The Midland Board decided 'to allow each society to frame its own regulations and that the printing of any General Local Rules is inadvisable'. Local societies, therefore, still retained most of their old regulations. Their independence, however, was considerably curtailed by the control of the District Boards, especially over financial matters and threatened disputes.

The right of all members to a voice in Association affairs was preserved through the medium of Delegate Meetings, which were to 'make all laws for the general government of the Association'.

The Association funds would provide weekly out-of-work and strike payments. Amalgamation would secure 'concentration of the energies and resources of the trade in all cases of dispute', which would not only achieve greater success in strikes, but also enable more equitable strike allowances to be paid. Strike hands would receive weekly three-fourths of the wages sacrificed for a period of six months (or, if they secured casual employment, would have their earnings made up to the wages of the town) and out-of-work allowance afterwards if still unemployed.

The Association did not, however, wish to encourage disputes. *The Times*, no doubt representing the views of many employers, accused it in 1846, during the great Edinburgh dispute, of being a 'conspiracy' to foment strikes and browbeat employers by 'tyrannical proceedings'.[1] It pointed out, in particular, 'the dangers of centralisation'.

Leave the towns or districts to themselves, to manage each its own affairs, and there is a strong probability that, however little squabbles might occur occasionally, no very important or permanent dissension would interrupt the relations of employer and employed. But introduce a foreign power—one that neither has nor can have that intimate knowledge of the feelings of the parties concerned without which the soundest judgement is liable to err—appeal to such a power as this, and all prospect of a compromise is at once shut out. The great central committee after deliberating in darkness, decides in folly; and issues a fiat that can hardly ... produce any other result than the widening of a breach which, if left to itself, might have closed itself.

There is not, however, the slightest shred of evidence to support such statements. As the *Typographical Gazette* pointed out, the Executive was

a power only appealed to when the towns *cannot* 'manage each its own affairs', that is, after remonstrance and a full local inquiry have failed to obtain an amicable understanding. ... The Association in no way interferes with master and man until ... the two have been found unable to settle their differences. ... The question in dispute is then submitted to the judgement of forty-five practical men working in London, Liverpool, Bristol, Edinburgh, and Dublin, nine in each city, besides officers, [and not to a] great central committee ... deliberating in darkness.

Neither did the Executive 'issue its fiat, decided in folly', but almost invariably adopted a cautious, moderate, restraining attitude, which often served to prevent serious disputes developing out of local feeling. The Association aimed, in fact, at 'the diminution of strikes', by placing strike decisions 'in the hand of a Committee, consisting of representatives of the whole Kingdom; thus rendering it impossible for any strike to take place upon an affair of trivial amount'.

The Association rule was that 'in any case of dispute occurring in any town connected with this Association, the secretary of the society shall communicate the particulars to the Board for that district, who shall

[1] *The Times*, 16 Nov. 1846.

determine whether it is necessary to require the general secretary to consult the whole of the Boards upon the question'. 'No society shall have power to declare any house unfair until it has been decided by the Executive.' Obviously it was the aim of the Association, by increased central control over local societies, to prevent trivial disputes developing into strikes. At the same time, of course, the Association aimed to provide the requisite funds to win strikes when they could not be prevented. Its establishment, as we shall see, aroused exaggerated hopes and was followed by an outbreak of disputes all over the country.

The second great object of the Association was the abolition of the tramp-relief system and substitution of weekly allowances to the unemployed. Each out-of-work member was to receive 6s. per week, casual earnings to be made up to 8s. No member was to be allowed any relief 'in travelling from town to town in search of employment—the object of weekly payments being to increase the comfort of unemployed members, and to supersede tramping'. But 'every member desirous of changing his locality may do so, by obtaining a certificate of membership, and a statement of his account, if any, addressed to the secretary of the town to which he is going', which would entitle him to free admission. Travelling members would, in fact, be entitled to draw their weekly unemployment allowance in whichever society town they happened to be located on a Saturday night. But the old tramp system was to be replaced by a system of labour direction along the lines laid down by 'Northern Unionist' in 1841, which would proportion the supply of hands to the demand in the various towns.

The new mode of relief would, it was hoped, keep men loyal to the Association, prevent 'ratting', render strikes more successful, and thus keep up wage rates. It would also do away with the moral and physical evils of the tramp system. To the objection that it would benefit 'the idle and ill-disposed', it was answered that 'the allowance proposed is not so great an inducement as to cause idleness'; but certain safeguards were imposed to see that unemployed and strike hands should work when possible and not defraud the Association. The usual warnings and penalties against 'ratting' were also enacted.

The meeting at Derby, which had 'unanimously agreed' upon the plan for a National Typographical Association, was primarily a Delegate Meeting of the Northern Union. Thirty-three of its members were present, as against three from London, one from Cambridge, two from Ireland, and one from Scotland. The initiative in the movement towards 'General Union' had, all along, come from the Northern Union. It remained, therefore, to secure the assent of London, Scotland, and Ireland to the proposed reorganization.

Scotland declared in favour of amalgamation at a Delegate Meeting in August, because of the 'many growing evils affecting the profession' which made 'a radical change' necessary. The S.T.A. had been completely defeated in a number of strikes. They also considered it 'the duty of each and all to sink minor differences in upholding the one great principle of Union'. Moreover, a remedy had been found for the evils of the tramp system and if they did not join the N.T.A. they would have to support their own unemployed and strike hands, who would no longer get tramp relief in England.

The London Union of Compositors also decided to participate. It was pointed out that, whereas the present Union had failed, the new Association promised great advantages. It would diminish the number of strikes and at the same time ensure success, by united action, in those which could not be prevented. It would also provide just compensation to strike hands and, above all, it would abolish the tramp system and give adequate relief to the out-of-work. The L.U.C.'s underlying motive, however, in supporting the proposed scheme was that it would reduce the influx of unemployed and strike hands from the provinces and thus keep up London wage rates—admittedly 'a selfish view of the question'.

Before the Association was actually established, however, another Delegate Meeting was held, in Manchester, in December 1844, to revise the proposed plan. A few alterations and additions were made, chiefly to prevent abuse of out-of-work payments, but the main principles remained unchanged. The Irish Union having decided in favour of amalgamation, the N.T.A. covered the whole United Kingdom.

Its launching fortunately coincided with the end of the long period of depression and the beginning of a trade boom, which brought increased employment in the printing industry. It could never have survived, in fact it could hardly have been established, but for this favourable trade situation. For a year and a half it was able to accumulate funds, in a period of comparatively full employment and few strikes; but when depression returned in 1846 it quickly collapsed.

At first, however, expansion was rapid. By June 1845 the Association had 59 branches and 4,338 members, increasing to 67 branches and 4,969 members by December. At the end of 1846 it had 74 branches[1]

---

[1] (i) SE. District: Aylesbury, Brighton, Cambridge, Hertford, Lewes, London, Oxford, Thames Ditton, Woking (2,417 members). (ii) SW. District: Bath, Birmingham, Brecon, Bristol, Cardiff, Cheltenham, Hereford, Leamington and

and 5,418 members, but had then been suffering from trade depression for about eight months. Unfortunately, there seems to be no third half-yearly report in existence. It is probable, however, that the Association reached its maximum membership in that period, perhaps 5,700.

Even so, it never included anything like all journeymen printers in the United Kingdom. In London the Pressmen and Daily Newspaper Compositors stood aloof, mainly from reasons of jealous independence. The Manchester Society also refused to join the Association, for similar reasons and because it considered the Association financially unsound.[1] In July 1846 a writer in the *Typographical Gazette* denounced the 'apathy, listlessness, and nonchalance exhibited by members of our profession in several cities and towns' in the south-western, southern, south-eastern, and eastern counties of England. 'Take, for instance, Norwich, Ipswich, Bury St. Edmunds, Exeter, and Plymouth. These are only a few; but . . . in almost all the towns where even the shadow of a printer is found, in the counties of Lincoln, Norfolk, Suffolk, Essex, Kent, Sussex (Brighton and Lewes excepted), Devon, and Cornwall, the same feeling of indifference seems to prevail.' In Wales the Association could number only three branches. These statements are confirmed by the Census Abstracts of 1841 and 1851, which show that scores of country towns containing printers were never included in the Association. Apart, moreover, from these non-union areas, there were, even in the very strongholds of the Association, a large number of 'unfair' offices and non-society men.

A few large cities formed the backbone of the Association. Nearly half its members were London compositors—2,200 out of 5,418 in December 1846. Edinburgh (580), Glasgow (353), Dublin (about 400), and Liverpool (320) accounted for another 1,653 members. The remainder were scattered among sixty-nine branches, fifty-four of which had less than thirty members each.

The Association's record for the first year of its existence was one of

Warwick, Newport, Stafford, Wolverhampton, Worcester (301 members). (iii) *Midland District*: Blackburn, Bolton, Bradford, Carlisle, Chester, Derby, Doncaster, Durham, Halifax, Huddersfield, Hull, Isle of Man, Kendal, Lancaster, Leeds, Leicester, Liverpool, Macclesfield, Manchester, Newcastle, Nottingham, Preston, Sheffield, South Shields, Wakefield, York (949 members). (iv) *Western District*: Armagh, Belfast, Carlow, Clonmel, Cork, Derry, Dublin, Galway, Kilkenny, Limerick, Nenagh, Newry, Omagh, Waterford, Wexford (687 members). (v) *Northern District*: Aberdeen, Dingwall, Dumfries, Dundee, Edinburgh, Glasgow, Kilmarnock, Perth, Stirling, Stranraer (1,064 members).

[1] A branch of the Association was eventually established in Manchester, but failed to attract more than about a quarter or a third of the old Society's members.

glorious success. The first half-yearly report showed a considerable surplus of receipts over expenditure in every district and a total balance in hand of over £900. The latter had increased by the end of the second half-year to nearly £2,000 and the report was full of self-congratulatory phrases. There were, however, ominous signs from Ireland, where heavy payments had been made to unemployed hands: expenditure there had exceeded receipts by over £150 and an appeal for assistance had been made to other districts.

It was the declared policy of the Association to diminish the number of strikes and it undoubtedly adopted a conciliatory, though firm, attitude. The various District Boards and the Executive kept a close control over the branches and sought to settle all disputes amicably—by deputation, negotiation, and mutual concessions. Their policy was mainly defensive. Even when it proved impossible to achieve a settlement by peaceful diplomacy, the Executive would not sanction a strike without a reasonable chance of success and required detailed information as to the state of trade, number of unemployed, non-members, and apprentices before coming to a decision.

Despite such cautious moderation, however, many disputes occurred. In the first half-year twenty-six were submitted to the Executive, in the second twenty-five, apart from those decided by individual Boards. It seems that the members, buoyed up by exaggerated belief in the strength of the new Association and assured of strike allowances, may have adopted a more independent, even aggressive, attitude towards employers. Moreover, trade was booming and the labour market favourable. In nearly all the disputes the Association secured victory or satisfactory settlements.

The disputes arose from familiar causes. The majority were due to the employment of an 'illegal' number of apprentices. There were several instances of employers attempting to reduce wage rates and one or two of their refusal to make payment for 'over-hours'. The transfer of matter from one office to another and the refusal of journeymen to compose matter for 'unfair' houses were also sources of dispute. Apart from these questions, the Boards were mainly concerned with excluding 'foreigners', insisting on the seven years' apprenticeship, fining 'unfair characters', punishing those guilty of 'misconduct', approving local rules, and extending the organization into unassociated towns. There is no evidence of the Association trying to raise wages.

John Backhouse viewed the Association's progress at the end of its first year with

the highest gratification. . . . The practicability of the Association has now been tested by experiment; and, notwithstanding the fears expressed by some, it has been found equal to its engagements in every point of view. Its strike-members, and those who have unfortunately been out of employment, have been supported. . . . The utility of the institution, in maintaining fair wages, restricting the number of apprentices, settling disputes, awakening the lethargic . . . reforming the vicious . . . is admirably and forcibly set before you in the Reports . . . and the moral influence of the Association, by producing temperance and good order will not . . . be questioned; and thus every fair and honourable employer may rely . . . on having steady and attentive workmen.

The hope was expressed that the Association would

not only ameliorate the present evils of the trade, but . . . elevate the professors of the noblest and most valuable art upon earth to that rank and to the enjoyment of that recompense to which their employment justly entitles them.

These extravagant hopes were doomed to rapid disappointment. Borne along on the crest of a trade 'boom', the Association had flourished. There had been few unemployed hands to support and contributions had flowed in steadily. The brisk demand for labour had enabled the Association to enforce its principles and there had been no strikes of any consequence. When the 'slump' came in the spring of 1846, however, the Association was soon hard hit and by the close of the year was in dire straits. The 'rot', as we have seen, began in Ireland in the autumn of 1845, as a result of the terrible potato famine. A similar dearth soon prevailed in England. In July 1846 it was reported in the *Typographical Gazette* that 'from a period of great activity we have descended to a time of almost unexampled slackness; and . . . the present lamentable state of trade in London, and in various other large cities in the provinces, in Scotland, and in Ireland . . . approximates closely to that which existed in 1841.' The country was, in fact, passing through another of those periodic commercial, industrial, and financial crises, which brought such severe suffering among wage-earners. Unemployment rapidly increased and with depression came more numerous attempts by employers to reduce wages and introduce apprentice labour. Strikes resulted, bringing an increasingly heavy burden upon the Association funds and reviving the problem of 'rat' labour.

The effects were already visible in the third half-yearly report.[1] There was still a balance in hand of just over £2,112, but expenditure had

---

[1] A financial summary is contained in the *Typographical Gazette*, No. 9, Nov. 1846.

begun to exceed income. Nearly £870 had been paid to unemployed members and over £515 to strike hands. Many societies had been forced to appeal for assistance. The number of disputes had increased: forty-six had been submitted to the Executive and many houses had been 'closed'. There were several demands for increased wages, but the Boards adopted an extremely cautious policy in view of the trade depression. Apprentice restriction was the main cause of disputes and 'closed' offices.

A Delegate Meeting was held in London at the end of March 1846. Being just prior to the slump, it resounded with self-congratulatory speeches. Very few changes were made in the rules, 'as the present position of the Association testifies that we have done well hitherto'. The chief result was a set of restrictive apprentice regulations for each district. The question of 'a limitation of the hours of labour' was also discussed, but it was deemed 'prudential' not to take any action, though regulations were made regarding payment for overtime and Sunday work. Non-society men were offered entry on easy terms in an effort 'to bring within our ranks every member of the profession'. There was a further tightening-up of the unemployment relief regulations: branches were to require 'proof that each claimant for the relief has made proper application for work'. There are several instances in the Midland Board's minutes of unemployed hands being ordered to move (or be deprived of relief) if there was no prospect of work in their own towns, but the Executive eventually decided that such men could only be required to move if employment was found for them. There seems to have been little labour direction by the Boards. Tramping practically disappeared in the first year or so of the Association's existence, but as soon as depression returned we find men 'on the road' again, searching for employment.

This meeting marks the apogee of the Association's fortunes. As depression descended in the following months, its position soon became critical. A growing number of unemployed had to be supported, disputes became more frequent, and scores of houses were 'closed', thereby increasing strike expenditure. Many local societies had to be assisted and the SE. and SW. Boards had to appeal for funds. In October, therefore, the Executive were forced to double the subscription for three months. Over £1,000 had been expended by the Association on unemployment relief in the previous quarter and strike payments were almost as heavy.

Strikes had everywhere failed. As soon as members were withdrawn, employers found many men ready and willing to take their places: 6s. per week could not prevent the out-of-work from 'ratting', while non-society men abounded. Many members, therefore, began to realize the futility of strikes 'in the present state of depression and of the Association's finances', advocating 'reason and argument . . . with the employer in place of force'. Expedients were also suggested for 'employing the unemployed' by providing 'more work', instead of strikes. Thus we get movements for co-operative production and abolition of the 'Taxes on Knowledge'.[1]

By the end of 1846 the Association was in a parlous condition. Income for the previous half-year, deducting branch balances, came to £3,372, while expenditure had been £4,507. Societies had forwarded only £592 to the District Boards and had been forced to claim therefrom £1,622, due to their heavy unemployed and strike payments—£1,996 and £1,261 respectively. The balance in the hands of the District Boards had consequently been reduced to £402 and the Executive were forced to continue the double subscription for a further period of three months. Ninety disputes had been brought before the Executive and numerous strikes had resulted, 'in which, through the unprincipled conduct of a number of men unconnected with us, we have not always been successful'. Members were warned that they must 'avoid and prevent strikes as much as possible' and fight only against 'flagrant instances of tyranny and injustice'.

There were ominous signs that employers had got the measure of the Association and realized its weaknesses. A Liverpool employer had proposed to give his men an increase 'if they would sign a document to disconnect themselves from the Association. If they refused to sign . . . they were to consider themselves under a fortnight's notice.' The same thing happened in London, where the hands on the *Morning Post* were required 'to sign a document, annulling their present rights and privileges'. But far more serious than either of these was the situation in Edinburgh, 'unparalleled in the history of the profession, wherein thirty-eight employers . . . the professed enemies of combination . . . combined to overthrow the Association'. The dispute was caused mainly by the Edinburgh branch's attempts at apprentice restriction. Friction had also arisen over certain of their working regulations, which the employers regarded as 'insolent interference' with the rights of management.[2] The

---

[1] See below, pp. 73 and 77.
[2] *The Times*, 16 Nov. 1846. An account of the origins and progress of this dispute is given in the *Typographical Gazette*.

outcome was that on 28 October 1846, at a meeting of Edinburgh master printers, thirty-eight subscribed their names to the following resolutions: '1. That no Journeyman shall be taken into employment who either leaves or threatens to leave his Employer on "strike". 2. That no Journeyman shall be taken into employment without producing a certificate from his last Employer. 3. That in all cases, Masters will prefer Non-Unionists to Unionists.'

It is obvious that the Edinburgh masters had decided to combine in an attempt to crush the 'insolent interference' and 'tyrannous dictation' of the Association. Their action was, in fact, 'an attack against the very existence of the Association itself'. The masters, knowing the Association's financial straits, deliberately aimed at overwhelming it by throwing over 200 men on the strike funds. Their resolutions were met in January 1847 by counter resolutions from the Edinburgh journeymen, refusing to knuckle under and threatening a strike unless the obnoxious ultimatum was withdrawn; but these were rejected and on 6 February, therefore, battle began. Over 200 men came out, involving a strike expenditure of more than £100 per week. It appears that twelve of the thirty-eight employers eventually withdrew their names from the resolutions, while a few of the strike hands secured situations elsewhere, but in April 1847 there were still 150 on the strike-roll. Their places were rapidly filled by 'rats' from London and by apprentices.

The Association was soon, therefore, in serious financial difficulties. Members fully realized that defeat in Edinburgh would mean the end of the Association and great efforts were made in nearly every town to raise funds, by voluntary subscriptions, collections, special meetings, concerts, and appeals to other trades. The various District Boards repeatedly forwarded money to Edinburgh and made urgent appeals to branches for grants from their local funds. The double subscription was again continued for another three months at the end of March and an additional contribution of 6d. per week 'during the continuance of the Edinburgh Strike' was also imposed. This, however, amounting to a 'treble levy' and coming after repeated renewals of the double subscription, aroused widespread opposition and had to be discontinued.

Unemployment was still widespread and branches were constantly appealing for financial assistance. Many were unable to pay the full amount of unemployed and strike allowances. There were frequent reports of desertion and arrears of subscriptions, while a number of smaller societies collapsed. A deficiency of over £90 in the Midland District accounts, discovered on the death of the Treasurer, caused angry feelings and division among members in Liverpool and discredited the Association generally. Principle was having to give way to expediency in disputes and the Association made repeated surrenders; but still petty strikes were numerous, mostly over apprentices. In London it proved utterly impossible to enforce the restrictions and the SE. Board was authorized to suspend them whenever expedient. This decision was very distasteful, however, to the Midland Board, which considered apprentice-limitation 'the most important feature of the national compact', abandonment of which would 'open the floodgates of abuse . . . to a ruinous extent'. There were constant recriminations between the various Boards, the Midland even threatening to secede from the Association when the Executive refused to close the *Liverpool Journal* office for non-payment of arrears. Similar ill feeling and dissension prevailed among local societies, several threatening secession or refusing to forward contributions.

This distress, these failures and divisions, formed the background to the great Edinburgh dispute. Obviously the Association could not cope with its pecuniary liabilities. Voluntary subscriptions proved insufficient and in June 1847 the treble levy was again imposed, to 'continue until the termination of the Edinburgh strike'. It merely served, however, to increase dissension and multiply desertions. The Association was consequently 'unable to implement its engagements to the strike hands', who therefore went back on the employers' terms. The Executive were forced to acquiesce and allow the Northern Board discretionary power to open the closed offices. The strike had ended in disastrous failure, after costing the Association about £2,000.

The 'Great Amalgamation' was now bankrupt and rapidly disintegrating, but a last attempt was made to save it by a Delegate Meeting held in Liverpool in August 1847 at which radical alterations were made in organization and finance. The office of General Corresponding Secretary was abolished, owing to constant friction between him and the District Boards and dislike of the 'absolute and irresponsible power' which he tended to acquire. In future the District Boards would communicate directly with each other. Increased powers were also given to the Boards, whose functions were now taken over by the local committees in London, Liverpool, &c. The general tendency, in fact, was towards decentralization, increased independence being granted to local societies. Subscriptions, it was also decided, were only to be raised in future by approval of the members, who were to be provided with more information about Executive action. Finally, to solve the financial crisis, it was decided to raise subscriptions and to make drastic reductions in out-of-work and strike payments.

These reforms merely prolonged the existence of the Association for a few more months. Members refused to pay their subscriptions and societies to forward their contributions. Soon strike and out-of-work payments had to be suspended. Branches broke up or seceded from the Association. Hundreds of members deserted. The Association was riddled with dissension and recrimination. All faith in amalgamation departed. The final collapse came early in 1848, when the SE. Committee (London) proposed that the Association be dissolved, to which the Midland Committee 'very reluctantly' agreed.

The chief cause of failure was, of course, the trade depression, though the Association might have survived this but for its weekly out-of-work and strike payments. National, geographical, and industrial differences had also contributed to the collapse. Feelings of local independence were still strong and the Amalgamation was regarded as unwieldy. Its collapse, therefore, resulted in a reversion to the *status quo*. The London Society of Compositors was re-established as a local society in 1848, the Northern Union as the Provincial Typographical Association in 1849, and the Scottish Typographical Association in 1852–3. Ireland was still in misery and chaos as a result of the famine, but the Dublin Society had reorganized itself and local societies in other towns managed to maintain a precarious existence. Amalgamation of all typographical societies in the British Isles has been frequently mooted since, but has never again been achieved.

V

SOCIAL AND POLITICAL ASPECTS OF TRADE UNIONISM IN THE PRINTING INDUSTRY IN THE FIRST HALF OF THE NINETEENTH CENTURY

THERE are two main but opposing social characteristics of trade union-ism among printers in this period. On the one hand, typographical societies still retained much of the exclusiveness of the craft gilds, small groups of skilled and well-paid artisans, separated from the 'masses' of manual workers: as such, they concerned themselves mainly with the regulation of their own craft and remained aloof from general Labour movements. On the other hand, as the printing industry developed and capitalist competition grew, as the old gild regulations decayed and the influx of apprentices broke down the barriers of exclusiveness, printers began to feel their interests at one with those of other workers whose customary standard of life was threatened by the same economic forces. Thus there is visible among them a growing solidarity with other sec-tions of the 'proletariat'.

Typographical societies were, as we have seen, affected by the general movement towards 'Greater Unionism' in the late twenties and early thirties, as a result of which the Northern Union was established in 1830. But, while in favour of national unions of workers in particular trades, they held strictly aloof from the movement to establish a general trades' union—of the workers, that is, in all trades—with its strands of Owenite idealism, revolutionary aggression, and direct-action syndicalism. When, for example, the Manchester Typographical Society received a letter from the committee of the 'National Association for the Protection of Labour', the general trades' union organized in 1830 by John Doherty, it decided 'that the subject be considered this day six months', and there is no further mention of the matter. Similarly they declined to join the 'Society for National Regeneration', organized in 1833 by Owen, Fielden, and Doherty for the achievement, among other things, of a general 8-hour day, regarding its objects as 'impracticable'. Typographi-cal societies also appear to have held aloof from Owen's 'Grand National Consolidated Trades' Union', in 1833-4, condemning its violent and revolutionary tendencies: though they sympathized with the workers fighting against capitalist exploitation, their attitude was one of critical superiority.

When, however, they felt their interests seriously threatened in common with those of other organized workmen, they would join in combined resistance. The famous trial of the five Glasgow cotton-spinners in 1837, for example, for conspiracy, violent intimidation, and murder, followed by the Parliamentary inquiry into workmen's combinations, brought printers into line with other trade societies and roused a sense of solidarity, especially as unionism in the Irish printing trade was particularly involved. Delegates were appointed to joint trades' committees and subscriptions raised for the cotton spinners' defence.

After the Parliamentary inquiry fizzled out, however, typographical societies returned to their erstwhile isolationist policy. They took no part, as we shall see, in the Chartist agitation of the following years. Neither did they participate in the renewed movement towards 'Greater Unionism' in the forties—the 'National Association of United Trades for the Protection of Labour'. The National Typographical Association sent two delegates to the first conference of the 'United Trades' in London at Easter 1845, but the new trades' union seems to have aroused no enthusiasm among printers, at that time busy establishing their own Amalgamation. It was decided, therefore, not to send a delegate to the postponed conference on 28 July, and when the question of joining the United Trades' Association was raised again, at the N.T.A. Delegate Meeting in the spring of 1846, it was 'not recommended by the Executive' and was eventually rejected by an overwhelming majority of the members.

The *Typographical Gazette* clearly expressed the attitude of most printers towards amalgamation with the United Trades' Association. Such action, it was considered, might lead to the collapse of their own Association, which had taken so many years to build up. It had been difficult enough getting the various typographical societies to unite: how, then, could an amalgamation of so many diverse trades be formed? The idea was utterly impractical. It would also lead to an outburst of strikes. Moreover, how could the 'United Trades' decide what was a fair price for printing? By joining that Association printers might have their wages reduced to the general level.

It is clear that, despite the moderate aims and prudent administration of the United Trades' Association, as compared with the 'Grand National' of 1834 and the Chartism of 1838–42, printers still regarded attempts at 'general union' as violent and revolutionary, of doubtful legality and 'savouring of a political character'. Workmen, it was considered, should confine themselves to organizing their own trades, using moderation and justice in dealings with employers instead of aggressive coercion. At the same time, they should be ever ready to help others in resisting oppression. Typographical societies did, in fact, make numerous grants to assist other trades in strikes against reduced wages, excess of apprentices, &c.—to builders, curriers, hatters, gold-beaters, boot and shoe makers, cotton spinners, carders, fustian cutters, weavers, miners, potters, and tin-plate workers, as well as to bookbinders and typefounders. But they refused to sacrifice their independence to any 'general union' or federation.

Owenite schemes of co-operation and socialism, however, did attract disciples among journeymen printers. George Mudie, a Scottish journalist and printer, who came to London in 1820, was editor of *The Economist* (1821-2), a weekly paper devoted to the propaganda of Owenite co-operation and denunciation of the capitalist system. He also organized among London journeymen printers an 'Economical and Co-operative Society' on Owenite lines, but it seems to have received no recognition from the London typographical societies and soon ended in failure.

An effort to establish a co-operative printing office in London in 1834, by 'friends of the exchange-labour system', also failed. Owenite ideas were taken up by such printers as Hetherington, Cleave, and Watson, but there is no indication that these men ever took any part in typographical trade unionism. By the time they had risen to play leading roles in working-class radical agitation they were employers with their own printing or publishing offices in London. As such, they and other Owenite leaders of the working class came in for criticism from the London Union of Compositors regarding wages on the *Poor Man's Guardian, Crisis,* and *Pioneer.* Typographical societies, however, strongly supported them in their campaign for liberty of the press and against the 'Taxes on Knowledge', and in their efforts to secure 'improvement' and 'enlightenment' of the working class.

John F. Bray, another of the early English Socialists, who effected, in his *Labour's Wrongs and Labour's Remedy* (1838-9), a synthesis of Owenite teachings and the anti-capitalist writings of such as Thomas Hodgskin, was a journeyman printer. During the thirties and early forties he worked in several provincial towns, mostly in Leeds, and appears to have been a member of the Northern Union.

Bray was a typical self-taught working man, roused by the propaganda of such as Owen and Hodgskin. Many journeymen printers, the *Typographical Gazette* informs us, were 'well-informed men, who, independent of their ordinary avocation as compositors, are conversant in social and political economy, in the arts and sciences, in language', as is also evidenced by some of the articles in their trade periodicals. But only a small minority, it would appear, imbibed the Owenite gospel. Journeymen printers were eminently practical in their trade organizations and critical, therefore, of the Utopian air about Owenite Socialism. Yet though they rejected schemes of community building and social revolution, many typographical societies were attracted by the ideas of co-operative production and working-class 'improvement'.

The efforts at co-operative production in 1820–1 and 1834 had not been supported by the typographical societies. In 1846, however, when the N.T.A. was collapsing amid widespread unemployment and strikes, many similar schemes were advocated in the *Typographical Gazette*, as a means of 'employing the unemployed' and an alternative to useless expenditure on strikes and out-of-work benefit. The outcome of these various proposals for 'co-operative printing offices', journeymen joint-stock 'typographical companies', a 'National Printing Office', or 'National Press', was the establishment in London of the *People's Newspaper*, a weekly newspaper, the first number of which appeared on 30 May 1847.

About twenty strike hands and fifteen out-of-work members were employed on this paper. Unfortunately, however, 'the discontinuance of the London trade subscriptions, which were absolutely necessary for the continuance of the paper, rendered it impossible to proceed beyond the fifth number, and it was most reluctantly abandoned', after incurring a net loss of about £100. It was taken over by a typographical joint-stock company, which, however, was only able to survive by receiving 'the loan of the strike hands of the Association upon credit'. The Delegate Meeting in August therefore decided to drop it. It had never received much support from the provinces, where many members objected to the appropriation of Association funds, intended solely for trade-union purposes, to the establishment of a newspaper, 'thereby bringing the employed into competition with the employer'.

Typographical societies were strongly influenced by the various movements for 'improvement of the moral and social condition of the working classes'. They deplored 'the instability and ignorance' of the masses and disapproved of violence, preferring 'moderation' and 'reason' and advocating the education and 'enlightenment' of the people. Among the objects outlined in one of the many plans for reorganization of printers' unions in the early forties, it was hoped 'to improve the physical and moral condition of the members . . . to discourage intemperance and immorality; to create a desire for, and a love of the practice of virtue; and thus to secure union, intelligence, and happiness'. For similar ends, 'Typographical Mutual Improvement Societies' were established in the forties, like that at Newcastle-on-Tyne, which included among its objects 'the mutual improvement of the profession generally' and 'the training of youth', and which aimed 'to promote a better knowledge of all matters appertaining to the trade, and to cultivate the moral, intellectual, and social well-being of all parties connected with it'. Lectures were given and a library was established. A 'Reading and News Room and Library' were also established in Manchester in 1849, 'where unemployed members of the Society may find an agreeable retreat during leisure hours, and thus be drawn from the temptation of the tavern, and where also the members generally may be enabled, after business hours, to assemble in a rational and desirable manner'.

This 'improving' tendency—the movement towards discussion societies, reading-rooms, and libraries—was closely linked with the temperance movement of the time. There are a number of articles in the trade periodicals denouncing the evils of drink, particularly those connected with society meetings in public-houses, which were both expensive and degrading.

That the evils depicted were not overdrawn is proved by the Manchester minutes and reports, with their evidence of drunken and disorderly behaviour and of the expense involved by ale at monthly meetings. In 1843, however, the society ceased to meet in a public-house and rented a 'Meeting Room': beer was no longer an item of expenditure. Several other large societies also removed from the 'pot-house' in this period.

Throughout these years typographical societies maintained a definite non-political attitude, or at any rate an attitude of non-interference in party politics. There was, as yet, no distinct 'Labour Party' in the country: workmen might be Radical, Liberal, or Conservative and the introduction of politics into a trade society would therefore create division and conflict. Moreover, most working men were excluded from the franchise, while both major political parties were aristocratic in composition and outlook, so that political action seemed rather futile. Workmen placed more trust in their trade unions than in party politics, which were felt to be unconnected with trade affairs.

The Union was, in theory at any rate, a democratic organization, in which every member had a vote. It enacted industrial laws and provided social securities. Most journeymen, therefore, looked to the Union, not Parliament, for protection and support. The State had abandoned the policy of industrial regulation for *laissez-faire*. Hence, the *Compositors' Chronicle* declared, 'to expect any interference on the part of the Legislature is futile'.

Denunciations of class legislation by a property-owning, capitalist Parliament are scattered throughout trade-union periodicals and reports in this period. 'Our legislators', it was declared, 'are wrong in not doing right to all. . . . They protect some, and leave us unprotected. What have we to do, then, but protect ourselves?' 'All trade societies are the results of that combination of property and influence which . . . governs the councils of the land—that legislative combination which, by directing its whole designs to the protection of capital, has left the working man no other resource but to combine for his own preservation.'

Obviously journeymen printers felt the existing political system to be unjust and even oppressive. As individuals they were, no doubt, greatly interested in current political questions and resented exclusion from parliamentary representation. The *Compositors' Chronicle* stated that it excluded politics from its columns 'not because we consider them unworthy of regard—for we think every working man should be a politician'. The growing liberalism of government was chiefly due to the fact that 'working men think more and know more of the policy of their rulers'. But from the prudential motives which we have already mentioned—the variety of political views and danger of internal conflict, the supposed non-connexion of politics and trade affairs, and also the violent and revolutionary air about working-class political movements in this period—typographical societies steered carefully clear of politics.

They appear to have played little part in the political agitation of the years 1830–2 to secure the passing of the Great Reform Bill. Neither did they participate in the Chartist Movement of 1838–42, the violent working-class protest against social oppression, which aimed to secure political power for the masses. It is probable that they regarded the movement as futile and doomed to failure, though many no doubt approved of the Chartist aims. They were also strongly opposed to its revolutionary character and advocacy of 'physical force'. Their general attitude approached closely to that of William Lovett, who, as a London cabinet-maker, also belonged to the class of skilled artisans. This is visible not only in their advocacy of 'moral force' as opposed to 'physical', but also in their desire for the education and 'enlightenment' of the working class.

Obviously the Chartist movement—with its violent talk and violent mobs of oppressed and degraded workers, with its tendency to 'physical force' and its loud-mouthed and scheming mob orators—could have little attraction for the more educated, skilled, and aristocratic sections of the working class, including printers. There are, in fact, very few references to Chartism in the literature of typographical societies. In a brief allusion in December 1841 the *Compositors' Chronicle* expressed its opinion as to the 'futility' of Chartist attempts at alteration of the political system: 'We expect to see the mummery of 1838 renewed with the same negative result.' The editor considered it imprudent, however, to make further comment, since 'it is never desirable to damp the efforts of those who are labouring in a good cause'. His forecast was correct, for the following summer saw strikes and 'plug plots' all end in failure and imprisonment. From these violent movements printers' unions stood aloof. It was stated in October 1842 that they could 'not be identified with the recent outbreaks which have characterised the actions of some trades' societies', that they had not been seized by 'the prevailing mania'. There had not been 'a single instance wherein a letter-press printer has either forfeited his liberty, or undergone an examination before any magistrate, for engaging in the recent tumults'. Printers were concerned solely with 'the maintenance of those generally recognised principles affecting the trade' and had 'no political aim or object in view, nor the slightest approximation to partisanship of the like nature'.

It is quite certain that printers had little love for Feargus O'Connor, the Chartist demagogue. As owner of the *Northern Star*, O'Connor was, in fact, denounced as an 'unfair' employer. When the paper was printed in Leeds the workmen had frequently to complain of irregularity in the payment of wages, and when it was transferred to London an excess of apprentices was employed—on a paper which advocated the claims of labour!

It is probable, however, that although typographical societies steered clear of Chartism on account of its revolutionary character and demagogy, they approved of its political aims. As we have seen, they undoubtedly shared the Chartist resentment against exclusion from political representation, against landed wealth, capitalist oppression, and class legislation. The Corn Laws were regarded as an obvious example of the latter. Typographical societies strongly supported the Anti-Corn Law League against 'landlords' monopoly'. The Manchester Society, for example, resolved unanimously in February 1839 to 'petition Parliament for a total and immediate repeal of the Corn Laws'. The *Compositors' Chronicle* contained all the stock arguments of the Abolitionists and urged members of the trade to strive 'by every legal and constitutional means' to get rid of the Corn Laws, so as to secure cheaper bread for the working classes, increase trade, and provide more employment.

Typographical societies were not, however, consistent in their application of 'free trade' ideas. Their interests were as narrow and selfish as those of the classes they denounced. Their trade policy was monopolistic and protective: their exclusion of 'foreigners', restriction of apprentices and regulation of wages and hours were undoubtedly opposed to the principle of *laissez-faire*. They only desired 'free trade' in so far as it would benefit themselves. They demanded the removal of all duties on articles of consumption such as corn, meat, and tea, but desired the maintenance of protection for British manufactures, particularly printing. They asked for abolition of the duty on paper, but sought to maintain that on foreign books.

The repeal of the newspaper stamp, paper, and advertisement duties and removal of restrictions on the size of newspapers would, it was hoped, cause a great expansion of the printing industry, increased employment, and higher wages. Typographical societies therefore made constant efforts to secure abolition of these obnoxious 'Taxes on Knowledge'. They repeated the arguments of those who wished to obtain cheap literature, education, and 'enlightenment' for the working classes. 'The labouring millions ought to be considered. By giving them a cheap press, you do that for their minds, which, in giving them a cheap loaf, you do for their bellies.' (*Typographical Gazette.*) Their real motives, however, were not 'improving' and educational, but self-interested and economic: to secure 'more work', 'employment for the unemployed', and higher wages.

In their political agitation typographical societies adhered strictly to 'legal and constitutional means', seeking to gain their ends by steady perseverance in petitioning Parliament. There was nothing violent or subversive in their actions. Such political action as they took, moreover, was almost invariably dominated by practical, economic motives, connected with their own industrial welfare. Normally avoiding political intervention, they felt that on questions vitally affecting their particular interests and devoid of 'party' colour they had a right to make their voices heard. This is illustrated not only by their agitation against the 'Taxes on Knowledge', but also by their opposition to the various Bills

introduced by Talfourd in the late thirties and early forties to extend the
period of copyright, which, they protested, would check 'the diffusion
of knowledge' and reduce employment in the printing trade. Typographical societies throughout the country therefore petitioned against
the Bills. They were even more alarmed, in common with other trade
unions, by the Masters and Servants Bill of 1844, which threatened to
increase the existing legal and judicial oppression of workmen. The
Printer strongly denounced the Bill and called on all journeymen to
petition Parliament against it. Their efforts doubtless helped to defeat
these measures.

Typographical societies seem to have suffered very little from legal or
judicial oppression after the repeal of the Combination Laws in 1824–5.
Quite frequently, in fact, they themselves appealed to the law, with success, against their employers, particularly to secure enforcement of the
customary fortnight's notice or wages on dismissal from a 'regular'
situation. The fact that they almost invariably restricted themselves to
'moral force' in pursuance of their aims and that the threat of a fortnight's notice was their only weapon rarely brought them under the
cognizance of the law. Moreover, despite many petty strikes, good relations existed on the whole between employers and employed.

PART II

THE TYPOGRAPHICAL ASSOCIATION
1849–1914

—·᚜✿᚛·—

VI

THE BACKGROUND TO TRADE UNIONISM
IN THE PRINTING INDUSTRY
1849–1914

THE second half of the nineteenth century witnessed a tremendous expansion of the printing industry, particularly the daily press, and an 'industrial revolution' resulting from the introduction of printing machinery and mechanical composition. The forces behind these great developments were the same as in the first half of the century: the enormous growth of industry and commerce, increasing population, spread of education, and development of political democracy.

The most important factor in the growth of the provincial printing industry, especially newspapers, was the repeal of the 'Taxes on Knowledge'. The abolition of the advertisement tax in 1853, the newspaper stamp duty in 1855, and the paper duty in 1861 resulted in a mushroom growth of newspapers—dailies were established; weeklies, bi-weeklies, and tri-weeklies multiplied—while magazines, periodicals, and books greatly increased in number and printed matter of every kind became cheaper and more abundant.

In 1846, according to *Mitchell's Newspaper Press Directory*, there were 551 newspapers in the United Kingdom, of which only 14 (London 12, Dublin 2) were dailies. By 1913 there were 2,456—London, 479 (25 morning and 7 evening dailies); English Provinces, 1,394 (42 morning and 81 evening dailies); Wales, 130 (4 morning and 4 evening dailies); Scotland, 274 (8 morning and 10 evening dailies); Ireland, 189 (10 morning and 8 evening dailies); Isles, 17 (4 dailies). The number of magazines, reviews, and periodicals had also gradually increased—to 3,099.

A similar expansion took place in the number of book and jobbing offices. Manchester, for example, which had about 70 offices in 1853, had over 150 by 1893, and Sheffield, with about 20 in 1853, had now over 40. The number of offices, in fact, in most towns had approximately doubled in the half-century and was still increasing.

Another feature of the trade in this period was the expansion of London book-houses into the provinces—where wages and other costs were lower—particularly after the construction of the railway and telegraph systems and the institution of cheaper and more efficient postal services. This exodus became very marked in the last decade of the century and by about 1907 many big London firms had established provincial branches.

This tremendous expansion of the printing industry is reflected in the Census figures. The number of people employed in the letterpress printing industry in England and Wales increased from about 23,000 (London 10,000) in 1851 to about 138,000 (London 43,000) in 1911. Expansion was less rapid in Ireland—from about 2,500 in 1851 to about 6,000 in 1911. London still contained in 1911 about one-third of the printers in the United Kingdom and also the largest firms, but provincial printing had greatly expanded.

Individual offices or 'works', as they were coming to be called, had also increased in size. Such firms as Wyman's (Reading), Hazell, Watson & Viney's (Aylesbury), Blacklock's (Manchester), Bemrose's (Derby), Petty's (Leeds), and many others now employed from 100 to 200 compositors and machinemen—not to mention lithographers, electrotypers, stereotypers, assistants, warehousemen, cutters, &c.—while many provincial daily newspaper offices had from 50 to 100.

There was also a growing tendency during this period for large firms to expand and establish or acquire offices in a number of different towns. McCorquodale's, for example, had offices in London, Glasgow, Leeds, Liverpool, Newton-le-Willows, Wolverton, and Crewe; Bemrose's in Derby, Watford, and London; Petty's in Leeds and Reading; while many London firms had provincial establishments. There was a similar development in the newspaper industry: individual companies came to control several newspapers in the same town and then in other towns. It was not, however, until the twentieth century that large-scale newspaper 'combines' came into existence, such as the huge groups built up by Edward Hulton, the Harmsworths (Viscounts Northcliffe

and Rothermere), and the Berrys (Viscounts Camrose and Kemsley).
The same tendency was visible in the publication of periodicals, as
illustrated by the Harmsworths' Amalgamated Press and Lord Iliffe's
publications.

The tendency towards joint-stockism in the printing industry began
soon after the company legislation of 1855–62, conceding limited liability. As the industry grew, as production expanded and firms increased
in size, as new buildings were erected and expensive machinery was
introduced, as more and more newsprint was required and sales organization expanded, the capitalist, joint-stock element became increasingly
pronounced. In place of the traditional 'family' concerns, owned by the
actual conductors of the business, there grew up limited liability companies, controlled by directors, and works run by managers.

These developments inevitably widened the gulf between employer
and employed. Company shareholders often had little or no practical
connexion with the business and were chiefly concerned with profits and
dividends, while directors, editors, and managers were interposed between wage-earners and proprietors. Instead of a master familiar to, and
little removed from, perhaps even working with, the journeymen, there
was now a distant, perhaps unknown, wealthy, and often titled proprietor. Apart, moreover, from this contrast in social position, this
separation of employer and employed, the workers felt themselves
threatened by the massed power of capital.

The T.A. noticed and deplored these tendencies. Trade unionism had
arisen in the printing industry long before the days of large works,
mechanization, and joint-stock companies; but there is no doubt that
these factors made the journeymen increasingly conscious of its necessity.

In spite, however, of the growing tendency to large firms and amalgamation, there still existed at the end of this period hundreds of small
offices employing only a few men. The great majority of printing firms,
in fact, remained private 'family businesses'. The great 'combines' had
by no means absorbed all provincial newspapers—there were still many
independent papers, dailies, bi-weeklies, and weeklies, devoted mainly
to county or local affairs—while small jobbing offices abounded. Book
printing tended, like newspaper publishing, to become concentrated in
the hands of a few large firms, but the printing of posters, bills, circulars,
tickets, and other commercial work was executed by a mass of small, as
well as large, businesses. According to the 1911 Census there were
5,675 employers and about 130,000 employees in the letterpress printing

industry of England and Wales, an average of about 23 workers in each office, while 1,339 were 'working on their own account'. The T.A. *Return of Journeymen and Apprentices in Recognised Offices* (1909) showed that the great majority of offices were still quite small, generally employing less than a dozen members, though a good many might have up to 50 or 60 and a few over 100.

Hand-presses and platens could be bought fairly cheaply. Salmon's, the Manchester manufacturers of printing machinery, were offering in the seventies to provide complete plant for a small jobbing office for £100 and upwards. Hence we find, throughout this period, journeymen continuing to 'set up for themselves'. In the Minutes of the Executive Council alone, from 1870 to 1900, the present writer has come across no less than fifty instances of T.A. members 'commencing business for themselves', some as proprietors of local papers, but most as small jobbing printers, and there are scores of other instances reported in the *Circular*. This habit of members becoming masters, however, was harmful to unionism in two ways: it resulted in a loss to the Association and an increase in the number of small 'unfair' offices. Small employers still remained the bane of the Association, which adopted, therefore, a policy of increasing disapproval towards them: offices which did not employ at least one journeyman for a portion of the year were not 'recognized' and excluded from the 'fair list', while it was demanded that small masters themselves working at the trade must retain honorary membership. Journeymen, on the other hand, who executed jobs on printing plant in their own homes, a practice strongly disapproved of by the Association, could not retain full membership.

Despite the T.A.'s antipathy to joint-stock company organization, workmen were much better off in the large firms than in the old-fashioned small offices: wages were higher, hours shorter, apprentices proportionately fewer, and working conditions healthier in the large works. The Children's Employment Commission, reporting on the printing and miscellaneous trades in 1866, condemned the long hours, exploitation of child labour, and unhealthy working conditions prevalent in many offices, and recommended that they should be brought under control. The Factory Acts Extension Act of 1867, therefore, brought printing offices under the system of factory inspection. It was mainly intended to restrict the over-working of women and children, but also led to improvement in general working conditions—greater cleanliness, better ventilation, and sanitation. Abuses still existed, of course, and the T.A. constantly complained that the number of inspectors was insufficient to make the Act effective. It is clear, however, that conditions were worst in the innumerable small offices. Large firms were not only, as a rule, more enlightened and considerate of their work-people than small struggling employers, but their works—large, prominent buildings—were more easily inspected than out-of-the-way offices in back-streets. The new offices erected in the last quarter of the nineteenth century by big newspaper and book-printing firms were well-built, large, and spacious, with plenty of windows, ventilation fans, improved lighting, and good sanitary arrangements. Large firms, moreover, began to establish provident, sick or welfare funds, social and sports clubs for their work-people, and voluntarily conceded holidays with pay. There is no doubt that journeymen in such firms were much better off than in 'the old days', despite sentimental reminiscences.

The tremendous expansion of the printing trade during the second half of the nineteenth century was accompanied, in fact made possible, by an 'industrial revolution' in both press and composing departments. An equally important factor, of course, was the increased production of paper. Paper-making machines and chlorine bleaching had, as we have seen, provided a greatly improved supply. The cost of paper was still further reduced by the reduction (1837) and abolition (1861) of the excise and customs duties upon it. The increased demand for paper, however, resulted in an acute shortage of rags and led, in the third quarter of the century, to experiments with rag substitutes and the manufacture of paper from straw, esparto, wood celluloses, and wood pulp. The result was a considerably cheaper and vastly increased supply of paper, which made possible the enormous expansion of the printing industry in this period.

Printing Machines

Printing machines were rapidly introduced into the Provinces after the repeal of the 'Taxes on Knowledge' and the resultant expansion of the industry, especially the newspaper press. During the period 1860–70, Hoe machines—sheet-fed rotaries, equipped with four, six, eight, or ten feeding stations—were more widely used than any other type by the principal London and provincial newspapers, but were then displaced by the reel-fed rotary perfecting press—printing from a reel or continuous web of paper and producing sheets printed on both sides. An American, William Bullock, invented such a machine in 1865, and the famous Walter Press, patented in 1866 and first used for printing *The Times* in 1868, was built on the same principle. Other firms soon came into the market with rotary machines such as the Hoe, Victory, and Prestonian.

During the following years rotary web machines of greater size and productivity were constantly introduced, as the circulation and size of newspapers increased. In these multiple web machines—printing from two, three, four, six, or eight reels of paper, single or double width (i.e. two or four pages wide): quadruple, sextuple, octuple, double sextuple, and double octuple machines—all the various operations of damping, feeding, printing (both sides), cutting, folding, counting, and delivery were purely automatic. Their output was enormous: a quadruple machine would produce 48,000 copies of eight pages per hour, a giant Hoe double octuple 50,000 copies of thirty-two pages, 100,000 of sixteen, or 200,000 of eight pages per hour.

These tremendous developments, however, were mainly confined to the great metropolitan and Manchester daily newspaper offices. The mass of provincial papers, especially the weeklies and bi-weeklies, with their much smaller circulations, continued for many years to use the old single-cylinders, two- or four-feeder flat-beds, and four-, six-, or eight-feeder Hoe machines. Most provincial dailies, however, and some of the larger general printing and book firms eventually installed rotaries.

Developments in machinery for jobbing and book-work were less spectacular. Many of the smaller offices continued, throughout this period, to use the old iron hand-presses—the Stanhopes, Albions, Imperials, and Columbians. From the sixties onwards, however, small platen machines, such as the Cropper, Arab, Minerva, Universal, and many others, either treadle or power-operated, were widely introduced for printing cards, circulars, and other small jobbing work. The double-platen machine was used for larger work.

It was for long thought that fine printing, such as book-work, could not be produced by cylinder impression, which was apt to be slurred or blurred, and platen machines or the hand-press were therefore used. But cylinder machines were eventually manufactured which were so accurate that they were able to produce quite as good work as the double platen, at increased speed, with less power. They could also print much larger sheets. Of these single-cylinder, flat-bed machines —improvements on those of Koenig, Cowper, and Applegarth— the most widely used were at first Main's 'Tumbler' and then the 'Wharfedale'. The latter, first manufactured in the mid-fifties, was built on the 'stop-cylinder' principle and was capable of about 1,000 to 1,500 impressions per hour, but printed one side of a sheet only. Perfecting machines were introduced, however, printing on both sides from two reciprocating type beds and two impression cylinders, the sheets being reversed in their travel between the two cylinders either by small drums or by grippers. Two-colour machines were also manufactured, generally single-cylinder, but with two formes and, of course, double-inking apparatus.

All these machines were brought into extensive use in the provinces after 1860. Towards the end of the century, faster two-revolution machines, such as the Miehle, capable of 1,500 to 2,000 impressions per hour, were introduced from America and soon became widely used, particularly for illustrated work. By a 'tandem' arrangement, two, three, or even four machines could be coupled together for colour work. To all the above classes of machines improvements such as automatic flyers and (later) feeders were added. Most of them were driven by steam engines or by gas, oil, and other internal combustion engines, but by the end of this period electricity was rapidly displacing other forms of motive power in the printing industry.

There are few references in the typographical literature of this period to labour displacement resulting from the introduction of printing machines. Mechanization was a gradual process, accompanied by rapid expansion of the industry. Printing machines, rather than displacing pressmen, who did not exist in the provinces as a specialized class, created a new section of the trade—'machine minders'—which more than absorbed all those previously engaged in press-work. At the same time they provided a vastly increased amount of work for hand compositors, whose craft was not mechanized to any considerable extent until after 1890.

Composing Machines

Attempts at mechanical composition in the first half of the nineteenth century had all proved failures and type-setting remained a manual art. Many inventors, both at home and abroad, patented designs for composing machines in the period 1850–65, but none was successful. The first machine to be of any practical use was that invented by Robert Hattersley. It was designed on the same principles as that of Dr. Church: the operator sat at a keyboard and, by pressing the appropriate keys, released letters from a type 'charge' in the upper part of the machine, whence they fell into a series of grooves and slid down into the composing stick. Hattersley also invented a justifying machine, but it proved a complete failure and justification had still to be done by hand. Each composing machine required two or more distributing machines (another of Hattersley's inventions) to keep the type 'charges' supplied.

Hattersleys were first introduced into the office of the *Eastern Morning News* at Hull in 1866 and into the *Bradford Times* office in 1868. By 1869 they were also in use at the offices of the *Hertfordshire and Bedfordshire Express* at Hitchin and the *Midland Gazette*, Sutton-in-Ashfield, in 1870 at the *Ulverston Mirror* and *Rochdale Pilot* offices. The *Southport Daily News* installed four Hattersleys in 1876, the first large Hattersley plant, and was followed by the *Bradford Observer* (1881), *Liverpool Courier* (1883), *Sheffield Independent* (1885), *Liverpool Daily Post* (1886), *Newcastle Journal* (1889), *Preston Guardian* (1890), and *Manchester Courier* (1891). This list is not exhaustive, but it shows that many of the leading provincial papers had adopted Hattersleys by 1890.

Hattersley claimed that his machine could set 8,000 ens per hour and average 6,000. But it appears that, although some operators could compose 5–6,000 ens in an hour, the average was about 4,000. The machine could, in fact, equal the output of two or three case hands. But it showed 'a predetermination to get out of order'. It damaged type and the working parts constantly needed repair or replacement. Moreover, justification had still to be done manually by the operator and distribution required two or three more hands. The type-setting advantages of the Hattersley were, in fact, outweighed by the inefficiency and cost of distribution, on which boys and girls had to be employed as cheap labour in order to work the machines economically. Obviously, the problem of mechanical composition was not yet satisfactorily solved.

The Thorne type-setting machine, introduced from America in the late eighties, was an improvement on the Hattersley. It was worked by a three-man 'team', consisting of an operator, justifier, and 'man behind'. The keyboard was of better design and required less 'thumping' than the Hattersley's, the justifier was furnished with mechanical appliances which expedited his work, and distribution was automatic, the distributing cylinder usually being looked after by a boy behind the machine. Based on the same mechanical type-setting principles as the Hattersley, the Thorne was liable to similar defects and stoppages, but its output was considerably higher. The average appears to have been about 6–8,000 ens per hour, though figures as high as 10–14,000 were achieved by expert operators. Thorne machines were first introduced into the offices of the *Bradford Observer* and the *Manchester Guardian* and *Evening News* in 1889 and into the *Belfast News Letter* office in 1892.

To gain maximum speed and efficiency, however, keyboard, type-casting, and line-justifying had to be combined. This was achieved in the Linotype and Monotype machines. The Linotype, designed by the American, Ottmar Mergenthaler, and first used in the office of the *New York Tribune* in 1886, is operated, like the other machines, by means of a keyboard, which assembles a line of matrices released from magazines similar to those of the Hattersley; these are automatically justified into a line; molten metal is then pumped in automatically and a bar or 'slug' for a whole line (a 'line o' type') is cast; the matrices are then returned to the magazines by a mechanical device, while the slugs can be remelted immediately after the forme has been printed from or stereotyped; distribution in the usual sense is thus entirely avoided.

Output averaged about eighty lines or 5–6,000 ens per hour, though much higher figures were reached. The first Linotype, known as the 'Blower', was liable to numerous breakdowns and stoppages, but improved models soon overcame most of the early defects. The Linotype therefore provided efficiency, speed, and economy and finally solved the problem of mechanical composition. It was particularly suited to newspaper offices, in which it rapidly displaced hand composition.

The *Newcastle Chronicle* was apparently the first office in this country to install a Linotype, in 1889, but was quickly followed by the *Nottingham Guardian, Sheffield Telegraph, Leeds Mercury*, and *Preston Guardian*. By 1902 there were 1,172 Linotypes and 87 Hattersleys in the various branches of the T.A. and hand composition was rapidly becoming a thing of the past in newspaper offices. A few case hands were still required to set up the most difficult matter, but improvements in design soon rendered the Linotype capable of casting every arrangement of type appearing in a newspaper.

The Linotype was not much used in this country at first outside newspaper offices. Book-printing and jobbing firms were very slow in taking up the idea of mechanical type-setting. Linotypes were thought to be unsuitable for better-class printing—though they and Intertype machines were used for book-work in America—their range of matrices was insufficient for more complicated work, corrections were apt to prove expensive (each one necessitating the recasting of a whole line), and Linotypes were economical only where rapid, continuous, and fairly straightforward composition was required. It was only in daily newspaper offices, therefore, that the Linotype had a revolutionary effect.

Towards the end of the century, however, the Monotype machine was introduced from America, where it had been invented by Tolbert Lanston in 1887. The Monotype is not, like the Linotype, a single unit, but two separate machines—the keyboard, or perforator, and caster. The keyboard operator, by tapping appropriate lettered keys, releases compressed air which causes metal punches to rise making perforations in a continuous paper roll or ribbon. Spacing and justification are also provided for automatically. The ribbon is then fed into the casting machine and dictates its mechanical action: molten metal is automatically pumped into the appropriate matrices by compressed air, the type sizes and spaces are automatically determined, and a justified line of separate types is cast.

The Monotype, with its independent keyboard and caster, its wide range of matrices, and its distinct letter-types, facilitating correction in proof, is admirably suited for book-work. By May 1902 there were 28 keyboards and 18 casters in T.A. branches, used mainly for books and magazines. Keyboard operators averaged 5,000 to 6,000 ens per hour on common matter. But mechanical composition did not make a rapid conquest of book-work and jobbing houses. In 1914 most jobbing work and perhaps also most books and better weekly periodicals and magazines were still set by hand.

The effects of this mechanical revolution in the printing trade were, on the whole, beneficial to the journeymen. As the T.A. General Secretary stated in 1901: 'At one time some were pessimistic enough to believe that the days of compositors were numbered, but . . . the position of the Association is stronger and the industrial status of those members who work Linotype machines better than in pre-Linotype days.' Gloomy forecasts were, indeed, made in the early nineties, when composing machines were rapidly displacing hand compositors and hundreds of men were thrown out of work. The situation was particularly bad during the trade depression of 1894–6. Other forces, however, were making for improvement. Mechanical composition, decreasing the cost and increasing the speed of production, resulted in more, cheaper, and larger newspapers, with extra editions and supplements, while the output of magazines and books was enormously increased. Moreover, the expanded production resulting from mechanical composition necessitated an increased number of hands for make-up and imposition. Thus displaced case hands were, to a great extent, absorbed in the expanding industry. Moreover, as we shall see, composing machines also resulted in increased wages, reduced hours, and improved working conditions.

The extent of the 'industrial revolution' in this period must not, however, be exaggerated. Hand composition had by no means been super-seded. Some case hands were still employed in newspaper offices and most of the composition in jobbing and book houses was still done by hand. The great majority of T.A. members, in fact, at the end of this period were still hand compositors.

Although the printing industry was rapidly expanding in this period and absorbing workers displaced by the new machinery, there was always a fairly large number of unemployed and casuals. Printing, in common with other industries, continued to suffer from periodic trade depres-sions. According to the Board of Trade's Abstracts of Labour Statistics, the lowest annual percentage returned as unemployed in the printing and allied trades was 1·3 (1873) and the highest 5·7 (1894), but in some months it rose as high as 8 or 9. Moreover, T.A. figures show that in slump periods about a quarter, or even a third, of the members were casually employed and that even in periods of good trade about a fifth to an eighth were casuals. Unemployment was, in fact, the greatest problem facing the Association.

VII

ESTABLISHMENT AND GROWTH OF THE
TYPOGRAPHICAL ASSOCIATION
1849–1914

THE movement towards a reincarnation of the old Northern Union had begun even before the last flickers of life had departed from the body of the National Typographical Association. After agreeing to the latter's dissolution in January 1848, the Midland Committee issued an 'Address' to members of their district, requesting their co-operation in reorganizing the old Northern Union; but division and recrimination still prevailed and on 30 May 1848 the Committee held its last meeting. Nevertheless, local societies still survived or were re-established in many provincial towns, between which correspondence continued, while the tramp system revived. The idea of provincial union also remained strong and as trade recovered in 1848–9 many proposals were made for re-establishment of the Northern Union.

The Manchester Society, founder of that Union, was the focus of provincial hopes: its criticisms of the 'Amalgamation' had been fully justified, and it had acquired increased wealth and power in its years of isolation. The Potteries Society therefore called on Manchester, as early as October 1847, 'to form another Northern Union'. But the Manchester committee, though regretting the situation which had resulted from the failure of the N.T.A., still clung to their isolationist policy and opposed any system of union except on the basis of local autonomy. They made the same reply to similar queries from Liverpool in November 1847 and Hereford in April 1848. In July 1848, however, a circular was issued by the Preston Society, 'calling upon various societies throughout the kingdom to form a general union, upon the principles of the late Northern Union'. At first the Manchester Society took no action, but in September, 'communications having been received from many important societies, expressing a desire that the Manchester Society would establish a system of union similar to the late Northern Union', the committee took the matter into consideration and eventually decided 'that a union, embracing many of the leading principles of the late Northern Union, be established'. Regulations for the establishment of a 'Provincial Typographical Union' were drawn up, printed, and distributed throughout the provinces in October 1848.

Differences arose, however, between the Manchester and Liverpool Societies. The latter took strong exception to the absence from the Manchester plan of a 'Central Government' and a tramp-relief reimbursement fund and therefore issued a circular proposing that these be added. But the Manchester committee was 'strongly of opinion that the system of control by a Central Board of Management is fraught with evils of great magnitude, uselessly expensive in its working, and tending . . . to produce dissatisfaction and disruption'. They still adhered, in fact, to the policy of local independence.

The Liverpool Society therefore issued proposals of its own and eventually invited delegates from provincial societies to a meeting at Sheffield on 4 June 1849 to consider the foundation of a 'Provincial Typographical Union . . . upon the general basis of the late Northern Union'. On that and the two following days, representatives from Liverpool, Sheffield, Preston, Nottingham, Halifax, Bolton, Wigan, and Wakefield met at the 'Fleur-de-lis' Tavern, Angel Street, Sheffield, and resolved upon the establishment of a 'Provincial Typographical Association'.

In their 'Address' issued after this meeting the Sheffield delegates outlined the evils which had resulted from the 'disunion' of the last two years—the multiplication of apprentices, reduced wages, and tramping abuses—evils which showed clearly that 'no locality is or can be safe under a system of isolation'. The new Association aimed 'to secure the co-operation of the entire profession in any movement calculated to advance our common interests' and to 'elevate our poverty-stricken but still noble profession'. In more precise terms, its objects were 'the limitation of the number of apprentices, restriction of the hours of labour, regulation of the standard of wages, and a general supervision of all matters affecting the interests of the printing profession'. The majority of its rules were word-for-word the same as those of the old Northern Union. The chief difference was that strike hands were to receive a weekly allowance—three-fourths of the wages of the town—for three months, instead of £4 and a 'backed' card. Opinion was also divided as to whether or not tramp relief should be replaced by an emigration fund, but a vote of the trade eventually decided in favour of tramping. Thus there was nothing novel about the Provincial Typographical Association : it was merely a 're-establishment' of the Northern Union and carried on where the latter had left off in 1844.

Delegates from eight societies had inaugurated the P.T.A. at Sheffield in June 1849. By the end of the first half-year it had nineteen branches and a membership of 481, mainly confined to Lancashire, Cheshire, and the West Riding, with a few outposts elsewhere. In the east, south, and south-west it had no branches whatsoever and only one, Waterford, in Ireland. Many provincial societies, once in union, now stood isolated— Birmingham, Blackburn, Bradford, Bristol, Derby, Hull, Leeds, Leicester, Manchester, and Norwich. After the Amalgamation had collapsed amid disillusionment, discontent, and recrimination, they preferred to hold aloof from any Association and rely upon their local resources. Many smaller societies had disintegrated or carried on a precarious existence as mere relief stations. In innumerable towns journeymen printers were completely unorganized.

By June 1914, however, the Association had 157 branches and 23,310 members, scattered all over England, Wales, and Ireland, and including every town of any importance except London and Dublin. This expansion took place in a series of forward surges, roughly corresponding with trade 'booms', in the years 1854–6, 1860–1, 1870–6, and 1887–93. In such times of increased employment and 'advance movements', when wages were being raised and hours reduced, the Association swept forward, attracting new recruits and storming non-union towns. But when trade slackened and depression set in, when hundreds were out of work and wages were reduced, enthusiasm waned, members fell away, and towns were lost. The Association was thrown on the defensive, striving to keep what it had won, forced here and there to retreat, but fighting strong rearguard actions and holding strong-points wherever possible. There were deserters and traitors, of course, while employers often broke right through where defence was weakest and overran territory previously won by the Association. Membership became stationary, sometimes fell, till trade revived, when the unionists, their spirits roused and strengthened by fresh reinforcements, sharpened their old weapons and took the offensive once again, reconquering lost terrain, sweeping over and beyond the old advance positions. After the appointment of 'organizers' in 1891 growth became steadier and more continuous, though still greatest in periods of busy trade, in 1898–1900, 1907, and 1912–14.

These offensives and this steady organizing had, by the end of this period, carried the union flag from the north of England into even the smallest towns of the midlands, east, south, and west, into Wales and all over Ireland. They were not revolutionary and ephemeral outbursts, followed by collapse, as in many labourers' unions in the nineteenth century, but steady, well-organized movements, resulting in permanent increase of membership.

This 'missionary' work was at first carried out chiefly by the branches. Large towns like Manchester, Liverpool, Sheffield, Birmingham, Newcastle, and Cardiff tried to 'organize' their surrounding districts, so as to restrict competition by low-paid or apprentice labour and prevent the influx of surplus hands from the small towns and country districts. They sent out deputations to address meetings, scatter literature, and, if possible, form sections of their branches in these outlying areas. Several had as many as eight or ten such sections under their wing which, as they grew stronger, developed into separate branches of the Association.

Much depended on the zeal and organizing ability of branch secretaries. Some enthusiasts accomplished a great deal, but the majority, working printers and spare-time officials, were too poorly recompensed, too tired, or too apathetic, to carry on the work systematically. The Delegate Meeting of 1853 therefore suggested that the Executive, which had so far merely issued printed 'addresses' to the trade, should send 'delegations' to non-union towns. The Executive, however, after planning an extensive tour by four delegates, eventually abandoned the idea as too expensive and issued another 'address' instead.

A number of branches were active in missionary work during the following years and the Association Secretary occasionally visited particular towns to address meetings. But the P.T.A. had, as yet, no full-time salaried officer and organizing was therefore scrappy and intermittent. Delegate Meetings, the *Monthly Circular*, and tramping helped, however, to bind the provincial trade together, and in 1863 a Relief Association was established which it was hoped would include all societies in the United Kingdom in one great tramping organization.[1] This was never achieved—London and Scotland stood aloof—but the R.A. brought many more provincial societies into union, both in England and Ireland.

Several Irish societies had applied to join the P.T.A. in 1849–50 and Waterford actually became a branch for a short time. But Ireland was in a state of chaos and the Sheffield Executive soon came to the conclusion 'that no English Executive can successfully manage an Association embracing branches so geographically distant, and so materially different in their regulations and their mode of remuneration, as those of the sister kingdom'. They recommended the Irish societies 'to establish a separate organization for their own country' and promised their co-operation. Attempts at Irish union failed, however, and the question of organizing Ireland was therefore taken up by the P.T.A. Delegate

[1] See below, pp. 273–4.

Meeting in 1861, which decided to send a delegation 'to assist our Irish brethren in instituting an Irish Association'. As a result, Dublin attempted to re-establish the Irish Typographical Union in 1863, but soon found it impossible to cope with the problems of apprentice labour, low wages, and indifference and was forced in 1867 to abandon the idea altogether. Ireland, therefore, relapsed into disorganization.

Meanwhile, however, the Relief Association had been established in England and a number of Irish societies applied for admission. The Executive decided to extend the R.A. to include the sister isle and nine Irish societies became branches in the years 1866–8: Belfast, Galway, Carlow, Castlebar, Cork, Kilkenny, Londonderry, Newry, and Wexford. Dublin, however, by far the largest society in Ireland, stood aloof.

The R.A. had, by this time, spread a network of relief routes over the English provinces. All recognized English provincial societies, except Leeds and Norwich, had joined by the end of 1863. By 1865, when the seat of government was transferred to Manchester, the R.A. had 61 branches, with a total membership of 2,549, including the 37 branches and 1,984 members of the P.T.A. The R.A., however, was merely a tramp organization, 'entirely unconnected with the objects of a trade union', and the Executive had no control over wages, hours, or apprentices in purely R.A. branches, which were often inclined to laxity in trade affairs. The Executive therefore recommended to the Delegate Meeting in 1877 that the R.A. should be extinguished as a separate organization, that R.A. branches should be offered membership of the P.T.A., and that, as a corollary, the rule restricting the latter's operations to England and Wales should be abolished. These proposals were adopted, the word 'Provincial' was dropped from the title and the Typographical Association came into existence. As a result, most of the purely R.A. branches in both England and Ireland applied to join the T.A.

By this time the Association was spreading all over the midlands and south of England. In this missionary work the branches were now assisted by a full-time Association Secretary, first appointed in 1865, but it was not until after the Delegate Meeting in 1872 that a really organized attempt was made to extend the boundaries of the Association. That meeting instructed the Executive 'to use vigorous efforts, by delegations or otherwise, to extend the principles of the Association' in non-union districts. During the next two years the Association Secretary made missionary tours all over England, visiting scores of towns, addressing meetings, distributing pamphlets, and establishing many new branches. At the same time, the large towns were vigorously pressing on with district organization.

The result of this outburst of missionary effort was a considerable numerical and geographical expansion of the Association. Between 1870 and 1876 the P.T.A. more than doubled its membership. At the end of 1876 it had 74 branches and 4,358 members. There were now thick clusters of branches in the industrial areas of Lancashire and Yorkshire, the north-east and midlands. The Association had also spread into hitherto unorganized areas, into the less industrialized districts and smaller towns of the eastern counties, the south, and south-west.

This expansion ceased as depression came in the mid-seventies. Membership rose considerably in 1877, owing to the accession of former R.A. branches, but in the following seven years it remained practically stationary. A number of the new branches collapsed, owing to lack of members, unemployment, apathy, and employers' hostility. The Association stood on the defensive, trying to consolidate its recent gains, to prevent wage reductions and combat unemployment. Missionary effort almost ceased. Little progress was therefore made: by the end of 1884 the Association had 85 branches and 6,170 members. That it actually grew, however, instead of contracting, during the 'Great Depression' was a considerable achievement.

Enthusiasm revived, with trade, in the mid-eighties. At a special meeting in August 1885 the Executive decided to inaugurate a great missionary campaign. They purchased copies of May's *Press Guide*, made a detailed examination of all the counties in England and Wales, and assigned towns and districts to the various branches for missionary purposes. They also printed several thousand propagandist pamphlets. A period of tremendous missionary activity followed. Almost every tiny town in the country was visited, meetings were held, tracts distributed, members enrolled, and new sections or branches established. There was also a campaign to open 'closed' offices and bring in non-unionists in the older society-towns. Deputations waited on employers, circulars were distributed, pressure was brought to bear through 'fair lists' and trades councils. The 'fair contracts' resolution, passed by many public bodies under political pressure from trade unions, had a powerful effect.[1] Many employers actually asked to have their offices recognized as 'fair' and undertook to run them on union lines.

[1] See below, p. 305.

The Association Secretary shared in this missionary work, but it was obviously impossible for him to be touring the country and, at the same time, dealing with the growing mass of central office work. Neither had branch secretaries much time or inclination for continuous missionary effort (unpaid). The Delegate Meeting of 1891 therefore decided on the appointment of full-time paid 'organizers'. The Executive at first appointed two, one for the northern, the other for the eastern and southern counties. The Delegate Meeting of 1893 added a third, for Ireland, and allocated definite districts to the two English organizers, north and south of a line drawn from Boston to Bristol. But the Representative Council of 1895, while agreeing to give the organizing work in Ireland another year's trial, decided to replace the two English organizers by an Assistant Secretary, whose services would, if necessary, be available for missionary work. It was felt that the organizing system was too expensive and that the work should be left to the branches.

This retrograde, mistaken step was soon retrieved, however, for the two English organizers were restored in 1896 (southern) and 1903 (northern), while the Irish organizer was retained. The Delegate Meeting of 1908, moreover, appointed another organizer for England and Wales.[1] These men, acting under Executive control, toured the country continuously, carrying out missionary work—visiting non-society towns, addressing meetings, distributing trade-union literature, interviewing men and employers, explaining the objects and methods of the Association, establishing new branches and sections, helping to maintain branch efficiency, and assisting in the settlement of disputes. To their work is mainly due the rapid and continuous growth of the Association up to 1914, particularly in the south of England. They were strongly assisted, however, by branch and district organizing.

As a result of these missionary efforts the membership and area of the Association rapidly expanded after 1884, particularly in the 'boom' years 1887–93. By the end of 1901 the T.A. had 133 branches and 16,600 members. Branches were now sprinkled all over southern England, particularly around London and along the south coast. The number of branches in Wales and Ireland had also increased and several more had been established in small towns in the old Association area. This expansion was steadily continued in the first decade of the twentieth century and by June 1914 the Association had 157 branches and 23,310 members.

[1] This was because G. H. Roberts, the southern organizer, had been elected to Parliament.

Geographical expansion was accompanied by large increases in branch membership, as shown by the following examples:

				1852	*1914*
Cardiff	.	.	.	15	440
Halifax	.	.	.	19	165
Liverpool	.	.	.	267	1,662
Manchester	.	.	.	293	2,553
Nottingham	.	.	.	20	532
Sheffield	.	.	.	57	590

This growth was natural, with increasing population and expanding industry, but it would have been impossible without branch loyalty and organization, steady maintenance of union principles, and vigorous missionary work.

The Association was not built in a day. It took years of patient organizing to overcome the obstacles to trade unionism in the provincial printing trade. The greatest was the industry's geographical dispersion, which entailed constant missionary effort and the establishment of branches and sections in towns all over the country. Another was the profusion of small offices, employing only one or two men, paying low wages, often mere apprentice 'nurseries', and very difficult to organize. The Association also had to face the hostility of employers, particularly in the outlying non-union areas, and apathy, indifference, or definite non-unionism among workmen.

How, in face of these tremendous difficulties, was the Association able to expand as it did? The problem of geographical dispersion was greatly lessened by the development of transport and communications, by the railway, penny post, telegraph, and telephone. The hostility of employers was reduced by a more general 'recognition' of trade unionism and its useful function in restricting 'unfair' competition and regulating industrial relationships. The apathy of members was often more apparent than real. Their unionism was, after all, the result of a common desire to protect and maintain their standard of life. There was a kind of basic brotherhood among them as working printers, an underlying loyalty, exhibited in innumerable strikes, though less apparent in ordinary times. Moreover, a 'rat' brought upon himself disgrace, a heavy fine, or even expulsion. The Association benefits also helped to maintain loyalty: members were loath to sacrifice unemployment, superannuation, and funeral benefits after contributing for several years.

Towards non-members the Association adopted a mixed policy of persuasion and compulsion. In non-society areas the advantages of union were placed to the fore: the Association, it was pointed out, would enable the men to secure fair wages and working conditions and to restrict the number of apprentices, in addition to providing friendly benefits—relief in unemployment, old age, and death. The Association also penetrated non-union areas and offices by a policy of infiltration, secretly introducing staunch unionists to 'leaven the lump'.

Such a policy of persuasive appeal was the only one possible in unorganized areas. But in strong union towns a different attitude was adopted—coercive, compelling non-unionists to come in—what we would nowadays call a 'closed-shop' policy. Before a man could start work in a 'recognized' office, he had to produce a union 'working card'.

This compulsion to join a trade union was opposed to the liberal idea of individual liberty. The Association appealed to this principle against antagonistic, non-union employers, asserting the right of individual workers to join without being victimized, but where it was strongly organized denied individuals any right *not* to join. Its policy was, in fact, based not on principle but expediency.

The Association was on stronger ground when using practical arguments. A man should not, it was maintained, be free to work for what hours and wages he pleased to the detriment of his fellow workers. A non-member in a society town enjoyed advantages gained for him by the union, to which, therefore, he should be forced to contribute. Moreover, a non-unionist element placed a powerful weapon in employers' hands and often caused the failure of strikes.

On these grounds compulsion was justified, but it must be 'moral compulsion only'. The Association had 'no sympathy with any attempt to coerce a man by physical force or social persecution', but members might refuse to work with non-members. Opposition to non-unionists, however, frequently went beyond this. As J. W. Crompton stated in 1860, 'opprobrious epithets' were flung at non-members and 'acts of petty tyranny and intimidation' committed against them.[1] If this 'moral suasion' failed, the unionists would approach their employer and ask for the non-member's dismissal, failing which they might threaten to strike.

To what extent had the Association succeeded in organizing journeymen printers by the end of this period? It had, as we have seen, spread from its original nucleus in Lancashire and Yorkshire, throughout the English provinces, Wales, and across the Irish Sea. London and Dublin

---

[1] Crompton, J. W., *Report on Printers' Strikes and Trade Unions since January 1845* (1860).

were, in fact, the only two cities of any importance in England, Wales, and Ireland outside its sphere. In many towns, particularly in the north, it had established powerful branches which included nearly all eligible members. Henry Slatter estimated in 1892, before the Royal Commission on Labour, that 'in the towns where we have branches ... we have at least four-fifths of the men in the trade as members of our Association'. But he was forced to admit that 'in the southern and the south-western counties there are a very large number of non-union men. They are nearly all non-union men.' The situation had improved considerably by 1914, as a result of organizing effort and the establishment of more southern branches, but there was still a great deal of missionary work to be done. Ireland was in the worst condition. A writer in the *Circular* in 1892 stated 'that in sixteen entire counties there is no branch or society of any kind in existence to look after the printer's interest'. Here, too, there was improvement by 1914, resulting from the organizing work of Hugh McManus, but the situation was still bad.

Obviously the Association was strongest in the large offices and big towns, weakest in the small shops and country districts. But even in staunch union towns there were 'unfair' offices. According to the *List of Society and Non-Society Offices in the various Branches of the T.A.*, published in 1893, there were 1,353 society and 260 non-society houses in the Association area. This list, moreover, ignored the numerous small towns in which there were no branches of the T.A., while, on its own admission, 'some of the offices classed as "Society" are not strictly so, but Members are permitted to work there'. Many, in fact, of these so-called 'Society' houses contained non-members. This is evident from the *Return of Journeymen and Apprentices in Recognised Offices* obtained in 1904, according to which there were 12,814 members and 1,788 non-members employed in so-called 'fair' houses. Allowing for the 'unfair' houses and non-society towns, it seems probable that not more than about two-thirds of the compositors and machinemen in the provincial printing trade belonged to the Association at the end of this period.

The Association never, like the labourers' or general unions, flung open its doors to all and sundry. Its growth was a steady organized process, not a series of mass enrolments: quality was never sacrificed to quantity. Much of the old craft gild exclusiveness still clung to the Association. It was composed of skilled tradesmen, from a craft steeped in tradition and in which the hereditary element was still strong, a craft which rigidly insisted upon a seven years' servitude and opposed dilution by unskilled or semi-skilled labour. Moreover, it was an Association axiom that the supply of labour must be restricted to maintain existing wage rates.

Hence none but legally qualified journeymen, able to produce indentures or proof of seven years at the trade, in receipt of the minimum standard of wages and working in 'fair' offices, could gain admission, while the applications even of 'legal' men were submitted to careful scrutiny. All new members had to pay an entrance-fee, while those guilty of past 'misconduct', such as 'ratting', or of 'holding aloof' from, or being 'antagonistic' to, the Association, were subjected to heavy fines, and notoriously 'bad' characters might even be refused admission. The Association also attempted to restrict the entry of incompetent workmen, who would lower the standard of the 'profession' and, more important, perhaps work at less than union rates or become a burden on the out-of-work fund.

Societies were subject to the same entry restrictions as individuals. The Executive required a copy of their rules, the names and 'antecedents' of members, the number of non-members and apprentices, the established wage rates and working hours, and the state of each office. If a society was not 'up to standard' in these respects it was refused admission.

Similar conditions governed the 'opening' of 'closed' offices. The Association was, in fact, a kind of exclusive trade club, membership of which was restricted to those possessing certain qualifications. Whereas some unions enrolled all and sundry and *then* attempted to improve their condition, the T.A. required that applicants should first reach a certain standard *before* being eligible for admission.

The Association was never able, however, to enforce these rigid rules. Insistence upon them would have prevented all expansion and quickly brought about the Association's collapse. It was only by the virtual suspension of the apprentice and minimum-wage rules that the Association was able to expand into non-union areas and open 'unfair' offices. The Association had first to get the men in and *then* gradually try to regulate wages, hours, and apprentices.

It also proved impossible, in innumerable instances, to enforce the rule against members and non-members working together. 'Open' or 'mixed' offices existed, in fact, in almost every branch. The Executive were also forced to adopt a very lax policy towards non-unionists, to admit them without fine and, during missionary campaigns, to 'throw open the books' to all applicants at the minimum entrance-fee. Moreover, among the new recruits there were undoubtedly many semi-skilled and incompetent workmen. The Association had to take anybody and everybody who applied so long as they had served a seven-years' apprenticeship, and even many who had not.[1]

The expansion and mechanization of the printing industry, the levelling influences of a common education, and the pressure of applicants for employment had, by the end of the nineteenth century, converted the typographical 'profession' into a 'trade'. But the T.A. still retained its essentially 'craft' characteristics. It had not expanded its ranks to absorb all workers in the printing industry, but remained an organization of skilled letterpress printers. Lithographers, bookbinders, stereotypers, and paper workers formed their own trade societies. The Association also excluded printers' labourers or 'assistants' from its ranks, the unapprenticed, semi-skilled, and lower-paid workers in the trade, who were not supposed to touch type or 'make ready' on machines. They, too, eventually formed unions of their own.[2]

In London differentiation and specialization were carried even farther, there being separate societies for compositors, readers, pressmen, machine minders, platen minders, and Monotype-caster attendants. The T.A., however, came to include all these sections: at first consisting of compositors and pressmen only, it began, towards the end of the century, to organize machinemen (platen, cylinder, and rotary) and, later on, caster attendants and readers.

The organization of machinemen and caster attendants will be dealt with later, when we come to the 'industrial revolution' in typography. Readers had for many years belonged to the T.A., being very often ex-compositors, but their membership was optional. Moreover, they must have served seven years' apprenticeship to the printing trade, which excluded many. The 1908 Delegate Meeting therefore decided to admit readers who had held situations as such for at least two years, provided they confined themselves strictly to their own department; but membership was not, as yet, compulsory. Employers were opposed to this extension of T.A. jurisdiction and secured the inclusion of a clause in the national 'Agreement on Rules' of 1911 expressly stating that readers' membership was 'permissive' only. This clause was strongly denounced, however, by the T.A. Delegate Meeting of 1918, which decided that membership of readers should be compulsory.

The Association kept its doors tightly closed against admission of

---

[1] See below, p. 185, for the breakdown of the apprenticeship system.
[2] See below, Chapter XII, for the other unions in the printing and kindred trades.

females. The entry of women into the trade would, it was feared, increase unemployment and lower wages, while there were also deep-rooted social and moral prejudices against it. The Association therefore adopted an uncompromising policy of non-recognition and exclusion of female labour, classing as 'unfair' any office in which women were employed on T.A. work.

Their opposition was not, however, entirely successful. According to the 1911 Census Abstracts there were in the provinces 464 females employed as hand compositors, 81 composing-machine operators, and 154 machine minders, while over 15,000 were simply described as 'others in printing'. The great majority of the latter were doubtless semi-skilled, not employed on 'craft' work, but the figures indicate the failure of T.A. efforts at complete exclusion. This failure is also evident from numerous references in T.A. records to women and girls employed at case or machine-minding, usually at about a third or half the men's standard rates.

The futility of the policy of exclusion, combined with the growth of feeling in favour of the 'equality of the sexes', induced the T.A. to alter its tactics. Instead of rigidly prohibiting the employment of women, they began to demand that women should, if employed, receive the union wage rates. The Conference of Typographical Societies in 1886, 'while strongly of opinion that women are not physically capable of performing the duties of a compositor', even recommended 'their admission to membership of the various Typographical Unions upon the same conditions as journeymen, provided always the females are paid strictly in accordance with scale'.

There is no evidence of the T.A. admitting any woman member, but it insisted upon the principle of equal wages, 'closing' offices where women were employed at reduced rates. The first instance of an office employing females being recognized by the Executive was in 1894, after Hazell, Watson & Viney's, of Aylesbury, had agreed to place their women compositors on the branch rate of wages. Similarly, in 1899, the Executive sanctioned the opening of the *Grimsby News* office, 'providing that the T.A. apprentice rules are complied with, females having served their apprenticeship to be paid full wages and work under identically the same conditions as the men'. But they 'did not think it advisable to admit females to membership of the T.A.'

T.A. opposition to the employment of women was clearly evident in regard to composing machines. Though forced to allow girls to distribute for the Hattersley, the Association rigidly opposed the employment of female operators and sought to restrict the keyboard to T.A. members and apprentices only. But many firms—particularly branch establishments of London houses in small provincial towns—employed women as keyboard operators, especially on the Monotype.

The T.A. adopted a similar attitude in regard to the employment of women on printing machines. They had no objection to females 'feeding', but were strongly opposed to their 'making ready' and minding. Despite T.A. hostility, however, many firms, including some of the largest general printing houses, employed women as minders, especially of platen machines.

The T.A. made no effort whatsoever to organize women in the industry, chiefly because this would entail recognition of their lower wages and thus threaten men's rates. The Association was in fact fundamentally opposed to the entry of women into the trade, fearing they would lower working standards.

Other unions, such as the National Society of Operative Printers and Assistants and the Paper Workers, undertook the work of organizing women, while a separate Society of Women Employed in the Bookbinding and Printing Trades was established, but the T.A. strongly opposed their attempts to organize females engaged on 'craft' work.

T.A. Finances

T.A. finances reflect, even more clearly than T.A. membership figures, the general trade situation. In periods of good trade, income from subscriptions rose, out-of-work expenditure fell, and the General Fund grew; but in trade depression, with a reduced income and heavy out-of-work payments, deficits resulted and, in the worst periods, bankruptcy threatened. The T.A.'s financial history is closely bound up with that of its out-of-work payments. A serious strike would also bring grave danger: hence the cautious and conciliatory policy pursued by the Executive, deprecating strikes and avoiding them whenever possible. Another important factor, in the later part of this period, was the Superannuation Fund, which took an ever-growing proportion of subscriptions and prevented adequate provision for the General Fund.

For its first thirty-odd years the T.A. had a precarious existence. Funds at the end of 1849 totalled £72 and were only £684 ten years later, after rising and falling uncertainly according to strike expenditure. The latter was, in these early years, the only Association benefit, tramp relief still being local and out-of-work, funeral, and superannuation benefits not yet established. The subscription was 2d. per week.

In 1861 the General Fund topped £1,000, so next year—this was a period of serious trade depression—the Executive temporarily halved the subscription, in response to branch requests. In 1863 the Relief Association was established, with a subscription of a penny per week, to provide 'mileage' relief to 'unemployed travelling printers', so the P.T.A. subscription was reduced by a halfpenny, to 1½d. per week. The R.A.'s income, however, proved to be less than half its expenditure, so its subscription had soon to be raised to 1½d. and benefits curtailed, while heavy loans had to be secured from the P.T.A., reducing the latter's General Fund to £793 at the end of 1863.

Trade was now improving, however, relief payments fell and the R.A. paid back most of its debt to the P.T.A. But the latter experienced a serious crisis in 1865 as a result of a strike at the Liverpool *Daily Post*, which reduced the General Fund to £337 by the end of the year and necessitated a levy. This brought it up to £949 by December 1866, but strike payments were again heavy in 1867, while further loans had to be made to the R.A. owing to a sharp trade depression, so that the Fund fell to £747. The P.T.A. subscription was therefore restored to the original twopence.

The next few years were very prosperous, a period of booming trade, 'advance movements', and reduced relief expenditure. The R.A. not only liquidated its debt to the P.T.A., but by the end of 1872 had a balance of nearly £1,100. The P.T.A. General Fund rose to £1,838 by December 1871, but in 1872 serious strikes for increased wages and shorter working hours in Birmingham, Liverpool, Nottingham, and Preston reduced it to £689. It recovered, however, in the following years to reach £2,302 by the end of 1877.

Prosperity, however, proved almost as dangerous as depression. The R.A. subscription, which had been raised to 2d. in 1869 to meet the heavy relief expenditure, was reduced to 1½d. again in 1871 as soon as the trade boom brought surpluses instead of deficits. Moreover, in 1872 weekly out-of-work benefits were instituted, payable by the R.A., without any increase in subscriptions, owing to strong opposition from some branches and E.C. shilly-shallying. All went well while trade remained good—the R.A. had a balance of £1,488 at the end of 1873—but as depression came in the following years and out-of-work and travelling relief expenditure mounted, this quickly went and a £500 grant had to be secured from the P.T.A. in 1876.

The 1877 Delegate Meeting dealt very inadequately with this serious situation. It merged the R.A. into the P.T.A., now the T.A., but only increased the combined subscriptions by a halfpenny, to 3½*d*., to which was also added another penny for the newly established Superannuation Fund, making a total subscription of 4½*d*. per week.[1] Moreover, the worst was still to come: the terrible depression of 1878–80. The Executive were consequently forced, in order to avert bankruptcy, to push through a new rule regarding levies. Hitherto they had only been able to impose a levy when 'imperatively necessary' and, after 1867, with the consent of the members. Now a levy was to be imposed whenever the General Fund fell below £2,500—a shilling per quarter on the fully employed and those earning more than three-fourths of the established wages and sixpence on those earning more than half, members earning half wages or less to be exempt—and was to be continued until the Fund was raised to that figure.

The new rule had soon to be implemented. Members refused to raise subscriptions, so the levy had to be continuously imposed in the years 1879–81, while drastic restrictions had to be made in out-of-work benefits.

The tide turned, however, in 1881 as trade revived and out-of-work payments fell. The next ten years were the most prosperous financially in the Association's history prior to 1914. The General Fund rose rapidly from less than £1,500 in 1879–80 to over £25,000 in 1892. This extraordinary rise made the new levy rule quite inappropriate and so it was altered in 1886, to make a levy necessary whenever the General Fund fell below £1 per member, further altered in 1908 to £1. 10s. per member.

Meanwhile, however, the actuarial shortcomings of the Superannuation Fund were beginning to make themselves felt. By 1888 nearly the whole of current income was being swallowed by current expenditure, without any provision for the enormous and increasing future liabilities. The members, however, could not be persuaded to pay increased subscriptions while the funds were so large and growing and things appeared to be going so prosperously. So an extra halfpenny was added to the Superannuation Fund allocation, making it 1½*d*., without increasing subscriptions: the General Fund, in other words, was raided to pay superannuation benefits.

The results of this short-sighted policy were soon seen, when trade depression returned in the early nineties and the effects of the introduction of Linotype machines also became serious, resulting in a large increase in the number of unemployed and casuals. A halfpenny was

---

[1] Raised to 5*d*. in 1879 by the addition of a halfpenny in place of the half-yearly funeral levy instituted in 1872. See below, p. 295.

added to the subscription by the 1891 Delegate Meeting for super-annuation purposes, followed by another halfpenny in 1895 to meet the swollen out-of-work expenditure, but benefits were extended and so half-yearly deficits continued. The General Fund remained stationary between £25,000 and £26,000 in the years 1892–4, then sank to just over £22,000 in 1896 and only recovered slowly, with improving trade, in the following years to reach nearly £26,000 again in 1900.

The 1898 Delegate Meeting raised the subscription to 7d. and, though strike payments due to 'advance movements' were rather heavier in these years, while out-of-work expenditure rose sharply after 1900, the General Fund began to increase steadily again. It suffered a set-back in 1904 due to a serious strike in Hull, but had reached nearly £37,000 by the end of 1907, despite the transfer to it of 'special grade' (incapacity) payments by the 1903 Delegate Meeting.

The 1908 Delegate Meeting increased the subscription to 9d.[1] Of this increase, 1¼d. went to the Superannuation Fund (whose allocation was now 3¼d.) and ½d. to the General Fund, out-of-work benefits being increased to meet the rise in the cost of living. This generosity combined with trade depression in the next few years to swell out-of-work payments so much that deficits again occurred and the General Fund was still little over £37,000 at the end of 1911. It increased rapidly, however, to over £42,000 in the years of good trade, 1912–14.

The 1913 Delegate Meeting, therefore, again extended out-of-work benefits, to meet which subscriptions were based on a graduated scale according to earnings, so 'that the burden should be placed on those best able to bear it'. This had often been advocated in the past, to relieve members in small towns where wages were low, but had hitherto been rejected on the grounds that the cost of living was higher in the large towns and that all members got the same benefits. The new scale ranged from 10d., for those whose wages were 40s. or over, down to 5d., for those who were unemployed or earning less than 15s. per week.

The history of the T.A. finances is rather a sorry tale of short-sighted-ness and stop-gap expedients. There was no consistent policy to build up the funds, but a cheese-paring economy blundering from one crisis to another. The fault lay almost entirely with the members. The E.C. were wiser and saw farther, but members and Delegate Meetings generally ignored their warnings and admonitions. The main concern of most T.A. members was to pay as little in subscriptions as possible,

[1] A farthing had been added in 1903 by the establishment of the Labour Representation Fund. See below, p. 310.

regardless of the consequences. It is a marvel that so much was achieved on such meagre resources.

Constitutional Development

The T.A. started off with a simple constitutional structure, as a federation of more or less independent societies, simply governed, subject to a few general rules made by occasional Delegate Meetings and to mild Executive strike supervision. But as the Association expanded this structure became more complicated. The larger branches evolved more intricate constitutional machinery, the Executive's functions and powers constantly developed, and new elements—voting papers, Representative Council, and districts or groups—were added. There was a steady tendency to increased centralization and uniformity: the Executive and paid officials became increasingly powerful and the branches were gradually restricted to routine local affairs. Association laws and benefits tended to replace local varieties and by the end of this period the Executive were negotiating national agreements with the employers. Nevertheless, the Association remained a democracy: the Executive and officials were, after all, but elected servants and, in the last resort, the 'will of the members', exercised in branch or Delegate Meeting or by voting paper, still remained supreme. The welfare of the Association, moreover, still rested on individual loyalty, on well-regulated chapels and branch efficiency.

The P.T.A. was, as we have seen, the old Northern Union re-established, with practically the same rules and constitution. Executive power was placed in the hands of a 'governing branch', chosen by Delegate Meeting and therefore 'removable'. The local committee of this branch was to form 'a council for the direction of the general Association business'. Its main functions were to exercise control over threatened disputes and, where a peaceful settlement proved impossible, to support the men with strike pay. It also exercised a vague supervision over tramp relief and administered a few general rules regarding wages, hours, and apprentices. The Association had no full-time paid official: it was considered advisable, 'especially with a view to economy', that the local branch secretary should also be Secretary of the Association, at a salary of £12 per annum. Like members of the Executive, he was a working journeyman—an amateur, spare-time official.

Local branches remained largely independent: they had merely united to gain added strength against employers and to systematize tramp relief. Each could 'frame laws for its local government', provided that they were not opposed to the few scrappy rules of the Association, fix its own subscriptions and tramp relief, run its own out-of-work, sick, and burial funds, print its own membership and working cards. An infinite variety of customs as to wages, hours, and working conditions prevailed among the different branches, even among the offices in each branch. In the event of a dispute, of course, a branch was supposed to inform the Executive, but the ambiguous strike rule of the Northern Union was re-enacted and the Executive frequently allowed large branches to use their own discretion. Some sacrifice of local independence was, of course, inevitable as a consequence of union, but under the original rules of the P.T.A. it was reduced to a minimum.

Local societies at the beginning of this period were still governed by committee and general meeting. This democratic constitution, which gave every member an opportunity of participating in society affairs, was well suited to small branches. But in such towns as Manchester, Liverpool, Birmingham, and Sheffield it became too cumbersome and unwieldy as membership grew. The Manchester Society therefore decided in August 1871 'that the time has arrived when the business of the Society shall be conducted by delegates', elected by the various offices and meeting each quarter. Annual general meetings, however, were still retained and special general meetings were occasionally held, while on important questions the opinion of the members had to be taken by voting paper. The election of the branch committee, hitherto in the hands of the members, was transferred to the delegates in 1871, but later restored to the members at their annual meetings.

Other large branches, such as Liverpool, Birmingham, Sheffield, and Newcastle, also established delegate meetings during the seventies and eighties. Direct government gave way to representative government. This change, though inevitable, tended to remove individual members from participation in branch affairs, to induce apathy and make union-ism a mere paying of subscriptions. Yet had not indifference and lack of interest in branch affairs always been characteristic of most members? Attendance and voting figures prove that this was so. As a rule, a mere handful of members turned up at branch meetings and very few wished to serve on branch committees. Official duties were troublesome and poorly recompensed, branch meetings a bore and a waste of time. Most members preferred football, cricket, or some other amusement, to parti-cipation in society affairs. So long as the subscriptions were not increased, why worry? Fines even had to be imposed to force members to vote. On several occasions it proved impossible to get a quorum of thirty out of more than a thousand Manchester members, even when important questions were involved. Of course, a movement to raise wages or reduce hours or a threatened strike might create excitement and arouse feelings, but as a general rule apathy and indifference prevailed, while a minority ruled.

Growth in branch membership had further effects. It combined with the temperance and educational movements to cause a transference of branch business from public-houses to private rooms and offices, where affairs could be conducted more efficiently and 'rational' recreation be provided. The Manchester Society established a 'Reading Room, News Room, and Library' in 1849, and during the fifties and sixties other branches, such as Hull, Liverpool, and Bristol, moved into 'society rooms' or 'institutes'. In 1900, however, about half the branches still had their headquarters in a local 'pub'.

Closely connected with this movement was another, the creation of full-time or 'permanent' secretaries. The Manchester Society was the first branch to appoint one in 1873. Bradford followed suit in 1894, Liverpool and Leeds in 1898–9, and other large towns in later years. Most branch secretaries, however, remained amateur, part-time officials, performing their duties in dinner hours and evenings.

Upon the branch secretary, to a great extent, depended the success and prosperity of the branch. There were numerous instances where a capable and energetic man almost created a strong society by his own efforts, while the carelessness, indifference, or dishonesty of others led to failure and even collapse.

As there was little competition for branch office, most secretaries were re-elected annually, many for twenty, thirty, or even forty years. They were also chosen, as a rule, to represent the branches at district and Delegate Meetings, so that there was a tendency for the Association to be 'run' almost entirely by its central and local officials.

A similar evolution was taking place in the Association's central government. Josephus Speak, 'finding it impossible, owing to the large increase of his duties as Association Secretary, to fill the office of local secretary', resigned the latter office in July 1855. The president, treasurer, and committee of the local society, however, still acted as officials and Executive of the Association. Speak was continuously re-elected Association Secretary by the Sheffield branch from 1849 to 1865; the treasurer and auditors also held office for terms of years and the same names keep recurring on the Executive Council. This permanence, of course, made for stability and continuity of policy, but there is evidence that it was also due to lack of candidates for such poorly paid yet responsible posts.[1]

The Association headquarters remained throughout these years at the Sheffield 'society house', the 'Dove and Rainbow', Hartshead. In accordance with the principle of a 'removable seat of government', the members were annually called upon to decide whether or not it should remain at Sheffield and on each occasion resolved that it should. By the end of 1862, however, if not before, the Sheffield men had had enough of Executive responsibility and they suggested that they were now 'entitled to some repose'. This suggestion the other branches ignored, so it was repeated in 1863, with the addition that members should 'consider nominating some other town for the future seat of government'. But there was again an almost unanimous opposition to removal, in spite of the clearly expressed wish of the Sheffield men: no other society seemed desirous of Executive honours. A special meeting of the Sheffield branch, however, absolutely refused to hold the management any longer and it therefore became necessary to choose some other branch.

Another question had also to be settled at this same time: whether or not a 'permanent' or full-time Association Secretary should be appointed, in view of his increasing duties.[2]

The final result of voting on these matters was 'that Manchester should be the future seat of Government; that a Secretary shall be appointed who shall devote his whole time to his duties, at a salary of £100; and that the appointment shall be made in the same manner as hitherto'.

The Manchester branch decided that the Association officers and Executive Council should be elected by branch voting papers and be 'distinct from the officers and committee of the Manchester typographical society'. Such a distinction was considered 'essential to the efficient management of the P.T.A.'. It was made necessary, like the 'permanent' secretary, by a great increase in Association business. It would also free the Executive, to some extent, from branch dictation and enable them to devote their whole attention to Association affairs.

The transfer of management from Sheffield to Manchester took place on 8 April 1865. Another change soon followed: removal of the Executive from public-house to private office. For the first year after the transfer the E.C. continued to meet in a public-house, the 'Seven Stars',

---

[1] The Secretary's salary was gradually raised from £12 to £40 per annum, the Treasurer's from £2 to £9. E.C. members each received 6d., later 1s., per meeting. The Council met about once a fortnight.

[2] Josephus Speak had for some years been working part-time only at the trade.

Withy Grove, but in July 1866 they moved into the Manchester Society's 'Typographical Institute'. This arrangement lasted until 1873, when it was decided to make the distinction between Executive Council and local committee complete, by renting separate offices for the former, in Colonial Chambers, 1 Cannon Street. In 1882 the headquarters were moved again to Market Buildings, Thomas Street, then in 1898 to Campfield Chambers, 312 Deansgate. In 1907, however, the E.C. moved back into the branch offices, the newly built 'Caxton Hall', in Chapel Street, Salford.

The Executive's duties and powers continued to grow and resulted in increasing centralization and uniformity. They gradually imposed their will on branches in regard to trade disputes: any matters likely to involve a strike, even trivial questions, had to be referred to them and unadvised action often resulted in refusal of strike pay. Similarly, an office could only be 'opened' by Executive permission. By their initiative power in legislation they expanded the Association rules into a detailed national code. The thirty-five meagre disjointed regulations of 1849, written on one side of a foolscap sheet, had developed by 1903 into fifty-eight methodically arranged rules, several of which had over a dozen sub-sections, contained in a forty-page booklet, covering almost every detail of Association government, friendly benefits, and working regulations. Branch rules had to be submitted to the E.C., to ensure that they were 'in conformity with those of the Association'. Association cards for membership, working, and travelling had replaced local varieties and the Executive exercised control over the admission and expulsion of all members. Association out-of-work, funeral, and superannuation benefits had also been established under close Executive supervision. The Association Secretary was constantly visiting branches, giving advice and settling disputes. Organizers, under Executive control, were appointed in 1891, and an Assistant Secretary was elected in 1896 to assist with the growing mass of central office work. The E.C. Minutes for 1853–65 were contained in one small book, but a large 500-page volume was needed for six months' minutes by the end of the century, while an increasing amount of correspondence, returns, and statistics from the branches piled up at headquarters. By this time, as we shall see, the E.C. were negotiating national agreements with employers' national organizations.

We find the same 'permanence' of officials after 1865 as before. They were, in fact, re-elected annually, usually without opposition, until they either died or resigned. The names of the General Secretaries were as follows: H. Roberts (1865–9), H. Slatter (1869–97), H. Hackett (1897–

1900), A. Jones (1900–1), H. Skinner (1901–34). The Assistant Secretaries were H. Hackett (1896–7), A. Jones (1897–1900), O. Waddington (1900–19). The early Secretaries had all the routine office work to do themselves, writing letters, reports, minutes, &c., by hand, but after the turn of the century, as the amount of this clerical work increased, first one and then more office assistants and typists were appointed. As a result, it became possible to reach the Association Secretaryships by two routes, either locally, as hitherto, via the offices of branch secretary and organizer, or centrally, by promotion from office assistant up to chief clerk. The General Secretary's salary rose, with increasing responsibility and rise in the cost of living, from £100 in 1865 to £225 in 1908, but was still little more than that of a skilled Linotype operator. The Assistant Secretary's salary was increased from £130 in 1896 to £156 in 1908.

The Association Treasurers were also virtually 'permanent', though still only amateur part-time officials, with a salary rising from £2 in 1849 to £50 in 1908. Their names were as follows: C. Corbitt (1849–51), J. Turner (1851–61), W. Clark (1862–5), T. J. Whitworth (1865–80), H. G. Pethybridge (1880–1900), P. Thompson (1900–15), and T. W. Mason (1915–29).

The General President, likewise, was a working journeyman. The office was mainly honorary (the salary was only £12 p.a. in 1908), a reward for long and meritorious service on the Executive Council. For many years the President was changed annually, but in the nineties he too tended to become 'permanent', R. Hackett holding the office in the years 1891 and 1893–6, O. Waddington 1899–1901, H. Matthewman 1902–7, J. H. Boothman 1908–12, and J. D. French 1913–34. The Vice-President also tended at one time to 'permanency', J. D. French holding the office 1908–12 and O. Connellan 1913–19.

The first English Organizers were appointed in 1892, H. Skinner and G. B. Beveridge, followed in 1894 by an Irish Organizer, H. McManus. The English Organizers were temporarily abolished in 1895, when an Assistant Secretary was appointed, but one was restored in 1896 and the other in 1903. The names of the Organizers were as follows. *English*: H. Skinner (1896–1900), A. Bottomley (1901–19), G. H. Roberts (1904–19),[1] and H. Matthewman (1909–23). *Irish*: H. McManus (1894–1910), and T. Cassidy (1911–37).

All these offices were open to annual election, but the same men were

---

[1] Roberts was elected T.A. Parliamentary Representative in 1906 and became an M.P., so that henceforth he did little 'organizing'.

always re-elected. The 1903 Delegate Meeting decided to give legal recognition to this virtual 'permanency' and at the same time provide the officers with greater security of tenure, by resolving 'that the Secretary, Assistant Secretary, Treasurer, and Organizers be made permanent officials of the Association, subject to three months' notice on either side'. The President, however, was still elected annually by the E.C. from their own number.

A further development came in 1918. The General President and Treasurer were by now only working part-time at the trade, owing to their increasing T.A. duties, so the 1918 Delegate Meeting decided to make them, like the General and Assistant Secretaries, full-time salaried officials, J. D. French and T. W. Mason, the then incumbents, being elected. The Vice-Presidency thus became the highest post in the Association to which an ordinary 'lay' member could aspire.

The professional officials gradually acquired great power. Their knowledge and experience gave considerable weight to their advice; they were skilled in handling both members and employers; they were continually travelling the country, negotiating settlements and addressing meetings; they edited the *Circular*; they suggested alterations in rules; they were frequently called upon to make quick decisions, without consulting the Executive, who almost invariably endorsed their action at the next Council meeting. But they were elected officials and might be removed if they adopted unpopular policies. They were also subject to the orders and control of a strong, practically permanent Executive.

E.C. members were, like the Association officers, continuously re-elected, often for fifteen to twenty years. They, too, gained knowledge, experience, and power. Moreover, although the full Executive Council consisted of eleven members, there existed from 1875 onwards a sub-committee, consisting of the President, Vice-President, and two or three others, whom the Association Secretary consulted on matters of urgency which arose between the ordinary meetings. They also dealt with financial questions, revision of branch rules and memorials, referred to them by the Council. The actions of this sub-committee were subject to approval by the full Council, but their decisions were hardly ever overruled. There was, in fact, a danger that they, together with the officials, would establish a centralized absolutism.

The chief safeguard against such a possibility was the Delegate Meeting. The Executive, it was laid down in 1849, 'shall be responsible for its decisions and management to a representative meeting'. But as such meetings were costly and ought only to be held 'when absolutely necessary', it had been left to the Executive to decide when a Delegate Meeting should take place, subject to a vote of the branches.

The E.C. referred several matters, such as tramp relief and emigration, to a vote of the branches during the next few years,[1] but in 1851 felt it to be 'their duty' to suggest a Delegate Meeting, 'in order to ascertain whether the present Association works well, whether the seat of Government can be advantageously moved, and whether any alterations in the rules of the Association are desirable'. A large majority of the branches, however, decided against a meeting.

The question was again submitted to them in 1852. The Executive pointed out that 'in previous organisations of the profession, it has been regarded as essential to their continued welfare, that Delegate Meetings should be held at least once in three years, in order that full enquiry might be made into the manner of administering the laws, and the continued adaptation or otherwise of those laws to the requirements of the profession'. Over three years had now elapsed since the last meeting, at the Association's establishment, and many questions required consideration. The Executive, therefore, strongly urged that a Delegate Meeting should be held.

Voting resulted in favour and the meeting was held in Manchester in March 1853. Representation was based on membership: 50 members or under, one delegate; 50–100 members, two delegates; 100–150 members, three delegates; 150–200 members, four delegates, the maximum allowed to any one society.

A number of important amendments and additions to the rules were made, but 'with a particular regard to the independence of local societies' and without increasing the powers of the Executive. It was suggested that the next Delegate Meeting should be held in May 1855.

Early in 1855, therefore, the E.C. consulted the branches with regard to a Delegate Meeting, pointing out, however, that there appeared to be no necessity for one. The branches concurred; nearly half of them could not even be bothered to vote.[2] Next year, however, the E.C. felt it their duty to resubmit the question and this time suggested reasons for holding a meeting. Again only about half the branches voted—in support of the Executive's suggestion.

The delegates met in September 1856 in Liverpool. They discussed many subjects and made several alterations in the Association rules, including one which made it 'incumbent upon the Executive annually

---

[1] Branch voting was by show of hands in general meetings.
[2] Similar apathy had been visible in earlier votes.

to take the sense of the branches as to the propriety of holding a Delegate Meeting'.

The Executive faithfully carried out this rule, but each year the members decided against a meeting. In 1860, however, the Executive pointed out 'that more or less frequent meetings are an inseparable element in an organisation like that of the P.T.A.'. It was the only way in which the scattered branches could be brought together to exchange opinions, discuss current problems, air grievances, criticize the Executive's administration, and establish harmony and unity. Moreover, a meeting was necessary to discuss policy in regard to the anticipated repeal of the paper duty. But the House of Lords rejected Gladstone's proposal and, as the immediate necessity had thus passed, the members decided not to hold a meeting.

Next year, however, the E.C. again urged the need for a meeting, pointing out that five years had elapsed since the last and that important questions required discussion and settlement. The branches therefore agreed to hold one in Manchester, in July 1861.

This meeting introduced an important new feature—the 'referendum'—into the T.A. constitution. It was decided that, 'in order more effectually to base the laws on the will of the members, and at the same time to enable the Association to make such alterations as experience may deem necessary, without having to call Delegate Meetings', all proposed alterations in rules should be printed in the *Circular* and then put to a ballot of the membership by voting papers. Thus, it was considered, not only would the heavy expense of Delegate Meetings be avoided, but Association government would also be made more democratic, based on the principle of 'direct legislation' by the members.

The Sheffield Executive, however, had no liking for the new system and made no use of it, still referring questions to branch votes. In 1864, when the question of removing the seat of government from Sheffield was under consideration, they suggested a Delegate Meeting, but the proposal was rejected and voting papers were now issued for the first time, after the Manchester branch had refused to take over without a legal ballot of the members.

During the Executive's sojourn in Sheffield the Association was, on the whole, democratically governed. Branches still retained local customs and independence, centralization had developed slowly, fairly frequent Delegate Meetings had been held, members had initiated and carried a number of new laws and amendments and had frequent opportunities of removing the seat of government, while the Executive had fully recognized that they were 'responsible to a higher tribunal for the faithful discharge of their duties'.

After 1865, however, Executive power and centralization rapidly developed in Manchester. It soon became obvious that the new Executive intended to dispense with Delegate Meetings and rule by the voting-paper system. First came a revision of the Relief Association rules. True, branch amendments were invited, but they were swamped in a long list of Executive propositions. The proposed amendments were first printed in the *Circular*, to give an opportunity for discussion, and then voting papers were issued. Members were asked to vote 'for' or 'against' a total of twenty-seven detailed amendments. Only about one-fifth of them voted and all the propositions, save one, were carried. The 'will of the members' was obviously cloaked in apathy and indifference. Most members could not be bothered even to read the two closely-printed pages of rather dull proposals, and many threw away the voting paper, or used it to light their pipes. It was clearly impossible to amend and harmonize laws in such wholesale fashion, by a simple 'yes' or 'no' on a voting paper, without discussion or amendment: a plebiscite is useless save for the simplest issues. Moreover, the Executive decided, after the sovereign 'will of the members' had been declared, that they had 'power to make alterations and amendments', and did so. They ignored practically all the branch proposals accepted by the members, but included all their own in the revised code of rules.

Even worse was to follow. The Executive decided in September 1866 that, as many of the P.T.A. rules were obsolete, 'an entirely new code' was essential. They accordingly prepared a new set of fifty-seven 'suggested rules', which were issued to the members in February 1867. Two months were then allowed for branch proposals, after which the whole lot, 105 propositions and amendments, were put before the trade, in a voting paper covering four closely printed sides of quarto. The result, of course, was farcical. About one-eighth of the members voted and every one of the fifty-seven suggested rules of the Executive was carried. About half the branch propositions were also carried, but the Executive, arbitrarily interpreting the 'will of the members', ignored these and merely printed their own suggested rules as the new Association code, which, they piously declared in the introduction, possessed 'the high prerogative of being "based on the will of the Members" '.

Rule by voting paper was further elaborated in the new code. It was laid down 'that the opinion of the branches shall be taken on any question affecting the fundamental or financial bases of the Association, and on all other matters the decision of which the Executive may consider too important for the exercise of their vested powers'. The Executive were to be 'responsible for their management to the collective judgement of the Branches of the Association only'. But it is difficult to see how this responsibility could be enforced, since only the Executive themselves could issue voting papers and regular Delegate Meetings had become a thing of the past. The only safeguard was contained in a clause stating that 'when a branch is dissatisfied with the conduct of the Executive, and deems a representative meeting necessary', it could require a vote on the question. But the Executive would issue the voting paper, with strongly biased emphasis on their own arguments. Executive absolutism was completed by a clause which gave them arbitrary powers of interpreting the rules and deciding any point not covered by them. Thus they would not merely administer, but also make and interpret the Association rules.

Criticism and dissatisfaction soon resulted. The Birmingham branch declared that revision of the rules by voting paper was a 'farce', that 'the Executive manufactured what rules they pleased for the Association', and that they had become 'insolent and irresponsible dictators'. Sheffield also strongly denounced the Executive's high-handed arbitrariness and the uselessness of voting papers for deciding important and complicated matters, which required deliberation by a Delegate Meeting and not simply a 'yes' or 'no'. The E.C., however, adhered to the strict letter of the rules and refused to call a Delegate Meeting. They easily secured the defeat of a motion of censure by their control of the *Circular* and remarks on the voting paper.

The Preston branch eventually (1870) hit on a solution to the growing discontent: that 'when a branch or branches comprising 300 members shall desire a Delegate Meeting to be called', the Executive must put the question to a vote. The E.C., aware of the general feeling, agreed to this proposal, which the members adopted by a large majority.

A Delegate Meeting was not, however, held under this new rule until December 1872, when the Rochdale branch secured one to discuss their proposal for an Association Provident Fund. Eleven years had then elapsed since the last Delegate Meeting.

There was considerable controversy at this meeting over an E.C. proposal that all alterations of rules by the delegates should afterwards be submitted to a vote of the members. Some considered that, as elected branch representatives, they were empowered to decide any questions; otherwise the meeting would be a mere talking-shop and waste of time.

Others, however, felt that the 'will of the members' must remain supreme. It was finally resolved, by a narrow majority, 'that the decisions of the meeting be final'; but the delegates later decided to submit proposals for out-of-work and funeral benefits 'to the approval of the members', on account of the increased subscriptions involved—though they abolished the rule whereby questions 'affecting the fundamental or financial bases of the Association' must be submitted to the members; only those 'not decided by a Delegate Meeting' were to be dealt with by voting papers. But, strange to say, the old rule reappeared, together with the new one, in the revised code. This can only be attributed to sharp practice by the Executive.

The delegates tried to check Executive power by a new rule that Delegate Meetings should be held every five years, which would prevent another long period of irresponsible government and ensure regular deliberation and discussion on all important questions affecting the Association. It was also decided that the Association Secretary should be nominated and elected annually by the whole of the members, as advocated in 1864–5, instead of by the governing branch, so that he need no longer be subservient to Manchester cliques.

In the interval between 1872 and the next Delegate Meeting in 1877 'the Voting Paper farce' continued, owing to the conflict and ambiguity of the rules. The Executive carried on, in fact, as before, submitting several matters 'decided' by the Delegate Meeting to a referendum. About a quarter of the members voted and all the Executive's proposals were carried by large majorities.

The Delegate Meeting of 1877 dealt with a large number of branch and Executive propositions. Several important decisions were made, such as abolition of the R.A. and establishment of a Superannuation Fund, as well as many minor amendments in the rules. Sound, consistent legislation could obviously be achieved far more effectively by representative meeting than by referendum. The general position of the Association and the work of the Executive were also reviewed. Moreover, the delegates had gained confidence and acted on their 1872 resolution that their decisions should be final: no voting papers were issued after the meeting and the new rules were printed 'as revised by the delegates'.

A storm of controversy followed this meeting. The delegates had decided on the establishment of a Superannuation Fund, which involved an increase in subscriptions of a penny per week. Several branches protested against such an 'assumption of power by the delegates' and de-

manded that, as the question affected 'the fundamental or financial basis of the Association', it should be submitted to the members by voting papers. Which was to be supreme, the 'will of the members' or that of the Delegate Meeting?

The Executive now switched sides. Hitherto they had upheld the sacred 'will of the members' against verbose, expensive, and useless Delegate Meetings: by this means they had imposed their own will on the Association. But now the 'general will' threatened to get out of hand and upset the Superannuation Fund, as designed by the Executive and passed by the delegates. The Executive therefore decided 'that the decision of the delegates cannot be reviewed or set aside either by themselves or any other power short of another Delegate Meeting', although they themselves had repeatedly reviewed and set aside questions 'decided by a Delegate Meeting'. They now proclaimed that only questions not so decided could be dealt with by voting papers. They positively refused to take 'the will of the members' on this matter and when branches protested fell back on their absolute power of interpreting the rules.

Their alliance with the delegates, however, was short-lived. Delegate Meetings were difficult to handle, too apt to criticize the Executive and assume supreme power, whereas by the voting-paper system the E.C. could rule the roost. In 1879, therefore, they decided to amend the rules —although 'decided' by the 1877 Delegate Meeting, whose supreme legislative power they had so recently defended! All their proposed amendments were, as usual, passed by the members, of whom only a quarter voted.

The Delegate Meeting rule was altered to suit the Executive. It was still laid down 'that a Delegate Meeting be held every five years', but if at that time there appeared to be 'no business of sufficient importance to justify the expense' of holding a meeting, they could put the matter to a vote. Moreover, 'all propositions adopted by the delegates involving an increased subscription . . . or affecting fundamental principles of the T.A. . . . must be confirmed by a vote of the whole Association . . . before such propositions can be incorporated in the rules'. Finally, these new regulations could only be altered by voting paper, so that no future Delegate Meeting would be able, like that in 1872, to assume supreme legislative power. Thus, it was asserted, the 'will of the members' would once more be sovereign.

The rule was again altered in 1882. Quinquennial Delegate Meetings were abolished: in future the E.C. were to take a vote every three years as to whether or not a meeting should be held. On each occasion,

however, when they took such a vote, they pointed out that there was no need for a meeting, that it would involve expense, and that all necessary amendments to the rules could be made by voting paper.

During these years the E.C. established a plebiscitarian dictatorship, boosting their own proposals but condemning others to which they were opposed, so that theirs were almost invariably carried by large majorities while those from branches were rejected. Voting papers were issued at such frequent intervals that few members knew what the rules were, while conflicting proposals were often carried. There was no possibility of deliberation or amendment; members had to vote for or against the motions as they stood. The result was scrappy, piecemeal legislation. The members were utterly apathetic: it was rare that more than a quarter voted.

The voting-paper system, therefore, failed in its intention to make Association government democratic. Instead, ironically, it gave the Executive almost absolute powers. Although by rule 'responsible to the collective judgment of the branches', the Council was a practically irresponsible body now that Delegate Meetings were no longer held and while members outside Manchester had no voice in their election.

From time to time, however, strong criticism was expressed against Executive absolutism and several proposals were put forward to make the Council either more responsible or more representative.[1] Some favoured moving the seat of government to another town, but when the question was first seriously raised, in 1877, the general feeling was against 'removal': it would cause expense and inconvenience; no other branch wanted to take over, while the Manchester men had acquired considerable experience and Manchester, it was felt, the stronghold of typographical trade unionism in the provinces, should remain the seat of management. Manchester itself had no great desire to retain the Executive and at the 1877 Delegate Meeting actually proposed its removal to Liverpool. But the delegates expressed complete satisfaction with Manchester's conduct of Association affairs and voted against removal.

Dissatisfaction grew rapidly, however, in the following years as a result of Manchester 'dictatorship', and although proposals for 'removal' were rejected, other schemes were propounded, either to make the Executive Council responsible to a representative council or to convert the Executive itself into a representative body. It was suggested, for

[1] The Association Secretary allowed fairly free criticism in the *Circular*, but he or some E.C. member usually demolished the arguments of correspondents.

example, that the various branches should be grouped into districts, which should send representatives to periodic meetings, to meet the Executive, review their management, and settle any important Association business. This idea was taken up by the Birmingham branch and discussed at a conference of branch secretaries in that city in July 1881. This conference, a result of local discontent with the non-representative character of Association government, recommended the establishment of an annual 'General Council', elected by districts, to review the work of the E.C. and examine proposed alterations or additions to the rules before they were voted on by the members.

Another scheme, propounded by the Southport branch, was for a representative Executive Council. With the growth of the Association and the development of rapid transport and communications, the system of a 'governing branch' was 'too primitive . . . to represent the trade'. Moreover, 'the democratic principle' demanded 'that every member should have a voice, directly or indirectly, in the election and control of the central committee'. The variety of customs in different parts of the country should also be represented on the Executive Council. At present, members and branches outside Manchester had no real share in Association government, and the result was indifference or discontent. It was therefore proposed that the E.C. should be elected from and by the whole membership. The full Council, however, would meet only once a quarter, business meanwhile being conducted by a sub-committee from Manchester and the nearest towns, whose decisions would be reviewed by the full Council meetings.

Both these schemes were criticized by the Executive as costly, cumbersome, and inefficient. They were therefore rejected by the members at the end of 1882 and fell temporarily into the background. But they revived and became increasingly popular towards the end of the eighties. In the forward surge of trade unionism after 1889 there was considerable criticism by 'New Unionists' of the narrow-minded, autocratic, and old-fashioned methods hitherto typical of most Executives, and a consequent demand for more democratic, representative government. The T.A. shared in this movement. During 1889–90 there was an increasingly loud demand for a Delegate Meeting. Many urgent problems, particularly the introduction of composing machines, required consideration by representatives of the whole Association. Voting papers were a farce, a blind for autocracy.

The Executive were forced to give way. They first of all invited representatives from a number of the largest branches to meet them in

Manchester, in February 1891, for a conference on composing machines. Then, in May 1891, they issued voting papers on the question of holding a Delegate Meeting. The result was an overwhelming majority in favour and the meeting was held in Manchester in September.

Fourteen years had elapsed since the last Delegate Meeting. Never, since the establishment of the Northern Union in 1830, had the trade been so long without one. It was now decided, however, that a Delegate Meeting must be held every five years and that any branch or branches of the Association, numbering in the aggregate not less than 1,000 members, could require the Executive to take a vote on the holding of a special meeting. The old voting-paper rules still remained in force, however, and all propositions adopted by the delegates involving an increased subscription or affecting fundamental principles of the T.A. must still be confirmed by a vote of the whole Association. The 'will of the members' remained supreme.

Proposals similar to those made in the early eighties were also put forward at the Delegate Meeting, with the aim of giving members more share in and control over the central government. But though delegates made numerous speeches in favour of representation and against auto-cracy, they could not agree on how the new ideas were to be put into practice and eventually came to the conclusion that representative councils would prove too costly and cumbersome and that it would be best to 'leave well alone'. They were, in fact, forced to praise the industry and ability of the Executive, however autocratic they may have been, and to give their confidence to Manchester once again.

The old autocratic government therefore continued. The Executive immediately overrode, for example, a decision of the delegates in re-gard to the new superannuation grade for forty years' members.[1] Dissatisfaction with the unrepresentative character of Association government therefore increased. In 1893, however, it was decided, on a proposal of the Executive, to hold another Delegate Meeting, especi-ally to consider the composing machine problem.

At this meeting, held in Sheffield in December 1893, proposals for a more representative form of government were again discussed and it was eventually decided to establish an annual Representative Council, composed of representatives elected by branches or groups of branches in the proportion of one to every 500 members. The Executive were to be 'responsible for their management to the Representative Council', whose first duty would be to review the half-yearly reports and balance-

---

[1] See below, p. 290.

sheets for the preceding twelve months. They would also elect the Association officers and Executive Council.

The Association Secretary would be nominated annually by the branches: if only one candidate was nominated, he would be deemed elected, but if there were more than one, the election would be made by the R.C. For the election of the Executive, the branch where the seat of government was located was to nominate not less than twenty-two candidates, including all retiring members willing to serve, and from this list the R.C. was to elect an Executive of eleven members.

This scheme certainly provided a more representative government and made Executive responsibility more of a reality. But it had obvious defects. The R.C., meeting once annually, would tend to be a mere reviewing body, without time or information enough to pass proper judgement on half-yearly reports and balance-sheets. The Executive, moreover, still remained a purely Manchester body and election by the R.C. was a farce. The delegates had obviously failed to realize their main aim —to give the branches a greater share in central government. The probability was that the Executive would retain most of their autocratic power.

The Delegate Meeting assigned no duties to the R.C. beyond consideration of the reports and balance–sheets and election of the Executive and officers. But in August 1894 the Executive decided 'that the branches should have an opportunity of submitting questions affecting the general welfare of the Association, upon which it is thought desirable that the members of the Representative Council should express their opinions'. As a result, branches forwarded a large number of propositions on wages, hours, apprentices, benefits, &c., just as they did for a Delegate Meeting. A lengthy agenda was drawn up and the meeting in September lasted three days. It debated a variety of subjects and passed a number of resolutions, only two of which were afterwards submitted to the members for ratification, although the Executive had stated that the Council would merely 'express their opinions'. The new Council had, in fact, metamorphosed from a mere reviewing and elective body into a legislative assembly.

The result was increased legislative confusion. Laws could now be passed by voting papers, by Delegate Meeting, or by Representative Council. The 'will of the members' still remained theoretically supreme, but was being consulted much less frequently than of late. Certain resolutions passed by Delegate Meeting or Representative Council were referred to the members, mainly as a matter of form, and were passed almost automatically.

Nevertheless, the members were liable, when dissatisfied or irritated, to assert their feelings strongly. They did so now. The R.C. had passed a resolution, unratified by the members, that superannuation claimants must produce a medical certificate as proof of incapacity before being eligible to benefit. The result was an immediate outcry against this 'monstrous injustice' and condemnation of the R.C. The latter were asked 'on what authority they passed such a resolution'. Nowhere were they given power to make or amend Association rules. Their action was 'a usurpation of power' and the question should be submitted to the members. The Executive, with a hornets' nest about their ears, had to acquiesce and the detested certificate was rejected by an overwhelming majority. The 'will of the members' evidently remained sovereign.[1]

The new system had aroused dissatisfaction in other ways. The Executive found it impossible to group the branches into equal electoral districts and hence there were complaints of unequal representation. Moreover, the system gave preponderating influence to one large branch in each group and caused discontent in smaller towns. Criticism was also directed against 'the utter absurdity' of the new mode of electing the Executive Council. There was practically no change either in the personnel or policy of the central government, which remained as unrepresentative and almost as autocratic as ever.

The R.C. did, however, perform some useful functions. It enabled branches annually to air their views and forward proposals for discussion by representatives of the whole Association. It gave them some voice in government and legislation. It brought representative men together at frequent intervals to exchange ideas, pool knowledge, and present grievances. It provided a sounder legislative instrument than the voting-paper system. The Executive Council were brought into touch with members, feelings, and customs outside Manchester and were given an opportunity of explaining their policy and receiving suggestions. The approval of the R.C. added weight to their decisions, particularly in regard to composing machines. They summoned a special R.C. meeting in May 1897 to discuss the proposals of the Linotype Users' Association and had also to submit the Linotype 'stab agreement arrived at with the L.U.A. to another special R.C. meeting in May 1899. Executive responsibility was thus made more of a reality.

---

[1] The R.C. was empowered by vote of the members in 1895 'to initiate or adopt legislative proposals', but any 'involving an increased subscription, or affecting the fundamental principles or change in the constitution of the T.A.', had to be submitted to the members by voting papers.

In many ways, however, the R.C. proved a failure. It failed, for example, to control the Executive, who on several occasions flouted its decisions with impunity. Review of half-yearly reports and balance-sheets proved a mere formality. Election of the E.C. meant simply the reappointment of retiring members. Appeals against E.C. decisions were almost invariably rejected. Moreover, annual representative meetings led to too frequent tinkering with the rules and created insta-bility. Soon, therefore, branches began to ask if it was worthwhile con-tinuing the R.C., since it had no real power and involved useless expense. Some suggested replacing it by triennial Delegate Meetings, while others urged the idea of a representative E.C.

Arguments for and against the R.C. occupied a large portion of space in the 1898 *Circular* and of the time of the Delegate Meeting that same year. It was eventually decided to maintain the R.C., but in future all branches were to have the right to make nominations for the E.C., though only from among the members of the Manchester branch. This was a ludicrous attempt to combine improved representation with ad-ministrative cheapness and efficiency. Outside Manchester practically nothing was known of the character or ability, or even the names, of most Manchester members. How, then, could other towns be expected to nominate Manchester men for the Executive? The result was inevit-able: the old names, the only ones known, were put forward and the same Executive continued in the saddle.

The delegates considered that the Executive had now been made 'subservient' to the R.C. They were soon proved wrong. The two came to a head-on clash over the Linotype Agreement of December 1898, and the Executive emerged triumphant after appealing to the members.[1] This humiliating blow spelt the doom of the Representative Council. It was now made completely subservient to the Executive, meeting mainly to hear the latter's report and act as a kind of electoral college. Official speeches dominated its debates. It became, in fact, a mere sound-ing-board for the Executive. Feeling therefore grew that it was unneces-sary and useless and the 1903 Delegate Meeting finally abolished it.

In its place there was established a District Executive Council, com-posed of thirteen members, five (including a machineman)[2] to be elected from the branch where the Executive was located, one from Ireland, one from Wales, and one from each of six grouped districts. Those elected

---

[1] See below, p. 201.
[2] Machinemen were first given special representation in 1893. See below, p. 218.

would, as previously, remain in office twelve months, retiring members to be eligible for re-election. The full Council would, except in emergencies, meet only once a quarter, while the five local members, together with the Association officers, were to meet fortnightly or as occasion required.

Thus a representative Executive Council was at last established which would give districts a real share in and control over central government. The chief dangers were that the Manchester sub-committee would still dominate and that the General Secretary might make the Association a 'one-man show'.

Association districts were not a new and artificial creation, but had grown up spontaneously over a long period. Yorkshire societies had started 'annual gatherings' as early as 1852. These consisted of 'outings', visits to places of interest, cricket matches, and other outdoor amusements during the day, with dinner, toasts, speeches, and songs in the evening. Their object was stated to be 'the cultivation of a spirit of union and friendship amongst the Members of the Printing Profession throughout the West Riding'. They were in no sense trade conferences, but trade affairs must have been discussed. They seem to have lapsed, however, after a few years and were not revived until 1881, still on lines of social conviviality. After that date they continued to be held annually.

Other districts followed suit. In 1882 the Lancashire branches held their first annual 'social gathering'. These Lancashire 'gatherings' seem to have lapsed after 1891, but were revived in 1904. The Midland branches were the first to establish district *trade* conferences, as distinct from annual dinners and drinking. The Birmingham branch secretary arranged in 1884 a conference with the Walsall, Wolverhampton, and Dudley secretaries, 'in order that the whole area of what is called the "Black Country" might be inquired into'. In 1889 another Midland conference was arranged and henceforth such meetings were held annually, genuine trade conferences, discussing wages, hours, apprentices, and other Association business, and making proposed amendments to Association rules. The Birmingham branch actively engaged in organizing and missionary work in this area, assisting 'advance movements' and trying to limit the employment of apprentices. A similar role was played in Yorkshire by the Sheffield branch and in Lancashire by the Manchester branch.

Newcastle was similarly active in the north-east. A conference of Northumberland and Durham delegates was first held in 1890, when it was decided to establish a North-eastern Typographical Federation and to hold annual conferences. The scheme failed temporarily, but was revived in 1900, when a Northern District was founded, including branches in the north-west as well as the north-east.

By this time an annual conference of southern branches had been established. In 1886 Bath suggested a conference of branch secretaries to discuss trade affairs in the south-west and co-operated with Bristol in missionary work. But the first conference of southern branches did not take place until 1894. It was expanded in 1895 into a conference of southern and south-western branches, henceforth held annually. It was an unwieldy district, however, covering a very large area, and was eventually (1910) divided into two separate groups, the Home Counties and SE. Group and the SW. Group.[1]

The first conference of T.A. branches in Ireland was held in 1897, as a result of efforts by H. McManus, the Irish Organizer, but no further Irish meetings took place until 1905, when separate annual conferences for Northern and Southern Ireland were established. In 1909, however, these were combined into an annual 'All-Ireland' conference.

The first annual conference of South Wales branches was held in 1899, after years of missionary work by the Cardiff branch, and by the end of this period the T.A. branches in North Wales were beginning to organize themselves.

All these annual district conferences had, by this time, become mainly concerned with trade affairs, though eating and drinking were not forgotten. District rules were established and district committees and officers appointed to carry on missionary or other work. Some groups also began to organize district wages and hours movements. Thus local societies, though sharing little in central government, were able to take a vigorous part in the work of their respective districts and, through the district conferences, to bring public opinion to bear on the Executive.

These districts or groups had for many years no recognized status in the Association rules. The districts established in 1903, for the purpose of electing the E.C., cut across them to some extent, but the 1913 Delegate Meeting adopted the older, more natural, divisions.

The criticisms of the new District Executive Council expressed at the 1903 Delegate Meeting proved justified. The sub-committee—the 'Manchester quintet'—meeting fortnightly, sometimes oftener, dealt with most of the Executive business, while the full Council, meeting only once a quarter, tended to become a mere reviewing body. The sub-

[1] The Home Counties Group had been formed, within the S. and SW. District, in 1903.

committee, moreover, was largely controlled by the General Secretary. This official—elected by the whole body of members, a professional administrator, dealing with Association business daily, fully acquainted with the rules and affairs of the union, constantly travelling, negotiating with employers, well known, and, after several years in office, possessed of great prestige and authority—tended to acquire dictatorial powers. His dictatorship was, of course, based on the 'will of the members', so that if he became exceptionally unpopular he might be turned out. Officially, moreover, he was merely the servant of the Executive Council and usually spoke in their name. But behind the scenes, by his advice, suggestions, and criticism, he dominated Association policy and Executive decisions.

Branch discontent, however, was mainly with the E.C., with continued Manchester rule and tiresome delays. Suggested reforms were brought forward at the 1908 Delegate Meeting, but abandoned owing to the negotiations then going on for typographical amalgamation. Dissatisfaction grew rapidly, however, in the following years, particularly as a result of the national agreement negotiated by the Executive with the employers in 1911.[1] This agreement, especially the modification of the apprentice rule, resulted in widespread revolt, similar to that against the Linotype Agreement of 1898. There is no doubt that the Executive had reason on their side: members failed to realize the difficulties involved in securing such national agreements; the Executive could not give a running commentary, divulge confidential information, and risk a breakdown of negotiations; agreements could only be reached by mutual concessions and the Executive made as good a bargain as possible. But branches and districts revolted against being 'left in the dark' while negotiations were going on at national level. At least the results should be submitted to a vote of the members and not simply be imposed upon them. Local autonomy had been gradually restricted throughout the preceding half century and these national agreements were, to many, the last straw.

Angry resolutions therefore poured in on the Executive Council. The Lancashire Group, for example, strongly protested against the Council's 'autocratic government', against their 'tying down' the branches and narrowing their powers. Yorkshire made a similar protest and complained that there was no indication in the *Circular* of the Executive's policy and what they were doing; while many districts and branches declared that the Council had no power to sign national agreements

---

[1] See below, p. 144.

affecting the 'fundamental principles' of the Association without submitting them to the members. There was a demand for a special Delegate Meeting to consider the agreement. But the Executive weathered the storm: they justified their actions in special circulars, pointed out the wasteful expense which a Delegate Meeting would involve, and secured its rejection in a vote of the members.

Dissatisfaction remained, however, and resulted at the 1913 Delegate Meeting in various constitutional reforms. The Executive Council was increased to fifteen members, three (instead of five), including one machine minder, to be elected from the branch where the Council was located, one each from branches with a membership of 750 and upwards, one from each of the six English groups, one from Ireland, one from Wales, and a machineman elected by the minders of the whole T.A. area. Thus Manchester's representation on the Council was reduced, while other large branches and the groups gained an increased share. The aim, of course, was to make the Council—which was now to meet every two months instead of three—as democratically constituted as possible. Moreover, the sub-committee was henceforth to consist not merely of the Manchester men, but also of six others elected by the Council from their own number. This change would result in greatly increased expenditure, but would democratize the central government.

The Executive were not to sign any national agreement 'without first submitting the proposed agreement to a vote of the members'. They were also, through the *Circular*, to 'keep members informed . . . of all matters affecting their welfare, and especially of negotiations with employers on national questions'. And they were to 'give attention' to all branch and group resolutions, which they had hitherto generally shelved or ignored.

It is clear that, despite tendencies to centralization and autocracy, members had not lost their voice in Association affairs. They were apt to get unruly and out-of-hand when dissatisfied and the Council and officials had to be careful to keep on the right side of them. Branches still managed their own local affairs (though these had been considerably circumscribed) and still negotiated (under Executive supervision) local agreements on wages and hours. They could also put forward propositions for discussion at Delegate Meetings and thus influence legislation. All such propositions were published in the *Circular* for members to see and discuss, so that they might instruct their delegates. A great many alterations and additions to the rules were made by the quinquennial assemblies, at which, however, the Association officials and Executive exercised a very powerful influence. All propositions adopted by the delegates 'involving an increased subscription . . . or affecting fundamental principles of the T.A.' had to be submitted to the members for ratification or otherwise, but were invariably passed by large majorities, while most members could not even be bothered to vote. The Executive also carried their views whenever ballots were taken on important questions arising between Delegate Meetings. Opportunities were undoubtedly available for members and branches to express their opinions and participate in Association affairs, but, as the T.A. grew and centralization developed, the individual and the branch tended to become less important. This tendency—and the indifference of most members—inevitably placed great power in the hands of the Executive and officials. But the latter at all times wielded this power for the welfare of the Association—to secure improved wages, hours, and working conditions, and, at the same time, to maintain industrial peace.

Throughout this period the T.A. remained an unregistered society. By the Trade Union Act of 1871 a trade union could become a registered society and thus acquire a kind of legal status or corporate existence, being able to sue or be sued or to invest funds through its legally appointed officers. It could also secure the summary conviction of any officer or member for fraud or misappropriation. And, finally, its provident funds could only be applied to the purposes for which they had been subscribed.

Many members wanted registration, especially to prevent the Association, in emergency, from laying hands on the Superannuation Fund. The Executive, however, were strongly opposed to registration. They considered that the new power of prosecution was not of much value, since they were already able to punish fraudulent officials in the ordinary law courts. They objected to the 'inquisitorial' supervision of the Registrar and the delays in getting rules or amendments passed. They also felt that, being first and foremost a trade union, they should be able to devote any of their funds to whatever purpose suited the 'will of the members'. These views they retained throughout this period. Registration was rejected on several occasions by vote of the members, Delegate Meeting, and Representative Council. The Association experienced some snags at first in regard to investments and prosecutions through its lack of legal status, but simple legal devices enabled it to overcome them and thereafter we find the Association investing funds and punishing fraudulent officials without any apparent difficulty. At the same time it preserved its cherished freedom of action.

VIII

RELATIONS WITH EMPLOYERS AND STRIKE POLICY

J. W. CROMPTON stated in 1860 that 'the leading unionists in the printing trade seem to be convinced that the interests of masters and men are mutual; and that what tends to the injury of the interests of either, must ultimately prove detrimental to both; and in combining to protect themselves from the unprincipled masters who would take advantage of the isolated position of an individual or a few, aim to regard the permanent interests of the trade as a whole'.[1]

The T.A. always asserted that it had no quarrel with 'fair' employers. Its motto was that of the old Northern Union: 'United to protect, but not combined to injure.' Its main aim, in fact, was to secure a fair standard of life for its members. It fought only against the unprincipled, grasping, tyrannical, and 'unfair' master printers, who exploited their men, injured 'honourable' employers by cut-throat competition, and lowered the standard of the trade. The Association imposed discipline upon its members, punished negligence or 'misconduct', and insisted upon a 'fair day's work for a fair day's wage'. It prevented strikes on trivial or unreasonable grounds and sought to preserve harmony and good feeling between masters and men by securing redress of grievances. It opposed violence, believing in conciliatory methods, and attempted to gain its ends by conference and reasoned argument rather than by wasteful disputes. Thus it promoted industrial peace. It also tried to reduce 'unfair' competition by standardizing wages, reducing boy labour, 'black-listing' non-union firms, and campaigning for 'fair contracts'. It pointed out not only the injustice, but also the false economy of boy labour, over-long hours, low wages, and bad working conditions, and by collective bargaining helped to establish rules and regulations for the good of the trade, substituting order and discipline for the chaos of competition.

Many master printers admitted the force of these arguments, sympathized with the men's aspirations, and did everything possible to provide for their well-being. Many granted wage increases or reduced hours voluntarily, or without demur when approached by the Association,

---

[1] Crompton, J. W., *Report on Printers' Strikes and Trade Unions since January 1845* (1860).

and Crompton discovered in 1860 that 'many masters seem to admit the necessity of limiting the number of apprentices in their offices'. The larger firms were also providing greatly improved working conditions. Many still carried on the ancient custom of providing an annual 'wayz-goose' for their men—usually a day's 'outing' to the seaside or some beauty-spot—and quite a number gave a week or fortnight's holiday each year, with pay. By the end of this period several firms had established welfare, sick, or pension funds for their employees, while a few had started profit-sharing and co-partnership schemes.[1] Employers, according to Crompton, 'generally admitted that society men in the printing trade are, as a rule, superior in ability and steadiness to non-society men'. Most firms found 'that if men are treated with fairness, considera-tion and firmness, it is possible, as a general rule, to carry on business pleasantly with society hands'.[2]

Good relations undoubtedly existed between employer and employed in many firms. But the antipathy between capital and labour was still there. In less enlightened establishments it was blatantly obvious and often resulted in open conflict. Unionism was the outcome of a real need, to protect workers from capitalist exploitation, to maintain and, if possible, raise their standard of living, threatened by unscrupulous, profit-seeking employers. Many employers detested union 'interfer-ence' in their affairs, particularly 'outside interference' by a branch com-mittee or distant Executive. They claimed, in accordance with 'free trade' ideas, to employ whomever they liked, pay what wages, work what hours, and have as many apprentices as they pleased, and objected to their men being coerced or inveigled into joining the union. Some, no doubt, objected on principle to what they regarded as unjust and arbi-trary regulations; others were driven to 'unfair' practices by cut-throat competition; but most were themselves undercutting and their 'free trade' cries were merely a cover for selfish, profit-making motives. The worst offenders were the smaller, struggling employers, who cut down wages, worked excessively long hours, and exploited boy labour in order to compete with larger firms.

Strikes were obviously inevitable. Some employers considered that unions tended to multiply strikes by 'agitating' and by placing in the hands of a central Executive the power to originate or sanction strikes

---

[1] Some of these schemes, however, were rather specious, aiming chiefly at keeping the men out of the T.A. Such firms often adopted a paternal 'we-can-best-look-after-your-interests' attitude and were opposed to union 'interference'
[2] *Sheffield Independent*, 2 April 1859.

in distant localities. These charges, however, cannot justly be laid against the T.A. One of its fundamental purposes was, undoubtedly, to give added strength through union, to build up a powerful reserve fund and support its members in strikes; but the latter were regarded as an evil, to be avoided whenever possible.

The old Northern Union strike rule was re-enacted in 1849. This rule, as we have seen, was an ambiguous one. Its intention was to give the Executive control over disputes, in order to prevent strikes through ill-judged, hasty, or prejudiced local action, but it failed to define Executive powers and left branches a good deal of independence. At first, indeed, branches regarded the Association merely as an assurance society from which they could secure funds in case of strike. They regulated their own wages and hours and only consulted the Executive when a dispute occurred. Even then the Executive frequently left matters entirely in local hands, merely promising financial support.

Gradually, however, the E.C. found it necessary to exercise closer supervision and control in order to prevent strikes and safeguard Association funds. This could not be done merely by correspondence, which involved delay and misunderstanding, so they started sending 'delegates', usually the Association Secretary, to make personal investigation into disputes. They also began to insist on being consulted before any 'extreme measures' were taken and to refuse strike pay when branches acted independently.

These practices were given legislative form in 1867. It was then laid down

that whenever a breach of the constitutional rules of the Association (apprentices, hours of labour, wages, &c.) occurs in an office, the Branch Secretary must at once transmit to the Association Secretary full particulars of the case, and summon the companionship immediately interested to a conference with the local Committee or officers, who, by deputation and other conciliatory means, shall endeavour to remove the grievance; but all action likely to compromise the interests of the Association must be avoided until the Executive have fully inquired into and decided upon the case. Should, however, local efforts prove dilatory or unsatisfactory, the Council shall send their Secretary or other representative to elicit from employer and employed all possible and necessary information, and obtain, through a general meeting, the verdict of the Branch; and such verdict, or the obstinacy or anticipatory action of an employer, shall be sufficient authority for the Executive closing a house and granting strike allowance.

But the Council was given 'discretionary power to defer action'.

The aim was obviously to prevent strikes by conciliatory means and Executive control, but branches still had a strong voice in strike decisions. In 1874, however, the clause with regard to obtaining the verdict of the branch was removed and it simply became the rule that 'if an amicable adjustment of the difficulty is found impossible, the Executive shall have power to close the office where the dispute exists'. No office, it was emphasized, could be closed without the Council's authority.

It was also made a definite rule in 1867 'that the opinion of the Executive shall be elicited before Branches initiate any movement for an advance of wages, reduction of hours, &c.; and no memorial or other document bearing on these questions . . . shall be issued to employers or the public without the knowledge and approval of the Board'. Branches guilty of 'unadvised action' would 'forfeit any participation in the Association funds' if a strike occurred. The Council considered that their functions were 'to advise and assist the Branches, and counsel against any high-handed and unreasonable demands on the part of the members, as well as to resist the encroachments of employers'.

Branches, however, were loath to lose their independence and during the years 1866–74 many initiated 'advance movements' without consulting the Executive. The latter were faced by a very difficult situation in this period, when all branches were clamouring to go in for increased wages and reduced hours. The Council could not cope with all of them at once, particularly as the Association funds were very limited, and had to postpone action in many instances. This restraint produced dissatisfaction and, not infrequently, revolt. But the Executive held the purse strings and were therefore able gradually to enforce their will. Cases of 'unadvised action' became less and less frequent in the following years and branches began to submit even the pettiest questions for Executive decision. Executive business expanded tremendously and the Association officials were constantly travelling the country to investigate disputes.

The Executive invariably adopted a conciliatory policy and were always prepared to compromise in order to avoid strikes. When an employer reduced wages, employed an excessive number of apprentices, or adopted other 'unfair' practices, repeated efforts were made to secure an amicable settlement by deputations from chapel, branch, and Executive. Moderate language and reasoned arguments were used and only in the last resort were 'extreme measures' adopted. When a branch applied for increased wages or reduced hours, its memorial was invariably couched in respectful terms, approved by the Executive, who took great care 'to avoid the use of any language which might be regarded as dictatorial'. The Council frequently reduced branch demands which they regarded as excessive or impracticable. They also considered whether or not the time was 'opportune' for an advance movement, having regard to the state of trade, the likelihood of opposition, the condition of the various offices (number of non-members and apprentices), and feeling in the branch. They often decided, for one reason or another, that the time was 'inopportune' and that the movement must be postponed. Even if the time was 'opportune', they favoured diplomacy and conference, rather than strike action, to attain their ends. Negotiations were often prolonged for weeks and months and branches were exasperated by the delays and excessive caution of the Executive. There is no doubt, however, that innumerable strikes were prevented by Executive diplomacy, particularly by the negotiating skill and tact of the General Secretary.

Trade competition for a long time prevented joint action among master printers. In its early years, therefore, the Association had to deal with individual and rival firms. When a demand was made for increased wages, it was addressed by the society concerned to all the employers in the town, but varying replies came back from individual offices, some conceding the terms asked for, some compromising, and others resolutely refusing. The society had then to adopt a kind of piecemeal diplomacy, sending deputations from chapels or branch committee to each opposing employer. The Association Secretary might also have to pay a visit. Eventually some sort of terms would be averaged out, though a few offices might reject them and therefore be 'closed'.

This lack of union among employers had, paradoxically, serious disadvantages for the men. As Henry Slatter pointed out in the *Circular* in 1875, 'one of the great causes of the severe and unprofitable competition now so prevalent in the printing trade is the want of a better understanding and greater unity of action amongst the employers'. This undercutting competition resulted in reduced wage rates and boy labour, made uniform trade regulations impossible, and produced a large number of 'closed' houses. 'We have, therefore,' Slatter declared, 'nothing to fear, but, rather, cause for hope in the possibility of greater union among the master printers.'

London master printers had combined in wages negotiations with the journeymen since at least as early as 1785 and formed successive associations, each lasting several years, in the following century. There is little evidence, however, of combination among master printers in any provincial town until the years 1866–74, when, during the numerous 'advance movements' by the journeymen, they frequently united to resist demands for increased wages and reduced hours. In some towns they formed permanent associations, the Manchester Association of Master Printers, for example, being established in 1874.

This united action by employers naturally suggested to the T.A. the idea of joint conferences to arrange settlements. Thus in 1866 we find the Executive recommending the Preston branch 'to solicit a conference with news employers, or their representatives, to agree to a scale of prices for morning papers, etc.'. The branch overtures appear to have been unsuccessful, however, and when they were repeated in 1869 it was expressly stated that 'the branch had failed to secure a conference with the employers'. When the Newcastle branch made a similar approach to the local master printers in 1866, regarding an advance of wages, 'only one attended a meeting to which they had been invited to discuss the matter'.

Many employers were loath to 'recognize' the local society or the Association by agreeing to joint conferences. They asserted their right to deal individually with their employees and rejected the idea of collective bargaining. Many shared the middle-class detestation of trade unions and were nauseated by the idea of discussing wage rates and hours with their men. But in several towns the advantages of joint conferences, in preventing strikes and establishing standard rates, proved stronger than these prejudices. In Sheffield, for example, as a result of branch demands in 1872 for increased wages and reduced hours, representatives of masters and men met in a series of conferences which finally resulted in a set of rules 'agreed upon by a joint committee of the employers and the branch'. A similar agreement on wages and hours was reached in Manchester in 1874 as a result of joint discussions. It became, in fact, the Executive's policy that, whenever difficulties occurred in regard to wage rates or hours, 'an effort should be made, by the holding of a conference between the representatives of the employers and the branch, to settle such difficulties in a pacific and conciliatory manner'.

Employers' associations were formed in many towns by the end of the century and negotiations between their representatives and those of the men became increasingly common. The next series of 'advance movements' in 1889–93 was remarkable for the number of such joint conferences and for the improved branch discipline under Executive control. All difficult negotiations were handled by the Association officials, although chapels and branches still played an important part in the early stages, in preparing and issuing memorials and in deputations to obstinate or hostile employers.

The result was a considerable reduction in the number of strikes. When masters and men got together, discussing questions in a fair and reasonable manner, they usually managed to agree on some compromise, though the Association frequently had to use the threat of strike action to gain its ends. These conferences were a means of mutual education, enabling masters and men to appreciate each other's point of view and to arrive at agreements which provided more settled working conditions and prevented wasteful disputes.

Employers seem rarely to have combined to bring about wage reductions or to increase the number of apprentices; most trouble still came from single firms, intent on reducing costs by a 'cheap labour' policy. As the employers' associations became more powerful they actually assisted the Association to enforce standard rates. Joint agreements and branch rules were signed by representatives of masters and men, to their mutual advantage. From the employers' point of view, these established rules tended to reduce undercutting in contracts and 'unfair' competition by low-paid or boy labour, while the men secured an agreed standard and rules which had been given force and durability by the employers' signature. The Association could therefore claim with justice at its jubilee in 1899 that it had 'secured redress of innumerable grievances, established rules and regulations for the trade, substituting discipline for chaos', and that 'in towns where they had branches . . . they found method, system, and a good understanding between the men and employers'.

By the end of the century a *national* agreement had been arrived at on rules for the working of Linotype machines.[1] It was natural that employers should follow the men in establishing not only local, but also national organizations. On the workers' side important negotiations were conducted by Association officials, backed by the funds of the whole union, whereas employers stood isolated or were organized in merely local organizations. In 1894, however, when the Association's demands in regard to working conditions on Linotype machines became, in the view of many employers, impossible, a 'Linotype Users' Association' was established, which eventually came to comprise a large proportion of the newspaper proprietors in the country. This organization opened up negotiations with the Executive of the T.A., which resulted, after prolonged correspondence, in the first national conference between

[1] See below, pp. 201–6.

employers and employed ever held in the printing trade, at the Queen's Hotel, Manchester, on 16 February 1897.

A provisional agreement on national lines was arrived at, but was considerably amended by a special meeting of the T.A. Representative Council in May 1897. The Executive were, in fact, greatly handicapped in their negotiations with the employers' Association by the necessity of securing the acquiescence of Representative Council, Delegate Meeting, and branches, who were loath to grant them plenary powers for settlement. Branches objected strongly to losing their independence and were apt to reject terms negotiated by the Executive, accusing the latter of compromise and surrender. Nevertheless, the Executive won their way and succeeded, after several conferences with the Linotype Users' committee, in negotiating national agreements for the working of Linotype machines on 'stab (1898) and piece (1903).

In the administration of these agreements in the various towns and offices, officials of the national Associations often met and negotiated settlements. Local master printers' associations tended, like T.A. branches, to refer disputes to their central executive. The Association officials therefore met frequently, formed mutual understandings and agreements, and usually managed to arrange friendly settlements. Strikes were very rare. The T.A. Executive emphasized 'the value of the good relations which exist between the two bodies', the 'mutual feeling of confidence', the tact and forbearance shown on both sides, which were producing 'permanent and satisfactory settlements' of difficult problems.[1]

A further development in employers' organization took place in 1900, when the 'Federation of Master Printers and Allied Trades of the United Kingdom of Great Britain and Ireland' was established. There had long been a tendency in the various towns to separate organization of news and jobbing proprietors (though many news offices had jobbing houses attached) and for the T.A. to negotiate with them separately. The newspaper proprietors were the first to form a national organization, the Linotype Users' Association, followed, early in the twentieth century, by the Federations of Northern and Southern Newspaper Owners and the Irish Newspaper Society. Now the local associations of employers in the book and general printing trade (letterpress printers, lithographers, bookbinders, &c.) also combined to form a national Federation.

A circular convening a meeting of the Manchester master printers in 1901 to consider federation stated 'that it had long been felt that local

---

[1] *Typographical Circular*, June 1900.

associations and individual employers were at a disadvantage in dealing with the highly organized forces of trade unionism, and that something should be done to enable employers to take into consideration labour questions with due regard to the conditions prevailing in the United Kingdom generally'. But the Federation vigorously denied that it was in any way antagonistic to trade unions. Its Secretary, H. Vane Stow, declared at the second annual meeting that 'their enemy was not the working man, but the man who will not pay enough for his work' and that their aim was 'to get a fair working profit for printers' by securing fair prices from the public and reducing competition in their own ranks, rather than by beating down wages. The Federation aimed, its President, Walter Hazell, declared, to establish 'a standard of reasonable conditions' or 'schedule of prices covering the chief items of printers' charges', upon which all estimates could be based, and to 'deal with those employers . . . who are injuring the workmen by paying sweating wages, and injuring their fellow-employers by unreasonably low prices'. In this way, 'reckless and ignorant competition' would be reduced and printing would be done 'under fair conditions and at a fair price'. The Federation would also provide trade information and watch legislation affecting printers. One of its chief aims, of course, was to place employers on an equality with the trade unions. The natural result of the men's collective action was that 'employers should meet them collectively'. But 'this need not be done in any antagonistic spirit. It is for the advantage of both employers and employed . . . that each of the parties to the bargain should be properly remunerated, and that the industry should be on a suitable footing.'

The *Typographical Circular*, commenting on this speech, applauded the Federation's proposed objects, pointing out that combination among master printers would be advantageous to all engaged in the trade, employers and wage-earners alike. T.A. officials had, in fact, frequently pointed out the necessity for increased union among master printers, so as to reduce 'unfair competition', which was equally harmful to employers and employed.

One of the rules of the F.M.P. provided that 'no step of general importance to the printing trade as a whole shall be taken by any federated association or individual member, without previous consultation with the council'. This centralizing policy naturally resulted in the Federation committee and officials being brought increasingly into negotiation with the T.A. Executive and its officers, not only to settle local disputes, but also to arrive at national agreements. It was not, however, until 25

October 1904 that representatives of the T.A. and F.M.P. met for the first time in national conference, at the Grand Hotel, Birmingham, to discuss regulations for working Monotype machines and the apprentice question. As a result of this and a further conference in Birmingham on 24 January 1905 an agreement was reached on 'stab and piece rules for the Monotype keyboard, though not for the Monotype caster, T.A. control being disputed by the Federation.[1]

These agreements with the L.U.A. and F.M.P. on Linotype and Monotype composing machines were a great achievement, placing the working conditions (wages, hours, &c.) of operators on a regular national basis. Irregularities still existed, of course, and disputes occurred, but the national agreements usually provided a means of friendly settlement. They also greatly increased and extended T.A. influence by securing the general adoption of 'fair' working conditions.

Settlement was still a long way off, however, in regard to the apprentice question, on which the Birmingham conference resulted in absolute deadlock. During the following years the F.M.P. repeatedly pressed for another conference but it was not until 1909 that negotiations were reopened, by which time the question of a revised apprentice scale had become part of a larger issue—that of securing a national settlement on the T.A. rules revised by the Delegate Meeting at St. Albans in 1908.

During the first decade of the twentieth century master printers had considerably strengthened their various national organizations. Officials of the F.M.P., L.U.A., and Newspaper Owners' Federations now took a prominent part in the settlement of local disputes. This development made for industrial peace, since T.A. officers were generally able to arrive at reasonable agreements with representatives of the employers' national organizations. But it also confronted the T.A. with a stronger and more united resistance to its demands. The F.M.P. and L.U.A. opposed the T.A. policy of piecemeal conquest. They refused, moreover, to countenance innovations or recognize rules established without their agreement.

As long ago as 1838 employers had protested against one-sided action by the men in laying down arbitrary rules for the trade without consultation with themselves.[2] But throughout the nineteenth century the T.A. continued to enact laws, by Delegate Meeting and voting paper, for the

---

[1] See the sections on Composing Machines and Apprentices for details of these negotiations.
[2] Select Committee on Combinations, Second Report (1838). Evidence by Mr. F. D. Finlay, Q. 5,445.

regulation of wages, hours, apprentices, and general working conditions. In the early years, before local master printers' associations were established, a kind of guerrilla warfare was carried on by chapels and branches to enforce these rules in individual offices. Later it became usual for branches to negotiate (under Executive control) with local employers' associations to secure recognition of branch rules, which, when agreement was arrived at, were usually signed by both sides. Many of the T.A. rules were nothing more than paper regulations, which could not be enforced locally. But the Association was constantly bringing pressure to bear on individual employers or on local master printers' associations in order to secure their acquiescence. Its rules, moreover, were continually changing and its demands becoming more extensive.

The F.M.P., L.U.A., and other national employers' organizations opposed a united front to these demands and refused to recognize rules which had never received their sanction. The T.A. Delegate Meeting of 1908, however, passed a whole series of new and altered rules in regard to wages and hours, limitation of overtime, apprentices, readers, machine-men, and mechanical indicators, which, after adoption by the members, were to be enforced upon employers in the usual fashion.

The F.M.P. and L.U.A. at once protested that these new rules would alter existing agreements and that, without their consent, such alterations would be invalid. All regulations, they claimed, affecting working conditions in their offices should be arrived at by 'mutual agreement', instead of being arbitrarily imposed by the Association. They could not recognize rules in the formation of which they had never been consulted. They therefore asked for a conference to discuss the new rules.

To this request the T.A. Executive agreed and a circular was issued to the branches asking them to use 'the utmost discretion' in attempting to enforce the new rules, pending negotiations with the employers' national organizations. Here was a new departure of great importance: never before had the T.A. rules regarding working conditions been submitted to a national body of employers for discussion and modification, though national agreements had been established on Linotype and Monotype rules. The E.C. now recognized, however, 'that it is better to get this matter of the new rules settled between the national bodies rather than to cause fifty or one hundred little difficulties' by negotiating at branch level, and that 'if we can come to a settlement, it will ensure industrial peace in the printing trade for many years to come'.

Separate negotiations were held with the F.M.P. and L.U.A. in 1909. The F.M.P. was mainly interested in securing the long-sought revision of the apprentice scale, which they considered must be settled before the other questions could be dealt with, and the three conferences between their representatives and those of the T.A. were confined almost exclusively to that subject.[1]

The four conferences between L.U.A. and T.A. representatives that same year covered a wider field. The L.U.A. stated at the first conference that they were 'in close relationship with the Federation of Northern Newspaper Owners, the Federation of Southern Newspaper Owners, and the Master Printers' Federation', so as 'to avoid overlapping', and the two Newspaper Federations sent representatives to the following conferences. They and the L.U.A. were, of course, solely concerned with questions affecting newspaper offices. The chief subjects discussed, therefore, were newspaper questions: the T.A.'s claim to control the rotary machine department, indicators on Linotype machines, and overtime on newspapers.

From the point of view of industrial relationships, the most interesting feature of the conferences was the L.U.A.'s attempt to secure permanent conciliation machinery for the settlement of disputes in the newspaper industry. The T.A. Delegate Meeting of 1891 had introduced an arbitration clause into the Association rules, but it was deleted by the meeting in 1908.[2] This the L.U.A. regarded as a retrograde step and wished to know if the T.A. was prepared to substitute some other method of settling disputes, so as to avoid strikes and lock-outs. They desired some agreement binding both employers and employed to exhaust all means of arriving at a friendly settlement before resorting to extreme measures.

The T.A. rejected arbitration, but was 'prepared to adopt the principle of conciliation in the settlement of any disputes that may arise in the newspaper trade'. A Conciliation Board had, however, recently been established by negotiation between the F.M.P. and the Printing and Kindred Trades Federation[3] and the T.A. Executive did not favour the establishment of other Boards for different sections of the industry, considering that there should be one Board for the whole. It was therefore agreed that newspaper owners, the L.U.A., that is, and the Northern and Southern Federations, should secure representation on this Board and that disputes in the newspaper industry should be referred to it.

On the other points discussed, however, on the rules for rotary machine minders, Linotype indicators, and overtime, no agreement was reached. The conferences with the F.M.P. on the apprentice question

[1] See below, p. 183.   [2] See below, pp. 146–7.
[3] See below, p. 256.

had also failed and the Master Printers refused to discuss the other rules until that was settled. Deadlock therefore resulted.

By this time T.A. branches were getting very restless and dissatisfied at the long delay and demanding that the new rules should be issued and enforced locally as in the past. It was now two years since the 1908 Delegate Meeting. On 7 May 1910, therefore, the Executive decided 'that the rules should be issued to the Branches with instructions to put them in force forthwith'. Copies of the rules were printed during the next three months, distributed to the branches, and presented to local employers and employers' associations with notice as to their enforcement.

This decisive action caused considerable alarm among employers and on 13 September a meeting of representatives from the F.M.P., L.U.A., Northern and Southern Newspaper Owners' Federations, and the Irish Newspaper Society was specially convened to consider the situation. They decided to inform the T.A. Executive that several of the rules issued by them were unworkable and could not be accepted, but that they were willing, if the rules were suspended, to meet in conference to arrange a general settlement. Meanwhile, individual employers were warned not to allow the new T.A. rules to be introduced in their offices. Some of the larger firms were 'gravely considering whether a general lock-out would not be a lesser evil than submission to the dictates of the Typographical Association'.

The T.A. Executive accepted the invitation to a conference and eventually advised branches to suspend local action, pending the result of negotiations with the employers' national organizations. Four national conferences followed between October 1910 and January 1911. Matters were complicated by the 48-hours' agitation being carried on concurrently by the Printing and Kindred Trades Federation.[1] The T.A. wished to treat the rules and hours agitations as 'two separate movements entirely' and to negotiate separately on the former. But the employers regarded the ballot on the hours question as a 'loaded pistol at our heads', and it certainly exercised a disturbing influence during the conferences and made it more difficult to arrive at a settlement. Discussion ranged over the whole of the new or amended T.A. rules—except that on wages and hours, which had to be excluded on account of the 48-hours' movement—including those on overtime, mechanical indicators, bonus-paid 'task-work', machine minders, readers, and apprentices. Agreement seemed within sight until the apprentice question was reached, but on that rock, as usual, the conferences foundered.

[1] See below, pp. 257–8.

The situation now, in mid-January 1911, was extremely critical. Not only had deadlock been reached on the T.A. rules, but a national strike threatened in the whole of the printing and kindred trades on the hours question. Whereas in the past local negotiations had involved innumerable local disputes, national negotiations now brought the dangerous possibility of national strikes. A great responsibility obviously rested on the shoulders of the national officials.

At this point the Board of Trade intervened. Here was a new phenomenon in industrial bargaining. The Government was being forced, in the national interest, to discard its *laissez-faire* ideas and mediate in these large-scale industrial disputes. A great deal of behind-the-scenes activity followed, in which the T.A. General Secretary, Herbert Skinner, and the L.U.A. President, Meredith T. Whittaker, were the leading actors, as a result of which further conferences were arranged on both the T.A. rules and the hours question at the beginning of March. A compromise agreement was reached on the hours question which was eventually accepted in a ballot of the provincial unions, but the rules conference again broke down over the apprentice ratio. Further negotiations followed between the officials, however, as a result of which a national 'Agreement on Rules' was finally arrived at and signed on 6 May 1911 between the T.A., on one side, and the F.M.P., L.U.A., and Northern and Southern Newspaper Federations on the other.

This agreement, as we have seen, produced much dissatisfaction in T.A. branches, which disliked being 'left in the dark' while the national Executives were in conference and national officials privately bargaining. They particularly resented having the agreement imposed upon them without a vote of the members. For a while it seemed likely that the E.C. would be hauled over the coals at a special Delegate Meeting, but they managed to maintain their authority in a ballot on the question. Nevertheless, the Delegate Meeting in 1913 enacted a rule that, in future, the Executive must 'not sign any agreement [with the employers' national organizations] without first submitting the proposed agreement to a vote of the members'.

The 1911 agreement, together with the Linotype and Monotype agreements, marks the change-over from local to national regulation of working conditions in the printing industry, from local variety to national uniformity. On many of their rules the T.A. Executive were forced to compromise in deference to the employers' point of view, but rules agreed to and signed by representatives of the F.M.P. and newspaper proprietors' national organizations were much more likely to be observed than the arbitrary, one-sided regulations which the T.A. had hitherto tried to enforce. Walter Hazell, first President of the F.M.P., had looked forward at the Annual Meeting in 1903 to the time 'when industrial disputes will give place to a better state of things in the form of industrial partnership'. This desirable state was brought considerably nearer now that representatives of employers' and workmen's national organizations were meeting on equal terms in friendly conference to agree upon working regulations for the whole industry.

Perhaps the most important feature of the 1911 Agreement was its establishment of a 'Committee of Reference' for the settlement of disputes by 'conciliation'. When negotiations with the L.U.A. and Newspaper Owners broke down in 1909 the T.A. Executive withdrew from the agreement regarding reference of disputes to the Conciliation Board. This matter was therefore pressed again with great urgency by the employers in the negotiations of 1910–11. They also asked for a Conciliation Board separate from that established with the P. & K.T.F., to settle disputes between T.A. members and themselves.

The T.A. eventually agreed to the establishment of a 'Committee of Reference', the rules for which were embodied in the treaty of 1911. It was laid down that 'in the event of any question or difference arising between an employer and members of the T.A. which proves incapable of settlement by the employer and the Branch concerned, no strike or lock-out shall take place and notices shall not be given by either side before reference of the question at issue has been made to a Standing Committee of employers and members of the T.A. Executive, which shall meet within six days of the matter being referred to it by either side'. The Standing Committee was to consist of eighteen members, nine nominated by the employers and nine by the T.A., of whom six were to be selected, three from each side, as far as possible unconnected with the dispute, to try to reach a settlement. It was also agreed that 'any difference arising as to the meaning, operation, or construction of this Agreement [the "Agreement on Rules"] or in relation thereto shall be referred in the first place to the Officials of the Employers' organisations and of the T.A., and failing a settlement by them shall be referred to the "Committee of Reference" '.

The Committee did not, however, prove very successful in the few years prior to the outbreak of war in 1914. Several local disputes were referred to it, nearly all concerned with the manning of printing machines under the rules laid down in the 1911 Agreement,[1] but on none of them

[1] See below, p. 225.

was a satisfactory settlement arrived at and eventually, towards the end of 1912, they were referred to arbitration. Both sides submitted a 'statement of facts' and sent representatives to argue their respective cases before the arbitrator, Sir Albert K. Rollit, who eventually gave a decision in favour of the employers. The T.A. Executive accepted this award, but immediately approached the employers for a conference 'with the object of securing the amendment of the Agreement on Machinemen's Rules'. The employers, however, refused to discuss amendment of the machine rules unless further amendment of the apprentice scale was also considered.

The T.A. Executive did not relish such a bargain and decided to leave matters to the 1913 Delegate Meeting. This meeting gave strong expression to local dissatisfaction with the 1911 Agreement, abrogating or altering not only the machine rules, but also those regarding Linotype indicators, overtime, and apprentices, and passing resolutions in favour of a 48-hour week and holidays with pay.

The employers were greatly indignant at this arbitrary, unilateral breach of the Agreement and relations deteriorated. Eventually, however, in June 1914, the T.A. Executive decided to submit the proposed changes in working conditions to the F.M.P., with a view to an agreed settlement. Before arrangements could be made for a conference, however, war broke out and the F.M.P. decided that negotiations must be postponed until after the war. The great National Agreements of 1919 were to be based on these pre-war precedents.

Conciliation was the keynote of T.A. policy throughout this period. But though the Association strongly favoured collective bargaining and agreed settlements, it was never very enthusiastic about arbitration, that is, settlement of a dispute by the decision of an impartial umpire, after representatives of both sides had argued their case before him. Arbitration involved 'outside interference' by 'non-practical' men, who were unfamiliar with printing technicalities and trade customs, and arbitration awards were apt to be unpalatable. On several occasions, therefore, the E.C. refused to permit disputes to go to arbitration.

Gradually, however, they modified this attitude, allowing arbitration when collective bargaining had broken down in order to prevent strikes. The 1891 Delegate Meeting decided that no office should be closed 'until the principle of arbitration shall have first been tendered'. Several disputes on wages and hours were settled by arbitration in the nineties and early years of the next century, but the Association still retained its aversion to it. The arbitration rule proved very inconvenient, since it hampered strike action. It was therefore abolished in 1908, leaving the question of arbitration in any dispute an open one. The E.C. agreed to arbitration on certain disputed clauses in the machinemen's rules in 1912, but the outcome only served to increase their dislike of it.

Although the T.A. Executive did everything possible to prevent strikes, they were often unavoidable, in order to fight 'unfair' employers or to enforce branch demands. The chief weapon used by the T.A. was the customary fortnight's notice, which allowed time for negotiation and compromise. The Executive refused strike pay to any member who left without proper notice, while, on the other hand, often taking legal action to secure a fortnight's notice or wages to men who had been summarily dismissed. Violent strike methods were consistently deprecated and rarely used. No employer before any of the various Royal Commissions or Parliamentary Committees in the nineteenth century ever accused typographical societies of using violence.

The Association relied mainly upon the 'closing' of 'unfair' offices, upon bringing out the hands employed and preventing others going in, so that the office in question would be unable to get out its papers or execute its orders and thus be forced to capitulate. It was a very difficult policy to carry out. In many offices non-unionists were employed, whom the T.A. could not bring out, while members not infrequently stayed in, owing to the difficulty of finding fresh situations, particularly in periods of trade depression. The 'numerous tribe of rats', who had broken so many strikes under the Northern Union, remained a menace to the T.A. throughout the century. The Association tried to enrol all non-unionists and to enforce discipline upon its members by fines, suspension from benefit, and expulsions, but 'ratting' continued undiminished, as evidenced by the frequently reported instances in the *Circular* and by the failure of innumerable strikes.

One of the main aims of the *Circular* was to furnish information as to strikes, 'closed' or 'unfair' houses, and 'rats'. At the head of every number it was announced 'that a penalty will be inflicted on members of the Association who apply for work in any town before consulting the local Secretary'. Any traveller arriving in a branch town was to report at once to the local secretary, lodge his card, and receive a list of 'fair' offices. If any member applied at an office where there was a dispute or which was considered 'unfair', he was to be reported to and dealt with by the Executive. Members were also warned against applying for advertised situations without first consulting the local secretary, so as to thwart 'unfair' employers, who frequently secured hands by advertising in papers all over the United Kingdom. 'Rats' were reported in the *Circular*, 'rat lists' were kept by a number of societies, and the Executive even tried to compile an Association 'Black Book', so as to ensure the punishment of 'unfair' hands.

The Executive were extremely loath to have dealings with 'rats' and non-unionists during strikes and realized that bribery of such men would cause an added influx. But they were often driven by force of circumstances to swallow their scruples and attempt to buy off 'rats' with offers of free membership, travelling cards, railway fares home, and money payments, so as to thwart the advertising and canvassing of employers and prevent hands from going in. They also inserted warning advertisements in rival papers, pointing out the facts of the dispute and appealing to journeymen printers not to be tempted by the employers' specious offers to betray their brethren. Picketing also became common in more serious strikes, but peaceful persuasion and bribery were the rule and violence was rare, though threats and personal abuse were common.

These were not the Association's only strike weapons. As early as 1845 we read of the Preston Society conducting a 'paper warfare' against an 'unfair' newspaper proprietor, 'posting' or 'placarding' him, so as to 'expose' his conduct to the public. This kind of 'paper warfare' had probably been waged for many years. It became increasingly common in the second half of the century. Whenever a strike broke out in any branch, the local society would issue thousands of handbills or circulars and stick up hundreds of posters all over the town, 'exposing' the practices of the proprietor concerned and appealing to the public, particularly the working class, for support, asking them to boycott 'unfair' newspapers and jobbing offices. Such appeals came to be made through the Trades Councils, which would hold public meetings and support the printers in their campaign. This mode of strike warfare was particularly effective against local newspaper proprietors, who relied largely on the working class for their limited circulation.

Branches also began to issue 'fair lists'. In 1847, for example, the Manchester committee decided 'that an address emanating from this society and circulated amongst the various trade and other societies (with a list of recognized offices appended), would be the means of increasing the work in fair establishments', and therefore had 200 such circulars printed and issued. Similarly, in 1853, the Liverpool Society decided on 'exposing the unfair employers' by publishing a poster, 'containing a list of fair employers, and also the chief employers among the unfair', together with an 'appeal to the public, particularly the operative class, who give a large amount of work to unfair houses, on account of the cheapness of it, calling upon them to support only those employers who pay a fair day's wage for a fair day's labour'. Soon all societies adopted this policy, until in 1887 a *List of Fair and Unfair Offices in the Various Branches of the T.A.* was compiled and printed in booklet form by the Executive. Several firms, however, instituted libel actions for use of the adjective 'unfair', so that the title was changed in 1890 to *Society and Non-Society Offices* and eventually the list was restricted to those printing firms 'recognized by the Association', unrecognized offices being conspicuous by their absence.

As the working class gained political power, the Association extended its policy by bringing electoral pressure to bear on local council and parliamentary candidates to make party newspapers 'fair', to have party literature printed in 'fair' offices, and to secure that public printing contracts should be given only to 'fair' houses.[1] Through the 'fair list' and the 'fair contracts' agitation the T.A. secured the 'opening' of many hitherto 'closed' offices.

It is difficult accurately to determine the success or failure of the Association's strike policy. The threat of a strike was undoubtedly a powerful weapon and frequently induced employers to make concessions. There were also numerous instances of firms being ruined and newspapers failing as a result of strikes. But more often employers managed to find a sufficient number of 'rats' and non-society men to break strikes and carry on their business. The Association was most successful in periods of good trade, when not only was there a scarcity of unemployed men available for use by employers, but strike hands more readily found employment in other offices or towns, thereby lessening the drain on Association funds. Moreover, when there was a likelihood of other employment the sacrifice demanded was smaller and fewer hands 'ratted' by staying in. In periods of bad trade, however, strikes almost invariably failed.

Strikes or 'disputes' in the printing trade were petty affairs. Half-yearly reports confirm J. W. Crompton's statement in 1860 that 'the strikes with which the Association has had to deal have invariably been local, and affecting only one office in the same locality at one time and for the same cause. . . . The number of men involved in each strike varies from one to twenty-six, five being about the average.' His statement was not quite true—some strikes had involved several offices in one

[1] See below, p. 305.

town—but it covered the vast majority of disputes, both before and after 1860. To the end of the century and beyond most strikes only concerned individual offices. The increase in the size of offices meant, of course, that a larger number of men were involved: in 1865, for example, over fifty men came out of the Liverpool *Daily Post*, in 1884 about forty were involved in a strike at Emmott & Co.'s in Manchester, and in 1901 nearly seventy came out at Butler and Tanner's in Frome. But the majority of strikes were in small offices and rarely involved more than about a dozen men.

Most of the T.A. strike payments, in fact, were made to individual members in the form of 'victimization pay'. Members prominent in society affairs, such as branch or chapel officials, were frequently marked by employers—who regarded them as agitators or trouble-makers—and dismissed, usually on some trivial pretext. Those who resisted 'encroachments on the privileges of the profession' or who took a leading part in advance movements were similarly 'weeded out' by employers.

These 'victims' were awarded strike pay by the Executive, but other men employed in the same office were not brought out to secure their reinstatement or to check further victimization. In 1891, however, a rule was enacted 'that where it is proved to the satisfaction of the E.C. that members are being discharged from their situations on account of any action taken in the interest of the Association, or for the purposes of intimidation, they shall have the power to withdraw the members, and declare the office closed'. But the Executive were loath to use this new power, as it might cause costly strikes, and still preferred to see individuals sacrificed. Consequently, we find branches urging 'that more drastic measures be taken with employers who habitually victimise members for the active part taken by them in the interests of the Association', and advocating strikes to secure the reinstatement of those victimized.

During the early part of this period negotiations with individual firms had produced many small disputes, but had precluded the possibility of large-scale strikes. But when societies sought wholesale wage increases and master printers began to combine in order to resist these demands, strikes tended to become more serious, involving many, or even all, offices in a town, or at any rate all the hands in one section of the trade, news or jobbing.

This was particularly evident during the advance movement of 1865–74. When, for example, the Liverpool branch memorialized the employers for increased wages and reduced hours in 1865, the proprietor of the *Daily Post* and several jobbing firms refused to concede the demand and nearly 110 men came out on strike. Similarly, when the jobbing employers of Birmingham refused in 1872 to grant the terms asked for in a branch memorial, about 170 men handed in their notices and eventually over 90 came out on strike. All the news hands of Preston (about 40) struck in the same year, when their request for increased piece rates was refused. A large-scale strike threatened in Manchester in 1874, when all the branch members tendered a fortnight's notice in order to secure their demands for increased wages and reduced hours, but a settlement was eventually reached by negotiation.

In the following years of trade depression strikes were on a very small scale, rarely involving more than one office. But in the period after 1889, when another great advance movement began, more serious strikes again occurred. In Leicester, for example, a strike involving several offices and over thirty men took place in 1891, and in 1896 over forty men came out in Blackpool. In the latter year a serious strike again threatened in Manchester, when twenty jobbing firms, employing about 125 hands, refused to grant a reduction of hours; the men tendered their notices and a strike involving about sixty members eventually occurred.

More strikes broke out in the renewed movement for improved conditions at the end of the century, mostly in jobbing offices. Disputes affecting from forty to sixty men occurred in Blackburn, Newcastle, and Norwich in 1899–1902, while in 1904 there took place the most serious strike in which the T.A. had ever been involved, when, as a result of the Hull jobbing employers' refusal to grant any wage increase, over 150 men came out. But, fortunately, as the half-yearly report stated, 'the great bulk of the employers with whom the Association has to deal from time to time are men of judgement and discretion, who fully appreciate the conciliatory policy which has always been a characteristic of the T.A. Hence the Executive Council rarely has to chronicle a dispute of the dimensions of that now in progress in Hull.' Even this 'extensive' dispute was purely local, involving only a portion of the jobbing section in one branch and less than 1 per cent. of the total membership. Compare this with the mass strikes and lock-outs in the mining, engineering, and textile trades and among dockers and general labourers!

During the years 1904–14 strikes were few and far between, despite the almost continuous local agitations for increased wages and reduced hours. The vast majority of disputes were settled by joint conferences (usually attended by officials of the national organizations) and mutual concessions. With the establishment, however, of employers' national organizations and the growing tendency towards negotiation on a national level, there obviously loomed ahead the possibility of a national strike in the printing industry. The danger was evident during the negotiations over T.A. rules and the 48-hours' movement in 1910–11.

By June 1914 the Association had expended about £44,000 in strike payments, or little more than it had paid out in mileage relief, rather less than its expenditure in funeral benefits, about a third of that on superannuation account, and only one-sixth of the total out-of-work payments. This did not mean, however, that the T.A. neglected trade affairs for friendly benefits: wages, hours, and apprentices occupied much more attention than anything else. The comparative smallness of strike expenditure was due to the Association policy of conciliation and the good feeling which generally prevailed between employers and employed. The effect of Executive control and collective bargaining is illustrated by the fact that annual strike expenditure in the decade 1901–10, excluding 1904, the year of the Hull strike, was little higher than it had been in the sixties, though membership was now ten times as great.

It was laid down at the establishment of the P.T.A. in 1849 that a strike hand should receive weekly from the General Fund 'three-fourths of the wages of the town for the period of three months'. If he obtained casual employment his earnings were to be made up to the established wages, but if he secured a permanent situation strike payments would cease.

At the Delegate Meeting of 1853 the period of strike payments was extended to six months: for the first nine weeks the strike hand was to receive three-fourths of the wages of the town; for the second nine weeks, half; and for the last eight weeks, one-third. In 1856, moreover, it was decided to grant extra payments to members over fifty, because of the greater difficulty which older men found in securing employment: such members were to receive thirty-six weeks' strike pay. Strike cards were also reintroduced for issue to strike hands on the expiration of their weekly payments, entitling them, as in Northern Union days, to double relief 'on the road'. These cards were abolished on the establishment of the R.A. in 1863, but a strike hand could still remove to another branch, to whose secretary the Executive would remit his weekly allowance.

The Executive also began to pay the removal expenses of strike hands who secured employment in other towns, to make loans to those wishing to remove in search of work, or to compound their strike claims, and also to pay lump sums in lieu of weekly payments to strike hands who desired to emigrate.[1] But it proved almost impossible to secure repayment of loans and so the Executive discontinued the practice, merely undertaking to pay the removal expenses of strike hands either 'obtaining or electing to seek employment in another town'.[2] It also became the rule that strike payments should only be compounded in the case of members wishing to emigrate, since it was found that many others who had received lump sums afterwards 'ratted'.

The Executive expected strike hands 'to use every legitimate endeavour to obtain work'. In 1867 it was laid down that strike hands must comply with the same regulations as out-of-work members, that is, sign the call-book and accept employment when offered. Furthermore, the E.C. were empowered to provide work for strike hands or to direct their removal to other towns where work was available. Strike payments were also altered. A strike hand was in future to receive £1 per week for twenty weeks while unemployed, but if he was above fifty years of age and had held his situation three years (altered in 1872 to one year), the allowance was to be continued for twenty-six weeks.

The period of strike payments was reduced at the Delegate Meeting in 1877—to fifteen weeks in the case of strike hands under fifty years of age and to twenty for those over fifty—owing to trade depression and the state of the Association funds.

The weekly payments were consecutive and included payments made in any weeks in which casual employment was secured. These provisions served to discourage attempts to find work, strike hands tending to sit back until the full fifteen weeks' allowance had been drawn. At the Delegate Meeting of 1891, therefore, it was decided that all strike hands should be entitled to a maximum compensation of £15 (£20 for men over fifty), which could be drawn in weekly payments, either full or partial, during the twelve months following a strike. This rule was still in force twenty years later, with an addition, made by the Delegate Meeting in 1898, empowering the Executive to grant an extension of strike benefit in cases where it might secure victory for the Association.[3]

A period of probation, at first six months, later a year, had to be served by new branches before their members were eligible for strike benefit. This proved a serious obstacle to the Association in 'missionary' work. Members of new branches, victimized for joining the union, could

---

[1] These practices were embodied in the rules in 1861.
[2] P.T.A. Rules (1867).
[3] The large branches usually supplemented or extended the Association strike allowance from their local funds.

expect nothing from the Association but moral support, except perhaps a travelling document. Many men, therefore, were afraid to join, or threw up their membership when threatened by their employers. The Association was consequently forced to adopt a more liberal policy and passed a rule in 1886 providing for compensation to new members who sacrificed their situations in efforts to form a branch. In the following years strike pay was frequently granted in such instances. Without this change of policy it is difficult to see how the Association could have expanded into new areas in face of the bitter hostility often displayed by employers.

It was forced to make a similar relaxation in regard to non-members in old-established branches. Many non-unionists were working in 'fair' offices and were a great source of weakness, especially in strikes. The Association, therefore, made constant efforts to get them into the union, particularly during advance movements, when disputes threatened. According to rule, however, these men had no prospect of strike pay and were therefore unwilling to join the Association or throw in their lot with the members. Hence the Executive were compelled, in spite of their principles and aversion to non-unionists, to ignore the rule and offer free membership cards, out-of-work pay, travelling documents, and even strike pay to such men, to induce them to come out with T.A. members. They were even driven occasionally, much against their will, to offer similar bribes to members working in 'unfair' or 'closed' houses, in an effort to 'open' them.

IX

WAGES, HOURS, AND WORKING
REGULATIONS

Two of the T.A.'s main objects, laid down in the rules at its establishment, were 'regulation of the standard of wages' and 'restriction of the hours of labour', or, in an oft-repeated phrase, 'a fair day's wage for a fair day's work'. Since 1815 this had meant standing on the defensive to maintain, in the face of generally falling prices, the wage rates and hours won during the French wars. In the second half of the century, however, in the years 1853–5, 1859–60, 1865–74, 1888–93, and 1898–1902, when trade was booming and prices were rising, the Association took to the offensive and won successive increases in wages and reductions of working hours. It also evolved a complicated mass of regulations, particularly for piece-work, to secure fair working conditions.

The most noticeable feature about wage rates and hours in the provincial printing trade in the second half of the nineteenth century was their increasing complexity and variety. Differences existed not only between the various towns, but between different offices in the same town and between different departments of the same office. In the first half of the century provincial printing consisted mainly of jobbing and weekly news work, for which there was generally one established wage rate and working week in each town. In the second half of the century, however, daily newspapers, morning and evening, sprang up in the provinces, with higher wage rates and shorter hours. Jobbing and book-work also tended to become differentiated. Compositors and machine-men, moreover, had different wage rates, and composing-machine operators became distinguished from hand compositors.[1] Finally, there were the different systems of piece and 'stab, which often co-existed in the same town or even in the same office. Attempts to achieve uniformity of wages and hours had, by the end of this period, done little to simplify the kaleidoscopic local variations.

The wage structure at the establishment of the P.T.A. was comparatively simple. In most towns the 'stab system prevailed and there was

---

[1] For the wages, hours, &c., of composing-machine operators and machine minders see below, Chapter XI. In this chapter we shall be dealing solely with hand compositors, who formed the main mass of T.A. members throughout this period.

rarely any difference between news and jobbing rates, no provincial dailies having yet been established. Wage rates varied considerably, however, between the different branches, from 21s. per week in the smaller, less organized, country towns to 30s. per week in large industrial cities such as Manchester and Liverpool. The established working hours were generally 59 per week.

During the years 1851–4 there was a general improvement in trade and the Crimean War broke out, increasing the demand for news and other printed matter, while at the same time the advertisement and supplement duties were abolished. Brisk trade, moreover, was accompanied by rising prices. In 1853, therefore, the Executive considered 'the propriety of some general movement for securing an advance in the wages of printers', in view of 'the improved and improving demand for journeymen, the enormous rise in the price of provisions', and the fact that other trades had secured increases. They decided, however, that a general movement would be unwise, owing to 'the yet superabundant labour market' and the danger of strikes, but were prepared to sanction memorials in certain instances, where a disparity existed with neighbouring towns. As a result, several branches gained slight increases.

There were a few more advances in 1859–61 and at the Delegate Meeting in the latter year the 'Short-Time Question'—the question of reducing the hours of labour—was discussed at great length. Several branches favoured an effort to secure a 9-hour day or 54-hour week and Saturday half-holiday. They pointed out that working hours had 're-mained unaltered for the past half-century' and urged that the Association should cease to be purely defensive and take action to secure for its members a fair share in the benefits arising from the repeal of the 'Taxes on Knowledge'. Other trades had already secured reductions in the hours of labour. Great advantages would accrue therefrom. 'Domestic enjoyment would be increased, and mental culture greatly promoted.' There would be an improvement of health and 'a diminution in the mortality of printers' due to the increased opportunities for physical and social recreation, while work would be provided for 'the present surplus labour'. The delegates therefore decided 'that the present is a fitting time for the various Societies making a vigorous effort by every legitimate means to obtain a reduction of the hours of labour or an advance in the rate of wages to such an extent as each Society may deem practicable'.

The early sixties were not, however, 'a fitting time' for such movements, since depression and cotton famine descended on the country as a result of the American Civil War. It was not, therefore, until 1864, when trade revived, that the great 'advance movement' began.

Meanwhile, the abolition of the 'Taxes on Knowledge' had led to the establishment of daily newspapers in many of the larger towns. The earliest of these was the *Northern Daily Times*, a morning paper, first published in Liverpool in September 1853. The Liverpool branch made inquiries from the Executive and other large branches 'as to what would be a fair remunerating wage for a provincial daily paper', bearing in mind the night work involved and the increased amount of composition during the day. The Executive recommended Liverpool 'to adopt the same difference between the prices on the dailies and other papers in Liverpool as exists between the London dailies and the regular [metropolitan] 'stab of 36/-', being 'convinced that that difference is by no means excessive for the arduous and incessant duties required on a daily paper, and for the wear and tear on the human system involved in the transformation of night into day'.

The Liverpool branch eventually passed a resolution 'that the number of hours per week should be sixty, inclusive of time for refreshment each night, and that the wages, for either day or night hands, should be £2. 2. 0. No apprentices allowed.' The proprietor refused these terms, however, and the Society therefore offered fresh ones: that work on daily papers during the day (from 8 a.m. to 7 p.m.) should be paid at the ordinary jobbing rate of 6d. per hour, that night work (after 7 p.m.) should be paid at 9d. per hour, that the regular hours should be 59, and that the usual number of apprentices should be allowed. These terms were also rejected by the proprietor, who would pay no more than 36s. per week to night hands. A strike therefore resulted, which the proprietor won by securing hands from all over the United Kingdom, particularly from Scotland and Ireland. In spite of the Society's warnings and appeals, Liverpool was 'perfectly inundated with tramps'. Nevertheless, it was partly due to the Liverpool Society's hostility that the *Morning News*, successor of the *Daily Times*, collapsed in 1859.

Meanwhile the *Mercury* and *Post* had become dailies, but the Society had failed to secure a standard rate of wages or uniform working hours. It was stated at the Delegate Meeting in 1861 that night hands in the *Mercury* office were receiving 9d. per hour after 6 p.m. and 6d., the ordinary rate, if required before that time. Their hours were 54 per week, seven of which were at 6d., so that their minimum wage was £1. 18s. 9d. The day hands were paid the ordinary wages of the town. In the *Daily Post* there was said to be 'no regularity of hours', and owing to 'the admixture of day with night hours' so-called night hands were only getting £1. 17s. 3d. per week of 58 hours. It was to take the Liverpool Society several years to establish uniform daily prices.

Manchester was next in the field after Liverpool and achieved greater success. During 1854–5 the *Guardian* and the *Examiner and Times* became dailies, while two or three other short-lived ones were established. A special committee appointed by the Society to draw up a morning paper rate of wages decided 'that the established wages for Daily Newspapers in Manchester be £2 per week for 54 hours' labour'. Meanwhile, however, advertisements had appeared in local papers for compositors 'at not less than 34s. per week' and a conflict appeared likely, but the Society eventually secured acceptance of the proposed wage rate and hours for night work and 34s. for 58 hours for day hands. Some of the night hands on the *Guardian* were stated in 1855 to be receiving from 54s. to 56s. per week. Compositors on the short-lived *Daily Telegraph* were put on piece at increased prices (long primer to minion, 9d. per 1,000; nonpareil, 9½d.; ruby, 10d.) and averaged £2. 10s., some getting as much as £3, for a 54-hour week.

In Sheffield the *Daily Telegraph* was established in 1855, followed soon afterwards by the *Morning's News*. The local Society at once held a special meeting to consider the scale of prices to be adopted. It was decided 'that an extra 'stab wage of 5s. per week be required, and an additional penny per thousand on the piece-prices, in all daily papers; retaining the threepence extra per hour for all hours worked from 10 p.m. to 5 a.m.'.[1] Hours were apparently to remain unchanged. After some opposition from the *News*, these wage rates were accepted by the proprietors, but a serious strike occurred in 1858–9, when a new paper, the *Daily Times*, refused to pay more than weekly rates. The Sheffield dailies were all put on piece and, at the advanced prices, the men were averaging £2. 2s. per week in 1861.

Similar negotiations and disputes took place in other branches where dailies were established. In each case increased wages and reduced hours were sought for the night work involved. In some cases an increase was secured on weekly news rates, piece or 'stab, in others an extra payment per hour after a certain time was made and the old-fashioned 'night-shilling' might also be paid, or there might be a combination of some or all of these. There were innumerable variations between different branches and offices. The Liverpool Society therefore urged at the Delegate Meeting in 1861 that the Association should attempt to secure

[1] This was the ordinary extra for overtime.

'some uniformity as to the hours and rates of remuneration' on daily papers. A special committee was appointed, but achieved nothing, so the Executive gave their views in the next half-yearly report. They suggested 'that no permanent settlement of the rate of remuneration be agreed to, excepting at an increase of 20 or 25 per cent. on the weekly scale, whether piece or 'stab'. Nothing was done, however, to assimilate the varying branch wage rates.

The year 1864 witnessed the beginning of a tremendous 'advance movement' for increased wages and reduced hours in both news and jobbing offices which lasted continuously for about ten years. Trade was prosperous, unemployment figures fell, and the situation favoured union demands, necessitated by the rising cost of living. The movement affected every branch at one time or another and in most there were two or three successive agitations, which gradually whittled down hours and pegged up wage rates. The period was one of tremendous activity on the part of chapels, branches, and Executive, a maelstrom of memorials, deputations, meetings, ballotings, conferences, and strikes. The Executive found great difficulty in imposing restraint on branch action and in co-ordinating so many different movements, but, on the whole, strikes were few: branch demands were conceded or compromises arrived at.

A number of branch memorials have been preserved. All proceed along the same lines, due to the directing influence of the Executive. It was pointed out that for nearly half a century the wages and hours of journeymen printers had remained unchanged. Comparisons were made with other trades, less skilled and requiring less intelligence than the 'art' of printing, in which increased wages or reduced hours had been granted, or with printers in other towns where concessions had been made. The demand for increased wages was further justified on the ground that the cost of living—prices of food, clothing, rents, rates, &c. —had greatly risen, with resultant hardships. Journeymen, it was also urged, had a right to some share in the benefits arising from the abolition of the 'Taxes on Knowledge', which had considerably increased employers' profits. Moreover, it was pointed out that 'a liberal remuneration of labour tends to increase the industry of intelligent workmen' and to attract a better class of youths to the trade, while low wages produce socially demoralized and incompetent workmen.

Reduced hours were claimed on the grounds of the sedentary nature and mental strain of compositors' employment, the unhealthy conditions, bad ventilation and gas light, particularly in the case of night-work. Stress was repeatedly laid on the recent medical report by Dr. E. Smith, which showed that the high death-rate among printers from lung diseases was due to long hours and bad working conditions.[1] Journeymen printers, it was urged, needed more leisure time for exercise and recreation. Employers would also benefit from the improved health and energies of their workmen. Another strong reason for reduced hours was that they would help to solve the out-of-work problem, by calling additional hands into employment. A more selfish, but powerful, motive was the extra pay which would result from increased overtime.

Employers met these arguments by complaints of competition from other towns, country printers, and 'unfair' houses employing 'boy labour' and paying low wages. They alleged falling profits and pointed out that they too were suffering from increased costs. They objected to paying higher rates to incompetent workmen. Many were opposed to union 'interference' and 'dictation'. On the other hand, however, some employers willingly conceded the men's requests.

The results of the 'advance movement' varied considerably. Some small country towns only got one or two shillings per week extra, while a few large towns got as much as eight: the average increase was three or four shillings. 'Stab wages now ranged from 24s. to 35s. per week for jobbing and weekly news and from 38s. to 44s. for morning news. Wage rates on evening newspapers, which had by now been established in many towns, were usually one or two shillings higher than those for weekly news and jobbing. Many newspapers, especially dailies, had gone over to piece-work and the men were generally earning considerably more than the 'stab rates. A farthing or halfpenny per thousand ens had been added to the piece prices in most towns during the 'advance movement'. They, too, like the 'stab rates, varied between small and large towns, prices per 1,000 ens (minion) ranging from 5¾d. to 8¼d. on weekly, from 6½d. to 8½d. on evening, and from 7d. to 9d. on morning newspapers. It is probable, however, that wage increases secured during the period 1849–74 hardly kept pace with the generally rising cost of living and that in real terms T.A. members were worse off, except those who had gone into daily newspaper offices.

Hours in jobbing and weekly news offices had generally been reduced to 54 per week—a 9-hour day, or 10-hour day and Saturday half-holiday —but they too varied, from 56 or 57 in some of the smaller towns to 50 in Liverpool. Evening news hours were usually the same as for jobbing and weekly news, an hour or two less in a few towns, but hours on

[1] Privy Council, Sixth Report of Medical Officer, 1863. Appendix by Dr. E. Smith.

morning newspapers, though the same as for jobbing in some cases, were usually from 51 to 53.

The years after 1874 were years of depression, in which the T.A. had to fight hard to preserve its previous gains. In many offices employers forced wage reductions or brought in non-society hands and additional apprentices. Numerous small strikes occurred, but, in spite of retrogression here and there, most branches succeeded in maintaining the rates won in 1864–74. As a result, 'real' wages improved considerably, for the period 1873–96, the period of the 'Great Depression', was marked by steadily falling prices. On the other hand, of course, unemployment was widespread, but was only really serious in the printing industry during the years 1879–81.

Towards the end of the eighties trade began to improve, unemployment figures fell, and another 'advance movement' began. In the years after 1888 the memorials, deputations, and negotiations of 1864–74 were repeated, but strikes were fewer owing to the frequent settlement of claims by joint conferences. The most noticeable new feature was the proposal for a 'Legal Eight Hours' Day', to be obtained by Act of Parliament, but though resolutions were passed in favour of action by the T.U.C., nothing came of them.

Meanwhile T.A. branches proceeded in the usual fashion with claims for reduced hours and increased wages. This movement, mainly affecting case hands, particularly in jobbing and weekly news offices, lasted from 1889 throughout the nineties, with a slight slackening in the depressed years 1894–5, into the early years of the twentieth century. A 48-hour week was rarely achieved in jobbing and weekly news offices, for the employers put up stiff opposition and a compromise of 50, 51, or, more often, 52 hours usually had to be accepted, though a number of strikes occurred. In many offices, however, enlightened employers voluntarily granted the 48 hours. Some of the smaller towns, on the other hand, were still working 53, 54, and 55 hours in 1905. On morning newspapers the hours of case hands now varied from 48 to 50. Evening news hours were generally still the same as for jobbing and weekly news, though an hour or two less in some towns and 48 in Manchester.

Most branches added another few shillings to their case 'stab rates. The average increase was again about three or four shillings for jobbing hands, but less in daily newspaper offices, from which hand compositors were being displaced by composing machines. There was also little change in case piece prices. Piece-work had never been common in jobbing and weekly news offices and there was now a reversion to the 'stab system on daily newspapers, as a result of the introduction of Lino types.

Ireland, which had only been brought into the Association in 1877, was still in a parlous condition, most of the branches (apart from Belfast) having wages as low as 21s. to 27s. and hours as long as 54 to 58 on jobbing and weekly news.

The 'advance movement' slackened off in the years 1903–5, due to trade depression, but revived thereafter until the next slump in 1908–10, after which it lasted continuously up to the outbreak of war in 1914 and beyond. The Edwardian era was, in fact, anything but calm and contented, as it is sometimes pictured in retrospect, but a period of working-class discontent, constant trade-union activity, and continual demands for increased wages and reduced hours. Nevertheless, Executive control and collective bargaining nearly always prevented strikes, though the threat of striking had often to be used. During this period there was a growing tendency towards district instead of branch wages movements,[1] while local P. & K.T. Federations more frequently co-operated, and in 1909–11 a great 48-hour movement was conducted by the National Federation.[2] Most wages movements, however, were still carried on by branches, under Executive supervision.

As a result of these various movements, jobbing hours were further reduced to 51 per week, less in some branches and offices, while amounts ranging from one to five shillings were added to weekly wages by 1914. The period 1896–1914, however, was one of generally rising prices, and wages, it would seem, hardly kept pace with the cost of living.

The 1913 Delegate Meeting still pressed for a 48-hour week, but, after the failure of the Federation movement, reverted to the idea of obtaining it by Act of Parliament, a policy which the T.U.C. was again advocating.

Let us now review the whole period, 1849–1914, and sum up the Association's achievements. Basic (jobbing) wage rates had on the average been raised by about 30 per cent. and now ranged from 28s. to 38s. 6d. There is no complete and scientifically accurate cost-of-living index for this period, but the available figures[3] do give some indication of the rise and fall in T.A. 'real' wages. During trade 'boom' periods money wages usually chased rising prices, lagging slightly behind. In

---

[1] See below, pp. 164–5.   [2] See below, pp. 257–8.
[3] Wood, G. H., 'Real Wages and the Standard of Comfort since 1850', *Statistical Journal*, 1909, pp. 91–103. Bowley, A. L., *Wages in the United Kingdom* (1900). Layton, W., and Crowther, G., *An Introduction to the Study of Prices* (1935).

trade depressions, however, when prices were falling, the Association succeeded, on the whole, in maintaining wage rates, so that those members who remained in work were better off; but unemployment, of course, was widespread. The net result of these ups and downs was a rise in 'real' wages of 25 to 30 per cent. by 1914. This, however, was considerably less than the average rise for all trades: jobbing printers had, in fact, lost ground relative to other workers; or perhaps it would be better to say that there had been a general levelling-up of wages.

T.A. members in daily newspaper offices, however, which had not existed in the provinces in 1849, were considerably better off. Morning news case hands were getting 20 to 25 per cent., evening news 5 to 10 per cent., more than jobbing 'stab rates. Composing-machine operators, as we shall see, were even more favourably situated, with a minimum of 12½ per cent. above the corresponding case rates. The pressure of work, however, was much greater in daily newspaper than in jobbing offices, and morning news hands, of course, were working at night.

The period had also witnessed a considerable reduction in working hours. Jobbing hours had been reduced from 59 to 51 or less, while most daily newspaper workers had got a working week of 48 to 50 hours, Linotype operators 44 to 48. The results, of course, were an increased amount of leisure time for amusement and recreation, improvement in health, decreased mortality and longer life.[1] Saturday afternoon became a holiday, except for evening newspaper workers, many of whom, however, were given some other afternoon off during the week. Many employers, moreover, had voluntarily granted an annual week's holiday with pay, while in 1891 the Manchester branch secured such a holiday for all compositors on morning and evening newspapers as part of a settlement on wages and hours. A similar demand grew up in other branches and the 1913 Delegate Meeting passed a resolution 'that all members shall be entitled to one whole week holiday per year, without loss of wages, provided such members have been in the employ of any one firm for a period of not less than twelve months'. The outbreak of war in 1914, however, caused negotiations with the employers on the holiday and other questions to be postponed.

Association Minimum Wages and Maximum Hours

There was a strong tendency during the second half of the nineteenth century, as a result of increasing centralization, towards Association standards and rules in place of varying local wage rates, hours, and

[1] See below, p. 296.

working regulations. The T.A. tried to secure increased uniformity or at least Association minima.

The delegates at Sheffield in 1849 laid down 'that fifty-nine hours per week be the maximum of working time for established wages'. This rule was expanded in 1867 to include the hours of piece hands. At the same time, moreover, an Association minimum wage was established: no society was to be eligible for admission that did not maintain a 'stab, or equivalent piece scale, of at least 24s. per week. The maximum hours were reduced to 56 in 1872, 54 in 1891, and 52 in 1908, while the minimum wage was raised to 26s. per week in 1891 and 30s. in 1908.

These rules were meant to apply chiefly to new branches and small towns and lagged well behind the hours and wages secured in the large cities. Even so, however, they could not be enforced. The Association was compelled to waive its rules in order to expand, to admit dozens of branches working longer hours and for less wages than the standard— in Ireland, for example, and the south of England. This was openly confessed in 1874, when the Executive were given a discretionary power to 'admit societies as Branches where it is not possible at that time to secure complete conformity to these rules'. The Association was, in fact, forced to relax its rigid standards and adopt a policy of first getting towns in and *then* attempting to improve their conditions. The Executive admitted in 1892 that the minimum wage was 'not an imperative rule, but a standard to be aimed at', and the General Secretary stated at the 1913 Delegate Meeting that 'it was a difficult matter to carry out'.

The difficulty was that the Association rules had never been recognized by employers' national organizations. The question of the Association standard wages and hours was excluded from the negotiations between the T.A. and the F.M.P. and L.U.A. in 1909–11, because of the concurrent 48-hours movement by the P. & K.T. Federation.[1] This movement resulted in a Federation agreement for a maximum working week of 51 hours. There was also an obvious likelihood of a T.A. national agreement on wages, like the Linotype and Monotype agreements of 1898–1905 and the 'Agreement on Rules' of 1911. Such an agreement was not, however, negotiated until after the 1914–18 war.

District Movements

The Association rules did little to produce increased uniformity of wages and hours. More progress was made in this direction by the efforts of large towns to raise wages and reduce hours in their surrounding

[1] See above, p 143.

districts. Such cities as Manchester, Liverpool, Birmingham, Sheffield, Newcastle, and Cardiff made repeated efforts to organize neighbouring towns, in order to reduce the competition which threatened their own wage rates and hours or prevented them from securing advances. Thus they gradually became the centres of districts, in which they tried to secure uniformity of working conditions. Their officers were constantly carrying out 'missionary' work and assisting smaller towns in advance movements.

Towards the end of the century the annual district conferences began to adopt the idea of standard wage rates and hours for their respective areas, and vigorous, though piecemeal, efforts were made to carry this policy into effect. A more ambitious movement was made by the newly established Home Counties Group in 1903, when a joint memorial was presented to the employers in this outer-London area and, as a result of negotiations with the F.M.P., a minimum 'stab wage of 31s. per week, minimum piece rate of 6½d. per 1,000 ens, and maximum working week of 54 hours were secured for all T.A. branches in the Group. Other districts followed suit, but it was not until the war years that group movements really got under way, most branches still acting independently.

Regulation of Hours and Overtime

It was no use having established hours and wage rates if employers were allowed to employ men beyond those hours without extra remuneration. Irregular hours and overtime were inevitable in the printing industry, on the publication nights of weekly, bi-weekly, or tri-weekly papers, in periods of seasonal demand, or when rush orders came in. But obviously extra payment should be made for the increased fatigue and night work involved.

The Northern Union had fought to secure an 'established' working *week* of 59 hours and overtime payment of 6d. per hour for all hours worked beyond these, with a 'night shilling' for any work between 10 p.m. and 5 a.m. The P.T.A., however, while adopting 59 hours per week as 'the standard of working time for established wages', left payment for overtime and Sunday work to local regulation. Neither did it attempt to regulate the hours of piece hands.

Most branches simply followed the old overtime rule. Several of the larger branches, however, began to demand 'that each *day* should stand by itself', that the working hours of each day should be 'fixed and defined' and that overtime should be reckoned as hours worked beyond the 'normal day', instead of the established week. The aims were, firstly, to prevent employers exploiting their workmen by over-long and irregular hours at ordinary pay, and, secondly, to reduce the amount of overtime worked, thus protecting the health of workmen, securing increased leisure time for physical recreation and mental improvement, and providing work for unemployed and casual hands. It was also pointed out to employers that excessive overtime impaired the mental and physical energies of their men and resulted in inferior work. An ulterior motive, however, with many men was to get more money through increased overtime payment.

The Sheffield Society appears to have been first in this field, securing an agreement with the employers as early as 1837 for 'an extra 3d. per hour for all hours worked after ten at night'. Other large societies, such as Liverpool, Birmingham, Manchester, and Leeds, got similar agreements in the forties and fifties, usually giving 2d. per hour extra for all hours worked outside the 'normal day', sometimes increased to 3d. after three or four hours' overtime.

It proved extremely difficult, however, to deal with the overtime problem. It was almost impossible to reduce the amount of overtime worked as it suited employers and was gladly accepted by most workmen because of the increased pay. It was also very difficult to establish the principle 'that each day (or night) should stand by itself' and to prevent the 'balancing' of lost time against overtime. Many employers refused to pay overtime rates until the full weekly hours had been worked. Any overtime worked one night would be 'taken out' next day and paid as ordinary time. Time 'lost' by a workman, through lack of work or through arriving late or as a result of sickness, was 'balanced' against any overtime which he might work later that day or week. Employers also objected to paying for overtime necessitated by the negligence, inefficiency, or even deliberate delay of their workmen.

The Sheffield, Liverpool, Manchester, and other large branches succeeded in their demand for a normal day and extra payment for overtime, but small towns were unable to effect any improvement. The Association, however, still left overtime to local regulation. Proposed rules on the subject were rejected by the 1856 and 1861 Delegate Meetings on account of the difficulty and danger of trying to enforce 'arbitrary laws', though the Executive promised to support local efforts at regulation.

A stiffening of attitude is visible after the removal of the Executive to Manchester. The revised rules of 1867 laid down 'that fifty-nine hours per week be the maximum of working time on piece or 'stab, local rules to define when a day's work begins and ends (providing for the day preceding the publication of newspapers) with a proportionate advance for overtime and Sunday work'. Apart from alteration of the maximum number of hours—to 56 in 1872, 54 in 1891, 52 in 1908, and 51 as a result of the 1911 Hours Agreement—this rule remained unchanged throughout this period. Payment for overtime continued, therefore, to be a matter of local regulation, and, like wages and hours, varied considerably from town to town; but under increasing central supervision a certain amount of uniformity was achieved. The Executive insisted rigidly upon a normal day—that 'each day (or night) should stand by itself'—and strongly opposed the 'balancing' of lost time against overtime. It remained, however, 'a common and recognised practice in branches of the T.A. for the staff employed on a weekly newspaper to work late on one night in the week, viz. publication night, at the ordinary rates on piece or 'stab'.

The 'normal day' varied in different towns and offices, but, whatever it was, it had to be 'fixed and defined'. The old 'night-shilling' gradually disappeared and was replaced by a fixed charge of so much extra per hour. It became a more or less general rule to pay 'time and a quarter' for the first three or four hours' overtime and 'time and a half' afterwards. Hands called in after having completed their regular day or night were entitled to 'call money', usually a shilling, in addition to overtime rates. Double time was usually paid on Sundays, Good Friday, and Christmas Day. Saturday afternoon also became a half-holiday (except on evening newspapers), work on which had to be paid for at overtime rates.

These regulations applied mainly to 'stab work. A very lax policy was adopted in regard to the hours and overtime of piece hands. The Association rule on working hours, enacted in 1867, covered both piece and 'stab, but was rarely applied to piece hands, who had often no defined day or week or higher rates for overtime. Moreover, distribution and 'standing time' were often not included in reckoning their working hours. Hence in many towns the prevalence of piece-work reduced the normal day to a nullity. Piece hands frequently worked for as long as 60, 70, or even more hours, though often, it must be admitted, voluntarily, in order to secure more pay.

During the eighties, however, an agitation began to secure 'that the working hours of piece-hands should be adjusted as strictly as those of time-hands' and to enforce payment for 'standing time'.[1] Several branches already had local rules defining piece hours and requiring extra

[1] See below, pp. 175–6, for the question of 'standing time' or 'slating'.

payment per hour for overtime in addition to matter set. In 1891, there-fore, a committee on piece-work appointed by the Delegate Meeting recommended a general rule that 'all hours worked by piece-hands before or after the ordinary time of commencing or leaving off work, or more than the recognized number of hours in any one branch, shall be rated overtime'. This was included in the Association rules in 1893. Together with the rule regarding payment for 'standing time', it went far towards making the regulation of hours on piece-work as strict as on 'stab.

These regulations were not, of course, everywhere enforced. Many employers vigorously opposed them, while members were often lax in their attitude. It is also doubtful whether they served to reduce the amount of overtime and provide work for the unemployed. The 'equali-zation of labour' was, however, persistently aimed at. It was considered that 'as large a number as possible should find regular employment, rather than that some should be totally unemployed while others are working late and early'.

Complaints against 'systematic overtime' multiplied during the nine-ties, when many hand compositors were thrown out of work by com-posing machines, and its abolition was frequently demanded. The Association at first considered that this could only be achieved 'by fixing the price for overtime at a prohibitive figure', so that, instead of working overtime, employers would be 'compelled . . . to put on extra men'. These efforts proved unavailing, however, due mainly to the 'selfishness' of many members, who were only too willing to increase their pay packets by working overtime.

In 1902, therefore, the Association decided to take a stronger line, by passing a rule 'that no member of the T.A. be allowed to work more than twelve hours' overtime in any one week, when casual labour is available'. But this rule, like many other of the T.A.'s restrictive regulations, could not be generally enforced, as is proved by the branch overtime returns secured prior to the Delegate Meeting of 1908. Excessive overtime was unavoidable at certain rush periods or on certain contracts, while members themselves were often glad of it. In certain cases, however, the rule is said to have resulted in the employment of more hands.

The delegates' remedy for non-enforcement of the rule was to make it even more restrictive, by enacting 'that no member . . . be allowed to work more than eight hours' overtime in any one week', whether or not casual labour was available. To this arbitrary and inelastic rule, however, the employers' national organizations strongly objected during negotiations with the T.A. in 1909–11, and the Association representatives were forced to admit the reasonableness of their arguments and allow numerous exceptions to the rule in the 1911 Agreement. This laid down that

the overtime limit shall be sixteen hours in any two consecutive weeks. . . . Such limitation shall not apply in cases of breakdown and emergency. In commercial houses it shall not apply to minutes of evidence, voters' lists, legal, parliamentary, and election work, and urgent railway work, nor in newspaper houses during periods of great pressure of work connected with their publications. When the publication of newspapers regularly enters into Saturday afternoons the overtime worked on Saturday afternoons shall not be reckoned as part of the sixteen hours. 'Emergency work' not enumerated above to be the subject of agreement between the house and the chapel.

These numerous exceptions made limitation practically a farce. The 1913 Delegate Meeting therefore re-enacted the 8 hours per week limit, but negotiations with the employers on this and other questions were suspended when war broke out. The T.A. had at least, however, secured from the employers a condemnation of 'continuous and systematic overtime'.

Wages Regulations

In 1849 the 'stab system was almost universal throughout the provinces. By the end of the century, however, piece-work was widely prevalent, particularly in daily newspaper offices, where rapid composition was essential. Some towns remained mainly 'stab, while others turned over almost entirely to piece, but in most the two systems were intermixed; they even co-existed in the same office. Generally speaking, jobbing and weekly news hands tended to remain on 'stab, while morning and evening papers went over to piece. In other words, where rapid and more or less straightforward composition was required the piece system was introduced, while for less urgent, more complicated, or artistic work 'stab hands were employed. But there was no uniformity: in some towns daily papers were done on 'stab, while in others jobbing hands were on piece.

The pros and cons of the two systems were constantly argued over throughout this period. The piece system, it was pointed out, put men on their merits and justly rewarded superior skill or extra effort, whereas 'stab put all men, idle and industrious, skilled and incompetent, on the same footing. Employers, moreover, were willing to employ less able or older men on piece, since a man only got what he earned, whereas on 'stab they tended to 'weed out' those who were incapable of earning the standard wage, by exercising close supervision, measuring individual output, and imposing a system of task-work. Employers had no incentive to cut down their staff on piece, since they had only to pay for matter composed; but they constantly strove to get their work done by fewer hands on 'stab, so as to reduce their wages bill.

Supporters of the 'stab system, however, argued that the piece system tended to employ fewer hands and create unemployment, since the men worked all hours and at high speed, so as to increase their earnings: piece-work was, in fact, selfish and 'opposed to the true spirit of unionism'. Alternatively, employers might have a large staff of piece hands to meet emergencies and keep most of them 'standing' for hours, waiting for copy. Moreover, the piece system gave rise to constant disputes over the giving out of copy, division of 'fat', property of piece and house hands, lifting of matter, payment for extras, casting up of founts, shortness of letter, robbing of cases, and so forth. No matter how detailed a piece-scale was drawn up, there were endless bickerings and strikes as to its interpretation and infringement.

The weight of attack was heaviest against piece-work. The Midland Conference actually passed resolutions favouring its abolition in 1896 and 1897, as did the Southern Conference in 1899 and the Representative Council in 1901. But the question was still arousing controversy in 1918, when the Delegate Meeting resolved that 'with a view to the abolition of piecework, no further extension of the system be allowed by the T.A.'. The introduction of composing machines, as we shall see, caused a general reversion to 'stab.

'Stab Regulations

Regulations for 'stab work were few and simple. Each branch had its 'established' minimum wage rates and maximum hours for the various sections—jobbing, weekly news, evening and morning papers. No office not conforming to these standards was to be recognized as 'fair' and no one receiving less than the minimum rate was to be admitted a member.

The Association defended a fixed minimum wage rate on several grounds.[1] It was considered that a man who had devoted seven years to learning a trade ought to get a reasonable wage, 'some recognized

---

[1] See, for example, the answers supplied by the P.T.A. to the questionnaire from the Royal Commission on Trade Unions (1868), printed in the Appendix to the Eleventh Report, and also *Trades Unions Defended* (c. 1868) by W. H. Wood, Secretary of the Manchester Typographical Society.

equivalent' for the time, money, and attention spent on his training. This however, could not be secured by free bargaining between employer and employed, since the latter was, as an individual, at an economic disadvantage. The Association therefore fixed a minimum 'upon the basis of an average workman's productive capabilities'. Moreover, 'that minimum is supposed to represent the lowest figure at which an intelligent operative of average ability can maintain himself and his family, and fulfil the duties of citizenship'. A fairly high minimum also attracted a better class of entrants to the trade and produced more intelligent and skilled workmen. An employer could always dismiss an inferior workman incapable of earning the minimum rate, or, to put it another way, 'the Society minimum was a very low one, and men not able to earn that had better apply themselves to some other occupation'. Finally, a minimum wage did not drag all men down to one level, for there was nothing to prevent an employer paying more to a superior workman.

The Association was not very successful, however, in maintaining its rigid standards. Strikes frequently failed to prevent wage reductions and 'unfair' houses were numerous. Employers objected to paying the standard rate to inefficient or aged workmen, considering that a man should get 'as much as he was worth'. Many employed 'improvers' at less than the full rate of wages. The Association's attitude—that of a skilled and exclusive craft—resulted in 'weeding out' and caused less efficient workmen either to remain unemployed or casuals, on tramp or out-of-work relief, or to enter 'unfair' offices at less than the recognized wages.

In many instances, therefore, the Association had to relax its rules or close its eyes to irregularities. It had to do so, as we have seen, in 'organizing' non-union areas and occasionally, with great reluctance, in order to secure the 'opening' of 'unfair' houses—usually, however, on condition that the men must make efforts to get the proper wages or leave the office after a certain time.

The Association minimum wage rates tended to become maximum. Many employers undoubtedly paid higher wages, particularly to superior workmen, but most would pay no more than the standard rate. Moreover, the payment of higher wages to individuals often caused jealousy and dissatisfaction among the men. The Association also opposed anything in the shape of bonus payments, since employers often engaged 'whips' at extra wages to 'make the running' for the other 'stab hands and thus increase output—a practice condemned by the Association as tending to produce 'racing' or competition between the men.

Many branches and offices adopted a deliberate 'limit system' on 'stab work, a policy of 'ca' canny' or 'go slow', restricting the amount of composition done by each man. This was intended to prevent 'slogging', to render individual comparisons abortive, and stop 'weeding out', while it would also secure employment for more hands, or more overtime. There is not, however, the slightest evidence of *official* support for such a system. The Executive's policy was always 'a fair day's work for a fair day's wage'. But they would never define what they considered 'a fair day's work' for 'stab wages and strongly objected to measurement of the matter set by individuals, on the ground that it would lead to task-work. They opposed, for example, the marking of copy with numbers or initials, the use of numbered clamps between each 'take', the 'slugging' of matter, and the use of time-sheets. They refused to recognize any number of lines per hour, day, or week as a 'fair' output, maintaining 'that no guarantee must be given as to output, nor must there be any restriction'.

Disputes were frequent on this question, employers maintaining, not without reason, that they had a right to measure individual output and to dismiss those who were not earning their wages. They also required statistics for costing purposes. The Association was forced, therefore, to relax its policy somewhat. It could not object to dockets filled in by overseers and was also forced to tolerate the system of individual time-sheets, provided that they were not used to impose task-work.

Piece-work Regulations

Piece-work regulations were numerous and complex. The piece rules of the Manchester Society, for example, in 1893, filled a booklet of thirty-one pages. They were divided into two sections, news and jobbing. Jobbing, in most branches, included book-work as well as posters, handbills, circulars, cards, tickets, and so on. Book-work, in other words, had not yet become an important and specialized branch of the provincial trade. Most of the book-work of the country was done in London and Edinburgh. Few T.A. branches, therefore, had special book-work scales. Newcastle had drawn up such a scale in 1880, modelled on that of Edinburgh, and Oxford had a scale based on the London one, as had several other extra-metropolitan societies. But, generally speaking, 'in the Midlands and the North, jobbing and book-work were considered to be one thing',[1] and such towns as had piece rules for book-work included them under the head of 'jobbing' regulations.

[1] 1903 D.M. Report.

Jobbing hands in the great majority of towns were on 'stab, but several of the larger branches had piece regulations. Jobs on piece were either paid for according to size or cast up at so much per 1,000 ens: if set in very large type, or displayed, they were usually charged according to size; if in smaller type, and not displayed, they were cast up. Extras were charged for script type, rules or borders, and other variations.

Book-work regulations were more complicated. First of all, there were the basic prices per 1,000 ens of the various type founts (brevier, minion, nonpareil, &c.) in the English language, common matter. Dictionaries, directories, catalogues, magazines, grammars, school books, technical works, music books, &c., were all paid varying higher rates. In addition there were multifarious extras for headlines, titles, dedications, footnotes, side-notes, column and tabular matter, contents and index matter, two- and three-line letters, rules and borders, &c., and various regulations and charges in regard to wood-cuts, stereo blocks, wrappers, &c. Works in foreign languages, of course, were charged higher rates.

It was not until the beginning of the twentieth century that the T.A. established a special book-work scale. Herbert Skinner stated in his annual reports as Southern Organizer in 1900 and 1901 that, owing to the growing tendency of London book-houses to establish branches in the extra-metropolitan area, 'the book branch of the trade is increasing very considerably in the provinces'. He therefore proposed that the Association should 'lay down a general set of regulations governing the working conditions of our members who are book-hands', as a basis for local book-work rules. 'At present', he stated, 'there is no uniformity whatever in that section of the trade, every establishment working according to a scheme greatly differing from that in operation in most other houses.'

The matter was pressed by the extra-metropolitan branches upon the Delegate Meeting in 1903, which instructed the E.C. to 'formulate a scale of prices for book-work'. The Guildford branch took the lead in drawing up a proposed scale, based on that of London, which the Executive approved, after a few amendments, and issued to the branches concerned in 1904 'as the basis for Book-work'.

Piece-work was much more common on daily newspapers in the provinces than in jobbing offices. It took the Association many years of hard fighting to establish anything like a uniform set of working regulations. There were endless disputes over piece prices, varying for weekly, evening, and morning news. Another frequent source of trouble was the unfair 'bastard' or 'thin' founts which some employers introduced, the Association having to devise new methods of 'casting up' or measurement to meet the various subterfuges practised by such employers.

A fair price was by no means the compositor's only concern. He also claimed that copy should be fairly distributed and that all should get a fair share of the 'fat' or 'advantageous' matter (leaded matter, standing headings, advertisements, table work, and small type, as contrasted with the 'lean'—solid matter, large type, short 'takes', and bad manuscript). Copy, it was demanded, must be either 'boxed' or 'clamped' and compositors should get 'takes' in turn from the box or clamp; there should be no selection by the overseer or giving out by hand.

This regulation, intended partly to prevent favouritism and jealousy, also aimed at preventing house or 'stab hands and apprentices getting an undue share of the 'fat' under the 'piece-'stab system', i.e. in 'mixed establishments', where both piece and 'stab compositors were employed.[1] In such offices the 'stab hands (on the fixed minimum wage) and apprentices often lifted copy some time before the piece hands, or while the latter were 'standing', and were also given most of the 'fat', while the piece hands were left with the 'lean'. On morning newspapers, a day 'stab staff was often employed on 'fat' matter, such as advertisements, and a night piece staff on solid composition. This was profitable to the employer, but grossly unfair to the piece hands.

A similar grievance was the transfer of piece hands to 'stab, and vice versa, without notice, according to the nature of the work. To prevent this, the Association re-enacted the old Northern Union rule, requiring a fortnight's notice of such a change, except for corrections or in an emergency. Piece hands called temporarily 'off their lines' were to be paid more than the ordinary time rate, in some towns as much as double time.

The evils of 'mixed establishments' were harder to remedy. The E.C. declared in 1854 that it was 'highly objectionable to introduce a system of mixed piece and 'stab work on newspapers, except so far as is necessary for providing for alterations in standing matter, corrections, etc.'. They made many similar protests in the following years, remonstrating against 'the unfair system of putting fat copy exclusively into the hands of 'stab men' and demanding 'a fair division of copy'. The question was discussed by the Delegate Meeting in 1861. Some delegates demanded 'that every paper in the provinces should be either altogether on piece

[1] Note that the term 'mixed' was also applied to (i) combined news and jobbing offices and (ii) offices in which both unionists and non-unionists were employed.

or altogether on 'stab', others 'that in mixed establishments . . . the piece hands take copy in the same manner as the 'stab, so that fat and lean shall be equally divided'. But the general opinion was that such rules could not be enforced and a mild resolution was eventually passed 'that, it seeming to be impossible to obviate the practice of mixed establishments, it be incumbent upon piece hands to claim their fair share of the "fat"'. The matter was, in fact, left to branch or chapel regulation.

The Executive began, however, to take more resolute action after the removal to Manchester. In 1872, for example, they resolved 'that a day staff in an office where a daily paper is produced on the piece system cannot be recognized', and 'that . . . 'stab hands should be kept only for making up, classifying advertisements, correcting house proofs, and work of that nature, and not for ordinary composition with the piece hands'. They began to demand, in fact, that as regards composition an office must be 'all piece or all 'stab'. Where this could not be secured, they insisted that, at least, 'stab hands and apprentices must lift copy at the same time as the piece hands and that copy must be 'boxed' or 'clamped' to prevent unfair distribution.

The Association's concession that 'stab hands might be employed on certain 'house' matter gave rise to frequent disputes as to just what matter belonged to the 'house' or 'establishment' and what to the piece hands or companionship. The 'house' usually claimed 'standing matter', such as advertisements, share lists, and other commercial tables, which only required slight alteration from day to day. All this, of course, was the fattest work and hence there were constant disputes as to what constituted 'standing matter'. Usually it depended on the proportion of new matter set: if, for example, more than three-fourths of the matter was new, then it should belong to the companionship. A similar rule usually governed matter 'lifted' from, say, an evening to a morning paper. The piece hands also claimed all standing heads, all blocks (if justified by the compositor), rules, and leads, other than those used in making-up. Articles set up solid by a piece hand and afterwards leaded by the 'house' were to be charged as leaded matter by the compositor.

Perhaps the greatest grievance of piece hands was 'slating', 'standing', or 'waiting for copy' without payment.[1] This might arise from the employment of 'stab hands and apprentices on 'fat' matter, from overstaffing, or from temporary lack of copy. As a result of 'slating' and

---

[1] The word 'slating' was derived from the practice of compositors writing their names on a slate when out of copy. This helped to ensure fair distribution, since 'takes' were in order of names on the slate.

unregulated hours on piece-work, men often had to put in 60, 70, or even 80 hours a week in order to earn a reasonable wage. To remedy this evil, the Association began to request payment for 'standing time'.

The matter was raised at the 1861 and 1872 Delegate Meetings, but it was considered impracticable to make an Association rule. In the following years, however, many branches sought, with Executive support, to enforce local regulations.

Closely associated with this demand was that for defined working hours and a guaranteed amount of composition per day (or night) or week. Branches sought to secure a guarantee of 5 or 6 hours' composition each day, from the time when copy was first lifted to when the 'line' was 'cut', compositors to be paid time (at overtime rates) in the event of 'slating' while the 'line' was 'on'. These aims, however, were difficult to secure. The Executive stated in 1892 that they were improvements 'which few branches have got'.

Another evil was that of short 'takes', sometimes of as little as two or three lines. These, involving considerable trouble and loss of time, were irritating and unprofitable to the compositor and most branches therefore passed rules defining the minimum number of lines which should constitute a 'take'. The Manchester rule, for example, in 1893, was that 'copy given out making less than ten lines (exclusive of leads) shall not be considered a take; if less, ten lines shall be charged', except in emergency or within one hour of going to press.

Piece-work 'extras' caused innumerable disputes. The principle was that difficult matter, involving extra trouble and work for the compositor, should be charged extra, over and above the prices for common matter. Manuscript copy, for example, illegibly written or interlined, matter in a foreign language, or English with archaic spelling, dialect, slang, or contractions, all took various extra charges. Italics, 'peculiar' matter consisting of names 'run on', or names and figures, such as prize lists, subscription lists, statistical returns, share markets, sporting results, &c., tabular and column matter, were also charged extra, as was matter with rules round it. Introductory matter was to take the same charge as the body of the article to which it belonged, and displayed advertisements were to be charged in whatever fount the bulk of the advertisements were set. These and other extras varied considerably from branch to branch and gave rise to constant disputes as to whether or not certain matter should take extra, or as to what the amount of extra should be. It was almost impossible to frame a scale covering all the varieties of newspaper composition.

During the eighties there was a growing demand for assimilation of the varying branch and chapel rules in regard to piece-work. The Executive, located in Manchester, mainly a 'stab town, were frequently criticized for lack of sympathy with, even antagonism towards, the piece system and inattention to its evils. But these criticisms were apt to ignore 'the extreme difficulty of establishing a general rule applicable to the complicated systems and customs in vogue, which are almost as numerous as the piece houses acknowledged by the Association'.[1] Moreover, there were peculiarities in composition which no hard and fast rule could regulate, and new ones were constantly cropping up.

Nevertheless, it was feasible to lay down certain general principles in regard to such matters as working hours, slating, property of piece hands, extras, and so on, leaving minor details to local regulation. The Delegate Meeting of 1891, therefore, appointed a special piece-work committee, which formulated a set of general regulations on these matters, which were endorsed by the next Delegate Meeting in 1893 and incorporated in the T.A. rules. In the next few years, however, case hands were rapidly displaced by composing machines in newspaper offices, where such hand compositors as remained were generally put on 'stab; but the principles laid down in these rules were embodied in the regulations for piece-work on composing machines.

[1] *Typographical Circular*, Oct. 1886.

X

APPRENTICES

ALL the old regulations in regard to apprentices were re-enacted at the establishment of the P.T.A. in 1849. There was the same limitation of the number of apprentices, insistence upon a seven years' servitude, and restriction of 'turnovers' as under the Northern Union. But the new Association was no more able to enforce these rigid rules than its predecessor, though it fought more battles over them than anything else.

The provincial printing industry expanded rapidly in the second half of the nineteenth century: the number of printers more than quintupled and many firms became of considerable size. The Association's outlook and rules, on the other hand, remained static, restrictive, and medieval. Its apprentice regulation laid down that 'the maximum number of apprentices in each recognized office shall be three': a small master employing two journeymen was allowed two apprentices, three when he had six men, but this was the maximum, so that a large firm employing over a hundred compositors was limited to that number.

The chief object of limitation was, as the rules put it in 1867, 'to adjust the balance of supply and demand, and maintain a fair remuneration for labour'. Throughout the century there were constant complaints of the 'superabundance of labour' caused by excess of apprentices. Not only were boys displacing journeymen, but an excessive number of workmen were being 'manufactured': hence unemployment, tramping, 'ratting', and reduced wages. This 'cheap labour' policy was considered grossly unjust by skilled printers, who maintained that 'whenever a journeyman has devoted a servitude to any particular trade . . . he naturally anticipates that he will be enabled to derive certain proportionate benefits when his time of service has expired'. The time, money, and attention devoted to it gave him 'a vested interest in that particular trade', a right to employment and a standard wage.[1] Apprentice restriction was thus essentially protective, savouring of the medieval craft gilds, aiming at the restriction of competition and maintenance of a certain standard of life.

[1] Wood, W. H., *Trades Unions Defended* (c. 1868).

The Association also pointed out that cheap labour was as harmful to capital—to the 'fair' and 'honourable' employer—as to labour. It was not profitable, for it merely led to 'trade war' between competing employers, in which reasonable profits were destroyed. It also resulted in 'cheap' and shoddy work and produced incompetent journeymen owing to inadequate training.

Many employers sympathized with the men and admitted the force of their arguments. But the majority refused to be bound by union restrictions. Some small employers were attracted by the premiums which were still customary in many places, particularly 'country towns', but the custom was dying out and competition was a greater incentive. Many employers found that, contrary to trade-union assertions, apprentices were both cheap and profitable, and therefore employed them in large numbers. The chief offenders were still the small masters. The Association, according to Henry Slatter, in his evidence before the Royal Commission on Labour in 1892, 'had very little trouble with the large establishments. Large establishments, as a rule, are not anxious to have apprentices, they do not find them profitable. It is only the small struggling employer who thinks it of advantage to have apprentices.' There is no doubt that a large number of such 'cock-robin' shops existed, in which apprentices were almost exclusively employed and which the Association found almost impossible to control; but many large and reputable firms also had an excessive number of apprentices, as is proved by the *Returns of Journeymen and Apprentices in Recognised Offices* secured in 1904 and 1909.

Slatter admitted that 'apprenticeship is the greatest difficulty we have with the employers'. It was, in fact, the cause of innumerable strikes, the majority of which proved failures. In hundreds of offices the Association maximum was exceeded; in many there were six, eight, a dozen, even twenty or more apprentices. Volumes of statistics from Executive minute-books, half-yearly reports, *Circulars*, and Delegate Meetings, endless complaints of excessive boy labour and a succession of futile strikes, all prove that apprentice restriction was a failure. Even in so-called 'fair' houses there was often a great excess.

The T.A. could not resist the forces of industrial competition and expansion. It might impose restrictive rules in the large towns, but it could not, in spite of 'missionary' and 'organizing' activities, control the myriads of small offices elsewhere. The Association's lop-sided limitation resulted, in fact, as an employer pointed out, in 'a large manufacture of journeymen in non-society offices'. The expanding industry was recruited, not from the large establishments, where apprentices were given a systematic training and trade-union feeling was usually strong, but from the small offices, the 'rat' houses and boy-labour 'nurseries', from the small towns and rural districts, in which neither trade unionism nor proper apprenticeship existed. There were constant complaints in the large towns against the excessive number of apprentices in country districts, who were turned adrift by their unscrupulous employers as soon as they began to ask for journeyman's wages and thence migrated, half-trained and ignorant of society principles, into the large towns. The Association attempted, at first, to impose restrictive penalties on entrants who had served their time in 'unfair' offices, but the influx was too great. 'How many', it might well be asked in 1878, 'of the present members of the T.A. were apprenticed in society houses?'[1]

The Association never gave up trying to enforce the rule, but had often to acquiesce in or ignore its violation. It was even driven, in the interests of 'missionary' effort, to wholesale relaxation. Many local societies could not cope with the boy-labour evil, but were barred from admission to the T.A. by the apprentice rule. Obviously, if the Association was to extend its boundaries and reduce the excessive number of apprentices, it would have to change its policy. The 1853 Delegate Meeting therefore exempted such societies from operation of the rule and made them eligible for admission, 'provided that efforts be made to reduce the number of apprentices to the prescribed scale'.

In the following years the Association accepted societies, particularly in the south of England and in Ireland, where apprentices swarmed, often outnumbering the journeymen. Even in the strongholds of the Association, moreover, it proved impossible to enforce restriction and the rule had to be relaxed. The E.C. were forced to allow separate sets of apprentices for combined news and jobbing offices, though they tried to stipulate that ownership must be distinct, or that the departments should be separate and not in the same building, and that there should be no interchange of journeymen or apprentices—restrictions which they were often unable to enforce. Separate sets of apprentices were also frequently allowed to owners of several newspapers or jobbing establishments in the same town.

Many proprietors also claimed a double set of apprentices for their composing and machine rooms. The latter occupied for many years an anomalous position. During the first half of the nineteenth century,

---

[1] *Typographical Circular*, Dec. 1878. The T.A. regulation was also rendered futile by the fact that in London there was practically no apprentice restriction.

before the great expansion and specialization of the provincial printing industry, apprentices were trained in all departments of the trade and when they became journeymen worked indiscriminately at press or case. Similarly, when printing machines were introduced they became 'twicers', trained to both case and machine. But with the increasing size of firms and the introduction of more complicated machines, specialization developed. The composing and machine rooms tended to become separate departments and machine minding required specialized training. In 1847–8, therefore, we find Messrs. Bradshaw & Blacklock of Manchester signifying 'their intention of binding apprentices to the machine printing', such apprentices to be 'confined exclusively to that department'. The Society was forced to allow this and, as a corollary, to admit 'persons who have served a legal apprenticeship to the machine printing only'. As a result, of course, similar claims were made for machine apprentices in other large offices and could not justly be refused.

The Executive permitted similar concessions in other towns, allowing extra apprentices 'if kept entirely to machine work' or 'exclusively employed in the machine room'. But 'twicing' remained the general practice in small offices throughout this period. Moreover, it was only in Manchester and one or two other large towns that machine rooms were regulated by the Society. In most branches the machinemen were unorganized and unbound boys were employed without limit.

During the eighties, however, the Executive launched a campaign to improve the condition of the machine department and tried to enforce a rule 'that only qualified journeymen or properly bound apprentices should be allowed to take charge of machines'. They also stipulated that where extra boys were allowed 'the apprentices in each branch (machine and composition) must be confined to that to which they were originally bound'.

At the Conference of Machinemen in November 1891 a general rule in regard to machine apprentices was established for the first time, allowing one apprentice to two machinemen and two to four or over. Thus a large firm could now have five apprentices—three at case, two at machine —'but on no account shall an apprentice change from machine to case, or vice-versa'. This last clause prohibited 'twicing', but many apprentices continued to be bound to both departments, particularly in small offices.

In spite of these various relaxations, the rule still remained too restrictive for the large firms, who repeatedly demanded its modification. This was considered by the Association on numerous occasions, but invariably rejected. The apprentice rule became, in fact, the T.A. totem—quite useless, but regarded with a kind of superstitious veneration, as an ancient palladium against all ills—against unemployment, low wages, 'illegal men', and incompetents.

The question of altering it came up at every Delegate Meeting and was a subject of constant controversy in the *Circular*. The General Secretary, many of the E.C., and other leading members realized its futility, in spite of innumerable strikes, and recognized its arbitrary and inelastic nature, that it was out of date with the great expansion of the industry and increase in the size of offices, and that it was resulting in a large number of 'unfair' houses and multiplication of apprentices in unorganized areas, particularly in small towns and offices. The E.C. were constantly forced to exercise their discretionary power in suspending the rule, while many branches allowed local relaxations. In strong society towns in periods of good trade the Association could often insist on rigid adherence to the rule, but where unionism was weak, and especially in trade depressions, it was forced to compromise and surrender. Even in the strongest union towns, the rule was extensively evaded. But the Association still clung to the rule and proposals for its amendment— for a sliding scale of apprentices according to the number of journey-men—were repeatedly rejected.

The main argument against relaxing the rule was that there was already a large amount of 'surplus labour' and that relaxation would still further 'flood the trade', make more incompetent workmen, increase unemployment, and reduce wages. It was also considered that, as the Association could not restrict the number of apprentices in 'unfair' offices and unorganized areas, it must at least limit them in 'fair' offices and society towns—though this was obviously unjust to 'fair' employers, since it meant that, while they were restricted to three apprentices, their non-society competitors could employ cheap labour *ad lib*.

Individual employers and local master printers' associations fre-quently protested against the unfair and absurd restriction of the T.A. rule, and in 1902 the question was taken up by the newly established Federation of Master Printers. The Federation considered it 'an inde-fensible position to argue . . . that a house employing only six journey-men may have three apprentices, yet one employing sixty may have only the same number'. They therefore asked for general recognition of the London rule, allowing one apprentice for every three journey-men.

The T.A. Executive, after long delay and evasion, stated that they 'could not depart from the present Association rule'. They were empowered, however, by the 1903 Representative Council meeting to confer with the employers' Federation and a joint conference was eventually held in October 1904. The employers considered the existing rule 'unjust and indefensible . . . arbitrary and irrational'. 'The rule was very old, and since its establishment great alterations had taken place in the printing trade. We had to-day offices with 60 to 100 compositors employed, and in face of this fact . . . there ought to be a revision.' They considered that the rule failed to provide a sufficient number of young journeymen to meet the demands of the expanding industry. As a result, it was extensively evaded and the industry was recruited from small 'unfair' offices and country towns, where apprentices were badly trained. The T.A. representatives, however, considered that any relaxation of the present rule would add to the number of unemployed.

No agreement was reached at this conference or at another in September 1905. The Association still clung conservatively to the rule first framed in 1834, a rule more suited to the hand-press and craft gild than to the needs of the modern printing industry.

The F.M.P. continued to press for revision throughout the years following, but the T.A. Executive adopted a policy of obstruction and delay. The Federation eventually became exasperated and forwarded a strong protest against these tactics, denouncing the present 'absurd and inequitable' apprentice scale and demanding that the T.A. Delegate Meeting of 1908 should empower the Executive to negotiate a settlement. To this the Delegate Meeting agreed, but the E.C. were only to concede a 'limited extension of the number of apprentices' in larger firms, while restriction was to be tightened in small offices so as not to increase the aggregate number of apprentices.

Three conferences with F.M.P. representatives were held in 1909, but each one proved abortive. T.A. fears of increased unemployment and lowered wages were the main obstacles to agreement.

The apprentice question now became inextricably entangled in the complicated negotiations between the T.A. and the various employers' organizations on the revised T.A. rules and the P. & K.T.F. movement for a 48-hour week.[1] It became, in fact, the crux of the whole question of national agreement on the revised rules, since the employers resolutely maintained that there could be no settlement without a satisfactory scale of apprentices. Several times negotiations broke down, but eventually,

[1] See above, pp. 141–4.

after numerous conferences and private meetings, after repeated proposals and counter proposals, supported by all the old familiar arguments, an agreed scale was arrived at, as follows:

Composing department			Machine department		
Apprentices		Journeymen	Apprentices		Journeymen
1	to	1	1	to	2
2	,,	3	2	,,	4
3	,,	8	3	,,	8
4	,,	18	4	,,	18
5	,,	40	5	,,	40
6	,,	60	6	,,	60
7	,,	80	7	,,	80
8	,,	100	8	,,	100

Eight apprentices to be the maximum allowed in each department.

This scale, however, was 'tentative only' and 'subject to review at the
instance of either party at the end of two years'. The employers were
greatly dissatisfied with it and when the 'tentative' period was drawing
to a close in April 1913, urged that a conference should be held to consider its amendment. But the T.A. Executive, while not wishing to evade
reconsideration of the scale, desired 'further experience of the action of
the rule in order to obtain clearer evidence on the effect of its working'.
They referred the matter to the 1913 Delegate Meeting.

This meeting considered 'that the number of apprentices allowed in
daily newspaper offices under the new agreement is excessive', as, 'owing
to the growth of machine composition such offices are not now suitable
for the training of boys in the compositor's trade'. Here was an old complaint in new guise: in the days of hand composition it was often declared
that apprentices in daily newspaper offices were made mere 'stamp-
lifters' and not taught the general trade; now they were made mere
machine 'operators'. Journeymen 'printers' deplored such specialization.[1]
It was therefore decided 'that in all newspaper offices where such
machines are employed the following be the scale of apprentices allowed,
viz. one to every three machines, two to eight, three to sixteen, four to
thirty, with a maximum of five'.

This resolution emphasized the conflicting viewpoints of the T.A. and
the employers. The conference proposed by the latter did not, therefore,
take place and a year later the Linotype Users' annual report stated that
'the vexed question of the number of apprentices to be allowed in an

[1] See below, p. 187.

office appears no nearer a settlement'. Soon afterwards negotiations were started on the various alterations in rules made by the T.A. Delegate Meeting, but were cut short by the outbreak of war. The employers were to press the apprentice question again after the war.

The Association was no more successful in maintaining its rule as to legal binding and a seven years' apprenticeship than in enforcing limitation. In the 'rat' houses, small offices, and country towns, where boys multiplied, many employers never bothered about indentures. Literally hundreds of instances were reported of unbound lads working at the trade. From the 'Apprentice Returns' secured in 1895 it appears that of the 2,368 apprentices reported, 893 were unbound. In several branches it was 'not the custom to indenture apprentices'.[1] The Executive were forced to concede 'that the indenturing of apprentices, though very desirable, is not imperative'. They tried to secure that an apprentice, if not actually bound, should serve seven years to the trade. In many instances unbound boys did serve the customary term, but a large number did not. Even indentured apprentices were not always bound for this period: the returns of 1895 show that in a number of branches they were bound for five or six years or 'until 21'. The situation was worst in the neglected machine department, where unbound lads, employed in feeding, flying, washing rollers, and other semi-skilled work, eventually became labourers or assistants and finally, by 'progression' within the trade, actual machine minders.

The T.A. could not, however, rigidly maintain its apprenticeship rule and refuse to admit these 'illegal' men, since it would have been foiled in negotiations or disputes with employers by a growing crowd of non-unionists. It was forced in many districts to admit practically all men actually working at the trade, whether they had been apprenticed or not, to 'open the books' periodically and take them in. Comparatively few of the early machine minders enrolled in the T.A. had served an apprenticeship.

It is evident that the system of indenturing and seven years' servitude was breaking down, but it still remained a fundamental part of T.A. policy to enforce it wherever possible. The Association relaxed its rule, however, at the Delegate Meeting in 1908, when it was decided that boys who remained at a higher elementary or technical school till fifteen or sixteen years of age need only serve an apprenticeship of six or five years respectively—the aim being to maintain or improve the quality of boys entering the trade and thus preserve the status of the printing

[1] The returns also showed a considerable number of 'turnovers'.

'profession'. At the same time the requirement of a seven years' servitude was waived in the case of readers.[1]

The 1918 Delegate Meeting decided that members need only have served 'a recognized apprenticeship'—not necessarily seven years. Readers, Monotype-caster attendants, machine minders, and even compositors, it was pointed out, often did not serve such a period. Nevertheless, some 'recognized apprenticeship' still had to be served.

Letterpress printers always prided themselves that theirs was a highly skilled trade, requiring no small degree of education and manual dexterity. Apprenticeship was meant to ensure that only trained and efficient workmen should enter the trade. The T.A. devoted considerable attention to this aspect. The *Circular* frequently deplored the fact that 'incompetent printers' were being created by neglect and evasion of the apprenticeship rule, that an 'inferior class of boys' were accepted as cheap labour, without regard to their educational qualifications, that they were given no proper supervision or training and were taught only a small portion of the trade or special class of work on which it was profitable to employ them. It pointed out the necessity for 'a closer supervision in the selection of apprentices, and a more searching inquiry into their educational attainments'. It also stressed the need for 'a system of education specially adapted to fit boys for apprenticeship to the printing trade', and even outlined the kind of education required and method of technical training. Some members urged that the Association should 'attempt something in the way of educating our apprentices', by appointing small committees in each branch to supervise their training, by instituting examinations and awarding certificates of proficiency. The interests of employers and employed were, it was pointed out, identical in this matter; but many masters, by taking on apprentices indiscriminately and in such numbers that they could not be properly trained, were producing inefficient workmen.

The Association was no doubt interested in securing good workmanship. But it had other motives. Bad selection and training produced a 'pool' of incompetent workmen, who either became a burden on the out-of-work fund or threatened union wage rates. The Association's interest in these matters was closely linked with its aim of restricting entry into the trade: they wished to impose educational and technical restrictions, under their own control if possible, as in other 'professions'.[2]

[1] See above, p. 101.
[2] Writers in the *Circular* often justified T.A. restrictions by reference to the medical, legal, and other professions.

Hence their early alarm at the teaching of typography in the newly established technical schools. At the Conference of Typographical Societies
in London in 1886 a resolution was passed 'that . . . the imparting of
technical knowledge in Technical or Board Schools should be confined
exclusively to duly-bound apprentices and journeymen printers . . . and
not imparted to all comers'. It was feared that employers would utilize
these schools to flood the trade with 'illegal' men and that the apprenticeship system itself was endangered. The Executive forbade members who
were instructors in such schools 'to teach the trade to any other than
properly-bound apprentices'. The latter, however, were encouraged to
attend the schools in many branches by grants and prizes. Soon we find
them taking the examination of the City and Guilds of London Institute.
At the conference with F.M.P. representatives in 1904 the T.A. delegates urged that boys should be allowed time to attend technical classes
during working hours.

The Association made frequent complaints during the second half of
the nineteenth century that apprentices were not, as in the past, being
taught the whole 'art and mystery' of printing. Many unscrupulous
masters did undoubtedly employ them as cheap labour on one particular
class of work and neglected to teach them a general knowledge of
the trade. But the Association was also fighting against the inevitable
specialization of the printing industry. Henry Slatter deplored the fact
in 1879 'that the division of printing offices (or "works", as it is now the
fashion to call them) into various departments limits the opportunities
of apprentices to acquire that complete knowledge of the trade which is
essential to a good printer'. This complaint was echoed by Herbert
Skinner in 1904, when he regretted that 'the close sub-division of work
and the tendency to keep boys to one section are responsible in many
cases for the production of inefficient journeymen'. News, jobbing, and
book-work were becoming specialized in the provinces, as they had long
been in London. The composing and machine rooms were also developing into distinct departments. And these divisions of the trade were
themselves becoming sub-divided, due to the industry's expansion and
the introduction of varied and complicated machines and processes.
Specialization was therefore inevitable. 'It was . . . no longer possible', an
employer considered, 'for a lad to be apprenticed to every department of
printing. It should be decided at the start what department the boy
would be placed in.' This became the general practice in large firms,
but in small jobbing offices apprentices still gained an all-round experience of the trade and 'twicing' remained common.

All aspects of the apprentice question discussed above—limitation of numbers, seven years' servitude, selection, and technical training—were closely linked. The T.A. constantly asserted that the excessive multiplication of apprentices, particularly in the smaller, less efficient offices, resulted in the production of incompetent workmen, that the breakdown of the old system of apprenticeship, the employment of ill-selected, unindentured boys and bad training, had the same result, and that this was bad for the trade. Many enlightened employers agreed with them. During the successive conferences between T.A. and F.M.P. representatives on the apprentice question in the first decade of the twentieth century the employers were at one with the men in deploring the decay of the apprenticeship system of industrial training, in view of the rapid technical development of the printing trade. Thus there was a promising possibility of the F.M.P. and T.A. getting together to preserve apprenticeship and with it the tradition of the trade for skilled workmen and fine workmanship.

It had been customary in the Northern Union and early typographical societies to admit apprentices during the last year of their time at half subscriptions, which entitled them to the privileges and benefits of membership on completion of their servitude. This policy was continued by the T.A. In 1891 apprentices were allowed to join during the last *two* years of their time and by 1914 the Association had 585 apprentice members. Strike pay was frequently awarded to apprentices who, on becoming journeymen, refused to accept less than the standard rate of wages.

XI

THE T.A. AND THE INDUSTRIAL
REVOLUTION IN LETTERPRESS PRINTING

Composing Machines

IN 1849, when the P.T.A. was established, composition was still entirely manual: by 1914 it was to a great extent mechanized, especially in newspaper offices. This 'industrial revolution' was extremely rapid, taking place mainly in the years after 1890. It presented by far the most serious problem which the T.A. has ever had to face.

It was not until a Hattersley machine was introduced into the office of the *Bradford Times* in 1868 that mechanical composition first affected the Association. The proprietors had brought in four extra boys to work the machine, one composing and three distributing and arranging the type. Opinion was divided in the Executive Council as to the policy to be adopted towards composing machines, 'whether to oppose their introduction; or, taking no heed of the question as one of machinery, solely to insist upon their being worked by journeymen or apprentices'. It was eventually decided to adopt the latter course: the Council, 'whilst unopposed to the introduction of composing machines', protested strongly 'against any but journeymen or legal apprentices operating upon or distributing for them'.

This was a momentous decision. Richard Hackett, the T.A. General Secretary, declared in 1900 that the Association's success in dealing with the introduction of composing machines was 'the result of the determination come to in the earliest stages . . . to secure an effective control over the working of these machines', instead of blindly opposing them.

The proprietors of the *Bradford Times* refused, however, to abide by the apprentice rule, a strike resulted, and the office was 'closed'. The same thing happened in several other offices in the early seventies. In 1876, however, the E.C. moderated their attitude when four Hattersleys were installed in the office of the *Southport Daily News*. As operation of the distributor was simply mechanical work, unfit for skilled journeymen, they agreed, as an experiment, 'to allow the employment of [unbound] boys at the distributing machine, on the condition that they are not taught or engaged in the general business of letterpress printers', i.e. provided that they were strictly confined to distributing type.

As regards wages, the Executive favoured the 'stab system until the capabilities of the Hattersley had been fully ascertained, but the operators preferred piece, as they were already getting much more than 'stab wages—being paid the full case rate of 9*d.* per 1,000![1] The machines were therefore allowed to remain on piece.

Association policy in regard to composing machines was discussed at the Delegate Meeting in 1877. The general opinion was 'that it would be unwise to oppose the introduction of machines', provided that fair working conditions were established. But, although the Executive's policy was approved, there was considerable opposition to the employment of unbound boys on distributing machines.

This question of 'irregular labour' soon afterwards became the subject of fierce controversy, especially when the E.C. allowed *girls* to work distributors. The Manchester Society strongly denounced this recognition of 'cheap boy and girl labour', maintaining that only qualified journeymen or apprentices should be allowed to operate either the composing or distributing machines, at the ordinary case rates, piece or 'stab. They demanded that a vote of the members should be taken on the subject.

To this the E.C. agreed, but in a special circular dated 4 October 1878 they pointed out the dangers of unreasonable restrictions on the working of composing machines, which might eventually supersede hand composition. Their main concern should be to see 'how such machines can be most advantageously worked in the interest of the journeyman printer, without prejudice or injury to that of the employer'. To ask for case piece rates or to prohibit juvenile labour on the machines might well be construed as opposition to their use.

A sharp controversy followed in the *Circular*. Many members were against any concessions, fearing that 'irregular labour' would swamp the trade and that composing machines would cause widespread unemployment among hand compositors. Others, however, were more enlightened, pointing out that it would be suicidal to oppose the machines, which would ultimately benefit the trade by increasing and cheapening output, providing more employment, and reducing hours.

The eventual outcome of the voting, after some E.C. management, was to leave matters in their hands, 'to deal with each case as it may arise', on the understanding that no opposition would be offered to composing machines provided that fair wages and working conditions were secured.

---

[1] This price was very soon reduced, however, first to 6*d.*, then to 5*d.*, but the operators still earned between £3 and £4 per week.

During the early eighties, Hattersleys were introduced into the offices of the *Bradford Observer*, *Liverpool Courier*, and *Sheffield Independent*. In each case girls were allowed on the distributing machines, provided that they were strictly confined to that work. Complaints soon arose from the case hands that the machines were kept going night and day, with the most remunerative type and the fattest copy, while the hand compositors frequently had to 'stand'. All the operators were at first put on the branch 'stab rate, but the proprietors were dissatisfied with the output. In the *Bradford Observer* office, therefore, the night machinist was put on piece at 3½*d.* per 1,000. The proprietor of the *Sheffield Independent* wished to adopt the same price, while the men on the *Liverpool Courier* were paid a bonus on work done. Meanwhile, the prices on the *Southport Daily News* had been reduced from 5*d.* per 1,000 to 4*d.* (night) and 3½*d.* (day). Employers were ascertaining the Hattersley's capabilities more accurately and bargaining on piece prices was becoming keener.

In 1886 the Liverpool branch drew up a set of piece-work regulations for composing machines and submitted it to the Executive. The latter decided to invite representatives from Liverpool, Sheffield, and Bradford to meet them 'with the view of drawing up a special Rule to deal with the question of Composing Machines'. This conference was held on 3 July 1886. It was followed by prolonged negotiations between the Executive, the Liverpool branch, and the proprietors of the *Courier* and *Daily Post*, which eventually resulted in an agreed code of rules. There was nothing novel in it. Composing machines brought no revolutionary change in working regulations. The fundamental principles of type-setting remained unchanged and the old rules and customs were merely adapted to the new mechanical element. This adaptability was, in fact, the secret of the T.A.'s success in dealing with composing machines. The Association was able to adjust itself to a rapidly changing environment and thus not only survived, but became stronger in the process.

The Liverpool rules—200 copies of which were printed by the Executive and distributed to other branches as a model code—were more or less stabilized by the end of 1889. They laid down 'that Type Composing Machines must be exclusively worked by Journeymen and duly recognized Apprentices, such Apprentices to be reckoned in the total number allowed to each office'. No compositor was to undertake piece-work on composing machines until he was able to earn the 'stab wage of the branch, 'which rate shall be guaranteed to him for three months after he is so employed'. If, after this time, a compositor was put on piece, he was to be paid 3*d*. per 1,000 for day and 3½*d*. for night work and was to be guaranteed four hours' composition per day or night, with payment for 'standing time'. Working hours and overtime regulations were to be the same as for case hands and the rules regarding payment for leads, heads, and blocks, and the various 'extras' for 'run-on' matter, tabular work, dialect, bad copy, &c., were also similar to those for hand composition. To protect case piece hands in offices where machines were introduced, the latter were not, it was laid down, to be given unduly long 'takes' and hand compositors were to be paid for 'standing time'.

The Association also applied to composing machines all the old regulations restricting output, with the aim of preventing undue displacement of hand compositors. Opposition was especially strong against the 'bonus system', which, since it encouraged men to 'slog', was denounced as 'task-work'. The Association also refused to allow marking of copy, slugging of matter, or any other means of measuring individual output. Employers, however, having installed expensive machines, were determined to get the most out of them and disputes were therefore frequent.

Another way of raising output was to go on piece-work, but piece prices were also a fruitful source of disagreement, employers regarding the T.A. demands as prohibitively high.

By 1890 composing machines were being rapidly introduced into many provincial towns. Matters were complicated, moreover, by the appearance of Thornes and Linotypes, with different mechanical arrangements, rates of output, and prices from the Hattersley. A number of branches, therefore, called attention to the varied and irregular manner in which composing machines were being worked in different towns and urged a conference to draw up uniform regulations. The E.C. eventually agreed and the conference was held in Manchester on 21 February 1891.

Despite denials at this conference of any intentions to oppose or restrict the working of composing machines, there was obviously a great deal of antipathy against them, motivated chiefly by fears of unemployment. There was also antagonism between hand compositors and operators. The latter were well off, night hands getting from £2. 5*s*. to over £4 per week of 48 to 52 hours, often on the 'bonus system'. This was strenuously denounced by the conference as a system of 'task-work' or 'sweating', as appealing to greed and selfishness and unfairly 'bolstering up' machines against hand compositors and throwing the latter out of work. Many operators, on the other hand, wanted to go on piece-work, in order to earn even higher wages, but employers were unwilling to pay the high prices demanded.

The conference failed in its aim of drawing up uniform regulations for the various types of machines. It merely reiterated that they were to be operated only by journeymen or duly-bound apprentices, and authorized the E.C. to frame rules for their working, with local wage rates based on those for hand composition, piece or 'stab. The 'bonus system' was to be 'strenuously discouraged with a view to stamping it out'.

The E.C. thereupon tried to draw up a general code of rules for composing machines, but nothing came of the attempt. The Delegate Meeting in September 1891 merely reaffirmed, for the most part, the resolutions of the February conference. In regard to working hours on composing machines, however, it was of opinion that, 'considering the nature of the employment', they should 'not exceed forty-eight per week, or an average of eight per day, either on piece or 'stab'.

From now on many branches sought to secure these reduced hours. Machine operating, they maintained, was more exhausting than hand composition. Moreover, 'labour-saving' machinery should give some benefit to the men and not merely increase employers' profits. The most powerful motive, however, was that reduced hours would lessen labour displacement and unemployment.

The next two years were occupied in constant negotiations regarding wages and working conditions on Linotypes, now being rapidly introduced into provincial newspaper offices. These negotiations were carried on in diplomatic and conciliatory fashion and no strike occurred. The machine operators almost invariably secured improvements on case rates and hours. There was continual dispute, however, over piece prices, particularly on Linotypes. Most firms were still dissatisfied with the output on 'stab and, since reasonable piece prices could not be obtained, persisted in the 'bonus system' or required operators to mark their copy or slug their matter, so as to ascertain the work done by each, and engaged 'whips' (often experts provided by the Linotype Company) to 'make the running'. The Association also continued to oppose these practices.

The rapid introduction of Linotypes resulted in an increasingly serious displacement of hand compositors, particularly older men. The Association could do little to prevent this, save by attempting to reduce hours and overtime and by restricting output on the machines. It also tried to protect case hands by demanding that operators should 'slate' with them and not be given preference in the supply of copy, and by securing payment for 'standing time'.

No general code of rules had as yet been drawn up to regulate the working of composing machines. Local agreements were negotiated by the different branches, with Executive assistance, as machines were introduced. The result was complete lack of uniformity. Linotype 'stab rates varied from 35s. to 40s. (day), and from 40s. to 45s. (night). Few Linotypes were as yet on piece; in Leeds, at 3d. per 1,000, operators were making over £3 per week, and Bolton, Hull, and Sheffield accepted the same price early in 1893. Hattersleys were mostly on piece at prices for night work varying from $2\frac{1}{2}d$. per 1,000 in Preston to $3\frac{1}{2}d$. in Liverpool, Manchester, and Sheffield. There was similar variety on the few Thornes in use. Hours varied from 48 to 54 per week.

In January 1893, therefore, the Executive instructed their sub-committee 'to prepare a code which should be generally applicable to the working of composing machines in any branch', and in March decided to convene a meeting of composing-machine operators to assist in framing these general rules, which 'would secure something like uniformity in the working of the same machines throughout the country'.

The conference produced little that was fresh. There was a general desire for an 8-hour day or 48-hour week for machine operators, less in the case of night hands. Marking of copy and the bonus system were again denounced. There was still resentment against machinery, particularly against what was called 'the dual system', the working of machines all-out on piece, with case hands doing corrections on 'stab, 'a most unfair bolstering up of machine as against hand labour'.

Immediately after this conference the Executive formulated a number of 'Rules and Regulations for the General Working of Composing Machines'. It was decided 'that the hours for composing machines be fixed at 48 for night and 50 for day work'. Where the machines were on 'stab, operators were to be paid 'not less than 5s. per week above the price paid for hand composition'. Machine piece prices were also to be based on the 'stab rate for hand composition: the minimum price for piecework on the Hattersley and Linotype machines to be 3d. per 1,000, where the case 'stab was 30s. or less; $3\frac{1}{4}d$., from 30s. to 36s.; $3\frac{1}{2}d$., above 36s. On the Thorne machine, which required two operators, prices were to be $2\frac{1}{4}d$. where the case 'stab was below 36s. and $2\frac{1}{2}d$. where it was above 36s. These prices were for day work. A halfpenny per thousand extra was to be charged for night work. The usual piece-work regulations in regard to 'standing time', 'extras', &c., were also passed.

Disputes multiplied in the following months. Employers were still greatly dissatisfied with output on the machines and there is evidence that several branches were adopting a deliberately restrictive policy, limiting the amount of composition to be done by each operator per day or night.

Many proprietors were eager to go over to piece-work in order to raise output, but considered the piece prices fixed by the Executive as much too high. There were also disputes over 'extras', payment for 'standing time', &c. The E.C. and most branches were, in fact, opposed to piece-work on composing machines, since, by increasing output, it created more unemployment.

The Executive also adopted an obstructionist policy in regard to tuition on composing machines. They rigidly insisted upon three months' training at 'stab wages before the introduction of piece-work, though employers pointed out that many men became quite proficient in a month. They also refused to permit case hands holding regular situations to learn the working of the machines in their leisure time, as being contrary to the 'smooting' rule—even though employers offered guarantees that matter composed by learners would be sent to the melting-pot and not used in the papers—and they forbade unemployed or casual hands to learn the machines without payment.

Several branches began to demand a Delegate Meeting on composing machines, but the E.C. tried first to arrive at an understanding with the makers, who, it was hoped, might then exercise 'a beneficial influence' on the users. Lengthy correspondence and interviews followed with representatives of the Linotype, Thorne, and Hattersley companies, but without any apparent result. The E.C. merely increased the existing confusion by putting forward wage proposals different from their recently formulated 'General Regulations'. They now suggested that 'stab operators should get 10 per cent. above the corresponding case 'stab rate and that machine piece prices should similarly be based on those for hand composition, e.g. Linotype day prices (minion) would range from $2\frac{1}{4}d.$ per 1,000 where the case price was less than $6d.$ per 1,000, to $3\frac{1}{4}d.$ where it was $8d.$ or over, with $\frac{1}{2}d.$ per 1,000 extra for night work.

The companies were willing to concede reduced working hours and increased wage rates, but maintained that the Association's demands were too high, especially its piece prices, and accused it, or at any rate some of its members, of restricting output. Nothing, therefore, came of the negotiations.

A Delegate Meeting was now held in Sheffield, in December 1893, at which a number of 'General Rules for the Working of Composing Machines' were drawn up. All machines were to be worked 'by journeymen members of the T.A. or duly recognized apprentices *in the last two years of their apprenticeship*, such apprentices to be reckoned in the number allowed by rule to each office'. In addition to securing the working of composing machines to T.A. members, the meeting wished to prevent employers bringing up their apprentices on the machines instead of training journeymen compositors. The aims were to prevent 'cheap labour', keep down unemployment, and ensure that apprentices received a proper seven years' training to the trade as a whole and not merely as operators. On the introduction of composing machines, branches were 'to arrange, as far as possible, for the working of the same by the members of the companionship into which they are introduced, to secure for them proper opportunities for tuition . . . and to use all legitimate means to lessen the displacement of members'. The rule regarding a three months' tuition period at the ordinary 'stab rate was re-enacted.

The meeting poured its wrath on 'stab hands who were 'slogging' at piece speed, in receipt of higher wages, bonus payments, or tips from composing-machine companies. A resolution was passed 'that no T.A. member shall accept work on composing machines on terms under which he is called upon to produce a fixed amount of composition, or on a system of payment (except piece-work purely and simply) which offers inducements to racing or undue competition between machine operators'. No machine operator, moreover, working on 'stab was to 'mark his copy, or assist in any method which may be suggested for the purpose of testing the amount of his composition'.

In regard to wages and hours the meeting made impossible claims. Hours, they decided, should be 48 (day), and 42 (night), minimum 'stab wage rates 40s. (day) and 42s. (night), piece prices $2\frac{1}{2}d.$ per 1,000 (day) and $3\frac{1}{2}d.$ (night) on Linotypes, overtime one-half extra.

To protect hand compositors, it was enacted that machines in piece offices should not be supplied with copy while case hands were idle. All copy was to 'be lifted in regular order by machine and case hands, each machine being allowed double the amount of "take" given to case hands'. The 'dual system' was also forbidden.

The next few years were filled with innumerable negotiations of chapels, branches, and Executive with individual employers. It soon became obvious that the terms laid down by the Delegate Meeting were impracticable and that to insist upon them would result in disastrous strikes and complete loss of control over composing machines. The Executive were therefore forced to bargain and compromise to secure the best terms they could. Their efforts were often thwarted by the fact of operators unadvisedly accepting reductions, but on the whole they were remarkably successful. Branch claims were invariably too high and the Executive, after experience in repeated negotiations with employers, had to exercise a moderating influence, to suggest terms which had a practical chance of being achieved, although this policy met with numerous complaints. Not a single strike took place over composing machines during all the complicated disputes and negotiations of these years.

The Executive did their best to protect the interests of case hands. They refused to sanction any lowering of wage rates or piece prices for hand compositors in order to meet machine competition. They also disapproved of 'short time' and tried to insist on payment of full 'stab wages. At the same time they sought to secure 'guaranteed' hours of composition for case hands and to enforce regulations with regard to lifting copy (ensuring hand 'comps' a fair share) and payment for 'standing time'. Any lowering of Association standards, they realized, would merely prolong the transition to mechanical composition and might gradually reduce compositors to the position of the old hand-loom weavers.

Many case hands voluntarily accepted 'short time' or put up with 'slating' in order to avoid discharge, but the inexorable progress of the Linotype gradually drove them out of newspaper offices. They were still employed on difficult matter, on corrections, setting up headlines, inserting two-line letters in advertisements, &c., but became, as it were, mere scavengers to the machines. The Executive, therefore, found it impossible to oppose the 'dual system', since it was obviously preferable to have these few remaining case hands on 'stab, even though the machines were on piece. The system also avoided the awkward problems in regard to division of copy and 'standing' by case hands. The Representative Council of 1894 endorsed the action of the Executive in deciding 'that the abolition of the dual system is impracticable'.

The Executive were also forced to modify their attitude in regard to the tuition of operators. Their policy—that a member learning machine composition must, for a probationary period of three months, be guaranteed 'stab wages, that case hands in regular employment must not learn the machines in their own time, and that unemployed or casual hands must not do so without payment—was obviously obstructive. Many employers objected to it and the Linotype Company took vigorous action to overcome it. They decided to establish 'schools' for the training of operators. In this way they hoped not only to speed the introduction of their machines, but also to reduce what they considered the ridiculously high prices demanded by the T.A. The first of their schools were established in London and Manchester in 1893-4 and soon advertisements appeared in the daily newspapers offering to train hundreds of young men gratis, in from one to six weeks, whether or not they were already in the trade.[1]

Here was a serious threat to the fundamental principles of the T.A. The Linotype Company threatened not only to flood the market with operators at reduced wage rates, but also to introduce 'non-union and non-practical men', who had never served an apprenticeship to the trade. When the Association protested the company replied that they had put up long enough with the union's unreasonable demands and obstructionist policy. They accused the Association of trying 'to check the spread of Linotype machines, because they supplant hand labour', and to keep the trade a 'closed borough' as in the past, 'and so be in a position to dictate to newspaper owners and printers, as well as to manufacturers of the printing plant, the whole terms and conditions upon which their businesses have to be conducted'.

To this the E.C. had no reply. There is no doubt that the Linotype Company's statements, though rather exaggerated, were for the most part true. The E.C. realized this and soon modified their policy. In their report on composing machines to the Representative Council in 1895 they pointed out the danger from the Linotype Company's 'schools' and 'the necessity of reconsidering our position with respect to the tuition of operators'. They suggested, in fact, that the various restrictions on the learning of composing machines should be removed.

This recommendation was accepted by the Representative Council and by the members in a subsequent vote. Members could now learn the machines in their own time and at their own expense. The Linotype Company's 'schools' in London and Manchester were soon 'opened' and operation of the machines also came to be taught in technical schools. The three months' probationary period was abolished and learners could be put straight away on piece. Some employers tried to keep operators on tuition terms (i.e. ordinary branch rates) for longer than three months, but the Executive insisted that machine rates must be paid after that

---

[1] See, for example, the *Manchester Guardian*, 17 Sept. 1894. The Association inserted a warning reply on 25 Sept., which the Linotype Company answered on 26 Sept.

time. Their policy was now, in fact, reversed: the tuition period might be *less* than three months, but must not be *more*. The Executive also experienced difficulty in enforcing the rule that only apprentices in their last two years should be put to learn composing machines and were frequently forced to sanction local relaxations. But by thus bending instead of being broken the T.A. was enabled, on the whole, to keep the working of composing machines in the hands of its own members and to exercise a salutary control over working conditions during this period of industrial revolution in the printing trade.

This is particularly evident in its policy regarding wages and hours. The Executive soon found it impossible to secure the terms demanded by the 1893 Delegate Meeting and adopted a policy of bargaining with individual employers for the best terms possible, without resorting to strikes. They successfully negotiated, or assisted branches and chapels to negotiate, numerous agreements regulating wages and working conditions, 'stab and piece, on composing machines. Linotypes were now being rapidly introduced and it needed great diplomatic skill to control the innumerable disputes which arose and to conduct negotiations simultaneously in many different branches and offices.

Employers strongly objected to what they considered the exorbitant demands of the Association, comparing the earnings of hand compositors with the excessively high claims made for machine operators, for whom, in addition, a considerable reduction in hours was demanded. The E.C. found it impossible in many cases to secure the minimum day 'stab rate of £2 laid down by the Delegate Meeting and therefore adhered as far as possible to the policy which they had suggested of a 10 per cent. advance on the ordinary 'stab wages. Day 'stab rates varied from 33s. to 40s. per week. The minimum night 'stab rate, on the other hand, was generally secured, night rates varying from 45s. to 50s. per week.

The Association was generally able to obtain a working week of 48 hours for day operators, but in most branches it proved impossible to get 42 hours for night operators, who usually had to be satisfied with 44 to 46. Neither could one-half extra be secured for overtime and 'time-and-a-quarter' had to be accepted.

It was over piece prices that there was most dispute. The E.C. were unable to get the maximum even in Manchester, but adhered rigidly to the minimum of $2\frac{1}{4}d$. per 1,000 ens. There was considerable variation in prices and earnings, from $2\frac{1}{2}d$. to $3\frac{1}{4}d$. per 1,000 and from 36s. to 65s. per week on day work, and from $2\frac{1}{2}d$. to $3\frac{3}{4}d$. per 1,000 and from 36s. to 70s. per week on night work. Employers wanted piece-work in order to raise output, but strongly denounced the Association's ridiculously high prices. On this question they began to combine. In February 1894 a deputation from the Linotype Company and several Linotype users, including the *Manchester Courier* and *Bolton Evening News*, met the E.C. 'to discuss the question of piecework on the Linotype machines', urging a reduction in prices. On 18 April 1894 a conference of Linotype users in provincial towns with a population of under 120,000 was held in Manchester and passed a resolution 'that where the scale for hand composition is 6½*d*. per 1,000 ens, the scale for the same sizes on the Linotype should be 2*d*. per 1,000 and *pro rata* for other towns and prices'. The aim, in other words, was to reduce Linotype piece prices in the smaller provincial towns. A deputation met the E.C. in April to discuss this resolution, stressing particularly the excessively high earnings of operators compared with those of hand compositors. The E.C. decided, however, 'that they had no power to go below the minimum piece rate fixed at the Delegate Meeting'.

Owing to the high piece prices demanded by the Association, the great majority, probably about three-quarters, of the Linotype machines in the provinces were worked on 'stab. But there was an obvious danger of conflict should the employers, in their desire for increased production, try to enforce piece-work at reduced prices.

The E.C. explained the situation clearly to the Representative Council in October 1895. The employers' objections were in many respects, they considered, well justified. The wage rates and hours laid down by the 1893 Delegate Meeting were impossible of attainment and, if not modified, would lead to widespread conflict and possible loss of T.A. control over the working of composing machines. The E.C. therefore urged acceptance of their own more reasonable proposals.

The R.C. agreed and so did the members in the ensuing vote. The E.C. were to aim in negotiations with employers at a 48-hour week for day operators with a reduction of at least two hours for night work. Machine 'stab rates were to be 10 per cent. above those for hand composition. Piece prices were to be proportioned to local case piece rates, the E.C. being given a free hand 'to treat with each branch according to the circumstances of the case'.

The complicated series of local negotiations therefore continued and further agreements were arrived at on the basis of the foregoing resolutions. In 1896, however, the 'Linotype Users' Association' was established and its committee at once suggested to the T.A. Executive that a general agreement should be negotiated, to remove local disparities.

Here was a new departure. Hitherto the Executive had bargained with individual employers or with local master printers' associations. Now they were approached by a national organization of employers and with the suggestion of a 'national agreement' instead of innumerable and varying local arrangements. They were at first opposed to this novel idea. Though 'not averse' to conferring with representatives of the Linotype Users' Association, they were 'not at present aware of any necessity for such a meeting'. They considered 'the varying conditions which prevail throughout the country seem to . . . preclude the possibility of fixing a hard and fast scale'. Negotiations at chapel or branch level had so far proved very successful.

The L.U.A., however, considered there was 'ample reason to justify a conference' and that 'in the interests of peace and equity, an uniform ratio of hours and wages for machine operators should be adopted which would be proportionate to the wages and hours prevailing in regard to hand composition before the introduction of the Linotype'. The E.C., therefore, though still dubious, agreed to a conference.

T.A. and L.U.A. representatives met for the first time in the Queen's Hotel, Manchester, on 16 February 1897, but it was not until December 1898, after several further conferences, two R.C. meetings, and a Delegate Meeting, that an agreement was finally reached. This agreement was met by an outburst of criticism and rejected by a special R.C. meeting in May 1899, but the E.C. managed to secure its acceptance by a vote of the membership.

It laid down 'Rules for Working Linotype Machines on 'Stab'—piecework, because of its complex variations, being left to local arrangement. All skilled operators were to be members of the T.A., and, on the introduction of composing machines into any office, preference was, as far as possible, to be given to members of the companionship for training as operators. The tuition clause was unchanged. Apprentices must have served three years before being put on the machines, and were not permanently to occupy machines beyond the proportion of one to each three in the office, or for more than one-third of the time the machines were worked. Linotype wage rates were to be $12\frac{1}{2}$ per cent. above the existing case rates in the various towns. Hours were to be 48 for day and 44 for night work, but operators might be required to work the same hours as case hands, 'to meet office exigencies', at ordinary machine rates.

This national agreement was a great achievement, producing order out of local chaos and putting an end to the constant guerrilla warfare over Linotype machines. Most employers, even those who were not members of the L.U.A., accepted its terms. The L.U.A. committee urged that 'disputes arising out of the agreement which cannot be settled locally, should in all cases be referred to the two executives with great advantage to the cause of peace'. A number of employers, however, including members of the L.U.A., still preferred to make their own local arrangements. In such cases, where employers violated the agreement, the T.A. Executive frequently protested to the L.U.A. committee, requesting that the latter should 'insist upon their members adhering to the Agreement', and redress was usually secured.

It was an undoubted advantage being able to negotiate with a body recognized by most newspaper companies and on the basis of an official signed agreement. Many local disputes were thus prevented. The T.A. itself was not, however, averse from bringing pressure to bear on individual firms: the Executive found it easier to out-argue and coerce individual employers than the representatives of the L.U.A. and were thus able to secure terms in advance of the agreement. In spite of the agreement, both branches and Executive still had a strong penchant towards negotiation at chapel or branch, rather than national level, particularly when demanding wage increases, and often refused to have local disputes submitted for judgement to the national Executives. On the whole, however, they found it advantageous to co-operate with the L.U.A. committee. In all difficult negotiations the secretaries of both Associations would be present, or would correspond with each other, on behalf of their Executives. Thus general understandings were arrived at and disputes which might have involved endless local controversy were simply and speedily settled.

There was considerable disagreement, however, over the interpretation and application of the agreement. In 1901, for example, the T.A. Executive protested to the L.U.A. with regard to certain members of that Association whose offices were non-union or who employed non-society men, contrary to the third clause of the Linotype Agreement. The L.U.A. secretary replied, however, 'that it was well known to the E.C. that at the time of the Agreement his Association was composed, and had always been composed, of offices employing both union and non-union labour'. In spite of T.A. protests, the L.U.A. continued to maintain the right of its members to employ non-unionists. This was obviously a violation of the agreement, but it is unlikely that the L.U.A. committee could have enforced the rule, even if they had tried, for many employers had a strong aversion to dictation on this matter and maintained their right to employ unionists and non-unionists alike. Nevertheless, the tendency of the agreement was to place the working of Linotype machines in the hands of T.A. members.

There was similar difficulty in securing enforcement of the apprentice clauses. Many employers disregarded the rule against boys being put on Linotypes in their first three years and that which limited the number of machines, or time on machines, to be allocated to apprentices.

As regards hours, some employers, particularly in the smaller branches, took advantage of the second clause in the agreement to work their operators for the same hours as case hands, but on the whole operators remained in enjoyment of a shorter working week.

The most serious disputes took place over interpretation of the clause concerning wage rates. The E.C. were able, with the support of the L.U.A., to secure fairly general acceptance of the Linotype rate, $12\frac{1}{2}$ per cent. above the case rate. But they maintained that there was an understanding at the conference of December 1898 'that the Agreement embodied *minimum* working conditions only, and that the existing rates on newspapers would not be disturbed', or, in other words, that members of the L.U.A. would not take advantage of the agreement to reduce wages or increase hours. This, however, was denied by the L.U.A. The agreement therefore produced varying results. In some branches a literal interpretation involved wage reductions and many employers, regarding its terms as *maximum*, not minimum, insisted on their strict enforcement. There is evidence that the L.U.A. instigated employers to reduce wages in this way, so as to secure a uniform standard.

This naturally caused great dissatisfaction among operators, and the E.C. supported branches in resisting any reductions. On the other hand, however, where they could get more than $12\frac{1}{2}$ per cent. they considered themselves 'at perfect liberty to do so', and frequently tried to force individual employers into paying higher rates. The L.U.A. opposed such coercion, insisting 'that the terms of the Agreement must be considered as establishing a Linotype rate in the different branches. . . . The $12\frac{1}{2}$ per cent. must be regarded as the established rate.' Individual firms were perfectly free to pay higher rates—and many did so—but they were not to be forced by the T.A.

There was also serious disagreement over interpretation of the words 'existing case rates', upon which the $12\frac{1}{2}$ per cent. advance for machine operators was based. In some towns different rates were paid for hand composition in the various offices and it was difficult to determine which was the 'existing' rate. Moreover, there was dispute as to whether Linotype rates should be based on the case rates 'existing' at any particular moment or on those 'existing' at the time the agreement was signed: in other words, should Linotype rates advance *pro rata* automatically when case hands secured an advance or were they fixed by the agreement? The L.U.A. upheld the latter view—a stupidly static one in that it failed to envisage the possibility of an advance in Linotype 'stab rates, which, according to their interpretation, were to remain fixed at $12\frac{1}{2}$ per cent. of the case rates existing in December 1898. A joint conference failed, however, to secure a settlement and the L.U.A. refused to submit the matter to arbitration. The result was a reversion to pre-agreement methods, to negotiations between branch, Executive, and individual employers, terminating in local agreements along the old lines. Unless the L.U.A. modified its attitude the national agreement obviously threatened to break down. The T.A., however, had reason on its side and was generally able, during the innumerable 'advance movements' of the following years, to secure local enforcement of its views.

Linotypes were used mostly in newspaper offices, particularly for morning and evening papers. In all except the largest jobbing offices hand composition still prevailed. Where Linotypes were introduced for jobbing they were governed by the same rules as in newspaper offices, but it became necessary to add a 'supplementary agreement' for jobbing offices where machines could not be constantly supplied with copy and operators were therefore often transferred to case. After a joint conference between T.A. and L.U.A. representatives it was agreed in July 1900 that in such cases the operator should receive Linotype rates for the half-day during which the change was made, from machine to case or vice versa.

Dispute soon arose, however, over interpretation of this agreement. The L.U.A. contended that an employer could transfer an operator from machine to case for an indefinite period at case rates when there was no machine copy available, but the T.A. maintained that such transfers could be made only for half days, or that a jobbing operator could be a case hand for only half his time so far as *wages* were concerned. A joint conference failed to produce agreement and the result was a reversion to settlement by local negotiation.

The conference of December 1898 had left the question of Linotype piece-work regulations to local bargaining. The Executive still tried to insist on the minimum price of $2\frac{1}{2}d.$ per 1,000 ens fixed by the 1893 Delegate Meeting, though they were occasionally forced to sanction $2\frac{1}{4}d.$ or even $2d.$ The L.U.A., however, had from its foundation protested strongly against what it termed the prohibitive T.A. Linotype scale and

unceasingly pressed upon the Executive the desirability of its modification. Many employers, dissatisfied with the high piece prices and exasperated by the innumerable piece regulations, changed to 'stab. But
others, equally discontented with output on 'stab, still demanded a revision of the piece scale. The question had merely been postponed in 1898,
pending a settlement of the 'stab rules. In October 1899, therefore, the
L.U.A. committee suggested another joint conference 'for the purpose
of considering the piece scale, with the view of arriving at a mutual
agreement thereon'.

The T.A. Executive recognized that modification of the present 'high
and almost prohibitive scale' was inevitable and agreed to negotiate if
the L.U.A. would forward detailed proposals. It was not, however, until
February 1902 that the L.U.A. committee next approached the T.A.
Executive. They were especially anxious to remove 'the unnecessary
complication with regard to extras' and suggested 'an inclusive rate'.
The T.A. Executive, however, were very dubious about the abolition of
'extras', which, they pointed out, had 'existed as long as piece-work
itself'. They therefore asked for further details.

The L.U.A. immediately forwarded draft proposals for a Linotype
scale. These were intended 'to simplify the scale so as to avoid many
small items which so often tend to irritate without any corresponding
advantage'. It was proposed to establish a 'universal machine piece rate',
with a simplified list of extras, including local increments for the higher
cost of living in large towns.

These proposals, however, were rejected by the T.A. Executive, who
clung conservatively to the old customs of hand composition. They made
no suggestions of their own and even positively refused at first to submit
any. Eventually, however, a special sub-committee drafted alternative
proposals which were approved by the 1903 Delegate Meeting. Conferences between the T.A. and L.U.A. representatives followed at the Midland Hotel, Manchester, on 29 September and 7 October 1903, and
'Rules for Piece-work on Linotype Machines' were agreed on.

The clauses of the 'stab agreement regarding operators' membership
of the T.A., tuition, and apprentices were to apply equally to piece-work.
Linotype piece prices were to be $33\frac{1}{3}$ per cent. of the 'current mean case
piece day rate' of the branch,[1] with a minimum of 2d. per thousand ens,
and 15 per cent. extra for night work. Piece-work hours were to be the

---

[1] This meant the mean or average of the hand piece prices for day work, e.g. if
the case rates were 6d. (brevier), $6\frac{1}{2}d.$ (minion), and 7d. (nonpareil), the mean
case rate would be $6\frac{1}{2}d.$ per 1,000 ens.

same as on 'stab, overtime to be charged 4*d*. extra for the first hour and 5*d*. per hour afterwards. Operators were guaranteed a minimum of 30 hours' composition per week, 'standing time' to be paid for at the machine 'stab rate. A long list of regulations was drawn up with regard to size of 'takes', charging of heads, leads, &c., and the customary 'extras'.

The E.C. had secured, from their own point of view, a very satisfactory agreement. The Linotype piece prices agreed on were, in most branches, little if at all less than those already being paid, for in small towns the old 2½*d*. minimum had never been generally enforced. As regards hours, they had cut out the compromising clause in the 'stab agreement concerning overtime, which, for piece operators, was to be reckoned as all time before or after the 'fixed and defined' day or night. The 'guarantee' of 30 hours' composition was a valuable achievement, in view of the tendency in morning newspaper offices to increase the number of machines and reduce the hours of composition, so as to get their papers out at a rush. The Executive had also secured most of their demands in regard to 'extras'.

Employers were greatly dissatisfied with the agreement which left piece prices practically unchanged and preserved nearly all the old obnoxious conditions and complications, particularly in regard to 'extras'. The result, as stated by the T.A. President in 1907, was that the new Linotype piece scale 'was not in operation in any office in the country', all Linotype users having adopted the 'stab system.

Linotypes, as we have seen, were mainly restricted to newspaper offices and mechanical composition invaded book and jobbing houses later and more slowly. In the last few years of the nineteenth century, however, Monotype machines started coming in. Their first mention in the minutes of the Executive Council does not occur until January 1902, after a letter had been received from the managing director of the Lanston Monotype Corporation. The Corporation considered that, as the number of Monotype installations in the country was rapidly increasing, 'the question as to what should be considered a fair wage as a minimum for work on the keyboard of the Monotype as compared with hand compositors' work, and mechanical work on the Linotype, is one which must be faced for our mutual benefit'. Some T.A. branches were claiming Linotype rates, but there was, the Monotype Corporation pointed out, a

marked difference in the strain which is placed upon the operators of the two machines. In the case of the Linotype the operator has not only to attend to the ordinary composition by manipulation of the keys, but has further to supervise the casting operation, the heating of his metal, the supply thereof, the distribution of his matrices, and, in general, the whole operation of composition and casting, whereas the Monotype operator has an independent keyboard, practically on all fours with a typewriting machine. He is removed not only from the noise and dirt, but also from the heat which is a necessary accompaniment to the casting machine.

The Corporation therefore suggested that Monotype operators' wages and hours should be 'somewhere about half way between hand work (52 hours a week) and Linotype work (48 hours a week)', and asked for the Executive's views.

The Executive decided to defer the matter until they had inspected the Monotype machine. A visit was arranged to the *Manchester Guardian* general printing works at Reddish, 'to get an insight into the working of the machines and to form an opinion as to their utility and productive capacity'. Branches were also asked for information concerning Monotypes, particularly by 'what class of person each Machine—the Perforating Machine and the Casting Machine—is worked, that is, whether by T.A. members or by others'.

These returns showed that, as yet, only a small number of Monotypes had been introduced. Some of them were in 'unrecognized' houses, and at Aylesbury a strike had occurred against the employment of 'cheap female labour' on the perforators; but as a rule qualified compositors—T.A. members in 'fair' houses—operated the keyboard. In practically every office, however, the casters were worked by mechanics or stereotypers. In Belfast, Birmingham, and Bristol, Monotype operators on day work were getting 34s. (52½ hours), 34s. 6d. (52 hours), and 35s. (52½ hours) respectively. At Belfast and Birmingham, in other words, they were being paid the same rates for the same hours as jobbing case hands, and at Bristol a few shillings more. In Liverpool and Manchester, however, they were getting the same pay and working the same hours as Linotype operators: 42s. (48 hours) and 39s. 6d. to 50s. (48 to 50 hours) respectively.

The Executive advised branches that, 'pending a Conference between the E.C. and the Lanston Monotype Corporation', they 'should endeavour to secure for Monotype operators the same conditions as apply to Linotype operators'. This policy was endorsed by the 1902 R.C. meeting, which also instructed the E.C. 'to endeavour to secure the work on the casting machine being done by members of the T.A.'.

Further correspondence between the Executive and the Lanston Monotype Corporation failed, however, to produce agreement. In July

1902, therefore, the Executive issued a circular to all branches asking them to carry out the policy approved by the R.C. meeting. They later instructed 'that full Linotype conditions should be obtained for the operator on the keyboard, and for the work on the caster not less than the case rate of the branch should be paid, and every effort should be made to retain this work in the hands of our members'. Branches now began to formulate local rules, approved and amended by the Executive, for the working of Monotype machines, just as they had previously done for Hattersleys, Thornes, and Linotypes, with all the familiar difficulties in regard to wage rates, hours, and apprentices.

Matters went on in this way until in September 1903 the Federation of Master Printers suggested a conference on the wage rates and working conditions on Monotype machines.[1] To this suggestion the T.A. Executive agreed, but it was not until 25 October 1904 that representatives of the T.A. and F.M.P. met for the first time at the Grand Hotel, Birmingham.

The T.A. representatives demanded the same conditions as on Linotypes, i.e. $12\frac{1}{2}$ per cent. increase on case rates and 48 hours per week. The employers, however, strongly opposed these claims, particularly any reduction of hours. The Monotype, they insisted, must be judged entirely upon its merits. It was not, they asserted, so profitable as the Linotype and working conditions were different. The Monotype could be worked easily, under better conditions than at case, and there was consequently no reason why operators' hours should be reduced. It was also impracticable to have different hours for operators and case hands in the same office. The T.A. was accused of trying to use a Monotype agreement as a lever to reduce case hours. The T.A. representatives alleged 'that fast-running machinery... caused greater mental and physical strain', but this the employers denied, pointing out that 'the machines are being worked in some instances by girls, and there is no evidence of strain, although... worked to the full number of hours'. An attempt by the T.A. to reduce hours might, in fact, 'facilitate the introduction of female labour'. The T.A.'s main motive in demanding a reduction of hours was that it would result in 'fuller employment and less payment of out-of-work benefit'. The employers would not, however, concede more than either (a) $12\frac{1}{2}$ per cent. advance in wages and $52\frac{1}{2}$ hours, or (b) 10 per cent. and 51 hours, and it was agreed that the T.A. representatives should take back these alternative proposals for consideration by the full Council, after which the conference would be resumed.

[1] The F.M.P. consisted of employers in the general printing and book trade, into which, mainly, the Monotype was being introduced.

The Executive decided to accept the first alternative and, with regard to the Monotype casters, instructed their representatives 'to try by every means to get the working of this portion of the machine into the hands of our members', but to avoid a deadlock.

The conference was resumed on 24 January 1905 with great success. Rules for working the Monotype keyboard on both 'stab and piece were agreed on. With regard to the employment of T.A. members on the machines, experience had shown in the case of Linotypes that it was impossible to compel firms to employ only society men and, as many members of the F.M.P. were non-union, it was decided that only 'in offices worked by agreement in conformity with the rules of the T.A.' should all operators be T.A. members. Keyboard operators on 'stab were to receive a minimum of 12½ per cent. above the case rates, those on night work 15 per cent. over the machine day 'stab rate. Weekly hours were to be 'as the case hours of the town, not exceeding 52½ for day work, and 48 hours for night work, the hours for each day or night's work to be fixed and defined'. In regard to overtime, it was laid down that 'all time worked before or after the defined hours shall be paid for at the rate of time and a quarter for the first three hours, and time and a half for any further hours worked each day or night'. The Linotype clauses in regard to tuition, employment of apprentices, and transference of hands from machine to case or vice versa were applied to work on the Monotype keyboard.

Piece prices, as usual, caused considerable difference of opinion. The T.A. representatives sought 33⅓ per cent. of the case rate, as on Linotypes, but could only get 25 per cent., with a minimum of 1½d. per 1,000, operators on night work to receive 15 per cent. extra. Operators were guaranteed a minimum of 35 hours' composition per week, compared with the 30 of Linotype operators, the 'stab machine rate to be charged for all time short of this figure. Hours were to be the same as on 'stab. Overtime was to be paid for at 4d. per hour extra for the first 3 hours and 5d. afterwards. Regulations very similar to those in the Linotype piece rules were adopted in regard to payment for 'lost time', the size of 'takes', the charging of headings, and the usual 'extras'.

No agreement was reached, however, on the Monotype caster. The T.A. representatives asked that their members should be given preference in working this machine in view of the labour displaced by the Monotype. They strongly opposed its being worked by non-printers, by outsiders over whom the T.A. would have no control. Compositors, they maintained, were better qualified than anyone else to work the casters and no one but a printer should handle type. The employers, however, held very different views. T.A. members, they considered, had no exclusive right to work the casters: no compositor's knowledge was required and mechanics, typefounders, or stereotypers were more suitable. Moreover, they could get caster hands from outside the T.A. at lower wages.

The T.A. Executive were greatly dissatisfied on this matter and asked for another meeting. The F.M.P. agreed, but the ensuing conference on 18 April 1905 failed to produce a settlement. The T.A. Executive were therefore indisposed to sign the keyboard agreement, but eventually did so in August 1905.

During the following years the T.A. temporarily abandoned its claim to control the working of the Monotype caster. The General Secretary stated at the Delegate Meeting in 1908 that there was 'no uniformity in the working of the Monotype caster. In a great many cases our members have got control of them. The Lanston Monotype Corporation has been training men and sending them out as caster attendants. In some cases, mechanics are in charge; in other cases, stereotypers and typefounders. In some instances, again, machine minders are in charge.' Monotype caster attendants might be members of the T.A., the Stereotypers' or Typefounders' Societies, the N.S.O.P.A., or some other printing trade union, among which 'demarcation' disputes were liable to occur. Casting was regarded by the T.A. as comparatively unskilled labouring work and the Association more or less recognized the Typefounders' claim to control it.[1] Proposals for the admission of caster attendants were rejected by the 1908 and 1913 Delegate Meetings. The 1918 Meeting, however, reversed this policy in favour of a renewed attempt to enrol such men and secure T.A. control over the working of the casters.

Meanwhile, the Monotype agreement of 1905 had operated very satisfactorily as a basis for the settlement of working conditions on the keyboard. As in the application of the Linotype agreements, there were a number of disputes, the T.A. regarding the terms laid down as minimum only, to be improved on locally if possible, while the F.M.P. tried to insist upon them as standard or maximum terms, occasionally forcing local reductions and resisting T.A. attempts to get beyond the agreement. As in the case of Linotypes, most firms worked their machines on the 'stab system. The agreement did not, of course, confine the working of the keyboard exclusively to T.A. members—though the Association tried to secure this—and many firms, particularly provincial branches of

[1] See below, p. 246.

London book-houses, employed not only non-members, but also female operators, at reduced wages, in spite of vigorous T.A. opposition.

The general adoption of 'stab work increased the controversy over output. Employers constantly complained of 'conspiracies' to limit output and resorted to all sorts of devices—such as the 'bonus system', 'slugging' matter, marking copy, and 'weeding-out'—to secure increased production. But the T.A. strongly opposed these practices, maintaining (as in the case of hand compositors) that no 'stab hand should be called upon 'to give an account of his lines or to assist in any system by which his individual earnings can be ascertained'. When employers devised methods of measuring individual output on Linotype machines without the co-operation of the operator—by the use of mechanical 'indicators' or 'clocks' which registered the number of lines cast—the Executive opposed these also, maintaining that employers were only entitled to ascertain aggregate output.

This attitude was strongly attacked by the L.U.A., who upheld the employer's right to ascertain both the quality and quantity of work produced by individual operators and considered that the T.A.'s policy was 'undoubtedly intended as a means of restricting the output of the machine'. *The Times* declared in a special article in December 1901 that 'both in London and in the provinces the policy of the "society" is to restrict the output from the machine, in order that it may not compare too favourably with hand work, and that the employer may be compelled to engage more men'. These charges were backed up by reference to the T.A. rules against 'task-work' and the 'bonus system' and to the restrictive system of 'extras' on piece-work.

Despite T.A. opposition, however, a number of firms began to fit indicators on their machines and the T.A. Executive, finding it difficult to refute the employers' claim to ascertain the output of each machine by purely mechanical means, were forced to modify their attitude. They decided in 1899 'that the simple registering of lines cannot be objected to; but that the introduction of the appliance must be guarded in such a manner as to prevent its misuse for the purposes of establishing any system of task-work'. This decision was endorsed by the R.C. in 1900 and 1901 and by the Delegate Meeting of 1903, but it is clear that the Association strongly disliked the indicators on the ground that they 'pushed' operators to increase their output.

Dissatisfaction grew in the following years as more indicators were introduced.[1] This system of checking output was regarded as 'little

---

[1] Numerous denunciatory articles appeared in the *Circular*.

better than espionage', as 'an attempt to sweat the workman of average ability', a system of 'slave-driving' which sought to get piece-work at 'stab wages by 'setting men against each other'. Moreover, indicators were apt to give inaccurate readings, while they took no account of the quality (as against mere quantity) of matter set, or of mechanical difficulties. They were injurious to the health of operators and to good feeling in an office. An overseer should be able, by ordinary means, to form an accurate enough estimate of the work done by each operator and employers should trust their workmen to give 'a fair day's work for a fair day's wage'. A strong motive, however, of this opposition to indicators was to prevent employers ascertaining individual output, which was undoubtedly restricted in many instances.

Closely related to this question was that of the 'bonus system', another method adopted by employers to secure increased output on 'stab. At the conferences on the Linotype piece-scale in 1903 the L.U.A. representatives expressed a desire to put this system on a recognized basis. They wished to secure 'the fullest results that the machines are capable of giving . . . and that those men who do more than what is a fair average day's work should be paid extra'. But the T.A. Executive regarded the bonus system as 'most objectionable' and one which they could not recognize, though they had, they asserted, no objection to expert operators being paid more than the standard rate. They regarded it as a 'sweating' system, which, like the use of indicators, encouraged 'slogging' or 'racing' and the employment of 'whips' or 'pace-makers', led to 'weeding out', and was liable to reduce standard wages and the number of men employed. The L.U.A. frequently urged the bonus system upon the T.A. in the following years, but the Executive refused to recognize any other method of working than ordinary 'stab or piece. If an employer wanted a high rate of output, he must put the men on piece and pay piece prices.

These questions were discussed by the Delegate Meeting of 1908, which passed a resolution 'that bonus-paid task-work, indicators, etc., or any system by which type-setting machine operators' output may be gauged shall not be permitted under the auspices of the Association; nor shall members accept work on composing machines on terms under which they are called upon to produce a fixed amount of composition, or on a system of payment (except piece-work pure and simple) which offers inducements to racing or undue competition between operators'.

The L.U.A. strongly denounced this 'complete reversal' of attitude as regards the use of indicators and the question occupied a prominent part in the joint conferences between representatives of the T.A. and the various employers' national organizations in the years 1909–11. The L.U.A. considered that the object of the new rule was 'to make it impossible for the management of any office to ascertain the output of individual operators', and Herbert Skinner, the T.A. General Secretary, admitted in two remarkable statements that it was merely an extension of an old principle, which the Association had long sought to maintain in hand composition, viz. 'that no individual record of the workmen's output should be kept' and that 'the employer has no right to know what a man does on 'stab work'. The T.A. representatives reproduced all the old arguments against 'task-work', &c., but the employers strongly maintained their right to ascertain individual output, to know whether a man was earning his wages, and to require a certain amount of work within a prescribed time; they also required statistics for costing purposes. They were prepared, however, to guard against abuses.

A compromise was eventually arrived at. The T.A. permitted the use of indicators on condition that grievances arising from their use should, in the event of non-settlement locally, be referred to the Committee of Reference, while the employers agreed to the remainder of the rule prohibiting bonus-paid work, slugging of matter, marking of copy, &c.

This compromise was rejected, however, by the T.A. Delegate Meeting in 1913, which unanimously passed a resolution 'that indicators on type-setting machines worked on 'stab should not be allowed in any circumstances'. The matter was now brought before the P. & K.T.F. and as a result of negotiations with the F.M.P. an agreed form of time-docket or time-sheet, to be filled in by individual workmen, was formulated in 1915 for use generally.

The trade was now beginning to settle down somewhat after the 'industrial revolution' wrought by composing machines in the nineties. This revolution was, of course, by no means complete, particularly in general printing offices, but national agreements had been drawn up establishing a sound basis for the regulation of working conditions in the industry. The T.A. had reason to be proud of a great achievement and could justly claim

that the manner in which we have dealt with this question . . . has been productive of results which may be described as unique in the history of trade unionism. . . . No organization outside the printing trade has been able to cope with the introduction of machines with the success which has marked our efforts. . . . In no other trade . . . has the working of machines been exclusively secured to members of the Union. . . . No other trade union has ever succeeded in obtaining so full and absolute recognition of what may be termed its restrictive rules, and no trade union has been able to so far maintain its position, in spite of adverse influences, as to render its assent an absolute factor in the settlement of working conditions.[1]

The T.A. had emerged from this 'industrial revolution' with enlarged membership and funds, increased wages, reduced hours, and improved working conditions—for case hands as well as operators—at the cost of few strikes and with a minimum of industrial unrest. Its power and prestige were, in consequence, enormously enhanced.

Printing Machines

The second half of the nineteenth century witnessed an 'industrial revolution' in the press as well as in the composing department, with the general introduction of printing machines. The T.A. was at first much less successful in dealing with this, chiefly because it failed to assert the same early control over printing as over composing machines and thus allowed them to slip out of its grasp. It took many years of hard work later to 'organize' machine rooms.

Comparatively few printing machines were to be found in the provinces in 1850. But the rapid growth of the provincial newspaper press in the second half of the century was accompanied by an equally rapid mechanization. Machines were also introduced, though more slowly, into jobbing offices and book houses.

The Manchester Typographical Society early realized the importance of these developments and tried to keep control over the working of the machines and to restrict 'irregular' labour, though it was forced, under pressure of industrial expansion and specialization, to recognize the machine-room as a separate department, with its specialized 'machine-men' or 'machine minders' and its own set of apprentices.[2] There was, as a result, a tendency to sectional division between machinemen and compositors; but the machinemen, though rather looked down on by the compositors, were eligible to join the Society. Moreover, rigid specialization was confined to a few large houses: in most offices 'twicing' was general, for smaller firms were unable to keep a machineman constantly employed, and many apprentices served their time to both machine and case, as they had previously done to press and case.

Outside Manchester, in other towns, machinemen were few in number and often excluded from the local typographical society.

[1] R.C. Meeting Report, May 1900.
[2] See above, pp. 46 and 181.

Compositors tended to regard them as an inferior class of mechanics. The result was that 'irregular' labour was often employed in machine-rooms, which were left completely unregulated as to wages, hours, apprentices, and general working conditions.

The P.T.A. adopted the old Northern Union rule that 'persons working at printing machines' who had not served a legal seven years' apprenticeship to the trade should be ineligible to join the Association. But this merely prevented 'illegal' men from becoming members: it did not prevent them from working the machines. Labourers and unbound boys were frequently employed, particularly to 'feed', 'take-off', and clean machines. When the Liverpool branch sought, in 1857, to enforce a local rule that only qualified journeymen or apprentices should be allowed to feed machines, the Executive refused their support, on the ground that this rule was 'opposed to the practice of nearly all other towns'. They recommended, however, that societies should 'adopt the general rule of requiring at least one practical printer to be in attendance on the working of each machine'.

The question was discussed at the 1861 Delegate Meeting, where it was stated that 'machines were greatly on the increase, and some regulation was highly necessary'. The Sheffield Society proposed 'that at every separate printing machine, at least one journeyman of the profession, or apprentice, shall be permanently in attendance when such machine is going'. But most speakers were opposed to such a rigid restriction. In many offices, it appears, a man would make the forme ready on one machine and then leave boys in charge while he proceeded to another. Moreover, mechanics and labourers were extensively employed. It was therefore decided to shelve the question by leaving it to local regulation.

Local regulation meant, as a rule, either no regulation or complete lack of uniformity. It was stated in the *Circular* in 1888, in regard to the position of machinemen, that 'custom varies very much in the different branches. In some, machinemen are expected to join in the same manner as compositors; in others, it is left optional; and in a third class no invitation is held out to machinemen, nor is any inducement offered them to join.' Some branches even refused machinemen admission. In many offices, particularly jobbing, unbound youths and, in some cases, girls worked the machines, and only in large offices were qualified machinemen employed to superintend, while 'twicing' was common in all branches. Many machinemen had served no proper apprenticeship to the trade and worked indiscriminately in 'fair' and 'unfair' houses. Even if they joined the society, they were in an insignificant minority among the compositors, who had little interest in their condition. There was, in fact, considerable antipathy between the two sections of the trade.

The Association began in the eighties to realize the dangers arising from this anomalous position of the machinemen. The latter became, with the continual introduction of larger and more complicated machines, highly skilled men, occupying a key position in the industry. By their adhesion or abstention they could often make or break a strike. The Executive, therefore, began to advocate 'the admission of all machine-men properly qualified by training and getting a certain rate of wages' and urged branches 'to use all legitimate efforts to induce such men to join'. But they tried to insist that only 'eligible' men, who had served a seven years' apprenticeship, should be admitted.

A special meeting of Manchester machine minders in March 1888 passed a resolution 'that all machinemen working in society offices should be compelled to belong to the branch in which they are working'. This resolution the Executive commended to all branches, 'in the hope that it may be found possible to establish a uniform system throughout the trade'. They considered 'that skilled workmen only should be allowed to have charge of machines, and that . . . machinemen should in all cases be allied with compositors'. Machinemen were recognized in T.A. rules for the first time in 1889, when it was laid down that members must have served 'a seven years' apprenticeship at case or machine'.

As the machinemen became more organized, they attempted to safe-guard their own interests. They tried, for example, to regulate the num-ber of machine apprentices and the employment of unbound boys. They were also strongly opposed to 'twicing', but the Executive decided that they could not interfere with the system.

The position of machinemen was considered by the 1891 Delegate Meeting. A proposal to abolish 'twicing' was overwhelmingly defeated on account of the 'number of small offices where it was impossible to employ a regular machineman', but other machinemen's grievances were favourably considered. Various delegates condemned the handling of machines by unbound boys and by 'mechanics who knew nothing about the printing trade, to which they had never served an apprenticeship'. Many felt that regulations should be made to govern working conditions in the machine department and it was therefore decided, in response to a memorial signed by 238 machinemen in various branches, that a special Conference of Machinemen should be summoned.

This conference, held in Manchester on 7 November 1891, passed a number of important resolutions, giving machinemen a fully recognized position in the Association and regulating their working conditions. It decided 'that all machinists obtaining employment in fair houses be compelled, if not already members, to join the Society'. No machineman, however, was to be admitted unless he had 'served his time in the business' or had been three years in charge of a machine. (Hitherto, apparently, in most towns, 'all a man had to do was to say he was a machineman, and he was admitted'.) It was even proposed that 'labourers or so-called machine assistants' on printing machines should be abolished and that only 'qualified men' should work them. The general opinion, however, was that 'they could not do without labourers in the machineroom', to feed, carry formes, wash rollers, and 'do all the dirty and heavy work', but that 'they must keep them in their places' and not allow them to 'make ready' or take charge of machines. The employment of mechanics and fitters as minders was strongly condemned.

The conference also dealt with the question of machine apprentices and the 'twicing' system.[1] It demanded that a man should be definitely identified as a compositor or machineman and kept exclusively to his own branch of the trade. E.C. members, however, pointed out the impossibility of enforcing such a rule in small offices and it was overwhelmingly rejected in the ensuing vote of the members.[2] The general feeling still prevailed that 'printers' had a right to work at any branch of the trade— at case, machine, or press.

A prolonged discussion took place at the conference as to the number of machines to be worked by one man. It was urged that no machineman should manage more than three platen machines, two single-cylinder machines from double demy downwards, or more than one perfecting, two-colour, or rotary machine. The conference eventually abandoned all reference to platens and rotaries, but passed resolutions 'that no machineman shall take the responsibility of more than two cylinder machines' nor countenance the practice of making machines ready and then leaving them in the charge of unbound boys. The conference also decided 'that machinemen shall not unduly be held responsible for breakages, spoilages, short paper, etc.', and should be awarded strike pay if dismissed for refusing to pay damages.

No regulations were made by the conference concerning wage rates. One delegate proposed that machinemen working larger machines than double demy, also two-colours, perfecters, and rotary machines, should receive extra remuneration, but the question was dropped. It appears

---

[1] See above, p. 181, for the regulation of machine apprentices.
[2] But a rule was passed against 'twicing' by apprentices.

that, except in Derby, machinemen were on 'stab and 'could generally command a few shillings per week more than the 'stab wage', particularly on the larger machines; but there was no general rule and wages were often left to individual bargaining. In many branches machinemen were working for less than the 'stab rate.

The machinemen, now that they were recognized as an integral part of the Association, claimed a fair representation on the Executive and at Delegate Meetings. For several years past there had usually been a machineman on the Council, but it was now demanded that a definite rule should be established, giving the machine section two out of the eleven Executive members. This claim was rejected in the subsequent voting, but the Delegate Meeting of 1893 decided that there must be at least one machineman on the Council. Machinemen were also granted a small representation at Delegate Meetings, were permitted to hold their own branch meetings and, in offices where there were seven or more machinemen, to form their own chapels, in order to protect and advance their particular interests.

These rules were little changed between 1891 and 1908. The 1897 R.C. meeting made the working regulations more stringent, so that in future no machineman should manage more than two single-cylinder machines, one perfecting, or one two-colour machine. The machinemen's repeated complaints against 'twicing' were also met by a rule that 'in all offices where two or more machinemen are employed, no compositor shall be allowed to change from case to machine, or to interfere with the legitimate work of machinemen; also, no machineman be allowed to change to case'—thus aiming at the abolition of 'twicing' in larger offices, but permitting it in small ones. In 1903 the E.C. decided to admit platen minders, considering 'that they were a part of the printing trade which should be retained and controlled by the Association', since 'the unorganised state of the platen hands was a source of weakness in many machine rooms'.[1]

But it was one thing to pass rules and another to enforce them. There still existed a good deal of ill feeling between the two sections of the trade and compositors had usually little interest in the condition of machinemen. Numerous offices, therefore, were classed as 'fair' in spite of non-society men, low wages, 'twicing', boy labour, and other abuses in their machine-rooms. These evils, however, were chiefly due to the apathy and indifference of the machinemen themselves, who remained

---

[1] In London there was a Platen Machine Minders' Society, established in 1891, distinct from the Printing Machine Managers' Trade Society.

disorganized for many years in most branches. In 1902 there were, in recognized offices alone, 513 non-unionist machinemen out of a total of 2,231. These figures take no account of the non-members employed in numerous 'unfair' houses. Many firms refused to recognize T.A. jurisdiction over the machine department. Labourers, youths, and girls were often in charge of machines, especially platens. Many machinemen, particularly rotary minders, had never served a proper apprenticeship: at first labourers or 'assistants', they eventually became minders by 'progression' within the trade and thus secured entry into the T.A. The apprenticeship rule could not, however, be rigidly enforced since it would merely create a large non-society element.

The E.C. also had to waive the rule that a man must be getting the minimum wage rate before admission. They had to 'organize' machinemen and then try to improve their wages.

These innumerable abuses would take years to eradicate. The 'organization of machinemen' was now, however, a leading feature of Association policy and improvement gradually resulted. By 1909 the Association had 2,751 machinemen members, though there were still 657 non-members in recognized offices, apart from those in 'unfair' houses. The T.A. had also assisted the National Society of Operative Printers' Assistants to establish provincial branches and organize the labourers or 'assistants' in newspaper rotary machine-rooms, whom the Association refused to admit on the ground that 'only men in actual charge of the machines could be accepted as members'. Moreover, the primitive regulations of 1891 had been considerably improved and expanded. A special sub-committee appointed by the E.C. in 1906, after consulting branch representatives and studying the London Machine Managers' rules, formulated a long list of revised regulations, which the 1908 Delegate Meeting approved almost without amendment.

The new rules were divided into two parts, dealing with general printing and newspaper rotary machines. Under the first heading it was laid down that 'all machinemen employed in recognised offices must be members of the Association' and that those admitted 'must, at the time of application, have served a seven years' apprenticeship to the business' (though apprentices, of course, could be admitted during the last two years of their time). Thus the alternative qualification of having been three years in charge of a machine was wiped out. The existing rule as to the number of machines for which a minder should be responsible was adopted almost unchanged, but with an addition that no machineman should take charge of more than three platens up to and including demy folio, above demy folio, two. It was also laid down that 'in all offices where platen machines are in use, it is the duty of members to regulate the supply of ink, change the gauges, and alter the impression, and in no case must girls or boys not apprentices perform this work'. The rule against 'twicing' was made more stringent, it being now forbidden in offices where one machineman was employed. The existing rules dealing with breakages and spoilt work, machine apprentices, and machinemen's organization remained practically unaltered. For the first time, however, minimum wage rates were laid down for machinemen in the Association rules. A machineman in charge of two single-cylinder machines, up to and including double-demy size, was to be paid not less than 3s. per week over the minimum 'stab rate of the branch; a machine with feeder attachment, not less than 3s. 6d.; a two-colour, double-revolution, gripper or tape perfecting machine, not less than 3s.; a rotary jobbing machine, not less than 25 per cent. over the minimum 'stab rate, for single-web rotary, and 5 per cent. extra for each additional web or cover. Where a night staff was employed, their remuneration was to be 'in accordance with the branch rate for night work', or, where no such rate was established, 'not less than 20 per cent. over the day rates'.

The greatest innovation, however, in the new rules was the special section dealing with rotary machine minders in newspaper offices. Rotaries had been mentioned at the 1891 conference, but had been left unregulated, with the result, as stated in 1908, that 'for many years the rotary minders throughout the Association area have been disorganised'. Rotary machines were mostly worked by non-members, mechanics and labourers, who had never served an apprenticeship to the printing trade, but had been recruited from outside. Rotary machine-minding 'was looked upon in the early stages as being entirely a mechanic's job'. But the T.A. gradually came to realize that it was really printers' work, that rotary minders were skilled craftsmen and should be members of the Association. Their inclusion, moreover, would greatly strengthen the union during disputes; rotary minders, in charge of intricate machines costing thousands of pounds, occupied a key position and could not easily be replaced. The Association had therefore begun to admit men in charge of rotary machines, regardless of apprenticeship.

It was now decided that 'all rotary machine minders employed in recognised offices must be members of the T.A.'. This rule implied, moreover, that they must have served a seven years' apprenticeship. The Association was, in fact, 'attempting what was at one time thought to be impossible . . . attempting to say that the rotary minder shall serve his time in the same way as a flat-bed minder'. The same apprentice scale was laid down for news as for general printing machine-rooms. An apprentice was not to take charge of a machine until the last two years of his apprenticeship.

The Association also tried to regulate the manning of news rotary machines. No member was to take charge of more than one single-width machine printing up to a 16-pp. paper, while a double-width machine printing three 8-pp., two 10-pp., two 12-pp., or two 16-pp. papers was to be manned by two machinemen. As in the case of general printing machinemen, rotary minders were not to be held responsible for breakages, spoilt work, neglect of assistants, &c.

Rotary wages and hours were also regulated. Branches were empowered to arrange local wage rates, with a minimum of 25 per cent. over the basic 'stab rate for day work and 20 per cent. over day machine rates for night work. Working hours were to be 'fixed and defined by arrangement between employers and employed, subject to the approval of the branch', and overtime rates were to be laid down.

These revised machinemen's rules became a fruitful source of dissension during negotiations with the employers' national organizations in the following years. Disagreement was greatest over the new rules for rotary newspaper machines. The Linotype Users' Association flatly refused, during the joint conferences of 1909, to recognize T.A. jurisdiction over this department. These rules, they considered, were 'an entirely new departure', an interfering innovation, an attempt to revolutionize present conditions in news machine rooms, to extend T.A. control over a body of men who had never previously been regarded as part of the union and for whom it had never legislated. They did not object to machinemen being members of the T.A., but they did object to any rule that T.A. members *only* should be employed and to the regulation of wages, hours, and working conditions by the Association. Many of their present machinemen, they pointed out, were mechanics or ex-assistants who had never served an apprenticeship to printing and were not T.A. members. They were not, in fact, under the new rules, eligible to join the Association. But they were skilled men whom the employers could not sacrifice. Moreover, the T.A. apprenticeship rule would prevent the advancement of assistants to take charge of machines and thus cause differences with the National Society of Operative Printers' Assistants, many of whose members had charge of machines, at lower wages than the T.A. demanded.

The employers' arguments were strongly resisted by the T.A. The

Association's claim to jurisdiction over the news rotary department was based on the fact that rotary minders were, like flat-bed machinemen, *printers*, not mechanics. The Association recognized the fact that most minders at present on rotary machines had never served an apprenticeship and was prepared, for some time at any rate, to admit all those who were actually in charge of machines, regardless of that qualification. The N.S.O.P.A. admitted that actual machine minders should belong to the T.A. and negotiations were afoot with that Society for an agreement on demarcation and transfer of members.[1] But the T.A. did desire 'the ultimate introduction of the apprenticeship system on rotary machines', so as 'to regularise the training of rotary machine minders'. They could not continue to allow 'the unskilled artisan or the unrecognised printer' to 'creep in' at a low rate of wages. An apprenticeship system, it was pointed out, would benefit employers as much as the Association, by providing properly trained and skilled workmen, instead of those who had merely picked up their knowledge haphazardly as labourers or assistants.

As regards the regulation of working conditions on rotary machines, the T.A. wished 'to come to a national agreement' with the employers like those for Linotype and Monotype composing machines. If the employers refused and things went on as at present, what would be the result? The Association would still adhere to its rules and try to enforce them in individual branches and offices. Thus there would be 'a hundred and one little difficulties with a hundred and one newspaper offices about the country'.

The L.U.A. was not, however, converted by these arguments and no agreement was reached. The utmost the T.A. could get was a statement that employers would not object to rotary minders being or becoming T.A. members. A similar result attended the conferences which followed in 1910–11 with the F.M.P., L.U.A., and other employers' organizations. The employers were determined to maintain 'the fullest freedom in the internal working of our offices' and refused to admit the T.A.'s 'right' to dictate 'how we are to man our machines and what number we should employ', to 'step into our offices and lay down certain rules and conditions under which these men are to carry on their work'. The regulations as to the manning of rotary machines they condemned as inelastic, unworkable, and over-costly: they would require (at least) a machineman to every machine, though all machines were rarely run together, many only for an hour or two each day and some only on particular days. They also rejected the wage rates fixed by the Association, being able to put

[1] See below, p. 244.

assistants on machines at lower rates. Finally, they were loath to strengthen the T.A.'s organization and power by conceding control over the rotary department. The utmost they would accept was a rule applying to machine minders similar to that in regard to readers, viz. that 'rotary machine-minders employed in recognised offices may be members of the T.A. provided always that the rule be regarded as of a permissive character'—though this rule was not to commit the T.A. to a recognition of the 'open house' system.

Thus the T.A. had failed to secure the desired national agreement on newspaper rotary machines. But it remained as determined as ever to assert its jurisdiction over this department, to organize and enrol all rotary minders and eventually to enforce its regulations as to wages, hours, and working conditions. Failing a national settlement, action would be taken locally.

Greater, though limited, success attended T.A. efforts to regulate the wages and working conditions of machinemen in jobbing and weekly news offices. Their proposed rules were argued over at great length during the conferences with the employers' national organizations in 1910–11 and eventually a 'hashed-up' set of rules was included in the 1911 Agreement. The employers refused to accept the rule that all machinemen employed in recognized offices must be members of the Association, for much the same reasons as in the case of news rotary minders. They had no objection to machinemen being T.A. members, but refused to be bound to the employment of T.A. members only. They were also strongly opposed to the T.A.'s demand that men working certain machines should receive more than the branch 'stab rate. They pointed out that the class of work was as important as the size or number of machines—it was often easier to work a large machine or several machines on cheap, straightforward jobs than one small machine on complicated and high-class work—that machines were not always working up to their size, that men were frequently changed about and not always kept to one class of machine, that conditions varied greatly in different offices and different parts of the country, and that they could not, therefore, accept 'any hard and fast arbitrary rule'. In many offices, they observed, skilled and experienced machinemen were already receiving more, often much more, than the 'stab rate and they considered that, in view of the 'varying conditions', payment of a higher rate should remain 'a voluntary act on the part of an employer'. It was agreed, however, that 2s. per week extra should be paid for an automatic feeder attachment, that jobbing rotary minders should get not less than 15 per cent. over the basic 'stab rate, and that where night staffs were employed they should be paid the branch rate for night work or, where no such rate had been fixed, not less than 15 per cent. over day rates, the same as Monotype operators.[1]

The employers strongly opposed the further restriction imposed by the new rule against 'twicing', because of its effect in small offices and on weekly newspapers, where there was not enough work to keep a machineman constantly employed, and the T.A. representatives agreed to restore the old rule.

They also accepted the employers' view in regard to breakages and spoilt work, that machine minders should 'not be held *unduly* responsible', but insisted that 'they should not be asked to *pay* for spoilt work'.

The greatest differences arose over the T.A.'s attempt to regulate the manning of machines and to dictate 'what shall be one man's work'. As in the case of news rotary machines, the employers insisted on the 'necessary freedom in the management of the business' and strongly opposed the T.A.'s 'endeavour to regulate what men shall be allowed to do or be called upon to do, in offices where the conditions vary . . . to very considerably regulate them according to a cast-iron rule, without reference to the exigencies or the practice of any particular office'. As in the case of wage rates, the difficulty and class of work were equally as important as the size or number of machines. Moreover, all machines were not kept constantly running: some were only used at rush periods or for a particular class of work. The hard-and-fast T.A. rules were therefore 'not elastic enough' for these varying conditions and requirements and would, in fact, be 'quite unworkable'. They would also incur 'very considerable extra expense'. The T.A., however, insisted that their rules were both fair and workable—drawn up by practical men as a result of practical experience—and that they were only asking for the same conditions as already existed in London and many of the best provincial offices. Many employers were making impossible demands on their machinemen and the Association was merely trying to define fair working conditions.

No real agreement was reached on these working regulations. The clause included in the 'Agreement on Rules' (1911) was very ambiguous. 'The proportion of machinemen, including apprentices', was 'to be one for each three platens, two single-cylinder machines including two-revolution machines of pony size (i.e. not exceeding double crown), and one for each two-revolution machine above pony size, two-colour machine,

---

[1] Jobbing night shifts were very rare at this time and few branches had night rates for jobbing.

or perfecting machine'. But this proportion was 'to be reckoned upon the number of machines actually employed', and, 'subject to the above proportion being maintained', the firm could 'regulate the manning of the machines to suit the requirements of the office'. Employers interpreted this to mean that, so long as they maintained the correct over-all proportion of men to machines in their offices, they had perfect freedom to arrange the manning of machines according to internal requirements and might put a man in charge of any number of machines. The T.A., however, disputed this interpretation and wished to add that no minder should 'at any time have charge of more than the number of machines mentioned'. But the employers refused to accept this addition and the agreement was eventually signed without the difference being settled.

The remainder of the agreement had reference to platens. The T.A. conceded that 'the manning of platen machines engaged in the regular production of Christmas cards and similar work shall be continued under the conditions existing in each office, but in offices not now engaged in this work the conditions as to manning machines shall be subject to arrangement between the firms affected and the local branch of the T.A.'; while the employers agreed that it was a machineman's duty 'to regulate the supply of ink, change the gauges, and alter the impression', and that 'in no case must girls or boys (not apprentices) perform this work'.

From the T.A. point of view this was in many ways an unsatisfactory agreement. But the Association had at least got a firm foot-hold in the machine department and secured recognition of this fact from the employers' national organizations. The agreement was a beginning which might be gradually improved on. The immediate gains, however, were meagre and doubtful. The ambiguous clause in regard to the manning of machines at once caused difficulties, which a conference in October 1911 failed to settle, and disputes soon broke out in various offices. These were referred to the Committee of Reference established by the 1911 Agreement, but no solution was reached and the question was therefore referred to arbitration. The decision of the arbitrator, Sir Albert K. Rollit, was in favour of the employers' interpretation. The T.A. Executive accepted this award, but at once approached the employers for a conference 'with the object of securing the amendment of the Agreement on Machinemen's Rules'. The F.M.P., however, would only agree to a conference if amendment of the apprentice scale, with which *they* were dissatisfied, was also discussed. The T.A. Executive did not relish such a bargain and referred the matter to the 1913 Delegate

Meeting, which reaffirmed the 1908 rules, rejecting the unsatisfactory compromise of 1911. The E.C. therefore approached the employers in 1914 for a new agreement, but negotiations had to be postponed because of the war. The 1918 Delegate Meeting again re-enacted the 1908 rules and added fresh clauses. A new agreement, much more favourable to the T.A., was to form part of the post-war settlement.

Machinemen, like compositors, were sometimes accused by employers of limiting output. *The Times*, for example, accused machinemen in 1901 of restricting output by a deliberate policy of 'go easy' or 'ca' canny', in order to 'make work' for others. In particular, it was asserted, they would not drive the new quick-running two-revolution flat-bed presses from America (which had a higher output than the Wharfedale) at their full speed. Some employers undoubtedly shared these views and began to fit electrical time-checking indicators or recorders on letterpress machines, which indicated in the manager's or overseer's office whenever a machine was stopped. To these 'contrivances' T.A. machinemen strongly objected, pointing out that it was often necessary to stop a machine when working difficult formes, so as not to spoil their work. They had no objection to counters or clocks which recorded the number of sheets printed—these, in fact, saved them the trouble of counting the sheets and gave a useful indication of machine speed: they regulated the work of the machines, not of the men—but they did object strongly to time-checking and the Delegate Meeting of 1908 passed a resolution against 'indicators or other mechanical contrivances' used for that purpose.

The question was discussed in conference with the employers' national organizations. The T.A. representatives declared that 'we as an Association do not desire to regulate the output or lower the output. . . . We desire to see the men do their level best.' But they objected to this system of 'espionage' by recorders. The employers at first maintained that they could not be prevented from checking the running of their machines by any method they might adopt, but eventually agreed that no new electrical indicators should be installed.[1]

---

[1] For no apparent reason this was not included in the 1911 Agreement.

XII

RELATIONS WITH OTHER UNIONS

THE T.A. was primarily concerned with its own affairs—the wages, hours, and working conditions of skilled men in the provincial letterpress printing trade. But outside itself there were other typographical societies, with which it was constantly brought into contact and with which it was often proposed that the Association should amalgamate or form reciprocity agreements. Furthermore, the 'typographical art' was merely one of a number of printing and kindred trades, containing many other unions with which the T.A. eventually federated. Outside the printing and allied trades, moreover, the T.A. became active in the British Labour Movement as a whole—in Trades Councils, the Trades Union Congress, and the Labour Party. It also came into touch with the international typographical and Labour world.

Relations with other Typographical Societies

The National Typographical Association had collapsed in 1847–8 amid ruin and recrimination, leaving behind it a strong aversion to amalgamation. The idea was not abandoned, but never again reached concrete form. The T.A. came, in the second half of the century, to include all provincial typographical societies in England, Wales, and Ireland, but London and Dublin stood aloof, while Scotland also re-erected its own Association.

Friendly feelings and co-operation still existed, however, between the various societies. The London Society of Compositors sent two representatives to Sheffield in June 1849 to give assistance and advice in establishing the P.T.A. Correspondence continued between them in regard to the admission of members: the T.A. would not, for example, admit a man who had 'ratted' in London. The different societies also continued to 'recognize' each other's cards. There were difficulties, however, concerning entrance fees and subscriptions. A provincial compositor, arriving in London, was permitted to place his name on the L.S.C. call-book and, on obtaining employment, had his card exchanged free, the London Society considering that 'a fair member should not be called on to pay more than one entrance-fee during his life'. The Scottish Association adopted the same policy. But London and Scottish compositors were charged entrance fees by provincial societies. The injustice of this was pointed out to the P.T.A. and the Delegate Meeting of 1856 passed a rule 'that no entrance-fee be charged on the cards of such recognised societies as reciprocate the advantage'.

The question of subscriptions caused much more trouble. It was laid down in 1856 that, when a member obtained a 'permanent' situation in a recognized society town, he must, if he wished to remain a member of the Association, pay the usual Association subscription 'in addition to the local requirement'. This meant that a member of the P.T.A. who secured employment in London must, if he wished to retain his P.T.A. membership, pay subscriptions to both the London Society and the Association. The same applied, of course, to a London member working in a provincial town. In the early days, men merely exchanged cards and allowed their old membership to lapse; but when valuable provident benefits were attached to membership, towards which they had contributed for years and which could only be secured by lengthy probation, they became very loath to throw it up. They strongly objected, however, to paying double subscriptions. As a result, we find T.A. members working in London or Scotland, and Scottish or London members working in provincial towns, refusing to pay subscriptions to the local society. This caused a good deal of ill-feeling between the various unions. Some reciprocal agreement was obviously necessary.

Typographical societies continued to assist each other in trade disputes. If, for example, a strike occurred in a recognized society town, T.A. members were warned in the *Circular* against accepting situations there and any who 'ratted' were liable to expulsion. Financial assistance was also given in serious strikes.

Tramping still formed a bond between the various societies, which continued to relieve each other's cards. But it also remained a source of ill-feeling. London constantly complained of the provincial influx, which tended to lower wages and cause unemployment. The provinces, on the other hand, felt that, by tramping, London was enabled to 'export' its out-of-work. There was also the old problem of 'equalizing' the burden of tramp relief: the P.T.A. felt, like the Northern Union, that London was not doing her fair share.

It was in order, partly, to remedy this inequality that the Relief Association was established in 1863, with a common Relief Fund and uniform weekly contribution. The Executive hoped to extend the new mileage system throughout the United Kingdom, but London, Scotland, and Dublin held aloof. The Relief Association, therefore, only gave half relief on 'non-conforming' cards. Considerable bitterness was aroused on both sides. London, Scotland, and Dublin continued at first to give tramp relief on the old system, but in the years 1878–81 the Scottish Association and the London Pressmen and Compositors abolished tramping altogether and replaced it by a system of removal grants. The T.A. therefore decided to discontinue relieving members of all independent societies. Thus the old tramp-relief reciprocity was ended.

There was a certain amount of co-operation during these years in 'missionary' work. In 1873, for example, the London Compositors voted £150 towards the P.T.A.'s campaign and appointed a representative to accompany the Association Secretary on a tour of various towns in Kent and Sussex. Later, they assisted the T.A. in attempts to establish branches at such places as Brighton, Hastings, Redhill, Beccles, Ipswich, Bury St. Edmunds, and Aylesbury. But the London men, while thoroughly approving of missionary work and even occasionally lending a hand, considered that it was 'work properly belonging to the P.T.A.' The L.S.C. stood, for the most part, in splendid isolation within a circle of 15 miles radius from the G.P.O. In this, the London area, it attempted rigidly to maintain its scale; outside, it had little interest. The T.A. frequently complained of London's lack of co-operation, indeed apathy, in regard to extra-metropolitan affairs and asked the L.S.C. committee in 1881 'whether the maintenance of this radius is beneficial or otherwise to the trade'. London was shortly to see the unwisdom of this isolationist policy.

Suggestions for amalgamation were frequently made during this period, usually at Delegate Meetings of the P.T.A. The latter, like those of the old Northern Union, were not mere provincial affairs, but general trade gatherings, attended by delegates from London, Scotland, Dublin, and other independent societies. Previous to the meeting in 1856 the Executive suggested that the profession might be brought 'into a closer and more efficient state of organisation', that the Association laws might be 'altered so as to meet the circumstances of the entire provincial trade'. But this, the Dublin Society observed, would amount to a revival of the 'Amalgamation', which they considered 'too extensive to be practically carried out'. The Scottish Association also felt 'that it would be much better to remain as a distinct body'. The Delegate Meeting therefore decided 'that the P.T.A. be continued on its present basis'.

A more definite proposition was put forward at the Delegate Meeting in 1861 by the Cork Society: 'that a general amalgamation of the trade be formed, with a central board, and using a uniform card'. But the meeting, while paying lip-service to amalgamation as ultimately desirable, considered that it was at present 'impracticable' or 'too comprehensive', that 'the peculiarities of the various districts could not be generalised', that there were too many different customs in regard to wages and apprentices to permit of amalgamation.

This attitude remained predominant. Henry Self, for example, Secretary of the L.S.C., spoke in 1868 of 'the differences of feeling, and the different modes of payment and customs of the provinces as compared with London'. Nevertheless, several suggestions were made during the seventies for amalgamation or federation. Alex Hunter, of Manchester, for example, writing in the *Circular* in 1874, urged that 'either a Federal Union or a United Typographical Association' should be established, that the different unions should overcome 'exclusiveness and isolation' and 'forget all distinctions of nationality, remembering only that we are working men who have but one object in common'. The peculiarities of the different districts could, he considered, be overcome by 'an elastic code of federation rules'. He pointed, by way of example, to the Amalgamated Society of Engineers and to the attempt then being made to form a federation of the engineering and shipbuilding trades. These ideas were supported by the Association Secretary, who advocated either a 'National Union of Printers' or a 'Typographical Federation of Great Britain and Ireland'.

The T.A. was by this time gradually absorbing all independent societies in the English provinces and in Ireland. But amalgamation with London and Scotland was no nearer. From 1872 onwards, representatives from independent societies were no longer invited to T.A. Delegate Meetings, which became purely Association affairs. In the late seventies, tramp-relief reciprocity was ended. There were also increasing difficulties in regard to the payment of subscriptions by members working outside the area of their own union. Mutual 'recognition' and co-operation, however, still continued, while reciprocal payment of strike benefits was established between the L.S.C. and the T.A. in the early eighties, a financial arrangement whereby members could receive strike benefit outside the area of their own organization. The idea of amalgamation, moreover, always kept cropping up. During the period 1879–82, when the question of a general federation of trade unions was again under discussion, Henry Slatter pointed out that 'the first necessity is unity in each different trade' and that in the printing trade there was 'too much sectional effort, too many societies content to remain in isolation, and too little done for the general good of the trade'. He considered, however, that 'the course of events is undoubtedly tending in the direction of a more thorough combination among existing societies'. Similar views were expressed by Charles Drummond, Secretary of the L.S.C. Attending the Annual Gathering of Yorkshire branches in 1883, he expressed 'a hope that at some not very distant date the whole of the typographical societies throughout the United Kingdom might be able to combine and work together in harmony for the good of the trade', and at a dinner of the Nottingham branch in the same year he stated that 'he would rejoice to see the day when their London and Manchester societies were amalgamated'.

These hopes were brought nearer to fruition in the years 1885–6. In January 1885 Drummond wrote to the T.A. Executive that the National Press Agency, an 'unfair' office in London, was supplying stereotype columns to various provincial papers and asked that the T.A. should prohibit their use in 'fair' houses. To this the Executive agreed, in accordance with their rule against the transfer of matter between 'fair' and 'unfair' offices. Shortly afterwards the T.A. itself had to make a similar appeal, when a strike occurred in the Belfast *Morning News* office and the proprietor secured matrices from Dublin and Glasgow. The Executive asked for co-operation against this practice and suggested 'that it might be desirable to hold a conference of the S.T.A., the L.S.C., the Dublin and Leeds Societies, and our Association, to consider the question'. To this suggestion the L.S.C. and Dublin agreed, but no reply was received from the S.T.A. and the question was therefore adjourned.

In the following year, however, a Delegate Meeting of the S.T.A. instructed their Executive 'to consider the propriety of holding a conference of representatives of the T.A., the S.T.A., and the L.S.C. on out-of-work payments, with a view to reciprocity'. Now that tramp-relief reciprocity no longer existed, the S.T.A. proposed reciprocal payment of out-of-work benefits—with a financial settlement between the unions at the end of each year—in order to enable men to look for work outside the area of their own union. The T.A. Executive favoured the idea and also asked 'whether it was not possible to enlarge the scope of the proposed conference so as to include other matters in which their organisations had a common interest'. This suggestion was accepted by the Scottish Executive, who further proposed that Dublin, Leeds, and the London Pressmen and Machinemen should also be invited and 'that the question of a united organisation might be considered with advantage'.

The conference was eventually held in London on 21 October 1886.

It discussed a large number of questions, including the use of stereotype in newspaper offices, reciprocity in relief payments, amalgamation and federation, missionary work, apprentices, machinemen, piece-work, overtime, female compositors, arbitration, and technical education. On most of these, pious resolutions were passed, pledging united action and mutual support; but it is obvious that there were many underlying differences. Little or no advance was made towards a more united organization. Although a resolution was passed 'that . . . a National Association of letter-press printers for Great Britain and Ireland', either by amalgamation or federation, 'should be the ultimate aim and object of the various typographical associations', no practical measures were taken. The conference could not even agree on a scheme of reciprocity in relief payments. Some felt that it would be reviving all the evils of the old tramping system, while the London men feared that it would increase the provincial influx. A committee was appointed 'to carry into effect the resolutions agreed to by this Conference . . . in order that rules and regulations may be framed to our mutual advantage', but it seems never to have met and the results of the conference were negligible.

Relations between the various typographical societies, therefore, remained unchanged. Leeds, the only remaining independent society of any importance in the English provinces, amalgamated with the T.A. in January 1895. The Dublin Society also considered amalgamation on several occasions, but each time decided against it. Between the T.A., London, and Scotland mutual recognition and support continued. Relations, on the whole, tended to become closer and more friendly. L.S.C. and S.T.A. representatives were, for example, again invited to attend T.A. Delegate and R.C. Meetings, especially to share in discussion on composing machines. The London Compositors and Machinemen were also represented at the conferences of T.A. southern branches.

Ideas of amalgamation and federation still persisted. The T.A. Delegate Meeting of 1891, for example, passed a resolution 'that immediate steps be taken to promote the amalgamation of the various typographical societies in the United Kingdom', and the Representative Council of 1896 instructed the Executive 'to negotiate with other typographical societies to bring about a closer alliance, if not federation, between them and the T.A.' In 1894 the S.T.A. was 'willing to consider some scheme of federation' with the T.A., 'whereby the two Associations would be better able to work hand in hand in the common cause', and in the following year the L.S.C. made a similar suggestion. But nothing came of these proposals. Deep-rooted differences still divided the various societies—differences in wage rates, piece-work regulations, apprentice rules, and other trade customs.

Relations were particularly strained with the London Printing Machine Managers' Trade Society (P.M.M.T.S.). As early as 1883, at least, that society was refusing to recognize provincial cards and placing other obstacles in the way of provincial machinemen securing work in London. Its aim, like that of the L.S.C., was to prevent an influx of provincial hands, who would compete with its members for work and perhaps lower wage rates. It complained, moreover, of the T.A.'s negligence in regard to the machine section, whereby many 'illegal men', who had never served an apprenticeship or were not proficient machine minders, gained admission. It also objected to the widespread system of 'twicing' by provincial compositors, regarding machine-work as a distinct and specialized branch. Finally, London machinemen refused to join the T.A. when in the provinces, since, if they wished to retain their London membership, they would have to pay two subscriptions.

The T.A. made repeated but useless protests against the hostility of the London society and finally, in 1891, decided to retaliate, by refusing to recognize its cards. An attempt was made at the Conference of Machinemen in that year to patch up the quarrel, but the meeting merely accentuated the differences. Hostilities continued in the following years. The London society even began to consider the establishment of provincial branches so as to form 'one machine-minders' organization for the whole country', a 'National Society of Machinemen'. A special committee on the subject was appointed in 1898, which condemned the indifference of the T.A. towards machine minders and their consequent disorganization. It deplored 'the great disproportion in wages' between London and most provincial towns, which tended to produce an 'overflow into London' and resulted not only in severe competition by provincial firms, but also in 'the opening, by London firms, of branch factories in the country': disorganization in the provinces was thus liable to cause lowered wage rates and unemployment in London. There was, therefore, a good case for 'the management of their own affairs by machine minders, and the establishment of branches in the provinces exclusively composed of them'. But there were difficulties: the problem of organizing the provinces and the hostility of the T.A. The committee therefore proposed a meeting with T.A. representatives to try to reach an 'amicable arrangement'.

A conference was duly arranged in January 1899. The London men explained their dissatisfaction 'that the interests of the machine section

. . . were not adequately cared for in the provinces', with results dangerous to their society. The T.A. representatives denied the charge of
negligence, however, pointing out the efforts being made to organize
provincial machinemen. The conference is said to have 'cleared away
several misunderstandings'.

Somewhat similar, though more friendly, differences existed between
the T.A. and the L.S.C. The latter, like the P.M.M.T.S., became increasingly alarmed at the low wage rates outside the London radius, the
consequent competition and exodus of London firms into the provinces.
They began to realize the error of their hitherto narrowly isolationist
policy and to take a growing interest in the extra-metropolitan area, particularly in those towns where London firms had established provincial
offices.

By this time, however, the T.A. had taken over all territory outside
the London radius, had appointed a special organizer, and established
numerous southern branches. In face of great difficulties, it was trying
to raise wages, reduce hours, and restrict apprentices. Thus the L.S.C.
could not now extend its radius without coming into conflict with the
T.A. At first, therefore, it adopted a policy of friendly co-operation. Its
secretary assisted the T.A. to establish new branches, attended T.A.
branch meetings and southern conferences, and took part in negotiations
with London-owned provincial firms.

The T.A. Executive greatly appreciated this assistance and instructed
its Southern Organizer to keep in close touch with the L.S.C. secretary.
But relations were tending, by the end of the nineties, to become rather
strained. The L.S.C. was demanding urgent action, but the T.A. was
doing all it could and pointed out that the only means of effecting an
improvement was slow, patient organizing effort.

The idea of 'reciprocity' in payment of benefits was frequently resur-
rected after the 1886 conference, but nothing was done until 1899.
Another conference on the subject was then held, in Manchester,
attended by representatives of the T.A., S.T.A., L.S.C., and P.M.M.T.S.
It succeeded in drawing up a scheme whereby any members 'temporarily
employed or travelling beyond the limits of their own organisation'
could receive out-of-work, strike, and (in the case of Scottish members)
sick benefits, in accordance with the rules of their parent Association,
through the society in whose area they happened to be—such payments
to be refunded by the parent Association. This scheme would, it was
hoped, not only be a boon to travelling members, but also enable 'proper
oversight' to be maintained over them, since they would have to report

to the secretary of the local society and observe its rules. If they secured work there they would have to become members of that society and pay its subscriptions. During the period of probation in the new society they would have to pay 4*d.* per week to the old one in order to secure continuity of benefit, but when probation was completed they could cease all payments to the old society, unless they wished to retain interest in its superannuation and funeral benefits.

Another conference in July 1900 ironed out a number of misunderstandings and the scheme came into operation on 1 January 1901. But differences in regard to the Outer London area became increasingly acute. The question was discussed rather heatedly at the reciprocity conferences, the London societies, especially the P.M.M.T.S., accusing the T.A. of negligence and pointing out the threat to their wage rates and working conditions of the unorganized extra-metropolitan area. The T.A. representatives replied, however, that they had been trying to organize the district for several years and that great difficulties had to be faced.

A special conference on the subject was held in London on 14 December 1900 between representatives of the T.A., L.S.C., P.M.M.T.S., and N.S.O.P.A. All the London representatives criticized the T.A. from a narrowly metropolitan standpoint. There is no doubt that conditions were bad in the Home Counties: many large London firms which were 'fair' in the metropolis had established 'unfair' branches in the country, employing non-unionists at low wage rates and cheap female and boy labour. The T.A. had been unable (or had neglected) to deal with these firms, which seriously affected the position of the London unions. But for years the latter had kept their heads in the sand, pursuing a narrow and selfish policy of isolation, while the T.A., from its nucleus in Lancashire and Yorkshire, had gradually, after half a century of patient organizing effort, established branches all over England and was doing its best to cope with the evils in the south—and yet these metropolitan societies now criticized the T.A. for the disorganization on their own doorstep! The injustice of this was pointed out by the T.A. representatives, who described the organizing work which had been done around London and suggested that the L.S.C. should appoint an organizer to help in the work. They also proposed 'that, in the event of London houses removing into towns where no branch of the T.A. exists, the Executive Councils of all the Societies concerned shall jointly agree upon the standard working conditions'. This proposal was accepted by the conference and the L.S.C. decided shortly afterwards to appoint an organizer.

In 1901, consequently, the L.S.C. and T.A. co-operated in wages negotiations at Gravesend and Dorking. But the L.S.C. remained dissatisfied and eventually, at the end of 1902, proposed an extension of their radius from 15 to 30 miles. Their main reasons were the rapid growth of the metropolis and the exodus of London firms to the provinces. They wished to retain control over these houses and to maintain the London scale of wages in the enlarged radius, so as to reduce competition. Work was being taken out of London, thus causing unemployment, while their membership was suffering from the provincial migration. But the effect of the proposed extension would be the absorption by the L.S.C. of about twelve branches of the T.A. and a serious weakening of the latter's position in the south of England. A joint conference (February 1903) merely aroused acrimonious feeling and the T.A. eventually rejected the London proposal.

The L.S.C. next initiated a movement of the Outer London (or Home Counties) branches of the T.A. to secure a standard rate of 34s. per week of 54 hours for all T.A. members working within 25 miles of the L.S.C. radius. But the T.A. was only able to get 30s. in negotiations with the F.M.P., and the L.S.C. therefore again pressed for an extension of the radius, feeling that they could do better than the T.A. Another conference (November 1904) failed, however, to produce agreement.

Further friction between the two unions resulted from the L.S.C.'s treatment of T.A. members migrating to London. The old dislike of a 'provincial influx'—as depriving L.S.C. members of employment and tending to lower wage rates—still existed and resulted in non-recognition of T.A. cards and attempts to prevent T.A. members securing situations.

Meanwhile, the T.A. was experiencing similar difficulties with the P.M.M.T.S., who contended, quite impracticably, that the T.A. ought to insist upon London wage rates being paid by London firms removing into the country. London machinemen ignored the reciprocity scheme in many T.A. branches, refusing to recognize the Association or pay its subscriptions. Moreover, the P.M.M.T.S. had no recognized radius and was guilty of 'poaching' in T.A. territory. It also adopted an exclusionist policy, like the L.S.C., refusing to recognize T.A. cards or charging entrance fees, trying to prevent T.A. members getting work in London, subjecting them to petty persecution, threatening to hand in notices if they were not dismissed, even damaging machines on which they were working. Its only justification seems to have been that T.A. members sometimes worked in 'unfair' London houses, for which, however, the

T.A. Executive would, if informed, inflict punishment. It also alleged that its members were boycotted in the provinces, but there is little evidence of this.

T.A. protests, a joint conference and drawn-out negotiations proved abortive and the P.M.M.T.S. decided in 1903 to withdraw from the reciprocity scheme. A further conference (April 1905) produced little improvement in relations and in May 1906 the T.A. threatened to take retaliatory measures against the P.M.M.T.S. for its treatment of T.A. members in London. By the beginning of 1907, however, the situation had become more serious: the P.M.M.T.S. was trying to establish branches in such towns as Watford, Guildford, Tonbridge, and Reading, while the L.S.C. had decided to extend its radius to 40 miles.

Matters had been brought to this crisis by the situation at Reading, where Wymans, the great London firm, had opened a large branch establishment, employing non-unionists at low rates and a large number of women, girls, and boys as cheap labour. For several years the T.A. took practically no action to organize the men employed there and the compositors eventually (1906) formed an independent society and applied for affiliation to the P. & K.T.F. The latter advised them to seek admission to the T.A. and also urged the various unions concerned to make every effort 'to bring the firm into line'. The T.A. Executive, therefore, now took active steps to organize the compositors and machinemen and approached the firm with a view to 'opening' the office. An agreement was eventually arrived at in February 1907 whereby the firm granted a wage advance from 28s. to 31s. per week and agreed to the gradual elimination of female labour and limitation of apprentices. This, however, was regarded as unsatisfactory by both the L.S.C. and P.M.M.T.S., who had meanwhile been seeking to enrol the men into their societies. Both were greatly dissatisfied with the T.A.'s inactivity and inability to raise wage rates in the extra-metropolitan area, both wished to retain control over what they regarded as 'London work' removed to provincial houses, and both therefore decided to expand their area of operations.

The L.S.C. committee declared in February 1907 that they were 'unable to recognise the claim set up by the T.A. to the exclusive control of England outside London' and recommended an extension of their radius to 40 miles. This proposal was accepted by the annual general meeting in March and the L.S.C., together with the P.M.M.T.S., which maintained it had no radius, now started active measures to establish branches in Reading and other towns in the Outer London area.

Conferences between the T.A. and P.M.M.T.S. (March 1907) and

L.S.C. (May 1907) failed to produce agreement. The T.A. strongly protested against the action of the London societies, particularly at Reading,
and pointed out that if persisted in it would lead to serious conflict. The
T.A. was prepared to co-operate with the London societies in dealing
with extra-metropolitan branch firms, but if they established provincial
branches the T.A. would establish a branch in London. The T.A. also
protested to the P. & K.T.F. and to the Parliamentary Committee of the
T.U.C. A special meeting of the P. & K.T.F. Administrative Council
(July 1907) failed, however, to produce agreement and open warfare
now broke out between the T.A. and the London societies. The T.A.
Executive at once established a branch in London, withdrew from the
reciprocity agreement with the L.S.C., and took vigorous steps to combat the London societies in the extra-metropolitan area. The L.S.C. and
P.M.M.T.S., meanwhile, formed branches in such towns as St. Albans,
Tonbridge, Watford, Letchworth, and Dorking and met the threat of a
T.A. branch in London by a counter-threat of further provincial expansion. The P.M.M.T.S. claimed, in fact, that theirs was a national society
and deleted 'London' from their title, while the L.S.C. changed its name
to 'The London and Provincial Society of Compositors'.

This internecine warfare between the T.A. and the London societies
was obviously harmful to unionism, to the trade, and to the men employed in it. The T.U.C. Parliamentary Committee therefore sought to
re-establish peace, after hearing representatives of the three unions
(August 1907), by recommending 'that the best solution of the difficulty
is the amalgamation of the three Societies into one national Society, so
as to control the whole trade of the country'. They pointed out 'that any
settlement of the question on the basis of a radius would not be permanent', as firms would move farther afield into lower-paid areas, and
that united action was needed to improve conditions in such districts.
They therefore urged the societies to meet together and try to arrange a
settlement on the basis of amalgamation.

As a result, a conference was held on 30 April 1908 between representatives of the T.A., L.S.C., P.M.M.T.S., and also the S.T.A., to consider the question of amalgamation. The principle was unanimously
adopted 'that the societies should amalgamate into one association' and
a constitutional framework was provisionally agreed on. There was to be
'one organisation, comprehending the whole of the United Kingdom',
under the control of a central Executive Council, elected on a representative basis. There was also to be a central fund, 'administered solely by
the Executive Council', and uniform subscriptions and benefits. There

would be 'one branch in each town', each branch to 'control its own local funds and have the administration of its purely local affairs'. Representation at Delegate Meetings was to be 'in proportion to numerical strength, with a maximum to be agreed upon'.

This scheme was approved by large majorities in subsequent ballots of the four societies and also of the London Correctors of the Press. Enthusiasm for the idea of amalgamation rose high. There were, however, serious obstacles in the way of its practical achievement—innumerable differences in rules, benefits and subscriptions, in wages, hours, and working conditions, apprentice regulations, and agreements with employers; ancient customs and prejudices, feelings of local independence, and personal jealousies of officials.

These difficulties were blatant in the ensuing conferences on amalgamation, in March, August, and December 1909 and September 1910. The most serious differences were on the question of 'local autonomy'. The London societies demanded sole control of their own funds and power not only to admit new members, fix entrance fees, deal with members in arrears and those acting contrary to rules—power which the T.A. eventually agreed to admit if 'subject to the endorsement of the Executive Council'—but also to negotiate with employers' organizations on questions of wages, hours, &c., to call strikes and award strike payments, without first consulting the Executive Council. They maintained that local differences in working conditions and trade customs necessitated local independence and that consultation of the Executive would involve delay and cripple their powers of negotiation with employers.

The S.T.A. made similar demands and also asked that Scotland 'be recognised, for purposes of local autonomy, as a branch'. What they and the London societies wanted, in fact, was that 'the various sections of the union . . . shall have full power to carry on all internal work of their individual unions through their own Executive Councils, but in all matters requiring joint action or movement entailing general action and expenditure for the betterment of the trade, such action shall then be subject to the ratification of the National Central Board'.

The T.A. refused to accept such proposals, pointing out that they were contrary to the terms of the provisional agreement—that there was to be a central fund 'administered solely by the Executive Council' and that each branch was merely to 'control its own local funds and have the administration of its purely local affairs'. The Executive could not possibly allow branches power to start strikes and expend money from the general fund without consulting them, but must have 'sole control of

the funds of the union'. The T.A. desired, in fact, genuine amalgamation, while London and Scotland wanted—though they did not say so—
merely federation. On this fundamental difference the scheme for a
'Typographical Union' foundered, though the idea remained alive.

The T.A. was still on good terms with the S.T.A., the reciprocity
agreement of 1900 remaining in force between them, but the questions
of radius and recognition of cards between the T.A. and the London
societies were as far off settlement as ever. The T.A. still maintained
its London branch and the L.S.C. and P.M.M.T.S. their provincial
branches, though neither side made much headway against the other.

Similar differences existed between the T.A. and the Dublin Typographical Society. The latter had on several occasions during the past
fifty years considered amalgamation with the T.A., but each time decided
to remain independent. Dublin occupied, in fact, a position in Ireland
similar to that of London in England and adopted much the same policy.
It also, like London, had an extra-metropolitan area where wages were
low, hours long, female and boy labour plentiful, and where Dublin
firms built branch establishments. Moreover, national feeling was strong
in Dublin. Relations between the T.A. and Dublin were quite friendly,
however, until about 1905. Differences then occurred in regard to 'recognition', Dublin members refusing to lodge their cards or pay local subscriptions when travelling in Ireland and often working in 'unfair'
houses, while similar complaints were made against T.A. members in
Dublin. The Dublin Society was also greatly dissatisfied with conditions
in the branch works of Messrs. Thom & Co. at Maynooth and in 1907
suggested a conference to discuss this and other grievances. It wished
to establish its jurisdiction over an area of at least 20 miles radius from
Dublin. This proposal the T.A. Executive refused to discuss and suggested that the question of amalgamation should be substituted. The
Dublin Society rejected this suggestion, however, and negotiations
therefore broke down.

Relations became even more strained in 1909, when T.A. members
working in Dublin requested the Executive to establish a branch or
chapel there (like that recently established in London) for the protection of their interests and payment of T.A. benefits, a request which was
supported by the first All-Ireland Conference of T.A. branches, held in
Dublin in April 1909. Dublin's answer was the threatened formation of
an 'Irish National Typographical Association'.

This dispute and that between the T.A. and the London societies in
regard to recognition of cards were referred to the annual meeting of the

P. & K.T.F. in 1911, which recommended that representatives of the societies concerned should meet and arrange settlements. The Federation Secretary accordingly convened a conference between representatives of the Dublin Society, the T.A., and S.T.A. (which also had differences with Dublin) in October 1911. This conference, held in Dublin, reached no agreement and the T.A. Executive once more came to the conclusion that the only satisfactory solution was amalgamation, to which, however, the Dublin Society was still opposed.

Conferences convened by the P. & K.T.F. to devise some scheme of reciprocity between the various typographical societies proved more successful. The first, in August 1911, was between representatives of the L.S.C., T.A., and S.T.A., but those following in 1912–13 were also attended by representatives of the P.M.M.T.S., the Dublin Society, and the London Association of Correctors of the Press. The old difficulty of double subscriptions was overcome by the idea of 'associate membership', whereby a member who moved into the area of another society need only pay 2*d*. per week as an 'associate member' (though he could become a full member if he wished), while retaining full membership of his original society, paying his subscriptions and receiving benefits through the 'adopted' society, to whose control he would be subject 'for Trade Union purposes'.

This was a great improvement on the previous reciprocity scheme. It solved the problem of dual membership: a man would no longer have to pay two subscriptions or resign membership of and lose benefits in his old society, while he would, for a nominal sum, acquire membership and be amenable to the authority of the society in whose area he was working.

This scheme was brought into operation between the T.A., S.T.A., and Dublin, but no agreement was reached between the T.A. and the London societies. The latter were willing to abolish their provincial branches if the T.A. would abolish its London branch; but the necessity for the latter still remained, in view of the treatment meted out to T.A. members seeking work there. The London societies, particularly the L.S.C., still maintained a selfish exclusionist policy, refusing to recognize the cards of T.A. members securing or seeking work in London while any of their own members were unemployed. These differences prevented agreement on reciprocity and in June 1914 the T.A. Executive decided to refer the whole matter back to the Parliamentary Committee of the T.U.C. The latter arranged conferences between the T.A. and L.S.C. in 1914–15, but without result.

In 1918, however, negotiations were reopened and in June 1919 agreements were at last effected with both the L.S.C. and P.M.M.T.S. The London radius was to remain at the old figure of 15 miles and the extra-metropolitan branches of the London societies were abolished, the T.A., in return, abolishing its London branch. The P.M.M.T.S. accepted the 1913 reciprocity scheme, with an associate subscription of 3d. per week, but the L.S.C. would not; T.A. and L.S.C. members obtaining or seeking work in the area of the other society must still become full members of that society. 'The signing of the Agreement', the L.S.C. Committee observed, 'will be the means of restoring perfect friendship between the two societies, and will take us one step nearer to amalgamation'.

Meanwhile, however, relations between the T.A. and the Dublin Society had deteriorated. Despite generous T.A. assistance during a strike in 1918, the Dublin Society decided to extend its radius to 35 miles, chiefly on account of the establishment by Messrs. Cahill & Co. of a branch office in Drogheda. It also revived the scheme of an Irish Association and refused to recognize T.A. documents. The T.A. therefore threatened to end reciprocity with Dublin and establish a branch there. Matters drifted along in this unfriendly fashion into the post-war years.

The T.A. had long been closely connected with such old-established societies as the L.S.C., P.M.M.T.S., S.T.A., and Dublin T.S. By the end of the century, however, other unions had been established in the letterpress printing trade—the London Association of Correctors of the Press, the London Platen Machine Minders' Society, and the National Society of Operative Printers' Assistants—with whom the T.A. came into contact.

The T.A. included readers and platen machine minders and thus the question of geographical demarcation arose between it and the London societies concerned, which, like the London Compositors and Machine Managers, tended to extend their jurisdiction over extra-metropolitan towns. Other questions, such as the reciprocal recognition of cards and transfer of members, also arose.

The Secretary of the Platen Machine Minders' Society wrote to the T.A. in June 1908 regarding the position of members who secured work in T.A. branches: 'If it is necessary that they should become members of the T.A., some agreement ought to be made as to their transfer.' The T.A. Executive decided 'that the Platen Minders' Society should be recognised, and its members admitted on the same terms as those of other recognised societies'. Differences soon occurred, however, owing to the fact that members of the Platen Minders' Society working in extra-metropolitan towns would not lodge their cards with T.A. branch secretaries and even formed branches of their own. Eventually, however, in April 1921, a reciprocity agreement was negotiated on the same lines as that with the P.M.M.T.S., with recognition of the 15-mile London radius, reciprocal payment of benefits, and associate membership.

Similar relations existed between the T.A. and the London Association of Correctors of the Press. The T.A. Executive decided in September 1909, after two London readers working in Colchester had applied for admission to the T.A., 'that their credentials should be accepted if clear with their Society, and that the General Secretary should endeavour to make arrangements with the Correctors' Society for the interchange of cards'. An understanding was apparently arrived at, but friction developed in 1918, when the A.C.P. decided to delete 'London' from its title and become a national Association, considering that the organization and interests of provincial readers had been neglected by the T.A., particularly in the Outer London area. It began organizing work and established branches at St. Albans and Tonbridge. The T.A. Delegate Meeting in that same year, however, decided to make the membership of readers compulsory, so that there was danger of the two unions coming into conflict. But joint conferences were arranged in the years 1918–21 as a result of which the A.C.P.—though turning down a T.A. suggestion of amalgamation—accepted an agreement similar to that between the T.A. and L.S.C., including recognition of the 15-mile London radius.

Demarcation problems and the question of transfers frequently arose between the T.A. and the National Society of Operative Printers' Assistants. This society, having organized printing machine (particularly news rotary) labourers or assistants in London, decided in 1903 to become a national union and gradually established branches in the chief provincial cities. The T.A. gave them considerable assistance in the work of organization. It was itself attempting during these years to organize machine minders and the two unions frequently co-operated to good effect. The question of demarcation and transfer of members, however, soon arose. There was as yet no general system of apprenticeship to machine minding, particularly on news rotary machines, and most machine minders were recruited from among the assistants (brake-hands, oilers, wetters, feeders, &c.). Many assistants, on becoming machine minders, retained their membership of the N.S.O.P.A. Assistants, moreover, were often put in charge of machines though not recognized or paid as minders. The T.A. claimed, however, that all machine minders must belong to the Association and that only recognized and properly paid minders should have charge of machines. Similar differences occurred in news reading-rooms, where N.S.O.P.A. members were employed as copyholders.

Conferences between T.A. and N.S.O.P.A. representatives were eventually held in December 1909 and March 1910 to discuss the transference of members, relations between members of the T.A. and N.S.O.P.A. working in the same offices, and demarcation of work. The T.A. urged 'the necessity for the members of the N.S.O.P.A. to become T.A. members on taking charge of news rotary machines and bill and platen machines'. But the N.S.O.P.A. representatives pointed out the serious loss this would cause to their Association and urged that transference should be optional. They also protested against the high entrance fees and long probation for benefits imposed on members joining the T.A. Furthermore, they objected to T.A. flat-bed minders being given charge of rotary machines. They also wanted all rotary minders to be recruited from assistants and were opposed to a system of apprenticeship on news rotary machines, which, as we have seen, was the T.A.'s ultimate aim. Machine apprentices would deprive their members of employment and opportunities of advancement. Their views, as members of a labourers' union, were different in this respect from those of the T.A., a skilled 'craft' organization.

Nevertheless, an agreement was eventually arrived at. It was agreed 'that members of the T.A. and members of the N.S.O.P.A. have equal rights to appointments as news rotary machine minders', and that any N.S.O.P.A. member placed in charge of a rotary machine should be transferred to the T.A., provided that he had been employed as an assistant for at least five years, had been in charge of a machine for a period of three months, and was receiving the minimum rotary rate fixed by the local branch of the T.A. Transferred members were to serve the usual probationary period for T.A. benefits. The same conditions were to apply to N.S.O.P.A. members promoted from copyholder to reader. Provision was made for settlement of disputes at workshop, branch, and national level, and the two unions agreed to co-operate in the work of organization.

Despite this agreement, however, differences still occurred. Many N.S.O.P.A. members objected to being forced to join the T.A. on obtaining charge of a rotary machine or becoming readers, while the question of demarcation still caused dispute: the N.S.O.P.A. was inclined to extend its sphere to include news rotary minders as well as assistants. In April 1912, therefore, N.S.O.P.A. branches declared against the above agreement being ratified and early in 1913 the Society's name was altered from the National Society of Operative Printers' Assistants to the National Society of Operative Printers *and* Assistants.

This change of title the T.A. viewed 'with some concern, if . . . intended as a prelude to an attempt to enrol in the N.S.O.P. & A. men who are eligible to join the T.A.' The Executive therefore requested an explanation of its object, asking if it was the intention of the N.S.O.P. & A. 'to enrol as members compositors, rotary machine minders, platen machine minders, and readers, who are or may be located within the area covered by the T.A.' The N.S.O.P. & A. denied that it had any such intention. It had, however, a number of members in various towns in the T.A. area who had been promoted to rotary machine minders and still retained membership of the N.S.O.P. & A. These members, it urged, should not be coerced into joining the T.A. It suggested that another effort should be made to arrive at agreement on the transfer of members. As a result, further joint conferences were held in August and October 1913 and another agreement was arrived at on much the same lines as the previous one.

This, however, failed to remove friction. Several T.A. branches, especially Manchester, complained of 'encroachment' by N.S.O.P. & A. members. Further conferences were therefore held in 1917–18 and the agreement was modified. It now applied to daily newspaper offices only, the T.A. regarding machine work in weekly newspaper and jobbing offices as its exclusive province. Moreover, only 'when a branch of the T.A. has no unemployed rotary machinemen in its own area' were T.A. flat-bed men and N.S.O.P. & A. members to have 'equal rights to fill vacancies as rotary machinemen' in such offices. Local joint committees were to deal with the promotion of assistants to minders. The T.A. agreed to halve the probation of transferred members. There was little change in the other clauses of the agreement, which, like the previous one, was also to apply to N.S.O.P. & A. copyholders becoming readers. Amalgamation had been suggested by the T.A., the Association to be divided into two sections, craftsmen and assistants, but nothing came of the proposal.

Relations with Allied Trade Societies

Demarcation problems also arose between the T.A. and allied trade societies, such as the Bookbinders, Lithographic Printers, Stereotypers, and Typefounders, particularly in smaller firms, where there was less sub-division and specialization. Relations with the Bookbinders and Lithographic Printers were generally very friendly and occasional differences were easily settled, but the Stereotypers constantly complained of 'twicing' by T.A. members. They strongly protested in 1901 against a proposal put before the T.A. Representative Council to admit stereotypers into the Association and the motion was therefore withdrawn; but T.A. members continued to do stereo-work in spite of protests from the Stereotypers, who therefore placed the matter before the annual meetings of the P. & K.T.F. in 1909 and 1910. The T.A. maintained, however, that 'twicing' or 'overlapping' was inevitable in small offices and that demarcation should not be too rigid—a view supported by the P. & K.T.F. annual conference on both occasions. 'Twicing', therefore, though deprecated in general terms by the Federation, continued. The Stereotypers, however, still wanted 'a line of demarcation' and in January 1914 asked the T.A. for a conference. This was arranged in February and the Stereotypers later submitted proposals for an agreement, but these the T.A. shelved on the ground that 'overlapping' was nowhere serious. Occasional differences continued to occur, though the two unions frequently co-operated.

Disputes between the T.A. and the Typefounders occurred over Monotype casters. When Monotype machines were first introduced the T.A. tried to secure control over the caster as well as the keyboard, on the grounds that it was part of the composing machine, but the F.M.P. refused to recognize exclusive T.A. jurisdiction.[1] Casters were worked not only by compositors, but also by mechanics, typefounders, stereotypers, and labourers, who might belong to any or none of several trade unions. The T.A. therefore abandoned its attempt to control them. When a proposal was introduced at the 1908 Delegate Meeting to admit Monotype-caster attendants, the General Secretary pointed out that the Typefounders' Society claimed control and the proposal was therefore rejected. A similar proposal was brought forward at the next Delegate Meeting in 1913, but the Typefounders protested against this threatened 'encroachment' and it was again rejected. In March 1914, therefore, we find the T.A. Executive recommending caster attendants in Manchester to join the Typefounders' Society. The T.A. still admitted them, however, as did other unions, and it was stated at the 1918 Delegate Meeting that there were now four societies catering for caster attendants—the T.A., Typefounders, N.S.O.P. & A., and the Printing and Paper

[1] See above, pp. 209–10.

Workers. The T.A. therefore decided to launch a campaign to enrol caster attendants and to approach the other unions 'with a view to securing an amicable arrangement for the transfer of these men to our Association'. There was obviously, however, danger of friction.

The Printing and Kindred Trades Federation

Attempts at amalgamation of the various typographical societies in the United Kingdom had failed, but a wider scheme—of federation in the whole of the printing and kindred trades—was to prove successful. The differentiation between London and the provinces was common to all of these—to bookbinders, lithographers, stereotypers, &c., as to letterpress printers—and there was also similar specialization and sub-division in each of the metropolitan trades. By the end of the nine-teenth century there were about twenty societies in the London printing and kindred trades, as compared with seven or eight in the provinces.

The letterpress printers, bookbinders, and lithographers had long established trade societies, but the stereotypers, electrotypers, printers' assistants, and labourers were still to a great extent unorganized, espe-cially in the provinces. Until the nineties they were ignored and looked down on by the aristocratic T.A., but Association policy and outlook then began to broaden. There was a more generous recognition of working-class solidarity: members began to feel that 'it was in har-mony with the new unionism that they should treat one another as brothers' and that skilled workers should assist labourers to organize themselves. In 1893, therefore, we find the Manchester T.S. taking the lead in establishing a Machine and Stereo Hands' Society in that city, including machine assistants, stereotypers, and stereotypers' assistants: members of the Manchester T.S. acted as its officers and its meetings were held in the Society's rooms. Later on the T.A. similarly assisted metropolitan societies to found national unions of such workers by the establishment of provincial branches—the Federated Society of Electro-typers and Stereotypers (1893), the National Amalgamated Society of Printers' Warehousemen and Cutters (1900), and the National Society of Operative Printers' Assistants (1903).

This tendency towards the formation of national unions by amalgama-tion of London and the provinces was also visible among the skilled workers and old-established societies. In 1910 London and provin-cial workers in the bookbinding industry amalgamated to form the National Union of Bookbinders and Machine Rulers, and a similar amal-gamation occurred among Lithographic Printers in 1912. An even more comprehensive organization was formed in 1914, the National Union of Printing and Paper Workers, by amalgamation of two national unions, the Paper Mill Workers and the Printers' Warehousemen and Cutters. Efforts to form a National Typographical Union, however, as we have seen, failed.

The T.A. had always been in closest relation with the corresponding letterpress organizations in London, Scotland, and Dublin, but frequently came into contact with allied societies. Many large firms combined letterpress and lithographic printing, stereotyping, electrotyping, bookbinding, and even typefounding, and the employers in these various branches of the trade were closely associated. It was only natural, therefore, that the various trade societies should federate to further their common interests. In the earliest *Circulars* we read of lithographers and bookbinders being present at social functions of T.A. branches, such as anniversary dinners. The kindred societies in some towns shared the same premises for trade meetings and soon began to co-operate in various trade movements. Towards the end of 1864, for example, a movement was initiated in Sheffield by the Letterpress and Lithographic Printers and Bookbinders, to reduce the hours of labour. Joint conferences were held, a joint memorial was issued, and a joint deputation waited on the employers.

There is, however, no other reported instance of such combined action until the early nineties, when the movement towards local federation became very marked. A letter appeared in the *Circular* of October 1888 from George D. Kelley, General Secretary of the Lithographic Printers, suggesting united action to secure a reduction of the hours of labour in the printing and cognate trades. He pointed out 'that in a large number of places the same power is used to drive the machinery employed in letterpress and litho. printing, bookbinding, &c. It is natural that the hours of each class of workmen should be the same, hence it is important that the question should be taken up by each trade simultaneously.' His advice was followed in a number of different towns. In 1890, for example, a local federation of allied trades in Manchester, including letterpress printers, lithographers, and bookbinders, presented a joint memorial to their employers, asking for a uniform 50-hour week. In 1891 a federation comprising workers in the printing and allied trades of Bradford, Halifax, Huddersfield, and Leeds launched a similar movement, as did a local federation in Rochdale.

These local federations naturally suggested a national organization. The T.A., Lithographic Printers, and Lithographic Artists each had their headquarters in Manchester, the Bookbinders in Bradford. The leading officials knew one another, met on various social occasions, and must have often discussed common problems. In March 1890, therefore, George D. Kelley, General Secretary of the Lithographic Printers, wrote on behalf of his Executive to the various unions, 'proposing a conference of printers and the allied trades, with the view of forming a federation'. The T.A. Executive eventually decided to send a delegate to the proposed conference, but 'without committing the Association to joining the federation'. There was still a strong tendency towards exclusiveness and isolation.

The conference was held in Manchester on 8 September 1890 and was attended by representatives from the following societies:

Typographical Association.
London Society of Compositors.
Scottish Typographical Association.
Leeds Typographical Society.
London Machine Managers' Society.
Amalgamated Society of Lithographic Artists, &c.
Amalgamated Society of Lithographic Printers.
London Society of Lithographic Printers.
Bookbinders' and Machine Rulers' Consolidated Union.
London Consolidated Bookbinders.

Kelley placed before the meeting a number of proposals, which were adopted with little amendment. The objects of the Federation would be 'to combine for trade purposes, and to secure unity of action among the various organisations established by the printing and kindred trades'. It would 'endeavour to obtain, as far as practicable, in each establishment uniform customs and hours of working in the different branches of the trades'. It would assist any affiliated union in 'maintaining its scale of prices and rates of wages, upholding its rules and customs, resisting an aggression on the part of the employers, or endeavouring to improve the social position of those affiliated'. It would 'resist any attack made by an employer upon any branch of the trades in detail, by withdrawing, if necessary, the whole of the workmen employed simultaneously'. Finally, it was proposed 'to recognise as fair employers only those who conform in every particular to the rules and customs of the whole of the several trades in the Federation'.

The Federation would not, however, be an aggressive strike organization or override the independence of the affiliated unions. It would only be 'of a mutual character, with no financial responsibilities attaching to any society, other than the claims of its own members, or the working expenses incurred'. It would 'not interfere in the internal management of any society'. All that was proposed, apparently, was that in the event of a dispute the various unions would refuse to assist the employer(s) concerned, and if the latter tried to introduce non-unionists then a conference of the affiliated unions would be called, with power 'to take what steps may be considered advisable'.

It was decided that the unions should place this scheme before their members as soon as possible, and, if it was accepted, that another meeting should be called to draw up a full code of rules and establish the organization. The T.A. Executive, however, adopted a very lukewarm and dilatory policy. They had not yet taken a vote of the members in December 1890 and required 'further time for consideration of the matter'. They had still not taken a vote when a circular was received announcing another meeting of societies in Manchester on 20 April 1891 and decided that the Association Secretary should attend only 'to watch proceedings'. They were obviously averse to any loss of independence under a federation or to any policy which might encourage strikes.

These objections were to a great extent removed by this second meeting. The Federation, it was stated, would interfere neither in the internal management of any union 'nor with its rules and customs'. It would 'prevent, as far as possible, the occurrence of strikes; and, in the event of disputes arising, encourage the settlement of such disputes by amicable means'. No strike of the Federation would be authorized 'without the consent of the executive committee of each union involved in the dispute being first obtained, and afterwards endorsed by the council of the Federation'. All the previously suggested rules were passed. The organization was to be known as the 'Printing and Kindred Trades Federation'. An annual conference or council of representatives was to be held, which would elect a president, treasurer, and secretary to act as a standing committee or executive.

The T.A. Executive decided to put the scheme before the Delegate Meeting in September 1891 and declined an invitation to another conference of societies in Newcastle that same month. The Delegate Meeting was strongly in favour of federation. A few die-hards thought that the Association ought to keep 'entirely independent of everybody' and were opposed to any 'levelling down to the condition of some of the other trades'; but the majority felt that 'the time has arrived . . . to federate with all kindred trades'. This opinion was confirmed by a subsequent vote of the members.

All the other provincial unions—the S.T.A., Edinburgh Machinemen, Dublin T.S., Litho Artists and Printers, and Bookbinders—came to a similar decision, but the London societies either refused to join or gradually fell away. Differences between London and the provinces were still too strong for a National Federation. The Printing and Kindred Trades Federation, therefore, became a purely provincial organization and the metropolis eventually formed its own Federation.

During the next ten years many T.A. branches co-operated with kindred trade societies to form local federations in Manchester, Bradford, Hyde, Middlesbrough, Belfast, Birmingham, Nottingham, Cardiff, Sheffield, Bolton, and other towns, where combined action was taken to secure reduced working hours. These movements were frequently referred, through the union executives, to the Federation committee, the General Secretaries of the three largest unions, who regularly conferred together, went on joint deputations to meet individual employers, or negotiated with representatives of masters' associations. The committee also took action to resist cheap female labour in Barrow, Dublin, and Glasgow, and launched a not very successful campaign to secure that houses recognized as 'fair' should be so in all departments. They always adopted a conciliatory policy and frequently averted strikes by cautious diplomacy.

There is no doubt that valuable machinery had been created for combined action in trade affairs. But the real powers were still the constituent trade societies. The Federation had practically no funds[1] and was therefore unable to back up its decisions, except through the various executives, which were apt to take an independent line. The Federation committee's powers were mainly consultative and negotiatory. They could arrive at no decisions and take no action without reference back to the individual executives. The various unions still shaped their own trade policies and relied mainly on their own powers to enforce them. Trade differences and mutual recrimination were also apt to hinder federated action. A speaker at the T.A. Delegate Meeting in 1898, therefore, considered that federation existed only 'on paper'.

In 1896 the Lithographic Artists suggested that the Federation should be given 'a financial basis', so that it could render more substantial assistance in any strike. The various executives, including the T.A., disapproved of this particular scheme, but the Federation committee were instructed to formulate alternative proposals. These, providing for the

---

[1] Each union in the Federation was required to pay a minimum affiliation fee of £2 per annum.

institution of levies during a dispute affecting any of the affiliated societies, were laid before the annual meeting in 1897, which referred them
to the various unions. Several societies adopted the new proposals, but
the T.A. Executive drew up another plan, for a 'National Federation of
Printing and Allied Trades'. They pointed out that a levy was meant for
emergencies only and that it would not meet future contingencies. They
therefore advocated 'a continuous subscription' of one penny per member per week, 'in times of tranquillity, as well as in the period of crisis'.
The 'Central Assurance Fund' thereby created would be a powerful
weapon in securing the objects of federation. It would, in particular,
enable a strike benefit of £1 per week to be paid for twenty weeks, to be
supplemented by the society concerned to the extent of 2s. 6d. per week.
In view of 'the great variety of working conditions obtaining in the
various trades' and in order to preserve 'the absolute autonomy of each
society', each union executive would determine the claims of its members to strike benefit. But an affiliated society must seek the advice and
assistance of the Administrative Council before entering on a serious
dispute. This Administrative Council, appointed annually and representative of each affiliated society, would meet 'from time to time, as
occasion requires, to transact the business of the Federation'. A Federation central office and secretary were also suggested. Annual conferences
would still be held and the Federation's objects would remain unchanged.

The proposed scheme would, it was pointed out, create 'no unneces-
sary machinery, the contribution would be at the lowest possible figure,
the entity of every society would be preserved'. It would, in fact, be little
more than 'an assurance association'. But it would be far more effective
than the present Federation, in view of its central fund and strike benefits. It was therefore hoped that all unions in the printing and allied
trades, London and provincial, would join in the scheme and make it
'national'.

These T.A. proposals were adopted by the annual Federation meeting
in 1898. The only important alteration was in the rate of subscription,
which was reduced to a halfpenny. It was decided to submit the scheme
to a vote of the members of the various affiliated societies. During the
following year the T.A., S.T.A., and Lithographic Printers accepted it
and the T.A. Executive drew up detailed rules, which were adopted at
the annual meeting of the Federation in 1899. These rules, together
with the proposed scheme, were submitted to all unions in the printing
and allied trades. The London Federation was urged to amalgamate and
thus form a great national organization.

Results were at first disappointing: by February 1900 only two societies, the T.A. and Lithographic Printers, had definitely accepted the new scheme, which threatened to prove abortive. Circulars were therefore issued pointing out that 'the Federation has not been formed with the object of encouraging disputes with employers, but rather to resist attack, and in case of a dispute arising, to encourage its settlement by amicable means'; and that it would 'in no sense interfere with the internal management of any Union, its main object being the establishment of a central fund for mutual assistance and support'. At the annual Federation meeting, however, in the following September, only one more society, the S.T.A., had decided to affiliate. The London societies were endeavouring to reform their own Federation.

It was therefore decided to postpone operation of the new scheme for another year and, meanwhile, to seek a conference with the London Federation on the question of amalgamation. A conference was duly arranged and held in London on 13 December 1900. It decided in favour of National Federation, but with a reduced subscription of 1s. per member per annum and a reduced strike benefit of 10s. per week, to be supplemented by the society concerned at not less than 5s. per week. These reductions were opposed by T.A. representatives, who contended that they would 'devitalize' their scheme and 'leave it little better than the existing Federation, whose mainspring is moral suasion'. But they considered that 'if the weakening of the financial proposals will result in the adhesion of the London Societies, a compensating advantage will have been secured'.

The new scheme, based on a mixture of the old Federation rules and those propounded by the T.A., was widely adopted: by the end of August 1901 thirteen unions, with a combined membership of 43,000, had decided to affiliate. The National Printing and Kindred Trades Federation was therefore established and at the beginning of 1903 consisted of the following societies:

Typographical Association.
Scottish Typographical Association.
London Society of Compositors.
Amalgamated Society of Pressmen.
Operative Printers' Assistants Society.
Stereotypers' Assistants Society.
Amalgamated Society of Lithographic Artists.
Amalgamated Society of Lithographic Printers.
London Society of Lithographic Printers.
Lithographic Music Printers.

Lithographic Stone and Plate Preparers.
London Consolidated Society of Journeymen Bookbinders.
Bookbinders' and Machine Rulers' Consolidated Union.
Vellum Binders' Society.
London Society of Machine Rulers.
National Amalgamated Society of Printers' Warehousemen and
    Cutters.

The formation of this National Federation among workers in the
printing and kindred trades was made urgent by the establishment in
1900 of the Federation of Master Printers and Allied Trades of the
United Kingdom. It was, in fact, part of the general process of consolidation then taking place in the forces of both capital and labour, part of the
tendency to substitute 'industrial' for 'craft' unionism. The Federation
was still, however, rather a weak and shadowy affair. Each union would
retain 'absolute autonomy'. The Federation would 'not interfere in the
internal management of any Union, nor with its rules and customs'.
Each union executive was to determine the eligibility of its members
for strike benefit: the Federation Secretary would automatically pay
out the money on receipt of a certificate from the union concerned.
According to the rules, an affiliated society was 'to obtain the advice and
assistance of the Administrative Council' of the Federation before entering on 'any dispute of a serious character', but this rule was frequently
ignored and, in any case, strike decisions rested with the individual union
executives. The chief object of the Federation, in fact, in the eyes of
most unions, was 'to establish a central fund for mutual assistance and
support' in strikes.

At first Federation affairs were managed by the Administrative Council, but at the second annual conference it was decided that an Executive
Committee should be established to 'manage the affairs of the Federation in the interim between the Annual and other meetings of the Representative Council'. Moreover, it was decided in 1908 that an affiliated
union must consult the Federation Executive, instead of the Administrative Council, before entering on a serious dispute.

The Federation Executive tried to assert control over all movements
likely to involve large strikes by threatening to withhold financial
support unless they were consulted and given an opportunity of seeking a settlement. Since all unions contributed to the central fund,
no one society should be allowed to endanger it by rash and unadvised
action. Moreover, a strike by one union might involve others. Hence
the need for Federation control.

Opinion was divided as to what powers the Federation Executive should exercise, but most unions were opposed to such control, as it would interfere with their 'autonomy', hamper their actions and involve delays. The T.A. Executive always referred serious disputes to the Federation Executive and frequently sought their advice and assistance in negotiations, but they never surrendered their absolute control over strike decisions, even in Federation movements, when the decisions of each society were supposed to be 'subservient to the majority votes of the whole of the Societies comprised in the Federation'. The T.A. remained, in fact, a perfectly independent body, deciding its own rules and constitution, initiating and conducting its own advance movements, negotiating its own agreements with employers, declaring strikes and awarding strike pay.

Despite, however, these tendencies to union independence and autonomy, the P. & K.T.F. proved an extremely useful and powerful organization. By the end of 1914 twenty-three societies were affiliated, with a total membership of over 82,000. In addition, thirty-seven local federations had been established and in many offices there were 'federated' or 'shop chapels'. Thus the Federation consolidated trade-union forces in the industry. The Federation Secretary and Executive lent valuable assistance in negotiations with employers, frequently preventing strikes by diplomatic means. Any affiliated union involved in a dispute was backed by the Federation's central fund, and members of other societies would lend assistance by confining themselves strictly to their own department and refusing to handle work done by imported non-union labour, or by coming out in sympathy, though a Federation strike could not be authorized 'without the consent of the Executive Committee of each Union being first obtained'. The T.A. was frequently assisted or gave assistance in this way.

A closely related object of the Federation was to secure that 'recognized' firms must be 'fair' in all departments. The various unions undoubtedly co-operated to exclude non-unionists and 'cheap labour' and to secure generally 'fair' conditions, but the ideal aimed at was far from being achieved by 1914. The T.A., for example, never made it a condition of inclusion in its 'Fair List' that firms should be 'fair' in every department, but was prepared to recognize any firm which employed T.A. compositors and machinemen at the standard wage rate.

The Federation was not, however, merely a strike organization. One of its main objects, in fact, was 'to prevent, as far as possible, the occurrence of strikes, and in the event of disputes arising to encourage the settlement of such disputes by amicable means'. On many occasions Federation assistance and advice prevented strikes. The Employers' Federation therefore proposed in 1907 that a conference be held to consider the formation of a permanent Joint Board of Conciliation for the Printing and Kindred Trades, 'to which body all disputes may be referred for settlement or arbitration'. The various unions agreed and the conference was held in May 1908, attended by a representative from each federated society. It adopted a resolution 'in favour of the principle of the formation of a Permanent Conciliation Board' and the appointment of a sub-committee to draft a scheme. The T.A. Executive endorsed this resolution, but stipulated that their representative 'should not consent to the total abolition of the power to strike'. They were not prepared to throw away their chief offensive and defensive weapon or to curtail their own powers in dealing with disputes.

A suggested code of rules was drawn up by the joint sub-committee and approved by the P. & K.T.F. Administrative Council in August 1908. It was agreed 'that a Permanent Conciliation Board be established', consisting of nine representatives of the F.M.P. and nine of the P. & K.T.F., to be elected annually. Its objects would be 'to adjust questions of dispute that may be referred to them with a view to an amicable settlement of the same'. No strike or lock-out was to be permitted 'until the matter in dispute has been referred to the said Conciliation Board'. This clause aroused considerable discussion. Several unions feared that it would deprive them of their freedom of action and the right to strike, but it was explained that, while the rule aimed at securing the friendly settlement of disputes, 'the rights and liberties of Societies to take extreme action, should they deem it necessary, will in no sense be interfered with'. Moreover, only serious disputes would be referred to the Board.

Affiliated unions were asked to take a ballot on this scheme. The T.A. voted in favour by an overwhelming majority, as did most other affiliated unions, and the Conciliation Board was therefore established. During the following years, however, disputes were rarely referred to it: the individual unions, including the T.A., clung to their autonomy and the right to strike, preferring to settle matters sectionally between themselves and the employers rather than by reference to the Board.

The P. & K.T.F. tried to settle disputes between affiliated unions, as well as with employers, to iron out 'demarcation' differences and promote amalgamations or reciprocity agreements. It was not always successful, however—failing, for example, to solve the differences between the T.A. and the London typographical societies.

Another important Federation function was to take action in the general interests of all affiliated unions. Thus it sent several deputations to the Financial Secretary to the Treasury and to the Controller of the Stationery Office, to urge enforcement of the Fair Wages Clause in Government contracts. It also arranged conferences with the Master Printers' Federation in regard to such general grievances as underpaid female labour and time-checking.

The most notable feature, however, of P. & K.T.F. history in this period was its activity, locally and nationally, in wages and hours movements. The T.A. and other unions still acted independently in most advance movements, but many were carried on by local federations, while in 1908–11 the National Federation waged a great campaign for a universal 48-hour working week.

The chief motive of the earliest local federations and of the first National Federation in 1890 was, as we have seen, to secure combined action in movements for reduced hours. Wages might vary in the different sections or trades, but it was only natural that hours should be uniform where all were working in the same establishment. The P. & K.T.F. Annual Meeting in February 1907, therefore, referred the question of a Federation movement for a general 48-hour week to the union executives.

The T.A. Executive strongly supported it. For many years a 48-hour week had been the Association's goal, but, in spite of numerous branch movements, it still seemed as far off as ever. Linotype operators had got it, of course, and a few firms had made it a general concession, but most branches had been unable to get less than 52 hours, while in many places 54 hours, or even more, were still worked. It had become obvious, in view of the united and determined opposition of employers, that 'something more than isolated Branch action is necessary' and that reduced hours could best be obtained either by 'movements embracing large districts' or by 'a movement comprehending . . . the whole of the organisations in the printing and allied trades of the United Kingdom'.

Most other union executives had come to the same conclusion and the P. & K.T.F. Annual Meeting of 1908 therefore decided that each union should ballot its members on the proposal. The result was a large majority in favour and the Annual Meeting of 1909 decided to present a memorial to the F.M.P.

Lengthy negotiations followed during the next two years, the employers resolutely refusing to come below 52 hours and the unions being divided on the question of strike action. The London societies were all for it, but provincial unions had to consider branches where 54 or more hours were worked and areas where organization was weak. The T.A., moreover, was at this same time engaged in important negotiations with the employers in regard to the Association rules and did not wish to wreck the possibility of settlement by rash action on the hours question.

The London societies eventually grew tired of Federation shilly-shallying and came out on strike in January 1911. The provincial unions, however, while lending them financial assistance, refused to be dragged in and further negotiations, assisted by the Board of Trade, prevented a national strike, an agreement being finally reached in March 1911. This brought about the gradual reduction of working hours in provincial offices to a uniform maximum of 51. Furthermore, it provided that subsequent changes in hours should be 'the subject of a National Agreement'.

This Federation movement for reduced hours is extremely interesting as the first step towards negotiation and agreement between the P. & K.T.F. and the employers' national organizations, rather than between the latter and the individual unions, or between union branches and local master printers' associations. This method of industrial bargaining was, of course, peculiarly applicable to working hours. It would be infinitely more difficult to apply it to the complicated and varied regulations governing wages and working conditions in the different unions. Nevertheless, the latter had, for the first time, subordinated their autonomy to a general Federation movement. The T.A., for example, refused to be drawn by the employers into negotiating separately on the hours question during the conferences on T.A. rules in 1909–11.

T.A. loyalty, however, was greatly strained by the system of voting at meetings of the Administrative Council of the Federation. The T.A. was numerically the most powerful of all the affiliated unions, having several times as many members as most others; but voting was 'by show of hands', each society being entitled to one representative, those with more than 5,000 members to another representative for each additional 5,000, but with a maximum of three. This rule obviously favoured the small unions, which could easily outvote the larger ones. It was later altered to give increased representation to the latter, but still greatly dissatisfied the T.A., who repeatedly demanded voting by card on the democratic basis of membership. The small unions, however, maintained that the P. & K.T.F. was 'not a federation of individuals but of societies', each with its own vital interests, and feared that in a card vote they would be swamped by the larger unions. They therefore rejected the principle, but after the T.A. had threatened to secede from the Federation a more liberal representation was agreed upon (February 1914), giving each society one representative; societies with a membership of 2,000, two representatives; 4,000, three representatives; and an additional representative for every 3,000 above that number, up to a maximum of ten for a society with 25,000 or more members.

Whatever system of voting was adopted, however, there was obviously a possibility of an individual union being outvoted and it was doubtful how far such a union would be prepared to acquiesce. The London societies, for example, had ignored a majority vote in taking strike action in the hours movement; while had that vote been in favour of extreme measures it is doubtful whether the T.A. and other provincial unions would have obeyed it.

Nevertheless, the Federation was becoming much stronger and unions were more frequently co-operating. There was even a movement in 1912–16 towards *amalgamation* of all the printing and allied trade unions. The London Federation arranged a conference in May 1912 to consider this question. Representatives attended from most unions in the P. &. K.T.F. and a resolution was passed approving 'the amalgamation of all the trade unions in the printing industry into one union' and recommending the various executives to ballot their members upon it. The T.A. Executive took no action, but agreed to send representatives to a special amalgamation conference in November 1912. They considered that before 'general amalgamation' was attempted efforts should be made to amalgamate different unions in the same section or trade, e.g. letterpress printing; but the conference resolved 'that all societies should amalgamate into one national union' and drew up a skeleton scheme for consideration by the union executives.

This enthusiasm for 'general' or 'industrial' amalgamation, however, gradually fizzled out in face of practical difficulties. Each union jealously guarded its autonomy, had its own particular rules, constitution, customs, and trade problems; some unions were 'craft', others 'non-craft'; some national, others local; while there were constant disputes between them in regard to 'demarcation'. Another amalgamation conference was held in May 1914, but the T.A. and several other unions sent no representatives. A committee was appointed to draft an amalgamation scheme and formulated new proposals for a 'National Union of Printing and Kindred Trades' divided into national and local trade sections, instead of general amalgamation. Further conferences were held to consider these, but it was eventually decided (September 1916) that the time was inopportune to proceed with the scheme.

The T.A. and General Trade Unionism

We have already seen how, in the first half of the nineteenth century, journeymen printers were tending towards solidarity with other sections of the working class and how the old craft gild exclusiveness was breaking down. This tendency was accentuated in the second half of the century as the industry expanded and became mechanized, as the printing 'profession' became a 'trade' and the printing 'office' or 'house' became a 'works', as 'the levelling influences of a common education and the pressure of applicants for employment tended to make the worker in the printing factory somewhere on a par with other people'.[1] Printers realized that many of their problems and grievances were common to all sections of the working class and that they could best be solved by united Labour action. Naturally, interest still centred mainly in the narrow concerns of the printing trade, but there was a gradual broadening of outlook. Printers came to participate actively in the affairs of Trades Councils and Trades Union Congress and to think seriously of Trades' Federation.

Throughout the period 1830–50 typographical societies had rendered frequent financial assistance to other trades during strikes and lock-outs or in periods of distress. This policy was continued and extended during the second half of the century. Individual societies made frequent grants and often entered into special voluntary subscriptions to assist their 'brethren' in other trades. The Executive frequently recommended certain cases to the 'favourable consideration' of the branches. They could not at first make grants to societies outside the Association, but in 1872 were permitted to grant money 'for the propagation of union principles'. Apart, however, from a £15 grant to the locked-out agricultural labourers in 1874, they continued for some years their previous policy of inserting all appeals in the *Circular* and recommending them to the branches; but from 1877 onwards their minute-books record a continual stream of grants to aid other unions in strikes or lock-outs, in addition to the much larger amount given by individual societies and offices. Between 1877 and 1897 the Association made well over a hundred such grants, totalling nearly £3,280, to engineers, builders, miners, textile workers, dockers—in fact, to any and every union which appealed for help. The grants were usually small, of £5 or £10, but in 1893 the

[1] *Typographical Circular*, Aug. 1902.

Executive gave £250 to assist the miners on strike against reduced wages, and in 1897, during the great lock-out in the engineering trades, a special levy was imposed and £2,235 was subscribed to assist the various unions involved, while a loan of £5,000 was granted to the Amalgamated Society of Engineers.

This financial assistance was reciprocated by other unions during printers' strikes. Typographical societies, moreover, frequently appealed to other trades to boycott 'unfair' newspaper and jobbing offices.[1] Realizing the advantages of such co-operation, they were often prominent in the establishment of Trades Councils, whose assistance they could seek in disputes. Trades Council deputations often met employers and tried to secure settlements; if these failed, they would assist in 'exposing' the offending proprietors by public meetings, hand-bills, and posters. Similarly, it was by agitation and political action through the Trades Councils that T.A. branches sought to enforce the 'fair contracts' clause on public bodies.[2]

It was from these local Trades Councils that the Trades Union Congress sprang in 1868, journeymen printers pioneering its establishment. William Dronfield, secretary of the Sheffield Typographical Society and also of the Sheffield Association of Organized Trades from its establishment in 1858, was the originator of the idea. He had for some time played a prominent part in general trade-union affairs and in 1866 he wrote out and issued the address calling together the 'Conference of Trades' Delegates of the United Kingdom', held in Sheffield in July, which, as he later pointed out, 'laid the foundation of the annual trades union congresses'.[3]

Dronfield had previously, in October 1865, read a paper in defence of trade societies before the annual congress in Sheffield of the Social Science Association.[4] His paper was omitted, however, from the official report, a great portion of which was devoted to arguments by other speakers against trade unions. This one-sided attitude was strongly denounced by Dronfield, who came to the conclusion that the working class must rely on their own efforts to secure justice. It was for this reason that he summoned the national conference of trade unionists in Sheffield in 1866, to consider such important questions as strikes and lock-outs, the establishment of courts of conciliation and arbitration, and reform of the law of master and servant.

---

[1] See above, p. 148.   [2] See below, p. 305.
[3] T.A. Delegate Meeting Report, 1877. See also the *Report of the Conference of Trades' Delegates*, Sheffield, July 1866.
[4] This was the time of the notorious 'Sheffield outrages'.

Dronfield's experience with the Social Science Congress prompted Samuel Nicholson, treasurer of the Manchester Typographical Society and president of the local Trades Council, to ask, 'Why not have a Congress of our own'? The idea was taken up by William Wood, secretary of the Manchester T.S. and of the Trades Council, and by other colleagues, with the result that in April 1868 the Manchester and Salford Trades Council summoned the first Trades Union Congress.

It is obvious that some journeymen printers were extremely active at this time—were, in fact, leaders—in the general Labour movement, with wide interests in all political and social questions affecting the working class. The Typographical Association itself, however, still retained much of its insularity. It had, somewhat reluctantly, appointed a delegate to attend the Sheffield Trades' Conference in 1866, but instructed him 'not to pledge the Association's adhesion to any plan that may be proposed'. This conference resulted in the establishment of the 'United Kingdom Alliance of Organised Trades' in 1867, a general federation of trade unions, whose council had power to impose a levy in support of any society locked out by their employers. William Dronfield was secretary of the Alliance until 1871. The T.A. Executive Council, however, did 'not feel themselves authorised to pledge the Association joining the proposed Trades' Alliance' and declined to send delegates to the ensuing conferences.[1] Similarly, when they received the circular from the Manchester and Salford Trades' Council in 1868, summoning the first Trades Union Congress, they decided that, while 'approving the objects contemplated at the proposed Congress', they were 'not invested with the power of incurring expense for such purposes'.

In November 1871, however, when trade-union agitation against the new Criminal Law Amendment Act was waxing furious, they decided that the Association Secretary should attend the Congress at Nottingham in January 1872. The question of representation at Trades Union Congresses was discussed by the 1872 Delegate Meeting. The Association President 'questioned whether we acted wisely in systematically keeping ourselves aloof from trade gatherings' and suggested that it was 'desirable to mix a little more with the other trades of the country'. Others pointed out that 'such congresses were convened for the common weal of the trades at large', that 'one branch of trade was intimately connected with another', and that the Association should therefore be represented. The chief objection was that Congress occupied itself too much with political questions, from which the Association should steer clear. It was

[1] Other unions held similar views and the 'Alliance' collapsed in 1871.

decided, however, that the Executive might send representatives in future.

Henceforward, T.A. delegates attended every Congress and the Association made small annual grants towards the expenses of the Parliamentary Committee.[1] Henry Slatter, the Association Secretary, was made a member of the Parliamentary Committee in 1877, to which he was annually re-elected until 1890, when he voluntarily resigned, after being treasurer for four years.

The Association was thus brought more closely into touch with the general political and social aspirations of the working class. But the T.U.C., mainly a political body, did practically nothing to overcome the narrow sectionalism characteristic of trade unions at that time. The T.A., like other unions, was still mainly concerned with its own problems of wage rates, hours, apprentices, and friendly benefits. Its attitude towards federation remained, throughout the century, the same as in 1834 and 1846; that inherent differences between trade and trade—in regard to wage rates, working conditions, apprentices, and strike policy—made general federation impracticable.

At the same time, however, the *idea* of federation was often applauded. When, for example, it was revived at the Trades Union Congresses of 1873–5, in answer to the recently established 'National Federation of Associated Employers of Labour', and a scheme for a 'Federation of Organised Trades' was drawn up by the Parliamentary Committee in 1875, the Association Secretary supported the idea, considering that working men should 'meet the combinations of capitalists by a more extensive and complete organisation of labour', and deplored 'the barriers of prejudice and ignorance' which too often divided them in their different trade societies. He was appointed by the Executive to attend the Federation Conference prior to the Trades Union Congress at Glasgow in October 1875, and was there elected treasurer of a provisional Federation committee. But the T.A. Executive, 'while sympathising with the objects of the proposed Federation', felt 'that it would be difficult for the P.T.A. to comply with the rules agreed upon for its government'—chiefly because they envisaged large-scale strikes—and therefore decided against joining. Other unions were similarly opposed to the scheme, which therefore fell through after an abortive meeting at Birmingham in May 1876.

The idea was raised again in 1879, prior to the Edinburgh Congress,

[1] The T.A. later began to send representatives to the annual conferences of the Irish T.U.C., to which it also paid a small affiliation fee.

but was once more rejected by the T.A. Executive, who were 'unable to see the practicability of any effective system of federating trade unions'. The *Circular*, while sympathizing with the 'fundamental idea' of general trades' federation, pointed out the conflicting interests, rules, and peculiar technical questions which prevented its practical achievement. What *was* feasible was federation or amalgamation of kindred societies. 'Each trade should endeavour to form among its own members a strong and healthy combination; and then by affiliation with Trades Councils in the various localities, and by representatives at the Trades Union Congresses, lend such help as it can to the common cause of unionism.' Until printers were 'much more united among themselves' it would be useless for them to join in general federation. When, therefore, the federation scheme adopted at Edinburgh was laid before the Executive, they 'unanimously agreed to decline participation in it'. It found little support in other trades and had therefore to be abandoned. Apart from the annual Trades Union Congresses, Trades Councils, and mutual assistance in strikes, sectionalism remained the dominant characteristic of trade unionism.

The wave of 'New Unionist' enthusiasm, which swept over the trade-union world in the late eighties, however, revived ideas of working-class solidarity. In 1890 the Federation of Printing and Kindred Trades was established. But printers still regarded general federation as impracticable. At the Delegate Meeting in 1891 Herbert Skinner 'feared the federation of all trades was somewhat remote, but the federation of kindred trades was both desirable and practicable'.

In the later nineties, however, the idea of general federation became increasingly popular, particularly after the great engineering lock-out and the Welsh coal strike in 1897–8. Great capitalist employers had combined to defeat even the most powerful of trade unions in what were described as 'national struggles'. National Trades Federation was therefore felt to be an absolute necessity and at the Birmingham Trades Union Congress in 1897 a special committee was appointed to formulate a suitable scheme. In addition to this, the 'official scheme', a number of others were propounded and federation became the great question of the day among all trade unionists.

It aroused considerable interest and enthusiasm among journeymen printers. The 1897 R.C. meeting considered 'that the time has arrived for the adoption of a scheme of federation for all organised workers in the United Kingdom', and many branches passed similar resolutions. The Executive therefore appointed a special committee in 1898 'to consider and report on the subject of Trades Federation'. This committee examined the various schemes of federation which had been put forward, but found them all unsuited to the printing trade, a view strongly supported by the Executive at the Delegate Meeting in 1898. They pointed out that while 'National Federation was the ideal' and was 'perfect theoretically', it was 'unworkable in practice'. The printing trade had experienced no such huge conflicts as the various federation schemes envisaged and would encourage; most of their strike payments were to victimized individuals, for whom no provision was made. The 'strike risks' in such industries as engineering and coal-mining were much higher than in the printing trade, so that the T.A. would have to pay out far more than it received—to a fund over which it would have practically no control. Members would refuse to pay the high contribution proposed—6*d.* per week—in addition to the T.A. subscription. Moreover, the Association must preserve its autonomy and not become lost in a great federation of miscellaneous trades, many of which would have no sympathy with certain fundamental T.A. rules. A federation, in fact, containing so many conflicting, even hostile, interests was quite impossible. The E.C. therefore 'reluctantly abandoned the idea in favour of a Federation of Kindred Trades', which might prove 'a stepping-stone to that greater union of the forces of Labour'.

These views, however, were opposed by most of the delegates, who strongly preferred general federation to the limited 'piece-meal federation' of kindred trades. They wanted 'one mighty, gigantic federation of labour' to face the combinations of capitalists, pointing out that 'when one trade was attacked, be it great or small, success or disaster in the struggle had a corresponding effect upon other trades'. The meeting, therefore, 'while agreeing with the federation of kindred trades as a secondary method', pledged itself to a 'National Federation of all Trades'.

The Executive accordingly sent a representative to the special Trades Union Congress on National Federation held in Manchester in January 1899, which adopted the 'official scheme'. But they still retained their former views and managed to carry them in a vote of the members in May 1899. The T.A. did not, therefore, join the newly founded 'General Federation of Trade Unions', but concentrated on the establishment of an effective Printing and Kindred Trades Federation.

The T.A. and International Trade Unionism

The gradual broadening of the T.A.'s outlook during the second half of the nineteenth century extended to international trade-union relations.

Most interest, of course, was taken in the doings of typographical societies abroad. As early as the forties and fifties communications had been
received from printers' unions in America, Canada, Australia, and
France, and the trade periodicals of this period had contained accounts of wages, hours, and working conditions in some of these countries. The letters came mostly from journeymen who had emigrated to
the colonies or the U.S.A. and were at first printed chiefly to encourage
further emigration from the overburdened labour market in the United
Kingdom. But the tone of these letters and Association policy changed
in the later fifties. Emigration schemes had proved a failure, while
colonial and American printers were opposed to an influx from outside
which threatened their wage rates. Their letters painted a picture of
strikes and wage reductions, high cost of living and housing difficulties.
The T.A. therefore began to discourage rather than encourage emigration and frequently printed warning notices in the *Circular*.

Assurances of support were also given by the T.A. to their 'brethren'
overseas. There was general agreement 'that union men should stand
loyally by each other whether at home or abroad' and that 'in cases of
dispute . . . it was their duty to give every support to their fellow trade
unionists' and to prevent emigration at the instigation of employers
which would damage kindred associations.[1] Frequent descriptions
of trade affairs in America and the colonies were given in the *Circular*
and there was a regular interchange of trade-union periodicals. Henry
Slatter considered that it was the duty of printers 'to recognise and
approve every effort which has for its object the improvement of the
status of the members of the craft, whether in Europe, America, or
Australia'.

When composing machines were being rapidly introduced into this
country from America during the early nineties, the T.A. Executive got
into touch with the International Typographical Union (U.S.A. and
Canada) as to working conditions 'over there'. There were frequent
comparisons in the following years of British and American methods,
working conditions, and trade-union action. In 1896 a representative of
the New York Typographical Union attended the British T.U.C. and
afterwards a meeting of the T.A. Executive Council, giving a summary
of the trade position in America and dealing especially with the working
of Linotypes. The T.A. accepted an invitation in 1902 to be represented
on the Mosely Industrial Commission to the United States, which was to

[1] Report of Reciprocity Conference, Manchester, Sept. 1899. (The representatives were discussing emigration to South Africa.)

study American methods of manufacture, but the General Secretary was eventually unable to go owing to ill health. The L.S.C. secretary went, however, as representative of the British printing trade and his report was given at length in the T.A. *Circular*. Herbert Skinner and G. H. Roberts attended the Annual Convention of the American Federation of Labour as representatives of the British T.U.C. in 1908 and 1911 respectively, when they met prominent members of the I.T.U. and learnt a good deal about conditions in the printing trade in America and Canada.

Friendly relations also existed between the T.A. and continental societies, but it was not until the nineties that much interest was taken in foreign typographical affairs. There seems to have been reciprocal 'recognition' and relief of cards between the T.A. and several continental unions, but the T.A. refused to give financial assistance during strikes or to arrange a mutual interchange of benefits, as suggested by the Paris Society in 1882.

The French *Fédération des Travailleurs du Livre* was represented at the Conference of Typographical Societies held in London in 1886. The ideas of international brotherhood and 'Universal Federation' of typographical societies were here applauded, but seem to have aroused little interest among T.A. members. When the T.A. was invited to send representatives to the first International Typographical Congress, held in Paris in July 1889, the Executive, 'while expressing sympathy with the objects of the Congress, did not think it necessary to be represented'.

During the nineties, however, under the stimulating influence of 'New Unionism', the T.A. somewhat broadened its outlook. In 1891 and 1896 it made grants of £10 in aid of printers' strikes in Germany and in 1898 sent £20 to the Antwerp Typographical Society. The Representative Council even passed a resolution in 1894 approving of 'the formation of an International Federation of Typographical Associations', but only 'for the purpose of preventing the execution of British bookwork and general printing in foreign offices by means of underpaid and unrecognised labour'. The aim was, in fact, not international brotherhood, but the prevention of 'unfair' foreign competition. It was thought that this could be achieved partly by raising the wages and social condition of workers abroad.

The T.A. took no practical steps, however, to bring about international federation and when an 'International Printers' Secretariat' was established at Berne in 1892, as a result of the Paris conference in 1889 —to provide mutual assistance in strikes and promote international typographical knowledge and co-operation—the T.A. did not become affiliated. It not only declined to join, but refused even to be represented at the International Congresses in 1896 (Geneva), 1901 (Lucerne), and 1907 (Paris). It continued, however, to assist continental printers in strikes, granting £10 to the French Printers' Federation in 1906 and £20 to the Italian Typographical Federation in 1908. Numerous articles, moreover, appeared in the *Circular* about conditions, wages movements, &c., among continental printers. The T.A. was undoubtedly influenced by 'the growing tendency towards the linking up internationally of the trade union movement'.[1] In 1912, therefore, the Executive accepted an invitation to be represented at the sixth International Typographical Congress, held in Stuttgart, and was considering the question of affiliation to the Secretariat when war broke out.

The 'New Unionist' sense of working-class solidarity produced a further widening of the T.A.'s mental horizon—a more general, though slight, realization of the common interests of all workers in all countries. There is no evidence that the T.A., or T.A. members, played any part in the Marxist 'International Association of Working Men', established in London in 1864 with the object of uniting the world's workers for the emancipation of labour from capitalism, or that they attended any of its annual congresses. The Association also held aloof from the later International Trades Union Congresses. When, for example, a circular was received in 1879 from the London Trades Council with regard to such a Congress, the Association Secretary was instructed 'to express sympathy with the object aimed at, without committing the E.C. to any action in the matter'. Similarly, when a circular was received in 1883 announcing an International Trades Union Congress to be held in Paris, 'no action was taken respecting it'. The next International Congress in 1886 was not even mentioned.

In 1888, however, the Association Secretary was deputed to attend the International Congress held in London and in 1896 T.A. members voted in favour of an International Trades Union Congress to be held the following year and of the Association sending delegates. There is no further reference to this proposed Congress, but the T.A. began at this time to render some slight assistance to continental workers during strikes. The first such grant to a non-typographical continental union was made in 1896—£5 to the dockers on strike at Hamburg. In 1899 the E.C. granted £10 to textile workers on strike in Austria and £20 to trade unionists locked out in Denmark; in 1900 £5 to the lace-makers of

[1] *Typographical Circular*, Nov. 1910.

Calais, resisting an attempt to enforce a 12-hour day; and in 1902 £5 to the diamond workers of Amsterdam, locked out for refusing to work with non-unionists. Several similar grants were made in the following years. In 1908 and 1911, moreover, as we have seen, Herbert Skinner and George Roberts attended the Annual Convention of the American Federation of Labour, as representatives of the British T.U.C. Roberts also visited continental countries on several occasions as a British Labour representative and articles on general working conditions in Europe began to appear in the *Circular*. There was an obvious broadening of outlook and interest, but the T.A. did not become affiliated to the International Trades Union Federation.

XIII

FRIENDLY BENEFITS

FRIENDLY benefits have always been a feature of trade unionism in the printing industry. Many T.A. branches originated as friendly or 'relief societies', providing for sickness and death and relieving tramps, but making little if any attempt to regulate trade conditions. Others, though 'trade societies' from the start, usually had friendly benefits as well.

The provincial unions—the Northern and P.T.A.—were mainly concerned with trade affairs. They merely gave added financial strength to resist unscrupulous employers and to support strikes. Tramp relief, their sole friendly benefit, was still left for the most part to regulation by local societies. The N.T.A. had tried to establish weekly out-of-work payments, but had collapsed in the trade depression of 1846-7, and tramp relief was restored under the P.T.A. in 1849.

In 1863 tramp relief was put on an Association basis by the establishment of the 'mileage system'. But a clear distinction was made between this friendly society element and the trade union by the creation of a separate Relief Association.

Meanwhile, a number of other trade unions, the engineers in particular, had established friendly benefits—unemployment, sick, superannuation, and funeral—on a national scale and printers began to feel that they 'should not be behindhand with other working men in that respect'.[1] A number of proposals for a general provident fund in the fifties and sixties culminated in a scheme put forward by the Rochdale branch in 1870, for an Association Sick, Burial, Out-of-Work, and Superannuation Fund. Other societies followed with similar proposals, which were discussed, together with the Rochdale scheme, at the 1872 Delegate Meeting. A general provident fund, it was urged, would 'make the Association worth belonging to'; it would unite branches more firmly to the Association and preserve the loyalty of members; it would bring in non-unionists and independent societies; it would prove to employers that the Association was not merely a strike organization; it would provide benefits which small local societies could not and make them 'general instead of local as hitherto', so that a member would not lose benefit by removing from one town to another. The main problem was that of cost.

[1] 1872 D.M. Report.

The Rochdale scheme—a 'wholesale introduction of what may be called the provident or friendly society element'—proved rather too large an order for the Delegate Meeting, which established out-of-work and funeral benefits only. During the next five years, however, more proposals were made for the establishment of superannuation and sick funds and the Delegate Meeting of 1877 decided in favour of the former. A sick fund was rejected on grounds of expense and possibility of abuse. Later proposals for a sick fund met with a similar fate.

The Relief Association was merged into the T.A. in 1877, so that the distinction between the trade and friendly elements became less clearly pronounced. A separate Superannuation Fund was established (contributions to which, however, were compulsory on all T.A. members), but travelling, out-of-work, and funeral payments came out of the General Fund.

Judged in the light of expenditure alone, friendly benefits tended in the following years to overshadow trade action, strike payments forming a relatively unimportant item. Such a judgement, however, would be decidedly misleading. The minute-books of the Executive Council show that trade questions—wages, hours, apprentices, composing machines, victimization, strikes, and so on—occupied far more attention than anything else. Important as were the payments on account of unemployed, superannuated, or dead members, most journeymen printers were far more vitally interested in wages and working conditions. Strike payments, moreover, form an inaccurate index of the ceaseless action by branches and Executive in trade matters: in the majority of cases settlement was arrived at by conciliatory means, without resort to extreme measures, and strikes, when they did occur, were usually small affairs.

Nevertheless, friendly benefits were of immense importance in these years, when the only alternative to starvation or poor-law relief was thrifty 'self-help'. Out-of-work payments were particularly important, for the problem of unemployment, the greatest with which the Association had to deal, was closely related to trade questions, to the regulation of wages and hours and the limitation of apprentices.

Payment of these friendly benefits imposed an immense burden on trade-union funds, though the allowances were miserably inadequate. Neither the State nor employers (with a few honourable exceptions) gave any assistance. Workers were apt to be regarded as mere units or tools, to be scrapped when worn-out, inefficient, or surplus. All obligations were discharged by the payment of wages. Economic writings encouraged this tendency to regard 'labour' as a mere 'factor of production', not as human beings and citizens.

By the end of this period, however, trade unions had come to realize that the burden of supporting their out-of-work, sick, and aged members was too great for them to bear and were claiming that the State should shoulder what was essentially a social responsibility. The first-fruits of these Socialist ideas and of the resultant political action by organized Labour were old-age pensions (1908) and the National Insurance Act (1911), with its scheme of sickness and unemployment benefits.

Unemployment Relief

Tramp relief had been abolished at the establishment of the N.T.A. in 1844 and replaced by weekly out-of-work payments, but the new system soon broke down under the burden of industrial depression and mass unemployment in 1846–7, and as the N.T.A. disintegrated tramps were reported in increasing numbers, roaming the country haphazardly, seeking relief on a variety of membership cards, indentures, notes, and forged documents. Soon, however, local societies revived and began to communicate with each other, issuing circulars offering reciprocal 'recognition' or 'honouring' of cards, 'with a view of establishing a mutual system of relief'.[1]

As tramping helped to forge the bonds of the Northern Union in 1830, so it played an important part in the establishment of the Provincial Typographical Association in 1849. The Liverpool Society, in its circular convening the inaugural meeting of 4 June, stressed the necessity for 'the establishment of some uniform system of relief, subject to central control', and tramping was one of the most important questions discussed at Sheffield.[2] Opinion among the delegates was divided: some wanted to reorganize the tramp-relief system, others to abolish it and substitute an emigration fund. All the old ground was gone over, all the old arguments for and against tramping reproduced, and it was eventually decided to submit the opposing propositions to a vote of the members. The result was a large majority in favour of maintaining tramp relief.[3]

The P.T.A. tramp rules were practically the same as those of the old Northern Union, relief being left almost entirely to local regulation and

[1] *Typographical Protection Circular*, Jan. 1849.
[2] *Address of the Delegates*, Sheffield, June 1849.
[3] See below, pp. 281–4, however, for the various emigration funds subsequently established.

varying, therefore, from town to town. The complaints against tramping, so frequent before 1844, were soon repeated. Tramps were denounced as idle, drunken, demoralized scoundrels, habitual 'roadsters', refusing to work, abusing society officers, forging cards, and often 'ratting'. It was chiefly to check these evils that the Executive decided in 1852 to issue a *Monthly Circular*, which was intended to provide a complete register of all cards issued, lodged, or renewed, and to publicize cases of forgery and other misconduct. For such offences and also for neglect of work, societies began to fine tramps, to refuse them relief, confiscate their cards, and even expel them, while in a few cases legal proceedings were taken against them.

Tramp relief figured prominently in the discussions at successive Delegate Meetings. The 1853 Meeting was 'anxious to see tramping of much less frequent occurrence, or, indeed, altogether abolished', but regarded it as 'a necessary evil' in the present state of the trade. Attention was called to the low rate of relief in most towns, which was insufficient to support a man or prevent him from 'ratting', and societies were urged to raise their relief and also to make provision for Sundays. A few did subsequently raise their payments, while the 'Sunday allowance', usually a shilling, became fairly general.

At the 1856 Delegate Meeting the abolition of tramping was proposed in favour of weekly relief to the unemployed, but was rejected, mainly on the grounds of expense. The insufficiency of tramp relief, however, was again pointed out: it averaged, apparently, little more than 9*d.* per day, and 'with such a miserable pittance as this a man could not support life'. Relief paid in small towns was quite inadequate, but societies there were bearing a proportionately heavier burden than large ones: in some nearly the whole of the members' subscriptions was expended on tramp relief. It was an old complaint and an old remedy was resorted to—reimbursement of small branches out of the Association funds, so that they might be able to raise their relief rates.

These reforms failed, however, to bring about much improvement and the next Delegate Meeting, in 1861, therefore decided to abolish the existing method of relief and replace it by the 'mileage system'. A detailed scheme was drawn up after the meeting and brought into operation at the beginning of 1863.

As one of the aims of the new scheme was 'to impart increased respectability to the profession', the old tramping system now became the 'Association for the Relief of Unemployed Travelling Printers', or, more briefly, the 'Relief Association'. All recognized typographical societies were invited to join. The new Association would be distinct from the P.T.A., so that they could become branches of the former without joining the latter. Both Associations, however, would be managed by the same Executive and officers.

Under the new system the 'travelling unemployed' were to be paid a penny per mile walked, up to maximum of 120 per week, making a total 'mileage' payment of 10s. Societies were also to provide suitable sleeping accommodation, or pay 6d. per night 'bed-money', and the by now customary 'Sunday shilling'. As previously, travellers would be relieved only once a year in each town.

A general Travelling Fund was to be formed, the subscription to which was to be a penny per member per week and out of which half-yearly reimbursements would be made to those branches which paid more than their due.

Thus the new scheme provided a more liberal, equitable, and systematic mode of relief in place of varying local payments. Moreover, it was hoped that it would encourage travellers to look for work in more remote districts, instead of 'trunk travelling' as rapidly as possible between society towns.

A man had to be a branch member for at least six months before being entitled to 'travelling document', which would last a year but might be renewed by the issuing society.

The aim of the P.T.A. Executive was 'to form the profession throughout the United Kingdom into one Association for the Relief of Unemployed Travelling Printers'. All English provincial societies save Leeds and Norwich joined, but London and Scotland held aloof, despite all appeals, and so, too, did Dublin. These 'non-conforming' societies, however, continued to relieve tramps in the old way and R.A. branches reciprocated by relieving their cards at a halfpenny per mile.

The Relief Association was undoubtedly an improvement on the old system, but it could not alter human nature. The new 'travelling printers' proved no better than the old 'tramps'. They adopted all sorts of subterfuges to secure large mileage claims, made false statements as to routes taken, cunningly arranged their itinerary so as to maximize their relief payments, altered entries, forged documents, got drunk, neglected work, and went into 'unfair' houses as frequently as of old. These offences were punished by fines, reduced relief, and suspension from benefit, but with little apparent improvement.

Rogues and vagabonds, however, were in a minority. Most men tramped the country unobtrusively, looking for work, which the R.A.

helped them to find. Travelling relief, despite its hardships and abuses, played an invaluable part in the periodic depressions and unemployment of these years. Except in the largest branches, it was the only alternative to the parish dole or workhouse.

The depression of the early sixties imposed a tremendous strain on the new Association. In 1863 nearly a third of the members were reported to be casuals or unemployed and hundreds tramped the roads vainly looking for work. The Association, moreover, had been established on a liberal scale of relief, without any reserve fund and with an inadequate subscription. Expenditure far exceeded income and the scheme would have foundered in the first half-year but for an advance of £430 from the P.T.A.

The R.A. subscription, therefore, had to be increased by a halfpenny, to 1½d. per week, while expenditure was reduced by abolition of 'bed-money' and an attempt was made, by a form of 'labour direction', to prevent fraudulent mileage claims, branch secretaries being instructed to write in each traveller's document the name of the town which he must next visit.

These reforms and a trade revival temporarily saved the situation. Deficits were changed to surpluses and the R.A. was able to pay back some of the money borrowed from the P.T.A. Hopes were even entertained of returning to the penny subscription. But depression came again in 1867, travellers multiplied, and there were more deficits, so the subscription had to be raised to 2d. Trade soon revived, however, and with the resultant surpluses the R.A. eventually paid off its debts to the parent Association. In 1870 it had a balance to its credit. Short-sighted policy therefore reduced the subscription to 1½d. again. All went well, however, while trade remained good.

Meanwhile, travellers had been subjected to further discipline. A 'route system' had been established, complete with maps marked with mileages, while the Executive had acquired control over the issue and renewal of all documents. To check 'the habit of perpetual tramping' without any effort to find work, the E.C. could refuse renewals or reduce them to half mileage, a punishment which was also inflicted on travellers guilty of neglecting or refusing work, while repeated offences were punished by suspension from benefit or even expulsion.

By this time, however, with cheap postage, advertising, and railways, tramp relief was obviously becoming out of date. It had for many years been attacked as useless and degrading and its replacement by weekly payments to the stationary unemployed had often been advocated. The experience of the N.T.A. in 1846–7 and chronic financial weakness had so far deterred the P.T.A. from adopting such a system, but the 1872 Delegate Meeting decided to do so. Tramp relief was still continued, however, so that the unemployed now had the alternatives of weekly out-of-work payments in their own towns or travelling relief.

Under the new scheme, out-of-work members would be paid 8s. per week for six weeks in each quarter, to meet which expenditure $1\frac{1}{2}d.$ would be added to the weekly subscriptions. There was such strong opposition, however, to this suggested increase that the E.C. decided to pay out-of-work benefits from the R.A. Fund without raising subscriptions—though the R.A. had been unable, in years of trade depression, to meet mileage payments alone. It is obvious what would happen in the event of another slump.

The Executive drew up various regulations to safeguard the Fund. Benefit would be paid only to those with at least a year's membership and clear with their subscriptions. Claimants must sign the 'call-book' or report to the branch secretary every morning and must be ready to take any work offered, while the Association Secretary could 'direct the removal' of out-of-work members to any branch where men were wanted. Anyone failing to sign the call-book or refusing to accept work would thereby lose benefit. It was also enacted later on that members who lost their employment 'through their own negligence or misconduct' would be debarred from benefit for a certain period.

The short-sightedness of policy in establishing out-of-work benefits without increasing subscriptions was quickly revealed in the depressed years after 1873. The R.A. was soon in serious financial straits and had to borrow from the P.T.A. again. The E.C. decided, however, to leave matters to the 1877 Delegate Meeting.

At this meeting they recommended not only that subscriptions should be increased, but also that the R.A. should be abolished as a separate organization and that out-of-work and mileage payments should be made out of the General Fund. As a corollary to this, they proposed that the operations of the P.T.A. should be extended to Ireland, so that the present R.A. branches there might be admitted. Their object in making these proposals was to abolish mere 'relief societies', which did little to regulate trade affairs and thereby (by failing, for example, to limit the number of apprentices) aggravated the unemployment problem.

These latter proposals were accepted by the Delegate Meeting. The R.A. was abolished and the T.A. came into existence, the word 'Provincial' being dropped. In dealing with the financial crisis, however, the delegates proved as short-sighted as their predecessors. They refused the Executive's request for increased subscriptions, attempting instead to reduce expenditure by imposing greater restrictions and penalties.

These reforms, however, were mere palliatives and as the trade depression deepened deficits grew. Mileage expenditure rose from £590 in 1873 to nearly £1,400 in 1879, while out-of-work payments soared from £145 to over £2,500. The Executive were therefore forced, since the members refused to raise subscriptions, to impose levies and restrict expenditure.

It would be tedious to go through all the complicated alterations of rules in the years 1878–81. Their outcome was as follows. The probationary or qualifying period of membership was progressively raised and graduated according to age—two years for those under 35, three for those between 35 and 45, and four for those over 45—older men being more likely to fall out of work. At the same time benefits were restricted. An unemployed member under 40 who received six weeks' benefit in one quarter was only entitled to four in the next, or ten in two consecutive quarters, in any one branch, after which he must, if he wished to remain on the fund, remove to another branch. His total benefits in twelve months were limited to £8. He was then suspended from benefit for a year, and if at the end of that period he had not had at least six months' regular or nine months' casual employment, he would be reduced to half benefit, which would be paid in alternate years until he could show the requisite amount of work. These regulations were relaxed somewhat for older members, who had greater difficulty in finding employment.

The penalties against neglect or refusal of work and against loss of employment through negligence or misconduct were also made more severe, while any member throwing up his situation 'without a sufficient or satisfactory cause' was liable to suspension from benefits.

These regulations applied equally to stationary and travelling unemployed. They amounted to this: that the Association, while aiding the temporarily unfortunate, would refuse to support the idle and incompetent. Many members, however, were out of work for long periods through no fault of their own.

These were drab, depressing years. The E.C. became absorbed in a narrow, parsimonious, and autocratic administration of benefits, constantly tinkering with the rules and wrapped up in petty details. But they succeeded, by rigid economy and without raising subscriptions, in bringing the Association safely through the years of bad trade. Moreover, though benefits had been curtailed, large payments had been made to the out-of-work, which must have considerably eased their hardships.

It was during these years that the old tramp-relief reciprocity with independent societies was ended. The S.T.A. abolished it in 1878, the London Pressmen in 1879, and the L.S.C. in 1881, substituting for it a system of removal grants. The T.A., therefore, while continuing to relieve its own travelling unemployed, ceased relieving those of other unions.

Trade began to improve towards the end of 1881 and out-of-work payments fell in the years 1882–4 to about £1,500 annually, mileage relief to below £400, so that the E.C. were able to dispense with levies. Until the next severe trade depression in 1893–7 affairs went along prosperously and the Association was able to build up its funds. Despite rapidly increasing membership, out-of-work expenditure averaged only about £2,200 annually in the years 1885–92 and mileage relief still less than £400.

From 1893 onwards, however, unemployment became more serious than ever before. Trade depression and the introduction of Linotype machines combined to throw hundreds out of work. Benefits were temporarily extended and levies had to be imposed again, while subscriptions were increased by a halfpenny in 1895, when the R.C. altered the rules, making length of membership instead of age the basis of benefits, on a graduated scale. As amended by the 1898 Delegate Meeting, the rules now entitled an unemployed member of less than ten years' standing to 8s. per week for five weeks in each quarter; ten to fifteen years, six weeks, fifteen years and upwards, seven weeks. After twelve months on the fund, a member of less than ten years' standing had to show twenty weeks' work or be reduced to 5s. per week; a ten to twenty years' member, sixteen weeks. Full benefit could only be regained by showing the requisite amount of work at the end of the following year, failing which the member would be suspended from relief for twelve months. Membership of twenty years or more gave exemption from these restrictions, which were also applied to travelling relief.

The rules had thus been made slightly more liberal, especially for the Association's veterans. This liberality and the serious trade depression caused expenditure to go up by leaps and bounds. But while weekly out-of-work payments grew rapidly—£4,500 in 1893, £6,800 in 1894, and £8,700 in 1895—mileage relief remained stationary round about £600 annually.

These figures showed that the tramp was disappearing and that the unemployed were remaining stationary in their own towns. Weekly out-of-work benefits were, of course, payable in any branch, but few men moved. The old custom of tramping the country during periods of bad trade, under great hardships, hopelessly looking for work, was now regarded by most as useless, degrading, and out of date. An unemployed member preferred to stay in his own town, with his family and friends, eking out existence on out-of-work benefit and what casual employment he could get, waiting for trade to improve. He could answer advertisements and travel by railway if he got work in another town, instead of tramping.

A special committee on the mileage relief system in 1901-2 recognized these facts and urged that 'the time has now arrived for a change'. But, though they condemned tramping, they could not bring themselves to end it, since it 'had been so long in existence' and still helped to make labour more mobile. It should be mended, they concluded, not ended.

The committee therefore proposed that the mileage system should be replaced by payments to travellers of 1s. 8d. *per day*, to encourage them to look for work instead of merely amassing mileage. Branch secretaries should also be given greater powers of 'labour direction'.

These proposals were adopted by the 1903 Delegate Meeting, but they merely prolonged tramping for a few years. Attacks upon it continued and the 1908 Delegate Meeting decided that it should be abolished at the end of 1913. In future, unemployed members who secured work in another town would be paid their railway fares by the Association.

Out-of-work payments, which thus completely replaced the travelling system, had meanwhile undergone little change. The weekly allowance was raised to 10s. in 1908, in view of the increased cost of living, and in 1913 the number of weekly payments was increased by one per quarter, while the required period of work to secure full benefit for a second year was reduced by four weeks.[1] This liberality combined with increased membership and unemployment to swell out-of-work expenditure considerably. From 1900 to 1908 it gradually rose, though fluctuating according to the state of trade, from about £9,000 to £11,000 per annum; then, in 1909-10, as a result of increased benefits and trade depression, it soared to over £15,000; but afterwards fell, as trade revived, to about £11,400 in 1913.

---

[1] The 2s. increase of 1908 was met by an additional ½d. per week subscription, while the extension of 1913 was made possible by the Board of Trade subsidy under Part II, Section 106, of the National Insurance Act. (See below, pp. 280-1.)

This was a very heavy burden for the Association to bear. The problem of unemployment was, indeed, the greatest which the union had to face in this period. The T.A. spent far more on out-of-work relief than on any other item—much more than on strikes. By the end of 1913 it had paid out nearly £36,000 in travelling relief and over £243,000 in out-of-work payments. Moreover, it constantly strove not only to relieve but also to reduce unemployment. Tramping and out-of-work benefits were, after all, merely negative: they eased suffering, but did nothing to prevent it. The effort to reduce unemployment is visible in almost every article of Association policy. By limitation of apprentices the Association sought to restrict entry into the trade and prevent 'surplus labour', while reduction of hours and overtime was largely intended to secure work for more men, as were the rules against 'smooting', the 'bonus system', and 'task-work'. The main reason why the Association fought so desperately to retain control over the introduction of composing machines was to check the displacement of members. For similar reasons they opposed the employment of 'cheap labour'—underpaid boys, girls, and women. The various attempts at industrial co-operation usually aimed to give employment to the out-of-work, while the emigration funds of the fifties were intended to remove surplus hands to other countries where work was available.

But in spite of all these efforts unemployment remained as great a problem as ever. In the nineties, therefore, many journeymen printers began to adopt Socialist theories and to urge that 'the proper solution of the surplus labour question is that the burden should be borne by the community as well as the Association'.[1] Hitherto trade unions had relied almost exclusively on 'self-help', on funds raised from the subscriptions of their members. Now they claimed that the State (more particularly, the capitalists whose wealth Labour had created) should assist them in relieving those whom the present industrial system had flung on the social scrap-heap. Some went farther, regarding relief as a mere palliative, which did not get at the causes of social misery: only by a reorganization of society, by collective ownership of the means of production, distribution, and exchange, could workmen secure 'full employment'.

Here were ideas portentous of vast future development. The National Insurance Act of 1911—resulting largely from political pressure by trade unions and the newly created Labour Party—was an early and striking embodiment of these ideas. The State had already granted meagre pen-

---

[1] 1903 D.M. Report. Speech by G. H. Roberts, Norwich B.S., later first T.A. Parliamentary Representative.

sions to the aged: now it produced a scheme for the relief of sickness and unemployment.[1] As regards the unemployment part of the Act, insurance was made compulsory only in certain trades—building, constructional, and engineering—but others could apply for inclusion. The T.A. preferred to maintain its own independent system of unemployment insurance, but took advantage of the clause (Part II, Section 106) whereby the Board of Trade could grant a subsidy of one-sixth of the amount (up to a maximum rate of 12s. per week) disbursed by a trade union in out-of-work benefits. It was thereby, as we have seen, enabled to grant an extra week's allowance in each quarter.

Call-books were still kept in the branch offices, though local labour exchanges offered facilities. The Association distrusted the new exchanges, fearing that they might be utilized to draft men into 'unfair' offices. It was felt that 'this mode of securing situations may be all right for unskilled labour, but if our members place themselves in the hands of Exchanges, who do not understand our trade, we shall find that our power as a great trade union has gone'. The exchanges were also felt to be rather degrading and appear to have been little used by T.A. members.

Emigration Schemes

Emigration is an age-old remedy for over-population. It was therefore taken up by trade unions in the nineteenth century as a means of solving the problem of 'surplus labour' and unemployment.

Dublin appears to have been the first typographical society to establish an emigration fund, already possessing such a fund in 1838. It was urged in the *Compositors' Chronicle* in 1841 that an emigration fund should be established in England, to 'provide an outlet for the superabundance of labour' and keep up wages. Money would be far more wisely spent on emigration than on useless strikes or tramp relief. Similar proposals continued to be made throughout the forties particularly in the years of distress after 1846, and there are several references to printers emigrating. Articles frequently appeared in the trade periodicals giving information about the state of trade and prospects in the colonies and U.S.A. But though Belfast, Glasgow, and one or two other towns soon followed Dublin's example, it was not until the fifties that active steps were taken in England to promote emigration in the printing trade. The subject was 'repeatedly discussed; but the enormous expen-

---

[1] Sickness and invalidity benefits (Part I of the Act) and the T.A. 'Approved Society' are dealt with below, p. 297.

diture that would be required to carry it out, and the slight diminution that would be made in the labour market, for a long time caused luke-warmness in the matter. Indeed the majority of societies, when the question was laid before them for their decision, voted against it.[1]

In the early fifties, however, the gold discoveries in Australia, the consequent rise in wages, and alluring accounts received from printers who had previously emigrated, created new interest in the subject. Emigration, as an alternative to tramp relief, was thoroughly discussed at the inaugural meeting of the P.T.A. in June 1849. Advocates of emigration pointed out that 'our profession has been overstocked with hands for a long period'; in every town there were out-of-work printers. Tramping from town to town was therefore useless: it was merely a palliative, providing relief, but doing nothing to remove surplus labour and reduce unemployment, while it was also open to grave abuses, encouraging idleness and destroying self-reliance. The only remedy was to find 'an outlet for this redundancy of numbers' abroad, in the colonies or U.S.A., where labour was needed: it was simply a case of equating supply and demand. Moreover, it was a waste of money to engage in strikes while the present 'superabundance of hands' existed. Emigration would benefit the unemployed, enabling them to get work and good wages and to live independent, useful lives abroad, instead of stagnating at home.

The E.C., however, while favourable to emigration, did not regard it as a sufficient substitute for tramping: many unemployed members would be unable or unwilling to leave the country. Voting therefore resulted in a large majority for continuance of tramp relief. But many members favoured a limited emigration scheme, co-existent with tramping, and the E.C. stated that when the new Association was in good working order they would be willing to receive proposals for such a scheme. In 1851, therefore, the Liverpool branch proposed the establishment of an Emigration Fund, 'as an auxiliary to, but not a substitute for, the present system of tramping'. The idea was favourably received, so rules for a 'Typographical Emigration Society' were drawn up and circulated by the E.C. Although management was vested in the P.T.A. Executive, all recognized societies in the United Kingdom were invited to join; membership of Association branches was optional. The subscription would be a penny per member per week and each emigrant would be paid £7 and travelling expenses to Liverpool, the port of embarkation. The scheme would be launched on 1 February 1852.

[1] *Typographical Protection Circular*, Jan. 1853.

The result was very disappointing. Only ten branches and one small independent society supported the scheme and not all their members contributed. It also proved very difficult to find willing emigrants. The final balance-sheet, published in July 1853, shows that only fourteen emigrants were sent out, to Australia and America, and of these ten came from the Liverpool branch, which had contributed £67 out of a total of £109. In spite of glowing accounts from Australia, the Society proved an utter 'flop'.

Meanwhile, the Liverpool branch, realizing that the Society's operations were on far too small a scale and that their effect on the labour market was utterly insignificant, took the initiative in another attempt to establish a 'National Printers' Emigration Society'. By this time Dublin, Belfast, Cork, Limerick, and other Irish towns had local emigration funds; so had Glasgow and (since September 1852) the L.S.C. It was therefore hoped to weld all these into 'a great amalgamated society'. The idea was unanimously adopted at the 1853 P.T.A. Delegate Meeting, which decided to wind up the existing Emigration Society and establish rules for the new national scheme. Contributions were to be bigger and graduated according to earnings, with a maximum of 3d. per week, so as to secure more funds and send out emigrants on an appreciable scale.

The result was again disappointing. 'The great mass of the profession proved apathetic.' There was practically no response from Scotland, Ireland, London, and southern England, while only eight P.T.A. branches joined. The main reasons seem to have been 'a cool and miserable calculation of the cost' and aversion to amalgamation after the recent failure of the N.T.A. The scheme proved 'a signal failure'. Almost all the contributions came from Manchester, Liverpool, and Sheffield. The so-called 'National' Society was therefore dissolved in December 1853, after an existence of only a few months. Its total expenditure had amounted to £91 and eight emigrants had been sent abroad.

Nevertheless, the emigration committee, still clinging to their faith, recommended a reorganization of the earlier provincial scheme, as a smaller but more efficient 'safety-valve for the surplus labour in the market'. This was done in the summer of 1854. It was considered, however, that the previous society's failure had been due to 'its being founded on a wrong principle, that of giving the money instead of lending it'. It was therefore decided to make loans instead of gifts to emigrants, of £12 for Australia and £4 for America, promissory notes to be given for repayment by monthly instalments after arrival out there. This 'would enable a continued stream of emigration to be kept up'.

Alas! for such hopes. The scheme proved as big a failure as its predecessors and had to be wound up after a year. Contributions had totalled £161, some of which was handed back, and seven emigrants had been sent out. The main cause of failure was again lack of support. Most members were unwilling to pay subscriptions for others to emigrate, while 'expatriation', the E.C. stated, was 'still regarded, by our profession at least, with something like dread'. News from Australia had also become less encouraging and the E.C. admitted that there had been 'some exaggerations in the descriptions of the prospects of journeymen printers in Australia'. Several emigrants had returned home, but refused to return the grants, while some even went into 'unfair' houses. The loan repayment scheme also proved a failure. Finally there had been a revival of trade at home and great things were expected from the repeal of the newspaper stamp duty.

The Association has never established another emigration fund, though the idea has continued to crop up. It still, however, makes provision for the emigration of strike hands. The idea was first adopted by the 1853 Delegate Meeting and it later became the rule that one-half the weekly strike payments should be paid to those wishing to emigrate. But this rule does not appear to have been much utilized.

Superannuation Fund

Competitive industry in the nineteenth century was no respecter of persons or grey hairs. The fittest survived and the weak went to the wall—to out-door relief or the workhouse. The printing trade, like others, had its human scrap-heap of aged or inefficient workmen. Age and inefficiency, it is true, did not invariably come together—some printers retained skill of hand and quickness of eye to an amazing age—and all masters were not Gradgrinds: there were numerous honourable instances of employers 'keeping on' their aged workmen, in spite of growing inefficiency, while a few philanthropists even rewarded long years of service with a small pension. But the general rule was 'too old at fifty', or perhaps fifty-five. Occupational ailments, such as failing eyesight and tuberculosis, told their tale and few employers would retain workmen who could not earn the standard wage rate which the union demanded. Younger hands, only too anxious for a 'sit.', were readily available in the ever-present surplus of the labour market. Once an ageing workman had lost a 'permanent' situation it was usually very difficult for him to find another. He fell as a rule into the ranks of the casuals and unemployed. Competition was keen even for casual labour and with increasing age came constant unemployment and misery.

Every journeyman printer was faced with this unpleasant prospect in later life. Few, as the saying went, had 'coffins under their frames'. What hope of remedy, then, was available? The State provided out-door relief or the workhouse; but to printers, members of an 'honourable profession', as to other 'respectable' workmen, the parish-dole and poor-law prison were abhorrent. The only alternatives were starvation or 'self-help'. Many, probably most, printers belonged to some friendly society. Their local trade-clubs, moreover, generally had a friendly society origin, making provision for sickness and unemployment. And, finally, there was the tramp-relief system. But tramping meant great hardship, with little probability for an older man of finding employment, while the local relief funds were intended for the temporarily, not the permanently, unemployed. Want and starvation, therefore, faced the aged journeyman.

It was to preserve those incapacitated by age from these misfortunes that trade unions established superannuation funds. A 'Printers' Pension Society' had been established in London as early as 1827. The earliest provincial scheme appears to have been the Liverpool 'Printers' Pension Society', founded about 1834, which paid superannuitants 5s. per week. This society, however, was wound up at the end of 1851. Manchester was next in the field, establishing a Superannuation and Benevolent Fund in May 1865 which provided a limited number of aged and incapacitated members with a pension of 8s. per week.

These funds, however, were local in character. The first union to establish a national scheme was the Amalgamated Society of Engineers in 1851. Other unions followed suit—the Boilermakers, Ironfounders, Stonemasons, and Carpenters and Joiners. The earliest proposal for a P.T.A. Superannuation Fund came from the Rochdale branch in 1870 and was discussed at the 1872 Delegate Meeting. It was rejected, however, by a narrow majority, firstly, because the Association was about to undertake the establishment of out-of-work and funeral benefits and could not stand the added expense of superannuation, and secondly, because of the actuarial dangers involved.

In the following years, however, articles continued to appear in the *Circular* in favour of a Superannuation Fund and many schemes were put forward for consideration at the next Delegate Meeting in 1877. None of them took sufficient account of the financial liabilities which such a fund would ultimately involve. Some branches even proposed giving pensions of 6s. to 10s. per week without any increase in subscriptions; none suggested more than 1½d. The Association had no accurate actuarial statistics, no reliable data as to number of members, average age, death rate, average age at death, &c. Reliance was placed chiefly on the example and experience of other unions, which themselves relied mainly on purely empirical methods and whose rules varied considerably.

Nevertheless, the 1877 Delegate Meeting decided in favour of a Superannuation Fund. Eligibility for allowances would depend on age and length of membership. The minimum age was fixed at sixty and benefits were to be as follows: thirty years' membership and upwards, 8s.; twenty-five to thirty years', 7s.; twenty to twenty-five years', 6s. Payments would not begin, however, for three years, so as to accumulate a reserve fund. The subscription was to be a penny per member per week. Detailed administrative rules would be drawn up by the E.C. and submitted to the members.

This scheme was obviously an actuarial farce. Payments would be started with hopelessly inadequate reserves, to members who had contributed next to nothing to the Fund. All members, young and old, would pay the same ridiculously low subscription. No calculation seems to have been made of future liabilities. But it was urged that the present generation of old men 'had worked hard in their earlier years, and the young men were now reaping the benefit of their exertions': they deserved, therefore, to be put on pension. It was also pointed out that many old members would be 'hale and able to work, and far too independent to fall upon the funds so long as they could help themselves', while the pensions were not of such size as to tempt men to retire. The advantages of a Superannuation Fund were extolled: it would preserve aged and incapacitated members from the hardships of unemployment; it would relieve the out-of-work fund; it would offer inducement to non-unionists and independent societies to join, and also preserve the loyalty of members.

The publication of this scheme resulted in a storm of controversy. Resolutions were passed by several branches strongly condemning it. The objections were not, however, that it was actuarially unsound, that it was over-liberal, but that it was not liberal enough. The qualifying age of sixty was considered too high: only one T.A. member in eight, according to death statistics in the *Circular*, would reach that age. Some urged, therefore, that the age should be lowered, others that years of membership and incapacity, whether by infirmity, accident, or age, should form the basis of eligibility. Strong criticism was also directed against the fact that membership of the Association alone would count, since this would exclude older men who had only recently become T.A. members, though they might have belonged for years to independent societies and would have to pay their quota to the newly established Fund. The compulsory nature of the scheme, in fact, raised strong opposition, since many members had already made provision for old age in friendly and assurance societies and objected against having to pay an additional penny subscription. Finally, there was a constitutional aspect: the Delegate Meeting had exceeded its powers in deciding upon the establishment of the Fund without taking a vote of the members.

The E.C., however, supported the Delegate Meeting's decision and refused to take a vote. As regards the basis of eligibility, they pointed out that superannuation was essentially a provision for old age, not for accidents, infirmity, or sickness. To widen the basis would prove too costly and open the door to fraud and imposition.

These views were supported by the majority of branches and opposition gradually simmered down. It revived, however, when the Executive issued proposed rules for working the Fund in December 1879. Most opposition was aroused by the clause that an applicant must produce evidence and answer questions before his branch committee concerning not only his age and length of membership, but also his 'inability to obtain or retain employment through incapacity'. A number of branches opposed the 'inquisitorial' character of this clause and urged that age and membership should be the only qualifications: they proposed, in fact, that the Fund should provide old-age pensions for all over sixty, regardless of capacity or incapacity to work. The Executive considered, however, that in view of the small subscription it was necessary to exercise the strictest economy. Their proposal was carried, but in the following years many branches were to give a lax interpretation to the rule.

Of the remaining clauses, one prescribed that any member who had worked in an 'unfair' office and had been expelled could only date his membership from his readmission. This, it was hoped, would keep men true to union principles, since expulsion would entail loss of benefits previously subscribed for. It was also laid down that a recipient would have to remain on the particular grade of payments to which he first made claim, 'no accumulating years of membership thereafter to count for any increased scale of payment'. This would tend to deter members from claiming on the Fund as soon as they were eligible for the lowest grade. No subscriptions would be required from superannuated members, who were to be put completely on the retired list and 'on no account, either on their own behalf or for an employer, to undertake any description of work pertaining to the duties of a letterpress printer; this restriction to include the reading of proofs'. Thus work would be provided for younger unemployed members. Finally, the E.C. attempted, by various administrative measures and the compilation of an Association register, to guard against abuse and imposition.

The establishment of the Fund was, as one correspondent put it, 'to a very large extent a "leap in the dark" '. For several years, however, all went well. By July 1880, when payments began, a reserve fund of £3,469 had been accumulated and this increased from year to year. The Association had only been established for 31 years, so that the number of claimants with the requisite length of membership was comparatively small—29 at first. Moreover, a good many members preferred to go on working rather than claim the small pittance from the Fund, while the 'incapacity' clause excluded others. Hence, income continually exceeded expenditure and the Fund grew.

Its very growth, however, soon brought danger. Many members, heedless or ignorant of future liabilities, saw only present prosperity. Some suggested increasing the weekly payments, others a transfer from the Superannuation to the General Fund, or an amalgamation of the two. The early eighties were years of depression, unemployment, and half-yearly deficits on the General Fund, to meet which the Executive were forced to impose levies. These produced considerable dissatisfaction and eyes naturally turned to the growing Superannuation Fund. The T.A., it was argued, was first and foremost a trade union and the Superannuation Fund might legitimately be used for general purposes. The Association was an unregistered society and there was nothing to prevent such a diversion if the members so decided.

The temptation to plunder or absorb the Superannuation Fund, however, was withstood. The Executive also secured the rejection of rash proposals to increase the scale of weekly payments, to lower the membership qualification, and to place 'wholly incapacitated' persons on the Fund, regardless of age and without any increase of subscriptions to meet the added expenditure.

For several years all went well, the Fund still increasing and apparently safe. A rude awakening came in May 1888, however, when the Association Treasurer pointed out 'that the expenditure is gradually approaching the point where it will exceed the income', that the superannuated members were steadily increasing in number, and that either the expenditure would have to be reduced or the income increased. By December 1887, in fact, the number of recipients had increased to 75, while expenditure had grown from £615 in 1881 to £1,345 in 1887 and was now absorbing nearly 95 per cent. of the income. Increase of membership—from 5,350, at the end of 1881, to 7,498, at the end of 1887—had alone prevented a large deficit. But the number of superannuitants was increasing in much greater proportion than membership and increased membership meant heavier future liabilities.

Most members failed, however, to see the danger: so long as present claims were met and a small balance left over, they were satisfied. They were particularly opposed to any increase in subscriptions. It was therefore decided that an additional halfpenny per member should be taken from the present weekly subscriptions for superannuation purposes: Peter was to be robbed to pay Paul. But this makeshift would not provide a permanent solution, as the E.C. pointed out:

The increased revenue which the Superannuation Fund will derive by the additional halfpenny per week will probably support the fund on its present basis for a few years longer, but it is impossible to ignore the fact that year by year the number of members qualified under the present rule to become recipients of the fund will naturally and steadily increase, and that the members of the Association will find (as members of other organisations have found in connection with superannuation) that considerably larger amounts will have to be set apart to guarantee the claims of their aged and infirm members.

In spite of this warning, several branches considered that the additional halfpenny would justify a lowering of the age limit and inclusion of permanently incapacitated members, regardless of age. These proposals were denounced by the E.C. and eventually rejected, but at the Delegate Meeting in 1891 similar proposals were again submitted. A special committee was appointed to deal with them. The committee's recommendations were adopted by the Delegate Meeting and afterwards confirmed by vote of the members. Another grade was created, whereby 'a contributing member for 40 years' would be entitled to 10s. per week, and also a 'special grade' for cases of confirmed paralysis or blindness, or permanent incapacity; such members might be placed upon the Fund without having reached the age of 60, provided they had been members for 30 years and upwards. To provide for these increased benefits, the Superannuation Fund allocation was raised from $1\frac{1}{2}d.$ to $2d.$, Association subscriptions being increased from 5*d*. to 5½*d*. The old grievance of injustice to members of one-time independent societies was again raised, but rejected.

A controversy now arose with regard to the phrase 'a contributing member for 40 years'. The special committee had undoubtedly intended it to mean a 40 years' contributing member to the Superannuation Fund, established in 1877, so that payments on the new 10*s*. grade would not commence until 1917.[1] The Executive decided, however, that membership of the T.A. was intended, and that the clause should therefore come into immediate operation. In spite of protests and relying on their power of interpreting the rules, they deliberately ignored the intention of the Delegate Meeting. They refused, moreover, to have the question decided by voting paper. It was raised again, however, at the Delegate Meeting of 1893, which decided by a large majority that the clause should not take effect until 1917. The Executive thereupon issued a voting paper. Naturally, the members were not interested in providing for posterity and declared for 'immediate benefit'. The result was further liability without any provision to meet it.

Liabilities had also been increased by a decision of the 1893 Delegate Meeting that membership of a formerly independent society should count towards eligibility, provided the branch and member claiming benefit had belonged to the Association since inauguration of the Fund in 1877.

As a result of the recent legislation and of trends previously apparent, the Fund was soon in a dangerous position again. Between 1887 and 1896 the number of superannuated members increased from 75 to 208 and expenditure rose from £1,345 to £4,034, rapidly overtaking income once again. A few members protested against going on in 'this hand-to-mouth fashion' and urged that the Fund should be placed on a firm and lasting basis by fixing a subscription large enough to meet future liabilities. The Plymouth branch urged that there should be an actuarial valuation of the assets and liabilities of the Fund, but the proposal was shelved by the Representative Council of 1894 and rejected by that of 1895, mainly on grounds of expense and distrust of actuarial statistics: as a writer in the *Circular* later put it, 'We don't . . . take kindly to actuaries, who are more mathematical than human, and don't understand trade union statistics.'

At the 1896 R.C. meeting, however, a special committee was appointed

[1] The intention was 'to induce young men to join the society'. *Typographical Circular*, June 1892.

to examine and report on the Fund. This committee came to the conclusion that the Fund had been floated with an insufficient reserve and inadequate contributions, that the institution of the 10s. and special grades had seriously added to its liabilities, and that only the large influx of new members since 1877 had saved the fund. They deplored 'the argument that because we have a respectable balance, therefore, the fund is perfectly sound and solvent', pointing out the enormous future liabilities and the rapid increase in expenditure as against income. They therefore proposed 'that a minimum reserve fund of £20,000 be established and maintained', that a grant should be made from the General Fund to create this reserve, and that whenever it fell below £20,000 the E.C. should be empowered to impose a levy of 6d. per member per half year. They also proposed that the weekly subscription to the Superannuation Fund should be raised to 3d. per member.

This Report was considered by the R.C. in October 1897. It was decided, however, that 'in face of the continued large yearly increase of the Superannuation Fund', the members could not be asked for further subscriptions; but it was agreed to accept the proposal for a guaranteed reserve fund of £20,000.[1]

Meanwhile a change was coming over the Fund. At its inauguration the rule had been clearly laid down that claimants must prove 'inability to obtain or retain employment through *incapacity*', as well as age and length of membership. But this rule had been systematically evaded in many branches on humanitarian grounds. A man over sixty might be of tolerably sound constitution and yet quite unable to secure employment. If the rule were enforced, he would be ineligible to benefit, despite grey hairs and long membership. Many branches, therefore, ignored incapacity and considered merely a claimant's 'inability to obtain or retain employment'. Superannuation tended to become a pension payable at sixty.

This laxity obviously resulted in greatly increased expenditure. The 1894 R.C. meeting therefore decided that all applicants must produce a medical certificate of incapacity. The result, however, was a loud outcry against such injustice to veteran members and the E.C. were forced to issue voting papers, when the obnoxious proposal was rejected by an overwhelming majority. The old rule as to incapacity still remained, but without any safeguard for its enforcement.

The 1898 Delegate Meeting widened the door to applicants still farther. At the inauguration of the Fund it was understood, though not

[1] The Fund stood at £18,462 at the end of 1896.

clearly expressed, that members with income from private means or from another trade should be debarred from superannuation. Here again, however, branches gave a broad interpretation to the rules. The special committee of 1896–7 therefore recommended a tightening-up in regard to 'the earnings of superannuitants, whether in business or otherwise'. But this, like the medical certificate, was considered by members a harsh and unjust proposal. It would constitute 'a tax on thrift'. When a man of sixty had paid for twenty or thirty years into the Fund, he was entitled to benefit, without inquiry into his private affairs. It was therefore decided at the Delegate Meeting in 1898 that a member, if otherwise eligible, should be 'entitled to superannuation benefit irrespective of any income he may derive from private means, or from any trade or calling not connected with the T.A.'

These acts of generosity accentuated the instability of the Fund. Between 1896 and 1902 the number of recipients increased from 205 to 348, while expenditure grew from £4,034 to £7,413 and in 1902 actually exceeded the income by £151. Several branches therefore urged an actuarial valuation or increased subscriptions. But most members, mesmerized by the size of the Fund and loath to pay more, deluded themselves into thinking all was well. Some branches even proposed raising the benefits.

A special committee appointed at the 1903 Delegate Meeting diagnosed the Fund's disease, but feared to apply the remedy. They rejected, of course, proposals for increased benefits, but dared not ask for increased subscriptions. Instead, they clung to the old policy of hand-to-mouth expedients, by suggesting that special grade (incapacity) payments to future claimants should be met for the next five years from the General Fund: again, it was a case of robbing Peter to pay Paul. The committee lamely admitted that 'this was only a temporary device for the purpose of just tiding over until they had a further opportunity of settling the question one way or the other'. It was argued, by way of justification, that the incapacity benefit could not be legitimately termed a superannuation allowance and ought, therefore, to be paid out of the General Fund; but no proposal was made to increase subscriptions. The committee dared not face facts and wished to postpone the evil hour. The delegates were equally timid and accepted the committee's proposals. At the same time they rejected a proposal for valuation, because 'if the fund was valued in the ordinary way it would place a condition of things before the members which would create more or less panic', and 'they would have to tell the members that they would have to pay 2d. or 3d.

per week more to meet expenses'. So the delegates kept their heads in the sand and hoped for the best.

The result, of course, was an increasing deficit—£727 in 1904 and £1,329 in 1905—despite the transfer of special grade payments to the General Fund. The Executive had therefore to ask members, at the end of 1905, to raise the contribution to the Superannuation Fund from 2d. to 2¾d. per week. This was agreed to, but by the time of the 1908 Delegate Meeting the resultant surplus was again dwindling. Another special committee was therefore appointed to examine the Fund. This committee, like its predecessors, came to the unanimous conclusion 'that the fund is in a very unsatisfactory condition': that, in particular, the income and reserve fund were insufficient to meet future liabilities. They therefore proposed that the contribution to the Fund should be increased by 1¼d. to 4d. per week; that when the reserve capital fell below £70 per superannuitant the E.C. should be empowered to levy 6d. per member per half-year until it reached that amount; that the fourth grade (twenty to twenty-five years' members) should be abolished (this not to affect present members); that the special grade should be permanently removed from the Superannuation Fund rules and established as an 'Incapacity Benefit', payable from the General Fund; and, finally, that the Fund should be actuarially valued. These proposals they regarded as the minimum essential to stability. But the delegates, as usual, thought them impossible. Now that there was no longer an actual deficit, they thought the Fund safe enough. They refused, therefore, to add more than ½d. to the contribution and reduced the reserve capital figure necessitating a levy to £50 per superannuitant. They accepted abolition of the fourth grade and conversion of the special grade into an 'Incapacity Benefit', but they (and the Executive) considered that there was no need for an actuarial valuation. Instead, the Executive were to issue a report prior to the next Delegate Meeting. The delegates still kept their heads in the sand and hoped for the best.

The inevitable followed. A large surplus in 1909 had almost disappeared by the end of 1912. The number of superannuitants (now 624) and the annual expenditure (now £13,715) were still increasing and the average age at death was rising, but membership was no longer growing so rapidly. It was therefore essential, the Executive stated in their report, that the income and reserve capital should be increased. At the Delegate Meeting in 1913 the usual special committee was appointed. Its chief proposal, for an actuarial valuation, was this time accepted, but its interim provision, that the contribution to the Fund should be increased by $\frac{1}{2}d.$ per week, was rejected. Moreover, the meeting decided that the clause requiring claimants to produce proof of their 'inability to obtain or retain employment through incapacity' should now be deleted. In future age and length of membership would be the only qualifications.

The old story was repeated after this meeting. An increased contribution having been rejected, the inevitable deficit resulted in 1914 and the Executive were forced to impose a levy, which, they pointed out, would have to be continued unless the subscription was raised. The outbreak of war and the resultant fall in income made matters worse, but the Executive deemed it inadvisable to continue the levy. They also decided in 1917 not to proceed with the actuarial valuation ordered by the Delegate Meeting, owing to the data required, high estimated cost, and war conditions. Deficits therefore continued, a problem to be dealt with by the Delegate Meeting of 1918.

We must not, however, judge the Superannuation Fund solely from an actuarial point of view. It was a laudable attempt at self-help in the years before old-age pensions were paid by the State. By 1914 annual expenditure on superannuation benefits was rapidly overhauling out-of-work payments and was soon to exceed that on any other benefit. It had risen from £616 in 1881 to £15,222 in 1914, by which time there were 739 superannuitants on the Fund. Moreover, the Association was now paying over £1,000 a year to incapacitated members. Since its establishment, the Fund had expended a total of £214,265 on these two benefits, a sum which must have helped considerably to relieve want and suffering among its aged members.[1]

The right of aged workers to a pension from the State was advocated by the T.A., in conjunction with other trade unions and the Labour Party, for a number of years before the Liberals passed the first Old-Age Pensions Act in 1908, which provided pensions of 5s. per week for those over seventy years of age. This Act met with considerable Labour (including T.A.) criticism, on account of the high qualifying age, the poor-law disqualification, and the fact that it penalized those who had already made provision for old age through trade unions or friendly societies. A T.A. superannuitant, for example, on the first grade, receiving 10s. per week, could get only a 3s. pension, or a combined maximum of 13s. Nevertheless, the important principle of State pensions for the aged had received recognition.

---

[1] Moreover, most large branches supplemented superannuation payments with a few shillings weekly.

Funeral Benefit

Funeral benefits, payable on the death of members or their wives, date back to the friendly society origin of numerous local societies. Naturally, therefore, they were prominent in the various schemes for an Association provident fund put forward in the early seventies. The Rochdale branch included burial payments in its proposals of 1870, which were discussed at the Delegate Meeting in 1872. They suggested a subscription of $1\frac{1}{4}d.$ per week and allowances varying from £4 to £10 according to length of membership, with similarly graduated, but smaller, payments on the death of a member's wife. This scheme was withdrawn, however, and a proposal from Wolverhampton carried: 'that for every death that may occur among the members of the P.T.A., each branch shall be levied $\frac{1}{2}d.$ per member', the Executive to advance the money, if necessary, until the branch half-yearly returns came in.[1]

This proposal was accepted by a large majority in the subsequent vote and the E.C. drew up a few simple rules for administration of the new benefit. The deceased must have been a T.A. member for twelve months, with subscriptions paid up on the last clearance day. The levy was to be imposed at the end of each half-year, its amount varying according to the number of deaths which had occurred.

It soon became evident, however, that the Rochdale scheme, of fixed allowances and weekly subscriptions, would have been much preferable to the one adopted. The funeral levy proved cumbersome, it lacked regularity, and was troublesome to collect. Moreover, there was no fixity or uniformity about the allowances, which, as membership grew, became proportionately larger. Finally, the scheme paid no regard to length of membership. A number of alterations were, therefore, soon made. The Delegate Meeting of 1877, while retaining the levy, fixed allowances on a sliding scale according to length of membership: one year's membership, £4; two years', £6; three years', £8; ten years', £10. The levy was abolished by voting paper in 1879 and replaced by a uniform subscription of a halfpenny per member per week. These rules remained in force to the end of our period.

Between 1873 and 1913 the total amount expended in funeral payments was nearly £45,000, rising from £97 in the first year to £2,064 in the latter.

Members' deaths were reported in the *Circular*. From these reports

[1] There was no provision for the death of members' wives. Suggestions for such an allowance were made on several occasions in the following years, but never adopted. Many branches, however, made local provision.

some interesting information can be derived about general causes of death and occupational diseases, and as to average age at death or average expectation of life. By far the commonest cause of death among printers, particularly younger men, was disease of the lungs: tuberculosis, phthisis, or 'consumption'. Long hours, night work, and lack of fresh air and exercise were the chief causes. Working conditions were often unhealthy, with bad ventilation, stifling, overheated atmosphere, dust, dirt, and lack of sanitation. From these various causes, the mortality rate from consumption among printers was much higher than that of the community as a whole.[1] A few deaths also occurred from poisoning, due to the lead, antimony, and arsenic contained in the type: the compositors inhaled type dust from the boxes, while many had bad habits of 'chewing type' while correcting and of eating food without previously washing their hands. The number of fatal accidents at work was increased by the introduction of power-driven machinery.

Nevertheless, the average age at death rose from 41·9 in the years 1874–84 to 51·2 in the years 1904–14. This improvement was due to a variety of causes: advance in medical science and improved medical services, shorter hours and more recreation, rise in wages and standard of living, and better working conditions.

Proposals for a Sick Fund. Establishment of the T.A. Approved Society (1912)

Sick funds, like funeral funds, had long been a feature of many local societies. Rochdale therefore included a proposal for the establishment of an Association Sick Fund in its general provident scheme in 1870. It was rejected, however, by the 1872 Delegate Meeting on the grounds of cost and liability to abuse, and since it would necessitate stringent control over admissions, taking age and physical fitness into account—restrictions more suited to a friendly society than a trade union. Moreover, many members were already covered by membership of local sick clubs or national friendly societies.

Proposals for a Sick Fund were again rejected by the 1877 Delegate Meeting, which decided that a Superannuation Fund would be preferable. This decision came in for a good deal of criticism, particularly from younger members. The Superannuation Fund, it was pointed out, 'will be of very little benefit for the members of the Association generally.... It is a good thing for the old members, certainly. But ... how many in our trade live to the age of sixty?' Very few. But almost every member

[1] As evidenced by the Registrar-General's returns.

was sick occasionally. Others, however, argued against a Sick Fund: it would be too costly, it would have to support unhealthy and aged lives, it would be open to fraud, and would introduce too much of the friendly society element into what was primarily a trade union.

The insuperable problem of cost, more than anything else, settled the question, and though the idea of a Sick Fund frequently cropped up again in the following years it never materialized.

In 1911, however, health insurance was made compulsory by the National Insurance Act. Under Part I of this Act, workman, employer, and State were to contribute 4*d.*, 3*d.*, and 2*d.* per week respectively towards a national insurance scheme, which would provide the insured person with sickness, invalidity, and maternity benefits. The trade unions, together with the friendly societies and industrial insurance companies, were made the agents for administration of these benefits,[1] so the T.A. at once formulated rules and applied for recognition as an 'Approved Society'. This was granted in July 1912 and by the end of the year over 12,000 (out of 22,000) Association members had joined the T.A. Approved Society.

Legal Aid

Association funds and Executive support enabled individual workmen —practically helpless legally against their more wealthy and influential employers—to fight for their legal rights. The Association frequently, for example, paid the legal expenses necessary to enforce claims for a fortnight's notice or wages. It also backed up members with legal aid in resisting wrongful deductions from wages for spoilt work. More important were the legal proceedings taken by the Association on behalf of members to secure compensation for injury while at work or for occupational diseases, such as lead poisoning, under the Employers' Liability Act of 1880 and the Workman's Compensation Acts of 1897 and 1906. Legal aid was also given to members prosecuted by employers as a result of trade-union action authorized by branch or Executive, to defend them against charges of libel, conspiracy, illegal picketing, intimidation, and suchlike.

[1] Medical benefit was administered by District Insurance Committees.

XIV

POLITICS AND CO-OPERATION

PRINTERS' trade societies maintained for many years after 1849 their traditional attitude of non-interference in politics. When, for example, the Manchester Society was asked in May 1867 to take part in a 'demonstration' for manhood suffrage organized by the National Reform League, it declined on the ground that 'that sort of thing was foreign to the objects for which the Manchester Typographical Society was formed'. The Reform Acts of 1867 and 1884-5 are not even mentioned in the T.A. *Circular*.

The sole example of political action by the T.A. until the late sixties was its continuance of the agitation for repeal of the 'Taxes on Knowledge'. This was a matter devoid of 'party' colouring and closely affecting their particular interests. Petitions were therefore sent to Parliament and contributions forwarded to the Repeal Society. P.T.A. branches were not, however, very active in the movement, the Executive frequently deploring their apathy.

A 'non-political' attitude remained characteristic of most trade unions in this period. It was in the new trades councils, rather than the trade unions, that workmen's political interests found expression. These councils, of course, were primarily intended for combined action in trade affairs, but they also became 'the political organs of the Trade Union world'.[1] William Allan, of the Engineers, Robert Applegarth, of the Carpenters, and other prominent officials of national societies formed a 'Junta' in the London Trades Council which adopted a policy of energetic agitation for political reforms. But the mass of trade societies, including the P.T.A. Executive and branches, took practically no interest and the 'Junta' therefore turned to the trades councils for support.

One of their chief provincial allies was William Dronfield, secretary of the Sheffield Typographical Society and also of the Sheffield Association of Organized Trades, whose activities in general trades unionism we have already noticed and who was for many years a leading figure in the T.A. Dronfield was very active in the working-class political agitation of the sixties and seventies—for the Franchise, amendment of the Master and Servant Law, new Mines Regulation Acts, National Education,

---

[1] Webb, S. and B., op. cit., p. 242.

and full legalization of trade unions. He was honorary secretary of the Sheffield committee for amendment of the Master and Servant Acts and attended the conference of trade-union representatives in London in May 1864 to organize and focus the agitation. He was one of those selected to bring the matter before the Home Secretary and also gave evidence before the Select Committee of Inquiry appointed by the Commons in 1865, as a result of whose report the new Master and Servant Act of 1867 was passed.

Meanwhile, however, the notorious 'Sheffield outrages' had occurred and a Royal Commission of Inquiry into trade societies had been appointed: trade unionism stood on trial. Dronfield took a prominent part in its defence, as secretary of the Sheffield Trades' Defence Committee and in evidence before the Royal Commission, proving that criminal acts such as 'rattening' were confined to a small number of Sheffield societies. He was entirely opposed to violent trade-union action, being a strong advocate of Courts of Conciliation and Arbitration and taking an active part in agitation during the fifties and sixties to secure the passing of parliamentary Bills for their establishment.

Dronfield was also a member of the Reform League and after participating in the Reform Bill agitation of 1866–7 was the first to ask A. J. Mundella to stand for Sheffield in the General Election of 1868 and acted as his honorary secretary during the campaign. Mundella, of course, was one of the most prominent middle-class leaders in the trade-union agitation for full legalization, which formed the main 'plank' in his election platform.

These were not Dronfield's only political interests. He supported the demands of the Yorkshire and North Derbyshire miners, whom he helped to organize, for legislative regulation of working conditions. He was also joint secretary of the National Education League, led by Joseph Chamberlain, which aimed at securing a national system of compulsory education and was largely responsible for the 1870 Education Act. His interest in public health legislation is evidenced by the fact that he became in 1871 one of the Sheffield sanitary inspectors under the Local Board of Health.

Dronfield was not alone in his political activities. The secretary and treasurer of the Manchester Typographical Society, W. H. Wood and S. C. Nicholson, who, as secretary and president of the Manchester and Salford Trades Council, were responsible for the summoning of the first Trades Union Congress in 1868, included among the proposed subjects of discussion such topics as the inequality of the law of conspiracy,

the Royal Commission on Trade Unions, the legalization of trade societies, Courts of Arbitration and Conciliation, factory inspection, and
technical education.

It is evident that some journeymen printers, as members of trades
councils, were taking a vigorous part in working-class political movements. But there is no evidence of any political action by typographical
societies, apart from petitions against the 'Taxes on Knowledge', until
the late sixties. It was not until the appointment of the Royal Commission on Trade Unions in 1867 that the P.T.A. began to take some
interest in political affairs, participating in the agitation of the following
years for legalization of trade unions. But this was not 'party politics':
it was a trade-union outburst for full legal recognition and justice. T.A.
political action was limited to that specific object.

There is no evidence that the Association was very active politically
until after the passing of the Trade Union and Criminal Law Amendment Acts in 1871. Its voice was then heard in the chorus of trade-
union indignation against legislative injustice and tyranny. The
Executive held a special meeting on 21 October 1871 to consider the two
Acts. The most prominent feature of the Trade Union Act was its
legalization of trade societies, which were no longer regarded as unlawful conspiracies. Under this Act, moreover, trade societies could secure
registration and thus legal protection of their funds against fraudulent
officials. But the conditions of registration required that the rules and
an annual statement of income and expenditure must be submitted to
and approved by the Registrar. These conditions the Executive regarded
as 'inquisitorial'. They were 'sufficiently conservative to consider that
there are matters affecting none outside the Association' and they repudiated 'the direct surveillance of Government officials in trade disputes
or agreements, wherein they never had, nor should have now, any concern'. The Executive could not, therefore, recommend registration, particularly as 'the power to punish delinquents already existed'. In any
case, 'the few questionable privileges' conferred by this Act were rendered useless by the Criminal Law Amendment Act. By the one Act
trade unions were legalized; but by the other all the usual methods
of peaceful trade-union action could be made criminal under such
undefined and comprehensive terms as 'molestation', 'intimidation', or
'coercion'. The Council therefore denounced the Act as 'unjust and
tyrannical', as an 'odious class enactment', and urged upon members
'the necessity of using all legitimate means to secure the repeal of this
obnoxious act'.

The Liberal Government, however, were deaf to the outcry and four years of political agitation followed. Printers joined in this campaign for abolition of the Criminal Law Amendment Act and amendment of the Conspiracy Law and the Master and Servant Act—forwarding petitions, taking part in 'demonstrations', and appealing to parliamentary members. The Executive also decided to send a delegate to the Trades Union Congress at Nottingham in 1872 and gave strong support to the Parliamentary Committee in its political campaign. But they were far too conservative to join the Labour Representation League or participate in the running of independent Labour candidates at the General Election of 1874.

The trade-union campaign eventually resulted in the parliamentary triumph of 1875. The Criminal Law Amendment Act was repealed and by the Conspiracy and Protection of Property Act definite and reasonable limits were set to the application of the law of conspiracy to trade disputes. Full legal recognition was at last given to collective bargaining and peaceful trade-union methods. Moreover, the Master and Servant Act of 1867 was replaced by the Employers and Workmen Act—'a change of nomenclature which expressed a fundamental revolution in the law'[1] —whereby employer and employed became two equal parties to a civil contract, breach of which was no longer punishable by imprisonment.

Thus the P.T.A. had achieved, in common with other unions, the aims set forth in 1867. But the Association had, it would seem, played a comparatively insignificant part in the political campaign. It was admitted in the *Circular* in 1875 that 'the operation of the objectionable laws recently repealed did not press so heavily upon printers as upon members of other trades; hence they [printers] have not taken so prominent a part as others in securing their amendment'. We have seen that typographical societies suffered little during the first half of the nineteenth century from legal or judicial persecution. The penal laws were 'rarely attempted to be put into force' and had become 'almost dead letter laws'.

The agitation of the years 1867–75 and the formation of the Trades Union Congress and Parliamentary Committee brought the Association more closely into touch with the general political and social aspirations of the working class. From 1872 onwards the P.T.A. was officially represented at the annual Congresses and its Secretary, Henry Slatter, was for many years a member of the Parliamentary Committee. The Trades Union Congress had arisen out of the political agitation of 1868–75 and

[1] Webb, S. and B., op. cit., p. 291.

retained the character then impressed upon it of 'an exclusively political body', whose chief use was to give weight to the Parliamentary action of the standing committee.[1] In the next fifteen years the Parliamentary Committee agitated for a wide variety of political and social reforms, such as employers' liability and workmen's compensation, extension of factory and workshop legislation, mines regulation, prevention of truck payments, establishment of arbitration and conciliation boards, land reform, reform of the jury system, regulation of the summary jurisdiction of magistrates, and abolition of the unpaid magistracy.

All these subjects were mentioned in the minutes and *Circular* of the T.A. and on many of them petitions were forwarded or deputations sent to Members of Parliament or the Home Secretary, most interest being shown in those questions, such as factory and workshop legislation, which closely affected their own working lives. But there is no evidence of any vigorous political action. The Executive were mostly content to leave things in the hands of the Parliamentary Committee and sign petitions when requested. There was, in fact, little sustained interest in political affairs, little imagination, little sense of the great social problems which required legislative interference. In 1878 the Manchester Society considered 'that the imperial legislation of the past few years has left on the statute book but few, if any, disabilities peculiar to working men', while Henry Slatter stated before the Royal Commission on Labour in 1893 that improved factory inspection was 'the only point' upon which the Association desired State intervention. The Association was mainly concerned with the narrow, sectional interests of the printing trade and had little concern in what the *Circular* called 'mere party politics'. As in the past, they put more trust in their union and collective bargaining than in legislative regulation.

But although printers took little sustained interest in parliamentary affairs, they were active in local politics. Henry Slatter, the Association Secretary, was the first working man appointed a magistrate, the date of his enrolment on the list of justices for the city of Manchester being 21 May 1885. He had already, in 1879, become a member of the Manchester School Board and was also on the committee of the Manchester Sanitary Association and chairman of another committee which provided cheap meals for poor children in the city. There are several other examples of journeymen printers, backed by local trades councils, being elected to town councils, local boards of health, school boards, and boards of guardians. At the anniversary dinners of many of the larger branches

[1] Webb, S. and B., op. cit., p 360

local notabilities were often present as guests, the mayor or councillors, or perhaps even a Member of Parliament. Organized printers were obviously becoming a recognized, respectable, even influential force in local society.

In spite, however, of spasmodic agitation for legislative reforms and individual participation in local government, the Association still eschewed 'politics'. At the Delegate Meeting of 1872, when representation at the Trades Union Congress was under discussion, several members expressed a hope that the Association would 'not be led away by political questions which were too frequently introduced at such meetings' and that it would 'steer clear of the political element'. The Association Secretary stated, in reply, that he and others had objected to the introduction of political questions at the Nottingham Congress and that they would, in future, be excluded.

Printers, in common with other workmen, felt that it was not 'politics' to agitate on questions closely affecting their trade or working lives, such as factory legislation or workmen's compensation. These, they felt, were devoid of political colour. By politics they meant 'party politics', which they persisted in excluding from their trade societies. It is a curious fact that they regarded the Parliamentary Committee's varied programme of legislative reform as non-political. But if party politics were introduced they immediately protested, as in 1887, when a resolution was unanimously passed, 'that this Council strongly condemns the action of the Trades Union Congress at Swansea in introducing party politics into its proceedings, believing that such discussion will cause a great amount of dissatisfaction and annoyance to the members of those societies who have voted funds and elected delegates under the belief that politics would be ignored, and that the interests of trade unionism would be the principal object of such Congress'.

The same non-party attitude was maintained in local politics. The *Circular* warned in May 1885 that trades councils must not be 'diverted from their legitimate purposes', the maintenance of trade interests, and that 'care should be taken . . . to prevent even the appearance of their being subordinated to the interests of any political party, though this need not prevent them rendering service in securing such legislative reforms as workmen of all shades of opinion are agreed upon'.

This 'non-political' attitude or political apathy was characteristic of most trade unions during these years. Ideas of political and social democracy had fallen into the background after the failures of Owenite Socialism and Chartism in the period 1830–48. During the political agitation of 1867–75 interest in politics had revived and a 'Labour Representation League' had been formed. At the General Election in 1874 thirteen 'Labour candidates' went to the polls and two, Alexander Macdonald and Thomas Burt, were elected as the first 'Labour members' of the House of Commons, followed in 1880 by Henry Broadhurst. But after 1875 political interest flagged. The Labour Representation League faded away about 1881. There was as yet no independent Labour Party with its own programme of social reform: the few Labour representatives in Parliament were 'Lib.-Labs.' The T.U.C. was lukewarm in its support of electoral reform and actually rejected manhood suffrage in 1882–3, though it assisted the Liberals to pass the Reform Acts of 1884–5.

New forces, however, were at work to change this somewhat apathetic political attitude. Trade unions were being permeated by Socialist ideas from the writings of Karl Marx and the propaganda of his disciples, H. M. Hyndman, William Morris, and others, and of the new Socialist organizations such as the Social Democratic Federation, Socialist League, and Fabian Society—propaganda which flourished in the prevailing depression and unemployment. The narrow, sectional, and non-political attitude of the 'old school' was attacked by 'New Unionists', who advocated political action to secure such 'progressive' reforms as legislative regulation of the hours of labour, land nationalization, and State and municipal socialism.

These ideas were reflected in the 'Address' issued by the T.U.C. Parliamentary Committee preparatory to the election of 1885. The Committee now advocated increased Labour representation in Parliament and on municipal and other local governing bodies, and suggested a fund to support Labour representatives in Parliament until payment by the State could be secured. The 'Address' demanded 'that all wealth which truly belongs to the nation shall be used for national purposes' and deplored 'the vast amount of poverty and wretchedness' in the great cities, 'the greater part of which is remediable'.

The T.A. was profoundly influenced by these ideas in the years after 1884, but absorbed them very gradually and without revolutionary tendencies. Political action by typographical societies developed naturally out of their trade action, out of their efforts to secure 'fair' working conditions. They had for many years practised the 'exposure' of 'unfair' employers by means of the 'fair list', and during strikes had appealed to the public, particularly the working class, for support by placards and hand-bills, through trades councils, and by public meetings.[1] Local news-

[1] See above, pp. 148–9.

papers were particularly vulnerable to 'exposure', which might reduce
their circulation and perhaps even ruin them. It might also have important political effects. Many newspapers were political party 'organs'
owned by Members of Parliament or local councillors, or supported by
Liberal or Conservative Associations. They were invaluable instruments
of political propaganda, particularly after the Acts of 1867 and 1884–5,
when they were used to catch the votes of the working class, for whose
welfare and prosperity both great parties usually professed concern, particularly at election times.

Typographical societies were thus in a very advantageous strategic
position. They could bring strong pressure to bear on newspaper proprietors and shareholders, on local party organizations and candidates,
to enforce 'fair' working conditions in their newspaper offices, under
threat of 'exposing' the difference between practice and profession and
appealing to the working class not to vote for any candidate whose
party organ was conducted on 'unfair' non-union lines. They soon
realized 'that in these democratic days, with an extended franchise, much
power was placed in their hands', which they should utilize for 'maintenance of the rights of labour'.[1]

This power was wielded widely and successfully in the years after
1884. Such a policy was not, however, really political: there was no party
bias or even interest in party politics as such, 'unfair' newspapers being
attacked 'on purely labour grounds'.

The same is true of the great campaign to secure a 'fair wages clause'
in public contracts. Here again the trade societies were able to utilize their
newly gained political power to put pressure on parliamentary and local
council candidates to support 'fair wages' and give contracts only to 'fair'
offices. This 'fair contracts' agitation went on ceaselessly from about the
mid-eighties. Typographical societies forwarded resolutions to town and
county councils, to school and poor-law boards, issued posters and
circulars, interviewed local officials and M.P.s, presented petitions to
Parliament, and sent deputations to the Treasury, the Home Secretary,
and other Ministers—all demanding that the principle of 'a fair day's
wage for a fair day's work' should be embodied in public contracts and
that 'sweating' should be discountenanced by public authorities.

Printers led the way in this agitation, for which they gained support
in the Trades Union Congress. The principle was soon adopted by other
trades, and, as a result of their pressure and the disclosures of a 'Sweating' Committee, the House of Commons passed on 13 February 1891 a

[1] *Typographical Circular*, April 1889.

'Fair Wages Resolution', expressing the opinion that 'it is the duty of the Government in all Government contracts . . . to make every effort to secure the payment of such wages as are generally accepted as current in each trade for competent workmen'.

This typographical and other trade societies were able to use as a lever to secure similar resolutions by local authorities. By 1898 over 200 town councils had adopted the 'fair contracts' principle, as well as many school and poor-law boards and some county councils. The Association Secretary considered that 'in recent years, no principle has done more to advance the position of trade unionism'.

Printers quickly discovered, however, that the 'fair wages clause' could best be enforced by direct political action, by labour representation on local public bodies. The Association Secretary had himself secured election to the Manchester School Board in 1879, and in the next twenty years many more journeymen printers were, with trades council support, elected to town councils, school and poor-law boards, usually 'on independent lines, irrespective of the exigencies of political parties'.[1]

It was a short step from labour representation on local bodies to labour representation in Parliament. The Association had hitherto stood aloof from 'politics' and taken no part in the work of the Labour Representation League. In 1884, however, the Birmingham Typographical Society 'made a new departure', by deciding, 'if a favourable chance occurs, to run a labour candidate' for Parliament. Many printers had at last come to the conclusion that 'it was no use sending a rich man to Parliament in the conviction that he was a representative of labour . . . they should send men from among themselves, men of the type of Mr. Broadhurst and Mr. Burt'. It was pointed out that 'until a practical printer is chosen as our Labour candidate, we can never expect to see a remedial change' in the condition of the trade.

The old non-political attitude, however, still remained strong. When a ballot of the Manchester Society was taken in 1892 on the question of joining the Labour Electoral Association, 452 voted against and only 251 for. The 'old school', moreover, still dominated the Executive Council, and Henry Slatter, who 'wanted to see trade unions carried on on the same sober and steady lines as in the past' and had resigned from the T.U.C. Parliamentary Committee after the triumph of the Socialist 'New Unionists' at the Liverpool Congress in 1890, remained Association Secretary until 1897.

[1] *Typographical Circular*, July 1892.

The first members of the T.A. to become parliamentary candidates, F. Maddison and T. R. Threlfall, were put forward by trades councils at the General Election in 1892.[1] Both failed, at Hull and Liverpool respectively, but Maddison was eventually successful, as a 'Lib.-Lab.', in the by-election in the Brightside division of Sheffield which followed the death of A. J. Mundella in 1897, thus being the first T.A. member to enter Parliament.[2]

Socialist ideas and the desire for independent labour representation were growing stronger. Birmingham was again to the fore. When a proposition was put before the branch in 1894 to sever connexion with the local trades council, 'because of the action of that body in bringing forward Independent Labour candidates, and of the Socialistic tone of the Council generally', it was defeated by an overwhelming majority. Strong approval was expressed of the council's policy and an 'Independent Labour Representation Fund' was established, with a weekly subscription of one penny, 'to finance Independent Labour Candidates'. It was considered 'necessary that working men should have proper representatives on all governing bodies. Hitherto they had been misrepresented by a class which, as a class, was opposed to the interests of working men.'

Socialist ideas also triumphed in the Nottingham branch, which forwarded the following resolution for consideration by the Representative Council in September 1894:

> That the R.C., whilst loyally adhering to the principles of trade unionism as hitherto interpreted and understood, is of opinion that in view of improved methods of production, the permanent solution of labour difficulties can only be found in the nationalisation of the means of production, distribution, and exchange, to be secured by direct labour representation in Parliament; and the R.C. further recommends the granting of a sum of money annually from the Association funds in aid of the election expenses of candidates who support the labour programme on independent lines.

This proposition was included in the printed agenda, but was not mentioned either in the minutes or reports of the meeting and was apparently 'only received with sarcasm'.

---

[1] These two men had for some years played a prominent part in local politics, at Hull and Southport respectively, both being elected town councillors.

[2] He was not, however, the first journeyman compositor to become an M.P. Michael Austin, a member of the then independent Cork T.S., was returned for West Limerick in the General Election of 1892. (*Typographical Circular*, Sept. 1892.) Both Maddison and Austin lost their seats in the 1900 General Election, but J. P. Nannetti, a member of the Dublin T.S., was elected.

Several branches established labour representation funds in the following years, but the 'Old Unionists' still clung to the Association helm: Henry Slatter did not resign until the end of 1897 and Richard Hackett, his successor, was of the same school. The T.A. belonged, moreover, to that group of highly organized, rather aristocratic, and conservative 'craft' unions into which the new ideas penetrated rather slowly. Nevertheless, letters in the *Circular* during the next few years show how opinion gradually swung round to Socialism and Independent Labour Representation.

Trade depression and composing machines combined in the nineties to produce a widespread problem of unemployment, which the old trade-union methods could not solve. 'Economic forces are continually throwing men out of work, and yet trade unionism (which has helped to advance wages and reduce the hours of labour) cannot stop its members from being unemployed.' Newspaper proprietors, however, were making fortunes out of the new machinery. The workers were being exploited by 'the rotten system of capitalism' and the only solution was nationalization, whereby the instruments of production would be 'owned by the people, worked by the people, for the benefit of the people'. The hardships resulting from the introduction of the Linotype machine were caused, like those resulting from the introduction of machinery in other trades, by 'the non-recognition of the right of the worker to the wealth which his labour has called into existence'. Nearly the whole of this wealth was swallowed up by capitalist exploiters, who used the legislative machinery to protect their profits and privileges. Trade unions should learn a lesson from the capitalists, 'capture the political machinery' and bring about 'collective ownership by the workers'. They must 'add politics to their trade unionism'; not the politics of aristocrats and capitalists, 'which divides the workers into two conflicting parties', but 'the politics of labour'. They should 'federate to return members of their trade unions apart from existing political parties'. Thus the unemployment problem would be solved, for the workers 'will then insist that the central Government and all the various local and municipal authorities shall provide work for those who desire it ... and the existing competitive method will gradually give place to a more rational and scientific mode of life, where the worker need have no fear of being out of a job'. There would, in fact, be 'full employment' under a planned Socialist economy.

But Collectivism would not come suddenly, by class war and violent revolution. It would be achieved 'by a slow constitutional process', by 'peaceful revolution'. It would be 'an agitating business', with 'plenty of hard work, self-sacrifice and contumely for a long time to come'.

These ideas gained increasingly wide acceptance, as evidenced by the large number of letters on Socialism and Labour Representation written to the *Circular*. A number of members, including several branch secretaries, joined the Independent Labour Party, and one, Tom Shaw, of Sheffield, was a member of the I.L.P. Executive. The election of A. W. Jones as Assistant Secretary in 1897 and General Secretary in 1900 was a triumph for the 'new school'. Jones 'believed there was no matter of social or political progress in which organised labour should not take its share'.[1] While Nottingham branch president, he was the leading spirit on the Labour Representation Committee of the Trades Council, and later, as Association Secretary, was an ardent advocate of labour representation both on local bodies and in Parliament. His successor, H. Skinner, held similar progressive views.

There was an obvious widening of interest throughout the Association, less sectionalism, more realization of common political and social interests. The *Circular* ceased, from 1899 onwards, to be a narrow trade organ and was opened to topics of general working-class interest, particularly labour legislation: the 8-hour day, factory legislation, workmen's compensation, housing, old-age pensions, poor-law reform, reform of taxation, education, and, above all, labour representation. T.A. representatives attended the Conference on Labour Representation held in London on 27 February 1900 in accordance with a resolution of the 1899 Trades Union Congress. The Labour Representation Committee established by that Conference was hailed in the *Circular* as a 'rallying point of the various sections' of the Labour movement and the idea of an independent 'United Labour Party' was applauded. Voting by the members resulted in 3,097 'for' and 1,077 'against' affiliation with this party. The General Secretary expressed disappointment, however, at 'the small number of votes cast on a question of such importance', for only a quarter of the members had voted. The greatest obstacle facing the new movement, like that confronting the old, was apathy among the rank and file.

The T.A. henceforth regularly sent representatives to the annual Labour Representation Conferences and paid an annual affiliation fee to the L.R.C. The Association was linked to the general Labour Movement in its two aspects, political and trade union, as embodied in the Labour Party and T.U.C. The two, though closely connected, remained

[1] *Typographical Circular*, Jan. 1902.

distinct. The General Secretary pointed out that, though Organized Labour had called Labour Representation to its aid, 'Trade-unionism should not be deserted for Labour politics; it must remain the base of industrial operations'.

It was not until 1902 that the Labour Representation Committee drew up a scheme to establish a fund for the maintenance of Labour members in the House of Commons and for assisting in paying election expenses. The decision of the Lords in the Taff Vale Case—depriving trade unions of the legal freedom which they had enjoyed since 1875 and crippling their powers of trade action, particularly picketing, by exposing them to heavy financial liabilities—had convinced many 'that a Labour party in Parliament is an absolute necessity'.[1]

The question was considered by T.A. representatives at the R.C. Meeting in 1902. They decided 'that labour representation in Parliament and on local governing bodies is urgently necessary' and requested that the matter be dealt with by the Delegate Meeting in 1903. Meanwhile, the members were to be asked if they were in favour of Labour representation in Parliament and on local public bodies, and if so, whether they were willing to pay an additional penny per month in support of this. Both questions were answered in the affirmative by large majorities. It was therefore decided, at the Delegate Meeting in 1903, to establish a 'Labour Representation Fund', to which each member of the Association in full employment should contribute one penny per month. The objects of the fund were 'to pay the necessary expenses incurred in running one candidate for the House of Commons; to pay such Parliamentary representative (if elected) a sufficient sum for maintenance and travelling expenses as may be hereafter decided by the members of the Association; to assist Branches in maintaining members who may obtain election to any local public body', for which purpose branches should retain one-quarter of their contributions to the Fund.

Each branch would have the right to nominate one member for election as Parliamentary candidate, election to be by exhaustive vote of all the members. Any member nominated as a candidate either for Parliament or a local council 'must sign an agreement to the effect that he will stand as an independent Labour candidate, and shall not be allowed to be nominated by either the Liberal or Conservative party'. He must, in fact, 'hold himself entirely free from both of these political parties'. The duties of the Parliamentary Representative would be 'to watch over the interests of the trade and all labour and other legislation affect-

[1] *Typographical Circular*, Oct. 1901.

ing the interests of the worker'. The main idea was, as one speaker put it, 'to secure the election of a representative of their trade union'. The Association's Parliamentary Representative would thus have to play a double role: financed by the T.A., to represent their trade-union interests, he would also be expected to represent a constituency. But plenty of Tories and Liberals were company directors and shareholders, with equally divided allegiance.

The T.A. representative would be 'independent', belonging to no political party, but devoted solely to working-class interests. The idea still persisted that Labour action had no connexion with party politics, that politics was a kind of Parliamentary game played by Liberal capitalists and Tory aristocrats. Some held that 'independent labour representation' meant uncompromising opposition to all other parties, but most held the more reasonable view that Labour representatives, while standing separate and unattached, avoiding entangling alliances and at all times supporting the Labour cause, should be free to co-operate with either Liberals or Tories to secure desirable reforms.

The Executive decided in November 1903 to contribute to the Labour Representation Committee's 'Maintenance Fund' on behalf of the Association. The contribution was at first 1d., raised in 1906 to 2d., per member per annum. The T.A.'s contribution, therefore, was just over £70 at first, rising to over £150 in 1906.[1] The T.A. was to choose its own candidate and the constituency for which he should stand and also pay his election expenses. If he was successful, moreover, the Association would pay his salary, but would receive £200 annually from the L.R.C.'s Maintenance Fund.

Nominations for the position of Parliamentary candidate were invited in June 1904 and voting resulted in favour of G. H. Roberts, who had recently been elected Southern Organizer, after being president and then secretary of the Norwich branch for several years. An ardent Socialist and member of the I.L.P., he had played a very active role in local politics as president of the Trades Council. He was the first Labour member to be elected (1899) to the Norwich School Board and had stood, unsuccessfully, as an Independent Labour candidate at the Parliamentary by-election in Norwich in 1904. It was decided that he should again stand as Labour candidate for Norwich, his candidature being endorsed by a large public meeting. The T.A. gave him strong support, providing an election agent, renting and furnishing a committee-room, printing election literature, paying travelling and other expenses, and sending

[1] This was in addition to the L.R.C. affiliation fee.

deputations to assist in the campaign, which resulted successfully in Roberts's election in January 1906 as the first T.A. Parliamentary Representative.[1]

Thus the T.A. shared in the great Labour electoral triumph of 1906 which established the party as a potent force in national politics. From now on political articles, usually of a strong Socialist flavour, occupied the most prominent position in the *Typographical Circular*, even to the exclusion of printing trade affairs: articles on current political questions, particularly social legislation and the activities of the Labour Party; articles denouncing the old political parties, the House of Lords, capitalist exploitation, and class privileges, demanding payment of M.P.s and election expenses, and urging such social reforms as the prevention or relief of unemployment, poor-law reform, old-age pensions, national insurance, slum clearance and new housing, improved education, meals and medical inspection for school-children, and so on—to be paid for by a graduated income-tax, increased death duties, and taxation of land values, unearned income, and excess profits—while the more extreme advocated nationalization of the means of production, distribution, and exchange. The T.A. was, in fact, carried along on the broad current of Labour politics. G. H. Roberts became widely known in the Labour movement as a vigorous propagandist on the I.L.P. platform. He was elected one of the party whips in the House of Commons and a member of the Executive Committee.

A substantial minority of T.A. members, however, had voted in 1900 against affiliation with the Labour Party and in 1903 against Labour Representation in Parliament. Many were still opposed to political action by trade unions. Many were Liberals or Conservatives and strongly objected to compulsory contributions to the support of the Labour Party and for the maintenance of a rabid Socialist as Parliamentary Representative. Against such dissentients, however, the Executive upheld the divine right of the majority to decide Association rules and policy and to override the opinions of a minority. They decided that any member who failed to pay the contributions due would be placed out of benefit and ultimately expelled.

[1] Other representatives of trade unionism in the printing trade who secured election in 1906 were T. Summerbell (of Sunderland, a T.A. member who had become a small master printer), C. W. Bowerman (L.S.C. Secretary), G. D. Kelley (General Secretary of the Litho. Printers and P. & K.T.F. Secretary), F. Maddison, and J. P. Nannetti. Prior to the election, the T.A. Executive called on all members in constituencies where there were Labour candidates 'to render all the support they can by working and voting for such candidates'.

In November 1908, however, the Court of Appeal granted an injunction to W. V. Osborne, a dissentient member of the Amalgamated Society of Railway Servants, restraining that union from making a levy on its members and from using any of its funds for political purposes, such as supporting the Labour Party or maintaining Members of Parliament—a decision upheld by the House of Lords in December 1909 in the famous Osborne Judgement. The A.S.R.S. was a society registered under the Trade Union Acts of 1871 and 1876, from which the judges drew their restrictive definition of the purposes of a trade union. But the T.A. was an unregistered society, to which, therefore, it might be held that this judgement did not apply. In April 1910, however, A. E. Buck, a member of the Derby branch, and S. Hassall, of the Stockport branch, instituted legal proceedings on behalf of all dissentient members to secure an injunction restraining the Executive from compelling members to contribute to the Labour Representation Fund and from using any of the Association's funds for Labour Representation purposes. As the Association was the first unregistered trade union against which proceedings had been instituted, the Executive decided to fight the case, which was heard before Vice-Chancellor Leigh-Clare in the Chancery division at the Manchester Assize Courts on 8 July 1910. The Vice-Chancellor decided, however, that non-registration did not affect the case and that he was bound by the Osborne Judgement and therefore granted the injunction.

It was useless to carry the case farther. Instead, the T.A. joined in the general trade-union outcry against the Osborne Judgement and in the demand that their right to political action, hitherto freely exercised, should be expressly recognized by the law. Until such legislative recognition could be achieved, the Executive had to rely upon purely voluntary contributions in order to maintain the Labour Representation Fund. They appealed to members 'not . . . to allow the Chancery Court's decision to prevent assistance being given to the Labour party in the good work that it is doing on behalf of Trade Unionism and the workers generally', and exhorted them 'to rise to the occasion by voluntarily contributing to the Labour Representation Fund at least as much as they have been doing in the past'. Members were also urged 'to use every means in their power to back up the Labour party in Parliament' in their endeavour to secure an alteration of the law giving freedom of political action to trade unions.

The Executive reported at the end of 1910 that 'comparatively few members have refrained from contributing to the Labour Representation

Fund', and the half-yearly Association balance-sheets show that annual contributions, which had averaged £873 in the years 1906–9, when they were compulsory, only fell to £829 in the years 1910–13, when they were voluntary. Clearly, the great majority of T.A. members were supporters of trade-union political action and of the Labour party, or were too timid or indifferent to refuse payment of the usual subscriptions.

Meanwhile, G. H. Roberts had held his seat at Norwich in the two General Elections of 1910, being strongly supported on each occasion by the Association. An important factor in his success was the appointment in 1906 of a permanent election agent, to carry on the work of registration and organization. It had been decided after the election of 1906 that Roberts should be allowed to retain the position of Southern Organizer, in view of the uncertainty attaching to tenure of a Parliamentary seat. His salary, as Parliamentary Representative and Organizer, was fixed at £350 per annum, £200 of which was recovered from the Labour Party's Maintenance Fund.

In 1911, however, Parliament conceded the payment of £400 a year to M.P.s. Considerable party funds were still necessary, of course, to win and hold seats—for organization, propaganda, registration, payment of election agents, and election expenses—and the Labour Representation Fund was therefore continued, but the Labour Party now ceased to pay its members and the T.A. decided that it would in future merely pay G. H. Roberts a retaining fee of £50 per annum as Organizer. As a result, Roberts tendered his resignation. He had no security as Parliamentary Representative, he feared that he would lose his position as Organizer (the duties of which office it was impossible for him to fulfil), and his expenses were so heavy that he was unable to make provision for the future—in fact he could not continue on his present income and could do better for himself and his family outside public life. It was eventually agreed, however, that the question of his salary should be referred to the Delegate Meeting in 1913, which decided 'that as Mr. Roberts was duly elected to the position of Organizer, which position has never been vacated, he receive the remuneration provided for the position in accordance with rule', i.e. £2. 5s. per week and, when travelling, 10s. per day for expenses, with third-class railway fare. The increased income proved satisfactory to Roberts, who therefore continued as T.A. Parliamentary Representative.

The Trade Union Act of 1913, resulting from the Labour outcry against the Osborne Judgement, empowered a trade union to include 'the furtherance of political objects' in its constitution—that is, the expenditure of money on the payment of election expenses, the holding of political meetings, distribution of political literature, and maintenance of political representatives—but only after a ballot of the members had been held and a majority of those voting had approved. Moreover, the payments were to be made out of a special political fund, from contribution to which any member could claim exemption. Such a member was not, through 'contracting out', to be excluded from any benefits of the union or placed under any disability or disadvantage as compared with other members. The rules for the political fund were to be approved and registered by the Chief Registrar of Friendly Societies, to whom a return was to be made each year, and to whom any member aggrieved by breach of the rules could complain.

A ballot of T.A. members under this Act was held in May 1914, the Executive urging them to vote in favour of political action in view of 'the great good that has been accomplished by means of Labour representation'. The result was 6,609 'for' to 3,793 'against' and rules for a T.A. political fund were therefore drawn up. These, approved and registered in January 1915, merely gave legal sanction to the existing voluntary fund, the subscription still remaining at the old figure of $\frac{1}{4}d.$ per week.

Co-operative Production

Typographical societies had been attracted by the idea of co-operative production in the 1840's, particularly as a means of 'employing the unemployed'. Various schemes for co-operative printing offices had been propounded and a short-lived *People's Newspaper* had actually been established. During the next twenty years, however, we hear little of such schemes. The P.T.A. devoted itself almost exclusively to purely trade-union affairs, to questions of wages, hours, and apprentices.

Interest in co-operative production revived, however, in the sixties. Henry Roberts, the Association Secretary, speaking at the Conference of Trades' Delegates in Sheffield in 1866, 'considered it an imperative duty to advocate the principles of Co-operation', which would enable the working classes 'to get the full benefit of their labour'. He especially urged that they should 'have a daily newspaper of their own to act as their organ'.

His successor, Henry Slatter, was also an ardent believer in co-operation. He was a prominent member of the Manchester and Salford Co-operative Society, chairman and honorary secretary at different times of the North-western Section of the Co-operative Board, and a regular attender at the annual Co-operative Congresses. He was also among the founders and for ten years president of the Co-operative Printing Society, established in Manchester in 1869.

This Society was founded by leading members of the Manchester Typographical Society and P.T.A. Executive Council who were also prominent in the Manchester and Salford Equitable Co-operative Society. Lancashire was the heart of the Co-operative Movement and they looked to the recently established Wholesale Society and numerous co-operative stores for the bulk of their trade. They also hoped to secure the printing of other working-class organizations, such as trade unions and friendly societies.

The C.P.S. was to be a labour co-partnership: the workmen were to hold shares and participate in the profits and management. Co-operative societies and trade unions were also invited to buy shares. In distributing profits, interest would first be paid on capital invested and the remainder would then be divided between shareholders and workmen.

As a business concern the Society proved extremely successful. Its share capital rose from £445 in 1869 to £16,631 in 1891, by which time it was employing 330 men and had an annual turnover of £63,149. In 1872 and 1886 it had established branches in Newcastle and London, while new buildings had been erected in Manchester. Shareholders were at first paid 7 per cent. per annum, plus a substantial bonus, while the workmen received a similar bonus in addition to their weekly wages. In 1872, however, the interest on share capital was raised to 7½ per cent. and the remaining profits were equally divided between shareholders, workers, and customers, the payment of dividend to the latter being intended to attract trade. Capital continued to take the lion's share of the profits. In 1891, for example, capital received 10 per cent. (dividend plus bonus) or 2s. in the pound, making a total of £1,627, while labour got only 5¾d. in the pound on wages and customers 4½d. in the pound on purchases, that is, £447 and £660 respectively.

This tendency to 'joint-stockism' was denounced by G. J. Holyoake:

The Manchester Printing Society gives 7½ per cent. to capital, where capital has small risk, seeing that the co-operative societies are at once shareholders and customers; and these well-secured, over-paid shareholders come in for a second share of profit with labour's one share, so that the workpeople have a shabby award insufficient to create pride, interest, or exertion on their part. This is imposture profit-sharing, but very good capital sharing.[1]

---

[1] Holyoake, G. J., *The Co-operative Movement Today* (1891), p. 133.

The Society was not, as its founders intended, a workers' co-partnership. At the end of 1892 the employees, who then numbered nearly 400, held only £700 out of about £17,000 share capital. They had also very little say in management, and discipline was enforced as in any other printing works. Moreover, the workers still needed to maintain their trade-union organization, though relations between management and workers were usually friendly and the Society was generally among the first to advance wages or reduce hours when approached by the Association. Working conditions were also good. The C.P.S. was, in fact, more like an enlightened, profit-sharing joint-stock company than a producers' co-operative association. The only difference was that the Society was 'organised by and for the advantage of the associations of consumers', which held most of the shares.[1]

No other typographical society appears to have succeeded in establishing a co-operative printing office like that in Manchester until the early nineties, though a few sporadic attempts were made and several articles on co-operative production appeared in the *Circular*. There is no sign that the mass of T.A. members had much belief or interest in the idea during these years.

The 'New Unionist' movement in the late eighties, however, with its Socialist leavening, revived enthusiasm for such schemes. Several T.A. branches founded co-operative printing offices in the early nineties. Nottingham, Hull, Leicester, and Blackpool established general printing offices. In Newcastle an *Evening News* was started to employ out-of-work members. Bolton and Bradford were making similar attempts in 1893 and the *Workman's Times* carried on a precarious existence for several years in Huddersfield, London, and Manchester. A Labour Press was also established in Manchester, mainly for the printing of political pamphlets.

These offices were usually established on labour co-partnership lines, but other societies were invited to buy shares. Their main purpose was to provide work for unemployed or strike hands. They were very small affairs, never employing more than about thirty men, usually much less, and many failed. Their chief problem was lack of capital and the 1898 Delegate Meeting therefore empowered the E.C. to invest Association funds in such undertakings.

As a result, several more co-operative printing offices were established in the new few years, at Darwen, Derby, Birmingham, and Norwich. The Executive invested £200 with the Labour Press and sums varying

[1] Webb, S. and B., *The Consumers' Co-operative Movement* (1921), p. 93.

from £50 to £160 with the Blackpool, Nottingham, Darwen, and Hull societies. But the Labour Press and the Darwen Printing Union collapsed in 1900–1 and the Association lost most of its investments. Co-operative societies were strongly opposed by private firms, they lacked capital, had management problems, and often succumbed to competition.

During the following decade, however, the co-operative printing societies in Nottingham, Hull, Leicester, Derby, Birmingham, and Norwich not only managed to survive, but slowly expanded, while others were established in Bristol, Plymouth, Portsmouth, and Swansea. In all of these the Executive invested loan capital, in sums varying from £50 to £550. In several it also placed a small amount of share capital, while it actually took over Norwich Printers Ltd. on its failure in 1908 and re-established it as the 'Caxton Press' with a capital investment of £345. All these societies, however, were small concerns, with capital of only a few hundred pounds, existing mainly on the printing of trade unions and other labour organizations. The co-operative vista was still a long way off.

PART III

THE TYPOGRAPHICAL ASSOCIATION
1914–1949

·꞉(❈)꞉·

XV

THE FIRST WORLD WAR
1914–18

APART from a few pacifist International Socialists, mostly members of the I.L.P., the T.A. adopted a whole-heartedly patriotic attitude on the outbreak of war. Articles in the *Circular* condemned German militaristic aggression, pointing out that the British Government had sought to avoid war, but that isolationist neutrality was impossible and that we must, in honour, defend Belgium. The T.A. thoroughly agreed with the Labour Party's decision to support the Government in waging the war. Thousands of T.A. volunteers joined the colours. By the end of 1914 there were nearly 2,000 in the Forces, over 6,000 by the end of 1916, and over 7,000 in 1917, after conscription, out of a membership of about 23,000. Over 800 T.A. members died during the war in the service of their country. Many also went into war work, particularly munitions.

The co-operation of the trade unions was vital to the war effort, and to secure it the Government had to accord them 'a *locus standi* in the determination of essentially national issues that was undreamt of in previous times. . . . In practically every branch of public administration, from unimportant local committees up to the Cabinet itself, we find the Trade Union world now accepted as forming, virtually, a separate constituency, which has to be specially represented.'[1] This development is clearly evidenced in T.A. history during the war years. We find the Executive of the T.A., or more usually the P. & K.T.F., being consulted or listened to by Government departments on all important questions affecting the printing trade, while T.A. representatives sat on National

---

[1] Webb, S. and B., op. cit., p. 645.

Service Committees, Labour Exchange Advisory Committees, War Pensions Committees, &c. G. H. Roberts, the T.A. Parliamentary Representative, entered Asquith's Coalition Ministry in 1915 as a Lord Commissioner of the Treasury; in the second Coalition Ministry formed by Lloyd George in December 1916 he became Parliamentary Secretary to the Board of Trade; and in the reorganization of Lloyd George's Government in August 1917 he was made Minister of Labour, with a seat in the Cabinet. Thus the T.A. shared in 'the revolutionary transformation of the social and political standing' of trade unions which resulted from the war.

The war, of course, had very serious effects on the printing trade and those employed in it. There was panic and dislocation at first: newspapers reduced in size, many publications suspended, general printing depressed, and the book trade hard hit. By the end of August incomplete branch returns showed 1,645 T.A. members unemployed and 7,600 on short time. So serious and widespread was unemployment that the Government had to make emergency grants. In a few months, however, trade recovered, to the slogan of 'Business as usual', while many members entered the Forces, munition works, engineering, and other trades where men were needed, with the result that, despite restricted supplies of paper, printing metal, &c., unemployment practically disappeared and gave way to labour shortage. Members employed on Government work or newspapers were exempt from military service, but general printing was regarded by the Government as a non-essential trade, workers in which should, as far as possible, be directed into the Forces, munition works, or some other national service. The result was that by the beginning of 1917 the number of men employed in the industry had been reduced by nearly 50 per cent. and there was such an acute labour shortage, particularly of machine minders and keyboard operators, that many firms had machines standing idle (between 30 and 40 per cent. of Monotype keyboards in the country were unmanned), while some had to close down.

Both Government and employers brought great pressure on the T.A. and other printing trade unions to relax restrictive rules and permit 'dilution', so as to release men for the Forces and munitions and, at the same time, meet the labour shortage. The problem was general and in many trades, particularly engineering, the unions agreed to a wholesale suspension of 'trade union conditions' for the duration of the war. The T.A., as we have seen, had built up a network of rules and customs, protective of the living standard and status of skilled printers, which might well be regarded as restrictive, even unpatriotic, in war-time: insistence, for example, on seven years' apprenticeship, exclusion of females, refusal to work with non-members, restrictive piece-work regulations, apprentice limitation, bans on 'twicing' and 'smooting', restrictions on overtime and the manning of printing machines.

Many employers sought to disregard these rules as labour shortage grew and the Government urged 'relaxation of rules and dilution of labour in order to release men for the armed forces and to enable the industry to be carried on'. More than anything else, they wished to introduce women, particularly on composing machines, for which they were considered especially suited: in other trades men had been satisfactorily replaced by women in far more difficult work. The whole question was brought before the P. & K.T.F., numerous meetings were held with Home Office and F.M.P. representatives, and the unions eventually agreed (July 1916) to 'such suspension of trade rules and customs as may be necessary to secure the carrying on of the trade', the details to be settled between employers and individual unions. 'This agreement', it was emphasized, 'shall be regarded purely as a war emergency, and pre-war conditions shall be reverted to when the war is over.' As a *quid pro quo* the employers guaranteed post-war reinstatement, 'where at all possible', of workmen joining the Forces.

A conference was now held between T.A. and F.M.P. representatives in October 1916, when an agreement was reached on relaxation of certain Association rules. Machine minders were now permitted to take charge of more machines than was customary prior to the war, provided they were paid specified extras. The 'twicing' rule was suspended, so that when no minders were available compositors might assist on machines, while compositor-readers could transfer to the composing department. When journeymen were not available, apprentices might work on Linotype and Monotype machines after the first two (instead of three) years of their apprenticeship. The limitation of overtime was suspended, together with the rule against 'smooting', so that there was now nothing to prevent members working whatever hours they liked or in different offices. The Association, moreover, had already allowed superannuated members to work at the trade, and urged that hand compositors should be trained to meet the shortage of operators. They had refused, however, the most urgent request of both employers and Government, for the introduction of females and unskilled labour: the agreement was 'to enable the trade to "carry on" with the efforts and assistance of *our members only*'. The Association was therefore accused of being unpatriotic:

all the concessions made, though they meant more work, would put more money into T.A. pockets, while they were insufficient to meet the existing labour shortage, which, it was hinted, the Association wished to maintain, since it gave them the whip-hand over employers in wage negotiations. The Association, on the other hand, asserted that the employers merely wanted cheap labour, that the entry of women and unskilled men would mean a lowering of standards and prevent a return to the *status quo* when the war ended: the Association was, in fact, holding the fort for members now in the Forces. They insisted that sufficient relaxation had been made, that qualified labour was available, members being unemployed in several branches, and, despite pressure by employers and Government and increasing labour shortage, rigidly maintained their exclusive attitude throughout the war. Many employers, however, did introduce females and 'diluted labour', though strikes often resulted, and the Monotype Corporation established schools to train women operators. Nevertheless, the T.A.'s stand was generally successful.

The Association maintained during the war its traditional attitude towards non-members and several strikes occurred against their employment, though 'mixed houses' were still common. The maintenance of minimum wages and apprentice-limitation also remained cardinal features of T.A. policy. Many apprentices joined the colours and employers wished to replace them, but the unions objected, since it might flood the post-war labour market. No agreement was reached until the war was nearly over, when the return of apprentices to civil life was the chief problem; the T.A. meanwhile would only permit replacement of apprentices who had reached the last eighteen months of their time prior to joining up, those with longer to serve still being counted in the apprentice ratio. The employers greatly resented this restrictive policy, which aggravated the labour shortage, particularly after conscription of eighteen-year-old apprentices: in many offices most or even all apprentices were called up. Disputes were therefore frequent.

The T.A., despite relaxation of certain rules during the war, never surrendered on fundamentals and was therefore in a strong position when war ended. The Association was fortunate in that printing was, generally speaking, less essential in war-time than, say, engineering, in which the number of workers and output had to be greatly increased, thus necessitating wholesale suspension of union rules and 'dilution of labour'.

By far the greatest space in T.A. minute-books during the war years is occupied by wages negotiations. The cost of living had been steadily rising for several years prior to 1914 and wages movements had been numerous; but when war broke out an industrial truce was tacitly agreed on. The T.A. Executive, under the general delusion that the war would soon be over, decided 'that all wages movements be deferred until after the war'. But soon, owing to the rapid rise in prices, branches were clamouring for wage increases or 'war bonuses' and in April 1915 the Executive decided 'to approach the employers nationally with a view to securing a war bonus of 15 per cent. on existing rates to those members in receipt of wages up to £2, and 10 per cent. to those in receipt of over £2'. This was an unprecedented step, all wages movements having hitherto been local: it foreshadowed the National Wages Agreement of 1919. A conference was arranged in June with the Federation of Master Printers and the Linotype Users' Association, but the employers refused to grant any bonus owing to reduced trade and rising costs. The T.A. Executive therefore advised branches that they 'should at once proceed with any local movements at present suspended'.

From now on the minute-books are a maelstrom of such movements, which, owing to the constant rise in the cost of living, went on unceasingly throughout the war years. At first advances of a few shillings were sought, as before the war, but by 1917–18 some branches were demanding increases of as much as 15s. per week. The growing labour shortage gave them the upper hand in wages negotiations and they usually secured most of what they asked for. On the other hand, employers generally appreciated the hardships caused by rising prices. Settlement was usually along the now traditional lines of conference and compromise, though strikes often threatened and did occasionally occur. Most branches secured four or five, some six or seven, increases during the war, either war bonuses or actual wage advances, so that by the end of 1918 wages were nearly double pre-war rates. In Manchester, for example, the minimum rate (including war bonus) had risen from 38s. 6d. to 70s., in Leeds from 37s. to 66s., in Exeter from 28s. to 60s., in Lincoln from 30s. to 61s. On average, allowing for differences in branch membership, wages had risen by about 90 per cent. above pre-war. The cost of living, however, had risen by about 120 per cent. so that members were considerably worse off than in 1914. In some of the smaller country towns, moreover, rates were as low as 50s., while in Ireland many printers were still only getting 30s. to 40s. a week.

During the earlier part of the war most wages movements were, as in the past, branch movements, though national officials usually took part and branches often participated in movements by local P. & K.T.F. federations. As the war progressed, however, there was an increasing tendency to action by groups, in order to elevate the lower-paid branches and sections, and it was decided at the Delegate Meeting in 1918 that in future 'all wage movements . . . shall be group movements', despite opposition by large branches such as Manchester, Liverpool, and Leeds, which clung to their local autonomy and disliked being held back by smaller, less strongly organized branches. By this time, however, the idea of a National Wages Agreement had been raised and, though it was rejected by the Delegate Meeting, the Executive were already in negotiation with the F.M.P. upon it.

The question of shorter hours and holidays fell into the background during the war. The General Secretary stated at the Delegate Meeting in 1918 that the Executive considered 'it is best to concentrate upon wages. . . . After all, it is the money our men want now; our members are less concerned about shorter hours and holidays than they are about better pay. All efforts should be centred upon getting higher wages, so that the members may live decently in the present difficult and distressing times.' Moreover, the acute labour shortage prevented any reduction of hours. During the last two years of the war, however, pressure grew increasingly strong for a 48-hour week and an annual week's holiday with pay, resulting in the National Hours and Holidays Agreement of 1919.

The question of agreement with the employers on the T.A. rules relating to machinemen, apprentices, indicators, &c., as revised by the Delegate Meeting of 1913, had also to be postponed until after the war. The Delegate Meeting of 1918, however, re-enacted and added to the 1913 rules and decided that they should become operative not later than 1 May 1919. Agreement on them was also to form part of the post-war settlement.

The pre-war national agreements on Linotype and Monotype machines continued to prove of great value during the war years, saving endless local negotiations on operators' wage rates. The T.A., however, generally ignored the clauses in the 1911 'Agreement on Rules' relating to the Committee of Reference: disputes were hardly ever brought before it, the Executive frequently using the strike weapon, despite protests from the F.M.P. and Newspaper Owners. Neither did the Association allow its strike action to be much fettered by affiliation to the P. & K.T.F.

T.A. membership suffered somewhat during the early years of the war, falling from 23,783 at the end of 1914 to 23,039 in June 1917, but then increased rapidly to 24,762 by the end of 1918. The number of branches also increased from 160 to 172 between December 1914 and

December 1918. Organizing work was very vigorous in the later years of the war, particularly in the country districts of east and south-west England, north Wales, and Ireland. Many men were attracted into the Association by the wage increases which it secured for its members, while the war-time labour shortage enabled the Association to put greater pressure on employers.

The war placed a severe strain upon T.A. finances, particularly as the Association exempted all Service members from subscriptions and paid their superannuation contributions out of the General Fund. The heavy loss of life also involved large funeral payments, while excessive unemployment at the beginning of the war was a great burden. Nevertheless, the Association overcame its difficulties and the General Fund actually rose from £43,637 in June 1914 to £61,900 in December 1918. This was due mainly to two things: firstly, the imposition of a war-time levy of 2d. per half-year, secondly, the practical disappearance of unemployment; out-of-work payments, which had averaged £10,000 to £15,000 annually in the years 1900–13 and rose to £17,000 in 1914, had fallen to £2,000 by 1918.

XVI

POST-WAR SETTLEMENT
1918–23

THE T.A. emerged from the immense trials and anxieties of the war years almost unscathed, with increased power and ready to face the problems of post-war settlement. The year 1919 was to be the most momentous in the whole history of the Association: the national agreements then reached have provided the framework of its later history down to the present day.

Demobilization and Reinstatement

Demobilization took place rapidly: by the end of 1919 there were only 759 T.A. members in the Forces. There was some increase in the number of unemployed and casuals, but most of the demobilized men were absorbed in the industry, which was participating in the post-war boom of 1919–20. The war-time relaxation of rules was ended early in 1919, now that plenty of labour was available. Agreements were concluded between the P. & K.T.F. and F.M.P., along the lines of the Government's post-war schemes, for the reinstatement of apprentices and for the training and employment of disabled ex-servicemen.

The Joint Industrial Council

Long before the war ended the air was full of schemes of 'Reconstruction'. Proposals for the 'Betterment of the Printing Trade' which appeared in the *Caxton Magazine* during the latter half of 1916 aroused considerable interest,[1] and a conference in London convened by the *Caxton* in April 1917 and attended by over a hundred master printers and trade union representatives endorsed 'the principle of greater co-operation between employers and workers for printing trade betterment' and urged the F.M.P. and P. & K.T.F. to meet with a view to agreement on a 'Betterment Scheme'.

Shortly after this conference the Government Reconstruction Committee issued the famous Whitley Report on 'Relations between Employers and Employed', recommending the formation of Joint Standing

---

[1] The idea was originated by James McQuitty of Belfast, writing under the pseudonym 'Q'. His proposals became known as the 'Q Scheme'.

Industrial Councils. The earlier 'Trade Betterment' schemes and the Whitley Report were therefore considered together and the eventual outcome, early in 1919, after many conferences and advice from the Ministry of Labour, was the establishment of a Joint Industrial Council.

The Joint Industrial Council of the Printing and Allied Trades of the United Kingdom was to be an association of members of the F.M.P.,[1] employing union labour, and trade unions affiliated to the P. & K.T.F. Its objects were to secure complete organization of employers and employees throughout the trade; to co-operate in the maintenance of fair prices and wages; to promote good relationship between employers and employed; to establish uniform working hours and conditions; to minimize unemployment; to insist upon clean, well-ventilated workshops and safeguard the health of workpeople generally; to consider the selection and technical training of apprentices; to improve processes, machinery, and standards of workmanship and secure the removal of restrictive practices; to deal with proposed legislation affecting the printing trade; to encourage social welfare activities—in fact 'to do all things possible for the betterment of the trade'. Perhaps its most important function would be 'to devise ways and means of settling any differences that may arise' between employers and employed. 'No strike, lock-out, or other aggressive or coercive action', it was laid down, 'shall take place in any locality until the matter in question has been placed before and been considered by the District Committee, and failing a settlement being arrived at, has been remitted to the National Executive, which shall meet to consider the question within six days.'

To carry out these objects there was to be a National Executive, consisting of equal numbers of employers and employees, with 'full power to consider all matters connected with the industry', and also District Committees, Works Advisory Committees, and a yearly National Assembly.

The first meeting of the J.I.C. took place in London on 1 July 1919, the proceedings being opened by G. J. Wardle, M.P., Parliamentary Secretary to the Board of Trade, who stated that this was the fortieth such Council to be established. The following sub-committees were appointed: Finance, General Purposes, Health, Conciliation, Unemployment, and Organization.

The J.I.C. did not meet the wishes of more extreme unionists, who had been demanding not only profit-sharing and participation in management, but even abolition of capitalism and establishment of guild socialism.

[1] The Newspaper Society was admitted in Jan. 1921.

It marked, however, a great improvement in industrial relationships. Whether it would succeed in carrying out its multifarious objects for 'Trade Betterment' and industrial peace remained to be seen. It also remained to be seen how far it would restrict T.A. autonomy, especially in regard to strikes: it obviously increased the powers of the P. & K.T.F. and tended towards treatment of printing trade problems on 'industrial' rather than 'craft' lines.

Hours and Holidays

It was through the P. & K.T.F. that the hours and holidays question was tackled after the war. A 48-hour week had long been the goal: the Federation movement of 1910-11 had failed, but the unions had never been satisfied with 51 hours.[1] Moreover, there was now a demand for an annual week's holiday with pay and payment for statutory holidays, such as Christmas Day, Good Friday, and Bank Holidays. Hours and holidays had fallen into the background at the beginning of the war, but in 1918 the Federation started to move again: there was a general demand for a 48-hour week, while some unions wanted 44 or even 40. Shorter hours would, it was hoped, reduce unemployment after the war, improve health, and provide more leisure time for mental and physical recreation. All the benefit of labour-saving machinery should not go to the employers.

The hours struggle of 1910-11 had been prolonged and bitter, with grave danger of a national strike. The post-war movement was short, however, the employers conceding almost all demands after friendly conferences at the beginning of 1919. The result was the National Hours and Holidays Agreement (January) and Daily Newspaper Offices Supplementary Agreement (March).[2] The working week was henceforth to be 48 hours in general printing and weekly news offices; 48 (day) and 45 (night) in daily newspaper offices; piece rates to be advanced proportionately to the reduction in hours. Holidays with pay were to be granted on Christmas Day, Boxing Day, Good Friday, Easter Monday, Whit Monday, and the first Monday in August. Except in the case of daily news hands, employees working on these days were to be paid time-and-a-half for Bank Holidays, double time for Christmas Day and the customary extra rates for Good Friday, with a minimum of time-and-a-half, besides which they would be entitled to a day's holiday with

[1] In many branches and offices the hours were already less, particularly in news offices.

[2] These agreements, negotiated with the B.F.M.P. and Newspaper Society, were later accepted by the I.M.P.A. in Ireland.

pay in place of the holiday worked; daily news hands working on any such holiday merely to have another day as substitute.[1] Finally, an annual week's holiday with pay was granted. Any disputes regarding the agreement were to be dealt with by a Joint Committee.

This agreement was generally acclaimed, but certain branches and sections were dissatisfied. Some of the large towns already had a 48-hour week and therefore got no reduction; but the Executive pointed out that the majority of branches had benefited. Daily newspaper hands, especially Linotype operators, were greatly discontented since the agreement left their hours unaffected.[2] They were also aggrieved at having to work on national holidays without being paid extra. About the latter grievance the Executive could, as yet, do little. In regard to hours, they had tried to get a reduction for operators, but had failed: the employers insisted on uniformity and it was difficult to combat their arguments. Moreover, it had always been a sore point with case hands that they had to work 51 or more hours and operators only 48. Further negotiations with the Linotype Users' Association also failed. In future, therefore, operators ceased to be a privileged section as regards hours.[3]

The ink was scarcely dry on the 48-hour agreement when the P. & K.T.F. decided, at its Annual Conference in April 1919, to move for a working week of 44 hours (day) and 40 hours (night): the 48-hour week, so long sought, was now felt to be out of date. A ballot showed an overwhelming majority in favour and negotiations were opened with the employers. Union officials, however, were rather lukewarm and found difficulty in refuting the employers' arguments at a conference in February 1920: that it was too soon to alter the 48-hour agreement; that, in the national interest, production must be increased; that labour was scarce and costs were rising. Moreover, the main question at the moment was increased wages, due to the high cost of living. The hours movement was therefore shelved. Hours were not, in fact, to be altered again until 1937.

National Wages Agreements

Since long before the T.A. was established, wages in the printing trade had varied from town to town and been settled locally. The T.A.,

---

[1] Workers on most daily newspapers published on these holidays were customarily paid ordinary rates. The employers maintained that this was part of the recognized conditions of employment on daily newspapers, for which the workers were compensated by higher wages.

[2] Linotype operators had secured 48 hours (day) and 44 (night) by the 1898 agreement.

[3] Except that their night hours remained at 44.

as we have seen, had tried to secure increased uniformity and latterly district or group movements had become common. There was still, however, an extraordinary variation. Moreover, the T.A. was only one of more than twenty unions affiliated to the P. & K.T.F., each with its own varying local wage rates. In some towns the different societies joined in local federation movements, but more often each acted independently. In wages matters particularly, the different unions clung to their autonomy. The result was utter confusion, rivalry, and lack of stability in wage rates, while endless time and labour were spent in local and sectional negotiations.

Towards the end of the war, therefore, the idea of a national wages settlement arose. There were two possibilities: either sectional agreements between employers and individual unions or a general agreement for the whole industry through the P. & K.T.F. The latter was already negotiating on hours, so why not on wages? Moreover, there was at this time a strong feeling in favour of amalgamation. At the Annual Conference of the Federation, therefore, in 1918, George Isaacs, N.S.O.P. & A. General Secretary, proposed the creation of 'A National Wage Committee for the printing trades, with a view of such committee dealing with all questions of wages covering all sections of the Federation in all areas.'[1] He condemned the existing chaos and proposed a national wage basis or 'standard rate from which all wages could be adjusted'. This would bring up wages in lower-paid sections and areas. The older, better-paid, craft unions, however, including the T.A., opposed the idea: they did not want 'levelling up' or to be 'tied down by a national wages standard'. Such a scheme would give too much power to Federation officials and limit the precious autonomy of individual unions. It would be too slow and cumbersome. It was opposed to ancient customs and prejudices and was therefore shelved.

The first suggestion for a national wages settlement came from the employers, towards the end of 1917. Sick of the endless round of branch and group movements, they proposed a conference either with the T.A. or P. & K.T.F. to discuss a national agreement. The T.A. Executive at first rejected the idea, but later agreed. Delays occurred, however, and the T.A. Delegate Meeting in June 1918 voted against a national wages movement, preferring the group system. Matters reached a crisis immediately afterwards, as a result of wages memorials from the T.A.

---

[1] In 1919 he proposed that a National Wage Committee should be set up within the J.I.C. This proposal is extremely interesting in view of present-day attempts to create a 'National Wages Structure' for the whole industry.

branches in Manchester and Liverpool. These branches had received an increase of nearly 10s. in January, but were now demanding a further 15s., which, of course, would soon set off other branches. The F.M.P., L.U.A., and Newspaper Owners therefore held a joint meeting on 20 June and decided 'to organise a most vigorous resistance to the memorials from the T.A. and other Unions in their present form', considering 'that the question of wages . . . should be dealt with as a national matter'. This put the T.A. Executive in a quandary, in view of the Delegate Meeting's decision. A serious strike or lock-out threatened, but eventually the Executive decided that, if the local movements in Manchester and Liverpool were first dealt with, they would be prepared to discuss the question of a national wages settlement. To this the employers agreed and, the Manchester and Liverpool dispute being settled, the first national wages conference was held in London on 1 August.

Meanwhile, in July 1917, the Linotype Users' Association had given notice to terminate the Linotype 'Stab Agreement of 1898. They particularly objected to the $12\frac{1}{2}$ per cent. over case rates fixed for operators. The T.A. Executive, however, strongly protested against such abrupt, one-sided termination of the agreement and instructed branches to resist any departure from it. In January 1918, therefore, the L.U.A. stated that they were prepared to meet in conference to discuss an amended agreement. The T.A. then asked for proposed amendments, but nothing more was heard. The revision of both the Linotype and Monotype agreements eventually became mixed up in the negotiations for a national wages scheme. In the conferences on this question the T.A. met representatives not only of the F.M.P. (including the Monotype Users' Association), but also of the L.U.A. and Newspaper Federations.

Little progress was made at the August conference. The T.A. Executive were not in a position to discuss a national wages scheme, in view of the adverse vote of the recent Delegate Meeting; but they promised to consider any proposals and submit them to the members. As soon as an outline scheme was received, the Executive took a ballot on whether or not they should discuss it with the employers. A large majority voting in favour, the Executive met the employers in conference again on 12 November. The employers suggested three or four wage grades covering the whole country, details to be dealt with by a joint committee. They also asked that local movements be suspended. To these proposals the Executive agreed and the joint committee held its first meeting on 4 December.

There were two main questions to be tackled: the actual wage grades and the classification of T.A. branches in those grades. Both sides submitted proposals: the employers proposed five grades, the highest 70s. and the lowest 60s.; the T.A. representatives six grades, ranging from 70s. to 80s. The T.A. scheme—'a gigantic memorial for increases for the whole of the country'—was unacceptable to the employers, but after numerous conferences in the first quarter of 1919 agreements were finally reached in April and accepted by ballot of the T.A. members.

By the National Wage Basis Agreement, which came into force in the week ending 24 May 1919, the branches in the T.A. area, apart from Ireland, were classified into six grades, according to size of town, importance as a printing centre, industrial character of the neighbourhood, and local cost of living. The basic 'stab case rates for jobbing,[1] weekly, and bi-weekly newspapers ranged from 60s. in the lowest to 75s. in the highest grade, with a difference of 3s. between grades. The case rates on evening and morning newspapers were 2s. 6d. and 8s. respectively above the basic minima.

On average, basic branch wage rates had now risen by about 105 per cent. above pre-war, the same as the cost-of-living index figure. But this is an 'unweighted' average, not allowing for differences in branch membership. While the position of the small, low-paid towns had been considerably improved, many now having wage rates 110 to 130 per cent. above pre-war, the large towns were not so well off, with wages only 90 to 100 per cent. higher. A 'weighted' average would give a figure of about 100 per cent. Most T.A. members, in other words, were still slightly worse off than in 1914.

Overtime rates were to be as follows: time-and-a-quarter for the first two hours; time-and-a-half for the next three; double time afterwards, until a rest of eight hours was given; Saturdays, time-and-a-half for the first five hours, double time afterwards; Sundays, double time; Christmas Day, Good Friday, and Bank Holidays as in the Hours and Holidays Agreement; members required to start work before the usual time to be paid time-and-a-half until the usual hour of starting. The last clause, however, and those regarding Saturdays and Sundays, did not apply to daily news hands. Those on evening papers would continue, in accordance with prevailing custom, to be paid ordinary rates for Saturday afternoons, and morning news hands double time on Sundays up to the usual hour of starting; but no provision was made for

[1] Day rates. No provision was made for jobbing night staffs at this time.

morning newsmen working on Saturdays or for evening newsmen on Sundays.

By the terms of the amended Linotype 'Stab Agreement day operators were to be paid extras ranging from 6s. in grade 6 to 8s. 6d. in grade 1 above the jobbing case rate, night operators from 7s. to 9s. 6d. above the night case rate.[1] These rates would apply to Linotype operators in both jobbing and news offices: no differentiation was made at this time. The agreement was anomalous, therefore, on certain points. For example, evening news operators would only get the same as those in jobbing and weekly news offices, all being on day work: they would not get the 2s. 6d. extra paid to evening news case hands, since their rates were based on the jobbing case rate. Similarly, no distinction was made between night jobbing and morning news operators: the only 'night case rate' established in the National Wages Agreement was, as we have seen, that for morning newspapers. Both this and the Linotype Agreement, in fact, neglected to provide for jobbing night staffs. These anomalies would have to be remedied by later negotiations.

The remainder of the new Linotype 'Stab Agreement, regarding hours, training, apprentices, &c., merely reaffirmed the original of 1898. The L.U.A. resolutely refused any reduction of hours for operators.

The Monotype 'Stab Agreement was similarly revised. Monotype operators would be paid the same rates as Linotype operators, but their night rates were reckoned on a different basis, being from 15s. to 17s. 6d. above the day case rates, whereas those of Linotype operators were based on the night case rates. Their hours were also the same as Linotype operators'—48 (day) and 44 (night).

The other clauses in the 1905 Monotype Agreement were little changed: the overtime clause was brought into conformity with the National Wages Agreement and it was laid down that in future 'all operators shall be members of the T.A.'

Piece prices, both of case hands and operators, were left unsettled, piece-workers meanwhile to receive the same advance as those on 'stab. Piece-work was now very uncommon in the provinces, except around London, and the Delegate Meeting of 1918 had passed a resolution that, 'with a view to the abolition of piecework, no further extension of the system be allowed by the T.A.'

Shortly after these national agreements had been concluded for England and Wales, the T.A. succeeded (July 1919) in negotiating similar

---

[1] Note that a flat rate replaced the old 12½ per cent. extra—to the great dissatisfaction of operators.

agreements for Ireland with the newly formed Irish Master Printers' Association.[1] The six Irish wage grades ranged from 51s. in the lowest to 70s. in the highest. The remainder of the Irish agreement, regarding evening and morning news rates, overtime, calls, &c., was the same as that for England and Wales, while the Linotype and Monotype Agreements were also applied to Ireland.

The National Wages Agreement provided for the establishment of a Joint Labour Committee, consisting of the T.A. Executive Council and a similar number from the employers' national organizations.[2] On either party giving notice of its desire to alter wage rates or other conditions of the Agreement, the Joint Labour Committee was to meet within fourteen days to consider the application and a decision was to be arrived at within thirty-five days, during which period no strike or lock-out was to take place. The Joint Labour Committee was also to deal with claims for reclassification or 'regrading' of T.A. branches. Thus all future wages movements were to be on a national basis.

These agreements were a great achievement, bringing national order out of local chaos.[3] They were not, however, accepted by T.A. members without considerable criticism. As in the case of the earlier national agreements, many members objected to being 'kept in the dark' while negotiations were going on and condemned the secrecy and dilatoriness of the Executive Council. Many branches, particularly the larger ones, disliked this further loss of autonomy, which tied them down to national agreements. There was also widespread dissatisfaction with the grading: there were too many grades, the difference between highest and lowest was too large, and most branches thought their grading too low. Moreover, though the agreement had secured an average wage increase of three to four shillings per week, many branches had only got one or two and most felt the increase woefully inadequate, in view of the rising cost of living. The loudest complaints—almost mutiny—came from the newspaper men, particularly Linotype operators, who, after thirty years of specially favoured treatment, had got practically nothing out of the agreements. Many threatened to strike unless they were given wage

---

[1] Belfast was not included in this agreement. For some time wages were still settled locally, until in Oct. 1921 it was agreed to place Belfast in grade 2 of the *English* Wages Agreement. The Belfast employers have continued, however, to claim a certain independence of English agreements.

[2] There was to be a separate J.L.C. in Ireland.

[3] The T.A. led the way in the establishment of national wages agreements in the printing industry. Similar agreements were negotiated in the next few months by other unions.

increases, shorter hours, and overtime on public holidays. Evening news operators also claimed the 2s. 6d. per week extra paid to case hands.

Under this pressure, the Executive were forced to take action. First of all, they approached the L.U.A. regarding the grievances of Linotype operators and newspaper workers generally, but at a conference in July 1919 the newspaper owners refused any material concessions. The Executive reiterated their demands, however, and in August drew up a national memorial requesting not only redress of the news hands' grievances, but also a general advance of 10s. on all wage rates and regrading of certain towns.

The employers at first refused any concessions and, after the failure of two conferences, referred the deadlock to the J.I.C. The latter brought the two sides together again and early in November an agreement was reached whereby all T.A. members, except those already getting 20s. above the minimum, received an increase of 7s. 6d. per week.[1] A proposal from the employers for a sliding scale of wages based on the cost of living was rejected, as was a suggested bonus scheme. In regard to regrading, it was agreed that a joint committee should be appointed to hold conferences in different towns.

The L.U.A. and Newspaper Society agreed to give evening news operators the 2s. 6d. per week extra paid to case hands and to pay double time to morning newsmen on Saturdays and to evening newsmen on Sundays. But they refused any additional increase of wages or reduction of hours to operators, considering that hitherto the latter had been unduly favoured compared with case hands. They agreed, however, that, where practicable, hours should be so adjusted as to give evening newspaper workers a half-day off per week and morning newspaper workers one night per fortnight.

These concessions far from satisfied news hands, some of whom refused overtime and threatened to strike unless increased wages and reduced hours were granted. The newspaper owners therefore agreed in December to give an increase of 4s. per week to all T.A. members on morning newspapers, but firmly refused any reduction of hours for Linotype operators, insisting on uniformity under the Hours and Holidays Agreement.

Agreement on T.A. Rules

The long-drawn-out, complicated bargaining on wages and hours in 1919 was accompanied by equally prolonged and intricate negotiations

---

[1] The same increase was secured in Ireland in March 1920. Other printing trade unions followed in the T.A.'s footsteps and got similar advances.

regarding T.A. rules. The 1911 agreement was now out of date, the T.A. Delegate Meetings of 1913 and 1918 having considerably altered or added to the Association rules. There was a particularly strong demand for revised machinemen's rules, and the position was now complicated by the introduction of intaglio or photogravure machines, which the T.A. claimed and for which the Executive drew up rules in 1919. The Association had also decided to enrol Monotype-caster attendants, for whom another set of rules was formulated. Readers' membership, more-over, was made compulsory, the old overtime restriction was restored, and differences still existed regarding apprentice limitation, indicators, and other matters. The Executive therefore asked the employers for a conference on the new rules.

The first conference was held in September 1919 and negotiations went on to the end of March 1920. The result was a new Agreement on Rules, which the Executive could justly claim was 'much in advance' of the previous one and completed the imposing structure of national agreements covering the wages, hours, and working conditions of T.A. members.[1]

Firstly, it dealt with the question of jobbing night staffs, ignored in the National Wages, Linotype, and Monotype Agreements. Night shifts and double day shifts were becoming increasingly common in general printing offices, owing to shortages of plant and labour. In regard to the former, it was agreed that wages should be 16s. 6d. above the jobbing day rates and hours 44 per week. No distinction was made, though the employers wanted it, between temporary and permanent night shifts. As yet they were mostly temporary, but permanent ones were soon to be established and jobbing employers would naturally object to paying higher rates than those for morning newspapers, which were only 12s. above jobbing day (case) rates.

No agreement was reached in regard to double day shifts. The T.A. asked for 10s. extra and a 42-hour week for each shift, but the employers refused and the matter had to be deferred. Failing agreement, the T.A. insisted on overtime rates for work before and after the ordinary hours.

As soon as the war was over and fear of unemployment returned, the old cry was raised for restriction of overtime. The 1911 agreement had limited overtime to 16 hours a fortnight, but with numerous exceptions, and the Delegate Meeting of 1913 had therefore re-enacted the rigid

[1] This agreement was negotiated with the B.F.M.P. and Newspaper Society. The T.A. failed to get a similar agreement in Ireland by negotiation with the I.M.P.A.

8 hours per week limit. This the employers could not accept and in the new agreement of 1920 the 16 hours per fortnight was restored, 'provided such overtime is not systematic'; but the numerous exceptions of 1911 were deleted, apart from cases of breakdown or emergency—emergency work to be the subject of agreement between house and chapel.

Mechanical indicators had long been a source of controversy, especially on Linotype machines: operators associated them with task-work, while employers insisted on their right to check output. Few firms, apparently, now used them and the T.A. secured the employers' agreement that 'indicators on composing machines shall not be permitted, and where such are at present in operation, they shall be withdrawn forthwith'. Moreover, the old prohibition against other forms of task-work and bonus-paid work still remained in force.

The Association also won its way in regard to readers' membership. The 1911 agreement had made their membership 'permissive', but the employers now agreed that all qualified 'men who are holding situations as readers . . . shall become members' of the T.A., except those specially engaged on foreign languages or special scientific or highly technical work.

No agreement was reached on apprentices. The T.A. was taking an increased interest in apprentices and wished to regulate not only their selection, training, and technical education, but also their wages.[1] Employers were very sympathetic towards these aims, but desired, as a *quid pro quo*, relaxation of the apprentice ratio. All the old arguments were reproduced, but no agreement was arrived at. The employers spoke of labour shortage and wanted an increase in the number of apprentices allowed to large firms, but the T.A. considered that the present scale met all the trade's requirements and pointed to their unemployed; they could only agree to an increase for large firms if there was a reduction in the small offices, which the employers considered impossible. The Association was dominated by fear of 'over-flooding' the labour market and causing unemployment: 'what we have in our mind is the pre-war condition of affairs, when 3,000 journeymen could not get a decent living.' Agreement proving impossible, the 1911 apprentice scale remained in force.

The Association secured its greatest triumph in regard to the machinemen's rules. In 1911 the employers had refused to recognize the T.A.'s control over the machine department and rejected most of the proposed regulations regarding manning and wage rates. Now they agreed that all machinemen, including news rotary minders, should be members of the T.A. and accepted a detailed code of machine regulations, though not, of

---

[1] See below, pp. 385–6.

course, without modifications. They repeated the arguments of 1911, demanding latitude in the manning of machines and accusing the T.A. of restricting output, of wanting 'to work less and be paid more'; but their opposition was now much weaker. There was a labour shortage and the T.A.'s grip over machine rooms had been greatly strengthened by organizing work.

Detailed regulations were drawn up in regard to the manning and wage rates of the various types and sizes of machines. Platen and flat-bed cylinder machines were arranged into a number of classes, with wage rates ranging from the minimum jobbing rate for a minder in charge of two or three small platens or a couple of Wharfedales of double-demy size or below, to 10s. extra for a man working a two-colour Miehle (any size) or gripper perfecter above quad demy, an additional extra of 4s. being paid for an automatic feeder or bronzing attachment—no minder to take charge of more machines than laid down in the different classes.

Various 'extras' were also established for rotary machines, of which many different types and sizes, for various classes of work, from half-tone and multi-colour to paper-bag and ticket printing, were being rapidly introduced into general printing offices. Minders in charge of rotaries used for jobbing, book-work, magazine, and weekly publications[1] were to be paid 12s. over the minimum rate, with another 1s. 6d. extra for each colour above two, and 17s. above the minimum on high-class publications, such as *Tatler* or *Motor Car*, with an extra 3s. 6d. for the minder in charge if the machine was manned by more than one. The wage rates, manning, &c., on small reel-fed rotaries, such as the Edler and Chambon, of which there was an increasingly large number, used for many special kinds of work, were left to future negotiations with individual firms and the J.L.C., on account of the difficulty of classifying them all.

A number of 'General Rules' were drawn up applying to all the above classes of machines. For the most part they merely repeated or tightened up existing rules, such as those regarding machinemen's duties, 'twicing', and breakages. The ambiguous addendum in the 1911 agreement about the manning of machines was deleted, but 'within the provisions of the above classifications' members could be transferred from one machine to another to suit the requirements of the office. It was provided that 'in the event of a question arising as to the classification of any machine or

---

[1] There was dispute as to what was meant here by 'weekly publications': the employers interpreted the words as meaning only such weekly magazines as *Ideas* and *Red Letter*, but the T.A. insisted that weekly newspapers were included.

class of work', it was to be reported to the Executives for settlement by the Joint Labour Committee.

A separate set of rules was drawn up for rotary machines in morning and evening newspaper offices. The wage rates of news rotary minders were to be 'not less than the 'stab rates paid to Linotype operators for night and day work in accordance with the National Agreement', an extra 2s. 6d. per week to be paid for machines with seal attachments. Their hours were also to be the same. The Association failed to get its proposed manning arrangements accepted, the question being left to negotiation between rotary chapel and management, subject to approval by the branch committee; failing agreement, the matter to be referred to the Joint Labour Committee. In the case of picture papers, however, like the *Daily Mirror* or *Daily Sketch*, those up to and including 16 pages, single width, were to have one minder; double width, two minders; with an extra machineman above 16 pages.

The new rules drawn up by the Executive in regard to intaglio or photogravure machines and Monotype casters were, for various reasons, not discussed with the employers at this time, but formed the subject of later agreements.

The T.A. Delegate Meeting of 1921 decided that all these rules regarding wages, hours, working conditions, &c., agreed on with the employers, should in future be printed separately from the purely domestic rules of the Association. The change was significant. Hitherto, ever since the Association's establishment, its rule-book had included regulations regarding not only its constitution, membership, subscriptions, benefits, &c., but also wage rates, hours, apprenticeship, and so on, which it arbitrarily enacted and tried, often vainly, to enforce without previous agreement with the employers. Now there was an agreed code, resulting from joint conferences, accepted by the national bodies on both sides and far more likely, therefore, to be effective. The T.A. did, in fact, frequently receive assistance from the employers' national organizations in securing observance of the agreed rules, while any differences could, if not settled locally, be referred for settlement to the Joint Labour Committee. Failing agreement there, the matter could come before the Joint Industrial Council. Thus there was ample machinery to secure effective regulation of the industry and prevent disputes.

Wage Increases, 1919–20

The years 1919–20 witnessed a prices-wages spiral similar to that of the present post-war period. Prices rose and trade boomed. Unions, therefore, faced by the rising cost of living and in a favourable labour market, made successive wage demands.

The ink had hardly dried on the National Wages Agreement of April 1919 when, as we have seen, the T.A. demanded a 10s. increase. The employers had conceded 7s. 6d. in November, on the understanding that, unless there was an extraordinary rise in the cost of living, the Association would not approach them again for six months. Prices, however, continued to rise rapidly and in March 1920, therefore, just as agreement was finally reached on the T.A. rules, the Executive launched another wages movement for a general advance of 20s. per week. Other printing trade unions put in similar demands.

A conference in May 1920, however, ended in deadlock. The employers were prepared to accept the Board of Trade cost-of-living index figure, which had risen from 125 in November 1919 to 138 in May 1920, and offered 6s. increase. The T.A. representatives, however, maintained that prices had risen far more than indicated by the official figures and also demanded an improvement of the 'status' of skilled printers above pre-war. They refused to have the matter referred to the J.I.C., or a court of inquiry, or arbitration, and made preparations for a strike.

Negotiations with other printing trade unions also having failed, the employers approached the P. & K.T.F., with the suggestion of a general wages agreement. The idea was favourably received by the Federation, which urged the affiliated unions to combine in reaching a general settlement. All agreed except the T.A., which clung jealously to its autonomy in wages matters and was opposed to the merging of 'craft' into 'industrial' unionism, with its inevitable levelling tendencies.

The Association refused to accept an agreement reached at a conference between the P. & K.T.F. and employers on 27 May, giving an increase of 10s. to men and 3s. 6d. to women, and continued to press its original demands. Notices were handed in and an overtime ban was imposed.

The T.A. had to fight not only the employers, but also the other unions in the P. & K.T.F., which refused to give financial support and urged the Association to fall in line. It was only, however, after several J.I.C. meetings and intervention by the Ministry of Labour that the T.A. finally, on 24 June, agreed to accept the 10s. increase and a national strike was avoided.[1]

---

[1] Immediately afterwards the E.C. opened negotiations with the I.M.P.A., which resulted in a similar increase for T.A. members in Ireland.

A large majority of T.A. members accepted the settlement, but not without considerable dissatisfaction. Feeling was bitterest in Manchester and Liverpool. These branches disliked the National Wages Agreement and hankered after their old autonomy, whereby they could make much larger gains. A flat increase for the whole country failed to take account of their higher cost of living. Now, therefore, without consulting the Executive, they presented a memorial to the local employers, asking for a 'bonus' of 10s. per week, and, getting a refusal, imposed an overtime ban, which practically stopped production of week-end newspapers.

A long and tedious dispute followed. The T.A. Executive condemned the action of the branches as unconstitutional, but could not get them to withdraw their memorial or overtime ban. The employers therefore threatened a national lock-out. Appeals and orders by the Executive, J.I.C. meetings, and conferences with the employers all failed to end the dispute and on 28 August the branch members stopped work without notice. Further J.I.C. meetings proved futile, but eventually, in mid-September, the T.U.C. Parliamentary Committee succeeded in getting the men back to work on condition that a national conference was immediately held between the T.A. Executive and employers to discuss wages, as affected by the new Rent Restriction Act and continued rise in the cost of living, and also the question of improvement in the journeyman printer's 'status'.

Thus ended 'the most regrettable and ill-advised action taken by branches in the whole history of the Association'. Unofficial strikes were rife at this time in many other unions. Members felt acutely the increased cost of living and were apt to think their Executives too weak and dilatory, not appreciating the difficulties involved in national negotiations and having little appreciation of the employers' viewpoint.

Meanwhile, in view of the new Rent Restriction Act and the continued rise in the cost of living, the P. & K.T.F. had initiated another federated wages movement. The T.A. again declined to join in, but put forward its own demands: 5s. for increased rents and rates, 7s. 6d. to cover the rise in the cost of living, and 20 per cent. on pre-war wages as improvement of status, making a total demand varying from 20s. for grade 1 to 18s. for grade 6 towns.

Several conferences with the employers followed in the next few months, resulting in November 1920 in an increase of 5s. per week, the same amount as that obtained by the P. & K.T.F. No greater sum could be secured owing to the slump which had suddenly hit the trade. T.A. wage rates now ranged from 82s. 6d. in grade 6 to 97s. 6d. in grade 1 towns.[1] These were 22s. 6d. above the May 1919 rates, the increases being 7s. 6d. in November 1919, and 10s. in June and 5s. in November 1920. On the average, T.A. rates were now about 165 per cent. above pre-war, while the cost of living, at its peak point in November 1920, was up by 176 per cent. Wages, in other words, had not yet caught up with prices and, in real terms, T.A. members were still worse off than in 1914.

T.A. branches had been clamouring during these years not only for wage increases, but also for regrading: more than half considered their grading too low. It had been agreed in November 1919 that a joint committee should hold regrading conferences in different parts of the country. Early in 1920, however, the P. & K.T.F. suggested collective regrading by the Federation, a suggestion strongly supported by the employers. Several unions agreed, but the T.A., as in the wages movements, preferred to act alone.

Eventually conferences were held in Manchester and Cardiff and a few towns were regraded. Meanwhile, however, scores of regrading applications were coming in and dissatisfaction was growing. At the wages conference with the employers on 4 November 1920, therefore, the T.A. asked that the whole grading scheme should be revised. The employers, however, succeeded in shelving the question.

The T.A. held conferences with the Bookbinders early in 1921, with a view to joint pressure for a revised scheme, but action had to be postponed owing to the trade depression. The T.A. Delegate Meeting in June 1921, however, voted for reduction of the number of grades to three.

Wage Reductions, 1921–3

By the end of 1920 the post-war trading 'boom' had ended and the country was entering a period of prolonged slump and unemployment. Thousands of T.A. members were soon out of work or on short time. The employers also had their troubles: high costs and reduced orders brought short time and financial losses and some firms had to close down. An obvious remedy was to cut costs by reducing wages—a course justified by the fall in the cost of living. The Board of Trade index figure, which had reached 176 in November 1920, had fallen to 128 by May 1921, approximately the same figure as in November 1919, when the first increase of 7s. 6d. had been given to the unions. The employers therefore approached the P. & K.T.F. suggesting a reduction in wages

[1] Owing to delay by the E.C., this 5s. increase was not secured in Ireland, so that at the end of 1920 Irish rates ranged from 68s. 6d. in grade 6 to 87s. 6d. in grade 1.

of 15s. for men and 5s. 6d. for women, 'in view of the serious condition of the industry'.

The T.A., however, and several other craft unions decided to act independently in resisting any reduction. Though they had justified their wage increase demands by the rising cost of living, they would not accept the falling cost of living as justification for any wage decrease. This attitude is understandable, but showed little appreciation of economic realities or the employers' difficulties.

Conferences and J.I.C. meetings failed to produce a settlement and the employers finally posted notices that the wage reduction would be enforced. A national strike therefore threatened, but at the eleventh hour the T.A. gave way and agreed to a reduction of 7s. 6d. in two stages, the last at the beginning of January 1922.[1] The P. & K.T.F. accepted the same terms for all the other unions except the L.S.C., A.C.P., and Stereotypers, which later negotiated a reduction of only 5s.

During the next few months the cost of living continued to fall rapidly and industry remained in a depressed condition. By February 1922 the Board of Trade index figure had fallen to 88, and the employers therefore proposed a further wage reduction. In order to secure some stabilization in wage rates, they suggested a sliding scale based on the official cost-of-living index. But neither the T.A. nor any of the other unions would accept the employers' proposals, which would have meant a reduction of over 16s.: the unions sought, in fact, to keep up their wage rates despite falling prices. The T.A. even demanded wholesale revision of the grading scheme, amounting to wage *increases* for 254 towns.

The employers were therefore forced to drop their sliding-scale proposals and concentrate simply on a wage reduction, in order, as they pointed out, to lower costs, reduce prices, stimulate demand, and reduce unemployment. They proposed a reduction of 15s. The T.A. representatives, however, refused any reduction until the regrading question had been settled. They would not accept the cost-of-living index, bitterly attacked the employers for taking advantage of existing unemployment to reduce wages, and blamed the capitalist Government and its backers for the trade depression.

The other unions put up a similar resistance, so the employers brought the situation before the J.I.C. at the end of April, threatening drastic

[1] The I.M.P.A. tried to secure a similar reduction in Ireland, but eventually, after prolonged negotiations, a threatened lock-out, and reference to the Irish Ministry of Labour, allowed the matter temporarily to drop. T.A. members in Ireland, it will be remembered, had not secured the last increase of 5s. obtained in England and were therefore strongly opposed to any decrease.

action unless a settlement was speedily negotiated. The workers' panel therefore recommended the various Executives to ballot their members on the employers' terms.

The result of the ballot was, in each case, an overwhelming majority against acceptance. The employers therefore decided to post notices of reduction on 12 June. Efforts by the P. & K.T.F. to prevent the crisis failed.

A national lock-out was prevented, however, by Ministry of Labour intervention. A J.I.C. meeting was held on 21 June, attended by Sir David Shackleton, as a result of which the employers, though refusing to withdraw notices, agreed to resume negotiations with the various unions next day.

Most of the London craft unions and the Stereotypers refused to negotiate, as committing them to a reduction, but the T.A. and other unions agreed. The conference between the T.A. and the employers failed, however, to solve the deadlock and it was therefore agreed, on the suggestion of Sir David Shackleton, to refer it to the Industrial Court, under the procedure of the Industrial Courts Act, 1919, notices being withdrawn.

The Industrial Court met on 4 July and heard evidence from both sides. Its decision was that a reduction of wages was clearly warranted by the depressed condition of the industry and the fall in the cost of living. Wages should be reduced by 12s. 6d., in three instalments of 3s., and one of 3s. 6d., the last as from the beginning of the first pay-week in January 1923.

The Court's decision was not legally binding, but both parties were expected to accept it. The T.A. Executive, however, had stated at the commencement of proceedings that, while they would in honour recommend the Court's decision for acceptance, they could not regard it as a final settlement, but must submit it to their members in accordance with the Association rules. The Court's decision was now, therefore, put to a ballot, but, despite the Executive's recommendation, was rejected by a large majority.

Who was to blame for this imbroglio? The employers insisted that the T.A. Executive had referred the question to the Industrial Court 'for settlement'. This was the wording of the Executive's telegram to the branches and this was the understanding in the minds not only of the employers, but also of Sir David Shackleton. The Industrial Court was a kind of arbitration court and its decisions should be honourably accepted. The T.A. Executive, on the other hand, had never accepted this view, being bound by the rules to put any national agreement to a vote of the members; but they admitted not having made their position quite definite.

The employers decided to enforce the Court's decision. A meeting of the J.I.C. on 19 July failed to avert the crisis, while the Ministry of Labour stated that they could do nothing more. The majority of employers therefore made the first reduction of 3s. on 22 July. T.A. members were instructed to regard this as terminating their engagements and 12,000 came out on strike. About 7,000 were still paid the old rate and allowed to stay in, while about 3,000 gave way and accepted the reduction. For the first time in its history the Association was involved in a national strike.

The P. & K.T.F. officials now intervened. The T.A., they pointed out, had ignored the Federation rule requiring an affiliated union to consult the Executive Committee before entering on a serious dispute. The Federation would, however, be expected to bear a large part of the financial responsibility. Other unions, moreover, would be involved in the strike. The Federation therefore proffered its assistance in trying to reach a settlement. This offer, however, the T.A. Executive turned down; they also refused to attend a conference of societies on 28 July to consider the situation. This conference recommended the various unions to carry on their own work during the T.A. strike.

More and more T.A. members went back to work at reduced wages as the strike continued, while many firms brought in non-union labour. Eventually, therefore, on 11 August, the T.A. Executive requested the employers for a conference to end the dispute. The employers agreed and the conference was held on 15 and 16 August. The employers took their stand on the Industrial Court's decision and the T.A. Executive could only secure variation of the dates and a stabilization clause. A provisional agreement was eventually reached, the Executive recommending a resumption of work pending a ballot.

The agreement was accepted by the members. It provided for a reduction of 12s. 6d., in four stages: 3s. immediately, 3s. on 9 September, 3s. on 11 November, and 3s. 6d. on 5 May 1923. Wages were to be stabilized until the end of 1923. The employers' organizations would recommend their members to reinstate T.A. men in their former positions, while the T.A. agreed not to expel those who had remained at or returned to work on the terms of the Industrial Court's award. As regards regrading, the employers agreed to consider genuine anomalies.

The strike, which lasted four weeks, cost the T.A. nearly £70,000.

A 20 per cent. levy on those remaining at work had brought in £22,000, but there was a loss of over £46,000 at the end of the half-year. Moreover, the strike had failed. It left behind it bitterness and discontent. Several hundred members lost their jobs. Many firms became non-union or 'open houses'. Many members refused to pay the strike levy or the heavy fines which the Executive imposed on those who had 'ratted', and there was a loss of several hundred in membership. The P. & K.T.F. decided that the T.A. had no claim to strike benefit, since it had ignored the Federation rules and acted independently. The result was a strong 'break-away' movement in the T.A. and a weakening of the Federation. All this would have been avoided had the Industrial Court's decision been accepted.

T.A. wage rates after 5 May 1923 ranged from 62s. 6d. in grade 6 to 77s. 6d. in grade 1 towns.[1] Thus they were still 2s. 6d. higher than in May 1919, although the cost of living was considerably lower, so that, despite the recent wage reductions, T.A. members in full employment were much better off than at that date. Moreover, their 'real' wages were now a good deal higher than in 1914: their money wages were about 108 per cent. higher, the cost of living only 70 per cent., so that in 'real' terms T.A. members were about 22 per cent. better off. On the other hand, unemployment and short time were widespread.

Meanwhile, those unions acting federally (the N.U.P.B. & P.W., N.S.O.P. & A., &c.) and the Lithographic societies had also accepted a 12s. 6d. reduction, but the London societies and the Stereotypers succeeded in negotiating a reduction of only 6s. after the T.A. strike.

It was out of the recent wages settlements that the questions of 'differentials' and 'parity' originated, which became so controversial in 1947-9. The T.A. first grade had been fixed at £3. 15s. in May 1919, while the minimum rate of the London letterpress craft unions was, about the same time, fixed at £3. 17s. 6d. During 1919-20 three general increases were given in the industry—7s. 6d., 10s., and 5s., making a total increase of 22s. 6d.—to all unions, London and provincial alike. As a result, the

[1] In Ireland there was a long struggle against wage reductions which proved surprisingly successful. Negotiations went on throughout 1922-3. On several occasions the Irish members rejected terms recommended by the Executive and the employers posted lock-out notices, but the members grimly refused to give way and the utmost the employers could get was a reduction of 5s. As a result Irish wage rates now ranged from 63s. 6d. in grade 6 to 82s. in grade 1 towns. There was, however, no town in grade 1, Belfast now being in grade 2 (74s. 6d.) of the English Wages Agreement, much to the dissatisfaction of Londonderry employers who were thus paying 2s. higher wages (76s. 6d., Irish grade 2).

T.A. grade 1 rate rose to £4. 17s. 6d. and the London letterpress craft rate to £5. The 'differential' thus remained 2s. 6d.

The wage reductions in 1921–3, however, were not uniform. The T.A. suffered two reductions, of 7s. 6d. and 12s. 6d., a total of £1, which reduced grade 1 to £3. 17s. 6d. The two reductions of the London societies, however, were 5s. and 6s., a total of only 11s., which brought their minimum rate to £4. 9s. Thus the 'differential' between the provinces and London was increased from 2s. 6d. to 11s. 6d.[1] The situation was made more galling to the T.A. by the fact that the Electrotypers and Stereotypers, a national union, had secured the same 11s. reduction as the London societies, so that their provincial members, working in the same offices as T.A. members, were now paid 9s. more. T.A. members could not forget that while they had fought the printing trade unions' battle in 1922, the others had stood watching, and that it was only after they had weakened the employers' forces that the London societies and Stereotypers were able to get more favourable terms.[2]

Nevertheless, wages had now reached stability—though no one could have imagined, after the turmoil of the past five years, that they were to remain stabilized until 1940.

[1] The difference was even greater between London and the T.A. extra-metropolitan branches, many of which were in grades 4, 5, or 6, and created intense dissatisfaction, particularly as most extra-metropolitan firms were London branch houses doing the same work as in London.

[2] Other unions, of course, such as the S.T.A., Lithos., N.U.P.B. & P.W., and N.S.O.P. & A., were also involved in this 'differentials' and 'parity' question.

XVII

T.A. GROWTH AND CONSTITUTIONAL DEVELOPMENT
1918–39

Industrial Background

THE printing industry continued to expand during this period. The number of persons occupied in it in England and Wales increased from 138,000 (London 43,000) in 1911 to over 190,000 (London 73,000) in 1931. London was still by far the greatest printing centre, containing over a third of those employed. Moreover, the census figures for Greater London do not include the extra-metropolitan area in which many new printing offices were being established. About 24,000 persons were employed in the printing industry in the SE. region outside London.

The industry was also expanding in other provincial areas. There were now nearly 28,000 occupied in the printing trade of Lancashire and Cheshire, over 19,000 in the West Midlands and 13,000 in the West Riding.

The average size of plants and businesses also increased during this period, but there was still great variety, from the large firm employing several thousand men to the one-man office. The most striking developments occurred in the newspaper industry, which became dominated by great combines and press lords, such as the Berry group (Allied Newspapers and Allied Northern Newspapers Ltd.), the Rothermere or *Daily Mail* group (Northcliffe Newspapers Ltd.), the Inveresk group (Provincial Newspapers Ltd.), the Starmer or Westminster Press Group, the Storey and several small groups. Most local weekly newspapers still remained independent family concerns, but the majority of morning, evening, and Sunday papers were controlled by the great combines.

As a result of this monopolizing process, a number of newspapers were bought up, amalgamated, or squeezed out of existence, with a consequent reduction in the total from 2,456 (89 morning, 114 evening) in 1913 to 1,888 (60 morning, 94 evening) in 1939.[1]

The number of magazines, reviews, and periodicals increased during this same period from 3,099 to 3,702, but many of these were published by large companies such as the Amalgamated Press, Iliffe & Co., &c.

Several large groups were also formed in the book-printing and

[1] *Mitchell's Newspaper Press Directory.*

jobbing trade, such as the Hutchinson, McCorquodale, Kelly, and Burrow groups, Universal Printers Ltd., and Associated Printers Ltd., while Mills & Rockley Ltd. controlled poster advertising businesses in many provincial towns. The great bulk of jobbing printers, however, were still small, independent concerns.

The 'industrial revolution' in the printing trade continued rapidly during this period. Improved Linotype machines were introduced, equipped with display founts and capable of setting newspaper advertisements. Monotype machines conquered the book-printing trade, with casters producing a wide range of type faces, &c. Machine, therefore, steadily displaced hand composition, as illustrated by the census figures, which show an increase in the number of machine operators in the English provinces and Wales from 3,156 in 1911 to 11,833 in 1931, while the number of hand compositors fell from 26,487 to 11,954.[1]

Even more revolutionary developments were presaged in the shape of photo-composing and teletype-setting machines. The latter caused considerable alarm among letterpress unions in the middle thirties, threatening to displace Linotype operators by telegraphic transmission and setting-up of news, but neither invention made much progress.

The most revolutionary developments in letterpress printing during this period occurred in the machine department. New and faster machines were introduced, both flat-bed and rotary. New attachments were added for automatic feeding, pile delivery, wax-spraying, interleaving, numbering, &c. Multiple-process machines were invented, combining many operations—cutting, scoring, punching, folding, &c., as well as printing—for the manufacture of paper bags, boxes, wrappers, cigarette packets, toffee papers, &c., printing from engraved steel rollers, using letterpress ink, or from rubber stereos, with aniline dyes, on waxed wrappings and cellophane as well as ordinary paper. Half-tone and colour printing developed considerably, while the new photogravure process made great strides. The volume and variety of production were enormously increased.

This increasing mechanization and these new processes were, together with amalgamation, part of the tendency to 'rationalization' in these years. Employers sought in such ways, and by careful costing and general tightening of control, to increase efficiency and lower costs of production. The T.A. recognized these developments as 'the natural evolution of things'[2] and made no attempts directly to impede them. But

---

[1] The census classification was very incomplete, but the figures are, nevertheless, significant.   [2] T.A. President at J.L.C. Conference, 6 Nov. 1923.

the employers considered that union regulations hampered progress: as soon as a new machine, attachment, or process was introduced, the unions clamoured for extras and restrictive working conditions. Increasing mechanization also led to union demands for reduced working hours.

The main reason for these claims was the unemployment which 'rationalization' helped to create. The chief cause of unemployment, however, was not mechanization but general trade conditions: the trade cycle, with its alternating booms and slumps. The printing industry did not, however, suffer as much as 'basic' industries like mining, engineering, shipbuilding, and textiles. During the twenties unemployment in the printing trade averaged about 5 per cent., while the general average was about 11; in 1932, in the depths of depression, it rose to nearly 11, but the general average went up to over 22 per cent. The situation was worst, of course, in the 'depressed areas' of the north and midlands; in the south, especially around London, where the trade was rapidly expanding, there was little unemployment. There was a steady, even increasing, demand for printing in industry, public administration, education, politics, literature, and entertainment, and the industry enjoys a large degree of 'natural protection'. Nevertheless, unemployment remained the T.A.'s greatest problem.

Working conditions continued to improve in this period. Factory inspection was now more effective, while the modern works built by large firms had plenty of space, light, and ventilation. The J.I.C. Health Committee also did much to investigate and circulate information about these matters and industrial diseases. Some of the continued increase in the printer's average length of life must be attributed to improved workshop conditions.

The worst conditions prevailed in small offices, which were the main seats of 'cheap competition'. Despite organization by the unions and F.M.P., an inquiry by the latter in 1938 'showed the existence of "unfair" conditions to be widespread and substantial. . . . Many members of the F.M.P. complained bitterly of cut-throat competition from houses working under "unfair" conditions', paying less than the standard rates, employing cheap female and apprentice labour, &c.

Growth in Membership

T.A. growth in the inter-war years, as in the pre-1914 period, was conditioned by the trade cycle. When trade was expanding, membership grew quickly; when depression came, it remained more or less stationary or fell slightly. Membership soared in the post-war boom from 24,762 in 1918 to 31,234 in 1920. It fell in the ensuing slump to 30,378 in 1923, after which it gradually rose with reviving trade to reach 34,098 in 1930.[1] Growth was again checked by depression in the early thirties, membership being 34,778 at the end of 1933. Thereafter it rose steadily as trade improved to 38,277 in 1939.

Thus T.A. membership had grown, though spasmodically, by 55 per cent. in the period 1918–39. Most branches had also increased in size. Some, such as Sunderland, Oldham, Sheffield, and Cardiff, in 'depressed areas', had grown very little or even declined; others, like Watford, Aylesbury, and Bristol, mostly in the south and especially around London, where new firms were established or expanding, had grown remarkably. Manchester was still the biggest branch, with about 3,000 members, followed by Liverpool, with 2,000. The great majority, however, were still small: over half had less than a hundred members. The total number of branches had increased from 183 in 1918 to 221 in 1939.

Growth in membership was a result of two factors: trade expansion and T.A. organizing. Both were most vigorous in the south, particularly in the Home Counties and South-eastern Group: established in 1903, with less than 1,000 members, this Group had over 9,000 by 1938, more than that of the North-western, hitherto the largest.

Organizing work was along now familiar lines. The three Organizers, two English and one Irish, constantly toured the country, aided in their work by groups and branches. Employers were interviewed, non-unionists were exhorted or forced to join, pamphlets were distributed, and 'fair lists' issued. One of the most effective organizing weapons was the 'fair wages clause': cases of non-compliance were reported to the Stationery Office and efforts were constantly made to secure its inclusion in the contracts of local councils. Customers were asked to withdraw work from 'unfair' or non-union firms: political parties were especially open to pressure. The T.A. often sought the co-operation of other unions or of the Printing & Kindred Trades Federation. Requests were also made to the Master Printers' Federation for assistance in stamping out 'unfair competition', and to the Joint Industrial Council, whose original ideal was to secure 'complete organization' of both employers and employed.

Many non-members were brought in as a result of organizing work, many 'closed' offices were 'opened', many 'black spots' disappeared, and extensive areas, hitherto outside T.A. control, were 'unionized'. The

[1] There was a slight fall in 1926–7 as a result of the General Strike.

Association also pressed forward with the organization of machine minders, readers, and Monotype-caster attendants; apprentices were brought into the union fold; new branches of the industry, such as photogravure, cinema printing, aniline and bag printing, were brought under T.A. control; while the Association maintained an uncompromising resistance to female labour.

There were still many non-union and 'unfair' offices in 1939, and many 'open houses' in which T.A. members were working with non-members. There were still many employers antagonistic to trade-union 'interference' and many men who 'held aloof'. There was still plenty of work for the Organizers to do. But the great majority of offices were now 'recognized' and the great majority of craftsmen in the provincial printing industry belonged to the T.A.

Statistics were collected by the E.C. in 1928–9, which, though far from complete, particularly as regards 'unrecognized' offices, do give a rough indication of the extent to which provincial printers were organized. In 'recognized' offices, according to these statistics, there were 22,000 members and 1,600 non-members, while a further 1,400 men were in 'unrecognized' offices (of which there were 567), making a total of 3,000 non-members: thus 88 per cent. of the journeymen were in the T.A.

These figures may be compared with those in the 1931 census reports. Classification was much better than in the 1911 census, but a great number were still vaguely described as 'printers' and 'other skilled workers', many of whom, no doubt, were ineligible for T.A. membership, as being semi-skilled or in some section of the trade other than letterpress printing. Including all these, however, with those listed as compositors, operators, and machine minders (litho. as well as letterpress), there was a total of about 42,000 journeymen printers in the provinces (England and Wales). The number of T.A. journeymen members at that time, excluding Ireland, was about 30,000: over 71 per cent. of this total. In actual fact, the Association probably included at least 80 per cent. of skilled letterpress printers. By 1939, moreover, as we have seen, it had expanded its membership considerably.

Finances[1]

T.A. finances, like its membership, grew considerably in the inter-war years, but were much more seriously affected by general trade conditions. When trade was good, fewer members were unemployed and

---

[1] We are primarily concerned here with the General Fund. The Superannuation Fund is dealt with separately below, pp. 400–1.

drawing out-of-work benefit, while more were paying full subscriptions: the Fund therefore grew. During depressions, on the other hand, many were unemployed, large sums were expended in out-of-work benefit, income was reduced, and the Fund fell. A large-scale strike, of course, would have a disastrous effect upon it, while the Superannuation Fund became an increasingly heavy burden, preventing adequate provision for trade purposes.

T.A. members, however, were very short-sighted financially, forgetting the old adage about saving in the fat years for the lean: not only did they repeatedly reject proposed levies for building up the Fund, but invariably voted increased benefits as soon as trade improved. Moreover, they seemed mesmerized by large figures: they did not seem to realize that £100,000 was only about £3 per head and would be quickly consumed in a national strike or serious trade depression.

The General Fund, which stood at nearly £62,000 at the end of 1918, grew rapidly in the post-war boom to over £101,000 by the end of 1920. This prosperity and the rising cost of living prompted increases in out-of-work and superannuation benefits, without any increase in subscriptions. When the slump came, however, in 1921–2, with a national strike against wage reductions, the Fund was quickly reduced to £29,000 and but for a strike levy the Association would have been practically bankrupt. A quarterly levy had to be imposed continuously in the following years.

The situation was so serious by the beginning of 1923 that the E.C. were forced to ask members either to increase subscriptions or reduce benefits. Voting was in favour of twopence on subscriptions. Payment of incapacity benefits was also transferred back to the Superannuation Fund and various administrative economies were made. Despite these measures, however, the General Fund had dwindled to less than £14,000 by the end of June, but the members refused to pay a proposed levy of a shilling per week. Only a revival of trade in the latter half of 1923 averted bankruptcy.

The Fund rose steadily with improving trade and reached nearly £56,000 by the end of 1925. The Delegate Meeting that year increased subscriptions by a penny, but took an extra twopence for Superannuation Fund purposes, so that the General Fund suffered. In 1926, moreover, there was the General Strike, which reduced the Fund to little more than £3,000, and since its assets were not quickly realizable, while branch returns did not come in till the half-year end, the Association had to secure an overdraft of nearly £21,000 from the bank in order to pay out-of-work benefits. By the end of 1927 there was a deficit of nearly £5,000, but the members refused to pay a temporary levy of 6d. per week proposed by the E.C., who had therefore to get a loan of £10,000 from the P. & K.T.F.

Trade was improving again, however, and by the end of 1928 there was over £7,000 in the Fund. But the P. & K.T.F. loan was still outstanding and the Association's financial position was obviously unsound. In 1929, moreover, there came another economic crisis, followed by the great depression of the early thirties.

Since members refused to pay levies or increase subscriptions, expenditure had to be cut. At the beginning of 1929, therefore, the E.C. pushed through a reduction of unemployment benefits, but the 1930 Delegate Meeting raised them again; subscriptions were increased by $3\frac{1}{2}d.$, but this went to the Superannuation Fund, which was in an equally critical condition. The result was that the General Fund, after growing to over £35,000 by the end of 1930, dwindled rapidly in 1931 as depression deepened. The E.C. therefore proposed an increase of 4d. in subscriptions and an overtime levy, but these were rejected. Unemployment benefits were reduced again and funeral benefits transferred to the Superannuation Fund, but this was not enough. By the beginning of March 1932 the Association again faced bankruptcy. Only an emergency levy could prevent it. The E.C. therefore summoned a special conference of Group Committees in Birmingham on 19 March, with whose support they managed to get the levy through: 9d. per week for grades 1 and 2, 6d. for grades 3 and 4, 4d. for grades 5 and 6. This saved the situation: by June 1933 the General Fund stood at nearly £44,000.

The 1932 Delegate Meeting took steps to stabilize T.A. finances. The special and ordinary levies were discontinued and subscriptions were increased by 6d., $3\frac{1}{2}d.$ for the General and $2\frac{1}{2}d.$ for the Superannuation Fund. Trade was at last recovering from the long depression and the General Fund grew with it. It rose rapidly in the next six years and was nearly £200,000 by June 1939. Subscriptions were raised again by the 1936 Delegate Meeting, chiefly, however, for Superannuation Fund purposes. They had been more than doubled in the inter-war years: whereas a man on the lowest 'stab rate paid 1s. 1d. per week in 1918, he was paying 2s. 4d. in 1939.

Since 1933, except for the years 1939–40, the T.A. has prospered. The trade situation has been very favourable: since the end of 1940 there has been full employment and acute labour shortage. An apparently enormous General Fund has therefore been built up. But prolonged depression or a national strike against wage reductions, if they should come, as they did after the First World War, would quickly dissipate it.

Constitutional Development

The T.A. changed very little constitutionally in this period. Its 'local government' was still carried on by chapels, branches, and groups, its 'parliament' was still the Delegate Meeting (made triennial in 1918), and its 'central government' the Executive Council and Association officers.

The Executive Council was still elected in much the same way. The largest branches had their own representatives, with a maximum (from 1932) of two; each group elected one, two, or three representatives, according to membership; and there were two special representatives for machinemen. The full Council met every two months, the Committee every fortnight, with special meetings as required. Manchester finally lost what remained of its predominance in 1921, when it was decided that the Committee should consist of any nine members elected by the Council from their own number.

It was decided in 1925 that the E.C., instead of being elected annually, should remain in office until the end of the year in which the Delegate Meeting was held. This would secure continuity of policy and make the E.C. more fully responsible to the Delegate Meeting. Retiring members were still eligible for re-election and many held their seats for long periods, sometimes twenty years or more. In 1936, however, a retiring age was established at 65.

The Association headquarters are still removable by Delegate Meeting, but have remained in Manchester. The E.C. continued for some time to rent offices from the Manchester branch in Caxton Hall, but the growing volume of business made this accommodation inadequate, so in 1923 they purchased a large private house, 'Beechwood', in Oak Drive, Fallowfield, which was converted into the headquarters office.

The tendency towards centralization was greatly increased by the series of national agreements in 1919–20, which resulted, of course, in a vast expansion of headquarters business. The E.C. had to deal with a multitude of questions: its special sub-committees and its minutes multiplied. In 1918 the General President and General Treasurer were made full-time officials: J. D. French and T. W. Mason, being virtually full-time already, were elected. H. Skinner and O. Waddington were still General and Assistant Secretaries, but Waddington died in 1919 and was succeeded by A. Bottomley, one of the Organizers. Mason died in 1929 and was followed as Treasurer by D. Lewis, then Chief Clerk.

Skinner, French, and Bottomley held office until the 1933 Delegate Meeting decided that Association officials and staff should retire on pension at 65. As a result of the subsequent elections, J. Fletcher (Chief Clerk) became General Secretary, H. Inglis (Liverpool B.P. and E.C. member) General President, and H. Riding (Organizer) Assistant Secretary. The Organizers during this period were H. Matthewman (1909–23), T. Cassidy (1911–37), T. Roberts (1920–9), H. E. Carss (1924–38), H. Riding (1929–34), F. B. Whitman (1935 onwards), and J. A. Bell (1936–41).

Not only was the number of full-time officials increased. There was also a growing staff of clerks and typists. The cellars at 'Beechwood' are stacked with the correspondence, circulars, forms, &c., of these years.

Branches inevitably lost much of their autonomy now that questions of wages, hours, and working conditions were settled nationally. There was, inevitably also, considerable criticism of the E.C. Some of the larger branches chafed at the bit: Manchester especially showed a strong tendency to independent action, not infrequently flouting E.C. decisions and national agreements. Such branches felt that they could get more by local action. Different sections also felt dissatisfied, considering their interests neglected, and there were numerous complaints against E.C. autocracy or delay.

Criticism 'agin the government' is inevitable in any democracy. One of democracy's greatest problems, in fact, is to harmonize individual and local freedom with efficient central government. On the whole, the T.A. achieved this fairly well. The E.C. and officials were elected by the whole membership and responsible to triennial Delegate Meetings. They kept members well informed of E.C. business through the *Circular*, by special circulars, and deputations to group and branch meetings. In cases of emergency—as in 1920, during the wages advance movement, in 1931, when bankruptcy threatened, and in 1933, when the employers demanded a wages reduction—they summoned special conferences of group representatives. They frequently co-opted members with specialized knowledge to assist them on difficult technical questions. They collated group and branch resolutions, as well as those of Delegate Meetings, and based their policy upon them. They did not, of course, always agree with these, and when they did were often unable to carry them out in the face of employers' opposition.

Democratic government did not mean weak government: the E.C. were not afraid of asserting their authority. Frequently, as any government must, they took unpopular action or acted decisively without consulting the members. But all major agreements were submitted, in accordance with rule, to ballot vote of the members. In most cases their actions were endorsed, though not without grumbling and criticism. The E.C. were always mindful of 'the will of the members', but aware, too, of their responsibility for the strength and welfare of the Association. In most cases, moreover, they were wiser than the members: when Delegate Meetings rejected their views it was generally for the worse. We shall see later on their statesmanship in negotiations with employers.

The Association officials, particularly the General Secretary, also acquired added power and responsibility. They were sometimes, in fact, considered dictatorial. They did, of course, exercise great influence, but were elected officials and responsible to the E.C. They were also able, sensible men, loyal to T.A. principles. The Association owes a great debt to officers such as Herbert Skinner and J. D. French.

It was decided at Aberystwyth in 1918 that Delegate Meetings should be held triennially. The next was therefore in 1921 (Hastings), but the two following were postponed to save expense, being held in 1925 (Lowestoft) and 1930 (Blackpool). Thereafter they were held triennially, in 1933 (Colwyn Bay), 1936 (Torquay), and 1939 (Eastbourne). These meetings considered all matters relating to the Association: constitution, finance, benefits, wages, hours, working conditions, &c., altering and adding to the rules and laying down policy. Criticism of the E.C. was freely expressed and their proposals were sometimes, though not usually, rejected. The main faults of Delegate Meetings were that they had too much on their agenda, that they passed too many and often impracticable resolutions, and that financially they were amateurish and inept. But they expressed T.A. opinion and kept up pressure on many questions: they formed, in fact, an essential part of democratic government.

The system of groups remained unaltered throughout this period, despite great variations in their size and activities. The work of branches and chapels also went on with little change. The majority of members continued to take little active interest in union affairs. Fines even had to be imposed for not voting on important questions, in order to force members to exercise their democratic rights!

A new feature of T.A. organization was the growing tendency to 'sectionalism'. We have already noticed, long before 1914, the increasing specialization in the industry: T.A. members were no longer journeymen printers, but compositors, operators, machinemen (flat-bed and rotary), Monotype-caster attendants, and readers, working on jobbing, bookwork, or news, letterpress or photogravure. As such, they developed sectional interests and began to set up their own organizations within the T.A.

We have seen how machinemen came to have their own chapels and branch meetings and special representatives on the E.C. and at Delegate Meetings. In 1918 a Machine Investigation Committee of the E.C. was established, specially to deal with questions in that department. Occasionally, as in 1891, 1916, and 1929, special national conferences of machinemen were held.

Other sections also began to organize, at first forming separate 'guilds' or 'associated chapels' in the branches and then national bodies. In 1919 there was formed the National Amalgamation of News Chapels and Machine Operators' Guild or, more shortly, the National News Guild, with its own committee, officials, and regular biennial conferences. Newsmen were greatly dissatisfied with the national agreements of 1919 and agitated continuously in the following years for improved wages, hours, and working conditions, as embodied in the 'Newsmen's Charter'. They made repeated demands for a separate News Section within the T.A., like that of the L.S.C., to deal with all newspaper questions. There was even a movement in favour of secession from the T.A. Newsmen felt they were being held in check by the jobbing section, the biggest in the Association, in which working conditions were quite different. At least, they demanded, they should have separate negotiations with the Newspaper Society and special representatives on the E.C. and at Delegate Meetings, and only newsmen should vote on news questions.

Both E.C. and Delegate Meetings, however, opposed such demands, deploring the tendency to sectionalism. But it was agreed in 1925 to establish a News Investigation Committee of the E.C., consisting of those who were newsmen and the permanent officials, 'with a view to securing direct negotiations between the newspaper owners and the E.C. on all questions affecting newspaper production'. It was not, however, until 1939 that the E.C. finally secured separate negotiations with the Newspaper Society. Meanwhile the National News Guild kept up pressure for improved conditions.

Jobbing compositors and readers also had their special interests and grievances and established their own sectional organizations, the Provincial Guild of Printers' Readers (1924) and the National Guild of Jobbing Printers (1926). Readers in some of the larger offices formed their own chapels, but the E.C. refused to recognize them and the 1936 Delegate Meeting condemned them, as tending to disunity: if readers had their own chapels, Lino. and Mono. operators would soon want them. A Jobbing Compositors' Investigation Committee of the E.C. was created, however, in 1936.

There was a possibility during this period, though never very strong, that Ireland might separate from the T.A. The main impulse came from Dublin, which was at times strongly nationalist and remained outside the T.A. There were serious differences between the Association and the Dublin Society in the years immediately after the war, when the latter tried to establish an Irish Typographical Union. The great majority of T.A. Irish members, however, proved loyal and the attempt failed. In the following years, Irish nationalists continued to urge a break away from the English trade-union movement, but trade-union solidarity proved stronger than racial differences.

Registration

Proposals continued to be made during this period that the T.A. should become a registered trade union, under the Trade Union Acts (1871 onwards), chiefly in order to secure exemption from income-tax on the Superannuation Fund interest and to prevent the possibility of that Fund being 'raided'. But the old objection remained strong that the Association's freedom of action would be hampered by the Registrar General's scrutiny. Eventually, however, when it was discovered that exemption from income-tax could be secured on *all* provident benefit funds, and that fears of inquisitorial control were greatly exaggerated, the 1939 Delegate Meeting decided that the Association should become registered. This was done in 1940, the T.A.'s registered number being 1576 T.

XVIII

RELATIONS WITH EMPLOYERS
1918–39

THE most outstanding feature in the history of industrial relations in the provincial letterpress printing trade during this period was the framework of national agreements on wages, hours, and working conditions elaborated in 1919–20 and amended or expanded in later years. These not only laid down a detailed code of industrial regulations, but also provided machinery in the Joint Labour Committee for regular consultation between the T.A. Executive and employers' national organizations on all matters affecting working conditions and for the friendly settlement of disputes. Innumerable J.L.C. conferences were held in the inter-war years, the reports of which fill many thick volumes. Only important questions, however, which could not be settled at chapel or branch level or by Executive correspondence, were brought before the J.L.C.

The J.L.C. usually succeeded in reaching a settlement, though negotiations were often prolonged over many years. Where agreement proved impossible and a dispute threatened, the question would be referred to the J.I.C. Conciliation Committee. At first, the T.A. was very averse to such outside interference, especially in regard to wage rates, since its autonomy was thereby threatened. But eventually we find the Executive accepting the J.I.C. Conciliation Committee as part of the normal machinery for settling disputes and even appealing to it on many questions. It was only on exceptional occasions, however, when all the ordinary resources of negotiation had been exhausted, that reference was made to the J.I.C. Moreover, the Conciliation Committee rarely made a definite decision, but usually recommended both sides to resume negotiations and formulate a compromise. Its function, according to the report for 1936–7, was 'not to settle differences, but to assist the parties to settle their own differences. The negotiating of hours, wages, &c., is not, and never has been, the function of this Council. The greater success which it has had in comparison with other Joint Industrial Councils is in a great measure due to the fact that it has refrained from acting as a negotiating body.'

The Joint Labour Committee, then, regulated working conditions in

T.A. offices. On the employers' side it consisted of representatives from both the Federation of Master Printers and the Newspaper Society. Hitherto, however, the T.A. had negotiated separately on newspaper questions with the Linotype Users' Association, now absorbed in the Newspaper Society, and T.A. newsmen soon began to agitate for the re-establishment of separate negotiations. Conditions, they pointed out, were different in news and jobbing offices, and jobbing employers were unqualified to deal with news questions; but their underlying motive was to secure higher wages and shorter hours. The employers refused to split forces, however, pointing out that many newspaper firms also had jobbing offices, that their interests were bound together, and that it would cause trouble and confusion to negotiate sectionally.

The matter was frequently argued over at J.L.C. meetings until in 1937 the T.A. Executive referred their claim to the J.I.C. Conciliation Committee, whose finding was in favour of separate negotiations on purely newspaper questions. Even so, the employers still created obstacles and it was not until 1939 that agreement was finally reached, while the first separate meeting with the Newspaper Society did not take place till 1945, on account of the war.

The national agreements with the B.F.M.P. and Newspaper Society covered England (apart from London) and Wales.[1] The T.A. had similar but quite separate agreements for Ireland with the I.M.P.A.[2] After the T.A. Executive's failure, however, to honour or enforce wages settlements in 1922–3, the I.M.P.A. held no further negotiations with them for many years. Meanwhile, numerous alterations or additions were being made to the English agreements. In 1931, therefore, the T.A. Executive approached the I.M.P.A. with regard to their application in Ireland. The I.M.P.A. stated, however, that before they would agree to meet the T.A. on any question, the 1923 agreement on wage reductions must be honoured.

There the matter rested until 1938, when the T.A. Executive again

---

[1] The London national newspapers publishing editions of daily and Sunday papers in Manchester did not belong to the Newspaper Society and conditions in their Manchester offices were settled by separate chapel agreements. Allied Newspapers Ltd. (now Kemsley Press) and the *Manchester Guardian* were in a similar position, although members of the Newspaper Society. Most of the London papers publishing in the provinces eventually (1941) formed themselves into the London Newspapers Provincial Association, for joint negotiation with the trade unions. See below, p. 422.

[2] Dublin was excluded, of course, and Belfast came under the English agreements, while the employers' associations in Cork, Limerick, and several smaller towns acted independently.

approached the I.M.P.A. A conference was held in November, but early in 1939 the I.M.P.A. rejected the T.A. request on the ground that conditions in Ireland were greatly different from those in England. Meanwhile, however, the Irish branches had, by local negotiations, secured many of the additions to the English agreements.

Industrial relations in this period, as in the past, were greatly affected by trade conditions. In the 'boom' years 1919-20, when prices were rising and there was practically full employment, the unions were very active and successful in securing wage increases. In 1921-3, however, during the trade depression, when thousands were unemployed, the employers were able to enforce wage reductions. All the machinery of J.L.C. and J.I.C. failed to prevent the T.A. national strike of 1922. This and heavy out-of-work payments seriously reduced T.A. funds and weakened its bargaining power. There was, therefore, a very noticeable stiffening in the employers' attitude to T.A. claims on such questions as machine rules and regrading.

In May 1926 there came the General Strike, when all T.A. members were ordered to stop work immediately in support of the coal-miners' fight against wage reductions. This event is unique in T.A. history. The Association had no quarrel with the printing-trade employers. Its action was dictated by 'loyalty to the organised Labour movement'. It was participating in what was felt to be the inevitable clash between the united forces of Capital and Labour. The printing-trade employers, on the other hand, regarded such action by the T.A. and other unions as a gross breach of agreements: there was no printing-trade dispute, no notice had been given, and the J.I.C. constitution had been ignored.

The strike was only short-lived, from 4 to 12 May, the *status quo* being restored by an agreement on 27 May, but it left a residuum of bitterness and distrust among employers very harmful to industrial relations in the next few years. Many firms refused to reinstate strike hands and went non-union, or became 'open houses', or established 'house unions',[1] to weaken trade-union loyalty and guard against future 'lightning strikes'. The anti-trade-union attitude became much stronger: many T.A. members were induced or forced, on threat of dismissal, to drop their cards, while the F.M.P. seems to have deliberately encouraged the 'open house' system.

The General Strike cost the T.A. about £55,000. The Association

---

[1] Like that of the *Manchester Guardian* and *Evening News*, which was now 'closed' and struck off the T.A. list of 'recognized' offices. It remained 'closed' to T.A. members till 1941, when an agreement was finally reached.

was now practically bankrupt and remained so until the end of the depression in the early thirties. It was in no condition, therefore, to enforce any of its demands on the employers. The latter, knowing that they now held the upper hand, steadily rejected T.A. claims in regard to Monotype casters, photogravure machines, regrading, and many other questions: on some the Association failed to get any agreement, while on others it was not until the years 1936–9, when trade was improving, that settlements were reached. On the other hand, the unions were able to resist the employers' proposed wage reductions in 1932–3.

On the whole, industrial relations were friendly and the period was one of 'stabilization', not without material improvement for T.A. members. The verbatim reports of J.L.C. conferences show representatives of both sides presenting their points of view in a reasonable and friendly way, with odd jokes and pleasantries. There was considerable respect and even friendly feeling on both sides: they got to know each others' point of view extremely well after meeting constantly over many years, and negotiations were conducted on a give-and-take basis. Conciliation and compromise continued, in fact, to be the keynotes in relations between the T.A. and the employers' organizations.

Innumerable petty disputes, of course, occurred in chapels and branches, but were usually settled easily. Strike payments averaged under £700 annually in the years 1928–39. Strike benefit was increased in 1918 from £1 to half the branch jobbing case rate per week; but it was decided in 1921 that if more than a quarter of the Association members were 'out', benefit would only be a third of the jobbing case rate.

Relations between employers and employed in this period were greatly improved by the J.I.C. Its work was not confined to settlement of disputes. Its Health Committee did much to better working conditions and prevent industrial diseases. The Costing or Fair Prices Committee tried to stamp out 'undercutting' and 'cheap labour'. Numerous proposals were made for an 'Enabling Bill', to secure legal enforcement of voluntary agreements in the industry, but there were objections on both sides. The unions disliked the idea of Government interference and feared the possible effects on union loyalty; they had no real wish to depart from the customary methods of industrial bargaining. Many employers, on the other hand, were non-union or objected to full trade-union recognition and compulsory observance of agreements. Nothing, therefore, came of the various proposals.

There were several other J.I.C. committees. The Organization Committee tried to secure the 'complete organization' envisaged in the J.I.C.

constitution, but without much success, mainly because most employers were opposed to compulsion. The Unemployment Committee also achieved little, beyond recommending the curtailment of overtime and institution of the double-shift system. The most interesting of its suggestions was that for an industrial pension scheme; but nothing came of it, mainly because of the employers' objections against the expense involved and compulsory trade-union membership. A Betterment Committee appointed in the late twenties made various suggestions for increasing production and employment and for reducing costs, but, while 'rationalization' was accepted, most unions opposed the piece system and bonus schemes or 'payment by results'. The Apprenticeship Committee, as we shall see, produced a valuable training scheme, but it was voluntary and was therefore ignored in many offices.

The J.I.C. did a great deal to improve industrial relations and promote the idea of 'betterment', but its work was largely educational. It had little but moral power and many of its committees therefore got nowhere beyond talking and issuing reports.

XIX

WAGES, HOURS, AND WORKING REGULATIONS
1923-39

THE main characteristic of this period—despite innumerable conferences, Delegate Meeting resolutions, the General Strike, and many smaller disturbances—was 'stabilization' on the basis of the post-war national agreements. Wages, except those of newsmen, remained unaltered till 1940, hours till 1937. There was ceaseless agitation for improved conditions, but the state of trade was for most of the period against successful union action, while the T.A. was too weak financially to take strong measures. Nevertheless, it did succeed, by patient negotiation, in securing valuable additions or amendments to the national agreements.

Wages[1]

News hands were greatly dissatisfied with the national agreements of 1919. Their discontent was little allayed by the wages improvements in 1920. They therefore got resolutions passed by the 1921 Delegate Meeting demanding reduced hours and night wage rates 25 per cent. above day. The E.C. were unable, however, for several years to shift the employers from their stand on 'stabilization', but eventually secured an agreement in 1925 giving graded increases to news hands. Evening news case rates were now 4s. 6d. in grades 6 to 3, 5s. 6d. in grade 2, and 6s. 6d. in grade 1—morning and tri-weekly newspapers 14s. in grades 6 to 3, 15s. in grade 2, and 16s. in grade 1—above the jobbing case rates. These rates remained unchanged throughout the remainder of this period.

The question of jobbing night staffs had not been properly settled in 1920. The employers objected to paying 16s. 6d. above day rates for both temporary and permanent staffs, since this was higher than morning news rates, and they rejected the T.A. claim for 25 per cent. above day rates for *all* night workers, news and jobbing. Negotiations dragged on for many years, agreements not being reached until 1931 (temporary) and 1936 (permanent). These provided that temporary night staffs (operating for a period of one complete week or more, but for less than

---

[1] Piece-work had practically disappeared from the provinces by this time. The General Secretary stated in 1938 that it was 'virtually dead'.

three months) should receive 16s. 6d. above the day grade-class rate for a week of 42½ hours, and permanent night staffs 12s. in grades 1, 2, and 3, and 11s. in grades 4, 5, and 6, for the same hours.

Agreement was also reached in 1931 regarding double day shifts: overtime rates were to be paid for any hours outside the normal working day.

The alterations in news and jobbing night rates necessitated revision of the Linotype and Monotype Agreements. This, however, was not finally achieved until 1937, when the anomalies of 1919 were removed by bringing the two agreements into line and making a clear distinction between news and jobbing. The minimum wage rates of both Lino. and Mono. operators were now fixed on the same basis. Jobbing and weekly news operators on day work received from 6s. in grade 6 to 8s. 6d. in grade 1 above the minimum grade rate, night operators the extras provided under the jobbing night staffs agreement. Evening news operators' rates were from 6s. in grade 6 to 8s. 6d. in grade 1 above the day case rates, morning news operators' from 7s. in grade 6 to 9s. 6d. in grade 1 above the night case rates.

Increases for news hands and operators added to the discontent of jobbing compositors. The 1919 National Wages Agreement placed them in the position of 'bottom dogs', the case rate being the basic minimum upon which all other sections got their various extras. They still formed, however, the majority of T.A. members and prided themselves on their craftsmanship. The National Guild of Jobbing Printers, therefore, at its inaugural conference in 1926, passed a resolution asking for 'the elimination of all terms in the National Wages Agreement which permanently establish the Jobbing members of the T.A. in an inferior status, with the object of establishing uniform minimum rates for all day and night workers'. At least, jobbing wages should be restored to 'a position comparable with other sections of the craft, and not less favourable than the 1919 National Wage Basis Agreement'. The conference therefore urged a movement to increase jobbing wages by 10s. per week.

The E.C. did nothing, however, considering there was no chance of the employers entertaining such proposals. When the Guild pressed them again in 1928, they stated that the matter could only be dealt with by a Delegate Meeting. The Guild therefore got the 1930 Meeting to pass a resolution supporting their demand for a 10s. wage increase; but as a result of the ensuing slump and the employers' demand for wages reductions, followed by the Federation movement for reduced hours, the matter was shelved. It was raised again, however, at the 1936

Delegate Meeting, which decided that a Jobbing Compositors' Investigation Committee should be appointed by the E.C., to secure justice for
'that neglected portion of our membership'; but the 'stabilization' clause
in the 1937 Hours Agreement and the movement for regrading forced
the E.C. to postpone action.

The question was beset with many difficulties. For the past fifty years
the Association had based its claims for extras for composing-machine
operators and machine minders on the additional skill and responsibility
required: how, then, could they now argue for equality for jobbing
compositors? To grant their demands would mean throwing all the
national wages agreements into the melting-pot. Moreover, the other
sections—news hands, operators, and machine minders—would immediately clamour for wage increases.

These problems were discussed in the *Circular* and at the 1939 Delegate Meeting, the E.C. admitting that they were 'stumped'. It was
therefore decided to elect a Jobbing Compositors' Commission to go
into the matter and report their findings to the membership. So matters
stood at the outbreak of war.

Readers were another dissatisfied section. They argued that, as the
majority of them were ex-compositors and their position was one of
great responsibility, they should therefore get more than the minimum
rate. At the Delegate Meeting in 1918 they asked for an extra 10 per cent.
and in 1921 for the same as Lino. and Mono. operators, but their motions were defeated. In 1925, however, their recently established Guild
secured a resolution demanding the Lino. rate for readers. This the
E.C. frequently but fruitlessly presented to the employers, who maintained that all readers did not have the same qualifications or responsibility and that men of special ability were already getting more than the
minimum rate. The question was still being pressed in 1939, successive
Delegate Meetings having backed the readers' claim.

Machinemen, too, had their special claims, which we shall look at
later. In addition to such sectional demands, there were several general
wages movements during this period. The first was in 1924-5. Trade
was improving after the slump and the cost of living rose slightly: many
branches therefore urged an advance movement and the 1925 Delegate
Meeting instructed the E.C. to 'take immediate steps to secure a flat
rate increase in wages of at least 10s. per week'. But the E.C. were
engaged in negotiations on regrading, machine rules, news rates and
hours, and in 1926 there came the General Strike. The question of a
wages advance therefore fell into abeyance.

In January 1932 the P. & K.T.F. Secretary received a letter from the employers referring to 'the serious effect on our industry of the prevailing depression'. There had been 'a very considerable falling-off of orders, resulting in a serious diminution—in many cases a total disappearance—of profits'. Customers were complaining of the high cost of printing and the employers therefore proposed a conference to find 'some means of reducing production costs'.

Asked for comments, the T.A. Executive reserved to itself 'the right to conduct its own negotiations with the employers, should at any time the necessity arise', but sent representatives to a Federation conference with the employers on 17 March. The employers' proposals were astounding: they wanted not only a wages reduction of 20 per cent., but also sweeping changes in agreements regarding Lino. and Mono. rates, machine rules, overtime, and apprentices. The Federation Executive pointed out that they could not negotiate on agreements made between individual unions and the employers' organizations: a conference of societies would have to be called.

This conference, which met on 18 April, empowered the Federation Executive to continue discussions. In the resumed talks in May the employers agreed to withdraw most of their other proposals if a wages cut of 15 per cent. was accepted; but the Federation Executive countered with demands for reduced hours and further limitation of overtime and apprentices, in order to reduce unemployment. They also condemned excessive competition and price-cutting, and pointed out that wages cuts would worsen the trade depression by reducing purchasing power. Moreover, they could not negotiate on wages agreements made with individual unions.

The employers, therefore, realizing that it was useless to continue negotiations with the Federation, now approached the individual unions. These, however, adopted deliberate delaying tactics. The T.A. managed to put off a conference till 15 November. The employers then repeated their proposals and arguments as to reduced orders, high costs, and falling profits, pointing out also that wages had remained unaltered since 1922, despite the fall in the cost of living, which was now only 43 per cent. above the pre-war level, while wages were 120 per cent. higher.[1] The E.C. informed the employers that their proposals would have to be put before a conference of group committees—which did not meet till 11 March.

[1] Actually, wages were about 108 per cent. higher on average (see above, p. 346), but the employers' argument was, nevertheless, well justified.

Meanwhile, further P. & K.T.F. conferences decided on joint resistance to the employers' demands. The E.C. therefore rejected all the employers' proposals, pointing out that the regrading question still remained unsettled; that the employers had steadily resisted all T.A. claims for the past twelve years on the grounds of 'stabilization'; and that the serious unemployment in the industry required a reduction of working hours, overtime, and apprentices. Moreover, statistics (supplied by the Labour Research Department from Somerset House) were produced showing that printing firms were not at all badly off financially and that a reduction of wages was not justified. Employers should stop price-cutting, cut down non-productive departments, and improve equipment. The T.A. could 'not be expected to accept any responsibility for the position of an industry over which we have never been allowed to exercise any control'.

The unions' stand was successful. In May 1933 the employers allowed the matter to drop, since a strike was the only alternative. Moreover, trade was now on the mend and improved steadily up to 1939. This improvement, in fact, together with the rising cost of living, led to a wages advance movement in the years 1937–9. Resolutions poured in from T.A. groups and branches and several unions proposed a P. & K.T.F. conference on the question. But the Federation Executive considered that the cost-of-living figures did not justify an advance movement. Such a movement, moreover, was not permissible owing to the 'stabilization' clause in the recent Hours Agreement. There was also the question of regrading to be settled. With these views the T.A. Executive agreed.

Thus wages, on the whole, remained stabilized throughout this period. Stabilization did not, however, mean that there was no change in the condition of T.A. members. While wages stood still, or rose slightly in certain cases, the cost of living fell. After the reductions of 1921–3, basic wage rates remained about 108 per cent. above pre-war, but the cost of living fell gradually from 70 per cent. (May 1923) to 36 per cent. (May 1933) above pre-war, and, though rising thereafter, was still only 55 per cent. above the 1914 level in August 1939. Thus the 'real' wages of T.A. members rose considerably during these years: they were about 22 per cent. higher than before the war in 1923, 53 per cent. in 1933, and 34 per cent. in 1939. Moreover, members now enjoyed an annual week's holiday with pay and shorter hours as a result of the agreements in 1919 and 1937. Thus their standard of living was a good deal higher than before the 1914–18 war. It was also higher than that of workers in most other trades.[1] Printing was, in fact, the only industry not to suffer wages cuts between 1922 and 1939.

These conclusions, of course, apply only to those who were fully employed. As we have seen, unemployment and short-time were widespread during this period, though not as serious in printing as in most other trades. But even the unemployed were better off than before the war, since they now got relief from the State as well as from the T.A.

There was constant agitation during this period for reform of the wage grading system. Under this system there were, as we have seen, six wage grades, ranging from 62s. 6d. to 77s. 6d., with London virtually a seventh, 11s. 6d. higher. These wide differences created intense dissatisfaction and there was a growing demand for 'equal pay for the same work'. The system encouraged the migration of large firms, especially from London, to small low-grade provincial towns, thus causing 'cheap competition'. Moreover, the actual grading system was full of anomalies, many important printing centres being unaccountably placed in the lower grades. No wonder, then, that grading was the greatest single source of irritation and unrest in T.A. branches during these years. Branch, group, and Delegate Meetings constantly pressed for either regrading or reduction in the number of grades.

At the time of the wage reduction in 1922 the employers had agreed to consider genuine grading anomalies. The E.C., therefore, at once appointed a special committee, which drew up a list of regrading proposals. The P. & K.T.F. Executive suggested joint action and summoned a special conference in November 1923 which agreed to form a Federation regrading committee, but the T.A. Executive decided to act independently. Conferences were held with the employers in April and June 1924, the T.A. submitting a long list of grading anomalies, affecting 140 towns and half the membership. This, the employers maintained, was merely seeking a general advance of wages; they wanted 'stabilization' and would only consider genuine anomalies. Moreover, they pointed out the difficulties of separate negotiations with the T.A. and P. & K.T.F. and suggested the establishment of a joint committee. The T.A. Executive accepted this proposal and the committee met in July, when it was agreed that sub-committees should be appointed to hold meetings and hear evidence in the different districts. First of all, however, the regrading proposals of the T.A. and the other unions had to be harmonized. This proved impossible, the T.A. strongly adhering

[1] See Cole, G. D. H., and Postgate, R., *The Common People, 1746–1946* (1949), pp. 639–47.

to its own list and opposing particularly a proposed extension of the London radius. In February 1925, therefore, the T.A. Executive reverted to independent action.

At a further conference in July 1925 the employers again rejected the T.A.'s wholesale regrading proposals and the T.A. eventually agreed to the establishment of a joint T.A.–F.M.P. committee of inquiry. Each district would be visited in turn and evidence would be heard, but there would be no actual regrading till the whole inquiry was completed. Thus the employers, in effect, shelved the whole question.

The 'Travelling Circus', as it was called, held numerous meetings in different parts of the country during 1924–6. The inquiry was then halted for two years as a result of the General Strike, but was resumed in 1928 and went on until 1931, after which matters stagnated for several years due to the trade depression, the employers' demands for wages reductions, and their resistance to any large-scale alterations in grading. When conferences on the question were eventually resumed in 1935 the employers declared that there was no point in carrying on with the inquiry since the evidence was now out of date, the industry needed 'stabilization' after the recent slump, and other important questions, such as hours and unemployment, were being considered. They also rejected a new T.A. proposal for reduction in the number of grades; they would only consider 'a few acute cases' of regrading.

Meanwhile, the P. & K.T.F. had started another regrading movement, but could make no headway without the T.A. Now that independent action had failed, however, the Association decided to join in the Federation movement. A joint committee was appointed in April 1936 and it was decided to ask for abolition of grades 4, 5, and 6. Action was delayed, however, by the hours movement, and negotiations with the employers on grading did not begin until 1938. The Federation now demanded not only elimination of the three lower grades, but also reduction of the differentials between the remaining three and between the first grade and the London rate.

These proposals the employers totally rejected. They considered the grading system 'as near to perfection as it could be made when . . . first introduced', and that conditions had changed little since 1919. The Federation was asking, not for regrading, but 'an all-round increase of wages' for provincial members, contrary to the three years' 'stabilization' clause in the 1937 Hours Agreement. A reduction in the number of grades to three would break the F.M.P. and cause many firms to go non-union.

This answer left the unions in a quandary, which they were still in when war broke out.

Hours

The Hours and Holidays Agreement of 1919, which had given the printing and kindred trades a working week of 48 hours (45 for night workers), by no means satisfied the unions. The most dissatisfied were the news workers, who had got nothing out of it and immediately began agitating for a reduction of hours. Their demand was for an '11-day fortnight': that hours should be reduced by eight a fortnight on morning newspapers, to give a night off, and by four a week on evening newspapers, to give a half-day off—in each case without reduction of pay.[1]

The E.C., acting on resolutions of the 1921 Delegate Meeting, presented these claims to the employers. The latter, however, put forward their usual arguments for 'stabilization'. They also pointed out that hours were covered by agreement with the Federation and that, in any case, the claims were impossible owing to shortage of operators. Eventually, however, after repeated conferences, a compromise was reached in 1925. In return for an increase of wages for news hands,[2] the E.C. accepted a 'balancing time' arrangement in regard to hours. The '11-day fortnight' was granted, but without reduction of hours: time taken off one week would have to be 'balanced' by extra hours the next.

News hands were greatly dissatisfied with this agreement, particularly as the employers contended that it did not apply to machine minders, but neither prolonged negotiations by the T.A. and P. & K.T.F. nor recommendations by the J.I.C. Conciliation Committee could move the Newspaper Society until the mid-thirties, when threatened strikes finally forced them to sign an agreement (May 1936) granting the 11-day fortnight without 'balancing time'.

Meanwhile very little had been done to secure a general reduction of hours since the failure of negotiations by the P. & K.T.F. for a 44-hour week in 1920. It was not until the thirties that the unions started to move again.

The T.A. Delegate Meeting of 1930 protested against Federation apathy on this question, pointing out that a reduction of hours would help solve the problem of unemployment caused by increasing mechanization and 'rationalization', and that it was called for by the speeding-up of production, which put a greater strain on the workers. Other unions

---

[1] This was one of the main articles in the 'Newsmen's Charter'.
[2] See above, p. 365.

held similar views and the P. & K.T.F. Administrative Council therefore decided at its annual meeting in 1931 that a special conference should be held. This conference, in January 1932, came to the conclusion that, in order to lessen unemployment and enable all to share in the benefits of increased output resulting from 'rationalization', there should be a reduction of working hours and further restriction of overtime and apprentices.

Just prior to this conference, however, the employers had dropped a bombshell by demanding wage reductions and sweeping revision of national agreements.[1] In view of this and the existing slump there was little likelihood of a successful hours movement. The unions were able, however, to use their claims as counters to the employers' proposals. They even raised their demands to a 40-hour week, 'in view of the continued unemployment'.

The P. & K.T.F. did nothing, however, but pass annual resolutions until 1935, when improving trade enabled stronger action to be taken. The final outcome, after prolonged negotiations, deadlocks, J.I.C. Conciliation Committees, and a threatened strike, was the 1937 Hours and Holidays Agreement, giving the general printing trade a working week of 45 hours (day) and 43 (night). In return the unions made certain concessions regarding overtime and accepted a 'stabilization' clause whereby it was agreed that, except in the event of a considerable increase in the cost of living or any national or international agreements regarding hours, neither side would request 'a major alteration of any Agreement which will materially affect the cost of production' during the next three years. This clause, as we have seen, proved a stumbling-block in the way of claims for increased wages and regrading.

A Daily Newspaper Offices Supplementary Agreement was signed at the same time, but gave no further reduction of hours to news hands, who were governed by the recent Eleven-Day Fortnight Agreement, their weekly hours averaging 44 (day) and $41\frac{1}{4}$ (night).

Overtime

The overtime limit fixed in 1919 was 16 hours per fortnight. But evasion was easy, owing to the 'emergency' clause and the desire of T.A. members for extra money. The rule failed, in fact, to prevent a large amount of 'systematic' and excessive overtime. Hence there were frequent demands for its rigid enforcement or a more restrictive rule, in order to reduce unemployment. Some proposed the total

[1] See above, p. 368.

abolition of overtime, but this was impracticable. The Delegate Meetings of 1933 and 1936 demanded reduction to 8 hours a fortnight, but the employers would not agree. In fact the overtime limit was *extended* by the 1937 Hours Agreement. The employers maintained that there would be insufficient skilled men to offset the shorter hours and the unions therefore agreed to increase the overtime maximum by the same number of hours as that by which the working week was reduced, i.e. to 22 per fortnight. It was mutually agreed, however, that 'avoidable overtime' was undesirable, the F.M.P. and Newspaper Society promising to discourage it.

Apart from minor alterations and new clauses such as those with regard to tea-money and meal-time working, the other overtime regulations in the National Wages Agreement remained unchanged during this period. On several occasions proposals were made to increase the overtime rates, in order to restrict the amount of overtime worked and thus reduce unemployment, but nothing came of them.

Another way of checking overtime was to impose a levy upon it of so much per hour. This was proposed at several Delegate Meetings, but was rejected on the grounds that it would be recognizing instead of reducing excessive overtime. Many branches, however, imposed local overtime levies, the proceeds going to assist the unemployed.

The Association continued to stand firm on the principle that 'each day should stand by itself', embodied in the 1919 Agreement, and refused to permit any 'balancing' of lost time against overtime. On this question they had a lengthy dispute with the employers in the years 1927–31, which they took to the J.I.C. Conciliation Committee, finally forcing the employers to give way.

Holidays

The 1919 Agreement caused great dissatisfaction among daily newsmen in regard to holidays as well as hours. They could still be required to work on Christmas Day, Boxing Day, and other recognized holidays at ordinary rates, for which substitute holidays with pay were insufficient compensation. During the war newspaper publications had been suspended on these days, but were resumed by many firms after the war, to the great discontent of news workers. On the recommendation of the Newspaper Society, there were no publications on Christmas Day, nor of morning papers on Boxing Day, but publication of evening papers on Boxing Day was left to local arrangement. This question was taken up by the P. & K.T.F. Executive, who secured an agreement in

1925 providing for the non-publication of evening newspapers on Boxing Day, except when it fell on Saturday or Monday.

Newsmen, however, still had to work on Bank Holidays[1] at ordinary rates, whereas jobbers were paid time-and-a-half. They therefore demanded the same conditions as the general printing trade. A resolution to this effect was passed by the 1936 Delegate Meeting and the E.C. pressed the matter on the P. & K.T.F., but the latter considered it unwise to take action in view of the recent Eleven-Day Fortnight Agreement and the negotiations on the 40-hour week. The demand was reiterated, however, by the T.A. Delegate Meeting in 1939.

The 1919 Agreement had given an annual week's holiday with pay. In the thirties the unions began to agitate for a fortnight, on the grounds that the workers should share in the benefits of increased production and that they needed longer holidays for health reasons, owing to the increased speed and mechanization of the industry. Moreover, it would help to absorb the unemployed. Resolutions to this effect were passed by every T.A. Delegate Meeting from 1930 onwards, but the P. & K.T.F. was unable to take action, first of all owing to more pressing matters of hours and regrading, and then because of the 'stabilization' clause in the 1937 Agreement.

Machine Rules

The revised machinemen's rules of 1920 were a considerable T.A. achievement. The Association had finally secured recognition by the employers of its control over all letterpress machines, flat-bed and rotary, jobbing and news, and had got a detailed code of regulations governing machine classification, wages, manning, and working conditions.

This agreement, however, did not end matters. New, faster, and more complicated machines were continually being introduced in this period and fresh branches of industry were opening up. The machine rules, therefore, had to be revised and expanded. This was the work of the Machine Investigation Committee of the E.C. established by the 1918 Delegate Meeting. This Committee was constantly at work, examining new machines or attachments and negotiating with employers regarding working conditions. There were so many makes and varieties of machines, often for specialized work, that it was almost impossible to bring them all into the national agreement, and local settlements were often made with individual firms. Where possible, however, new rules were devised to cover them.

[1] There was usually no publication on Good Friday.

The T.A. generally sought to secure increased rates or 'extras', basing their claims chiefly on the extra skill required, added responsibility, and increased output, in the profits of which it was considered the workers had a right to share. The employers countered with arguments as to the cost of new machines, their simpler operation, and T.A. restriction on mechanical development. These pros and cons are to be found in all the innumerable conference reports of these years.

It was stated at the 1921 Delegate Meeting that machine minders all over the country were dissatisfied with the recent national agreement on machine rules. Wage rates and manning of news rotaries, for example, had been left to chapel negotiation; the principle of 'one man, one machine' had not been achieved for flat-bed minders; and there was a widespread demand for increased extras for the different classes of machines. The delegates therefore drew up a revised code. Their proposals, however, were turned down by the employers, who insisted on 'stabilization'.

The 1925 Delegate Meeting expressed 'intense disappointment' at this outcome and instructed the E.C. to negotiate further. But the employers again rejected the proposed amendments, which they considered were 'an attempt to obtain higher remuneration for practically all the machinemen in the country and would also mean a further limitation in the number of machines which your members are working'. The industry could not stand the increased cost, in view of competition from 'office machines' and reduced orders.

The Delegate Meeting of 1930, however, after a national machinemen's conference the year before, made claims for even higher rates and more restrictive manning regulations. These were reaffirmed by the Meetings in 1933 and 1936, but the E.C. were so much occupied with other business that they did not present them to the employers until 1938. The employers' reply was much the same as in 1927: that 'the T.A.'s proposals cannot be entertained as they are tantamount to a general increase of wages so far as minders are concerned', and therefore contrary to the stabilization clause in the 1937 Hours and Holidays Agreement. This the E.C. disputed and they were still pressing for revision when war broke out.

Although the E.C. failed to carry through a wholesale revision of the machine rules in this period, they did succeed in getting some important additions for new machines and attachments—though often only after long years of haggling with the employers and, in some cases, threatened stoppages and reference to the J.I.C. Extra payments were secured for many different kinds of machines—6s. for an Edler check-book rotary, for example, 8s. for a Cossar machine, 10s. for a weekly news rotary, 15s. for a tandem Miehle, and 24s. for an Iris four-colour chromo-rotary—while further 'extras' were added for automatic and semi-automatic feeders, bronzing attachments, numbering and anti-setoff devices. The most important agreement was that finally reached in 1934 for small reel-fed rotaries such as the Chambon and similar multiple-process machines for cutting, creasing, scoring, punching, and folding, as well as printing, bags, cartons, wrappers, &c. A minder in charge of such a machine with a printing cylinder width of less than 17 in., but not less than 12 in., or of two machines below that size, was to receive the minimum grade rate; 5s. extra for a larger machine; and 2s. 6d. extra for each additional machine of any size. No manning limitations were laid down in the agreement, but the 1936 Delegate Meeting decided that four should be the limit for one minder, while the E.C. later advised that it should be three.

A new problem with which the T.A. was faced in this period was that of 'office machines'. Not only were wax-stencil duplicating machines such as the Roneo and Gestetner extensively introduced, but also small letterpress machines such as the Gammeter Multigraph and Adana and small off-set machines like the Rotaprint and Multilith, which were capable of producing high-class work. Many public bodies, large business firms, insurance companies, and banks installed such machines, worked by girls, owing to the high cost of print.

These machines were regarded by both employers and unions in the printing industry as 'a menace to the trade'. The employers, as we have seen, referred to the competition from them in rejecting the T.A.'s revised machine rules in 1927. They did so again in 1932 when proposing wage reductions. Their method of coping with the problem was by reducing costs. The T.A., however, sought to secure the working of such machines by its members. They approached various firms and public bodies and also the machine manufacturers, but without much success. They discussed the problem with the F.M.P. and P. & K.T.F., but neither could suggest effective action. Such machines were regarded by makers and users as purely office equipment, outside T.A. control, easily and cheaply operated by girl labour.

The organization of letterpress machinemen was steadily continued during this period. Returns collected in 1928-9 showed that in recognized offices there were 6,073 members and 515 non-members, while in unrecognized offices (for which, however, the returns were very incomplete) there were 323 non-members. A good deal of 'cheap labour' (females and unapprenticed youths) was still employed, particularly on platens, while the T.A. occasionally came into conflict with non-craft unions (the N.S.O.P. & A. and N.U.P.B. & P.W.) in regard to the manning of various types of machines, particularly those used for box and bag making.[1]

Photogravure Machines

By 1918 intaglio or photogravure machines had been introduced into several T.A. branches. As soon as their possibilities were realized, the Association tried to secure control of their working. The Machine Investigation Committee collected a great deal of information and drew up a set of rules. Intaglio machines, it was laid down, should be manned only by T.A. members. Wage rates should be high, as the work was 'unusually unhealthy because of the chemical ingredients of the inks used in the process'. Charge-hands should receive not less than 15s. over the ordinary 'stab rate on sheet-fed machines, 25s. on reel-fed machines, with 20s. extra for the second hand. For two-sided rotaries (double cylinder) these rates should be increased by 10s., machines more than 40 in. in breadth should be charged 5s. extra, and a further 5s. was to be paid for accessories such as folding, slicing, or other automatic attachment. No extra apprentices would be allowed: machine apprentices were to be trained in both letterpress and photogravure departments, but should not be allowed on intaglio machines until they had completed five years of their apprenticeship.

These proposed rules were placed before the employers in the national conferences towards the end of 1919. Matters were complicated, however, by the rival claims of the Lithographic Printers. The employers would not recognize that any particular union had an exclusive right to work the machines. It was eventually agreed to refer the matter to the P. & K.T.F. for decision as to which union had the better claim. The P. & K.T.F. decided, however, 'that the machine cannot be allocated to the Letterpress or Lithographic sections as it does the work of both', and advised that the unions should confer to form an agreement on wages and working conditions.

This proposal the T.A. rejected, claiming sole manning of the machines. Conferences were held with the P.M.M.T.S. and S.T.A., who agreed to co-operate in securing letterpress control. The E.C. instructed members to claim the working of intaglio machines when introduced into

---

[1] See below, pp. 390–1.

any recognized office. Conflict occurred with the Lithos. in several places, but returns collected in 1927-8 showed that in most branches T.A. members were working the machines.

The E.C., meanwhile, had resubmitted their proposed rules to the F.M.P. at a J.L.C. conference in April 1924, only to have them turned down again. Consequently agreements had to be sought with individual firms. By 1929, however, the F.M.P. had come to recognize that the manning of photogravure machines should belong to the letterpress unions, though not exclusively, and were prepared to discuss working conditions. The T.A. and P.M.M.T.S. therefore had further meetings to draw up agreed proposals and decided to meet the employers jointly.

Conferences were held with the F.M.P. Photogravure Committee in 1931, but made no headway. The employers refused to concede exclusive letterpress control and there were wide differences on manning and wage rates. The F.M.P. proposed that the existing agreements for letterpress machines should be applied to photogravure, which, they asserted, actually required less skill and attention, since there was no make-ready, registering, &c. The unions' demands, they considered, were excessively high and would hamper photogravure development.

Negotiations consequently lapsed for another three or four years. Further conferences were held with the P.M.M.T.S., the two unions agreeing to continue joint action, but the employers refused to meet them jointly again. Eventually, therefore, they agreed to negotiate separately, but to keep each other informed.

Numerous conferences with the F.M.P. Photogravure Committee in the years 1935-8 finally resulted in an agreement in March 1938, giving the T.A. exclusive control over the manning of photogravure machines and laying down regulations as to wages, manning, and apprenticeship. It was based on that for letterpress machines, but secured higher wage rates.

All photogravure machine minders were to be T.A. members or apprentices, but the latter were not to be made minders on reel-fed rotary perfecter machines until they had served three years of their apprenticeship. The photogravure minimum wage rate was to be 5s. above the letterpress: on this basis varying rates were fixed for the different types and sizes of machines. Wage rates for minders on sheet-fed photogravure machines ranged from the minimum on a double royal or below, to 12s. extra on a two-colour or perfecter (any size), with additional 'extras' for automatic and semi-automatic feeders as in the letterpress agreement. Rates for reel-fed rotary perfecters similarly ranged from 8s. above the minimum on a machine with a web-width of 17 in.

up to but not including 24 in., to 20s. extra for the minder in charge of a machine with more than one unit and a web-width of 24 in. and over, when more than one minder was employed; while additional 'extras' varying from 3s. to 15s., according to the size of machine, were fixed for variable folders. Rates for small reel-fed rotaries such as the Alma, Chambon, Goebel, &c., were almost identical with those for the same kind of letterpress machines, except that the minimum was the photogravure rate. For single-sided rotaries (non-reversible) the photogravure minimum was to be paid, with 3s. extra for each unit above one.

Manning regulations were also laid down for reel-fed rotary perfecter machines, according to the number and width of the cylinders. Thus while one minder could manage a two-cylinder machine (any size) without a folder, four must man a machine of over 60 in. maximum webwidth with seven or eight cylinders and a folder.

A separate set of apprentices was allowed to the photogravure department, on a sliding scale according to the number of journeymen employed, much the same as that for letterpress machine-rooms.

The Litho. Society had now reluctantly to recognize T.A. control over photogravure machines, the Association agreeing not to disturb those Litho. members (only 19) at present engaged in this work.

Monotype Casters

The Delegate Meeting of 1918 having decided to admit Monotype-caster attendants, with the object of getting them all into the Association and securing control over the working of these machines, the Executive proceeded to draw up a set of rules. All fully qualified caster attendants in recognized offices, it was laid down, must be T.A. members, the qualification being 'an apprenticeship in the letterpress departments and to the casting machine'. Those at present employed as caster attendants who had not served such an apprenticeship might be admitted after four years on the machines. An apprentice ratio was laid down for the casting department: one caster attendant, one apprentice; three or more, two apprentices. In regard to manning, where more than one machine was installed a caster attendant must be employed, who might take charge of up to three machines, but above that number there was to be a caster attendant to every two additional machines. A man in charge of one machine was to receive not less than the branch minimum rate (news or jobbing); more than one machine, the keyboard rate.

These rules were submitted to the Monotype Users' Association in 1921. The position was complicated, however, by the rival claims of several other unions: the Typefounders, N.S.O.P. & A., and N.U.P.B. & P.W. The two latter had actually concluded an agreement with the employers in 1919, providing for a caster wage rate 3s. below the T.A. minimum and five years' training for 'learners'. A large number of labourers and 'runners' were, in fact, employed on Monotype casting, which was regarded as comparatively unskilled work, not requiring craft training. On the other hand, a good many caster attendants had actually served an apprenticeship in the composing or machine departments. When, therefore, the T.A. protested against the recent agreement, the N.S.O.P. & A. suggested demarcation between printer and non-printer caster attendants.

This was the line taken by the employers, who refused to recognize exclusive T.A. control or pay the T.A. rate, regarding the work as unskilled. They were also opposed to any restrictions on the manning of the machines. Neither were they agreeable to an all-round training for caster attendants, in composing or machine work as well as casting, preferring specialization. They were also unwilling to eliminate assistants and runners in favour of craftsmen and apprentices. What they wanted, in fact, was to keep things as they were, to employ whomever they liked, on as many machines and at whatever wages they liked. Their policy was 'divide and rule', by playing off the different unions against each other.

T.A. differences with the N.S.O.P. & A. and N.U.P.B. & P.W. were not, however, very serious. These unions had only a few Monotype caster members and were willing to transfer them to the T.A., especially if the latter could secure better wages. The conflict with the Typefounders was on different grounds and more serious. The Typefounders agreed with the T.A. in regarding Monotype casting as craft work and in striving to secure proper conditions; but they insisted that it belonged to typefounders, not printers, as the T.A. claimed, especially as the Monotype caster was superseding the type-foundry; over three-quarters, in fact, of their members were caster attendants and prior to 1918 the T.A. had recognized their control over Monotype casters. They claimed, therefore, to be the national society catering for caster attendants. The T.A., however, had now reversed its policy and was claiming to organize and control such workers in the provinces. About three-quarters of the Typefounders' members were in London and the majority of provincial caster attendants, as proved by branch reports, belonged to the T.A. The Typefounders should therefore, the T.A. considered, confine themselves to London, like the L.S.C., P.M.M.T.S., and A.C.P., and a reciprocity agreement should be arranged between them. The Association, being a much bigger union with a stronger grip on provincial printing offices, was more capable of organizing these men. The Typefounders, however, stuck firmly to their claims, rejected reciprocity, and denounced the T.A.'s coercive attitude. Numerous conferences and P. & K.T.F. arbitration failed to settle the differences and the Typefounders eventually (1937) enlarged their name to the 'Monotype Casters and Typefounders Society'.

Conferences with the Monotype Users' Association dragged on interminably throughout this period. At times the T.A. almost threw up the sponge in favour of joint action with the other unions. But eventually, after the Association had threatened strike action and the matter had been referred to the J.I.C. Conciliation Committee, an agreement was concluded in 1939. The T.A. secured the grade case rate for all caster attendants and recognition of apprenticeship in the casting department, but the manning of machines was more or less left to the employers. Those caster attendants who were qualified compositors could be interchanged freely between the caster and composing departments, provided that they were paid the appropriate wages. Non-printer caster attendants, who had not served an apprenticeship in the composing department, were only allowed to break up formes (including the clearing and storing, but not distribution, of type matter, &c.) and to pull galley proofs. The apprentice ratio in the caster department was one apprentice to one journeyman, two to three, and three (the maximum) to eight or more.

The N.S.O.P. & A. and N.U.P.B. & P.W., meanwhile, had agreed to transfer their caster attendants to the T.A. Friendly relations had also been established with the Typefounders: a temporary 'working agreement' was reached in 1938, the two societies agreeing to recognize each other's cards pending discussions on amalgamation.

Returns collected from the branches in 1934 give some idea of the extent to which the T.A. had organized caster attendants. There were 444 T.A. members, 119 belonging to other unions, 152 non-unionists, and a considerable number of boys and assistants. Moreover, these returns were from 'fair' offices only. Obviously there was still a good deal of organizing to be done in this department.

Readers[1]

There was continuous disagreement with the employers during this period regarding interpretation of the readers' rule in the 1919 Agree-

[1] See above, p. 367, for readers' wages.

ment.[1] The employers took advantage of the wording to maintain, firstly, that it referred only to men and did not prevent them from employing women readers, and secondly, that it permitted employment of part-time male readers who were not T.A. members, since membership was only compulsory for fully qualified men who had held such a position for at least two years.

The T.A. Executive strongly opposed such interpretations and tried repeatedly to get the rule redrafted. The question cropped up continually at conferences of the Joint Labour Committee, but the employers remained adamant. The difficulty was that in most offices reading was part-time work done by the proprietors, members of their family, reporters, and clerks, as well as by compositors.

The T.A.'s main concern at first was with the elimination of female readers. Twice they took the matter to the J.I.C. Conciliation Committee and secured findings in their favour, but the employers, though replacing women by men in particular cases, refused to give way on the general principle and female readers, though fewer in number, were still employed at the end of this period.

The T.A. Delegate Meetings in 1936 and 1939 demanded the exclusion not only of women, but also of men who had not served seven years to the trade either as compositors or copyholders,[2] in order to prevent 'outsiders' getting in after only two years as readers. They also demanded that specialist readers, at present exempted, should become members after holding such situations two years. These demands, however, were also rejected by the employers.

T.A. figures collected in 1925 showed that out of 907 readers, 752 were T.A. members, 30 belonged to other unions, and 125 were non-unionists. There were also 42 females employed. These figures did not, however, include the large number of part-time readers in smaller offices.

Apprentices

The T.A. was much more successful during this period in maintaining its apprentice regulations, and 'the apprentice problem', which loomed so large in the nineteenth century, receded into the background. There were several reasons for this: the falling birth-rate, stronger union organization, increasing mechanization, and wider recognition by employers of the value of apprenticeship and sound technical training.

[1] See above, p. 337.
[2] See below, p. 385, for the question of N.S.O.P. & A. copyholders and revisers.

The old fears still persisted, however, and the Association could only with difficulty be persuaded to relax its restrictive regulations to meet the needs of the expanding industry. When the employers suggested an extension of the apprentice scale in November 1920, the E.C. refused as 'the country would be flooded with newly-fledged journeymen', thus increasing unemployment.

At the beginning of 1926 the F.M.P. complained to the P. & K.T.F. of 'the inadequate number of apprentices . . . now being trained in various sections of the industry' and suggested a conference of all the unions concerned. The T.A. Executive, however, were 'not prepared to make any alteration in the present agreement'. They even tried to enforce a more restrictive rule passed by the 1913 Delegate Meeting in regard to apprentices in news composing rooms,[1] but the employers refused to accept it.

In 1927 the F.M.P. approached the T.A. directly for an increased ratio of apprentices and negotiations dragged on for over three years. The employers used not only their own statistics, but also those of the Balfour Committee on Trade and Industry, to prove the necessity for a larger number of apprentices. The T.A. Executive, however, secured branch returns which showed that no increase was necessary: many offices did not have their full quota under the present scale, while, on the other hand, many were exceeding it, especially small unrecognized offices. There were arguments also about the average length of working life and wastage due to deaths and retirements. Whose figures were right it seems impossible to say; but the T.A. could adduce the one incontrovertible fact that over a thousand members were out of work and many others casually employed or on short time. The Executive therefore rejected the employers' proposals, and, as trade depression deepened, the F.M.P. allowed the matter to drop. The T.A., on the other hand, began to urge further limitation of apprentices in order to reduce unemployment. The Delegate Meetings of 1930, 1933, and 1936 all passed resolutions to this effect, but the E.C. were too busy with other matters to take any action. The apprentice scales for composing and machine rooms therefore remained unaltered. The T.A. did, however, as we have seen, eventually concede separate sets of apprentices for the photogravure and caster departments.

The seven years' apprenticeship rule remained a cardinal feature of T.A. policy, except that boys who stayed at school till fifteen or sixteen years of age were allowed a shorter period, terminating at twenty-one.

[1] See above, p. 184.

To prevent employment of adult labour at apprentice rates, the Association secured the employers' agreement in 1938 not to apprentice boys over 16½ years of age.

The seven years' rule seems to have been generally observed, but the Association did not succeed in introducing the apprenticeship system into news rotary-machine rooms. It was precluded from doing so by its agreement with the N.S.O.P. & A. Boys entered news rotary departments first of all as 'learners' or 'junior assistants' and then became 'assistants' (brake-hands, oilers, &c.), joining the N.S.O.P. & A. Not until they were in charge of machines could they join the T.A. On several occasions we actually find the E.C. forbidding apprenticeship in news rotary rooms. Some rotary minders, however, were recruited from among T.A. flat-bed men, under the fifty-fifty agreement with the N.S.O.P. & A., and these, of course, had served an apprenticeship.

A similar system prevailed in regard to readers in daily newspaper offices. Boys were brought in as learners and progressed gradually to copyholders and revisers, being members of the N.S.O.P. & A. Not until they had been five years as copyholders and/or revisers after the age of twenty-one were they eligible for T.A. membership. In general printing offices, however, a man could join the T.A. after two years as a reader, though about half the readers were ex-compositors.

The Association continued its efforts to secure the proper indenturing of apprentices. The question was brought before the J.I.C., and the F.M.P., though not agreeable to compulsory indenturing, did recommend use of the model indenture form drawn up by the Apprenticeship Committee. It was stated at the Delegate Meeting in 1936, however, that 'the form of legal indentures has gone by the board . . . there are comparatively few branches of the Association where the indenturing of apprentices is now in operation'. This would appear to be an exaggerated statement, but it does indicate that in many places the old system was dying out.

The T.A.'s increasing interest in apprentices is illustrated by the decision of the 1918 Delegate Meeting to admit them at sixteen years of age, on reduced subscriptions, in the hope that they 'would be imbued with the principles of trade unionism in their early years'. This Meeting, moreover, adopted a new principle by drawing up an apprentices' wage scale, varying from one-fifth of the branch rate in the first year to one-half in the last. Considerable attention was also given to the selection, technical education, and training of apprentices, over which the Association claimed some control, in accordance with the recommendations of the Whitley Report.

The Association made vigorous efforts in the inter-war years to secure these objects. T.A. officials played a prominent part in the establishment, through the J.I.C., of a scheme for the selection and training of apprentices, as recommended in the Whitley Report and encouraged by the Ministries of Labour and Education. This scheme took several years to formulate, being finally adopted in October 1924. It provided for the establishment of 'Local Printing and Allied Trades Joint Apprenticeship Committees', composed of equal numbers of employers and employed. These, acting in close concert with the local Advisory Committees for Juvenile Employment and the Local Education Authorities, were to secure the selection of suitable boys for apprenticeship and a sound education and training both in the workshop and at technical school.

This scheme was a great step forward, but it was purely voluntary and was not for many years brought into anything like effective operation. In many towns no local committees were established, many employers objecting to outside interference, and in many offices training remained very defective. The more enlightened employers, however, particularly the large firms, strongly supported the scheme, realizing the increasing necessity for sound educational and technical training as machines and processes became more complicated.

The E.C. approached the F.M.P. on the question of an apprentices' wage scale in 1920, but the employers countered with a proposed increase in the number of apprentices and negotiations broke down. The F.M.P., however, published a suggested list of apprentices' wage rates, varying from 15 per cent. of the journeyman's rate in the first year to 45 per cent. in the seventh, which many firms accepted.

No further action was taken until 1937, when a special P. & K.T.F. conference decided to seek an agreement on apprentices' wages, with the idea of preventing cheap labour. The proposed scale varied from 15 per cent. of the journeyman's rate in the first year to 60 per cent. in the seventh. When, however, the F.M.P. were approached in 1939, they refused to recognize the right of trade unions to interfere in this question, as being one entirely between employer, boy, and parent.

The number of T.A. apprentice members rose to 2,865 by 1932 as a result of the 1918 decision to admit them at sixteen years of age. The 1936 Delegate Meeting, however, decided to revert to the old system of only admitting apprentices in the last two years of their time, since only then could it be ascertained whether or not they would make efficient journeymen and worthy T.A. members. But this retrograde step was retrieved in 1939, when it was decided to take in boys at the commencement of their apprenticeship and organize them into a 'Guild of Young Printers', so as to kindle the trade-union spirit in youth and secure youthful enthusiasm for the Association.

Female Labour

The T.A. Delegate Meeting of 1918 strongly reaffirmed the policy of opposition to the employment of women on craft work and this policy was maintained throughout this period. The Association took active steps not only to prevent their entry, but also to eliminate those already in the trade. Where employers refused to dismiss them, agreements were often secured that they should be replaced by men on leaving.

There were some differences at first with non-craft unions such as the N.S.O.P. & A. and N.U.P.B. & P.W., who wished to organize all women workers. The T.A. strongly opposed any such recognition of female labour on craft work and the other unions came to accept this viewpoint.

This exclusive policy was on the whole successful. There was no large-scale entry of women into the craft section of letterpress printing. Quite a number, however, were still employed. According to the 1931 census figures there were in the provinces 285 female hand compositors, 236 composing-machine operators, 1,559 machine minders (letterpress and litho.), and 4,804 described simply as 'printers' or 'other skilled workers'.

XX

RELATIONS WITH OTHER UNIONS
1918–39

Printing and Kindred Trades

INTER-UNION relations in the printing and kindred trades in these years present much the same features as in the earlier period: co-operation on many trade questions, reciprocity agreements, and proposals for amalgamation; but also friction over demarcation and other problems.

Relations were most strained with the London Society of Compositors. Strife was only temporarily allayed by the radius agreement of 1919. As soon as trade depression and unemployment came in the latter half of 1920, the L.S.C. returned to its old exclusive policy, refusing to recognize T.A. cards or let T.A. members start work in London. The T.A. Executive at once protested and threatened retaliation, but failed to move the L.S.C. Conferences in 1922 proved a failure and a T.A. member, J. W. Holland, therefore took legal proceedings against the L.S.C., on the ground that it 'did wrongfully and maliciously prevent the plaintiff from taking up and following his legitimate occupation'. The action failed, however, on legal technicalities.

Meanwhile, the L.S.C. had withdrawn from the radius agreement and the T.A. therefore re-established its London branch. A T.A. proposal for an amalgamation conference, as 'the most feasible solution of the difficulty', was rejected by the L.S.C. The latter made no attempt, however, to extend the 15-mile London radius. The dispute was solely on recognition of cards: the L.S.C. considered that migration of T.A. members to London should be prevented while so many of their own members were out of work; but the T.A. maintained that trade-union members should be recognized and allowed to seek work anywhere.

The T.A. now submitted the question to the T.U.C. again. The case was heard by the T.U.C.'s Disputes Committee in October 1924, but the decision went against the T.A., 'in view of the large amount of unemployment that now exists among members of the L.S.C.' An appeal having failed, the T.A. Executive instructed branches to exercise discrimination in acceptance of L.S.C. cards and to charge entrance fees.

Another conference with the L.S.C. in October 1930 also proved abortive and the L.S.C. rejected another T.A. proposal for amalgamation. The T.A. Executive therefore told branches not to admit any L.S.C. members while T.A. members were unemployed. A conference of letterpress societies convened by the P. & K.T.F. in January 1938, to deal with the general question of recognition and reciprocity, also failed to solve the problem, mainly on account of L.S.C. intransigence.

A similar example of L.S.C. exclusiveness was their refusal to handle type set in provincial offices and transferred to London, unless they were paid for it. They objected to such transfer as 'unfair competition' or 'undercutting', though the work was done in offices recognized as 'fair' by the T.A. They had no objection, of course, to exporting type and stereo blocks from London to the provinces. The T.A. might well denounce such an attitude.

The London Association of Correctors of the Press also adopted an exclusionist policy, despite the agreement of 1921, and the T.A. was forced to retaliate. Relations with the London Machine Managers, on the other hand, were very friendly, both sides adhering to the reciprocity agreement of 1919. The two societies frequently co-operated in trade affairs—on automatic feeders, for example, and photogravure machines —and an amalgamation conference was held in 1923, but nothing came of it.

T.A. differences with the Dublin Typographical Society in Ireland were similar to those with the L.S.C. in England, complicated by nationalist feeling. In 1920 the D.T.P.S. tried to establish an Irish Typographical Union, but failed. Dublin, like London, refused to admit T.A. members owing to unemployment in the city and the T.A. therefore retaliated. Meetings and correspondence failed to solve the dispute and so did reference to the Irish Labour Party and T.U.C. in 1927. In 1931 the T.A. suggested revival of the reciprocity scheme, but the D.T.P.S. refused. At a conference in September, however, a better understanding was reached and friction lessened thereafter.

Relations with the Scottish T.A. were very friendly, based on the reciprocity agreement of 1900. There was also good understanding and frequent co-operation with the National Society of Operative Printers and Assistants. Negotiations on amalgamation with the N.S.O.P. & A. were reopened in 1920, the T.A. again proposing division into two sections, craft and non-craft. Conferences were held in 1920–1 and a joint committee recommended amalgamation 'at the earliest possible moment' and drew up preliminary regulations. Negotiations then lapsed, however, until July 1924, when the N.S.O.P. & A. invited both T.A. and

S.T.A. representatives to an amalgamation conference. Several meetings were held in the next two years and an amalgamation scheme was formulated, but it eventually foundered on the question of S.T.A. recognition of female compositors.

The 1918 agreement with the N.S.O.P. & A. caused numerous difficulties, especially the 'equal rights' clause.[1] The T.A. Executive's interpretation was that, when no unemployed T.A. rotary machinemen were available, vacancies should be filled alternately by T.A. flat-bed minders and N.S.O.P. & A. members, i.e. on a fifty/fifty basis. The N.S.O.P. & A., however, considered that it meant equal opportunities and that it was for employers to determine the filling of vacancies: they objected to flat-bed minders being brought in. A conference in January 1924 failed to settle these differences and inquiries in 1933 showed that in practically all the large towns except Manchester the agreement was a dead letter: nearly all news rotary vacancies were filled by promotion of assistants, sometimes with only two or three years' experience. After further conferences it was agreed to instruct branches to establish local joint committees, in accordance with the agreement, to deal with rotary promotion. Thereafter, the T.A. Executive frequently insisted on observance of the fifty/fifty clause.

Similar differences occurred in news reading departments regarding the promotion and duties of N.S.O.P. & A. copyholders and revisers. A separate agreement was eventually reached in August 1936 along the same lines as that for the rotary department, and a demarcation line was drawn to prevent revisers doing readers' work.

Differences with the N.S.O.P. & A. in regard to the organization of females and Monotype caster attendants were easily settled. The N.S.O.P. & A. also agreed in 1930 that proof-pulling was T.A. work. Many N.S.O.P. & A. members, however, were employed as machine minders on platens, bag-making machines, aniline printing, &c. The greatest difficulties occurred at E. S. & A. Robinson's, of Bristol, and had to be referred to the P. & K.T.F. Arbitration Board in 1937, which decided that the bag-making department belonged to the N.S.O.P. & A.

The National Union of Printing, Bookbinding and Paper Workers, formed in 1921 by amalgamation of the Bookbinders and Machine Rulers with the Printing and Paper Workers, was now much the biggest union in the printing and kindred trades. An example of 'general' as opposed to 'craft' unionism, comprising paper-mill workers, printers' warehousemen and cutters, bookbinders, machine rulers, and, after

[1] See above, p. 245.

1924, platen minders,[1] it showed a strong tendency to encroach on the work of the craft unions. Its members were often found working platens in provincial offices, despite the agreement with the Platen Minders in 1921, on proof (especially galley) presses, and sorting and storing type matter, which employers regarded as unskilled work. There were also difficulties over process proving, which both unions claimed; the organization of females on T.A. work, which the T.A. strongly opposed; and Monotype casters.[2] The most serious differences, however, arose in regard to the new multiple-process machines, mass-producing paper bags, cardboard boxes, cartons, wrappers, and packets of all kinds.[3] Printing was merely one process on these machines, which also did cutting, scoring, creasing, punching, &c., hitherto performed by N.U.P.B. & P.W. members, who were consequently displaced. Moreover, the printing attachment was very simple, practically automatic, and not needing the attention of a skilled minder. Box- and bag-making was, in fact, covered by a Trade Boards Act, which recognized it as semi-skilled or unskilled work, with wage rates much lower than those of the T.A. The N.U.P.B. & P.W. therefore claimed these machines, but the T.A. maintained that any machines doing printing must be managed by its members.

Three conferences were held with the N.U.P.B. & P.W. in 1924, under P. & K.T.F. auspices, but no agreement was reached. The P. & K.T.F. Executive made another attempt at settlement in 1930–2, three more conferences being held, attended by representatives of the T.A., P.M.M.T.S., S.T.A., N.U.P.B. & P.W., and N.S.O.P. & A., but again without success. Eventually, however, in 1936, the T.A. reached agreement with the N.U.P.B. & P.W. regarding bag-making machines at the C.W.S. works in Warrington. A division of labour was agreed on: a T.A. member would look after the printing attachments on four of the simpler machines—less where there was two-colour printing—while Paper Workers would manage the bag-making. A similar arrangement was

---

[1] The London Platen Minders amalgamated with the N.U.P.B. & P.W. in 1924. They had previously approached the T.A. in regard to amalgamation, but the E.C. had raised difficulties about entrance fees and probation.

[2] See above, pp. 387 and 381, for female workers and Mono. casters. An agreement in regard to process provers was reached in 1927, whereby T.A. members on such work should become associate members of the N.U.P.B. & P.W., but it was virtually a dead letter, the T.A. continuing to claim process proving.

[3] Note that on many of these points of demarcation the T.A. also had differences with the N.S.O.P. & A. Both these non-craft unions, which overlap to some extent, have a tendency to encroach on the work of craft unions like the T.A.

made at Messrs. Gregory's, of Liverpool, in 1939: on each battery of six bag-making machines there were to be two T.A. members in charge and four Paper Workers, but without any demarcation between printing and bag-tackling.

There was a long-drawn-out dispute between the T.A. and the Type-founders' Society during this period, arising out of their rival claims to provincial Monotype casters.[1] Many conferences were held, the P. & K.T.F. trying repeatedly but unsuccessfully to arrange a settlement. By 1938-9, however, relations had taken a more favourable turn and suggestions of reciprocity or even amalgamation were in the air.

There was also a lengthy dispute with the Lithographic Printers, both unions claiming control of photogravure machines.[2] The T.A. eventually won the day and the Lithos. had reluctantly to recognize the fact. On other questions, however, the two societies co-operated: on rates for automatic feeders (1926) and anti-setoff devices (1938), and in trying to secure control of Rotaprint 'office machines'.

Differences arose between the T.A. and the Process Workers in regard to photogravure 'planning' or 'layout'. The T.A. considered this akin to letterpress imposition or layout, but eventually recognized it as belonging to the Process Workers.

Other new processes and machines also caused trouble with rival unions: photo-composition with the Litho. Artists and Process Workers, teletype-setting with the Press Telegraphists. If these developed they would almost certainly cause serious inter-union disputes.

Demarcation disputes also occurred with the Stereotypers, in regard to the imposing and mounting of stereo plates and T.A. members doing actual stereotyping. The P. & K.T.F. Executive arranged several conferences in 1923, but no agreement was reached until 1932, and even then the question of mounting plates remained unsettled. Moreover, the agreement had to be relaxed somewhat to allow of T.A. members doing stereotyping in small offices, where there was insufficient work for a stereotyper.

The P. & K.T.F. Executive, as we have seen, strove constantly in these years to settle demarcation disputes between the various unions. The T.A. and several other unions, however, liked to settle their own differences: they would accept the Federation's good offices, but strongly opposed anything in the nature of compulsory arbitration, particularly on what they regarded as fundamental matters. The P. & K.T.F. Administrative Council in May 1928, however, passed a new rule providing

[1] See above, pp. 381-2.   [2] See above, pp. 378-80.

for reference of inter-union disputes to an Arbitration Board, whose decisions should be binding, if the unions themselves could not reach agreement. This was accepted by a majority of the affiliated unions, but rejected by the T.A. The Association persisted for several years in refusing to accept it, but eventually acquiesced and allowed several disputes to be settled in this way, e.g. with the Typefounders over the super-caster machine (1931) and with the N.S.O.P. & A. over the Adrema machine (1934) and bag-making (1937). This procedure certainly lessened inter-union disputes, but was apt to create dissatisfaction. The more usual way of settling differences, therefore, was by getting the parties themselves to agree.

Despite innumerable differences between unions in the printing and kindred trades, there was a general feeling of solidarity and common interest, which brought them closer together. The idea of amalgamation remained alive throughout this period. It had fizzled out during the war, but was revived in 1919. At conferences arranged by the P. & K.T.F. in 1919–20, however, the old differences reappeared between advocates of sectional (craft) and general (industrial) amalgamation, while most unions were loath to sacrifice their autonomy. No progress, therefore, was made.

In 1923 the T.U.C., in accordance with its policy of 'organization by industry', arranged a conference on amalgamation in the printing and kindred trades, but failed to secure agreement. Another attempt in 1928 met with the same fate.

Lip service was often paid to the ideal of amalgamation in the following years, but nothing practical was done till 1938, when the P.M.M.T.S. invited the L.S.C., T.A., and N.S.O.P. & A. to an amalgamation conference. It was then agreed to ask the S.T.A., A.C.P., N.U.P.B. & P.W., and Typefounders to participate. These agreed and another conference was held, but the whole scheme foundered when the L.S.C. and S.T.A. withdrew.

Amalgamation, then, was no nearer in 1939 than in 1919. The P. & K.T.F., however, had considerably strengthened its organization and was playing a wider, more active role. More local federations and federated chapels had been established to secure unity in branch and workshop, while the Federation Executive tried to get national co-operation in the industry as a whole. The T.A., however, and most other unions clung jealously to their autonomy and continued to negotiate independently with the employers on wages and other matters. Nevertheless, the Federation gradually encroached on T.A. independence. It already dealt with hours and holidays,[1] and during this period we find the Association eventually surrendering to it the conduct of negotiations on regrading, the newsmen's 11-day fortnight, and apprentices' wages. The T.A. refused to hand over wages agreements, but the Federation, nevertheless, played an important part in the negotiations of 1919–23 and 1932–3. The Federation also exercised an important control over strike policy, though the T.A. sometimes acted independently. Action on general questions such as legislation for the printing industry, workmen's compensation, national health and unemployment insurance, &c., was usually through the Federation. The Federation, moreover, constituted the workers' side of the J.I.C., which dealt with such questions as settlement of disputes, apprentices' training, health, unemployment, betterment, and fair prices.

Obviously, the Federation was playing an increasingly bigger part in the regulation of working conditions in the industry. At times, however, T.A. relations with the Federation were rather strained. During the wages movements of 1919–23, for example, the T.A. found Federation restraints very irksome and disliked its levelling tendencies. And when the Federation refused strike benefit for the T.A. national strike in 1922, there was a strong movement for secession. This 'betrayal' rankled in T.A. minds for many years. There was a widespread feeling that the T.A.'s craft interests suffered in an organization controlled by the larger numbers of unskilled and semi-skilled workers. The Federation's unwieldiness, jealousies, and delays were also criticized.

The T.A. did not, however, secede: 'unity' and 'brotherhood' carried the day and relations gradually improved. More and more the T.A. came to realize the necessity of federated action. 'Methods are changing in matters of industrial policy', the General President stated at the 1939 Delegate Meeting, 'and unity of action is required on our side to meet the difficulties confronting us in our relations and negotiations with the employers. Is it not wise and timely to consider the simultaneous presentation to the employers of a carefully planned programme of wage increases and a standard of working hours, backed by the united determination of the whole industry, rather than the sporadic negotiations by individual unions?'

General Trade Unionism

This period was also marked by increased solidarity in the sphere of general trade unionism. Though the T.A. refused to affiliate to the

[1] Its most important achievement in this period was the 1937 Hours and Holidays Agreement. See above, p. 373.

General Federation of Trade Unions, it supported the principle of mutual aid in industrial disputes. In May 1922, for example, the Executive approved the T.U.C. scheme of 'joint defence for the preservation of trade-union standards', and in May 1926, acting on the instructions of the T.U.C. General Council, the T.A. joined in the General Strike to support the miners in their fight against wage reductions: 'a wonderful manifestation of loyalty to the organised Labour movement',[1] costing the T.A. over £50,000. At the Trades Union Congress in 1934, moreover, we find the T.A. delegates urging the raising of funds for national disputes.

The T.A. Executive continued throughout these years to assist other unions on strike with monetary grants, totalling about £1,700, and in 1921 loans of £5,000 and £1,000 respectively were made to the Yorkshire Miners and the Furnishing Trades.

The Association regularly paid its affiliation fees and sent delegates and resolutions to the T.U.C., while its General Secretary, H. Skinner, was for many years a member of the General Council, but the Association did not play a very important part in general trade-union affairs.

International Trade Unionism

The T.A. had been considering affiliation to the International Typographical Secretariat when war broke out in 1914. The question came up again after the war. The Secretariat was revived at a conference in Lucerne in 1919, but no British representatives were present. The British P. & K.T.F. was therefore asked to affiliate and a representative of the Secretariat attended the annual conference in May 1921, which decided to send a 'fraternal delegation' to the next international congress in Vienna in September 1921. The T.A. President, J. D. French, was sent and reported on his return that he had 'become an Internationalist'. The 1922 P. & K.T.F. annual conference therefore recommended typographical unions to affiliate to the Secretariat.

The P. & K.T.F. itself could not affiliate, since it was composed of all unions in the printing and kindred trades, whereas there were separate international secretariats for typographers, lithographers, bookbinders, and journalists. The British urged an amalgamation of all these into one international organization for the whole industry, but without success. It was therefore left to the individual unions to decide whether or not they would affiliate to the respective Secretariats.

In the following years the T.A. Executive repeatedly turned down

[1] H. Y. Report, June 1926.

invitations either to become affiliated with or to attend conferences of the International Typographical Secretariat. Insularity was still very strong. The P. & K.T.F. made another attempt in 1930 to form the separate Secretariats into 'an International Industrial Federation for the printing industry', and international conferences were held in London (December 1930) and Berlin (August 1931), but nothing came of them. The continental Secretariats were mainly interested in getting the individual British unions to affiliate, but very few of them would do so.

In the later thirties, however, greater interest began to be taken in international typographical affairs and the T.A. sent its President to attend the Secretariat's congress in Copenhagen in August 1939. On his return he strongly recommended the Executive to consider affiliation, but war once again intervened.

There is only one instance in this period of a T.A. grant to foreign printers: £200 to the Belgians in 1925, to assist them in a strike against reduced wages and increased hours. The Association had very little contact with printers outside Europe.

Since such little interest was taken in international organization in the printing industry, it is only to be expected that even less was shown in general international trade unionism. The T.A. was indirectly connected with the International Federation of Trade Unions through T.U.C. affiliation, but would have no truck with the Communist International. Occasional grants, totalling over £1,300, were made to assist foreign workers on strike or in distress, or suffering under totalitarian rule.

XXI

FRIENDLY BENEFITS
1918-39

Out-of-work Benefits

THE T.A. continued throughout this period to relieve its unemployed members and also to administer the various State Unemployment Insurance Acts. Unemployment was still, in fact, the Association's biggest problem, bringing it more than once to the verge of bankruptcy.[1]

Under Part II, Section 106, of the 1911 National Insurance Act, the Association only received a Government subsidy of one-sixth of its out-of-work payments, State unemployment insurance being limited as yet to a few selected trades. In 1920, however, it was extended to include nearly all wage-earners, and trade unions were empowered to administer the new Act, along with friendly societies and insurance companies. The T.A. decided to do so, but still continued its own out-of-work benefits: in future, unemployed members would receive both Association and State benefits.

We obviously cannot discuss here details of the 1920 and later Unemployment Insurance Acts. Later on we shall examine certain problems and grievances which they created, but first we will trace the history of the T.A.'s own out-of-work benefits.

In 1914 Association out-of-work payments were as follows: those with less than ten years' membership, 10s. per week for six weeks in each quarter; ten to fifteen years', seven weeks; over fifteen years', eight weeks. If, at the end of a year, they had not worked for a requisite number of weeks (sixteen weeks for those with less than ten years' membership, twelve for ten to twenty years' members), they would be reduced to half benefit; and if, after another year, they had still not done enough work, they would be suspended for a year, after which they would again be dealt with as at the end of the first year. Those with twenty years' membership, however, or over sixty-five years of age and ineligible for superannuation, were exempt from this clause.

Unemployment increased somewhat when the war ended: the number of T.A. casually employed rose from about 700 in 1918 to 1,500 in 1919, and out-of-work payments from £2,000 to over £9,000. But

---

[1] See above, pp. 352-4.

this was less than before the war. There was, in fact, a post-war trading boom. In 1920, therefore, the unemployment benefit, which had been raised to 13s. during the war, was raised again, first to 18s. and then to 20s. per week, and extended by one week per quarter, while members who had completed six months' probation were granted 5s. per week for four weeks in each quarter.

In 1921, however, there was a severe slump. The number of casuals, many of whom were totally unemployed, rose to over 3,200, about 10 per cent. of the whole membership, and out-of-work expenditure soared to more than £59,000. There was little improvement in 1922 and subscriptions had to be increased by 2d. at the beginning of 1923 to maintain the existing benefits.

The situation improved as trade revived in 1923, but out-of-work payments continued to be heavy. In 1925 over £31,000 was expended and there were still about 2,000 casually employed. Things got worse again in the years 1926-8, payments averaging about £44,000 annually and casuals about 2,500.

In 1929, therefore, and also as a result of the 1927 Unemployment Insurance Act, the E.C. carried through an alteration of the out-of-work rules. Hitherto, T.A. benefit had been paid for only a limited number of weeks, varying according to length of membership, in each quarter. Now it had to be paid for each day of unemployment, as in the case of State benefit. Daily rates were fixed as follows: less than ten years' membership, 1s. 10d.; ten to fifteen, 2s.; over fifteen, 2s. 2d.; while probationary members and those not otherwise entitled to benefit would get 6d. per day. The amount of benefit per week was thus reduced, but the sum total per quarter was about the same.

These changes hit those who were unemployed for only a few weeks per quarter. The 1930 Delegate Meeting therefore revised the rates again: they now fell gradually from 3s. to 1s. per day the longer a man was unemployed in each quarter. The increased benefits, however, combined with trade depression to swell out-of-work payments, below £26,000 in 1929, to nearly £65,000 in 1931. The E.C., consequently, had to get them reduced again: five years' membership, 8s. per week; five to ten, 10s.; ten to fifteen, 12s.; over fifteen, 13s.[1] Conditions were also made more stringent: no relief for less than four days' unemployment in one week, longer qualifying periods of work, &c. Even so, expenditure was only slightly reduced in 1932, when there were over 4,000 casuals, most of them totally unemployed.

[1] Weekly benefits were restored as a result of legislative change.

Matters were little better in 1933, but improved slowly in the following years as trade revived. Even in 1938, however, the Association spent nearly £35,000 in out-of-work payments. Benefits had been increased by a shilling in 1937.

The amounts paid out by the T.A. in State Unemployment Benefits varied, like Association expenditure, with the state of trade.[1]

	£			£
1921	. . 45,671	1930	. . 48,800
1922	. . 39,228	1931	. . 89,379
1923	. . 33,705	1932	. . 90,401
1924	. . 27,313	1933	. . 81,867
1925	. . 27,003	1934	. . 76,024
1926	. . 39,466	1935	. . 59,227
1927	. . 39,176	1936	. . 50,886
1928	. . 34,186	1937	. . 41,596
1929	. . 28,027	1938	. . 45,167

The T.A., in administering the Unemployment Insurance Acts, provided valuable protection for its members. Insurance officers frequently refused claims on the grounds that men had left their employment 'without just cause', or had been dismissed for 'misconduct', or were 'not genuinely seeking work'. The T.A. held no brief for genuine malingering or misconduct: it had, as we have seen, its own regulations against such abuses, while branches and groups were active in trying to find situations for out-of-work members. But claims were often rejected where men had refused to work in 'unrecognized' offices, with non-members or females, or at less than the T.A. minimum wage rate, or where they had been thrown out of work by a trade dispute. Many appeals, both written and oral, were made to the Court of Referees and to the Umpire by the T.A. Insurance Manager, J. W. Lowe, J.P., who frequently secured favourable decisions.

Lowe was first Vice-President and then President of the Trades Union Unemployment Insurance Association and was very active, with E.C. support, in agitating for legislative reforms. Feeling was particularly strong against the 'Means Test', especially as trade-union benefits were taken into account by Public Assistance Committees in assessing members' needs for 'transitional benefit' or 'unemployment assistance', after they had 'run out' of insurance benefit. In 1934, moreover, payment of unemployment assistance was taken out of the hands of trade unions. The T.A. therefore got protest resolutions passed by the T.U.C. in 1937

[1] The rates and periods of benefit similarly varied.

and the General Secretary and Insurance Manager formed part of the deputation which presented them to the Unemployment Assistance Board and Ministry of Labour. The outcome was successful: the first 5s. of trade-union benefits would in future be disregarded in assessing means, and trade unions got back the right to administer unemployment assistance.

Superannuation Fund

This Fund was in parlous condition by the end of the First World War. Since it had been established on such an unsound basis, with hopelessly inadequate subscriptions and reserve fund, its condition got progressively worse as more and more older members came upon it.

By the time of the 1918 Delegate Meeting the number of superannuitants (now nearly 800) and the annual expenditure (over £16,000) were increasing rapidly, income was insufficient, and deficits were piling up. This meeting therefore decided to increase subscriptions to the Fund from 3¼d. to 6d. per week and to continue the levy of 6d. per half year until the reserve fund contained £75 per superannuitant; but, at the same time, it increased benefits by 25 per cent., in view of the rising cost of living. Two years later, moreover, the E.C. had them raised again, by 2s. 6d., while in 1923 it was decided to transfer payment of incapacity benefits back to the Superannuation Fund, in order to relieve the General Fund.

Nevertheless, with the increased subscriptions, all seemed to be going well in the next few years. The Fund increased from about £28,000 at the end of 1918 to nearly £85,000 by the end of 1925. But the annual gains, at first very large, gradually dwindled and finally disappeared. By 1925 annual expenditure had grown to nearly £40,000 and there were over 1,100 on the Fund. The Delegate Meeting that year therefore increased contributions by 2d., but only raised Association subscriptions by a penny, so that the General Fund suffered. It was the old expedient of robbing Peter to pay Paul.

By the end of 1928, however, there were nearly 1,500 superannuitants, annual expenditure had risen to over £51,000, and there was again a deficit. The E.C. therefore appointed a special committee, which, after exhaustive investigation, produced several alternative schemes, involving either considerably increased subscriptions (the Superannuation Fund allocation would ultimately, it was calculated, have to be raised from 8d. to 1s. 6d. per week to maintain present benefits) or reduced benefits or both. These they decided to put to ballot vote, together with a proposed new grade providing 5s. per week for twenty years' members not less than sixty years of age. But there was such a loud outcry that they had to drop the idea. The Delegate Meeting in 1930 rejected all their proposed schemes, except the new grade. Instead, contributions were increased by 3½d., of which 1½d. was to meet immediate demands and 2d. to build up a sinking fund of £100,000.

Alas! for such hopes. Deficits continued and in 1931 the E.C. had to use the 2d. allocated to the sinking fund for payment of present benefits. At the same time, the General Fund being practically bankrupt, they transferred payment of funeral benefits to the Superannuation Fund. By June 1933 there was again a deficit and the Delegate Meeting therefore increased contributions by 3d., discontinuing the half-yearly levy, and put funeral payments back on the General Fund. The 1936 Delegate Meeting, however, was confronted by the usual deficit. There were now nearly 3,000 superannuitants and annual expenditure had reached £100,000, more than the whole Fund. The latter was therefore given another 4d. from subscriptions, which, however, were only increased by 2d., the General Fund being raided again for the other 2d.

Things now went well for a few years, but became critical again during the war, when levies and transfers from the General Fund were needed to save the situation. Members might well begin to ask if the Superannuation Fund was worth it.

Incapacity Benefit

Incapacity benefit was increased from 8s. to 10s. per week in 1918, and then to 12s. 6d. in 1920, to meet the increased cost of living. It remained at this figure until 1936, when it was reduced and graded according to length of membership: thirty years or over, 10s.; twenty-five to thirty, 7s. 6d.; twenty to twenty-five, 5s. In 1939, however, the first grade was restored to 12s. 6d. By that date there were 115 incapacitated members on the Fund and payments totalled over £2,300 annually.

Funeral Benefit

Funeral benefits were increased by 50 per cent. in 1921, owing to the rising costs of interment, and were now as follows: one year's membership, £6; two, £9; three, £12; and ten, £15. In 1931, however, during the financial crisis, they were reduced and the qualifying periods of membership lengthened, in order to cut expenditure. Payments were now on the following scale: one to five years' membership, £3; five to ten, £5; ten to fifteen, £7. 10s.; fifteen to twenty, £10; twenty and upwards, £15.

Expenditure on funeral benefits gradually increased from £3,432 in 1919 to £6,958 in 1939. Average age at death, which had risen to 51·2 in the years 1904–14, rose still farther to 63·5 in 1937–9, which is evidence of improvement not only in medical science, but also in living standards and working conditions. T.A. members were now living, on average, over 21 years longer than in the 1870's.

Legal Aid

The Association was called on to provide legal aid during this period in an enormous number of compensation cases. Accidents grew alarmingly with the increasing mechanization of the industry, and without union backing individual members would frequently have failed to get any or adequate compensation from insurance companies.

A comprehensive scheme was formulated in 1938 for the provision of legal aid in cases not only of accident at work and industrial illness, but also of road accidents involving members or their families. Moreover, free legal advice would be provided on *any* matter, a facility which members found extremely helpful in innumerable problems. In the twelve months following establishment of this scheme, the Association's legal department dealt with nearly 400 cases.

T.A. Approved Society No. 301

The T.A. Approved Society No. 301 continued to administer benefits payable to members under the National Health Insurance scheme with laudable efficiency. By the end of 1938 it had expended altogether over £360,000 in sickness, disablement, maternity, dental, optical, and other benefits. Quinquennial Government valuations showed its financial position to be extremely sound and it was able to pay considerably above average benefits. The Society's aim was to secure 100 per cent. membership, but only 15,000 members, less than 50 per cent., had joined by 1939.

Its work was not confined to payment of cash benefits. Its manager, J. W. Lowe, who was a member of the National Association of T.U. Approved Societies' Executive, the T.U.C. Social Insurance Committee, and the N.H.I. Advisory Council, strove constantly to secure legislative reforms, such as increased old-age pensions and a more comprehensive national health service, and to better working conditions, prevent industrial diseases, and improve workmen's compensation.

Several proposals were made for a T.A. sick society, but not adopted. Many branches, however, still had their own sick or benevolent funds.

XXII

POLITICS AND CO-OPERATION
1918–39

BY 1914 the T.A. had its own Labour Representation Fund and Parliamentary Representative, was affiliated to the Labour Party, and taking an active interest in general political affairs.

The Association strongly supported the Coalition Government during the 1914–18 War and its Parliamentary Representative, G. H. Roberts, M.P. for Norwich, rose to become Minister of Labour in Lloyd George's Government in August 1917. His relations with the local party, however, were very strained. He had broken with the I.L.P. at the outbreak of war and was labelled a renegade by his old associates for supporting the recruiting campaign, entering the Coalition Government, changing his mind on conscription, and supporting various 'reactionary' measures. Open rupture came in 1917, when he was opposed by the Norwich Labour Party in the by-election following his appointment as Minister of Labour, but managed to keep his seat.

Roberts could justly claim that he was merely following the national Labour Party policy and he was staunchly supported by the T.A. There is no doubt, however, that he was drifting to the Right and that antagonism was developing between him and the Labour Party. He resigned from the Executive at the beginning of 1918, 'on account of the work entailed in his Ministerial office', and was again repudiated by the local party in June, but the T.A. continued to support him. The final break, however, was soon to come.

Immediately after the Armistice a special conference was held in London to consider Labour policy. T.A. delegates were instructed to vote against withdrawal of Labour Members from the Coalition Government, but the conference decided that the Party should resume its pre-war independence. Roberts, however, together with several other Labour ministers, refused to resign; yet he determined to stand again for election at Norwich.

What policy should the T.A. now adopt? An inquiry was sent to Labour Party headquarters, as to 'what would be the position of the T.A. with the Labour Party if they supported the candidature of Mr. Roberts', to which an answer came warning them against 'acting in contravention of the London decision'. The E.C. decided to explain the position to the members and take a vote on whether or not Roberts should be given financial support in the election; but then, despite a small majority in his favour, decided to toe the Party line. Even so, and despite the running of an opposing candidate by the local Labour Party, Roberts topped the poll at Norwich in December 1918. The E.C. informed him, however, that he had broken the rules by not standing as an independent Labour candidate and had therefore ceased to be the Association Parliamentary Representative. He was also forced to resign his position as T.A. Organizer.

Meanwhile, the T.A. had secured another Parliamentary Representative. The 1913 Delegate Meeting had decided that the Association should run 'one or more additional Labour Parliamentary Candidates' as soon as the funds were sufficient. In July 1917, therefore, the E.C. decided on the election of a second candidate. Another Roberts, F. O. Roberts, J.P., Secretary of the Northampton branch, member of the E.C., and prominent in local politics, was chosen and eventually elected for West Bromwich in December 1918.

After G. H. Roberts' demise another candidate was elected, O. Connellan, J.P., President of the Leeds branch, T.A. Vice-President, and member of the Leeds City Council; but he was unsuccessful in the North Bucks. Division in the General Election of 1922.[1] The T.A. therefore continued to have only one Parliamentary Representative, F. O. Roberts being re-elected for West Bromwich.

In view of its increased political commitments, the Association had, in 1920, raised the contribution to the Labour Representation Fund from $\frac{1}{4}d.$ to $\frac{1}{2}d.$ per member per week. Out of this it was decided to pay Roberts a maintenance allowance of £150 per annum and £50 for a railway contract.

Roberts was re-elected for West Bromwich in the General Election of December 1923 and became Minister of Pensions in the first Labour Government. Though this Government fell in October 1924, he still retained his seat. He was again re-elected in 1929 and reappointed Minister of Pensions in the second Labour Government from 1929 to 1931. When Ramsay MacDonald betrayed the Labour Party in the crisis of 1931, by going over to the Conservatives and forming a 'National Government', Roberts resigned office, 'standing with the Labour Party against the new Government and in opposition to the proposed reduction of unemployment benefit'. In the subsequent 'landslide' he was narrowly defeated at West Bromwich.

[1] Connellan resigned in 1923, owing to ill health, and died soon afterwards.

The procedure for election of a Parliamentary Representative remained the same as in 1906: election of a T.A. candidate by ballot vote of the members; choice of a suitable constituency, with the assistance of the Labour Party national agent; adoption as prospective candidate by the local Labour Party Executive; election as M.P. by a majority of the constituency in the Parliamentary Election. A great deal, of course, depended on the local Labour Party organization and support of the National Executive, but the T.A. footed most of the bill: renting an office, paying an election agent, and meeting most of the campaign expenses. The elected member, moreover, was not merely a Labour Party member and M.P. for West Bromwich; he was in a real sense the T.A. Parliamentary Representative and was expected to support its special interests in the House of Commons; he had to keep in touch with his constituents in the T.A. as well as in West Bromwich. Generally speaking, however, the T.A. followed the Party line and its Parliamentary Representative acted under the directions of the National Executive. The Association was pledged to Labour political action and loyal to the idea of a united and independent Labour Party: it merely, for the most part, helped to provide funds and organization for the election and maintenance of one or two Labour M.P.s, whose duty it was to forward the general interests of Labour and not merely the particular interests of the T.A. The Labour Party is largely, of course, the embodiment of trade-union solidarity in the political sphere.

The Trade Disputes and Trade Unions Act passed by the Conservatives in 1927 sought not only to prevent general and sympathetic strikes, but also to drive a wedge between the trade unions and the Labour Party and weaken the latter's finances: whereas previously, under the 1913 Act, political contributions had been levied on all members unless they 'contracted out', now they could only be collected from those who 'contracted in'. The T.A. participated in the campaign against the Bill, and after it was passed members were exhorted to 'contract in' so as to maintain the Association's Political Fund. The majority did so: annual contributions, which had averaged £1,680 in the years 1921–7, only fell to £1,420 in 1928–34: about 65 per cent. of journeymen members 'contracted in'.

Expenditure from the Political Fund was mainly on four items: Labour Party affiliation fees, maintenance of the Parliamentary Representative, agent's salary, and election expenses. Labour Party affiliation fees rose with increasing membership from £274 in 1920 to £377 in 1938, and, in addition, the T.A. made several grants, varying from £50 to

£250, in response to special Labour Party electioneering or campaign appeals. The Parliamentary Representative was paid £200 annually for maintenance and travelling expenses. The election agent's salary from 1922 onwards was £337. 10s. per annum, while there were many miscellaneous expense items. An election cost from £500 to £700. To run a second candidate, of course, meant doubling these expenses, which proved impossible after 1923.

In 1932, however, the E.C. decided to make new financial arrangements with the West Bromwich Trades and Labour Council. An interview with the National Agent of the Labour Party revealed that the T.A. had been doing far too much in financing the local division: the local party should be responsible for the candidate, appoint and pay the agent, &c., not the T.A. New arrangements were accordingly made: T.A. payments to the local party were gradually reduced to £100 per annum (later raised to £150) and an election grant of £400.

A second candidate could now be run. F. O. Roberts was again elected prospective Labour candidate for West Bromwich and H. Inglis, president of the Liverpool branch and E.C. member, was chosen for Blackburn, where a similar arrangement was made with the local party.

F. O. Roberts, meanwhile, was in financial straits. Having resigned from the Government and lost his seat in Parliament, like many other deposed Labour M.P.s 'he did not know what he was going to do for a job', but was hoping that the T.A. would retain his services. For four months he was out of work, with no income whatsoever. The E.C. eventually granted him £150 per annum as prospective Parliamentary candidate, but he still had a struggle to make ends meet on account of his expenses.

The whole position was considered by the 1933 Delegate Meeting, which decided that election grants were not to exceed £300 and that a maintenance allowance of £150 should be paid to Association M.P.s, who, in the event of losing their seats and failing to secure full-time employment, should receive a grant of £200 per year for two years. The E.C. decided that the latter rule should be applied prospectively to F. O. Roberts, whose allowance would otherwise have ceased. Even £200 proved insufficient, however, and in response to an appeal the E.C. made him a grant of £50 and a loan of £200 in 1935.

H. Inglis resigned his position as Parliamentary candidate in 1934, having been elected T.A. President. His successor was G. H. Walker, Kendal branch secretary, E.C. member, and president of the Westmorland Divisional and Kendal Labour Parties. In the General Election of

1935 Roberts regained his seat at West Bromwich, but Walker was unsuccessful at Blackburn. He was re-elected second Parliamentary candidate in 1936, however, and became prospective Labour candidate for Rossendale the following year.

The new financial arrangements made with the West Bromwich Labour Party meant that the latter, no longer spoon-fed by the T.A., had to raise money to pay the election agent and general expenses. This it proved incapable of doing: although the agent's salary was reduced, he was owed over £300 arrears by 1938, when he resigned. In 1941, however, T.A. political relations with West Bromwich ceased, when F. O. Roberts was forced to resign owing to ill health, after being T.A. Parliamentary Representative for 23 years.

Other T.A. members, apart from the official Association candidates, fought Parliamentary elections in the inter-war years. In the 1918 election four T.A. members were put up by local Labour parties, but failed at the polls. Two of these, A. E. Stubbs and W. F. Toynbee, tried repeatedly but in vain in various constituencies at every succeeding General Election. The E.C. usually helped them with grants of at first £50 and then £100.

T.A. members in Ireland were also active politically. R. S. Anthony, of Cork, secured election to the Dail Eireann in 1927 and held that seat until 1938. The E.C. made him a grant of £50 in the 1927 election, but turned down later appeals since the rules of the Political Fund only provided for election of representatives to the House of Commons. The T.A. All-Ireland Conference in 1932 therefore requested that they be amended to include candidates for the Dail Eireann and Northern Ireland Parliament and that the T.A. should become affiliated to the Irish Labour Party. This request, however, was rejected by the 1933 Delegate Meeting, which considered 'it would be far better for us in England not to interfere in Irish politics'. Nevertheless, the E.C. made a grant of £25 to the Irish Labour Party in 1937 and another to the Northern Ireland Labour Party in 1938.

Many T.A. members actively participated in local politics, several securing seats on local councils and a few even becoming mayors. A quarter (after 1939 a half) of the political contributions was retained for local purposes by the branches, which were generally affiliated to the local Trades Council and Labour Party.

Numerous articles appeared in the *Circular* on current political events and members were constantly urged to support the Labour Party and buy the *Daily Herald*. The Association also became affiliated to the Workers'

Educational Association and the National Council of Labour Colleges, and a number of members attended their classes or took their correspondence courses.

T.A. political interest extended to foreign as well as domestic affairs and the growth of Fascism and Nazism in the thirties was viewed with alarm. Grants totalling over £600 were made, mostly to the National Council of Labour's International Solidarity Fund, to assist Austrian refugees, Spanish workers, wounded and dependants of the International Brigade, Czechoslovakian relief work, and aid to China.

The only example of threatened industrial action by the T.A. on a political question during this period was in the field of foreign affairs, in 1920, when the British Government looked like intervening in the Russo-Polish War. The T.A. Executive sent representatives to attend the conference convened in August by the 'Council of Action' of the Labour Party and T.U.C., to consider the question of a general strike to prevent war. They strongly supported this 'calling together of the National Political and Industrial Forces of the Country' and would support 'any action ... to prevent the country going to war'—a resolution to this effect being forwarded to the Prime Minister and Secretary of State for War.

The danger passed, however, and there is no further instance of threatened strike action on any political question. Generally speaking it was disapproved of, reliance being placed on constitutional action by Labour Party representatives in the House of Commons.

Co-operative Printing

There is little to add for this period to the earlier account of co-operation in the printing industry. Several new co-operative concerns were established, which the T.A. Executive assisted with share or loan capital, so that by 1939 there were societies of 'co-operative printers' at Birmingham, Bristol, Cardiff, Derby, Gloucester, Guildford, Hull, Leicester, Nottingham, Plymouth, Portsmouth, Swansea, and Watford, while the C.P.S. had offices in Manchester, London, and Newcastle, and the C.W.S. also had several printing establishments. The Association had invested over £5,000 in them, but the majority of shares belonged to individual members, branches, other unions, and co-operative societies.

The C.P.S. and C.W.S. did a large amount of printing, the former's annual turnover being £355,000 in 1938. The other more purely T.A. societies were much smaller concerns, although the Leicester and Birmingham societies had turnovers of £87,000 and £38,000 respectively in 1938.

XXIII

THE SECOND WORLD WAR
1939-45

T.A. HISTORY in the Second World War was remarkably similar to that
in the First. The printing trade was faced with much the same problems:
dislocation and heavy unemployment at first, followed by gradual adjustment to war conditions, with shortages, Government rationing and control of raw materials and printing; conscription into the Armed Forces
and transfer, even compulsory 'direction', of labour from printing, a
'less essential' trade in war-time, into munitions and Civil Defence, resulting in a growing labour shortage and the necessity for relaxation of
trade-union rules and 'dilution' of labour; rising costs of production;
rising cost of living and incessant union demands for wage increases;
problems of replacing apprentices and post-war reinstatement.

The printing industry was more seriously affected, however, by the
Second than the First World War. Shortages of materials were more
acute, Government control and rationing more stringent, and labour
shortage greater, while air raids destroyed or damaged a great number
of printing offices and killed or injured many civilians: 1939-45 was, in
fact, much more a 'total' war than 1914-18. On the other hand, people
were better prepared in 1939 than in 1914: with the experience of World
War I, the printing industry, like the nation as a whole, got down to
war-time conditions more quickly and efficiently.

We cannot, in this short space, give anything like a full picture of the
T.A.'s multifarious war-time activities, in regard to labour-supply,
wages, hours, overtime, and working conditions, with the problems of
conscription, reservations, deferments, apprentice replacements, relaxation of rules, transfers, dilution, &c.; air raids, black-out, fire-watching,
and civil defence; disablement, rehabilitation, compensation, insurance,
and income-tax; paper supply and salvage; innumerable Government
controls, interviews with Government departments, boards, panels, and
committees; incessant travelling, conferences, inquiries, and circulars;
and then, towards the end of the war, the problems of post-war reinstatement and reconstruction.

Much of this work was done through the P. & K.T.F. or J.I.C.
War brought the unions much closer together and the Federation came
to represent and negotiate for the whole industry as never before, while

the J.I.C., in consequence, became increasingly important, its War Emergency Standing Committee dealing with innumerable problems. This was largely due to the requirements of the Government: it was necessary, on the grounds of time and expediency, that the various Ministries should be able to deal with one organization representing the whole industry, instead of seventeen different unions. Moreover, the unions themselves realized that 'complete unity of purpose and action . . . was vital to their welfare'.[1]

T.A. history, therefore, during these war years merges to a great extent into the history of the Federation. The Association still remained, of course, a separate entity with its own peculiar interests and often acted independently, but most of the industry's major war problems affected all unions alike and were dealt with by the Federation: witness the series of War Agreements dealing with short time, air raids, relaxation of rules and labour dilution, transfer of workers, apprentice replacements, wage increases, and working hours. The increased importance of the Federation is shown by the fact that John Fletcher, the T.A. General Secretary, resigned that post in 1941 to become P. & K.T.F. Secretary, the key post on the trade-union side of the industry.[2]

Despite this war-time unity, however, the underlying sectional interests remained. When a proposal was made at the P. & K.T.F. Annual Conference in 1943, for 'the complete amalgamation of the whole of the separate Unions now operating in the industry', it was defeated, mainly through the opposition of the L.S.C., S.T.A., and the smaller specialized unions.[3]

As in 1914, the T.A. was staunchly patriotic, strongly supporting the T.U.C. and Labour Party in their policy of co-operation with the Government in waging the war. The great majority of T.A. members felt that this was a fight against tyranny and oppression, to preserve our freedom and way of life: the fate of trade unionism, co-operation, and socialism under Nazi and Fascist rule was well known. A few Communists inveighed against capitalist imperialism, till Hitler attacked Russia in 1941, and there was also a number of conscientious objectors, whose rights the T.A. protected; but the great mass of T.A. members devoted themselves to the war effort. Large numbers volunteered or were

[1] G. A. Isaacs, M.P., P. & K.T.F. President, in the foreword to *Team Work* (1944) by J. Fletcher, the Federation Secretary. This booklet gives an excellent account of the Federation's war-time activities.

[2] Another T.A. member, G. G. Eastwood, NW. Group Secretary and T.A. Vice-President, was elected P. & K.T.F. Assistant Secretary in 1943.

[3] The T.A. supported the proposal.

conscripted into the Forces, while many went into Civil Defence or munitions and armament factories, leaving a gravely depleted labour force, mostly of older men, to produce the essential war-time printing, under difficulties of air raids, black-out, and fire-watching. By 1944 there were nearly 13,000 members in the Forces and about 4,000 on full-time Civil Defence (A.R.P., N.F.S., &c.) and munitions, out of a total membership of 40,000. Over 600 T.A. members died on active service during the war, while many were killed in air raids at home.

The Government again discovered, in war-time, that the co-operation of the trade unions was essential to solve man-power problems, prevent disputes, and boost production. Again we find trade unions represented in practically every branch of public administration, from local committees up to the Cabinet itself, and consulted on all questions of labour and production. The Federation, as we have seen, represented all unions in the printing and kindred trades in relations with the Government. Its activities are illustrated by the Secretary's summary for 1943: 'Nineteen meetings, conferences, or interviews took place covering eight Ministries, and twenty-two meetings of Appeal Boards and Industrial Transfer Panels were held', not to mention the mass of official correspondence. The T.A. Executive and officials were also constantly having to deal with different Government departments, while branch secretaries had to cope with innumerable Government orders and forms. Not only did the Association continue to protect the rights of its members with an eye to 'after the war', but, like other unions, greatly assisted the Government in marshalling, directing, and controlling labour in war-time.

The immediate effect of war on the printing industry in 1939, as in 1914, was a terrific slump: cancelled orders in the general printing and book trade, publications suspended, advertisements curtailed, newspapers reduced in size, firms going on short time, dismissing men, or closing down, and a growing shortage of paper, printing metal, and other materials. Thousands of T.A. members were thrown into unemployment or on short time, and the out-of-work rules had to be relaxed so that assistance might be given. Pre-war programmes and proposals regarding grading, overtime, machine rules, readers, jobbing wages, &c., resolutions of the 1939 Delegate Meeting—all these, of course, had to be shelved, most of them 'for the duration'. Inter-union squabbles had also to be laid aside and war-time reciprocity agreements, permitting free transference of members, were made with the L.S.C. and A.C.P. and later with other unions.

Despite the initial chaos, the industry was better prepared for the emergency than in 1914. Both sides, employers and employed, were now more strongly organized and accustomed to co-operation through the J.I.C. At the request of the employers' organizations (the B.F.M.P. and Newspaper Society), the P. & K.T.F. Executive agreed to a joint meeting on 30 August, four days before war broke out, when an Emergency Agreement was drawn up, which, though strongly criticized, did act as 'the vehicle of transition from conditions of peace to conditions of war'.[1] Provision was made for transference of work and workers to other districts; rearrangement of hours so as to permit of work being done during daylight; payment of wages for time lost in air-raid alerts; short time by mutual agreement in each establishment; and the setting up of a joint War Emergency Committee. These conditions would, of course, apply only in war-time, assurances on this point being secured from the employers.

The T.A. Executive endorsed this agreement, but warned members that 'whilst adjustments are made it is our duty to preserve generally the working conditions and standards of our industry intact during this difficult period'. There was to be no relaxation of Association rules other than provided for in the Emergency Agreement and mutually agreed on in each office. The agreement did not, for example, abrogate all overtime rules or permit dismissals without proper notice. Moreover, 'all attempts to introduce dilution of labour—women, labourers, &c.—must be resisted'.

There was not much likelihood of the latter during the short time and unemployment of 1939-40. The chief merit of the Emergency Agreement in the eyes of the T.A. Executive was that it helped to prevent wholesale dismissals and unemployment by permitting short time and thus 'spreading out' available work. But, though most employers interpreted it fairly, a good many sought to exploit its provisions regarding short time and hours. There was also dispute about overtime payment on short time, while employers objected to paying full wages for hours spent in the air-raid shelters. Moreover, conditions were now changing as more and more workers left the industry for the Forces, Civil Defence, and munitions. Negotiations on amending the agreement having failed, it was therefore cancelled after lasting nine months. Thus working conditions were restored to the *status quo*, except in so far as chapels agreed to rearrangement of hours, short time, &c.

A new arrangement was quickly made by the Federation regarding payment for time lost during air raids, the employers' liability being

[1] *Typographical Circular*, Jan. 1940.

reduced to half wages, except for the first hour lost in each day, for which full wages were to be paid. This arrangement, however, was only temporary. Owing to the loss of production caused by stoppage in enemy air attacks, many of them merely 'nuisance raids', the Government began to urge all essential industries to 'work after the siren' until warning of 'imminent danger' was given by 'roof-spotters'. Moreover, employers were dissatisfied even with their reduced wage-payment obligations. A new agreement, therefore, War Agreement No. 2, was arranged between the P. & K.T.F. and employers' organizations in September 1940, along the lines suggested by the Government. As the time spent in the shelters would now be much less, employers guaranteed full wages. Other clauses made provision for suspension of work through air-raid damage, for transference of workers to other districts, and rearrangement of working hours so as to utilize as much winter daylight as possible. Thus printing-trade workers were brought into the industrial front line.

As enemy bombing grew more severe, 'fire-watching' was enforced in January 1941. This and the 'black-out' and all the other war-time difficulties added to the hardships of workers left in the industry.

Another problem which the unions had to face was that of the replacement and reinstatement of apprentices called up into the Forces. This had arisen before the outbreak of war with the Military Training Act, but it became much greater as the war years went by. Reinstatement, of course, could not really be settled till the end of hostilities came in sight. Replacement was the immediate problem. The T.A., like other craft unions, was greatly concerned to prevent wholesale replacement, since this would flood the post-war labour market: failure to get an agreement in 1914-18 had no doubt contributed to unemployment between the wars.

A special joint committee, representative of the P. & K.T.F. and the employers' organizations, was set up in December 1939—there being, meanwhile, a 'moratorium' on apprentice replacements—and an agreement was reached in March 1940. This stipulated that an apprentice serving with the Forces should not be replaced until the date on which he would normally have finished his time; till then he was still to be reckoned in the firm's apprentice complement. Firms could, however, claim replacements under a 'special hardship' clause. This agreement was regarded as very satisfactory by the unions, since it regulated and considerably restricted replacements.

The situation in the printing industry changed dramatically after

June 1940. The 'phoney war' ended with the German conquest of Denmark, Norway, Holland, Belgium, and then France: after Dunkirk Britain stood alone with her back to the wall. The Government, having acquired emergency powers, began vigorously to regulate national industry, making great efforts to step up production of munitions, armaments, and aircraft, and restricting 'less essential' trades. From now on Government control of paper, metals, inks, and all forms of printing became increasingly severe. At the same time the industry was urged to transfer men to war work. This question was discussed at a conference on 5 June 1940 between representatives of the Ministry of Labour, the employers' organizations, and the P. & K.T.F., with the result that an 'Urgent Appeal to the Printing Industry' was issued by the J.I.C. for transfers to war work. The printing unions readily co-operated in the J.I.C. scheme, especially as it would solve the problems of unemployment and short time. The T.A. even made special grants of 10s. per week, in addition to those paid by the State, to members undergoing training in Government establishments.

More and more men were required by the Government, not only for war work, but also for the Forces. The 'reserved' age for printing trade workers, hitherto thirty, was raised to thirty-five in December 1940, many occupations were dereserved in July 1941, while another revised schedule in December provided for the gradual abolition of almost all reservations: only individual cases would now be considered, while fewer 'deferments' would be granted. Men over military age (forty-one) came under the Registration for Employment Order and might be directed to war work.

The result was that thousands of T.A. members left the printing industry for munitions and Civil Defence or were conscripted into the Forces. By the end of 1940 their numbers had already reached 3,390 and 8,137 respectively, rising to 3,984 and 12,773 by mid-1944, a total of 16,757, while the number of members employed in printing fell from 31,899 before the war to 20,592 by the end of 1940 and 16,891 by June 1944, a reduction of nearly 50 per cent.

Thus unemployment and short time in the first year of the war gave way to labour shortage by the end of 1940 which became increasingly acute in 1941. Despite Government restrictions on paper and printing, there was still a good deal of 'essential printing' to be done. At the same time, however, the Government was clamouring for more men for the Forces and munitions.

To solve the man-power shortage, both Ministry of Labour and employers urged relaxation of restrictive trade-union rules and 'dilution of labour'. The alternative was Government compulsion. War Agreement No. 3 was therefore negotiated between the P. & K.T.F. and the employers' organizations in February 1941, permitting agreed 'variation of trade agreements, Trade Union rules, and customs', on certain conditions. The agreement, it was stressed, was 'solely one to meet the war emergency', after which pre-war conditions would be re-established. Relaxation would apply 'only when and for so long as the Unions are unable to supply labour'. Employees going into the Forces or other national service were as far as possible to be reinstated after the war. Where women were introduced to take the places of men reasonable preference was to be given to those already in the trade. If an employer had to reduce his staff he must dispense first with 'dilutee' labour.

On the basis of this general agreement, the individual unions entered into negotiations with the B.F.M.P. and Newspaper Society. The T.A. was anxious to do its best to help the industry and the country in the critical war situation, 'but the occasion must not', it considered, 'be used for unnecessarily encroaching upon our conditions'. Its main endeavour, as in 1914-18, was to carry on the trade as far as possible with the depleted labour force of its own members, by relaxing working rules, with as little 'dilution' as possible, especially by women; for 'dilutees' might be kept on after the war, to the exclusion of T.A. members who had gone into the Forces or munitions; they might create post-war unemployment, provide 'cheap labour', and have a deteriorating effect on wage rates and working conditions, so laboriously built up and so zealously guarded.

Under War Agreement No. 3A, concluded between the T.A. and the employers' organizations in April 1941, local joint committees could, with Head Office approval, when (but only when) no unemployed T.A. labour was available, arrange relaxation of rules in regard to such matters as the manning of machines, overtime, interchangeability between departments ('twicing'), lending of men from one office to another ('smooting'), apprentices' duties, and employment of superannuated members.[1] Moreover, to facilitate the filling of vacancies and transfer of labour from one part of the country to another, the T.A. Executive had established a central register of unemployed members, while by War Agreement No. 4 (February 1941) the employers undertook to pay a weekly subsistence allowance of 24s. 6d. to workers transferred away

---

[1] Note, too, that the wages settlement of Nov. 1941 provided for extension of working hours See below, p. 418.

from home. When (but only when) all such transfers, relaxations, longer hours, and harder work failed to provide sufficient labour, substitution of men from other printing trade unions or, if necessary, from outside the industry might be permitted. Such dilutees would receive short periods of training (six to nine months), but on completion were to be paid full T.A. rates.

A deadlock, however, was reached on the question of women dilutees, which was therefore referred to a joint committee of the P. & K.T.F. and the employers' organizations. The main difference was in regard to wages, the employers refusing to pay men's rates to women. Eventually, however, in July 1941, an agreement was reached, whereby women dilutees would, after a period of training and reaching the journeyman's standard, get the man's 'rate for the job'; but if not of the required proficiency, two-thirds, or, in the case of keyboard operators, three-fourths. This was followed by more detailed agreements with individual unions as to periods of training, wage rates, &c.

The T.A.'s aim, in the case of both male and female dilutees, was to restrict their training[1] and keep them to a particular class of easy work, yet at the same time to secure full union rates; thus it was hoped to preserve T.A. standards during the war and prepare for the exclusion of dilutees when it was over.

Branches and chapels were urged to secure the strict observance of all the conditions and safeguards in these agreements and to resist unauthorized innovations. There were to be no relaxations of rules or introduction of dilutees without Executive sanction. Some employers, of course, evaded or ignored the agreements, but on the whole the Association kept a firm control, assisted not only by the Federation, but also by the good faith and co-operation of the employers' organizations.

Wages Movements

Relaxation of rules and labour dilution were very important. Wages, however, were of much greater concern to most T.A. members. The cost of living rose rapidly during the war, while income tax was increased, with the result that there was a constant clamour for wage increases.

Prices jumped sharply in the first months of the war, the cost-of-living index figure (July 1914 = 100) rising from 155 on 1 September to 173 by 1 December 1939. Branch resolutions therefore poured in urging action to secure either a wage increase or a war bonus. Prospects

---

[1] The period of training for women dilutees varied from nine to eighteen months.

were not very bright, with widespread slump, unemployment, and short time, but the Executive considered a claim justified by the rise in the cost of living. As, however, the question came under the stabilization clause of the 1937 Hours and Holidays Agreement, it was referred to the P. & K.T.F.—a novel procedure for the T.A., which had always insisted hitherto on conducting its own wages negotiations.

Other unions also favoured joint action and a conference of societies was therefore held on 28 November under P. & K.T.F. auspices, when it was decided to ask the employers for a flat-rate war bonus of 10s. per week for men, 7s. 6d. for women, and 4s. for juveniles. Conferences with the employers followed in January and February 1940, but the unions' claim was completely rejected, mainly on account of the trade depression. The matter was therefore brought before the J.I.C. in May, but it failed to solve the deadlock, and another conference with the employers in June also proved fruitless.

It was now just after Dunkirk and the Minister of Labour, Ernest Bevin, acting under the Emergency Powers Act, had just established the National Arbitration Tribunal for the settlement of labour disputes. The P. & K.T.F., therefore, to preserve industrial peace in so critical a period, referred the wages question to the new Tribunal—unpopular though arbitration had always been. The case—the first to come before the Tribunal—was heard on 13 August. The award was 5s. per week to men, 2s. 6d. to women, and 1s. 6d. to juveniles.

Most unions were dissatisfied with this award. The cost-of-living index figure was now up to 185 and continued to rise in the following months, reaching 199 by May 1941. It was not long, therefore, before another wages movement was started: the Federation Executive were already considering it by February 1941. This time, however, it was decided to ask not for a flat-rate, but for a graded increase, giving greater amounts to the lower-paid towns; indirectly, in fact, this movement was for regrading as well as for a wages increase. Regrading had been dropped temporarily on the outbreak of war, but was now raised again. Government rationing and price control, which tended to level living costs over the whole country, accentuated the unjust inequalities of the grading system—the difference of 15s. between T.A. grades 1 and 6 and the further 11s. 6d. between grade 1 and the London rate.

After several conferences and a final meeting of union executives on 22 July, the Federation presented its claims to the employers. Wage increases were asked for varying from 6s., where the basic grade rate was 90s. or over, to 14s. where it was under 60s., with proportionate advances for women and juveniles. The employers refused, however, in the ensuing conferences, to accept these proposals, but offered flat increases of 5s. for men, 3s. 6d. for women, and 2s. for juveniles, on condition that employers might, if necessary, extend regular working hours from 45 to 50, paying overtime rates for the extra five hours.[1] This offer was accepted by a conference of societies in November. (War Agreement No. 6.)

The settlement caused intense dissatisfaction, however, in the T.A. and other unions with similar wage grades. A storm of protest arose: the grading system was bitterly attacked and many branches threatened 'non-co-operation' with the employers regarding overtime, labour dilution, and other relaxations under War Agreement No. 3A. There was a widespread feeling that the National Wages Agreement must be 'mended or ended': if grading was not altered, branches and groups would revert to local action to get wage adjustments.

The P. & K.T.F. also came in for a great deal of criticism. When, therefore, it summoned a conference of societies in January 1942 to consider another approach to the employers for improvement of low-grade wages, the T.A. Executive decided not to be represented, but to act independently. An application was thereupon submitted to the employers for graded wage increases, varying from 5s. in grade 1 to 15s. in grade 6. The other unions with the six-grade system (the Stereotypers, N.U.P.B. & P.W., N.S.O.P. & A., and Women Workers) also acted separately, putting in similar requests.

The employers now, at last, faced by threatened abrogation of the National Wages Agreement, realized that there must be 'some adjustment in the present system of grading', which would raise the wages of lower-graded workers. They would not, however, waste time in separate negotiations with individual unions, but submitted their proposals to the Federation Executive (May 1942). These were that towns in grades 1, 2, and 3 should remain unchanged, that those in grade 4 should be raised to grade 3, and those in grades 5 and 6 to grade 4: thus the two bottom grades would be abolished and 'rough justice' would be done to the lower-graded workers.[2]

The T.A. Executive at first protested to the employers that they were 'the only body competent to discuss a revision of the wages of T.A. members', but soon agreed to join in negotiations through the Federa-

---

[1] This was to help meet the labour shortage.
[2] The differentiation between existing grades was 3s., so that grade 6 towns would get 6s. increase, grades 5 and 4, 3s.

tion. These went on for several months and ended in deadlock. The employers suggested reference to the N.A.T., but this was rejected by the unions, who threatened guerrilla warfare throughout the industry. Eventually, however, at the end of July, the J.I.C. officers succeeded in getting a compromise accepted by both sides.

By this agreement (War Agreement No. 7), which came into force in September 1942, the six provincial wage grades were reduced to four. The effects on T.A. wage rates were as follows:

Previous grade and wage			New grade and wage			Increase	
	s.	d.		s.	d.	s.	d.
1	87	6	1	87	6		
2	84	6	2	86	0	1	6
3	81	6⎱	3	83	0	1	6
4	78	6⎰				4	6
5	75	6⎱	4	80	0	4	6
6	72	6⎰				7	6

This agreement undoubtedly benefited lower-graded workers, but it could only be regarded as a half-way house in the regrading struggle. The difference between top and bottom T.A. grades had, indeed, been halved to 7s. 6d., but that of 11s. 6d. between T.A. grade 1 and the L.S.C. rate remained unaltered. A more immediate grievance was the fact that London and grade 1 towns had got nothing and grades 2 and 3 only a paltry 1s. 6d. Moreover, wages in the printing trade had not kept pace with those in other, especially 'war', industries, or with the rising cost of living, even as indicated by the official index figure, which was universally scoffed at. It was not long, therefore, before the unions were 'at it again'.

By the end of 1942 resolutions for a further wage increase were coming in from many branches, while early in February 1943 T.A. chapels in Manchester put in claims for £1 per week, without consulting the E.C. There was similar agitation in other unions and the P. & K.T.F. therefore called a conference of union executives on 16 February, when it was agreed to make joint application for an increase of £1 a week for all adult workers, with proportionate increases for apprentices and juniors.

The P. & K.T.F. Executive met the employers' Joint Labour Committee on 30 March and 21 April. John Fletcher, the P. & K.T.F. Secretary, presenting the unions' claim, pointed out the 'inferior position' into which they had fallen financially since the outbreak of war, in comparison with workers in other industries: according to the *Ministry of Labour*

Gazette (January 1943), the average level of wage rates in all industries had risen by about 33 per cent. since October 1938, but in the printing industry by only 15 per cent., much less in the case of the big cities and more highly skilled workers. Most printing could now be classed as 'essential', and labour was in short supply. Furthermore, most firms were making good profits. The unions' claim was intended to bring the printing industry 'much nearer, relatively, the good position it held in peace-time'.

The employers, however, rejected this claim absolutely, without any counter offer. Their chairman, Colonel Fletcher, pointed out that there had been no material change in the cost of living since the 5s. increase in November 1941.[1] Printers had been fortunate in their 'superior position' pre-war as regards wages and hours, and could not now expect to get the same proportionate increases as trades like mining and shipbuilding, which, after suffering severe depression and wage-cuts in the inter-war years, had suddenly boomed owing to war conditions; even so, they were hardly in an 'inferior position', being fifth out of sixteen industries in the Ministry of Labour's table of average weekly earnings.[2] Many firms were *not* making good profits, production had fallen enormously since the war began, paper supplies had been drastically cut, further withdrawals of labour were threatened, and an increase in costs might put some firms out of business and cause more loss of work to office printing machines.

The deadlock was referred to the J.I.C. on 29 April, and then, failing settlement, to the National Arbitration Tribunal, which heard the case on 17 June. Its award, published on 22 June, totally rejected the men's claim for £1 a week, but gave 4s. to women.

This decision created feelings of bitter resentment, injustice, and anger throughout the industry. It resulted in a storm of protests and widespread unrest. The N.A.T. was denounced as a pro-capitalist instrument created by the Government to keep down wages, the union executives expressed their 'complete dissatisfaction' at a meeting on 6 July, branches clamoured for action, chapels imposed overtime bans and

[1] The Ministry of Labour index figure had remained at about 200, i.e. about 30 per cent. above that for August 1939.

[2] On the other hand, the average weekly earnings of men employed in the printing industry, which had been well above all others in October 1938 (£4. 4s. 3d., as compared with the general average of £3. 9s.), had only risen by about 28 per cent. up to January 1943, compared with the general average of nearly 65 per cent., and were now only £5. 7s. 6d., as compared with the general average of £5. 13s. 9d. (*Ministry of Labour Gazette*, June 1943). Most industries, however, were working considerably more overtime than printing.

adopted a general policy of 'non-co-operation', while the executives of individual unions, including the T.A., approached the employers' organizations separately for wage increases: unless some satisfaction was quickly secured, strife threatened in every printing office in the country. There is no doubt that the T.A. and other union executives encouraged aggressive local action, despite agreements and the J.I.C. constitution, as proof of 'widespread dissatisfaction' with the N.A.T. awards and to force concessions from the employers' organizations.

Government arbitration had proved as unsatisfactory and unpleasant in 1943 as in 1922. The N.A.T. might be backed by War Emergency powers, it might be recognized by the T.U.C. and union executives, but that was no guarantee that its arbitrary fiat would be accepted, any more than Government policy against inflation. Association members were convinced that their living standard was falling, and, having the whip hand in the prevailing labour shortage, intended using it.

The employers were forced to give way. A meeting of their Joint Labour Committee on 27 September decided to invite the P. & K.T.F. Executive to resume wages negotiations on behalf of the individual unions, provided that all aggressive or coercive action was withdrawn. To this the P. & K.T.F. Executive agreed, though without committing the unions, and a conference took place on 11 October, when a proposed settlement was reached, giving an increase of 7s. 6d. to men, another 2s. 6d. to women, and 3s. to male juveniles (female juveniles having recently been given a 3s. increase). There was, however, an important condition, that wages thus increased should be 'stabilized', no further collective increases to be asked for during the period of the war and for twelve months after, so long as the cost of living remained at its present or approximately its present figure.

These terms were accepted by a meeting of union executives next day and later by ballot vote of the members, coming into force on the first pay-day in November 1943 (War Agreement No. 8).

At the same time an agreement was finally reached on the wages of apprentices, after prolonged negotiations by the P. & K.T.F. Executive. This was a landmark, in that the employers at last recognized the unions' jurisdiction over apprentices' wages, hitherto unregulated except for a scale recommended by the employers' organizations. The new agreement based them on a sliding scale, rising from 20 per cent. (first year) to 60 per cent. (seventh year) of the journeyman's minimum rate.

Wages remained generally stabilized until after the war, under War Agreement No. 8, but this did not prevent several sectional alterations.

The most notable of these concerned the national newspapers published in Manchester. Hitherto, conditions in these offices had been regulated by separate agreements between individual managements and chapels, but in 1941 the London Newspaper Proprietors formed a provincial organization, the London Newspapers Provincial Association, for collective bargaining.[1] When, therefore, early in 1943, T.A. members employed in the Manchester offices put in a claim for a war bonus of £1 per week, the L.N.P.A. refused to negotiate either with individual chapels or branch, but insisted on 'national' agreement with the T.A. Executive. A negotiating committee was eventually established consisting of E.C., branch, and chapel representatives, but negotiations broke down in January 1944, owing to the L.N.P.A.'s refusal to concede any general wages increase, and the E.C. left matters to branch and chapel action. The result was an overtime ban at the *Express*, answered by a threatened lock-out on all national newspapers, which stood firm on the principle of collective bargaining. The T.A. Executive therefore resumed negotiations and a 'national' agreement was eventually reached in June 1944, though it took several months to get it accepted in the *Express* and *Herald* offices.

Basic wage rates were to be as follows:

	£	s.	d.
Rotary machine minders	7	1	0
Linotype operators	6	18	0
Stone hands and makers-up	6	14	6
Ludlow operators	6	10	0
Case hands and readers	6	7	6

These wages were based on an 11-day fortnight, with an average working week of $41\frac{1}{4}$ hours. Men working on Saturdays for Sunday newspapers would be paid double-time rates and 'call money' and get an extra night off during the week (for which, however, one-sixth of their basic weekly wage would be deducted) and an additional annual holiday allowance, according to the number of week-ends worked. The agreement also included several special extras, for headline machines, seals, &c.

[1] The Association included the four 'national' dailies printed in Manchester (*Daily Express, Daily Mail, Daily Herald*, and *News Chronicle*) and the Sunday papers printed in the same offices (*Sunday Express, Sunday Dispatch, People*, and *News of the World* respectively). It did not include the Kemsley Newspapers, nor the Manchester edition of the *Daily Telegraph*, printed in the Kemsley Buildings, nor the *Manchester Guardian*. Conditions in these offices continued to be regulated by agreements with the Newspaper Society and by 'house' agreements.

The Commission which had been established by the 1939 Delegate Meeting, to inquire into the wages status of jobbing compositors, met and reported in 1940. Acting on its recommendations, the E.C. eventually (1944) got the employers to agree to the substitution of 'grade rate' for 'case rate' in the National Wage Basis Agreement, so that the jobbing compositor's rate ceased to be the basic minimum. Although no attempt was made to alter the existing wage rates, an important principle had been secured.

The only other alteration in wage rates of any significance during the war was that in 1944 changing the flat-rate extra of double-day staffs to a percentage of the normal weekly wage: 10 per cent. for a week of 40 hours, $12\frac{1}{2}$ per cent. for 41, and 15 per cent. for 42.

Ireland

We will now turn to consider war-time conditions in Ireland. Eire, of course, was neutral, and there was no conscription in Northern Ireland, which also escaped the air-raids and was not in other ways so seriously affected by the war as England. Nevertheless, industry (especially printing) was greatly dislocated, while the cost of living rose more steeply in Eire than in England.

The various English War Agreements, which we have previously described, did not apply to Ireland, apart from Belfast, the T.A. still negotiating separately with the I.M.P.A. Difficulties and dangers of travel across the Irish Sea led to the establishment in 1940 of an Irish Advisory Board, consisting of the newly appointed Organizer, J. P. Forristal, and the two Irish E.C. members.

Eire's neutrality and the trade-union and wages policy of its Government tended to create a split in the T.A.'s Irish membership. There was, in fact, a possibility of Eire being cut off from the T.A. The Eire Trade Union Act of 1941 was not merely restrictive of trade-union functions, but designed to cripple, or at any rate handicap, unions with headquarters in England. There were strongly nationalist sentiments in the Eire Government and among some of the Irish trade unions, as illustrated by the report of the Commission on Vocational Organization (1944), in favour of Irish national trade unions and exclusion of any English control, and by the split in the Irish trade-union movement on this question in 1944–5.

The T.A. Executive were strongly tempted to throw up Eire as being more trouble than it was worth, especially as many Irish members were heavily in arrears with their subscriptions. There was not a scrap of truth, so far as the T.A. was concerned, in Irish statements about English domination. The Association had only taken in Ireland in 1877 at the repeated request of Irish societies, because Dublin had failed to organize an Irish Typographical Union and conditions in the printing industry were so bad. It had always given Irish branches a great deal of independence in trade matters and deliberately refrained from any interference in Irish political affairs. On repeated occasions the T.A. membership in Southern Ireland had expressed their loyalty to the Association.

Such resolutions came in now from almost every Irish branch, and it was in response to urgent Irish requests that the E.C. agreed to take out a negotiating licence (for which £1,200 had to be deposited with the Eire authorities) under the new Act. The Act was strongly attacked by T.A. branches in Ireland, which also opposed the nationalist split in the Irish trade-union movement. At the T.A. All-Ireland Conferences, which continued to be held throughout the war, trade-union solidarity was the keynote.

The Eire Government restricted trade-union action much more grievously, however, by its Emergency Powers (No. 83) Order in June 1941, which decreed a 'standstill' or 'freeze' in wages. In November 1940, following the National Arbitration Tribunal award of 5s. in England, the T.A. had got the same increase from the I.M.P.A. for all Ireland, after a threatened strike. The new Order, however, meant that the Association would no longer be able to conduct wages movements in Eire, despite the rising cost of living, though it would not, of course, be precluded from such action in Northern Ireland.

The 'Standstill Order' was relaxed in September 1942 by Emergency Powers (No. 166) Order, but wages still remained under close Government control. Unions could now make application (preferably with, but if necessary without, the employers' agreement) to the Minister for Industry and Commerce for a Bonus Order, permitting wage bonuses according to the rise in the cost of living. The bonus was not to exceed 1s. (6d. for apprentices) for each increase of five points above the cost-of-living figure 225 (July 1914 = 100), with a ceiling of 265, i.e. a maximum bonus of 8s.

This Order had to be modified in October 1943 by Emergency Powers (No. 260) Order, due to the continued rise in the cost of living. The ceiling was raised to 294, but the bonus rate was reduced to 1s. for each ten, instead of five, points rise above 264, so that the maximum bonus would now be 11s.

The T.A. secured the whole of this bonus in several instalments in the years 1942-5, but wages in Eire were left well behind those in England, while grading remained unaltered.

In Northern Ireland, on the other hand, wages kept pace with those in England, though with a time-lag, exasperating to Northern Ireland members, of several months. There was first of all the 5s. increase in November 1940; then, by separate negotiation with the I.M.P.A.'s Northern Alliance, a further 5s. in July 1942, back-dated three months; reduction of grades to three in May 1943 by raising the lower-paid branches; and finally, an increase of 7s. 6d. in March 1944,[1] back-dated a month, with the same stabilization clause as in England.

In November 1944 the E.C. secured an apprentices' wages agreement for the whole of Ireland. Unlike that recently made in England, however, this was not a percentage scale, based on journeymen's wages, but a list of fixed rates, rising from 12s. 6d. in the first year to 50s. in the seventh.

Strike Payments

It is a great tribute to the tact, negotiating skill, and conciliatory policy on both sides of the printing industry that, despite the innumerable war-time difficulties and wages movements, there were hardly any strikes. T.A. strike payments dwindled from £1,007 (1939) to £428 (1940), £165 (1941), £44 (1942), £33 (1943), £6 (1944), and finally nil (1945).

Membership and Finances

T.A. membership increased but slowly during the war years, as was only to be expected in view of the reduction in printing. That it did not fall was due to the loyalty of those who went into war work and Civil Defence. The Association continued its organizing work and was able, as a result of the war-time labour shortage, to unionize many 'open houses' and even notoriously 'black spots'. Membership therefore rose from 38,277 at the end of 1939 to 41,000 by the end of 1945.

The Association's constitutional machinery was able to function normally during the war, except that the Delegate Meeting due in 1942 was postponed till 1944 (Rhyl). When J. Fletcher, the General Secretary, became P. & K.T.F. Secretary in 1941, H. Riding, the Assistant Secretary, was elected in his place, the Assistant Secretaryship being secured

---

[1] Londonderry got only 7s., to equalize it with Belfast, in grade 2 of the English Wages Agreement. The three grades in N. Ireland were now the same as the English grades 2, 3, and 4.

by H. E. Joseph, then Chief Clerk. J. P. Forristal succeeded T. Cassidy (retired 1937) as Irish Organizer in 1939, and J. A. Bell (died 1941), Organizer in southern England, was succeeded by E. F. Andrews (resigned 1943) and J. Codling.

The Association finances suffered severely in the first year of the war. Owing to the widespread unemployment and short time, out-of-work payments[1] rose from £35,000 in 1938 to £58,000 in 1939 and £74,000 in 1940. At the same time income was considerably reduced as a result of the decision to exempt Forces members from payment of subscriptions. Both General and Superannuation Funds therefore suffered heavy losses: the former was reduced from nearly £200,000 to £158,000 by the end of 1940, the latter from £130,000 to £119,000.

As, however, unemployment gave way to labour shortage in 1940-1, the Association's financial position improved. Out-of-work payments fell rapidly to £8,500 in 1941 and were less than £1,000 by 1945. The General Fund therefore rose by leaps and bounds to over £292,000 by the end of 1945. The Superannuation Fund, however, fell to £104,000 in June 1941 and the Executive had to ask members not only to pay a general levy of 4d. per week and an overtime levy of 2d. per hour, but also to permit the transfer of money from the General Fund. These proposals were accepted and saved the Superannuation Fund from threatened collapse. Despite the levies, however, and also the fact that a good many superannuated members returned to the trade, £13,500 had to be transferred from the General Fund in 1942. The situation was worsened by cessation of the overtime levy, after legal action by the Manchester news workers,[2] and although the members agreed to increase the ordinary levy from 4d. to 8d. per week, regular transfers from the General Fund were still necessary: £5,685 in 1943, £13,500 in 1944, and £11,500 in 1945. The Superannuation Fund increased to nearly £149,000 by the end of 1945, but its financial position was obviously unsound.

---

[1] Exclusive of State Unemployment Insurance and Dependency Benefits.

[2] Who objected to imposition of the levy on their week-end earnings on Sunday newspapers. The whole amount paid, £13,619, was reimbursed out of the General Fund.

XXIV

POST-WAR SETTLEMENT
1945–9

Post-War Reconstruction Schemes

THE return to 'normal' peace-time conditions has been much slower after 1945 than after 1918. The country's economic position is fundamentally more serious and Government control has been more prolonged. Industry has been faced with greater difficulties in replacing plant and machinery and with severer shortages of labour and raw materials. Nevertheless, the country has enjoyed a trade 'boom' far longer than that following the First World War. At home there has been a greater amount of work to make up for losses and sacrifices in the war, while abroad foreign competition has taken longer to build up. The years 1945–9, therefore, have been marked by 'full employment' and increased production.

Long before the war ended the air was full, as in 1917–18, of schemes for 'Post-War Reconstruction' in every sphere, national and international. The T.A. Executive appointed a special committee in January 1943, but its plans were eventually incorporated in a P. & K.T.F. Report on Post-War Reconstruction for the whole industry, compiled in 1943–4. A wide variety of subjects were covered. There was first of all the question of employment after the war, with the problems of rebuilding, replacement of machinery, shortage of raw materials and labour, reinstatement of those in the Forces and Civil Defence, and rehabilitation of the disabled. Wages and hours also loomed large in post-war plans: there was a widespread demand for increased wages, reduction in the number of grades, a 40-hour 5-day week, and limitation of overtime, while the T.A. had its sectional claims in regard to the wages of jobbing compositors, machine minders, readers, operators, and news hands. Apprenticeship and technical training were also considered.

The unions also aimed to improve working conditions—cleanliness, lighting, heating, ventilation, sanitation, welfare facilities, &c.—with the aim of preventing industrial sickness, disease, and accidents. They devoted considerable attention, too, to the Beveridge Report and the Government's Social Security proposals, with special regard to their effects on trade-union sickness, unemployment, and superannuation schemes. The question of a national pension scheme for the industry was also kept in view.

Relations between unions in the printing industry were also considered. If amalgamation (general or sectional) was not possible, there should at least be closer working, some co-ordination of policy and organization. Friction on demarcation and other questions should be eliminated. Unity and strength were the watchwords. Most of the post-war problems concerned the whole industry and would be affected by Government legislation and control. They would be best dealt with, therefore, by the Federation, which had proved so effective during the war. This raised the important question as to whether or not the unions should continue their war-time unity in negotiations on wage rates and working conditions.

On many of these post-war problems action through the J.I.C. was recommended. A scheme was, in fact, put forward to strengthen and widen the authority of the J.I.C., to endow it with 'extensive powers of control over the whole industry', in order to secure 'complete organization' of employers and employed and complete recognition of trade agreements. The idea was to maintain and develop the industry's tradition of 'self-government', rather than to bring in an Enabling Bill, though this was seriously considered. Many unionists went farther, demanding a greater share in the control and profits of the industry. A majority of the unions, however, decided in the end to leave the powers of the unions and J.I.C. exactly as they were.

The printing trade unions were not alone, of course, in their post-war planning. Every industry was concerned with post-war reconstruction. Most of the problems, in fact, were national ones and therefore dealt with by the Government in consultation with the Employers' Confederation and T.U.C. There resulted legislation on such questions as reinstatement in civil employment, rehabilitation of disabled persons, interrupted apprenticeships, and social security, while Government control continued over industry and trade.

The printing trade had to fit its post-war reconstruction plans into this general framework of Government legislation and regulation. Most of the work was done through the J.I.C., which continued its war-time representation of the whole industry.

Demobilization took place fairly rapidly after the war, but the labour shortage remained acute and War Emergency Agreements Nos. 3 and 3A, in regard to relaxation of rules and 'dilution' of labour, had therefore to be continued and are still in force. The Association is careful, however, to safeguard the interests of full members under these agreements, to prevent unnecessary dilution and ensure that 'dilutees' go first in the event of dismissals. Dilution would, in fact, have a 'cushioning' effect on fully trained craftsmen in a trade depression. Hence some have preferred it to a larger intake of apprentices, who would become regular journeymen.

The Disabled Persons (Employment) Act, 1944, imposed on every industry a liability for the training and employment of a certain quota of disabled persons, the Government paying training allowances. Details were to be arranged by negotiation in each group of trades. A special J.I.C. committee was appointed in the printing and kindred trades, to formulate a scheme for approval by the Ministry of Labour. The unions again, as in 1918, adopted a very exclusive attitude, trying to restrict the scheme as far as possible to disabled persons previously employed in the industry and insisting that any outsiders admitted must be reckoned in the apprentice ratio. The employers eventually agreed and a Vocational Training Scheme was formulated, approved by the Ministry of Labour in September 1946.

The reinstatement of apprentices returning from war service was another problem dealt with by the J.I.C. The Government was prepared to provide financial assistance under approved schemes prepared by individual industries to enable apprentices to complete their training. The J.I.C. had already made provision for reinstatement under War Agreement No. 5, which was now supplemented and partly replaced by an Interrupted Apprenticeship Scheme, approved by the Ministry of Labour in March 1945. Apprentices who, at the time of call-up, had only one year to serve were to be considered journeymen; those with longer to serve had the unexpired period reduced by one-half their period of war-service, and would be paid journeymen's wages from the date on which the apprenticeship would normally have ended, the Ministry of Labour paying one-third.

The J.I.C. scheme for the Recruitment and Training of Apprentices[1] was part of the post-war reconstruction in the printing industry. A J.I.C. Committee was also established on Employment and Production, to deal with such problems as rebuilding, replacements of machinery, supply of labour and raw materials, and increased production. Another serious post-war problem has been the winter 'fuel crises', resulting in power cuts and stoppages of production, and necessitating staggered hours and night shifts to 'spread the load' on electricity power stations.

[1] See below, pp. 458-9.

The worst was in 1947. The P. & K.T.F. arranged emergency measures with the employers in January, followed by a full agreement in August, which has had to be put into operation in succeeding winters owing to continued coal shortages.

The main post-war concern of the unions, however, has been with wages and hours, especially the former, owing to the ever-rising cost of living.

Wages and Hours

The wages stabilization clause in War Agreement No. 8 (November 1943) had stipulated that 'no further collective increases shall be asked for during the period of the war and twelve months thereafter, so long as the cost of living remains at its present, or approximately its present figure'. The Ministry of Labour cost-of-living index figure had then stood at 199 (July 1914=100), round about which it remained throughout 1944. By July 1945, however, it had risen to 207 and the P. & K.T.F. Executive therefore consulted the unions as to whether they should proceed with an application for a general wages advance. The unions agreed and a conference was arranged with the employers (B.F.M.P. and Newspaper Society) on 26 September.

By this time, however, the cost-of-living index figure had fallen to 203. The Federation Executive therefore decided to base their claim not so much on the increased cost of living as on the argument that the total increases during the war in the printing industry compared unfavourably, except in the lower graded areas in the old schedule, with the total advances in other industries. They did not state any specific amount of increase desired, but pointed out that the average increase since 1939 to employees in the printing industry was 17s. 6d., as compared with sums ranging from 23s. 6d. in the electrical to 28s. in the engineering industry.

The employers gave their answer at a further conference on 31 October. They agreed that wage increases in other industries during the war had exceeded those in the printing trade, but suggested that what had happened was a levelling up. Whereas printing wages had remained stabilized between 1922 and 1939, despite the fall in the cost of living, there had been considerable wages cuts in other industries. Printers, moreover, had enjoyed a 45-hour week since 1937. Nevertheless, the employers offered an increase of 7s. 6d. for men, 5s. 6d. for women, and 3s. 6d. for boy and girl learners; apprentices, of course, to get an appropriate percentage on journeymen's minimum rates.

This offer was considered by a conference of union executives summoned by the Federation Executive on 13 November, when it was decided to press for better terms. The Executive therefore requested a further conference with the employers. At this conference, on 3 December, an agreement was reached, the employers improving their offer to 8s. 6d. for men, 7s. 6d. for women, and 4s. for juveniles. Wages were to be stabilized until 30 June 1947, provided that the cost of living did not materially alter. A joint committee was to be set up to watch unemployment in the industry and, if need arose, devise means of dealing with the problem before substantial unemployment occurred.

The agreement was accepted by a large majority in a ballot vote of union members and came into force on the first pay-day in January 1946.

The stabilization clause in this agreement applied to wages only and did not preclude an approach to the employers for reduced working hours and increased holidays, for which there was growing pressure in all the unions, including the T.A. In February 1946, therefore, the Federation Executive approached the B.F.M.P. and Newspaper Society for revision of the 1937 Hours and Holidays Agreement, to make provision for a 44-hour, 5-day working week and a fortnight's annual holiday with pay.

The unions' case was presented at a joint conference on 1 May. It was 'based principally upon the need and legitimate desire of the workers . . . for increased leisure time', in order to enjoy 'recreational and social activities'. They should get some of the benefits of increased production due to new methods and faster running machinery, which imposed a greater strain upon them, especially in newspaper production. Another motive, in the background, was that shorter hours and more holidays would provide work for more people; the unions had not forgotten the unemployment after the post-war boom of 1918-20. They could see no reason why their claims should not be conceded. Employers were making 'very substantial profits', while increased costs could be passed on to the consumer in higher prices. There was no scarcity of labour, and shortage of paper and other raw materials precluded any very great expansion in production. Besides, printing being 'a sheltered industry', it was in a different position from those called on to boost exports. Finally, improved health and contentment among the workers would increase efficiency and expand output.

The employers gave their reply at a further conference on 28 May. They completely rejected the unions' claim, on the grounds that 'it would be damaging not only to our industry, but also to the nation', and 'would be entirely out of harmony with the needs of this country today'. The Government was making urgent appeals for increased production and the printing trade had a vitally important part to play, not only as 'an essential service' in industry, administration, and education at home, but also in the export drive; no industry could consider itself 'sheltered'. The 'main difficulty' was the acute labour shortage: the industry's labour force was only two-thirds pre-war strength. To grant the unions' claims would mean, not more leisure, but more overtime, if the industry was to meet the demands made upon it, thus increasing the already high costs of printing, with consequently greater danger from 'office machinery' and foreign competition. As regards the union argument about technical improvements and faster running machinery, there had been few new developments in the last ten years, and employers were having great difficulty in getting new machinery; in fact output per man-hour had fallen compared with pre-war.

The deadlock now came before a Conciliation Committee of the J.I.C. (26 June), then a special meeting of the full J.I.C. (11 July), and finally the J.I.C. Committee on Employment and Production (16 July), but no solution was reached. The unions therefore threatened to strike and prepared to impose an overtime ban after conciliatory intervention by the Ministry of Labour had failed to end the dispute.

The B.F.M.P. remained adamant, however, refusing to come below 43½ hours, and urged the Minister of Labour to refer the dispute to arbitration or to any independent tribunal or court, 'or to institute an immediate inquiry into the situation'. The Minister, George Isaacs, ex-N.S.O.P. & A. General Secretary, therefore, after a last fruitless effort to secure agreement, decided to appoint a Court of Inquiry under the 1919 Industrial Courts Act.

The Court held its meetings in late August and early September and its Report was published as a White Paper (Cmd. 6912) on 24 September. The main question at issue, it stated, was 'the practicability of the claims of the Trade Unions at the present time', having regard to the labour available and the need for maintaining production. The Court came to the conclusion 'that in the General Printing Section of the Industry the demands on production are at present very large and, so far as we can see, are likely to continue to be very large for some appreciable time to come'. They agreed with the employers that there was a serious labour shortage and that 'there will be a substantial loss of production if the claims of the Trade Unions are granted in full'. On the other hand, 'some shortening of hours would be beneficial to the productive capacity of the individual worker'. Hence, it was concluded, although a 40-hour week was not practicable at the present time, 'some reduction' of hours and a fortnight's annual holiday with pay were practicable. There was no clear definition of what reduction the Court thought feasible; it preferred to leave this controversial point to be settled by negotiations between the two parties. Finally, various suggestions were made for removing labour shortage difficulties in the industry. These were mainly due to the 'subnormal intake into the Industry during the six years of war' and would have to be met chiefly 'by recruitment to the Industry', by increasing, for example, the apprentice ratio and training not only disabled but also non-disabled adult men. The report also suggested consideration of shift work and methods of remuneration, meaning 'payment by results' under bonus systems or on piece-work.

Meanwhile the unions had imposed their overtime ban and balloted overwhelmingly in favour of strike action. The B.F.M.P. refused, however, to negotiate under duress and the dispute dragged on. The Ministry of Labour therefore had to intervene again and eventually, after prolonged discussions towards the end of September, succeeded in getting the two sides to negotiate an agreement, the unions finally accepting a 43½-hour week, together with a wages increase.

By this Hours, Holidays, and Wages Agreement, which came into effect on 4 November 1946, the unions secured two weeks annual holiday with pay, in addition to Bank Holidays, a 43½-hour, 5-day working week, and acceptance of the principle of a 42½-hour week 'when the necessary adjustments for adequate recruitment into the industry have been made with the unions concerned, and when the labour situation has sufficiently improved to enable the industry to meet its obligations to the community'.[1] Wage increases of 10s. per week were given to male craftsmen, 8s. to other adult males, 7s. 6d. to adult women, and appropriate percentage increases to apprentices and juveniles, while the wages stabilization clause in the wages agreement of January 1946 was cancelled.

A similar agreement was negotiated with the Newspaper Society on 17 October. A 5-day 5-night week was introduced in provincial daily newspaper offices as from the beginning of April 1947, reducing the working hours of day hands (evening newspapers) to 40 hours per week and those of night hands (morning newspapers) to 37½ hours.[2]

There is no doubt, in the light of the present-day position in the

---

[1] The overtime limit was raised to 25 hours in any two consecutive weeks.
[2] Night Linotype operators and rotary machine minders, 36½ hours.

industry, that the employers were right in their stand against any reduction of working hours below 43½. There is still today (1949) a serious
labour shortage, heavy overtime is still required, the industry is unable
fully to meet the demands made upon it, there are large arrears of work,
and printing costs are excessively high. They would have been far higher
had the unions had their way, for even more overtime would have had
to be worked. Employers were, in fact, justified in denouncing the union
claims as, in reality, an attempt to get bigger wage packets regardless of
the public interest. There is still among trade unions—despite recognition of their role in the regulation of industry, despite the growth of
Socialism—a nineteenth-century mentality, a tendency merely to grab
what they can in the way of shorter hours and increased wages, without
any sense of responsibility, heedless even of their own Labour Ministers.

The unions agreed in this settlement on hours, holidays, and wages to
consider with the employers the Court of Inquiry's suggestions for
removing labour shortage difficulties in the industry. These matters
were immediately considered by the J.I.C. Committee on Employment
and Production, which set up special sub-committees to examine the
various proposals. These sub-committees made several recommendations. They supported 'payment by results' on piece-work or bonus
systems in order to increase output. They advocated 'wider use of double
day shifts and night shifts . . . to obtain the fullest production possible
from the plant available'. And finally, they recommended a reduction
in the period of apprenticeship, owing to the school-leaving age having
been raised to fifteen and in view of National Service. On these recommendations the full Committee decided in February 1947 to seek the
views of both sides of the industry.

The T.A. Executive's replies show, again, that they were much more
concerned with getting what they could out of the industry than with
what they put in; wages mattered to them far more than production.
Piece-work and bonus systems had for years been condemned by the
Association, as 'offering inducements to racing or undue competition
between members', as 'task-work', as being 'opposed to true unionist
principles', appealing to selfish desire for gain, and creating unemployment. The Association had also continued to oppose any mechanical
methods of time recording and checking of individual output. Workers
remembered pre-war days and feared 'working themselves out of a job'.
The existing labour shortage enabled them to secure better wages and
working conditions. Why, then, should they try to end it? Production
was the employers' worry; why should they work harder to increase

capitalist profits? True, Labour Ministers were crying out for increased production, but despite warnings of 'Work or Want', economic crisis, inflation, &c., things didn't seem so bad; in fact, most workers had never been so well off. The cost of living was still rising, however, and other unions were after wage increases, so the T.A. should join in.

That was how most members felt. The General Secretary, Harry Riding, introduced another question, that of 'differentials' and 'parity', dating from the wages reductions of 1922. The E.C. adopted a reply he drafted. While 'not opposed to exploring the principle of bonus-paid work', they considered that 'before such incentives to increased production are considered, the overall wage basis of the industry should be revised'. T.A. members had been 'aggrieved at their invidious wage position in comparison with . . . other sections of the industry' ever since the wages reductions following the strike in 1922; these were 'still a source of bitter resentment' and 'undoubtedly responsible for a spirit of non-co-operation and a drag on that full production which is so essential today'. What the T.A. wanted was 'parity' with the Stereotypers, at present getting 9s. more, and a reduction of the 'differential' of 11s. 6d. between grade 1 and London. The removal of these 'fundamental injustices in the wage scales of the industry' would do much more to increase production than 'piecemeal "patching up" by individual or departmental incentives'.

There is no doubt that this question was a 'traditional grievance' among T.A. members, but it had lain practically dormant until after Harry Riding became General Secretary. He had brought it up in the wages negotiations in 1942 and now pressed it again. In the inter-war years after 1922 the T.A. had been mainly on the defensive, but now, with the existing labour shortage, it could take strong action to enforce its claims and get back parity.

In regard to the other proposals of the Employment and Production Committee, the E.C. were 'in favour of an extension of shift working', but considered that shift rates should be revised if the workers' co-operation was to be secured. In fact, they had been considering for some time an increase in the extras paid to double day and night shifts. The former, put on a percentage basis in 1944, were now regarded as insufficient, while the latter, the pre-war flat-rate extras, were quite inadequate proportionately to the increased basic wage rates and cost of living, and ought to be changed to improved percentage extras. Moreover, shift work hours should be reduced in view of the recent reduction in ordinary hours.

The question of shift working was taken up by the P. & K.T.F. and, after conferences of union representatives, a joint application was made to the B.F.M.P. in May 1947 for 33⅓ per cent. extra (double day shifts) and 50 per cent. extra (night shifts) above basic day rates, with a working week of 37½ hours in each case.

Shortly afterwards (June 1947), as the result of a T.A. proposal and a conference of union representatives, the P. & K.T.F. made a similar application to the Newspaper Society on behalf of the T.A. and four other unions with members in provincial daily newspaper offices. Morning and evening newspaper extras, being flat rates, had depreciated like those of jobbing night shifts, due to increases in basic wage rates and the cost of living. The unions therefore claimed the following increased percentage extras above weekly newspaper rates: 15 per cent. for evening and 33⅓ per cent. for morning news workers.

Meanwhile, resolutions were pouring in for the T.A. Delegate Meeting in June 1947. Many of these were concerned with wages: some for a general wage increase or for regrading, others sectional demands by jobbing compositors, machinemen, monotype-caster attendants, and readers, which had been relegated during the war. The General Secretary, however, persuaded the E.C. that, instead of dissipating energy in sectional movements, the Association should concentrate on regaining the 9s. lost in 1922, to get back 'parity' with the Stereotypers and restore the 2s. 6d. 'differential' between T.A. grade 1 and the L.S.C. minimum.

This wages policy—'nine bob or bust'—was accepted by the Delegate Meeting. The E.C. did not, it was stated, intend to break away from Federation movements—they would wish to participate in any general wages increase—but this 'parity' question was regarded as a peculiarly T.A. affair and they would therefore negotiate independently with the B.F.M.P. and Newspaper Society upon it. When, however, the N.U.P.B. & P.W. proposed a Federation movement for a general wages increase of £1 per week they decided not to participate, but to press on with their own application for a 9s. increase. Yet this question of 'parity' and 'differentials' really involved all the unions: how could the T.A. Executive secure the desired revision of 'the overall wage basis of the industry' by isolated action? It was, in fact, independent action by individual unions, especially the T.A., which had wrecked federated action in the post-1918 period and created the 'fundamental injustices in the wage scales of the industry' which the T.A. Executive now denounced.

During the war the unions had generally acted together in the Federation to get wage increases. But the old autonomous tendencies still persisted: London still retained its exclusiveness, Scotland its national and geographical differences, and the craft unions, while jealous of each other, were intent on preserving the differentials between skilled and unskilled. Flat-rate increases tended to reduce all proportionate differences and the craft unions therefore favoured independent action. Wages negotiations in the post-war years are riddled with the narrow selfishness and petty jealousies of the unions.

John Fletcher, the P. & K.T.F. Secretary, had put forward as part of the Post-War Reconstruction scheme a suggested 'Minimum Wages Pact', in which he urged that united action should be continued after the war in order to prevent a recurrence of the chaos of 1922, which had created all the present irregularities in the wages scales. Only by agreement and united action could they hope to remedy these evils and create a rational scale of minimum wage rates, having regard to skill, nature of the work, and geographical situation, with a final settlement of the grading problem. Other industries, building for example, already had such a scheme whereby minimum rates, 'though varying, are moved generally and not through sectional effort', while they themselves had for years adopted the principle in regard to hours and holidays.

This plan was rejected, however, mainly due to opposition from the craft unions. So, now, was the N.U.P.B. & P.W. proposal for a federated wages movement. During the summer of 1947, therefore, almost all the unions put in individual applications for wage increases, though in regard to shift work and daily newspaper wages, as we have seen, there was united action through the Federation.

The B.F.M.P. and Newspaper Society, confronted by these numerous and varying claims, drew up a joint statement which they sent on 14 October to all the unions concerned and the P. & K.T.F. They considered 'that it would be against the best interests of the industry, and against the national interest, to endeavour to deal separately with a long list of varying claims from individual unions, involving lengthy negotiations and the possibility of a series of sectional disputes which might disrupt the industry and interfere with the primary target which has been put before every industry by the Government—namely to increase production without increase in costs'. Furthermore, the unions were reminded of Government statements urging that wage claims should not be pressed in the present economic crisis, so as to check inflation and keep down export prices on which so much depended. The P. & K.T.F. was therefore invited to negotiate on behalf of all the unions.

The Federation Executive immediately asked the unions whether they should accept the invitation and 'meet the employers in a purely exploratory capacity'. Replies being favourable, the Executive agreed to a conference on 12 November, but 'only to hear what the employers have to say' and 'without prejudice to the existing claims of the Unions and the Federation'.

At this conference the employers put forward proposals for a 'general settlement' of the various union claims, very much along the lines of the T.A. application. They were 'prepared to close the gap between the compositor and the stereotyper in the provinces and in Scotland', so as to establish a uniform minimum rate for all craftsmen in each grade. This would mean 'a general uplift of about 9s. in the minimum basic rate for all craft sections [in the provinces] except the stereotypers and the Litho artists'. There would be difficulties in London, where there was less uniformity in craft rates, but these could be dealt with. Various machine extras, such as those for feeders, anti-setoff devices, &c., should now be abolished, since these attachments were no longer innovations, but everyday appliances.

The basic non-craft rate, it was suggested, should be 80 per cent. of the craft minimum, which would give increases varying from about 5s. 6d. to 6s. 6d. in different grades and categories.

As regards shift work, they were prepared to grant some increase in wage rates, but no reduction of hours. They would also put forward proposals on daily newspaper rates. Finally, they again pressed for a reduction in the period of apprenticeship on account of the new school-leaving age and National Service, and also for removal of the top limit on apprentice quotas.

The employers made these proposals on the understanding that they would lead to increased production, and they asked the unions to accept without delay the principle of 'payment by results'.

The unions were urged to settle their differences and work together for a general settlement. 'We must', the employers' chairman, J. Hubbard, declared, 'sooner or later get an understanding between the two sides which will provide a solid basis for wages negotiations, taking into account the variety of occupations and the differing degrees of skill which are to be found in an industry like ours.'

The T.A. naturally accepted the employers' proposals as a basis for further negotiation and settlement, but they were rejected by all the other unions, and the P. & K.T.F. therefore informed the employers that they could not enter on joint negotiations. The employers thus had no alternative but to meet the unions separately, though they refused to negotiate with those taking aggressive action to enforce their claims. (The S.T.A. and L.S.C. had imposed overtime bans and the latter was also threatening strike action.)

The T.A. Executive met the employers on 9 December, when an agreement was reached within the framework of the employers' proposed 'wages structure' for the whole industry. Thus the Association got the desired 9s. increase, giving them 'parity' with the Stereotypers and the old 2s. 6d. 'differential' between grade 1 and London. In return they accepted the employers' apprentice proposals[1] and agreed to the establishment of a joint committee 'to formulate a scheme for the introduction of incentive payments in T.A. departments', in view of Government statements on the need for increased production, the Court of Inquiry's Report, and the introduction of such schemes in other major industries.

This agreement was ratified by the members and came into force in the week commencing 19 January 1948. Obviously, however, its stability would depend on the employers getting their proposed 'wages structure' accepted by the other unions, which was not at all likely. The T.A. had clearly pointed out that the newly restored 'parity' and 'differentials' must be maintained, so that if, for example, the Stereotypers or L.S.C. got an increase, the T.A. would want the same.

The employers were by this time involved in a serious dispute with the L.S.C., who threatened to strike for a 22s. increase. The dispute was eventually referred by the Minister of Labour to the National Arbitration Tribunal, which awarded an increase of 15s. (14 January 1948), chiefly on the ground that 'in recent years the traditional differential between the rates paid to compositors in London and in the Provinces, respectively, as expressed in terms of a percentage has progressively declined'.

This award ignored the fact that the original 'differential' established in 1918 was only 2s. 6d. and that the increase to 11s. 6d. in 1922 had always been regarded by the T.A. as an injustice. It was hardly likely to be accepted by T.A. members as establishing a 'traditional differential' between London and the provinces. There was, in fact, a strong demand for one 'rate for the job', regardless of geographical differences.

There was also deadlock between the employers and the Lithographic Printers. A special J.I.C. meeting therefore recommended that

[1] See below, pp. 457-8.

another attempt should be made to negotiate a general wages settlement at a conference in London on 27 January.

Both sides accepted this recommendation. At the conference the employers put forward proposals for a general wages settlement broadly on the basis of a 15s. increase for craftsmen in London, according to the L.S.C.'s recent N.A.T. award, and 9s. in the provinces, except to Stereotypers, as in the T.A. settlement, with proportionate increases for non-craft workers. The idea was to secure uniformity in the wage rates of both craft and non-craft workers in London and the provinces.

The unions put forward counter proposals for the establishment of uniform minimum rates for craftsmen of £7 in London and £6. 10s. (grade 1) in the provinces, the L.S.C. agreeing to waive their claim to the 17s. 6d. differential established by the N.A.T. award; stereotypers in provincial newspaper offices to get the Linotype rate; the existing monetary differentials between craft and non-craft wages to be maintained. These proposals would mean an increase of 22s. 6d. to many of the craft workers in London and an overall increase of 16s. 6d. (less 9s. in the case of the Stereotypers and T.A.) to provincial craftsmen. There was little likelihood, therefore, the employers' chairman stated, of their being accepted.

The conference was adjourned for a week so that the employers might consider the unions' counter proposals. When it was resumed on 4 February there was an adjournment until the evening, in view of the Government's White Paper, the *Statement on Personal Incomes, Costs and Prices* (Cmd. 7321), being introduced in Parliament that afternoon. When the conference reassembled the unions pressed for immediate resumption of negotiations, but eventually agreed to the Ministry of Labour being consulted as to whether or not the White Paper would apply to the proposed wages increase. An interview next morning, however, failed to produce much satisfaction.

When negotiations were resumed in the afternoon the employers would not go beyond their previous proposals, except for minor amendments. These, however, were unacceptable to most of the unions and the attempt to form a 'wages structure' for the industry, therefore, again broke down.

It was now left for individual union executives to decide their own action. The Litho. Printers' dispute was referred by the Minister of Labour to the N.A.T., while agreements were negotiated between the employers and the other unions, the Stereotypers getting an increase of 8s. 6d. in grade 1, with 8s., 7s. 6d., and 7s. in grades 2, 3, and 4 respectively.

Thus the T.A. had quickly lost their recently restored parity with the Stereotypers, while the differential between London and the provinces had been increased to 17s. 6d. The Association had, however, made it quite clear in their original claim that their demand was for 'parity with the best' and abolition of the injustices of the 1922 wages revisions. Now, therefore, in April 1948, they reiterated this demand, claiming the same increases as the Stereotypers had just secured.

Wages parity was put at the very forefront of Association policy. There is little evidence of any regard by the E.C. for the Labour Government's White Paper on Personal Incomes, endorsed by the T.U.C. As the B.F.M.P. *Members' Circular* remarked, 'this does not appear to count for anything on the union side, and the Government's efforts to impress on the man in the street that there is an economic crisis seem to have failed completely'. The T.A. justified its action by the argument that the parity claim had been put in long before the White Paper came out and was intended to remedy a grievance twenty-five years old. Moreover, several wages settlements, including the Stereotypers', had been made after publication of the White Paper. Furthermore, while the Government was exhorting wages stabilization, it seemed to be doing little to restrict profits and prices.

That wages mattered far more to the Association than increased production is again obvious from the response in April 1948 to a Ministry of Labour proposed scheme for training able-bodied (in addition to disabled) adults for the industry, in view of the serious labour shortage. The E.C., fearing future unemployment, rejected the proposal, considering that 'the problem could be solved only by satisfactory adjustment of wages forthwith', on the grounds that this would remove dissatisfaction, improve output, and attract recruits to the industry. They also decided in June that 'unless the T.A. received wage parity there would be no incentive scheme or apprentice adjustment allowed', the agreement of January 1948 being conditional upon that.

An Incentives Committee had already been appointed to collaborate with the employers in working out a scheme, but its report was dominated by the old fears of unemployment, 'racing', 'task-work', and over-specialization. Piece-work was still opposed as being 'cut-throat', and bonus payments, it was considered, should be on a 'pooled', not an individual, basis. There must be no reduction of staff as a result of an incentive scheme; no such scheme should be introduced while unemployed labour was available, and as soon as unemployment appeared incentive schemes should be revised or scrapped. The old dislike of output measurement remained very strong and 'time and motion study' was regarded with suspicion. Moreover, it was felt that quality ought not to be sacrificed to quantity. The main concern, in fact, of the Committee was not to increase production but to devise safeguards.

The T.A. case for wages parity with the Stereotypers was presented at a conference with the employers on 14 June. The employers gave their reply at a further conference on 27 July. They could not grant any increase. Costs of production, they insisted, must be kept down, not only as a duty to the nation, in response to the Government's White Paper, but also in the interests of both sides of the printing industry itself. The sellers' market was changing and customers were refusing to pay ever-increasing prices. Any further increase in costs would stimulate the development, already serious, of office printing machinery. Increased wages could not, as the T.A. claimed, be paid out of profits without raising prices: T.A. figures of profits were very misleading, the firms chosen not being representative and no account being taken of taxation, depreciation, re-equipment, &c.; employers were also having to face increasing costs of paper and other materials. The employers strongly favoured payment by results, which would increase production and earnings without increasing costs and prices. If the T.A. claims were granted it would result in a spate of claims from other unions and the industry would be in turmoil again. The T.A. had agreed, in the unions' proposed wages structure of 27 January, to the Stereotypers being paid the Linotype rate, and this was the basis of their recent increase. It was pointed out that 'any question of adjustment of wage structure or clearing up of anomalies between unions cannot be settled in discussion with one union alone. There can only be a co-ordinated approach to such problems.' The unions were to blame for the breakdown of attempts to form a wages structure for the industry.

In reply Harry Riding expressed the T.A.'s disappointment and determination to secure parity. Unless this was granted they would refuse to operate the January agreement in regard to incentive schemes and apprentices; they considered basic rates 'far more important than bonus payments'. The T.A.'s acceptance of the Linotype rate for stereotypers had been conditional on the employers agreeing to the unions' proposed wages structure; in rejecting it the employers were responsible for the present situation. It was also pointed out that each union had autonomy in wages matters. Rejection of the T.A. claim would create a dangerous possibility of dispute. There was strong dissatisfaction among the union members and the E.C. would have to consider 'strong action'; they could cause considerable trouble without overstepping the Conditions of Employment Order. They were, in fact, determined to 'fight this out'.

The conference having ended in deadlock, the T.A. Executive decided on 18 August to give notice of termination of the clauses concerning payment by results and apprentice ratios in the agreement of January 1948 and also of the jobbing night and double day staffs sections of the National Agreement.[1] These were the first steps in a policy of pressure by 'withdrawal of co-operation' without creating a dispute, thus avoiding reference to the National Arbitration Tribunal under the Conditions of Employment and National Arbitration Order, S.R. & O. No. 1305 (1940). Moreover, the Executive wished to avoid a repetition of the disastrous 1922 national strike.

The employers quickly protested against such unilateral termination of sections in the National Agreement, pointing out that the proper procedure was to ask for a meeting of the Joint Labour Committee. To this the T.A. agreed, but a conference on 31 August merely confirmed the existing deadlock, which the employers therefore referred to a Conciliation Committee of the J.I.C. This met on 14 September and decided that as the dispute arose out of the general wages structure and might involve the whole industry it should be brought before the full J.I.C. at its meeting on 13 October.

At this meeting the B.F.M.P. President again urged the necessity for a wages structure covering the whole industry. Separate negotiations with individual unions led to constant friction and strife, a 'vicious circle' of 'leap-frogging' wages movements. The only sensible way out was a co-ordinated wages structure. It was therefore suggested that both sides should get together, perhaps informally, to discuss the matter.

Many of the unions, however, especially the London ones and the Stereotypers, which were comparatively well off and unlikely to get much out of a wages structure, still clung to their autonomy; petty jealousies and narrow selfishness still prevailed. Nevertheless, it was decided that 'the advisability and practicability of a wages structure' should be referred to both sides of the industry.

Meanwhile, negotiations with the Newspaper Society in regard to

---

[1] The wages and hours of jobbing night and double day shifts, it will be remembered, had been the subject of a P. & K.T.F. application to the employers (see above, p. 436). After prolonged negotiations, however, the Federation had failed to secure satisfactory terms and the matter was now, therefore, left to the individual unions.

increased extras on provincial daily newspapers had also reached dead-lock.[1] The employers had agreed, after long delay, to a conference on 29 June, when they offered 3s. per week extra to evening news and 9s. to morning news hands, but with conditions objectionable to the unions. Another conference on 30 August failed to produce a settlement, but eventually, after reference to a J.I.C. Conciliation Committee, the Newspaper Society withdrew their conditions and an agreement was concluded on 15 November. The basic rates on provincial daily news-papers were now as follows: evening newspaper rates, 7s. 6d. in grades 3 and 4, 8s. 6d. in grade 2, and 9s. 6d. in grade 1—morning newspapers 23s. in grades 3 and 4, 24s. in grade 2, and 25s. in grade 1—above the minimum grade rate.

The question of a wages structure was now, once again, being con-sidered by both sides of the industry. The T.A. Executive, though 'resentful of the interminable delay in reaching finality on our claim', was in favour of a wages structure, 'providing this will "level out" the anomalies at present obtaining'. A conference of union executives on 15 November was unanimous on the 'desirability' of a wages structure, but dubious as to its 'practicability', and therefore decided that a special committee should investigate the practical problems involved. Its report, presented to a further conference of union executives on 15 December, contained concrete proposals for a wages structure, with basic rates for craft, non-craft, and women's sections in both London and the provinces.[2] A letter from the B.F.M.P. was also submitted to the conference, repeating the proposal for an informal meeting in regard to a wages structure, but stressing the need for increased production and payment by results to offset any wage increases and prevent price rises.

The unions decided to accept the employers' invitation to an informal talk, but only provided it was 'purely exploratory' and did not commit any union to the policy of a wages structure. Union differences re-mained unsolved: the main obstacle was the autonomous attitude of the London craft unions and the Stereotypers, who were chiefly con-cerned to maintain their craft status and differentials, which they feared would be endangered in an industrial wages structure, since they would

---

[1] These, it will be remembered, were being conducted by the P. & K.T.F. See above, p. 436.

[2] *Craft rates*: provinces, £6. 15s.; London, £7. 5s. (7½% above provinces). *Non-craft rates*: provinces, Class 1 (90% of craft rate), £6. 1s. 6d., Class 2 (85% of craft rate), £5. 14s. 6d.; London, Class 1, £6. 10s. 6d., Class 2, £6. 3s. *Women* (75% of craft rate): provinces, £5. 1s.; London, £5. 9s. These proposals would mean abolition of grading in the provinces.

be outvoted by the larger unions—the T.A., N.S.O.P. & A., and N.U.P.B. & P.W.—of which the two latter were non-craft. Controversy therefore centred round the system of Federation voting, on which a special committee was appointed.

Little headway was made at the informal meeting with the employers on 4 January 1949, the two sides arguing over incentives and increased production, grading, differentials, extras, &c. It was eventually suggested that a small joint committee should be set up to formulate a scheme.

The union executives met again on 27 January, but could not agree on what steps to take. Several unions were obviously not enamoured of a wages structure. Neither had the voting question been settled. The whole problem was therefore referred back to the union executives for further consideration, but their replies were so various and conflicting that the Federation Executive decided on 28 February that it was 'unable to proceed with the movement for a wages structure for the industry'.

This meant a return to the *status quo*, to the position in the previous September, when the dispute over the T.A.'s parity claim had been referred to the J.I.C. The result was an immediate joint approach to the employers by the T.A., Lithos., N.S.O.P. & A., and N.U.P.B. & P.W.—comprising between them over three-quarters of the total P. & K.T.F. membership—all of which were suffering from similar grievances in regard to 'parity' and 'differentials' arising out of the wages reductions in 1922. They informed the employers of the great urgency of the matter and the danger of revolt among union members owing to the interminable delay.

A final effort by the employers to secure a general settlement at a special J.I.C. meeting on 5 April having proved abortive, a conference was held on 12 April between representatives of the B.F.M.P. and Newspaper Society and the four unions. The latter expressed their determination to secure a speedy remedy of their 'invidious relative position'. They regretted the failure of attempts to form an industrial wages structure, but pointed out that 'if agreement is reached with the four unions here today (who are representing over three-quarters of the workers employed in the industry) it should not be difficult for you, in later negotiations . . . with other Unions, to fit them into the scheme'. They therefore submitted proposals for a wages structure practically the same as those drawn up by the special P. & K.T.F. committee in December 1948, with basic rates for craft, non-craft, and women workers in London and the provinces and abolition of grading, which was now out of date and 'riddled with anomalies'. If the employers would not accept this proposed wages structure, then the unions would revert to the demand for parity. A demand was also made for a jobbing night rate 50 per cent. and double-day rate 33⅓ per cent. above the day rate, for a week of 37½ hours in each case. Unless, it was pointed out, wages were improved considerably the industry would fail to attract recruits and the existing labour shortage would grow more serious. Before the war printing had comfortably headed the Ministry of Labour's list of industrial wage rates, but this was no longer so, and workers were therefore leaving printing for other trades. The unions' most powerful argument, however, was the growing dissatisfaction of their members and the threat of disputes. Their patience was practically exhausted and if satisfaction was not speedily secured they would have to consider strong action.

It was not, however, until 5 July that the employers gave their reply. Though they could not accept the unions' proposals, they agreed with them on the necessity of a wages structure, with adjustments in basic rates to remove anomalies. But this, they insisted, must be accepted by *all* the unions in the industry (to each of whom copies of the employers' new proposals had been sent), otherwise it would not be feasible. The employers could not agree to the elimination of provincial grading, though they were prepared to reduce the number of grades from four to three. They adhered firmly to the principles of the Government's White Paper of February 1948. It was necessary, if wages were to be raised, to increase production so as to keep down costs and prices; yet the unions had done little or nothing to implement the recommendations of the Court of Inquiry in September 1946 regarding recruitment, apprentice ratios, shift-work, and payment by results. They had been almost completely preoccupied with wages, without regard to increasing efficiency and lowering costs—'those very things which would justify and make possible the adjustments in basic rates and increased earnings which your members desire'. The employers expected that, if their offer was accepted, the unions would agree to a speedy settlement on these points and removal of 'restrictive practices'.

The employers' proposals were, briefly, as follows: the craft rate was to be raised to £7. 2s. 6d. in London, except for binders and cutters (£6. 14s. 6d.), and to £6. 11s. (grade 1), £6. 5s. 6d. (grade 2), and £6. 2s. (grade 3) in the provinces, thus restoring the differential between London and the provincial grade 1 to 11s. 6d. and reducing provincial grades to three. Similar proposals were made regarding non-craft rates, ranging from £5. 17s. in London to £4. 18s. 6d. in provincial grade 3, and also for women workers.

These proposals had several serious objections from the union point of view. Not only were the increases less than had been asked for, but 'extras' were to be reduced and grading was to be maintained; and though the number of grades was reduced to three, the gap between top and bottom was increased from 7s. 6d. to 9s.[1] The unions also disliked linking wage increases with increased production, incentives, and additional recruitment, since employers were already making increased profits and there was no guarantee of full employment being maintained. Finally, the proposals were made conditional on acceptance by all the unions in the P. & K.T.F., though this was most unlikely in view of their recent differences. The Litho. Printers, in fact, considered the proposals quite unacceptable and decided to withdraw from the joint negotiations.

The other three unions met the employers again on 4 August, when Harry Riding presented their objections. The employers, however, still insisted on all unions coming into the wages structure. To make an agreement with the three unions would lead at once to demands from the others, and so the old vicious circle would go on. They must settle things now, by a conference with all the unions, or, failing agreement, by Ministry of Labour inquiry or arbitration. The unions, on the other hand, stated that they could delay no longer, as the members were on the point of revolt. All hope of a wages structure would end in chaos unless they soon got something. The employers should make an agreement with them—representing as they did three-quarters of the industry—and then present it to the other unions; if these were dissatisfied they could be forced into the N.A.T. The employers would have 'to decide who they wanted to have trouble with'.

The conference proved inconclusive. The employers wished to wait until they had answers from the other unions; they still hoped that a wages structure could be negotiated by 'co-ordinated discussion on the whole subject'. T.A. patience, however, was now exhausted: for two years they had been trying to get parity with the Stereotypers, but were no nearer. A special E.C. meeting on 11 August therefore decided that, as 'normal methods of industrial negotiation' were getting them no-where, they would have to put stronger pressure on the employers. They did not, however, want a national strike like that in 1922, nor reference to the N.A.T., whose decision would be determined by the Government's

[1] The Litho. Printers already had three grades, with an overall difference of only 5s.

White Paper. To avoid an actual 'dispute', therefore, under the meaning of Order No. 1305, the following proposals were adopted: (1) Negotiations with the employers to be terminated unless the claim for parity with the Stereotypers was conceded by 10 September. (2) Abrogation of the National Wage Basis Agreement and War Agreement No. 3A (relaxation of rules and dilutees). (3) Withdrawal from the J.I.C. (4) Encouragement to branches to take local action, short of striking, to force employers individually to meet their demands. Chapels could 'withdraw co-operation and goodwill' by, for example, refusing to work shifts or overtime, by 'going slow', or even refusing to work for less than the desired rates. The prevailing labour shortage would enable great pressure to be exerted in this way. What was proposed, in fact, was a return to pre-1919 conditions of guerrilla warfare by branches and chapels.

These proposals were put to ballot vote of the members. Meanwhile, the B.F.M.P. and Newspaper Society, having received replies from the other unions on their proposals for a wages structure, requested a meeting with officials of all the federated unions on 29 August. The unions agreed, but the conference proved completely abortive. The employers' proposals for a wages structure were unacceptable and the unions refused to give up their autonomy on wages matters.

The B.F.M.P. and Newspaper Society immediately, therefore, reported the deadlock and 'apprehended dispute' to the Ministry of Labour, requesting action to prevent dislocation of the industry and assistance in solving the dispute. At the same time they urged their members to stand firm against aggressive local action by the T.A., on the principle of refusing to negotiate under duress.

During the next few days Sir Robert Gould and other Ministry officials made repeated efforts to solve the dispute by bringing the two sides together. Harry Riding refused, however, to participate in further negotiations unless the employers made a 'firm offer' and unless representatives of the N.S.O.P. & A. and N.U.P.B. & P.W. were also invited. He maintained that there was no dispute under the terms of Order No. 1305: the T.A. was merely balloting on the proposed termination of national in favour of local wages negotiations, a return to pre-1919 conditions. The employers, on the other hand, regarded the T.A. ballot and the proposed coercive measures as 'duress' and as threatening, in actual fact, a national dispute; the T.A. was merely trying to disguise this so as to avoid reference to the N.A.T. and to force employers to concede their terms.

No progress was made towards settlement by 10 September. The T.A. ballot resulted in an overwhelming majority in favour of the E.C. proposals and so on 12 September the Association formally withdrew its wage claim and gave a fortnight's notice of termination of the national agreements.

The employers refused to accept a fortnight's notice as 'valid termination' of the national agreements and sought an interim injunction 'to restrain the Typographical Association and its members from acting as though valid notice had been given'. This, however, was refused by Mr. Justice Devlin in the Vacation Court on 21 September.

On the same day the Ministry of Labour announced that the T.A.'s action in terminating its national agreements could not be interpreted as a trade dispute under the terms of Order No. 1305, in view of its wage claim having first been withdrawn. But great care had to be exercised by branches, chapels, and members to avoid local disputes and reference to the N.A.T. Numerous cases of local aggressive action were reported by employers to the Ministry and in many the T.A. had to withdraw the action complained of. The only legal way of evading the Order was by individuals handing in notice, without stating any reason.

The fortnight's notice terminating the national agreements ended on 26 September and wages negotiations reverted to branches and chapels. On 29 September, however, the Ministry of Labour Conciliation Officers at last succeeded in getting officials of the two sides to an informal meeting, when a formula of settlement was agreed on. The T.A. officers therefore sent telegrams to all branches the following morning, instructing them to suspend all aggressive action and resume normal working conditions, as negotiations were to be resumed at national level.

The T.A. Executive met the Joint Labour Committee of the B.F.M.P. and Newspaper Society on 4 and 5 October, when a new National Wage Basis Agreement was drafted. The greatest differences were in regard to grading, which the employers wished to retain and the T.A. to abolish. The T.A. emphasized that rationing and price control had practically evened out the cost of living over the whole country; but the employers, while opposing the T.A. contention, insisted that other factors—such as a town's importance as a printing centre and the effect on smaller towns of competition from the big cities—must also be considered. The T.A. eventually agreed to four grades, but with a considerable amount of up-grading. Most of the large towns formerly in grade 2 were raised to grade 1, all branches in grade 3 were brought into grade 2, while many previously in grade 4 were raised to grade 3.

Moreover, the whole question of grading anomalies was to be investigated by a joint committee.

The new grades were the same as those proposed by the employers to the four unions on 5 July, with the insertion of an additional grade: grade 1, £6. 11s.; grade 2, £6 5s. 6d.; grade 3, £6. 3s. 6d.; grade 4, £6. 2s.

The new hourly rate for jobbing night shifts would be 25 per cent. above the basic day hourly rate, for a week of 41 hours;[1] double day shifts, 20 per cent. for a 42-hour week.

The 'extras' for machine compositors and machine minders were reduced in accordance with the employers' recent wage structure proposals. Linotype and Monotype operators would now get only 5s. above the appropriate case rates, jobbing and weekly news, evening and morning news. Machine extras were also considerably reduced. As regards platens and flat-bed cylinder machines, the old class 2 (3s. extra) was merged into class 1 (minimum rate), so that class 3 (6s. extra) now became class 2 (5s. extra) and class 4 (10s. extra) became class 3 (7s. 6d. extra), while the extras on tandem Miehles and Cossars were reduced by 2s. 6d. and 3s. respectively. The extras for rotaries used on jobbing, book-work, weekly periodicals, and high-class magazines were cut by 4s. 6d., on weekly news rotaries by 5s. Other machine extras (for feeders, sprayers, &c.), however, remained unchanged.

These reductions in 'extras' were, of course, part of the concessions which the Association had to make to secure the desired increases in basic rates. This was in accord with the wages policy of the 1947 Delegate Meeting, which had endorsed the General Secretary's opinion that 'in the past far too much energy . . . has been dissipated in seeking sectional advantages for one part of the membership or the other', instead of going in for general increases. It went a good way towards satisfying the long-standing grievance of the jobbing compositors in regard to their inferior wage position.

Other concessions had also to be made. Not only did the Association concede a 'bonus' of 200 apprentices,[2] but also agreed 'to co-operate in taking all practicable steps which make for greater productive efficiency', such as introducing schemes of 'payment by results', including both individual and group bonus methods. A special joint committee on incentive schemes was to be set up and joint consultative committees

---

[1] This would apply to *all* night shifts, temporary and permanent.
[2] Apprentices were also allowed to work composing machines after two instead of three years.

were recommended in offices where such schemes were introduced. It was also agreed that 'the working of reasonable overtime as occasion arises is . . . a necessity to meet the production requirements of the industry', and War Agreement No. 3A was restored. (This, being temporary, with provision for withdrawal of dilutees in the event of slump, was regarded as preferable to a permanent increase in the apprentice ratio, which the employers had asked for.) Finally, the employers insisted on a clause in the new Agreement providing for six months' notice of its abrogation.

This agreement was accepted in a ballot vote of the membership by 21,283 votes against 10,859 and was signed on 7 November 1949. Obviously there was a good deal of dissatisfaction with it. Most of this, no doubt, came from operators and machine minders strongly opposed to cuts in their 'extras'. The actual increases gained were regarded by many as miserably inadequate after such long-drawn-out agitation and in view of the rise in the cost of living. Many members were also greatly dissatisfied at maintenance of the grading system, particularly as the differential between top and bottom had been increased from 7s. 6d. to 9s. Moreover, although the long-sought parity had finally been secured, how long would it last? The London craft unions and the Stereotypers would inevitably put in for increases to maintain their differential advantages and thus 'leap-frogging' wages movements would go on— though the employers had got a clause in the new Agreement that 'the rates of wages paid to any other Union shall not be the basis of a claim for a wage adjustment'. The question of a wages structure for the whole industry was bound, therefore, to be raised again. It also remained to be seen how T.A. members would react to incentive schemes for increasing production, so 'clearly a departure from traditional Association policy'.[1]

Negotiations with the Newspaper Society

Since the end of the war the T.A. has had separate conferences with the Newspaper Society to deal with purely newspaper questions. Agreements have been reached regarding the 'long day' or 'late night' in weekly newspaper offices, extra remuneration for members employed in offices publishing four or more separate weekly newspapers, and stop-press printing on Bush machines. But the Association has been unable to stop jobbing work in daily newspaper offices or the transfer of matrices and stereos.

[1] *Typographical Circular*, Dec. 1949.

Manchester Daily Newspapers

The London 'national' dailies published in Manchester—the *Daily Express, Daily Mail, News Chronicle,* and *Daily Herald*—and the Sunday newspapers printed in the same offices did not, as we have seen, belong to the Newspaper Society, but were organized separately in the London Newspapers' Provincial Association or, as it became in the post-war period, the Newspaper Proprietors' Association (Northern Group). Kemsley Newspapers and the *Manchester Guardian* were members of the Newspaper Society, but also had 'house' agreements giving substantial extras.

In 1944 the L.N.P.A. had succeeded in negotiating an agreement with the T.A. for all their Manchester offices.[1] Towards the end of 1945, however, as a result of the 8s. 6d. Newspaper Society increase, the L.N.P.A. offices began to agitate not only for a similar rise, but also for a 5-night week and fortnight's annual holiday with pay. The P. & K.T.F. tried to secure joint action by all the unions concerned, both in London and Manchester, but the T.A. chapels refused to participate. The L.N.P.A. granted the wage increase and fortnight's holiday in return for P. & K.T.F. co-operation in the establishment of joint conciliation machinery (to prevent sudden stoppages) covering all affiliated unions. Efforts by both the P. & K.T.F. and L.N.P.A. failed, however, to bring in the T.A. chapels; the most that could be secured was an assurance from the E.C. against extreme action by the Manchester news section.

The T.A. chapels also refused to join in a further P. & K.T.F. application for a 5-night week in both London and Manchester daily newspaper offices. The L.N.P.A. pointed out in vain 'that the broad principles of any post-war adjustments of agreements cannot be expeditiously and satisfactorily dealt with by negotiations with individual unions and cannot be considered except in relation to all the employees in national newspaper offices', and that 'therefore the best course . . . is that matters of common interest should be dealt with in conference with the P. & K.T.F.'. The T.A. chapels clung jealously to their independence.

The L.N.P.A. also tried in vain to get Kemsley Newspapers into a five-office agreement. The Kemsley management was willing, but the T.A. Kemsley chapels refused, as their independence enabled them to secure the cumulative advantages of Newspaper Society, L.N.P.A., and 'house' agreements.

The outcome was a separate T.A. agreement for L.N.P.A. offices,

[1] See above, p. 422.

fitting, however, into a general wages structure negotiated with the other unions. This, the Memorandum of Principles (Wages and Hours Agreement) of January 1947, gave to all T.A. members concerned (rotary machine minders, Linotype operators, stone hands and makers-up, Ludlow operators, case hands, and readers) a minimum wage of £8. 0s. 6d. for a 5-night (or day) working week (37½ hours night, 40 hours day). Men working Saturday night on Sunday papers would get in addition £3. 8s. 3d. (composing department) and £4. 18s. 7d. (machine department), with a night out during the week, for which one-fifth of the weekly wage would be deducted. Most of the special extras were also increased.

This agreement was only in broad outline; a full agreement on all the details of working conditions was to be negotiated later. Negotiations went on throughout 1947 and a draft agreement was ready for signature when (March–April 1948) trouble broke out over a wages claim of £1 per week by T.A. members in L.N.P.A. offices, following the 9s. increase conceded by the B.F.M.P. and Newspaper Society. In support of this claim it was pointed out that L.N.P.A. members had received an increase of only 33⅓ per cent. on pre-war wages, compared with 58 per cent. (grade 1) in the general trade, and that their rates, which before the war were the highest in Manchester news offices, were now less than those of Kemsley Newspapers and the *Guardian*. Moreover, the cost of living had increased by 6 per cent. since the agreement of January 1947.

The N.P.A., however, rejected this claim outright. They refused to be influenced by Newspaper Society agreements or to upset their general wages structure. They objected to having Kemsley's and the *Guardian* played off against them. They also rejected the principle of maintaining percentage 'differentials', as this would make their rates disproportionately high; other daily newspapers were gradually coming up to their standards. Neither would they accept the principle of basing wage increases too closely on the cost of living, but wanted some stabilization. Finally, they were suffering from increased costs of newsprint, transport, &c.

The outcome, after several months' fruitless negotiation, was a refusal by T.A. chapels to work Saturday nights on Sunday papers, the aim being to force the N.P.A. into concessions without a full-scale strike and reference to the National Arbitration Tribunal. The employers, however, regarded this as terminating the whole contract, for daily as well as Sunday newspapers, and a stoppage of the Manchester national newspapers ensued on 31 July. 'The Associations' most belligerent section had clashed with the employers' strongest section.'

The N.P.A. refused to negotiate under duress and referred the dispute to the Minister of Labour. Ministry officials at once tried to mediate, but the stoppage was not ended until 12 August. Lengthy negotiations followed until an agreement was signed in January 1949.[1] As a result the minimum weekly wage of T.A. members in N.P.A. Manchester offices was raised to £8. 8s., with £4. 0s. 9d. (composing) and £5. 13s. 9d. (machine) for Saturday night, a total increase, allowing for the deduction for the night out, of 15s. 3d. (compositors) and 18s. 3d. (rotary minders) per week.

The N.P.A. had again tried to get Kemsley's into the agreement, but the chapels refused. The Kemsley management therefore withdrew from the Newspaper Society and terminated their 'house' agreement, with the intention of equalizing their rates with those of the N.P.A. The *Manchester Guardian* also refused to pay more than the N.P.A. Thus there would be uniform wage rates for all Manchester daily newspapers.

Ireland

The war-time division of T.A. affairs in Ireland, corresponding with the political split, has continued in the post-war period. Wages and hours in Northern Ireland have remained closely related to those in England: a wage increase of 8s. 6d. per week was secured in January 1946; another 10s. in November 1946, together with a fortnight's annual paid holiday and 5-day working week (43½ hours, later reduced to 42½, an hour less than in England); another 9s. in January 1948; and negotiations are now (December 1949) again in progress for the same increase as that recently secured in England.

T.A. members in Eire were the first to get a fortnight's annual holiday with pay, by an agreement with the I.M.P.A. in October 1945. A further 4s. was also secured early in 1946 by a 'Bonus Order' under the Government's Emergency Powers (No. 260) Order restricting wage increases. This war-time 'Standstill Order' was revoked in September of that year after the passing of the Eire Industrial Relations Act. This left the unions free to bargain with the employers for wage increases, but established a Labour Court in which agreements could be registered and to which threatened strikes or lock-outs could be referred. Registration would secure legal enforcement of wages agreements, but would restrict trade-union action since application for wage increases would have to be made to and be approved by the Labour Court. The T.A. therefore decided against it in order to recover independence in wages movements.

---

[1] This was again part of a general settlement with all the unions, though the T.A. still negotiated independently.

The Association soon made up the leeway resulting from the war-time wages restriction, getting an increase of £1 per week in December 1946, together with a 5-day week as in Northern Ireland, and another 12s. 6d. in November 1947. Wages were then stabilized until the end of July 1948 and the T.A. agreed to discuss a proposed sliding scale of wages based on the cost of living. The employers' proposals were rejected, however, in the ensuing conference (December 1947).

The Government was now threatening another 'Standstill Order' unless the unions exercised restraint in wages claims. The Irish T.U.C. accepted the principle of restricting wage increases to a percentage of pre-war rates, according to the cost of living, but the T.A. decided to contract out of the T.U.C. proposals in order to preserve its freedom of action. The Association has refrained, however, from further wage claims until recent months. Negotiations are now in progress (December 1949) not only for another increase in view of the rise in the cost of living and increases in other trades, but also for a reduction in the number of grades, of which there are still five in Eire as compared with three in Northern Ireland. The ideal aimed at, as in England, is for the complete abolition of grading and one basic rate for all T.A. members.

The political division between Northern Ireland and Eire has not caused a complete split in Irish trade-union affairs. The T.A. still covers the whole country and still holds its All-Ireland Conference. The employers' organization, the I.M.P.A., also covers the whole island. Though negotiations on wages and hours have been separate for north and south, on certain questions agreements have been reached for the whole country, on apprentices' wage rates, for example, and the late night in weekly newspaper offices. The Ireland Act of 1949, whereby Eire ceased all allegiance to the British Crown and became completely independent, has not so far caused any change in the T.A.'s position in Ireland.

Machine Questions

As soon as the war ended the E.C. again took up the question of re-classification of machines and rates. But these and other sectional matters were dropped in 1947 as a result of the decision to press first and foremost for general wages parity with the Stereotypers. The eventual result, in fact, of this wages policy was a reduction, instead of an increase, in machine 'extras'.[1] Moreover, War Agreement No. 3A still remains in force, permitting relaxation of the manning regulations.

[1] See above, p. 450.

Rapid developments in printing machinery, however, have called for special attention by the E.C. The 1938 Photogravure Agreement soon became out-of-date and the 1947 Delegate Meeting instructed the E.C. to secure its revision, especially in regard to manning and the duties of minders. A Photogravure Investigation Committee has therefore been appointed, with power to co-opt expert minders, and has formulated detailed proposals for presentation to the employers.

Aniline printing has developed enormously in the production of paper and cellophane bags, wrappers, &c., some machines printing up to eight colours. The T.A. has made vigorous attempts in the post-war period to organize aniline printers. Like the early letterpress machine minders, most of the men on this work have been recruited from outside the industry and have served no proper apprenticeship to printing. The E.C. have had to admit them in order to assert control over this department, but the ultimate aim is to train apprentices in aniline printing. They have also been trying to negotiate agreements with the chief firms on wage rates and manning, with hopes eventually of a national agreement. Matters have been complicated, however, by the fact that bag-making comes under a Trade Board Wages Council and by the rival claims of the N.U.P.B. & P.W. and N.S.O.P. & A.

One of the greatest problems facing printing firms and trade unions in the post-war period has been the increasing introduction of 'office printing machines'. Large private firms, banks, insurance companies, and town corporations, faced by the high cost and delays of printing, have installed Gammeter Multigraph, Multilith, Rotaprint, and other 'office machines', which are capable of producing even high-quality multi-colour work.

It is proving extremely difficult to secure control over these machines. There are no accurate statistics as to how many firms and corporations have installed them, and they are often worked by girls, or by men who may belong to non-printing unions such as N.A.L.G.O. or the Municipal and General Workers. The problem has been before the P. & K.T.F. and J.I.C., but without much progress being made, and the T.A. Executive have therefore decided to admit male operators, with the idea of creating a separate section.

It is in the machine department that the most revolutionary developments have occurred in the past forty years. There are, however, possibilities of even more revolutionary changes in the composing room in the near future, with the development of teletype-setting and photo-composition. A considerable amount of technical research has been devoted to these in the post-war period, and though not yet of very great practical importance, they are regarded by the T.A. with not a little trepidation.

Apprentices

Apprenticeship has been considerably affected in the post-war period by the raising of the school-leaving age to fifteen and by National Service. The T.A. had already, as long ago as 1908, sanctioned a shorter period of apprenticeship for boys staying at school after the age of fourteen up to 'sixteen plus'. Further provision had now to be made for National Service.

War Agreement No. 5, negotiated by the P. & K.T.F., still covered the replacement of apprentices called up for National Service, but its reinstatement clauses had been superseded by the Interrupted Apprenticeship Scheme subsidized by the Ministry of Labour. The latter, however, decided to terminate this scheme for apprentices called up after 31 December 1946.

These various questions were brought before the J.I.C. Another matter referred to it was the recommendation of the Court of Inquiry on the hours dispute in September 1946, for increased recruitment into the industry in view of the serious labour shortage due to the 'subnormal intake' during the war.

The J.I.C. Committee on Employment and Production recommended early in 1947 that, the school-leaving age having been raised to fifteen, the period of apprenticeship should be reduced to 'six years in the case of apprentices who did not undertake compulsory National Service and five years plus any period of National Service' for those who did, but no apprenticeship to terminate before twenty-one years of age. The period of apprenticeship, however, and apprentice ratios were matters for agreement between the employers' organizations and individual unions, to which, therefore, the J.I.C. proposals were submitted.

That the T.A. had not greatly changed its attitude on these questions is shown by the 1947 Delegate Meeting resolution instructing the E.C. to press for a reduction in the number of apprentices in composing rooms. The Association was fearful of slump and unemployment as in pre-war days. The employers, on the other hand, were urgently demanding an increase on account of the serious labour shortage, and the E.C. had to make concessions in order to secure wages parity. In the agreement of January 1948 they accepted the J.I.C. recommendation for a reduced apprenticeship period and also agreed to remove the top limit of eight apprentices to a hundred journeymen in composing and machine departments, one apprentice being allowed, in future, for each additional twenty journeymen. The limit was not, however, removed in the Monotype-caster department: the E.C. would only permit a fourth apprentice when eighteen or more men were employed.

When the wages parity question again became acute in August 1948 the E.C. threatened to cancel these concessions, but eventually withdrew notice. There was some argument over interpretation of the J.I.C. recommendation regarding a reduced apprenticeship period, but agreement was eventually reached in December 1948. So long as the school-leaving age remained at fifteen, apprenticeship was to be for six years including any period of National Service, provided that at least five years of actual craft training was carried out; no apprenticeship to terminate before twenty-one. If a boy remained at school after the age of fifteen the period of his extended schooling might be deducted from the six-year period of apprenticeship, provided that the other conditions were observed; but no boy was normally to be apprenticed after reaching seventeen years of age.

A new Interrupted Apprenticeship Scheme was also concluded in February 1949, on the basis of an agreement negotiated in 1947–8 by the P. & K.T.F. This was on exactly similar lines to the previous Ministry of Labour scheme, the employers agreeing to pay full wages for the extended period of apprenticeship.

The employers were still seriously concerned at the continuing labour shortage and pressed strongly in the wages conference with the T.A. Executive in October 1949 for increased apprentice quotas. The E.C. were loath, however, to make a permanent alteration in the apprentice ratio to meet what they considered a temporary scarcity. Instead they agreed to grant the employers a 'bonus' of 200 apprentices and to restore War Agreement No. 3A (relaxation of rules and dilution of labour).

A great deal of attention has been directed in the post-war period to the selection and training of apprentices. This question was brought before the J.I.C. long before the war ended by a communication in September 1942 from the Ministry of Labour. A special sub-committee was appointed, the result of whose work was a report on the 'Recruitment and Training of Apprentices' in the printing industry, approved by the full J.I.C. in April 1945. The scheme was not, however, finally adopted by both sides of the industry until April 1947. It was a development of that formulated after the First World War. Together with supplementary memoranda, it covered in great detail the questions of selection, indenturing, training (workshop and technical college), examination, and certification of apprentices, the scheme to be administered by a J.I.C. Apprenticeship Authority and Local Apprenticeship Committees. The aim was to secure the best type of boys for the industry, to ensure a sound technical training, and to preserve and develop craftsmanship. The unions tried to make the scheme compulsory, but, like its predecessor, it was voluntary and would depend for its success chiefly on the energy of the local joint committees.

The T.A. 'Guild of Young Printers' has proved a great success in arousing and organizing the interest and enthusiasm of apprentice members. The Association has tried not merely to kindle the trade-union spirit among them, but to develop pride in craftsmanship and in the printing trade generally.

Relations with Other Unions

During the war the unions in the printing and kindred trades had been forced to drop their differences, shelve their autonomy, and act together in the Federation. The P. & K.T.F. Report on Post-War Reconstruction expressed anxiety that this unity should be maintained and even improved. Amalgamation had been rejected by the 1943 Annual Conference, so the Report merely recommended the establishment of Joint Consultative Committees on a sectional basis, to secure 'closer working between unions'.

Such committees were established by the Federation Executive in 1946, after consultation with the unions, but have proved abortive. We have already seen, in the post-war wages movements, how strong the feelings of autonomy still are and how numerous the differences—of geography, trade sections, craft and non-craft—among the seventeen unions in the P. & K.T.F. All the old squabbles over demarcation have revived after the war.

The T.A.'s War Emergency Agreements with the L.S.C. and A.C.P. were cancelled in 1946, London returning to its policy of exclusion and refusing reciprocal recognition and entry. The quarrel with the Monotype Casters and Typefounders Society, temporarily settled by the 'working agreement' of 1938, has also revived, the T.A. reasserting its claim to jurisdiction over all provincial caster attendants.

Radius difficulties have occurred again with the Dublin Typographical Society over rival claims to Dun Laoghaire, the dispute being referred eventually to the Irish Labour Court, whose finding (May 1947) was in favour of the Dublin Society: that the boundary of County Dublin should be recognized as 'the line of demarcation between their present areas of organisational activity'.

Continual difficulties have also occurred with the N.S.O.P. & A. regarding interpretation of the fifty-fifty agreement on rotary promotions. In daily newspaper offices this agreement had never been much observed before the war, except in Manchester, and now, with the post-war shortage of newspaper rotary minders, many more N.S.O.P. & A. members are being promoted. The N.S.O.P. & A. strongly opposes the introduction of T.A. flat-bed minders under the 'equal rights' clause, and newspaper proprietors are unwilling to place expensive machinery in charge of men without rotary experience. Moreover, the T.A. is unable in most instances, owing to the labour shortage, to provide men for the vacancies. The result is that about 95 per cent. of them have gone to N.S.O.P. & A. members.

This is very distasteful to T.A. craft feelings and vigorous demands have been made for full observance of the agreement. Moreover, it has been proposed that a limited apprenticeship system should be introduced in newspaper rotary departments, so that the Association might be able to provide properly qualified minders. The N.S.O.P. & A., however, opposes this as endangering the position and prospects of its members. Negotiations for a tripartite agreement between the T.A., N.S.O.P. & A., and Newspaper Society have so far proved fruitless. The fifty-fifty agreement with the N.S.O.P. & A. was amended somewhat in June 1948, but without solving the differences between the two unions. Meanwhile the T.A. has been forced to accept existing facts and admit a large number of N.S.O.P. & A. members promoted to rotary minders.

Differences between the T.A. and N.U.P.B. & P.W. have similarly revived since the war. That in regard to the organization of process provers was referred to a P. & K.T.F. Arbitration Board, which decided in favour of the N.U.P.B. & P.W. (February 1946). A more serious problem has been the manning of multiple-process machines making and printing paper and cellophane bags, wrappers, &c. Several friendly conferences have been held and a fifty-fifty manning arrangement for 'bag-tackler-printers', without demarcation of work, has been proposed, but so far no agreement has been reached. The problem is complicated by the fact that at Messrs. E. S. & A. Robinson's, of Bristol, these machines are manned by N.S.O.P. & A. members.

These differences between the various unions should not, however, obscure their underlying unity and constant co-operation on innumerable matters through the P. & K.T.F. In post-war reconstruction, in wages and hours movements, in organizing, and on the J.I.C. the Federation has played a tremendously important role. The developments, in fact, of the past fifty years have been steadily in the direction of increased unity and ultimate amalgamation.

International Trade Unionism

Increasing unity has also been a feature of international trade-union organization in the printing and allied trades. The T.A. Delegate Meeting in 1944 expressed its 'earnest desire to assist in the revival of a strong printing Trade Union Movement on the Continent at the conclusion of hostilities', but urged the creation of one international organization in place of the three Secretariats for the letterpress, lithographic, and bookbinding sections.

The question was taken up by the P. & K.T.F. and it was as a result mainly of its efforts that the International Graphical Federation was formed in 1949, to which the T.A. is affiliated.

The T.A. was also affiliated, through the T.U.C., to the World Federation of Trade Unions until the recent withdrawal owing to Communist domination. An international organization of Free Trade Unions is now in the making.

Finances and Membership

These post-war years, despite all their difficulties, have been the most prosperous in the T.A.'s whole history. As a result of 'full employment', out-of-work payments have averaged only £5,000 annually, compared with £40,000 before the war. This reduced expenditure has brought about an unprecedentedly rapid increase in the General Fund from £277,000 (June 1945) to £525,000 (September 1949). Membership has also increased from 40,308 to 46,866.

Constitutional Changes

The T.A.'s constitutional framework has been little altered in the post-war reconstruction. Several minor changes, however, were made by the 1947 Delegate Meeting as a result of E.C. proposals. The basis of the E.C. constitution is now one representative to approximately 2,500 members. This has meant only one, instead of two, representatives each for Wales and Ireland and abolition of special representation both for the large branches and for machinemen. The group system, however, remains unaltered: proposals for alteration of geographical areas, full-time Group Secretaries instead of Organizers, and decentralization have been rejected. Instead, annual district conferences of branch secretaries, attended by E.C. members and Officers, have been instituted, to provide closer contact with Head Office, stimulate interest in branch work and organization, and increase administrative efficiency.

The number of Head Office officials has been increased by the creation of a second Assistant Secretary, while the General Treasurer has been transformed into the Financial Secretary.

Several changes in official personnel have occurred. D. Lewis, the General Treasurer, retired in 1948 and was succeeded as Financial Secretary by H. Taylor, one of the Head Office clerks. H. Inglis, the General President, was succeeded on his retirement in 1949 by F. C. Blackburn, Bristol B.S. and for several years an E.C. member. J. M. Bonfield, of Letchworth, became second Assistant Secretary in 1948. H. Riding and H. E. Joseph are still General and Assistant Secretaries respectively.

Of the Guilds, only the National News Guild has remained active, still trying, though without success, to secure separate representation for newsmen and pressing extravagant claims in regard to wages and hours. The E.C. has withdrawn recognition of the Guild after its 'treachery' in trying to negotiate separately with the Newspaper Society during the recent wages crisis (September 1949).

Superannuation Fund

The Superannuation Fund was only saved from collapse during the war by levies and transfers from the General Fund. The 1944 Delegate Meeting therefore instructed the E.C. 'to formulate a scheme that will stabilise the Fund over a number of years', the levy to continue meanwhile.

The present position of the Superannuation Fund was, as we have seen, the culmination of mistakes made ever since its establishment in 1877. It had been started with practically no reserve funds and hopelessly inadequate subscriptions, paying benefits after three years to members who had contributed little or nothing, without any regard to future liabilities. It had changed from a benefit payable only to old and incapacitated members to a pension for all at sixty. Additional grades had been created and benefits increased.

The dangers had long been evident, but successive Delegate Meetings had closed their eyes and hoped for the best, not daring to face up to their responsibilities and place matters squarely before the members. Instead they patched things up with odd pennies and halfpennies, leaving the ultimate burden to posterity. Rapidly increasing membership had enabled the Fund to meet current liabilities, without any adequate provision for future claimants. But now 'complete organization' was approached and the burden of the increasing number of superannuitants was becoming unbearable. It was increased, moreover, by the falling death rate and longer life of T.A. members. The 3¼d. weekly allocation to the Fund of 1918 had increased to 1s. 6d. out of 2s. 5d. total subscription (grade 6) by 1939 and an 8d. levy was also payable, while £58,000 had been transferred from the General Fund during the war. Present members were having to pay for the pensions which past members had drawn; young members were supporting old ones who had never paid their proper share, contributing to a Fund of doubtful future benefit to themselves.

The Fund possessed other objectionable features. If a member died before retiring on the Fund nothing was paid from it to his widow or relatives, though he might have contributed for twenty, thirty, or forty years; and over half the members died before the age of sixty. Those who joined the Association late in life, after forty-five years of age, had little prospect of ever drawing any superannuation benefit, except perhaps the lowest grades, yet were forced to contribute to the Fund. This fact, together with the high subscriptions, added considerably to the difficulties of organizing. The Fund had, in fact, in the opinion of many, become a millstone round the Association's neck. It was swallowing up the greater part of the subscriptions, it was a heavy drain on the General Fund, and prevented the building up of financial reserves for trade-union purposes. It was making the T.A. more a glorified friendly society than a trade union.

Criticism was intensified after publication of the Government's Social Insurance Scheme early in 1946. Not only were old-age pensions, or retiral allowances, to be increased from 10s. to £1. 6s. for a single man and from £1 to £2. 2s. for a married couple, thus reducing the need for trade-union benefit, but National Health and Insurance contributions would be raised ultimately from 2s. 1d. to 4s. 7d., so that opposition to the additional burden of T.A. subscriptions would be increased.

Defenders of the Superannuation Fund, mostly older members, spoke of the valiant work of the veterans who had built up the T.A. and who richly deserved the benefits of the Fund. They accused those who wanted to abolish it of betraying the older members, forgetting that it was past short-sightedness and failure to face up to responsibilities which had brought things to the present pass. Those who neglected to join the Association till late in life did not, it was considered, deserve any benefit

—even though they might have been living in an unorganized area—and were rightly forced to pay towards the pensions of those who had borne the heat and burden of trade-union strife. The Superannuation Fund had proved of great assistance in organizing, offering valuable and tangible benefits. It also helped to preserve the loyalty of members in times of crisis, since they did not want to lose the benefit of past contributions nor the future safeguard of a superannuation pension. To abolish it would be to jettison the sheet-anchor of the Association and would be especially dangerous in view of the numerous pension schemes being introduced by private firms. Moreover, it would result in members continuing at work to a greater age, thereby reducing the opportunities of younger members and increasing unemployment, thus throwing a heavier burden on the Out-of-Work Fund.

The E.C., in accordance with the 1944 Delegate Meeting's instructions, appointed a special committee to formulate a scheme for stabilizing the Fund. There were several alternatives: either to increase contributions, or reduce benefits, or raise the qualifying age, or combine all these. The special committee eventually recommended that contributions (at present 2s. 2d., including the levy) should be increased by 4d. per week.

Meanwhile, however, the Government's Social Insurance Scheme came out, so the E.C., realizing the strong opposition there would be to any increase in Association subscriptions, decided to reconsider the whole question. Another special committee was appointed which produced three alternative schemes, the first two involving either increased subscriptions or reduced benefits and a qualifying age of sixty-five, the other, which was recommended, abolition of the Superannuation Fund and its replacement by a retiral or funeral benefit, providing lump sums at retirement or death, according to years of membership.

The E.C. adopted this proposal, but decided, in view of the importance of the matter, to take a vote on the question of holding a special Delegate Meeting. The voting being in favour, the meeting was held at Cambridge on 27 and 28 August 1946. It showed that the Association was completely divided, a struggle developing between those who wanted to abolish the Superannuation Fund and those wishing to preserve it—a struggle, broadly speaking, between the younger and older members. Forces were evenly divided and the meeting accomplished nothing, all resolutions and amendments being rejected.

The E.C. now decided to take a ballot vote of the membership on three proposals: firstly, that the Fund be wound up; secondly, that benefits be reduced and the qualifying age raised to sixty-five; thirdly, that a retiral or funeral benefit be instituted. Many branches put forward amendments, but the Executive got them to agree to their being grouped under the three main proposals.

The outcome, after several ballots, was a decision by a large majority at the end of 1947 'that the Superannuation Fund be wound up; the payment of benefits from the Fund discontinued, and the scales of contributions reduced accordingly; and that the Fund be shared out amongst the members on a *pro rata* basis', according to years of membership. A number of ex-superannuitants took legal action to challenge this decision as invalid under the Association rules, but the action, heard in the Chancery Court, London, on 28-30 July 1948, failed. The E.C. therefore proceeded to distribute the Fund, at the rate of 6s. $4\frac{1}{2}d$. for each complete year of membership.[1]

The *Circular* was full during these years of arguments for and against the Superannuation Fund and much bitterness was roused. There seemed little doubt that the Fund had to go. The E.C., fearing that the loyalty of members would be weakened, wished to replace it by a retiral benefit, but the attraction of reduced subscriptions was too strong.[2] Moreover, members could get better terms from insurance companies and friendly societies. It was undoubtedly best that pensions and insurance should be left to these agencies and to the State. The latter, now increasingly providing for sickness, old age, and death, was taking over the friendly society functions of the trade unions, as they had so long advocated it should.

It is easy, in going over the history of the Superannuation Fund, to criticize the stupidity and short-sightedness of Executive, Delegate Meetings, and members, lost in the maze of actuarial statistics. But one can only applaud their aims in establishing the Fund: a monument to thrift, self-help, and humanitarian motives.

The winding up of the Association's Superannuation Fund has created greater interest in the idea of an industrial pension scheme. Many progressive firms already have their own pension funds and the Newspaper Society has a wider scheme. But the unions are inclined to regard these with suspicion, as weakening trade-union loyalty. A draft scheme for the whole industry was drawn up by the J.I.C. in the years

[1] At the end of 1947 the Fund stood at about £235,000 and there were 4,245 members on it. The expenditure in 1947 on superannuation and incapacity benefits was nearly £145,000.

[2] Subscriptions were reduced by 2s. 2d. and now ranged from 1s. per week in grade 4 to 1s. 3d. in grade 1.

1935-7, but dropped owing to differences regarding cost and trade-union membership. It has now been revived, however, and taken up by the P. & K.T.F. in 1948-9. The proposal will soon, it appears, be brought before the J.I.C. again. The establishment of such a scheme in Eire has already been discussed between T.A. and I.M.P.A. representatives.

Other Benefits

As a result of the National Insurance Act (1946), brought into operation in July 1948, trade unions have ceased to administer State Unemployment Insurance Benefits. Out-of-work members must now attend at employment exchanges to make claims for benefit, prove unemployment, and receive payment. (The exchanges will supply proof of days of unemployment to unions making out-of-work payments from their own funds, and T.A. vacant books are now lodged there to be signed by members at the time of their attendance.) Under the Control of Engagement Orders of 1945 and 1947, however, trade unions have been recognized as 'Approved Employment Agencies'. Thus T.A. branch officers have recovered their pre-war function of placing out-of-work members in employment in the printing industry.

Unions have also ceased, as a result of the National Insurance Act, to administer National Health (sickness and medical) benefits. Their Approved Societies have been wound up and taken over by the Ministry of National Insurance. Thus the T.A. '301' ceased to exist and its manager, J. W. Lowe, who had done such sterling pioneer work since 1912 in the development of the 'Social Services', went into retirement, dying shortly afterwards.

Despite increasing State provision for unemployment, sickness, and death, the T.A. has continued its out-of-work and funeral benefits and branches their sick funds. The rules for out-of-work benefit have remained unaltered. Owing to the acute labour shortage there has been very little unemployment and annual payments have averaged only about £5,000.

The scale of funeral benefits was altered by the 1944 Delegate Meeting so as to base it more fairly on years of membership, with £1 for each year up to a maximum of £20. As a result, annual payments have risen to over £10,000 annually.

Politics

Since the resignation of F. O. Roberts in 1941 the T.A. had had no representative in the House of Commons. The Association shared, however, in the Labour Party's electoral triumph of July 1945, when, for the first time, both its official candidates, G. H. Walker and W. A. Wilkins, were successful, in the Rossendale and Bristol South Divisions respectively. The veteran campaigner A. E. Stubbs, now a superannuated T.A. member, was also elected, for Cambridgeshire, but R. B. Collingson was unsuccessful in the Eye Division of Suffolk.

As a result of the ensuing increase in M.P.s' salaries to £1,000 per annum, the Association's grant to its representatives was, at their suggestion, reduced to a token figure of £50 a year.

Another result of Labour's triumph was the Trade Disputes and Trade Unions Act (1946), repealing the 1927 Act and restoring the position to that under the 1913 Trade Union Act, with 'contracting out' instead of 'in' as regards contributions to trade-union political funds. Contributions to the T.A. Political Fund have thereby risen somewhat. Before the war (1936-9), with a membership of about 37,000 and only a quarter of the contributions retained by the branches for local purposes, they averaged about £1,500 annually. Now, with a membership of about 46,000 and half the contributions retained by the branches, they are about the same.[1]

Political contributions are generally collected only from fully employed journeymen members. Of those liable to contributions (about 36,000), therefore, nearly a quarter have 'contracted out'. As an organization, however, the T.A. has continued its staunch support of the Labour Party. The lively interest taken in political affairs is reflected in the pages of the *Circular*.

In Eire, R. S. Anthony won back his seat in the Irish Parliament in 1943 as the representative of Cork City, and after being narrowly defeated in 1948 was then elected to the Senate. He was given financial assistance by the E.C. in his election campaigns, being a candidate of the Irish Labour Party.

The Association has strongly supported the T.U.C. and Labour Party in opposition to Communist infiltration. A discussion on this question by the E.C. in December 1948 showed that 'the Council was unanimously opposed to Communism' and that 'there was no evidence of any branch in the Association being troubled with a disruptive Communistic element', though 'small groups here and there endeavoured to belittle the authority of branch officials by disparagement'. But, as the T.U.C. was informed, 'the Association does not enquire into a member's political views, and under the present rules of the T.A. there is nothing to debar a Communist from appointment' to official positions.

[1] The contribution is still ½d. per week.

Conclusion

So we come to the end of the T.A.'s first hundred years of history. But 1949 marks the end only of this written story; it is merely a milestone, though a notable one, in the course of events. As the writer pens these final words we are *in medias res*.

Nevertheless, we may stand a moment and look back over the past hundred years and mark the growth and achievements of the Association, how patiently it has organized towns and offices throughout the country, how its democratic constitution has developed, how wages have been increased, hours reduced, apprentices limited, working regulations formulated, how the Association has faced the 'industrial revolution' in printing, how national negotiations have developed with employers' organizations to regulate the industry, improve working conditions, and prevent industrial strife, how the Association has grown in the wider framework of general trade-union and political affairs.

It has been impossible in this history to pay tribute to the countless individual members who, in chapel, branch, group, and Executive Council, have played loyal and stalwart parts in creating and building the Association. As in every democratic organization, many, in fact most, members have been content merely to pay their 'subs.' and occasionally criticize, but a minority, endowed with courage and enthusiasm, have striven against great difficulties to better the lot of journeymen printers, to secure a fair standard of living, freedom, and social justice. Great success has attended their efforts. The pioneers of 1849 'builded better than they knew'. The T.A. is immensely bigger and more powerful and its members are enjoying better conditions than they can ever have hoped for.

Today the position, problems, and responsibilities of trade unions are different in many ways and greater than they were a hundred years ago. The pioneering hardships, the struggle for recognition and fight for fair conditions, are largely past in this country. Unions today are immensely powerful bodies with a recognized share in the control of industry. As such they bear far greater responsibilities and must exercise far greater foresight, wisdom, and restraint than in the past. They must adopt constructive policies and not merely go for what they can get out of industry. They must, for example, consider the greatly changed position of this country in the world economy. They must not regard what they have won as theirs by inherent right, but as something still to be worked for and maintained, not merely by traditional trade-union methods, but by efforts to improve technical efficiency and increase production. These are no longer matters merely for the 'bosses'. They must be seriously considered nowadays by the trade unions as well. A great deal of re-thinking is called for, a broader outlook, and greater statesmanship. There are, however, hopeful indications that these qualities are not lacking in the leaders of the trade-union movement today.

APPENDIX

SUMMARY OF BENEFITS PAID BY THE T.A.

1849–1949

NUMBER OF MEMBERS

Year	Members	Year	Members	Year	Members
1849	481	1883	6,281	1917	23,583
1850	603	1884	6,533	1918	24,762
1851	634	1885	6,919	1919	29,567
1852	911	1886	7,449	1920	31,234
1853	964	1887	7,919	1921	31,099
1854	1,127	1888	8,164	1922	30,716
1855	1,288	1889	8,830	1923	30,378
1856	1,395	1890	9,556	1924	30,906
1857	1,439	1891	10,836	1925	31,918
1858	1,364	1892	11,939	1926	32,190
1859	1,351	1893	12,736	1927	31,953
1860	1,473	1894	13,202	1928	32,557
1861	1,922	1895	13,593	1929	33,499
1862	1,927	1896	13,906	1930	34,098
1863	1,940	1897	14,405	1931	34,495
1864	1,964	1898	15,075	1932	34,598
1865	1,992	1899	15,854	1933	34,778
1866	2,181	1900	16,179	1934	35,163
1867	2,262	1901	16,600	1935	35,784
1868	2,246	1902	17,243	1936	36,482
1869	2,266	1903	17,698	1937	37,183
1870	2,430	1904	18,230	1938	37,974
1871	2,687	1905	18,752	1939	38,277
1872	2,812	1906	19,103	1940	39,447
1873	3,402	1907	19,733	1941	40,030
1874	3,752	1908	20,254	1942	39,865
1875	3,902	1909	20,783	1943	39,931
1876	4,638	1910	21,436	1944	40,011
1877	5,612	1911	21,768	1945	41,000
1878	5,675	1912	22,078	1946	43,381
1879	5,487	1913	22,925	1947	44,321
1880	5,699	1914	23,783	1948*	46,511
1881	5,717	1915	23,617		
1882	6,031	1916	23,236		

* To March 1949.

STRIKE OR VICTIMIZATION PAYMENTS

	£	s.	d.		£	s.	d.		£	s.	d.
1850	101	19	2	1884	710	3	4	1918	419	11	10
1851	39	6	10	1885	509	1	0	1919	969	2	9
1852	152	1	7	1886	786	13	5	1920	5,036	1	2
1853	217	18	9	1887	231	15	1	1921	2,421	9	7
1854	204	14	6	1888	752	8	0	1922	70,565	7	4
1855	380	17	0	1889	245	10	7	1923	3,040	9	11
1856	264	4	2	1890	148	4	6	1924	360	17	2
1857	61	2	10	1891	501	18	8	1925	303	3	2
1858	528	13	6	1892	448	1	11	1926	55,647	11	8
1859	118	4	2	1893	1,022	10	3	1927	1,199	15	1
1860	150	6	11	1894	1,052	2	0	1928	160	11	5
1861	104	5	2	1895	1,056	10	7	1929	145	13	0
1862	106	17	2	1896	1,792	19	7	1930	664	8	6
1863	148	0	2	1897	951	7	7	1931	562	11	8½
1864	207	7	9	1898	1,024	8	1	1932	641	13	3½
1865	1,899	1	1	1899	1,866	12	6	1933	433	15	4
1866	442	2	3	1900	1,560	1	8	1934	922	3	11½
1867	544	0	2	1901	1,097	5	5	1935	979	16	0½
1868	404	16	5	1902	1,313	15	5	1936	353	15	5
1869	192	13	10	1903	549	16	10	1937	1,353	14	0
1870	124	19	4	1904	4,582	0	8	1938	787	3	10
1871	316	2	5	1905	1,201	17	0	1939	1,007	12	11
1872	1,942	5	6	1906	366	1	0	1940	428	10	2
1873	538	12	11	1907	697	5	3	1941	165	7	6
1874	876	11	4	1908	625	4	2	1942	44	9	9
1875	600	19	6	1909	439	16	10	1943	33	14	4
1876	360	19	4	1910	462	3	9	1944	6	0	0
1877	284	18	5	1911	1,948	16	4	1945	—		
1878	414	14	11	1912	1,391	9	1	1946	67	14	9
1879	990	14	9	1913	672	13	6	1947	58	15	2
1880	265	0	7	1914	399	19	1	1948*	2,192	10	8
1881	217	0	6	1915	1,073	7	5	Total £197,857		12	1
1882	133	8	0	1916	447	14	1				
1883	307	4	2	1917	1,330	5	1				

* To March 1949.

TRAVELLING RELIEF PAYMENTS

	£	s.	d.		£	s.	d.		£	s.	d.
1863	1,165	8	8	1882	374	12	7	1901	771	11	5
1864	702	10	5	1883	372	1	1	1902	740	15	3
1865	574	18	1	1884	325	5	9	1903	697	10	9
1866	699	9	3	1885	432	5	6	1904	565	0	11
1867	1,090	6	2	1886	394	8	10	1905	498	5	1
1868	875	1	9	1887	382	19	5	1906	570	5	0
1869	1,030	4	0	1888	634	4	8	1907	423	3	5
1870	873	4	1	1889	380	8	0	1908	525	10	4
1871	684	3	9	1890	353	14	7	1909	812	9	5
1872	674	11	2	1891	330	2	5	1910	850	18	11
1873	589	19	8	1892	361	10	10	1911	824	4	11
1874	841	18	8	1893	560	19	0	1912	870	17	7
1875	1,101	6	10	1894	486	12	8	1913	838	14	4
1876	1,374	2	9	1895	532	6	11				
1877	1,252	13	8	1896	806	14	2		Total £36,011 16 7		
1878	1,242	13	3	1897	523	13	4				
1879	1,397	7	6	1898	607	10	4		*Travelling Relief*		
1880	990	11	7	1899	657	11	5		*discontinued,* 1913		
1881	538	17	5	1900	805	19	7				

OUT-OF-WORK PAYMENTS

	£	s.	d.		£	s.	d.		£	s.	d.
1873	144	18	2	1899	6,961	10	11	1925	31,179	2	11
1874	361	5	7	1900	8,706	17	5	1926	44,189	0	8
1875	567	17	6	1901	9,470	9	6	1927	45,921	2	9
1876	1,028	12	1	1902	10,055	13	0	1928	42,113	1	0
1877	1,185	18	8	1903	9,153	5	0	1929	26,685	11	11
1878	1,992	1	11	1904	10,104	19	7	1930	35,013	12	0
1879	2,537	1	4	1905	10,699	6	10	1931	64,744	4	0
1880	2,248	14	8	1906	10,699	5	2	1932	59,260	11	6
1881	2,354	3	0	1907	9,908	13	10	1933	52,677	19	8
1882	1,499	2	11	1908	10,865	13	2	1934	44,744	11	4
1883	1,535	9	5	1909	15,123	15	1	1935	39,989	19	10
1884	1,614	7	9	1910	15,506	4	1	1936	36,565	18	9
1885	1,942	10	3	1911	13,236	15	0	1937	32,479	17	9
1886	2,108	8	10	1912	13,515	9	10	1938	34,811	7	9
1887	2,271	0	5	1913	11,384	18	3	1939	57,718	6	2
1888	2,659	6	6	1914	17,081	13	0	1940	74,097	4	1
1889	2,220	9	0	1915	14,260	9	1	1941	8,498	3	9
1890	2,354	0	5	1916	6,951	7	7	1942	3,339	15	8
1891	2,037	8	5	1917	3,031	11	2	1943	2,326	18	6
1892	2,342	4	11	1918	2,093	16	10	1944	1,539	3	4
1893	4,568	11	5	1919	9,252	17	6	1945	996	0	4
1894	6,813	13	1	1920*	13,664	15	9	1946	3,721	4	8
1895	8,714	5	5	1921	59,230	1	10	1947	7,324	3	9
1896	8,841	15	2	1922	56,755	1	1	1948†	8,273	13	9
1897	7,048	11	7	1923	45,131	9	3				
1898	6,924	11	11	1924	33,302	7	4		Total £1,262,275 13 10		

* Exclusive of State Unemployment Insurance and Dependency Benefits from 1920. † To March 1949.

FUNERAL PAYMENTS

	£	s.	d.		£	s.	d.		£	s.	d.
1873	97	10	0	1900	1,496	10	8	1927	5,216	12	4
1874	368	0	0	1901	1,264	0	0	1928	5,242	18	8
1875	420	0	0	1902	1,379	13	3	1929	6,272	8	5
1876	441	4	6	1903	1,735	1	10	1930	4,720	16	6
1877	381	17	6	1904	1,228	0	0	1931	5,812	0	0
1878	432	13	4	1905	1,658	19	5	1932	5,375	5	0
1879	628	0	0	1906	1,839	1	3	1933	5,598	0	8
1880	510	0	0	1907	1,664	0	0	1934	5,394	6	6
1881	628	0	0	1908	2,063	10	1	1935	5,914	10	6
1882	570	0	0	1909	1,879	19	3	1936	6,393	10	0
1883	565	9	6	1910	2,074	0	9	1937	6,252	0	9
1884	581	2	9	1911	1,901	8	10	1938	5,849	15	0
1885	600	0	0	1912	1,782	0	0	1939	6,598	5	0
1886	666	0	0	1913	2,064	3	2	1940	7,511	18	10
1887	817	10	0	1914	2,122	0	0	1941	7,323	10	0
1888	802	0	0	1915	2,496	0	0	1942	6,931	12	7
1889	718	0	0	1916	3,502	7	8	1943	7,652	17	9
1890	1,098	0	0	1917	4,912	10	0	1944	8,349	10	0
1891	968	11	7	1918	5,042	6	11	1945	10,311	0	2
1892	899	4	0	1919	3,432	8	0	1946	10,484	0	0
1893	1,150	5	0	1920	2,678	10	0	1947	10,845	0	0
1894	1,020	10	0	1921	2,460	10	0	1948*	14,198	1	1
1895	1,265	7	8	1922	4,320	13	9				
1896	1,234	0	0	1923	4,486	0	0				
1897	1,250	14	8	1924	4,363	0	0				
1898	1,276	0	0	1925	4,645	0	0				
1899	1,571	9	0	1926	5,146	9	5				

Total £242,838 13 6

* To March 1949.

SUPERANNUATION PAYMENTS

	£	s.	d.		£	s.	d.		£	s.	d.
1880	274	18	0	1904	8,581	12	8	1929	54,865	19	4
(6 months)				1905	9,271	15	0	1930	59,907	7	5
1881	616	5	0	1906	9,802	8	0	1931	66,517	15	3
1882	699	6	0	1907	10,237	12	0	1932	75,287	3	4
1883	777	14	0	1908	10,675	6	0	1933	82,449	0	0
1884	866	8	0	1909	10,871	4	0	1934	89,406	12	8
1885	1,076	9	0	1910	12,155	16	0	1935	95,863	12	10
1886	1,176	10	0	1911	12,558	11	0	1936	101,010	12	8
1887	1,345	10	0	1912	13,714	11	0	1937	106,353	14	2
1888	1,441	17	0	1913	14,402	7	6	1938	113,824	11	5
1889	1,611	11	0	1914	15,221	16	0	1939	116,792	0	8
1890	1,721	4	0	1915	16,410	15	0	1940	121,652	1	6
1891	1,840	2	6	1916	17,483	12	8	1941	120,744	6	7
1892	2,094	18	5	1917	16,733	11	0	1942	117,566	7	8
1893	2,472	0	0	1918	16,110	3	4	1943	116,691	17	2
1894	2,676	6	6	1919	21,093	19	10	1944	119,026	1	0
1895	3,078	0	0	1920	25,236	9	7	1945	121,693	14	11
1896	4,034	10	0	1921	29,194	9	3	1946	136,725	12	9
1897	4,528	0	0	1922	29,976	15	7	1947	144,734	2	10
1898	4,919	9	0	1923*	32,296	13	6	1948	391	12	9
1899	5,118	5	0	1924	35,672	6	1				
1900	5,794	16	0	1925	39,414	15	10	Total £2,578,962 14 6			
1901	6,761	1	0	1926	42,703	18	5				
1902	7,413	5	0	1927	46,309	1	9				
1903	7,927	3	7	1928	51,063	7	7				

* Includes Special Grade and Incapacity Benefit Payments since July 1923.

SPECIAL GRADE AND INCAPACITY PAYMENTS

	£	s.	d.		£	s.	d.		£	s.	d.
1904	65	12	0	1912	900	0	0	1920	1,576	17	11
1905	193	12	0	1913	1,032	4	0	1921	1,960	9	2
1906	268	4	0	1914	1,004	16	0	1922	1,986	16	1
1907	381	12	0	1915	1,030	0	0	1923*	1,087	2	0
1908	462	8	0	1916	1,088	3	4	(6 months)			
1909	606	16	0	1917	1,058	9	6				
1910	755	4	0	1918	1,053	4	0	Total £18,751 12 9			
1911	836	0	0	1919	1,404	2	9				

* Payments of Special Grade and Incapacity Benefits made from Superannuation Fund since July 1923.

RAILWAY FARES TO UNEMPLOYED MEMBERS

	£	s.	d.		£	s.	d.		£	s.	d.
1914	230	8	3	1927	344	18	7	1940	247	2	1
1915	101	16	11	1928	301	16	9	1941	204	5	2
1916	46	3	7	1929	284	13	3½	1942	126	16	4
1917	52	17	10	1930	347	6	2	1943	59	19	10
1918	62	14	8	1931	321	6	10	1944	27	18	4
1919	137	11	2	1932	457	15	10½	1945	29	14	10
1920	181	4	6	1933	490	15	0½	1946	58	13	9
1921	196	2	0	1934	470	9	5	1947	28	10	5
1922	403	2	4	1935	543	17	10	1948*	38	6	0½
1923	293	6	0	1936	582	7	8½				
1924	278	13	7	1937	580	19	4	Total £9,074		8	9¼
1925	215	1	6	1938	602	12	10½				
1926	254	11	10	1939	470	8	1½				

* To March 1949.

INDEX